TRACKatlas
of
Mainland Britain

TRACKmaps

TRACKatlas
of
Mainland Britain

Contents

Published in the United Kingdom by
TRACKmaps
Little Court
Upper South Wraxall
Bradford on Avon
BA15 2SE
www.trackmaps.co.uk

© TRACKmaps 2009

ISBN 978-0-9549866-5-0

All cartography in this book is generated from the National Network Map © 2009 ESR Cartography Ltd.

Produced by ESR Cartography Ltd, Woodley, Reading RG5 3LE
Cover design by Pastiche Art Studio, Swindon SN6 8TZ
Cover Photography © Rail Images, Leigh-on-Sea SS9 4AL
Printed and bound by 1010 Printing International Ltd

Acknowledgements

Many people have contributed to this Atlas. The original cartography was created at ESR Cartography Ltd from an idea by Mike Bridge and drawn digitally by cartographers Chris Fry, Dave Jones, Bob Lewis, John Gill, Jo Grant, Kathy Szwenk and Anne Rayski, led by Dave Padgett. The current work reflects editorial by Mike Bridge and Bob Lewis, cartographic artwork by Kathy and John Szwenk and other artwork by Jo Grant. Throughout the life of this Atlas, Dave Padgett has had a major influence on both the cartography and the layouts for which the Publisher is extremely grateful. The basic information incorporated comes from industry sources and a number of industry insiders have assisted over different layouts and reviews. The Publisher also wishes to thank Richard Groves and Chris Salisbury from NDC Consultants who kindly provided the milepost images from a vast array they have acquired while undertaking a full telecoms survey of the network for the infrastructure owner. Finally, special thanks go to Gerald Jacobs for his contribution of the Railway Mileages article. To every one of the helpers, with significant input or with small, your efforts are greatly appreciated.

Every effort has been made to ensure that the information in the book is as accurate as possible at the time of going to press. Notwithstanding, the Publisher welcomes corrections on errors and omissions.

Preface

Although my first interest in the railways was probably listening from a distance to the clanging of empty coal trucks being collected by a Bulleid Q1 from the Charrington's siding at Worcester Park station before getting up for school or perhaps waiting on the platform at Wimbledon for the train home as the occasional Merchant Navy passed through at speed, it was never an obsession. Only in recent years has it become such with my work with ESR Cartography's supply of bespoke maps for the Industry or becoming publisher for the Quail Track Diagram series of books. This Atlas is a result of that burgeoning obsession with both maps and the railway.

My primary object is to show today's railway network on mainland Britain in its geographic context and at a level of detail which allows readers to understand where they might be in railway terms and the implications of the trackwork in front of them.

The Atlas has been seven years in the making. To be truthful, when work started on the original Network map, the idea was not to produce an atlas but more to provide over-view mapping for railway management. Its origin, therefore, is in a series of maps drawn by the team at ESR Cartography Ltd from available industrial sources and produced on a bespoke basis to meet specific projects in the Rail Industry. Many of these maps can be found in control rooms and in maintenance, operations or planning offices throughout the UK. However, once the whole of the Network had been drawn and some breath had been taken, it became clear that an atlas at track level detail would be of great interest to a large number of people, enthusiast and Industry alike. This is that Atlas.

Mike Bridge, Publisher and Managing Editor

About this Atlas

The detail shown here started life as geo-referenced centrelines and from there, using industry sources for the track layout detail, the line work was drawn over. However, if drawn at true scale, it is likely that an atlas would require several hundred pages to show the detail at readable size. Indeed, many of those pages would show very little information as countryside lines can be both long and devoid of infrastructure.

To overcome this problem, a schematic approach has been taken to detail and one could call the result a Geo-schematic Map. It does have an underlying scale from the original geo-referenced centrelines but the infrastructure has been 'pushed and pulled' to enable sufficient detail to be shown. Therefore, the maps can be considered to have a Notional Scale only which, for the main part, is 1:210,000. To help the reader understand if such pushing and pulling has been used, a 5 mile marker symbol has been added to the maps. If, in any run, the markers are wider apart than elsewhere, it means detail at the beginning and end of the section has been moved to make space for detail in-between.

There are one or two other aspects that the reader needs to be aware of. For example, to help with the geographic context, rivers and urban sprawl have been shown. These are essentially true-scale. However, the points at which rivers cross track routes should not be taken as evidence of the actual crossing point.

Sidings have also been an issue due to scale. To give some substance to the information, the majority have been described by name rather than by detail but it is admitted there is no consistency about this. Finally, the reader should be aware that little is included on heritage or private systems except where they may interface the main network.

In principle, the maps show the passenger and freight routes which represent the national rail network together with their track formations including connections, crossovers and infrastructure. All stations appear with most signal boxes, junctions and tunnels including their names and railway mileages. Most level crossings that affect signaling are included together with information describing their type. Where the maps become very complex in conurbations, specific areas are shown as larger scale insets. These appear towards the back of the book.

The reader will note that, unlike most other atlases but following industry practice, the Trackatlas indicates not only the name of an asset but also gives it a reference in miles and chains; the railway mileage. Railway mileages are subject in their own right and are discussed on the next page.

RAILWAY MILEAGES

A Brief History
By Gerald Jacobs

One of the key aspects of managing the Railway Infrastructure is detailed knowledge of the location of the assets. Throughout the UK rail system this is expressed as the Railway Mileage and, like our sister publications, Quail Track Diagrams, this Atlas shows the railway mileage with the asset. Most of the infrastructure assets identified in this Atlas have a railway mileage expressed in miles and chains (eg, 146m 39ch). This may seem archaic to some but has a history as old as the Railway itself. It needs some explanation.

In the beginning
In the days when the Railway was being first built, Parliamentary approval was given on plans which were intended to show not only the routes but also the major constructions on the way. These major constructions and other fixed items all had to be referenced in some way and initially, their positions would be related to items of lineside furniture such as telegraph poles, plaques, statutory obelisks and posts. Generally, these features have disappeared now. Telegraph poles, for example, were once commonplace carrying telegraph or telephone or control lines linking signalling equipment in signal boxes which have generally moved underground. These features would be used to provide unique identities for signal posts, gantries, equipment cupboards, lineside telephones, bridge and viaduct numbers and gradient posts which mark the changes in the gradient of the track.

To maintain some commonality, the Railways Clauses Consolidation Act of 1845 (section 94) stated railway companies "...*shall cause the length of the railway to be measured, and milestones, posts, or other conspicuous objects to be set up and maintained along the whole line thereof, at the distance of one quarter of a mile from each other, with numbers or marks inscribed thereon denoting such distances*". As a consequence, the idea of measuring the railway linearly along its route became the norm (as opposed to the eastings and northings used elsewhere for geographic spatial position) and the railway milepost, including quarter, half and three-quarter posts, became a statutory measure point for railway locations.

For increased accuracy, it became practice to use chains for smaller measure. The Chain (22 yards, 20 chains per quarter mile, 80 chains to the mile) has much older origins than the Railway and was the fraction of a mile used most commonly in land surveying for 2 centuries before the 1845 Act. As a consequence, present day mileposts and the use of miles and chains measure have such distant origins that they have become rooted in railway history and geography.

How are mileages applied?
Railway measurement in this form would have been familiar to everyone before the 1923 Grouping of Railways. In the simplest terms, it required the 'planting' of a milepost (other than a Zero) along a line of route to indicate a 'measured' distance from a critical point of origin. There was no standard practice governing whether the mileposts were placed on one side of the line or the other and each company normally adopted one or the other throughout their system. Some companies, the L&YR for example, placed full mileposts on each side of the line.

Distances were usually measured from the buffer stops at the terminal station or from a junction of origin. Distances attributed to intermediate stations were normally calculated at a mean point from the extremities of the down and up platforms. A point of origin may generate miles which proceed along more than one route.

Why is it not that simple?
Notwithstanding the apparent simplicity in the method of measurement, following a route by mileage can occasionally mislead the reader. Take start or zero points, for example. Following the 1923 Grouping, each of the 'Big Four' acquired multiple routes with different start points. This is probably best illustrated by the table below with reference to the principal pre-grouping companies.

Great Western	London, Paddington
Southern Railway	
L&SWR	London, Waterloo
LB&SCR	London Bridge (Central)
SER	London, Charing Cross
LCDR	London, Victoria
LNER	
GNR	London, Kings Cross
GER	London, Liverpool Street
GCR	Manchester, London Road
NBR	Edinburgh, Waverley
GNofS	Aberdeen
LMSR	
L&NWR	London, Euston
Midland	London, St. Pancras
L&YR	Manchester, Victoria
Caledonian	Carlisle
G&SWR	Glasgow, Bridge Street
Highland	Perth

With expansions and amalgamations of railways, re-measurements were inevitable. There are various examples of the effect on mileages. For example, the South Eastern line would have been measured in its earliest form from London Bridge to Dover via Redhill; currently this route is measured from London, Charing Cross via Sevenoaks to Dover.

On the former Midland Railway, all distances were measured from Derby; this still applies to the routes which head to Birmingham and the south west but with the opening of their London, St. Pancras terminal all northbound routes were re-measured from that point.  When different routes from London met, usually the route with the lesser mileage went forward. As the Midland Railway was a fascinating tapestry of routes, interpreting mileposts can be a little bit bewildering. However, there is a trail which links St. Pancras right through to Carlisle, even if there are gaps where tracks have been removed.

On the former Great Western Railway, the primary route continues to be known as the Main Line and has a mileage sequence which runs from Paddington to Penzance via Bristol. The mileage of the later alternate route via Newbury, however, expires at Cogload Junction, near Taunton.

Longer distances create more opportunities for confusion and neither the East Coast nor the West Coast Main lines have continuous mileage sequences. On the WCML, the mileage originating from Euston starts with a negative value because of platform extensions and finishes at 187m 76ch at Golborne Junction, north of Warrington. A new mileage which has originated from Newton-le-Willows, on the former Grand Junction line goes forward as far as Preston from whence another sequence runs to Lancaster. Another sequence then runs to Carlisle to link with the Caledonian mileage which goes forward to Glasgow and Aberdeen.

On the ECML, the GNR mileage runs from London, Kings Cross to York, albeit the final 28 miles are over the metals of the former North Eastern Railway. York is a mileage origin point for a number of routes, including one that takes the ECML to Newcastle and then another from Newcastle to just north of Berwick where a mileage which has originated at Edinburgh and running south to Berwick completes the route.

Other peculiarities become obvious when studying the sequences of miles. When a new line was built and made a junction with a former one, it is the latter's mileage which usually goes forward. Gaps in sequences may occur when a 'joint' line arises, that is one managed by more than one company and only one sequence of miles will be evident. Sometimes mileages are reversed at a junction and may then either increase or decrease over the branch line. In a rare case, two mileages may actually apply over a common section of line.

We also need to make a distinction when apparently conflicting mileages may appear in print. In the context of this article, we have been referring to what may be described as track engineering mileages. Other compilations of mileage tables and information may have been constructed to suit passenger and freight requirements and may be referred to as computed mileages for special purposes.

What about the modern age?
Nothing stays the same. Eventually miles and chains will change to kilometres as new lines develop or outside forces come into play but at the moment this is limited. London Underground lines (which do not appear in this Atlas) were converted to kilometres in 1972 and measured from Ongar. Kilometre 'overlays' exist on both the WCML and ECML, also between Newcastle and Sunderland and kilometres prevail on the Channel Tunnel Route Line. Most recently of all, kilometres are supplanting miles on the Cambrian lines in preparation for the introduction of European Rail Traffic Management Systems (ERTMS).

In summary, railway mileages form an interesting sub-division of railway knowledge. They can inform, they can confuse and they can infuriate. However, steeped in history and with logic of their own, they will be with us for quite a while.

Editor's note: a table equating chains with yards and a equivalent kilometre measurement is provided on the Key page. This will also help the reader calculate tunnel lengths where the maps give only the portal mileages.

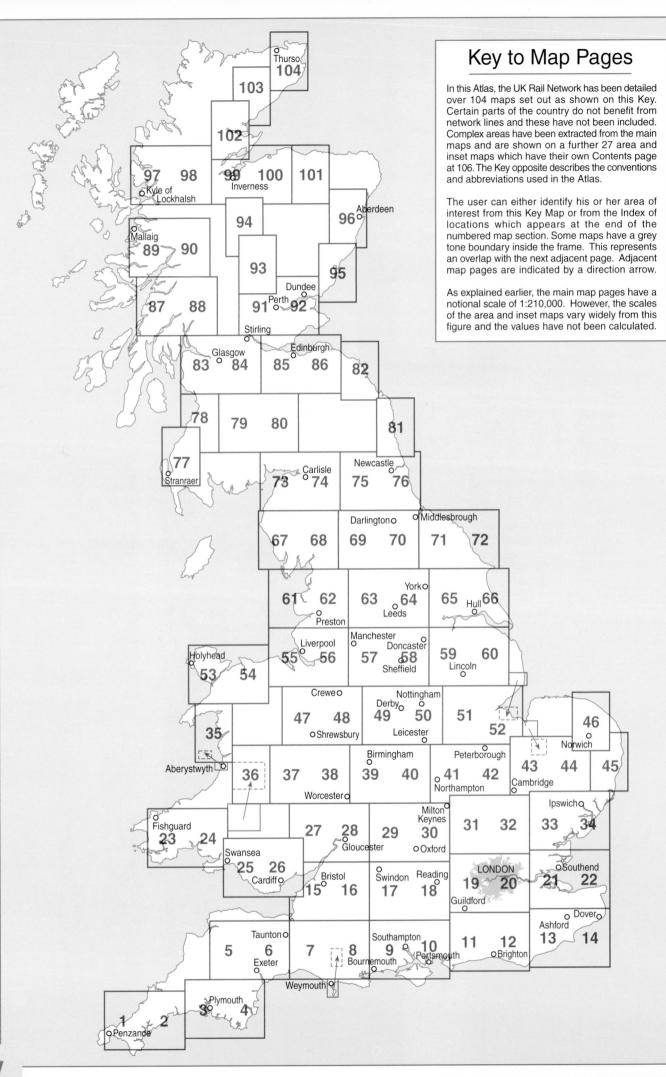

Key to Map Pages

In this Atlas, the UK Rail Network has been detailed over 104 maps set out as shown on this Key. Certain parts of the country do not benefit from network lines and these have not been included. Complex areas have been extracted from the main maps and are shown on a further 27 area and inset maps which have their own Contents page at 106. The Key opposite describes the conventions and abbreviations used in the Atlas.

The user can either identify his or her area of interest from this Key Map or from the Index of locations which appears at the end of the numbered map section. Some maps have a grey tone boundary inside the frame. This represents an overlap with the next adjacent page. Adjacent map pages are indicated by a direction arrow.

As explained earlier, the main map pages have a notional scale of 1:210,000. However, the scales of the area and inset maps vary widely from this figure and the values have not been calculated.

Thurso 104
103
102
97 98 99 100 101
Inverness
Kyle of Lochalsh
Aberdeen
94 96
Mallaig
89 90
93 95
Dundee
87 88 91 Perth 92
Stirling
Glasgow Edinburgh
83 84 85 86 82
78 79 80 81
77
Stranraer
Carlisle Newcastle
73 74 75 76
Darlington Middlesbrough
67 68 69 70 71 72
York
61 62 63 64 65 66
Preston Leeds Hull
Manchester
Liverpool Doncaster
55 56 57 58 59 60
Sheffield Lincoln
Crewe Nottingham
Derby
47 48 49 50 51
Shrewsbury Leicester 52
46
35
Norwich
Birmingham Peterborough
Aberystwyth 43 44 45
36 37 38 39 40 41 42
Worcester Northampton Cambridge
Milton Ipswich
Keynes
Fishguard 27 28 29 30 31 32 33 34
23 24 Gloucester Oxford
Swansea
25 26 Bristol Swindon Reading LONDON Southend
Cardiff 15 16 17 18 19 20 21 22
Guildford
Dover
Ashford
Taunton Southampton 11 12 13 14
5 6 7 8 9 10 Brighton
Exeter Bournemouth Portsmouth
Weymouth
Plymouth
3 4
1 2
Penzance

IV

Key to Map Symbols

■ .... Station
24m 51ch/39.650km...... Station Mileage/Signal Box Mileage
27m 00ch/43.452km .... Junction Mileage
12m 06ch/19.433km .... Crossing &Tunnel Mileage
• .... 5 Mile Marker
—————— .... Running Lines
—————— .... Electrified Overhead
—————— .... Electrified 3rd Rail
—————— .... Electrified 4th Rail

——— ...... Electrified, overhead & Conductor Rail
——— .... Light Rail
.... Line under construction
}—--{ .... Tunnel
——+—— .... Level Crossing
see table for abbreviations
oou .... Out of Use
⊠ .... Signal Box
■ .... Signal Room (CTRL)
▢ .... Platform Out of Use

Level Crossing and Other Abbreviations

ABCL .... Automatic Barrier Crossing, locally monitored
AHB .... Automatic Half-Barrier
AHB-X .... Automatic Half-Barrier which works automatically for wrong direction movements
AOCL .... Automatic Open Crossing, locally monitored
CCTV ....Closed Circuit Television
OPEN .... Open
MCB .... Manually Controlled Barriers by Signaller or Keeper
MCG .... Manually Controlled Gates by Signaller or Keeper
RC .... Remote Controlled
R/G .... Miniature Red/Green warning lights
R/G-X .... Miniature Red/Green warning lights which work automatically for wrong direction movements
TMO ....Traincrew Operated
UWC .... User Worked
FP .... Footpath

NB: Unabbreviated crossings are locally operated by signaller, crossing keeper or privately, but telephone equipped.

ASC .... Area Signalling Centre
COM .... Change of Mileage
EGF.. Emergency Ground Frame
EMD.................................... Electric Maintenance Depot
GF .... Ground Frame
GSP .... Ground Switch Panel
IECC.................... Integrated Electronic Control Centre
Jn.. Junction
LC .... Level Crossing (manned or open)
MOD .... Ministry of Defence
SC.. Signalling Centre
SCC .... Signalling Gontrol Centre
TMD ....Traction Maintenance Depot
UG/DG.. Up/Down Goods
UGL/DGL .... Up/Down Goods Loop

Chains to Yards Conversion Table

80 chains = 1 mile

Chains	Yards	Km equivalent	Chains	Yards	Km equivalent	Chains	Yards	Km equivalent
1	22	0.020	28	616	0.563	55	1,210	1.106
2	44	0.040	29	638	0.583	56	1,232	1.127
3	66	0.060	30	660	0.604	57	1,254	1.147
4	88	0.080	31	682	0.624	58	1,276	1.167
5	110	0.101	32	704	0.644	59	1,298	1.187
6	132	0.121	33	726	0.664	60	1,320	1.207
7	154	0.141	34	748	0.684	61	1,342	1.227
8	176	0.161	35	770	0.704	62	1,364	1.247
9	198	0.181	36	792	0.724	63	1,386	1.267
10	220	0.201	37	814	0.744	64	1,408	1.287
11	242	0.221	38	836	0.764	65	1,430	1.308
12	264	0.241	39	858	0.785	66	1,452	1.328
13	286	0.262	40	880	0.805	67	1,474	1.348
14	308	0.282	41	902	0.825	68	1,496	1.368
15	330	0.302	42	924	0.845	69	1,518	1.388
16	352	0.322	43	946	0.865	70	1,540	1.408
17	374	0.342	44	968	0.885	71	1,562	1.428
18	396	0.362	45	990	0.905	72	1,584	1.448
19	418	0.382	46	1,012	0.925	73	1,606	1.469
20	440	0.402	47	1,034	0.945	74	1,628	1.489
21	462	0.422	48	1,056	0.966	75	1,650	1.509
22	484	0.443	49	1,078	0.986	76	1,672	1.529
23	506	0.463	50	1,100	1.006	77	1,694	1.549
24	528	0.483	51	1,122	1.026	78	1,716	1.569
25	550	0.503	52	1,144	1.046	79	1,738	1.589
26	572	0.523	53	1,166	1.066	80	1,760	1.609
27	594	0.543	54	1,188	1.086			

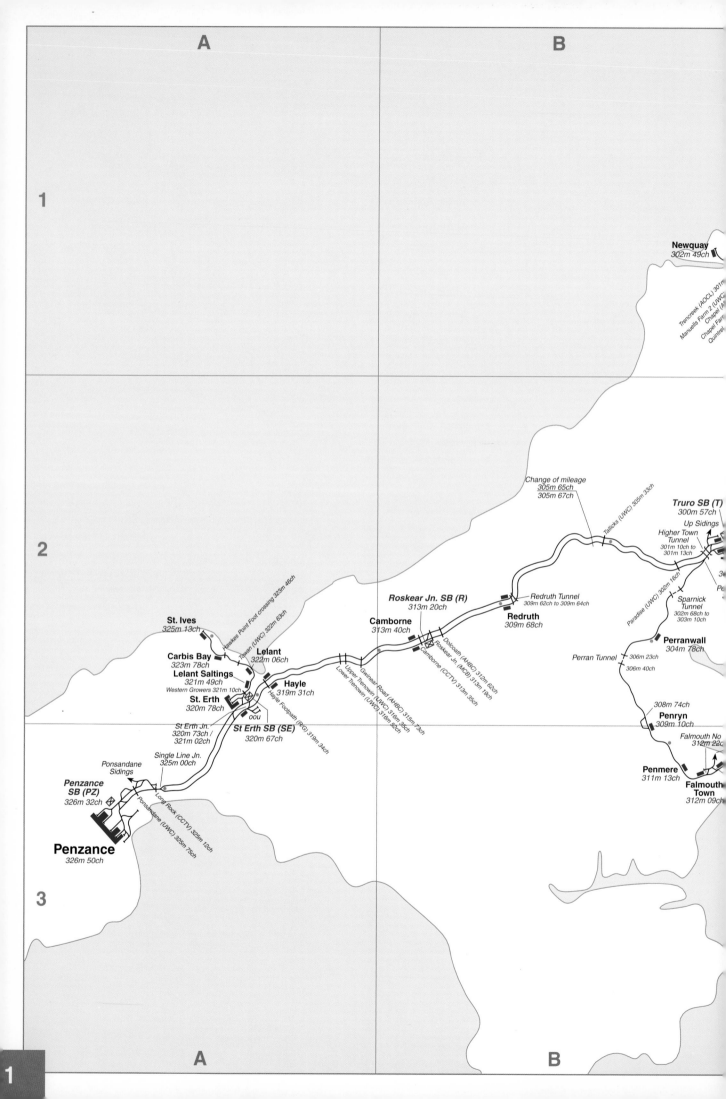

1

A

B

1

2

3

Newquay
302m 49ch

Trencreek (AOCL) 301m
Manuells Farm 2 (UWC)
Chapel Farm (A
Chapel Farm
Quintrel

Change of mileage
305m 65ch
305m 67ch

Tallicks (UWC) 305m 33ch

Truro SB (T)
300m 57ch

Up Sidings
Higher Town
Tunnel
301m 10ch to
301m 13ch

Pe

Paradise (UWC) 302m 16ch

Sparnick
Tunnel
302m 68ch to
303m 10ch

St. Ives
325m 13ch

Hawkes Point Foot crossing 323m 46ch

Towan (UWC) 322m 63ch

Roskear Jn. SB (R)
313m 20ch

Redruth Tunnel
309m 62ch to 309m 64ch

Redruth
309m 68ch

Perran Tunnel

Perranwall
304m 78ch

Perran Tunnel   *306m 23ch*
306m 40ch

Camborne
313m 40ch

Dolcoath (AHBC) 312m 62ch
Camborne (CCTV) 313m 19ch
Roskear Jn. (MCB) 313m 35ch

Carbis Bay
323m 78ch

Lelant
322m 06ch

Lelant Saltings
321m 49ch

Western Growers 321m 10ch

Hayle
319m 31ch

St. Erth
320m 78ch

Hayle Footpath (R/G) 319m 34ch

308m 74ch

Penryn
309m 10ch

oou

Upper Trenowin (UWC) 316m 36ch
Lower Trenowin (UWC) 316m 52ch

Gwinear Road (AHBC) 315m 73ch

St Erth SB (SE)
320m 67ch

Falmouth No
312m 22c

St Erth Jn.
320m 73ch /
321m 02ch

Penmere
311m 13ch

Falmouth Town
312m 09ch

Single Line Jn.
325m 00ch

Ponsandane
Sidings

Penzance
SB (PZ)
326m 32ch

Long Rock (CCTV) 325m 12ch

Ponsandane (UWC) 325m 75ch

Penzance
326m 50ch

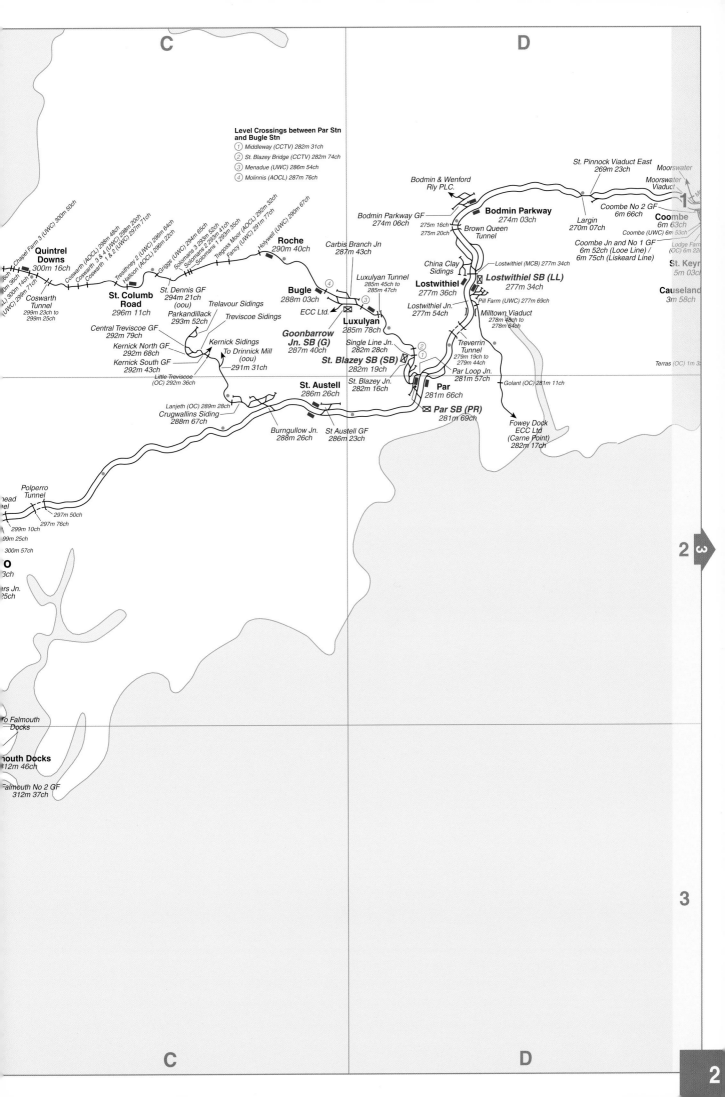

C

D

Level Crossings between Par Stn and Bugle Stn
① Middleway (CCTV) 282m 31ch
② St. Blazey Bridge (CCTV) 282m 74ch
③ Menadue (UWC) 286m 54ch
④ Molinnis (AOCL) 287m 76ch

St. Pinnock Viaduct East
269m 23ch

Moorswater

Moorswater Viaduct

Bodmin & Wenford
Rly PLC.

Bodmin Parkway GF
274m 06ch

Bodmin Parkway
274m 03ch

275m 16ch
275m 20ch

Brown Queen
Tunnel

Coombe No 2 GF
6m 66ch

Largin
270m 07ch

Coombe
6m 63ch

Coombe (UWC) 6m 53ch

Lodge Farm (OC) 6m 22ch

St. Keyr
5m 03ch

Coombe Jn and No 1 GF
6m 52ch (Looe Line) /
6m 75ch (Liskeard Line)

**Quintrel
Downs**
300m 16ch

Chapel Farm 3 (UWC) 300m 50ch

Coswarth (AOCL) 298m 48ch

Coswarth 3 & 4 (UWC) 298m 20ch

Coswarth 1 & 2 (UWC) 297m 71ch

Tresithney 2 (UWC) 298m 23ch

Halloon (AOCL) 296m 22ch

Griggs (UWC) 294m 65ch

Solomans 3 293m 52ch

Solomans 2 293m 41ch

Solomans 1 293m 35ch

Tregoss Moor (AOCL) 292m 32ch

Fancy (UWC) 291m 77ch

Holywell (UWC) 290m 67ch

Roche
290m 40ch

Carbis Branch Jn
287m 43ch

Luxulyan Tunnel
285m 45ch to
285m 47ch

China Clay
Sidings

Lostwithiel (MCB) 277m 34ch

Lostwithiel
277m 36ch

⊠ **Lostwithiel SB (LL)**
277m 34ch

**St. Columb
Road**
296m 11ch

St. Dennis GF
294m 21ch
(oou)

Parkandillack
293m 52ch

Trelavour Sidings

Treviscoe Sidings

Bugle
288m 03ch

④

③

ECC Ltd.

⊠

Luxulyan
285m 78ch

Pill Farm (UWC) 277m 69ch

Lostwithiel Jn.
277m 54ch

Milltown Viaduct
278m 48ch to
278m 64ch

Central Treviscoe GF
292m 79ch

Kernick North GF
292m 68ch

Kernick South GF
292m 43ch

Kernick Sidings

To Drinnick Mill
(oou)
291m 31ch

**Goonbarrow
Jn. SB (G)**
287m 40ch

Single Line Jn.
282m 28ch

②
①

Treverrin
Tunnel
279m 19ch to
279m 44ch

Par Loop Jn.
281m 57ch

Little Treviscoe
(OC) 292m 36ch

St. Blazey SB (SB)
282m 19ch

St. Blazey Jn.
282m 16ch

Par
281m 66ch

Golant (OC) 281m 11ch

Terras (OC) 1m 33

St. Austell
286m 26ch

⊠ **Par SB (PR)**
281m 69ch

Lanjeth (OC) 289m 28ch

Crugwallins Siding
288m 67ch

Burngullow Jn.
288m 26ch

St Austell GF
286m 23ch

↘ Fowey Dock
ECC Ltd
(Carne Point)
282m 17ch

Polperro
Tunnel

297m 50ch

297m 76ch

299m 10ch

299m 25ch

300m 57ch

...head
...el

...O
...3ch

...ers Jn.
...25ch

To Falmouth
Docks

...mouth Docks
...12m 46ch

*Falmouth No 2 GF
312m 37ch*

2 ►❸

C

D

3

❷

2

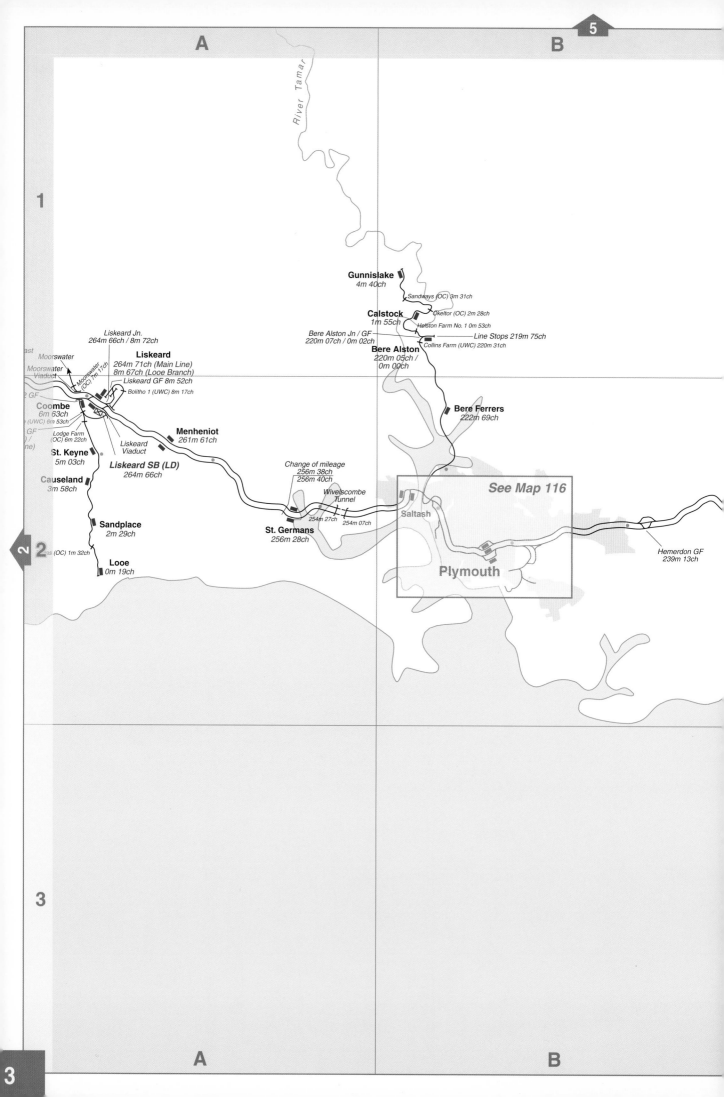

A

B

River Tamar

1

Gunnislake
4m 40ch

Sandways (OC) 3m 31ch

Okeltor (OC) 2m 28ch

Calstock
1m 55ch

Helston Farm No. 1 0m 53ch

Bere Alston Jn / GF
220m 07ch / 0m 02ch

Line Stops 219m 75ch

Collins Farm (UWC) 220m 31ch

Bere Alston
220m 05ch /
0m 00ch

Liskeard Jn.
264m 66ch / 8m 72ch

Moorswater

*Moorswater
Viaduct*

Liskeard
264m 71ch (Main Line)
8m 67ch (Looe Branch)

*Moorswater
(OC) 7m 17ch*

Liskeard GF 8m 52ch

2 GF

Bolitho 1 (UWC) 8m 17ch

Coombe
6m 63ch

Bere Ferrers
222m 69ch

(UWC) 6m 53ch

*Lodge Farm
(OC) 6m 22ch*

St. Keyne
5m 03ch

*Liskeard
Viaduct*

Menheniot
261m 61ch

*GF
) /
ne)*

Liskeard SB (LD)
264m 66ch

Causeland
3m 58ch

*Change of mileage
256m 38ch
256m 40ch*

*Wivelscombe
Tunnel*

See Map 116

2

Sandplace
2m 29ch

as (OC) 1m 32ch

254m 27ch   *254m 07ch*

St. Germans
256m 28ch

Saltash

*Hemerdon GF
239m 13ch*

Looe
0m 19ch

Plymouth

3

A

B

Lympstone
Village
7m 28ch

Powderham (SWO) 200m 50ch

Starcross
202m 36ch

Exmo
9m 32

204m 12ch   204m 13ch

204m 55ch   Dawlish Warren
                   204m 34ch

End of Line
4m 46ch

ECC Ballclays
3m 54ch

Heathfield 4m 00ch

Heathfield Branch Jn.
213m 75ch / 0m 14ch

Barrow crossing (WL) 206m 13ch

Newton Abbot East Jn.
218m 50ch

① Dawlish
206m 07ch

Teigngrace 2m 28ch

②

209m 10ch   207m 19ch
                   207m 42ch
③
④

Teignbridge (TMO) 1m 51ch

0m 55ch
(Branch oou from this point)

Parsons Tunnel

Teignmouth
208m 70ch

1

Watts Blake Bearne
Ball Clay Siding
0m 53ch

Hackney Engineers
Sidings

Newton Abbot
214m 05ch

Newton Abbot
West Jn.
214m 43ch

Former Aller Jn.
215m 09ch

Barrow crossing (WL) 208m 78ch

① Kennaway Tunnel
   206m 34ch to
   206m 43ch

② Coryton Tunnel
   206m 53ch to
   206m 63ch

③ Phillot Tunnel
   206m 66ch to
   206m 69ch

④ Clerks Tunnel
   206m 72ch to
   206m 75ch

217m 63ch
217m 76ch

Dainton Tunnel

Torre
219m 12ch

To Buckfastleigh
6m 73ch
(South Devon
Railway)

Totnes
222m 66ch

Totnes East
222m 39ch

Torquay
219m 79ch

Marley
Tunnels

228m 22ch 227m 62ch

Paignton SB (PN)
222m 12ch

Paignton
222m 12ch

Paignton North (CCTV) 222m 04ch

Paignton & Dartmouth
Steam Railway (P&DSR)

Paignton South (TMO) 222m 23ch

231m 58ch
231m 61ch

Aish Emergency Crossovers
230m 37ch

Wrangaton
Tunnel

Paignton
Crossover GF
222m 25ch

Goodrington
Yard Sidings

Ivybridge
234m 27ch

To
Kingswear
228m 64ch
(P&DSE)

2

3

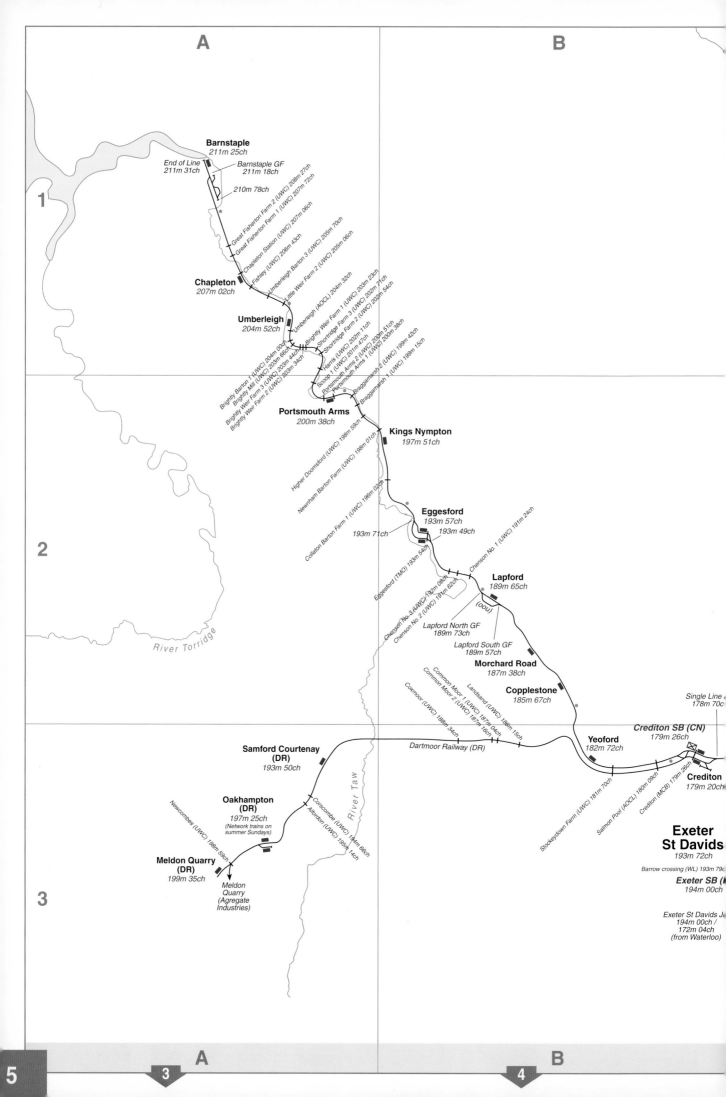

Barnstaple
211m 25ch

End of Line
211m 31ch

Barnstaple GF
211m 18ch

210m 78ch

Great Fisherton Farm 2 (UWC) 208m 27ch
Great Fisherton Farm 1 (UWC) 207m 72ch
Chapleton Station (UWC) 207m 06ch
Fishley (UWC) 206m 43ch

Chapleton
207m 02ch

Umberleigh Barton 3 (UWC) 205m 70ch
Little Weir Farm 2 (UWC) 205m 40ch

Umberleigh
204m 52ch

Umberleigh (AOCL) 204m 32ch
Brightly Weir Farm 1 (UWC) 203m 23ch
Shortridge Farm 3 (UWC) 202m 71ch
Shortridge Farm 2 (UWC) 202m 54ch

Brightly Barton 1 (UWC) 204m 00ch
Brightly Mill (UWC) 203m 66ch
Brightly Weir Farm 3 (UWC) 203m 44ch
Brightly Weir Farm 2 (UWC) 203m 34ch

Harris (UWC) 202m 11ch
Scoop 1 (UWC) 201m 47ch
Portsmouth Arms 2 (UWC) 200m 51ch
Portsmouth Arms 1 (UWC) 200m 38ch
Braggamarsh 2 (UWC) 199m 42ch
Braggamarsh 1 (UWC) 199m 15ch

Portsmouth Arms
200m 38ch

Higher Doomsford (UWC) 198m 59ch
Newnham Barton Farm (UWC) 198m 01ch

Kings Nympton
197m 51ch

Collaton Barton Farm 1 (UWC) 196m 02ch

Eggesford
193m 57ch
193m 49ch

193m 71ch

Chenson No. 1 (UWC) 191m 24ch

Eggesford (TMO) 193m 54ch
Chenson No. 3 (UWC) 192m 08ch
Chenson No. 2 (UWC) 191m 62ch

Lapford
189m 65ch

(OOU)

Lapford North GF
189m 73ch

Lapford South GF
189m 57ch

Morchard Road
187m 38ch

Landsand (UWC) 187m 04ch
Common Moor 1 (UWC) 186m 15ch
Common Moor 2 (UWC) 187m 16ch
Coxmoor (UWC) 188m 34ch

Copplestone
185m 67ch

Single Line
178m 70c

Crediton SB (CN)
179m 26ch

Yeoford
182m 72ch

Dartmoor Railway (DR)

Samford Courtenay
(DR)
193m 50ch

Stockeydown Farm (UWC) 181m 70ch
Salmon Pool (AOCL) 180m 09ch
Crediton (MCB) 179m 26ch

Crediton
179m 20ch

Oakhampton
(DR)
197m 25ch
(Network trains on summer Sundays)

Newcombes (UWC) 198m 59ch
Corscombe (UWC) 194m 66ch
Allordon (UWC) 195m 14ch

Exeter
St Davids
193m 72ch

Barrow crossing (WL) 193m 79c

Exeter SB (
194m 00ch

Meldon Quarry
(DR)
199m 35ch

Meldon Quarry (Agregate Industries)

Exeter St Davids J
194m 00ch /
172m 04ch
(from Waterloo)

River Torridge

River Taw

A   B

1

2

3

5

3   A   4   B

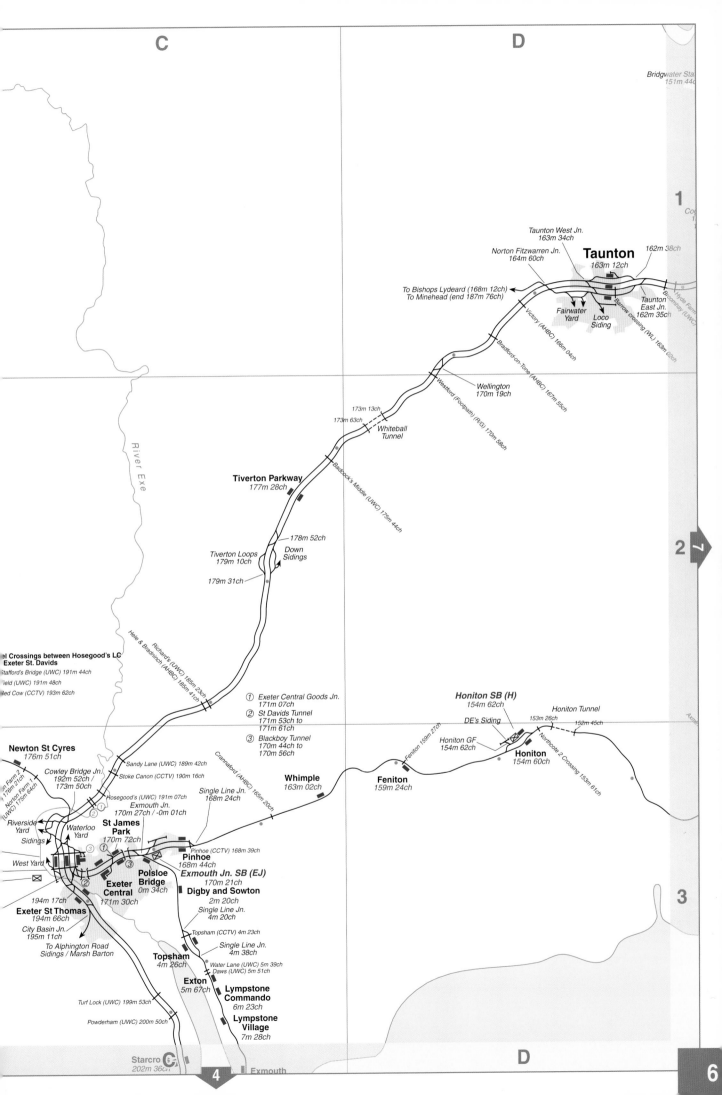

C   D

Bridgwater Sta.
151m 44c

1

Taunton West Jn.
163m 34ch

Norton Fitzwarren Jn.
164m 60ch

Taunton
163m 12ch

162m 38ch

To Bishops Lydeard (168m 12ch)
To Minehead (end 187m 76ch)

Victory (AHBC) 166m 04ch

Fairwater
Yard

Loco
Siding

Barrow crossing (WL) 163m 02ch

Taunton
East Jn.
162m 35ch

Bloomfield (UWC

Bradford-on-Tone (AHBC) 167m 55ch

Hyde Farm

Westford (Footpath) (RVG) 170m 58ch

Wellington
170m 19ch

River Exe

173m 13ch

173m 63ch

Whiteball
Tunnel

Tiverton Parkway
177m 28ch

Badcock's Middle (UWC) 175m 44ch

2 ⬇

178m 52ch
Down
Sidings

Tiverton Loops
179m 10ch

179m 31ch

Hele & Bradninch (AHBC) 185m 41ch

Richard's (UWC) 185m 23ch

el Crossings between Hosegood's LC
Exeter St. Davids

...tafford's Bridge (UWC) 191m 44ch
...field (UWC) 191m 48ch
...ed Cow (CCTV) 193m 62ch

① Exeter Central Goods Jn.
   171m 07ch
② St Davids Tunnel
   171m 53ch to
   171m 61ch
③ Blackboy Tunnel
   170m 44ch to
   170m 56ch

Honiton SB (H)
154m 62ch

Honiton Tunnel

153m 26ch   152m 45ch

DE's Siding

Axmi

Honiton GF
154m 62ch

Honiton
154m 60ch

Northcote 2 Crossing 153m 61ch

Newton St Cyres
176m 51ch

Sandy Lane (UWC) 189m 42ch

Feniton 159m 27ch

Cowley Bridge Jn.
192m 52ch /
173m 50ch

Stoke Canon (CCTV) 190m 16ch

Whimple
163m 02ch

Feniton
159m 24ch

...on Farm 2
176m 21ch
Norton Farm 1
175m 64ch
(UWC) 175m 11ch

Hosegood's (UWC) 191m 07ch
Exmouth Jn.
170m 27ch / -0m 01ch

Cranniford (AHBC) 165m 20ch

Single Line Jn.
168m 24ch

Riverside
Yard

Waterloo
Yard

St James
Park
170m 72ch

Sidings

Pinhoe (CCTV) 168m 39ch

Pinhoe
168m 44ch

West Yard

Exmouth Jn. SB (EJ)
170m 21ch

✉

Polsloe
Bridge
0m 34ch

Exeter
Central
171m 30ch

Digby and Sowton
2m 20ch

Single Line Jn.
4m 20ch

194m 17ch

Topsham (CCTV) 4m 23ch

Exeter St Thomas
194m 66ch

City Basin Jn.
195m 11ch

Single Line Jn.
4m 38ch

To Alphington Road
Sidings / Marsh Barton

Topsham
4m 26ch

Water Lane (UWC) 5m 39ch
Daws (UWC) 5m 51ch

Exton
5m 67ch

Lympstone
Commando
6m 23ch

Turf Lock (UWC) 199m 53ch

Powderham (UWC) 200m 50ch

Lympstone
Village
7m 28ch

3

Starcro⊙
202m 36ch

⬇ **4**   ▮ Exmouth

         D

6

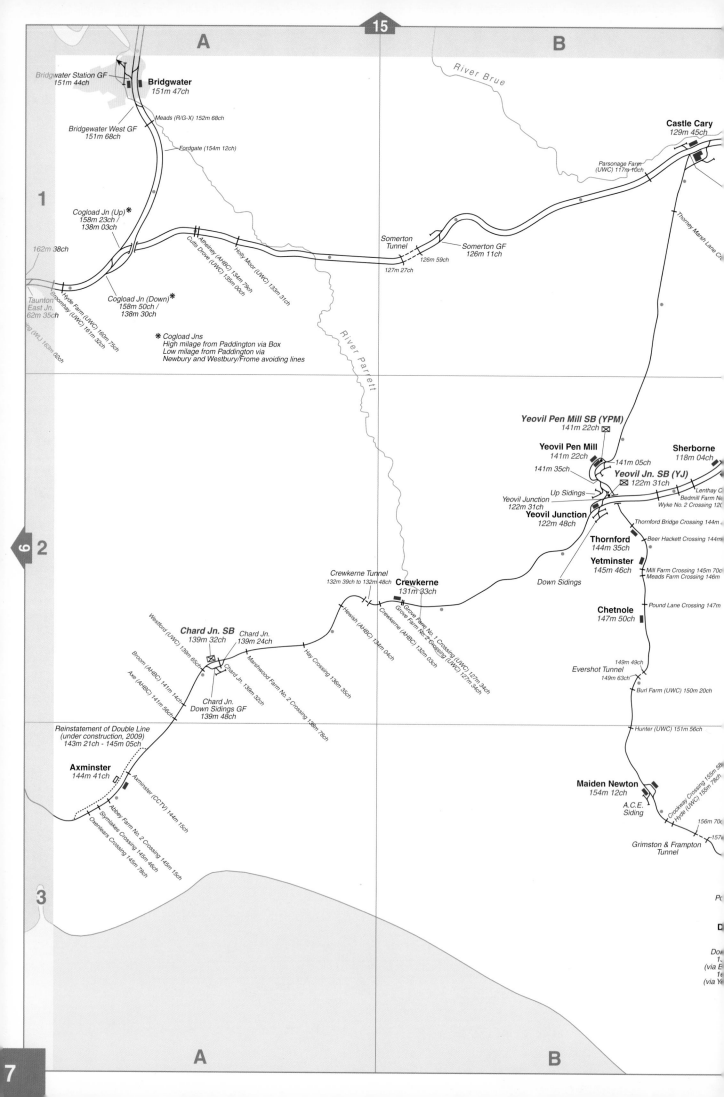

A   B

River Brue

Bridgwater Station GF
151m 44ch

Bridgwater
151m 47ch

Castle Cary
129m 45ch

Meads (R/G-X) 152m 68ch

Bridgewater West GF
151m 68ch

*Parsonage Farm
(UWC) 117m 10ch*

Fordgate (154m 12ch)

1

Cogload Jn (Up) ✱
158m 23ch
138m 03ch

*Somerton
Tunnel*

*Somerton GF
126m 11ch*

Thorney Marsh Lane Cr

162m 38ch

Athelney (AHBC) 134m 79ch

Cutts Drove (UWC) 134m 79ch

Holly Moor (UWC) 135m 00ch

126m 59ch

127m 27ch

*Taunton
East Jn.
162m 35ch*

Hyde Farm (UWC) 160m 75ch

Broomhay (UWC) 161m 32ch

Cogload Jn (Down) ✱
158m 50ch /
138m 30ch

(WL) 163m 02ch

✱ Cogload Jns
High milage from Paddington via Box
Low milage from Paddington via
Newbury and Westbury/Frome avoiding lines

River Parrett

Yeovil Pen Mill SB (YPM)
141m 22ch ✉

Yeovil Pen Mill
141m 22ch

Sherborne
118m 04ch

141m 05ch

141m 35ch

Yeovil Jn. SB (YJ)
✉ 122m 31ch

Up Sidings

Lenthay C

*Yeovil Junction
122m 31ch*

Bedmill Farm Ne

Wyke No. 2 Crossing 120

6

2

Yeovil Junction
122m 48ch

Thornford Bridge Crossing 144m

Beer Hackett Crossing 144m

Thornford
144m 35ch

*Crewkerne Tunnel
132m 39ch to 132m 48ch*

Crewkerne
131m 33ch

Down Sidings

Yetminster
145m 46ch

Mill Farm Crossing 145m 70c

Meads Farm Crossing 146m

Pound Lane Crossing 147m

Hewish (AHBC) 134m 04ch

Westford (UWC) 139m 66ch

Chard Jn. SB
139m 32ch

*Chard Jn.
139m 24ch*

Grove Farm No. 1 Crossing (UWC) 127m 34ch

Grove Farm No. 2 Crossing (UWC) 127m 34ch

Crewkerne (AHBC) 130m 03ch

Chetnole
147m 50ch

Broom (AHBC) 141m 14ch

Chard Jn. 139m 32ch

Marshwood Farm No. 2 Crossing 138m 78ch

Hay Crossing 136m 35ch

149m 49ch

Axe (AHBC) 141m 56ch

**Chard Jn.
Down Sidings GF
139m 48ch**

Evershot Tunnel
149m 63ch

Burl Farm (UWC) 150m 20ch

*Reinstatement of Double Line
(under construction, 2009)
143m 21ch - 145m 05ch*

Hunter (UWC) 151m 56ch

Axminster
144m 41ch

Axminster (CCTV) 144m 15ch

Maiden Newton
154m 12ch

Crockway Crossing 155m 58c

Hyde (UWC) 155m 78ch

*A.C.E.
Siding*

156m 70c

Abbey Farm No. 2 Crossing 145m 15ch

Slymlakes Crossing 145m 46ch

Oxenhears Crossing 145m 78ch

157

*Grimston & Frampton
Tunnel*

3

Pc

D

*Do
1,
(via E
1
(via Y*

A   B

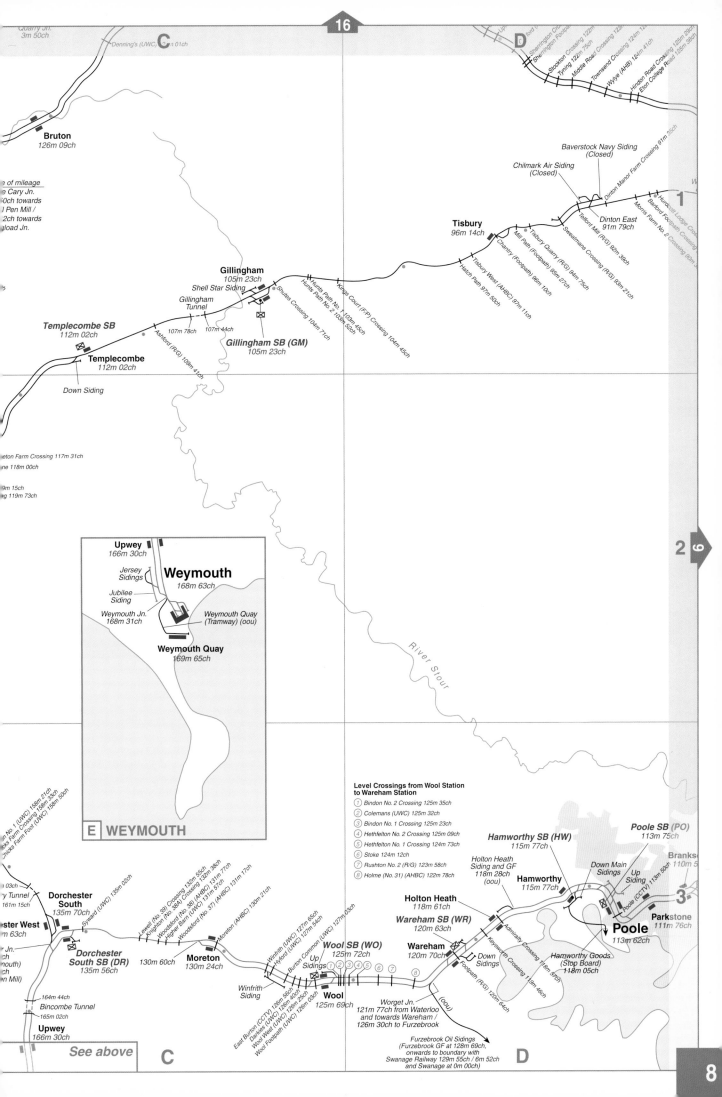

Quarry Jn.
3m 50ch

Denning's (UWC) 0m 01ch — C

Bruton
126m 09ch

e of mileage
e Cary Jn.
0ch towards
l Pen Mill /
2ch towards
load Jn.

Templecombe SB
112m 02ch

Templecombe
112m 02ch

Down Siding

Ashford (R/G) 109m 41ch

107m 78ch   107m 44ch

Gillingham Tunnel

Shell Star Siding

Gillingham
105m 23ch

Gillingham SB (GM)
105m 23ch

Shutes Crossing 104m 45ch

Hunts Path No. 2 103m 52ch
Hunts Path No. 1 103m 45ch

Kings Court (F-P) Crossing 104m 71ch

Tisbury
96m 14ch

Hatch Path 97m 50ch
Hatch Path 97m 11ch
Mill Path (Footpath) 96m 10ch
Chantry (Footpath) 95m 27ch
Tisbury West (AHBC) 97m 11ch
Tisbury Quarry (R/G) 94m 75ch
Sweatmans Crossing 93m 39ch
Mill Path (R/G) 93m 39ch

Tellont Mill (R/G) 92m 39ch
Dinton East
91m 79ch

Chilmark Air Siding
(Closed)

Baverstock Navy Siding
(Closed)

Dinton Manor Farm Crossing 91m 35ch

Hurleatt Lodge Cross
Barford Footpath Crossing
Morris Farm No. 2 Crossing 90m 3

1

Stockton Crossing 122m
Tyning 122m 75ch
Middle Road Crossing 122m
Townsend Crossing 124m 41ch
Wylye (AHB) 124m 41ch
Hindon Road Crossing 125m 29c
Eton College Road 125m 38c

D

Sherrington Cro
Sherrington Footpa

eton Farm Crossing 117m 31ch
ne 118m 00ch

9m 15ch
g 119m 73ch

Upwey
166m 30ch

Jersey Sidings

Jubilee Siding

Weymouth
168m 63ch

Weymouth Jn.
168m 31ch

Weymouth Quay
(Tramway) (oou)

Weymouth Quay
169m 65ch

E WEYMOUTH

2 6

River Stour

Level Crossings from Wool Station to Wareham Station

① Bindon No. 2 Crossing 125m 35ch
② Colemans (UWC) 125m 32ch
③ Bindon No. 1 Crossing 125m 23ch
④ Hethfelton No. 2 Crossing 125m 09ch
⑤ Hethfelton No. 1 Crossing 124m 73ch
⑥ Stoke 124m 12ch
⑦ Rushton No. 2 (R/G) 123m 58ch
⑧ Holme (No. 31) (AHBC) 122m 78ch

Poole SB (PO)
113m 75ch

Branks

Hamworthy SB (HW)
115m 77ch

Holton Heath
Siding and GF
118m 28ch
(oou)

Down Main
Sidings

Up
Siding

Hamworthy
115m 77ch

Poole (CCTV) 113m 50ch

3

Holton Heath
118m 61ch

Wareham SB (WR)
120m 63ch

Admiralty Crossing 118m 57ch

Keysworth Crossing 119m 46ch

Hamworthy Goods
(Stop Board)
118m 05ch

Poole
113m 62ch

Parkstone
111m 76ch

110m 5

No. 1 (UWC) 158m 21ch
ks Farm Crossing 158m 33ch
Chicks Farm Foot (UWC) 158m 50ch

03ch
ry Tunnel
161m 15ch

Dorchester
South
135m 70ch

ster West
63ch

Jn.
(mouth)
nouth)
n Mill)

Dorchester
South SB (DR)
135m 56ch

164m 44ch
Bincombe Tunnel
165m 02ch

Upwey
166m 30ch

See above

C

Syward (UWC) 135m 02ch

Lewell (No. 39) Crossing 132m 55ch
Knighton (No. 38A) Crossing 132m 38ch
Woodsford (No. 38) (AHBC) 131m 77ch
Higher Barn (UWC) 131m 57ch
Woodsford (No. 37) (AHBC) 131m 17ch

Moreton (AHBC) 130m 21ch

Moreton
130m 24ch

130m 60ch
Up
Sidings

Winfrith (UWC) 127m 65ch
Hyford (UWC) 127m 54ch
Burton Common (UWC) 127m 03ch

Winfrith
Siding

Wool SB (WO)
125m 72ch

① ② ③ ④ ⑤ ⑥ ⑦   ⑧

East Burton (CCTV) 126m 56ch
Darkies (UWC) 126m 40ch
Wool West (UWC) 126m 25ch
Wool Footpath (UWC) 126m 03ch

Wool
125m 69ch

Worget Jn.
121m 77ch from Waterloo
and towards Wareham /
126m 30ch to Furzebrook

Wareham
120m 70ch

Down
Sidings

Footpath (R/G) 120m 64ch

(oou)

Furzebrook Oil Sidings
(Furzebrook GF at 128m 69ch,
onwards to boundary with
Swanage Railway 129m 55ch / 6m 52ch
and Swanage at 0m 00ch)

D

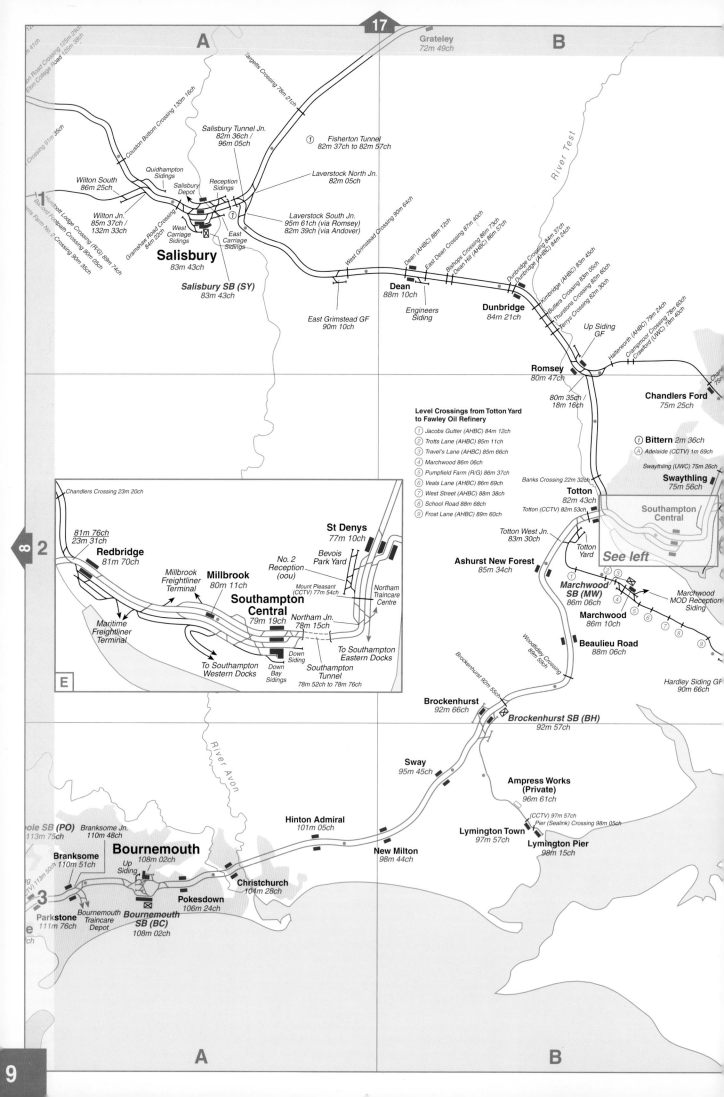

Grateley
72m 49ch

A

B

Couston Bottom Crossing 130m 16ch

Targetts Crossing 78m 21ch

Salisbury Tunnel Jn.
82m 36ch / 96m 05ch

① Fisherton Tunnel
82m 37ch to 82m 57ch

Laverstock North Jn.
82m 05ch

Quidhampton Sidings

Reception Sidings

Wilton South
86m 25ch

Salisbury Depot

Laverstock South Jn.
95m 61ch (via Romsey)
82m 39ch (via Andover)

Wilton Jn.
85m 37ch / 132m 33ch

West Carriage Sidings

East Carriage Sidings

Gramshaw Road Crossing 84m 22ch

①

West Grimstead Crossing 90m 64ch

Dean (AHBC) 88m 12ch

East Dean Crossing 87m 40ch

Bishops Crossing 86m 73ch

Dean Hill (AHBC) 86m 57ch

Dunbridge Crossing 84m 37ch

Dunbridge (AHBC) 84m 24ch

Kimbridge (AHBC) 83m 45ch

Butlers Crossing 83m 05ch

Thurstons Crossing 82m 60ch

Terrys Crossing 82m 30ch

Salisbury
83m 43ch

Salisbury SB (SY)
83m 43ch

East Grimstead GF
90m 10ch

Engineers Siding

Dean
88m 10ch

Dunbridge
84m 21ch

Up Siding GF

Romsey
80m 47ch

Halterworth (AHBC) 79m 24ch

Crampmoor Crossing 78m 60ch

Crawford (UWC) 78m 40ch

Chandlers Ford
75m 25ch

80m 35ch / 18m 16ch

Level Crossings from Totton Yard to Fawley Oil Refinery

① Jacobs Gutter (AHBC) 84m 12ch
② Trotts Lane (AHBC) 85m 11ch
③ Travel's Lane (AHBC) 85m 66ch
④ Marchwood 86m 06ch
⑤ Pumpfield Farm (R/G) 86m 37ch
⑥ Veals Lane (AHBC) 86m 69ch
⑦ West Street (AHBC) 88m 38ch
⑧ School Road 88m 68ch
⑨ Frost Lane (AHBC) 89m 60ch

① **Bittern** 2m 36ch
Ⓐ Adelaide (CCTV) 1m 69ch

Swaythling (UWC) 75m 26ch

Swaythling
75m 56ch

Banks Crossing 22m 32ch

Totton
82m 43ch

Totton (CCTV) 82m 53ch

Southampton Central

See left

Totton West Jn.
83m 30ch

Totton Yard

INSET (E):

Chandlers Crossing 23m 20ch

St Denys
77m 10ch

81m 76ch / 23m 31ch

Redbridge
81m 70ch

Millbrook Freightliner Terminal

Millbrook
80m 11ch

No. 2 Reception (oou)

Bevois Park Yard

Mount Pleasant (CCTV) 77m 54ch

Northam Traincare Centre

Maritime Freightliner Terminal

Southampton Central
79m 19ch

Northam Jn.
78m 15ch

To Southampton Western Docks

Down Siding

Down Bay Sidings

Southampton Tunnel
78m 52ch to 78m 76ch

To Southampton Eastern Docks

E

Ashurst New Forest
85m 34ch

Marchwood SB (MW)
86m 06ch

② ③

④

⑤ ⑥

Marchwood MOD Reception Siding

Marchwood
86m 10ch

⑦ ⑧

Beaulieu Road
88m 06ch

⑨

Hardley Siding GF
90m 66ch

Woodfidley Crossing 89m 55ch

Brockenhurst Crossing 92m 55ch

Brockenhurst
92m 66ch

Brockenhurst SB (BH)
92m 57ch

River Avon

River Test

Sway
95m 45ch

Ampress Works (Private)
96m 61ch

(CCTV) 97m 57ch
Pier (Sealink) Crossing 98m 05ch

Hinton Admiral
101m 05ch

Lymington Town
97m 57ch

Lymington Pier
98m 15ch

ole SB (PO)
113m 75ch

Branksome Jn.
110m 48ch

New Milton
98m 44ch

Bournemouth
108m 02ch

Branksome
110m 51ch

Up Siding

Christchurch
104m 28ch

Pokesdown
106m 24ch

Bournemouth Traincare Depot

Bournemouth SB (BC)
108m 02ch

Parkstone
111m 76ch

A

B

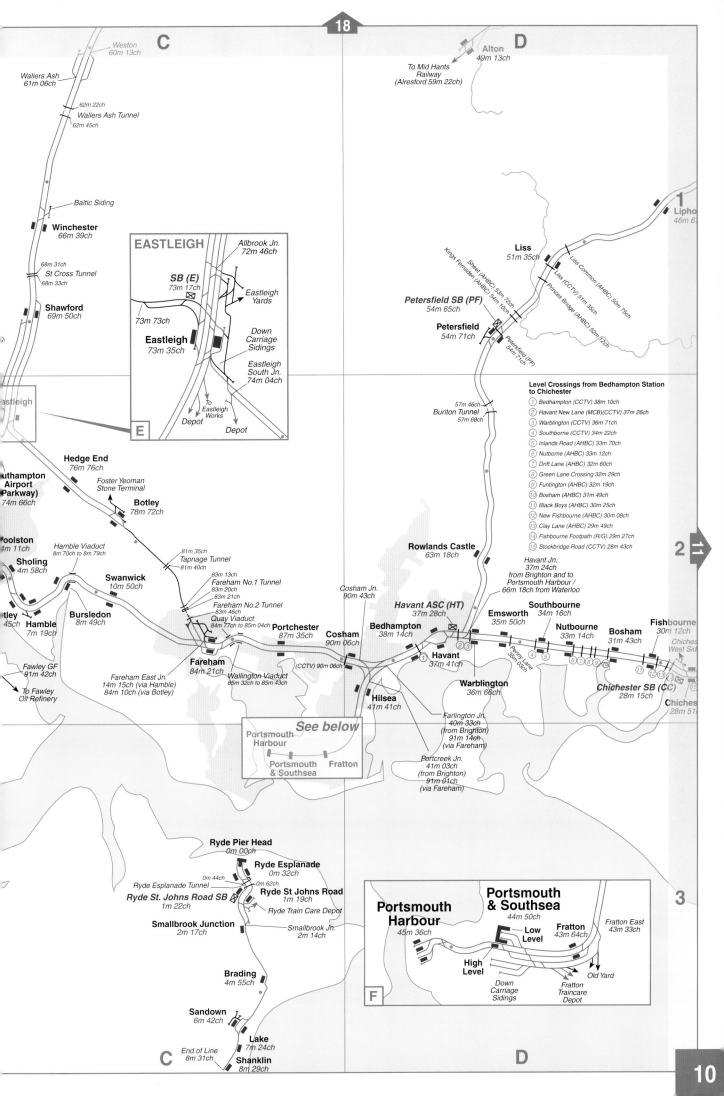

Weston
60m 13ch

Wallers Ash
61m 06ch

62m 22ch
Wallers Ash Tunnel
62m 45ch

Baltic Siding

Winchester
66m 39ch

68m 31ch
St Cross Tunnel
68m 33ch

Shawford
69m 50ch

C

EASTLEIGH

Allbrook Jn.
72m 46ch

SB (E)
73m 17ch

Eastleigh
Yards

73m 73ch

Eastleigh
73m 35ch

*Down
Carriage
Sidings*

*Eastleigh
South Jn.*
74m 04ch

*To
Eastleigh
Works*

Depot   *Depot*

E

astleigh

Hedge End
76m 76ch

Foster Yeoman
Stone Terminal

Botley
78m 72ch

uthampton
**Airport
(Parkway)**
74m 66ch

oolston
m 11ch

Sholing
4m 58ch

Hamble Viaduct
8m 70ch to 8m 79ch

81m 35ch
Tapnage Tunnel
81m 40ch

Swanwick
10m 50ch

83m 13ch
Fareham No.1 Tunnel
83m 20ch
83m 21ch
Fareham No.2 Tunnel
83m 46ch

tley   **Hamble**
45ch   7m 19ch

Bursledon
8m 49ch

Quay Viaduct
84m 77ch to 85m 04ch

Portchester
87m 35ch

Fareham
84m 21ch

Fareham East Jn.
14m 15ch (via Hamble)
84m 10ch (via Botley)

Wallington Viaduct
85m 32ch to 85m 43ch

Fawley GF
91m 42ch

To Fawley
Oil Refinery

Cosham Jn.
90m 43ch

Cosham
90m 06ch

(CCTV) 90m 06ch

Hilsea
41m 41ch

See below

Portsmouth
Harbour

Portsmouth
& Southsea   Fratton

Farlington Jn.
40m 33ch
(from Brighton)
91m 14ch
(via Fareham)

Portcreek Jn.
41m 03ch
(from Brighton)
91m 01ch
(via Fareham)

D

Alton
49m 13ch

To Mid Hants
Railway
(Alresford 59m 22ch)

1

Lipho
46m 6

Liss
51m 35ch

Liss Common (AHBC) 50m 75ch

Liss (CCTV) 51m 35ch

Princes Bridge (AHBC) 50m 12ch

Sheet (AHBC) 53m 72ch

Kings Fernsden (AHBC) 54m 10ch

Petersfield SB (PF)
54m 65ch

Petersfield
54m 71ch

Petersfield
(PF)
54m 71ch

57m 46ch
Buriton Tunnel
57m 68ch

**Level Crossings from Bedhampton Station
to Chichester**

1. Bedhampton (CCTV) 38m 10ch
2. Havant New Lane (MCB)(CCTV) 37m 26ch
3. Warblington (CCTV) 36m 71ch
4. Southborne (CCTV) 34m 22ch
5. Inlands Road (AHBC) 33m 70ch
6. Nutborne (AHBC) 33m 12ch
7. Drift Lane (AHBC) 32m 60ch
8. Green Lane Crossing 32m 29ch
9. Funtington (AHBC) 32m 19ch
10. Bosham (AHBC) 31m 49ch
11. Black Boys (AHBC) 30m 25ch
12. New Fishbourne (AHBC) 30m 08ch
13. Clay Lane (AHBC) 29m 49ch
14. Fishbourne Footpath (R/G) 29m 27ch
15. Stockbridge Road (CCTV) 28m 43ch

Rowlands Castle
63m 18ch

Havant Jn.
37m 24ch
from Brighton and to
Portsmouth Harbour /
66m 18ch from Waterloo

Havant ASC (HT)
37m 28ch

Emsworth
35m 50ch

Southbourne
34m 16ch

Nutbourne
33m 14ch

Bosham
31m 43ch

Fishbourne
30m 12ch

Chiches
West Sid

Bedhampton
38m 14ch

Havant
37m 41ch

1 2 3

4 5

Penny Lane
35m 03ch

6 7 8 9 10

11 12 13 14

Chichester SB (CC)
28m 15ch

Chiches
28m 51c

15

Warblington
36m 66ch

2

3

Ryde Pier Head
0m 00ch

Ryde Esplanade
0m 32ch

Ryde Esplanade Tunnel
0m 44ch

0m 62ch

Ryde St Johns Road
1m 19ch

Ryde St. Johns Road SB
1m 22ch

Ryde Train Care Depot

Smallbrook Junction
2m 17ch

Smallbrook Jn.
2m 14ch

**Portsmouth
Harbour**
45m 36ch

**Portsmouth
& Southsea**
44m 50ch

Low
Level

Fratton
43m 64ch

Fratton East
43m 33ch

**High
Level**

*Down
Carriage
Sidings*

Fratton
Traincare
Depot

Old Yard

F

Brading
4m 55ch

Sandown
6m 42ch

Lake
7m 24ch

End of Line
8m 31ch

Shanklin
8m 29ch

C   D

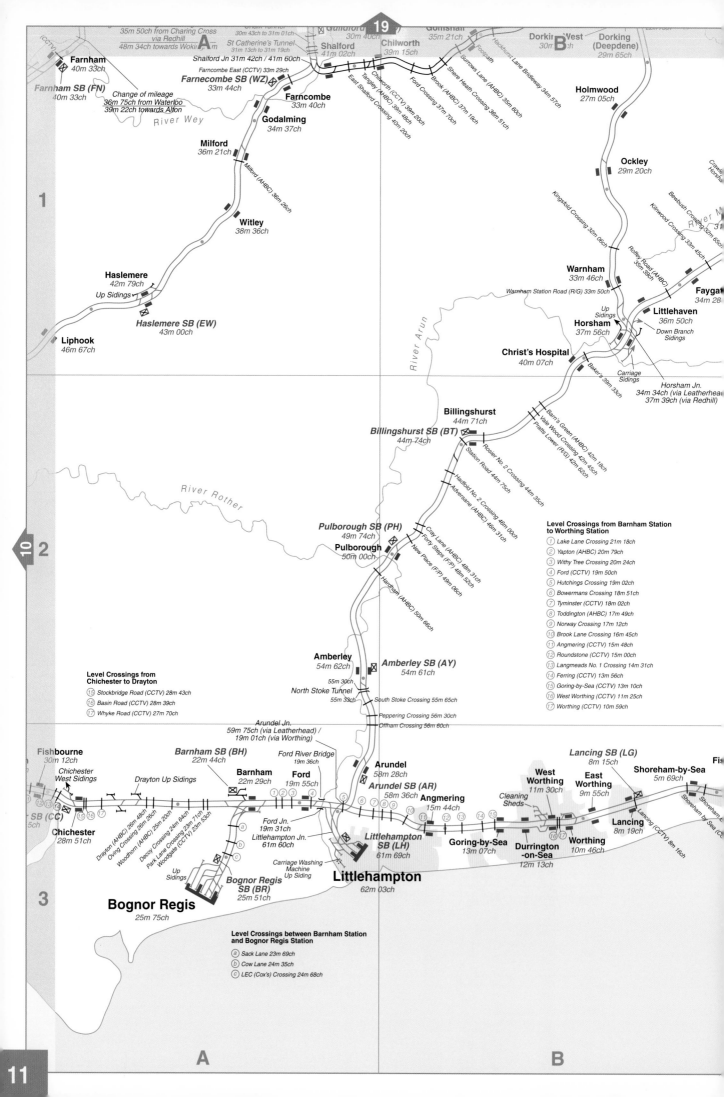

Farnham
40m 33ch

Farnham SB (FN)
40m 33ch

35m 50ch from Charing Cross
via Redhill
48m 34ch towards Woking

Chalk Tunnel
30m 43ch to 31m 01ch
St Catherine's Tunnel
31m 13ch to 31m 19ch

Shalford Jn 31m 42ch / 41m 60ch

Change of mileage
36m 75ch from Waterloo
39m 22ch towards Alton

Farncombe East (CCTV) 33m 29ch

Farnecombe SB (WZ)
33m 44ch

Farncombe
33m 40ch

Godalming
34m 37ch

River Wey

Milford
36m 21ch

Milford (AHBC) 36m 26ch

Witley
38m 36ch

Haslemere
42m 79ch

Up Sidings

Haslemere SB (EW)
43m 00ch

Liphook
46m 67ch

Guildford
30m 40ch

Shalford
41m 02ch

Chilworth
39m 15ch

Gomshall
35m 21ch

Chilworth (CCTV) 39m 20ch
Tangley (AHBC) 39m 48ch
East Shalford Crossing 40m 20ch

Ford Crossing 38m 20ch

Brook (AHBC) 37m 70ch

Shere Heath Crossing 36m 51ch

Burrows Lane (AHBC) 35m 60ch

Footpath

Hackhurst Lane Bridleway 34m 57ch

Dorking West
30m

Dorking (Deepdene)
29m 65ch

Holmwood
27m 05ch

Ockley
29m 20ch

Crawl
Horsha

Bewbush Crossing 33m 65ch
Kilnwood Crossing 33m 45ch

Kingsfold Crossing 32m 06ch

Roffey Road (AHBC) 35m 39ch

River M

Warnham
33m 46ch

Warnham Station Road (R/G) 33m 50ch

Up Sidings

Horsham
37m 56ch

Faygat
34m 28

Littlehaven
36m 50ch

Down Branch Sidings

Carriage Sidings

Horsham Jn.
34m 34ch (via Leatherhea
37m 39ch (via Redhill)

Baker's 39m 33ch

Christ's Hospital
40m 07ch

River Arun

Billingshurst
44m 71ch

Billingshurst SB (BT)
44m 74ch

Barn's Green (AHBC) 42m 18ch

Vale Wood Crossing 42m 45ch

Pratts Lower (R/G) 42m 62ch

Rosier No. 2 Crossing 44m 35ch

Station Road 44m 75ch

Hadfold No. 2 Crossing 46m 00ch

Adversane (AHBC) 46m 31ch

River Rother

Pulborough SB (PH)
49m 74ch

Pulborough
50m 00ch

Cray Lane (AHBC) 48m 31ch

Forty Steps (F/P) 48m 52ch

New Place (F/P) 49m 06ch

Hardham (AHBC) 50m 66ch

Level Crossings from Barnham Station to Worthing Station

1. Lake Lane Crossing 21m 18ch
2. Yapton (AHBC) 20m 79ch
3. Withy Tree Crossing 20m 24ch
4. Ford (CCTV) 19m 50ch
5. Hutchings Crossing 19m 02ch
6. Bowermans Crossing 18m 51ch
7. Tyminster (CCTV) 18m 02ch
8. Toddington (AHBC) 17m 49ch
9. Norway Crossing 17m 12ch
10. Brook Lane Crossing 16m 45ch
11. Angmering (CCTV) 15m 48ch
12. Roundstone (CCTV) 15m 00ch
13. Langmeads No. 1 Crossing 14m 31ch
14. Ferring (CCTV) 13m 56ch
15. Goring-by-Sea (CCTV) 13m 10ch
16. West Worthing (CCTV) 11m 25ch
17. Worthing (CCTV) 10m 59ch

Amberley
54m 62ch

Amberley SB (AY)
54m 61ch

55m 30ch

North Stoke Tunnel
55m 33ch

South Stoke Crossing 55m 65ch

Peppering Crossing 56m 30ch

Offham Crossing 56m 60ch

Level Crossings from Chichester to Drayton

15. Stockbridge Road (CCTV) 28m 43ch
16. Basin Road (CCTV) 28m 39ch
17. Whyke Road (CCTV) 27m 70ch

Arundel Jn.
59m 75ch (via Leatherhead) /
19m 01ch (via Worthing)

Fishbourne
30m 12ch

Chichester West Sidings

Drayton Up Sidings

Barnham SB (BH)
22m 44ch

Ford River Bridge
19m 36ch

Barnham
22m 29ch

Ford
19m 55ch

Drayton (AHBC) 26m 48ch
Oving Crossing 26m 26ch
Woodhorn (AHBC) 25m 20ch
Decoy Crossing 24m 64ch
Park Lane Crossing 23m 71ch
Woodgate (CCTV) 23m 53ch

① ② ③ ④

Ⓐ
Ⓑ
Ⓒ

SB (CC)
5ch

Chichester
28m 51ch

15 16 17

12 15 16
17

Arundel
19m 05ch

Arundel SB (AR)
58m 36ch

⑤

⑥ ⑦ ⑧ ⑨

⑩

Angmering
15m 44ch

⑪ ⑫ ⑬

⑭ ⑮

West Worthing
11m 30ch

East Worthing
9m 55ch

Cleaning Sheds

Lancing SB (LG)
8m 15ch

Shoreham-by-Sea
5m 69ch

Fi

Shoreham
Shoreham
Shoreham-by-Sea (Co

Lancing (CCTV) 8m 16ch

Lancing
8m 19ch

⑯ ⑰

Worthing
10m 46ch

Goring-by-Sea
13m 07ch

Durrington-on-Sea
12m 13ch

Ford Jn.
19m 31ch
Littlehampton Jn.
61m 60ch

Littlehampton SB (LH)
61m 69ch

Carriage Washing Machine Up Siding

Up Sidings

Bognor Regis SB (BR)
25m 51ch

Bognor Regis
25m 75ch

Littlehampton
62m 03ch

Level Crossings between Barnham Station and Bognor Regis Station

Ⓐ Sack Lane 23m 69ch
Ⓑ Cow Lane 24m 35ch
Ⓒ LEC (Cox's) Crossing 24m 68ch

A

B

10
2

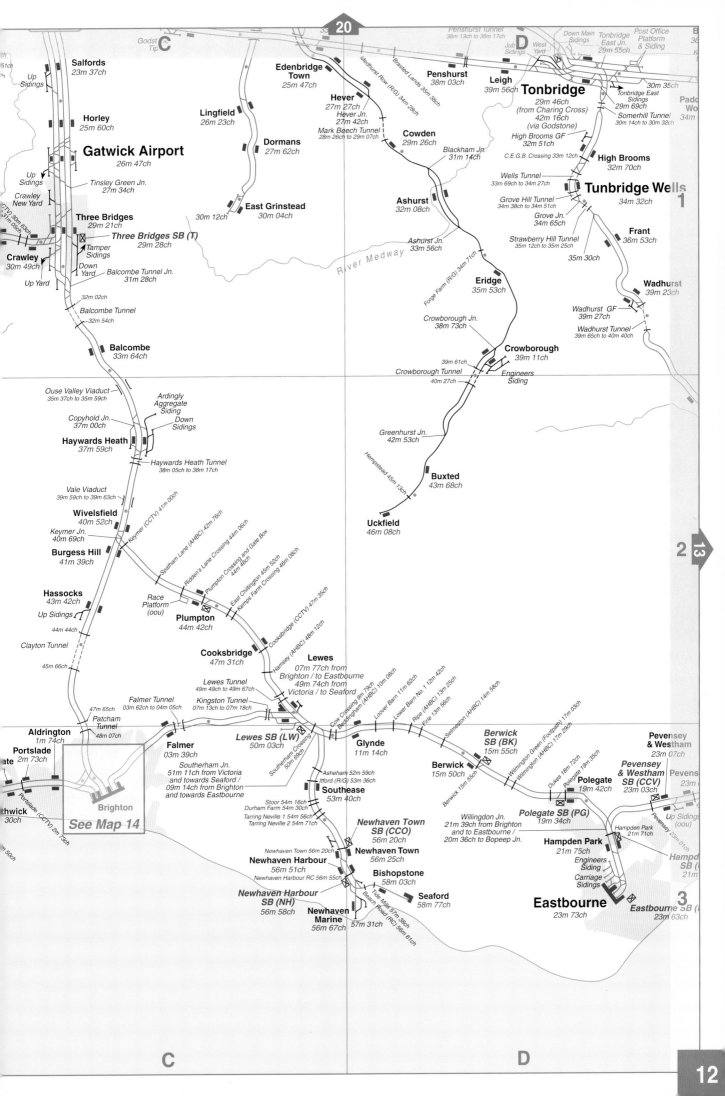

Godst Tip **C**

Salfords
23m 37ch

Up Sidings

Horley
25m 60ch

Gatwick Airport
26m 47ch

Up Sidings

Crawley
New Yard

Tinsley Green Jn.
27m 34ch

Three Bridges
29m 21ch

Three Bridges SB (T)
29m 28ch

Tamper
Sidings

Crawley
30m 49ch

Down
Yard

Balcombe Tunnel Jn.
31m 28ch

Up Yard

32m 02ch

Balcombe Tunnel
32m 54ch

Balcombe
33m 64ch

Ouse Valley Viaduct
35m 37ch to 35m 59ch

Copyhold Jn.
37m 00ch

Ardingly
Aggregate
Siding

Down
Sidings

Haywards Heath
37m 59ch

Haywards Heath Tunnel
38m 05ch to 38m 17ch

Vale Viaduct
39m 59ch to 39m 63ch

Wivelsfield
40m 52ch

Keymer Jn.
40m 69ch

Keymer (CCTV) 41m 00ch

Burgess Hill
41m 39ch

Hassocks
43m 42ch

Up Sidings

44m 44ch

Clayton Tunnel

45m 66ch

Spatham Lane (AHBC) 42m 76ch

Ridden's Lane Crossing 44m 06ch

Plumpton Crossing and Gate Box
44m 46ch

East Chiltington 45m 52ch

Kemps Farm Crossing 46m 08ch

Race
Platform
(oou)

Plumpton
44m 42ch

Cooksbridge
47m 31ch

Cooksbridge (CCTV) 47m 35ch

Hamsey (AHBC) 48m 12ch

Lewes
07m 77ch from
Brighton / to Eastbourne
49m 74ch from
Victoria / to Seaford

Lewes Tunnel
49m 49ch to 49m 67ch

Kingston Tunnel
07m 13ch to 07m 18ch

Aldrington
1m 74ch

Portslade
2m 73ch

Falmer Tunnel
03m 62ch to 04m 05ch

Patcham
Tunnel
48m 07ch

Falmer
03m 39ch

Lewes SB (LW)
50m 03ch

Southerham Crossing
50m 69ch

Southerham Jn.
51m 11ch from Victoria
and towards Seaford /
09m 14ch from Brighton
and towards Eastbourne

Brighton
See Map 14

Portslade (CCTV) 2m 73ch

hwick

Asheham 52m 59ch
Itford (R/G) 53m 36ch

Southease
53m 40ch

Stoor 54m 16ch
Durham Farm 54m 30ch
Tarring Neville 1 54m 56ch
Tarring Neville 2 54m 71ch

Newhaven Town
SB (CCO)
56m 20ch

Newhaven Town 56m 20ch

Newhaven Town
56m 25ch

Newhaven Harbour
56m 51ch

Newhaven Harbour RC 56m 55ch

Newhaven Harbour
SB (NH)
56m 58ch

Bishopstone
58m 03ch

Tide Mills 57m 38ch

Beach Road (RC) 56m 61ch

Newhaven
Marine
56m 67ch

57m 31ch

Seaford
58m 77ch

Glynde
11m 14ch

Cow Crossing 9m 79ch
Beddingham (AHBC) 10m 08ch
Loover Barn 11m 62ch
Lower Barn No. 1 12m 42ch
Ripe (AHBC) 13m 25ch
Fitle 13m 56ch

Selmeston (AHBC) 14m 58ch

Berwick
SB (BK)
15m 55ch

Berwick
15m 50ch

Berwick 15m 55ch

Wilmington Green (Footpath) 17m 03ch
Wilmington (AHBC) 17m 29ch

Pevensey
& Westham
23m 07ch

Pevensey & Westham
SB (CCV)
23m 03ch

Pevensey

Pevensey 23m 07ch
23m

Polegate
19m 42ch

Dukes 18m 72ch
Polegate 19m 35ch

Polegate SB (PG)
19m 34ch

Willingdon Jn.
21m 39ch from Brighton
and to Eastbourne /
20m 36ch to Bopeep Jn.

Hampden Park
21m 75ch

Hampden Park 21m 71ch

Engineers
Siding

Carriage
Sidings

Up Sidings
(oou)

Hampd
SB
21m

Eastbourne
23m 73ch

Eastbourne SB (
23m 63ch

Penshurst Tunnel
38m 13ch to 38m 17ch

Down Main
Sidings

Tonbridge
East
29m 55ch

Post Office
Platform
& Siding

D

Jub
Sidings

West
Yard

Medhurst Row (R/G) 34m 28ch

Brasted Lands 35m 36ch

Edenbridge
Town
25m 47ch

Hever
27m 27ch
Hever Jn.
27m 42ch

Mark Beech Tunnel
28m 26ch to 29m 07ch

Penshurst
38m 03ch

Leigh
39m 56ch

Tonbridge
29m 46ch
(from Charing Cross)
30m 14ch
(via Godstone)

30m 35ch

Tonbridge East
Sidings
29m 69ch

Somerhill Tunnel
30m 14ch to 30m 32ch

Lingfield
26m 23ch

Dormans
27m 62ch

East Grinstead
30m 04ch

30m 12ch

Cowden
29m 26ch

Blackham Jn.
31m 14ch

Ashurst
32m 08ch

Ashurst Jn.
33m 56ch

River Medway

Forge Farm (R/G) 34m 71ch

Eridge
35m 53ch

High Brooms GF
32m 51ch

C.E.G.B. Crossing 33m 12ch

High Brooms
32m 70ch

Wells Tunnel
33m 69ch to 34m 27ch

Grove Hill Tunnel
34m 38ch to 34m 51ch

Tunbridge Wells
34m 32ch

Grove Jn.
34m 65ch

Strawberry Hill Tunnel
35m 12ch to 35m 25ch

35m 30ch

Frant
36m 53ch

Wadhurst
39m 23ch

Wadhurst GF
39m 27ch

Wadhurst Tunnel
39m 65ch to 40m 40ch

Crowborough Jn.
38m 73ch

Crowborough
39m 11ch

39m 61ch

Engineers
Siding

Crowborough Tunnel
40m 27ch

Greenhurst Jn.
42m 53ch

Hempstead 45m 13ch

Buxted
43m 68ch

Uckfield
46m 08ch

C **D**

A

East Farleigh
42m 75ch

Wateringbur SB (WB)
39m 72ch

Yalding
38m 19ch

37m 34ch

East Peckham Engineers Tip Siding

Beltring
36m 50ch

Keylands Sidings

Yalding (ABCL) 38m 15ch
Wards 37m 73ch
Ballast Hole 37m 45ch
Stoneham 37m 27ch
Beltring (AHBC) 36m 52ch

30m 35ch

Paddock Wood
34m 67ch

Engineers Siding

Old Hay 35m 51ch

Marden
39m 31ch

Staplehurst
41m 70ch

(a) Wagon Lane (AHBC) 35m 60ch
(b) Swatlands (AHBC) 35m 29ch

Cranmore Loop

Headcorn
45m 20ch

Fishers (Footpath) 42m 09ch

Church (Footpath) 44m 56ch

New Bridge Lane (Footpath) 46m 00ch
East End 46m 11ch

Lenham SR 77.2

B

Charing
53m 11ch

Sandway Tunnel 74.18km to 74.35km

Lenham Crossover 75.59km to 75.88km

Lenham Loops

77.09km

Charing Crossover 79.38km

Hothfield Sidings

Leacon Lane Tunnel 82.45km to 82.57km

Wye Cross

Spring Gro

Ashford IECC (AD) (NK)
56m 21ch

Ashford West Jn. 88.31km
88.55km

Pluckley
50m 35ch

Chart Crossing 54m 00ch

Chart Leacon Repair Shop & Inspection Shed

Ashford International

Ashfield Jn. 55m 54ch (via Tonbridge) / 58m 61ch (via Maidstone)

Hastings Line Jn. 56m 20ch

Newtown Sidings
56m 09ch

1

e Wells
2ch

nt 53ch

Wadhurst 39m 23ch

Stonegate
43m 66ch

Crowhurst Bridge (AHBC) 45m 36ch

Etchingham
47m 34ch

Etchingham (CCTV) 47m 40ch

Down Siding

Robertsbridge
49m 47ch

Robertsbridge 49m 53ch

Robertsbridge SB (RB)
49m 54ch

Mountfield Tunnel 51m 46ch to 51m 70ch

Riverhall (CCTV) 52m 36ch
Battle Road (AHBC) 52m 52ch

Mountfield Sidings GF 51m 78ch

Mountfield Sidings

Battle
55m 46ch

Marley Lane (CCTV) 55m 31ch

Coopers & Farmers (AHBC) 76m 47ch
Haystacks 77m 05ch
Snailham (Accom) 76m 59ch
Coopers (UWC) 76m 21ch

Merrick No. 3 (Accom) 75m 71ch
Merrick No. 2 (Accom) 75m 21ch
Mail No. 2 (Accom) 73m 73ch

Doleham
77m 43ch

Doleham 77m 60ch

Crowhurst
57m 50ch

Ore GF 81m 46ch

Up Sidings

Three Oaks
78m 65ch

Ore Tunnel 80m 26ch to 81m 10ch
81m 28ch

Hastings SB (EDL)
82m 24ch

Bopeep Tunnel 60m 71ch to 61m 51ch

Park Sidings

Ore
81m 42ch

Mount Pleasant Tunnel 81m 50ch to 81m 60ch

Rye
71m 36ch

Rye SB (RY)
71m 34ch

Winchelsea
73m 22ch

Winchelsea (AOCL) 73m 16ch

Warehorne (AHBC) 62m 60ch
Kenardington (AHBC) 63m 73ch
Appledore (AHBC) 64m 45ch

Ham Street
61m 51ch

Appledore
64m 50ch
64m 53ch

Ashleys 65m 03ch
Snargate 65m 73ch
Grove Lane (OPEN) 66m 30ch
Bowdell (OPEN) 66m 50ch
King Street (AOCL) 66m 71ch
Brooklands (OPEN) 67m 20ch
Boarmans (OPEN) 67m 45ch
Tillery (OPEN) 67m 59ch
Fielders (OPEN) 67m 7
Mountain (OPEN)

Beckett's (AHBC) 66m 47ch

Coldharbour

Barts (Accom) 68m 77ch

Cooks No. 1 (Accom) 69m 29ch
Bakers (Accom) 69m 33ch
Star (AHBC) 69m 40ch
Pear Tree (Accom) 69m 77ch
East Guldeford (AHBC) 70m 19ch
Cookes (Accom) 70m 36ch
Grove Road (CCTV) 71m 24ch
Ferry Road (CCTV) 71m 46ch

Midl

2

◄12

Hastings
Change of mileage 62m 33ch (from Charing Cross via Battle) / 82m 34ch (from Charing Cross via Rye)
Hastings Tunnel 61m 59ch to 62m 15ch

West St. Leonard's
60m 59ch

Bexhill GF 29m 77ch

Carriage Cleaning & Stabling Depot

Bexhill SB (CCW)
29m 61ch

Cooden Beach
27m 53ch

Collington
29m 04ch

Bexhill
29m 69ch

St. Leonards Warrior Square
61m 55ch

Bopeep Jn. SB (BJ)
32m 72ch

Bopeep Jn. 60m 69ch (via Tunbridge Wells) / 32m 76ch (via Willingdon Jn.)

Pevensey & Westham
23m 07ch

Havensmouth 26m 00ch

nsey stham (CV) 03ch

Pevensey Bay
23m 68ch

Pevensey Sluice (AHBC) 26m 56ch

Normans Bay
25m 77ch

Wallsend 26m 73ch

Up Sidings (oou)

Pevensey 23m 01ch

3

Hampden Park SB (CDB)
21m 71ch

stbourne SB (EB)
23m 63ch

A

B

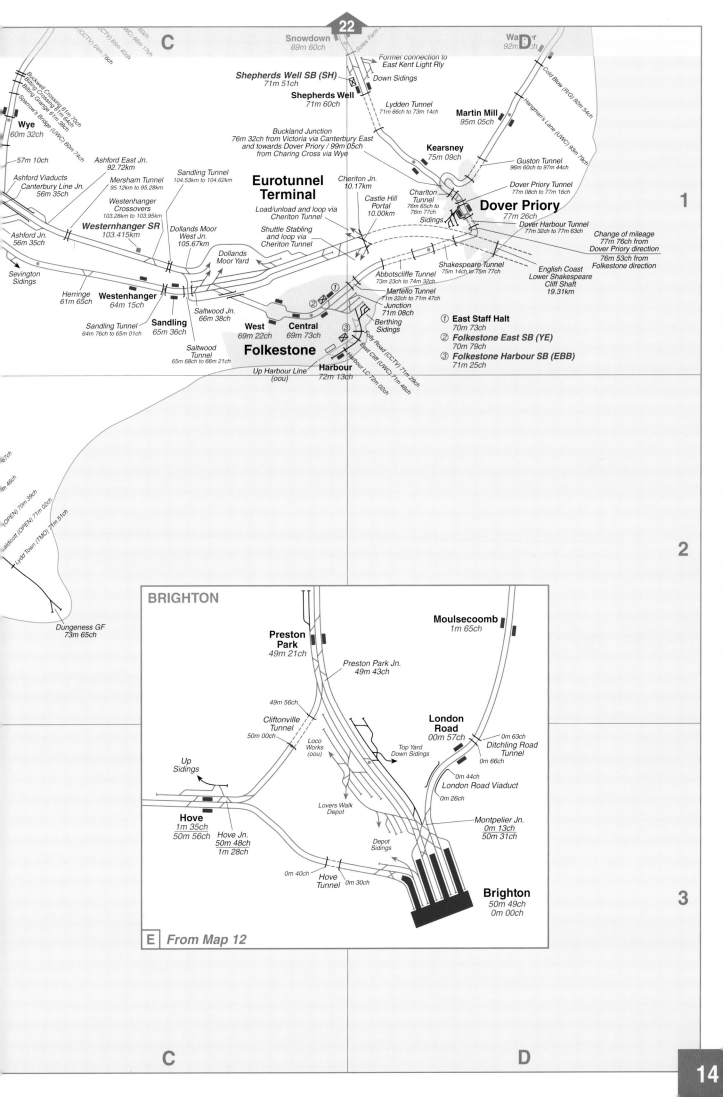

C

Snowdown
69m 60ch

Wa**D**or
92m ?ch

Buckwell Crossing 61m 70ch
Billing Crossing 61m 64ch
Billing Grange 61m 39ch
Sparrow's Bridge (UWC) 60m 74ch

(CCTV) 64m 76ch
(UWC) 66m 17ch
60ch

Shepherds Well SB (SH)
71m 51ch

Former connection to
East Kent Light Rly

Cold Blow (R/G) 92m 54ch

Wye
60m 32ch

Shepherds Well
71m 60ch

Down Sidings

Hangman's Lane (UWC) 93m 79ch

Martin Mill
95m 05ch

Lydden Tunnel
71m 66ch to 73m 14ch

~57m 10ch

Buckland Junction
76m 32ch from Victoria via Canterbury East
and towards Dover Priory / 99m 05ch
from Charing Cross via Wye

Kearsney
75m 09ch

Guston Tunnel
96m 60ch to 97m 44ch

Ashford East Jn.
92.72km

Mersham Tunnel
95.12km to 95.28km

Sandling Tunnel
104.53km to 104.62km

Cheriton Jn.
10.17km

Eurotunnel
Terminal

Charlton
Tunnel
76m 65ch to
76m 77ch

Dover Priory Tunnel
77m 08ch to 77m 16ch

Ashford Viaducts
Canterbury Line Jn.
56m 35ch

Westenhanger
Crossovers
103.28km to 103.95km

Load/unload and loop via
Cheriton Tunnel

Castle Hill
Portal
10.00km

Dover Priory
77m 26ch

Westernhanger SR
103.415km

Dollands Moor
West Jn.
105.67km

Shuttle Stabling
and loop via
Cheriton Tunnel

Sidings

Dover Harbour Tunnel
77m 32ch to 77m 63ch

Change of mileage
77m 76ch from
Dover Priory direction

Ashford Jn.
56m 35ch

Dollands
Moor Yard

76m 53ch from
Folkestone direction

Shakespeare Tunnel
75m 14ch to 75m 77ch

English Coast
Lower Shakespeare
Cliff Shaft
19.31km

Sevington
Sidings

Abbotscliffe Tunnel
73m 23ch to 74m 32ch

① *Martello Tunnel*
71m 22ch to 71m 47ch

② *Junction*
71m 08ch

Herringe
61m 65ch

Westenhanger
64m 15ch

Saltwood Jn.
66m 38ch

Berthing
Sidings

① **East Staff Halt**
70m 73ch

Sandling Tunnel
64m 76ch to 65m 01ch

Sandling
65m 36ch

West
69m 22ch

Central
69m 73ch

③ *Folly Road (CCTV) 71m 29ch*

② *Folkestone East SB (YE)*
70m 79ch

③ *Folkestone Harbour SB (EBB)*
71m 25ch

Saltwood
Tunnel
65m 68ch to 66m 21ch

Folkestone

East Cliff (UWC) 71m 46ch

Up Harbour Line (oou)

Harbour
72m 13ch

Harbour LC 72m 02ch

67ch
m 46ch
(OPEN) 70m 39ch
aldicott (OPEN) 71m 02ch
Lydd Town (TMO) 71m 51ch

2

Dungeness GF
73m 65ch

BRIGHTON

Moulsecoomb
1m 65ch

Preston
Park
49m 21ch

Preston Park Jn.
49m 43ch

49m 56ch

Cliftonville
Tunnel

50m 00ch

London
Road
00m 57ch

0m 63ch

Ditchling Road
Tunnel

Loco
Works
(oou)

Top Yard
Down Sidings

0m 66ch

0m 44ch

Up
Sidings

Lovers Walk
Depot

London Road Viaduct

0m 26ch

Hove
1m 35ch
50m 56ch

Hove Jn.
50m 48ch
1m 28ch

Depot
Sidings

Montpelier Jn.
0m 13ch
50m 31ch

0m 40ch

Hove
Tunnel

0m 30ch

Brighton
50m 49ch
0m 00ch

E | *From Map 12*

C

D

1

3

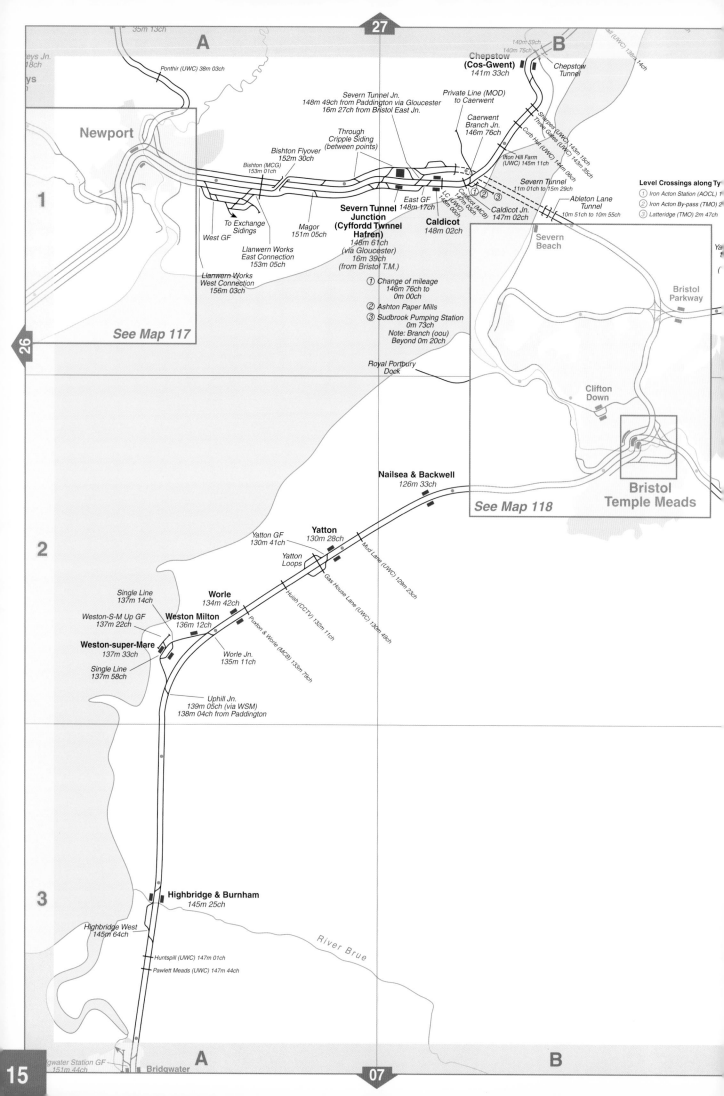

A   B

Ponthir (UWC) 38m 03ch

35m 13ch

eys Jn.
18ch

ys

Newport

140m 59ch
140m 75ch

**Chepstow
(Cos-Gwent)**
141m 33ch

Chepstow
Tunnel

(UWC) 139m 14ch

Severn Tunnel Jn.
148m 49ch from Paddington via Gloucester
16m 27ch from Bristol East Jn.

Private Line (MOD)
to Caerwent

Through
Cripple Siding
(between points)

Bishton Flyover
152m 30ch

Bishton (MCG)
153m 01ch

Caerwent
Branch Jn.
146m 76ch

Sharpes (UWC) 143m 15ch
Three Gates (UWC) 143m 35ch
Curtis Hill (UWC) 144m 06ch

Ifton Hill Farm
(UWC) 145m 11ch

To Exchange
Sidings

West GF

East GF
148m 17ch

LC (UWC)
148m 00ch

Caldicot (MCB)
147m 03ch

Caldicot Jn.
147m 02ch

Severn Tunnel
11m 01ch to 15m 29ch

Ableton Lane
Tunnel
10m 51ch to 10m 55ch

**Severn Tunnel
Junction
(Cyffordd Twnnel
Hafren)**
148m 61ch
(via Gloucester)
16m 39ch
(from Bristol T.M.)

Caldicot
148m 02ch

Magor
151m 05ch

Llanwern Works
East Connection
153m 05ch

Llanwern Works
West Connection
156m 03ch

See Map 117

① Change of mileage
146m 76ch to
0m 00ch
② Ashton Paper Mills
③ Sudbrook Pumping Station
0m 73ch
Note: Branch (oou)
Beyond 0m 20ch

Royal Portbury
Dock

Level Crossings along Ty
① Iron Acton Station (AOCL)
② Iron Acton By-pass (TMO) 2
③ Latteridge (TMO) 2m 47ch

Severn
Beach

Bristol
Parkway

See Map 118

**Bristol
Temple Meads**

Clifton
Down

Ya

26

Nailsea & Backwell
126m 33ch

Yatton GF
130m 41ch

Yatton
130m 28ch

Yatton
Loops

Mud Lane (UWC) 129m 23ch

Gas House Lane (UWC) 130m 49ch

2

Single Line
137m 14ch

Weston-S-M Up GF
137m 22ch

Worle
134m 42ch

Weston Milton
136m 12ch

Hush (CCTV) 132m 11ch

Puxton & Worle (MCB) 133m 79ch

Weston-super-Mare
137m 33ch

Single Line
137m 58ch

Worle Jn.
135m 11ch

Uphill Jn.
139m 05ch (via WSM)
138m 04ch from Paddington

3

Highbridge & Burnham
145m 25ch

Highbridge West
145m 64ch

River Brue

Huntspill (UWC) 147m 01ch
Pawlett Meads (UWC) 147m 44ch

A   B

gwater Station GF
151m 44ch   **Bridgwater**

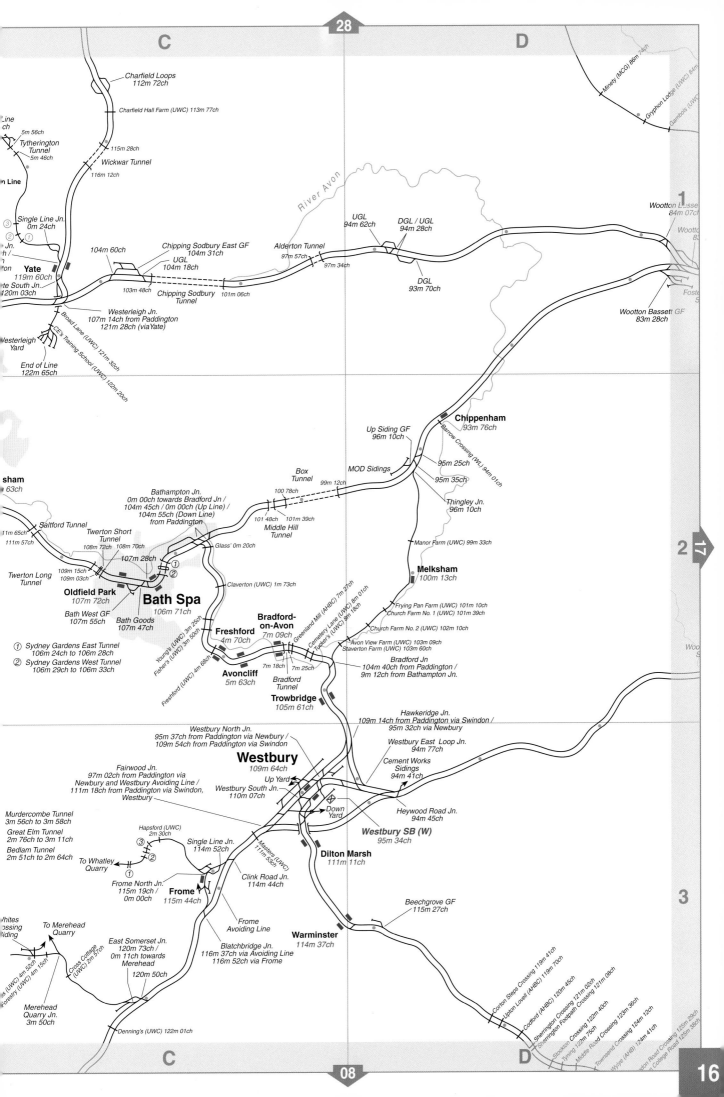

C   D

Charfield Loops
112m 72ch

Charfield Hall Farm (UWC) 113m 77ch

Line
ch

5m 56ch
Tytherington
Tunnel
5m 46ch

115m 28ch

Wickwar Tunnel
116m 12ch

n Line

Minety (MCG) 86m 74ch

Gryphon Lodge (UWC) 84m

Wootton Basset
84m 07ch

Wootto
83

Single Line Jn.
0m 24ch

③
②
Jn.
①

104m 60ch

Chipping Sodbury East GF
104m 31ch

UGL
104m 18ch

Yate
119m 60ch

te South Jn.
120m 03ch

103m 48ch

Chipping Sodbury
Tunnel   101m 06ch

Westerleigh Jn.
107m 14ch from Paddington /
121m 28ch (via Yate)

Broad Lane (UWC) 121m 32ch

GE's Training School (UWC) 122m 20ch

Westerleigh
Yard

End of Line
122m 65ch

UGL
94m 62ch

DGL / UGL
94m 28ch

Alderton Tunnel
97m 57ch

97m 34ch

DGL
93m 70ch

Foste
S

Wootton Bassett GF
83m 28ch

River Avon

Chippenham
93m 76ch

Barrow Crossing (WL) 94m 01ch

Up Siding GF
96m 10ch

MOD Sidings

95m 25ch

95m 35ch

Thingley Jn.
96m 10ch

Box
Tunnel

99m 12ch

100 78ch

sham
63ch

Bathampton Jn.
0m 00ch towards Bradford Jn /
104m 45ch / 0m 00ch (Up Line) /
104m 55ch (Down Line)
from Paddington

101 48ch   101m 39ch
Middle Hill
Tunnel

Saltford Tunnel

Twerton Short
Tunnel

1m 65ch
111m 57ch

108m 72ch   108m 70ch
              107m 28ch

109m 15ch
109m 03ch

Twerton Long
Tunnel

Oldfield Park
107m 72ch

Bath West GF
107m 55ch

Bath Goods
107m 47ch

① Sydney Gardens East Tunnel
   106m 24ch to 106m 28ch
② Sydney Gardens West Tunnel
   106m 29ch to 106m 33ch

①
②

Glass' 0m 20ch

Claverton (UWC) 1m 73ch

Bath Spa
106m 71ch

Young's (UWC) 3m 25ch
Fisher's (UWC) 3m 50ch

Freshford
4m 70ch

Freshford (UWC) 4m 68ch

Avoncliff
5m 63ch

Bradford-
on-Avon
7m 09ch

7m 18ch   7m 25ch

Bradford
Tunnel

Greenland Mill (AHBC) 7m 27ch
Cemetery Lane (UWC) 8m 01ch
Tucker's (UWC) 8m 18ch

Avon View Farm (UWC) 103m 09ch
Staverton Farm (UWC) 103m 60ch

Bradford Jn.
104m 40ch from Paddington /
9m 12ch from Bathampton Jn.

Manor Farm (UWC) 99m 33ch

Melksham
100m 13ch

Frying Pan Farm (UWC) 101m 10ch
Church Farm No. 1 (UWC) 101m 39ch

Church Farm No. 2 (UWC) 102m 10ch

Trowbridge
105m 61ch

Hawkeridge Jn.
109m 14ch from Paddington via Swindon /
95m 32ch via Newbury

Westbury North Jn.
95m 37ch from Paddington via Newbury /
109m 54ch from Paddington via Swindon

Westbury East Loop Jn.
94m 77ch

Westbury
109m 64ch

Cement Works
Sidings
94m 41ch

Fairwood Jn.
97m 02ch from Paddington via
Newbury and Westbury Avoiding Line /
111m 18ch from Paddington via Swindon,
Westbury

Up Yard

Westbury South Jn.
110m 07ch

Down
Yard

Heywood Road Jn.
94m 45ch

Westbury SB (W)
95m 34ch

Murdercombe Tunnel
3m 56ch to 3m 58ch

Great Elm Tunnel
2m 76ch to 3m 11ch

Bedlam Tunnel
2m 51ch to 2m 64ch

Hapsford (UWC)
2m 30ch

③
②

To Whatley
Quarry

①

Single Line Jn.
114m 52ch

Frome North Jn.
115m 19ch /
0m 00ch

Frome
115m 44ch

Masters (UWC)
111m 53ch

Clink Road Jn.
114m 44ch

Dilton Marsh
111m 11ch

Frome
Avoiding Line

Beechgrove GF
115m 27ch

hites
ossing
iding

To Merehead
Quarry

Cross Cottage
(UWC) 2m 57ch

East Somerset Jn.
120m 73ch /
0m 11ch towards
Merehead
120m 50ch

Blatchbridge Jn.
116m 37ch via Avoiding Line
116m 52ch via Frome

Warminster
114m 37ch

s (UWC) 4m 52ch
Forestry (UWC) 4m 15ch

Merehead
Quarry Jn.
3m 50ch

Denning's (UWC) 122m 01ch

Corton Steps Crossing 119m 41ch
Upton Lovell (AHBC) 119m 70ch

Codford (AHBC) 120m 45ch

Sherrington Crossing 121m 02ch
Sherrington Footpath Crossing 121m 08ch

Stockton Crossing 122m 40ch
Tyning 122m 75ch
Middle Road Crossing 123m 36ch

Wylye (AHB) 124m 12ch

Townsend Crossing 124m 41ch

ghton Road Crossing 125m 29ch
College Road 125m 38ch

C   D

1

2 17

3

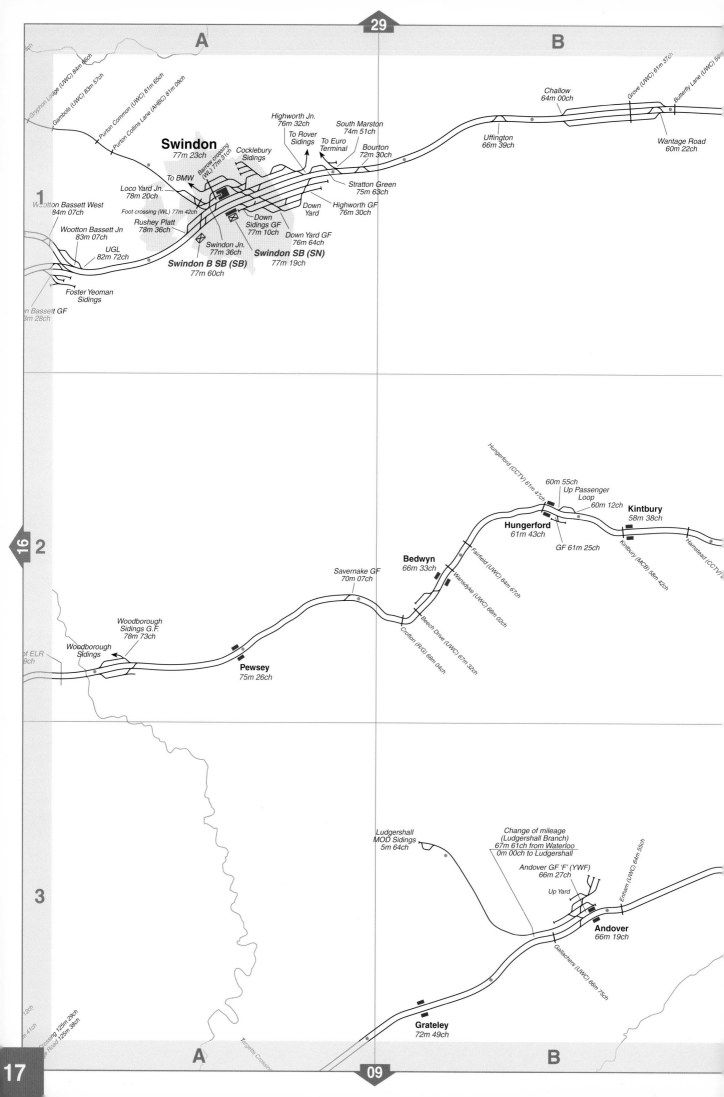

A

B

Gryphon Lodge (UWC) 84m 66ch

Gambols (UWC) 83m 57ch

Purton Common (UWC) 81m 65ch

Purton Collins Lane (AHBC) 81m 09ch

Swindon
77m 23ch

Barrow crossing (WL) 77m 31ch

Cocklebury Sidings

Highworth Jn.
76m 32ch

To Rover Sidings

South Marston
74m 51ch

To Euro Terminal

Bourton
72m 30ch

Challow
64m 00ch

Grove (UWC) 61m 37ch

Butterfly Lane (UWC) 59ch

Uffington
66m 39ch

Wantage Road
60m 22ch

To BMW

Loco Yard Jn.
78m 20ch

Stratton Green
75m 68ch

Foot crossing (WL) 77m 42ch

Down Yard

Highworth GF
76m 30ch

1

Wootton Bassett West
84m 07ch

Rushey Platt
78m 36ch

Down Sidings GF
77m 10ch

Down Yard GF
76m 64ch

Wootton Bassett Jn
83m 07ch

UGL
82m 72ch

Swindon Jn.
77m 36ch

Swindon SB (SN)
77m 19ch

Swindon B SB (SB)
77m 60ch

Foster Yeoman
Sidings

n Bassett GF
8m 28ch

Hungerford (CCTV) 61m 47ch

60m 55ch
Up Passenger Loop

60m 12ch

Kintbury
58m 38ch

Hungerford
61m 43ch

GF 61m 25ch

Kintbury (MCB) 59m 42ch

Hamstead (CCTV)

Savernake GF
70m 07ch

Bedwyn
66m 33ch

Fairfield (UWC) 64m 67ch

16 2

Woodborough
Sidings G.F.
78m 73ch

Wansdyke (UWC) 66m 02ch

Woodborough
Sidings

Beech Drive (UWC) 67m 32ch

Crofton (R/G) 68m 04ch

of ELR
9ch

Pewsey
75m 26ch

Ludgershall
MOD Sidings
5m 64ch

Change of mileage
(Ludgershall Branch)
67m 61ch from Waterloo
0m 00ch to Ludgershall

Andover GF 'F' (YWF)
66m 27ch

Enham (UWC) 64m 55ch

Up Yard

3

Andover
66m 19ch

Gallachers (UWC) 66m 75ch

2ch

ss 125m 29ch

e Road) 125m 38ch

Targetts Crossing

Grateley
72m 49ch

A

B

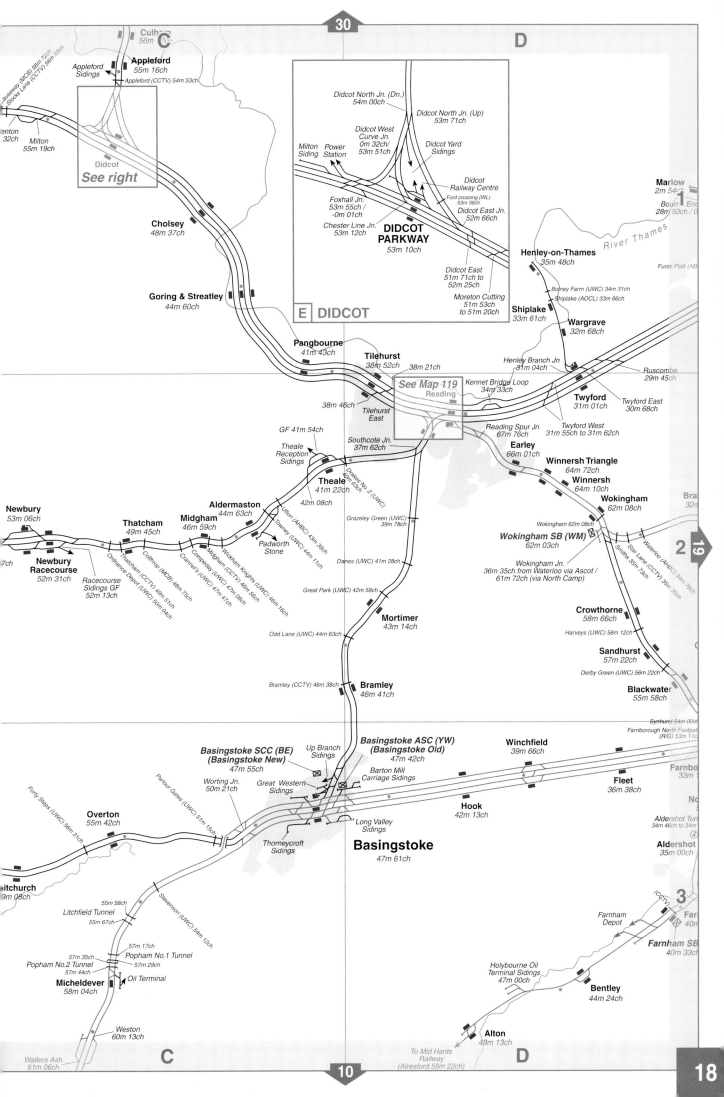

D

Culham
56m

Appleford
55m 16ch

Appleford
Sidings

Causeway (MCB) 56m 72ch
Stocks Lane (CCTV) 56m 68ch

Appleford (CCTV) 54m 53ch

-enton
32ch

Milton
55m 19ch

Didcot
See right

DIDCOT

Didcot North Jn. (Dn.)
54m 00ch

Didcot North Jn. (Up)
53m 71ch

Didcot West
Curve Jn.
0m 32ch/
53m 51ch

Milton
Siding

Power
Station

Didcot Yard
Sidings

Didcot
Railway Centre

Foot crossing (WL)
53m 06ch

Foxhall Jn.
53m 55ch /
-0m 01ch

Didcot East Jn.
52m 66ch

Chester Line Jn.
53m 12ch

**DIDCOT
PARKWAY**
53m 10ch

Didcot East
51m 71ch to
52m 25ch

Moreton Cutting
51m 53ch
to 51m 20ch

Cholsey
48m 37ch

Goring & Streatley
44m 60ch

E | **DIDCOT**

Marlow
2m 54ch

Bourne End
28m 50ch / 0

River Thames

Furze Platt (AB

Henley-on-Thames
35m 48ch

Bolney Farm (UWC) 34m 31ch
Shiplake (AOCL) 33m 66ch

Shiplake
33m 61ch

Wargrave
32m 68ch

Pangbourne
41m 43ch

Tilehurst
38m 52ch

38m 21ch

Henley Branch Jn
31m 04ch

Ruscombe
29m 45ch

38m 46ch

See Map 119
Reading

Kennet Bridge Loop
34m 33ch

Twyford
31m 01ch

Twyford East
30m 68ch

GF 41m 54ch

Theale
Reception
Sidings

Tilehurst
East

Southcote Jn.
37m 62ch

Reading Spur Jn
67m 76ch

Twyford West
31m 55ch to 31m 62ch

Earley
66m 01ch

Winnersh Triangle
64m 72ch

Drakes No. 2 (UWC)
40m 63ch

Theale
41m 22ch

42m 08ch

Grazeley Green (UWC)
39m 78ch

Winnersh
64m 10ch

Wokingham
62m 08ch

Aldermaston
44m 63ch

Ulton (AHBC) 43m 39ch

Towney (UWC) 44m 11ch

Wokingham 62m 08ch

Newbury
53m 06ch

Midgham
46m 59ch

Wickham Knights (UWC) 46m 56ch

**Padworth
Stone**

Danes (UWC) 41m 28ch

Wokingham SB (WM)
62m 03ch

Compedley (UWC) 47m 47ch

Midgham (CCTV) 46m 16ch

Br
32

Thatcham
49m 45ch

Colthrop (MCB) 48m 75ch

Crannel's (UWC) 47m 08ch

Great Park (UWC) 42m 58ch

Wokingham Jn.
36m 35ch from Waterloo via Ascot /
61m 72ch (via North Camp)

**Newbury
Racecourse**
52m 31ch

Ordnance Depot (UWC) 49m 51ch

Thatcham (CCTV) 49m 51ch

Compedley (UWC) 50m 04ch

Odd Lane (UWC) 44m 63ch

Mortimer
43m 14ch

Star Lane (CCTV) 35m 73ch

Waterloo (AHB
35m 30ch

Smiths (UWC) 35m 30ch

Crowthorne
58m 66ch

Harveys (UWC) 58m 12ch

7ch

Racecourse
Sidings GF
52m 13ch

Sandhurst
57m 22ch

Derby Green (UWC) 56m 22ch

Bramley (CCTV) 46m 38ch

Bramley
46m 41ch

Blackwater
55m 58ch

Synhurst 54m 00ch

Farnborough North Footpath
(R/G) 53m 11ch

Winchfield
39m 66ch

Farnbo
33m

***Basingstoke ASC (YW)
(Basingstoke Old)***
47m 42ch

No

***Basingstoke SCC (BE)
(Basingstoke New)***
47m 55ch

Up Branch
Sidings

Barton Mill
Carriage Sidings

Fleet
36m 38ch

Aldershot Tun
34m 46ch to 34m

Worting Jn.
50m 21ch

Great Western
Sidings

Aldershot
35m 00ch

Parlour Gates (UWC) 51m 15ch

Hook
42m 13ch

Overton
55m 42ch

Forty Steps (UWC) 56m 31ch

Thorneycroft
Sidings

Long Valley
Sidings

Basingstoke
47m 61ch

(CCTV)

Far

Farnham SB
40m 33ch

itchurch
9m 08ch

Stevenson (UWC) 54m 12ch

55m 58ch

Litchfield Tunnel
55m 67ch

Farnham
Depot

57m 17ch

Popham No.1 Tunnel
57m 29ch

Holybourne Oil
Terminal Sidings
47m 00ch

Bentley
44m 24ch

57m 35ch

Popham No.2 Tunnel
57m 44ch

Micheldever
58m 04ch

Oil Terminal

Weston
60m 13ch

Alton
49m 13ch

To Mid Hants
Railway
(Alresford 59m 22ch)

Wallers Ash
61m 06ch

C

D

2

19

3

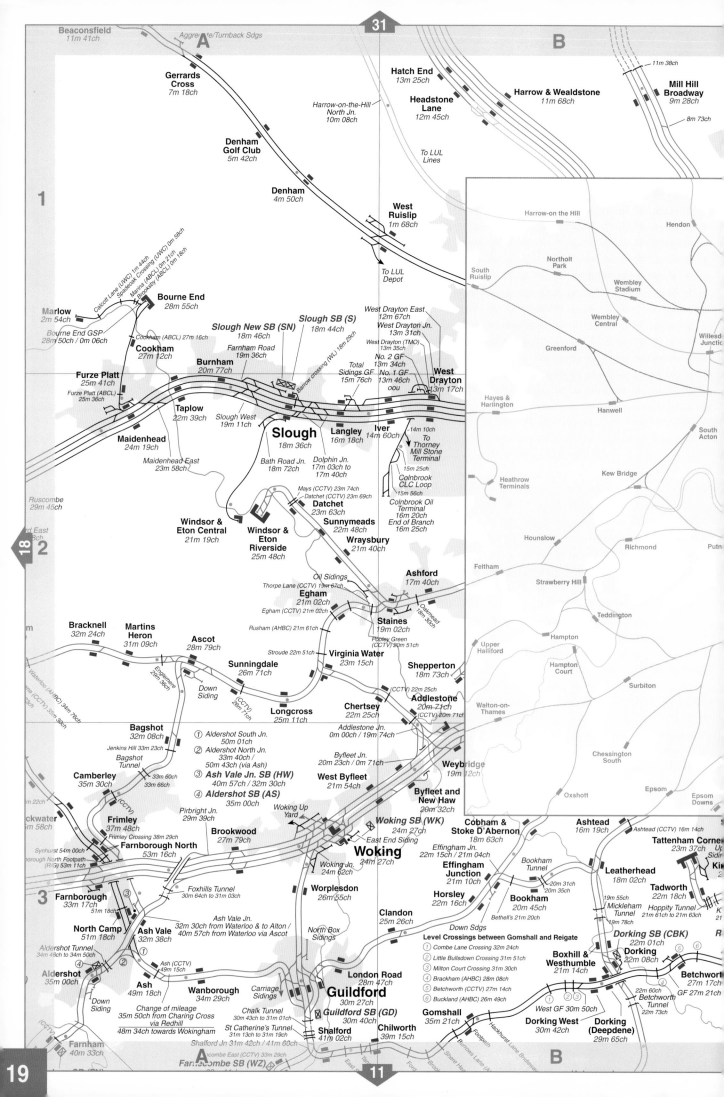

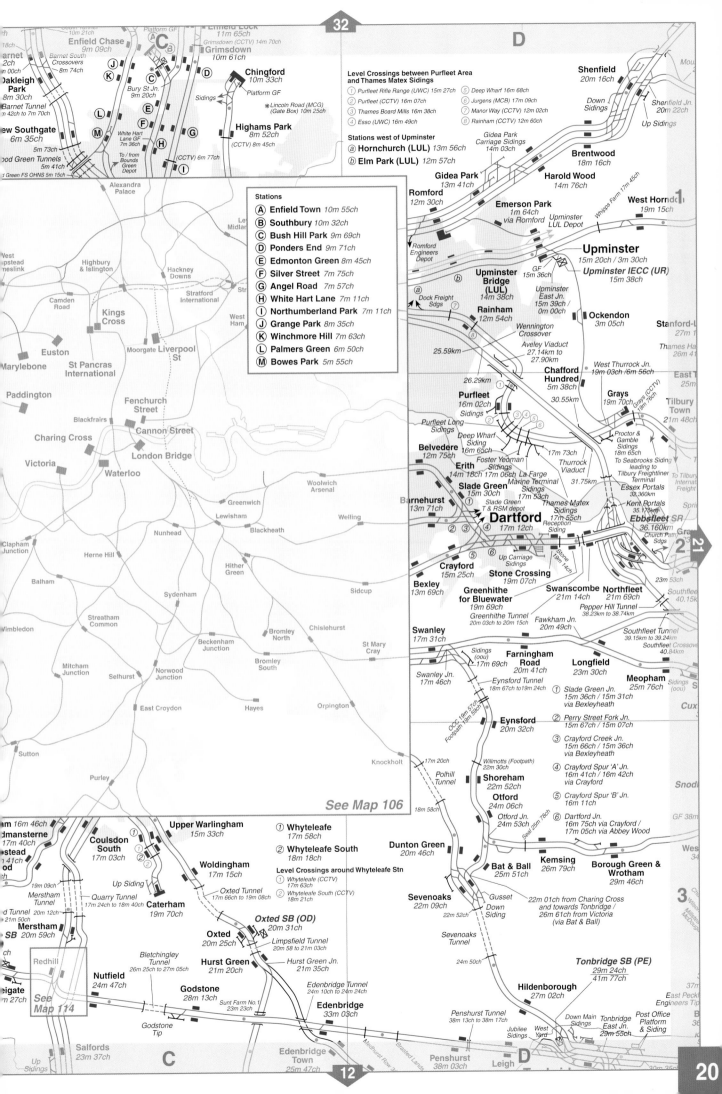

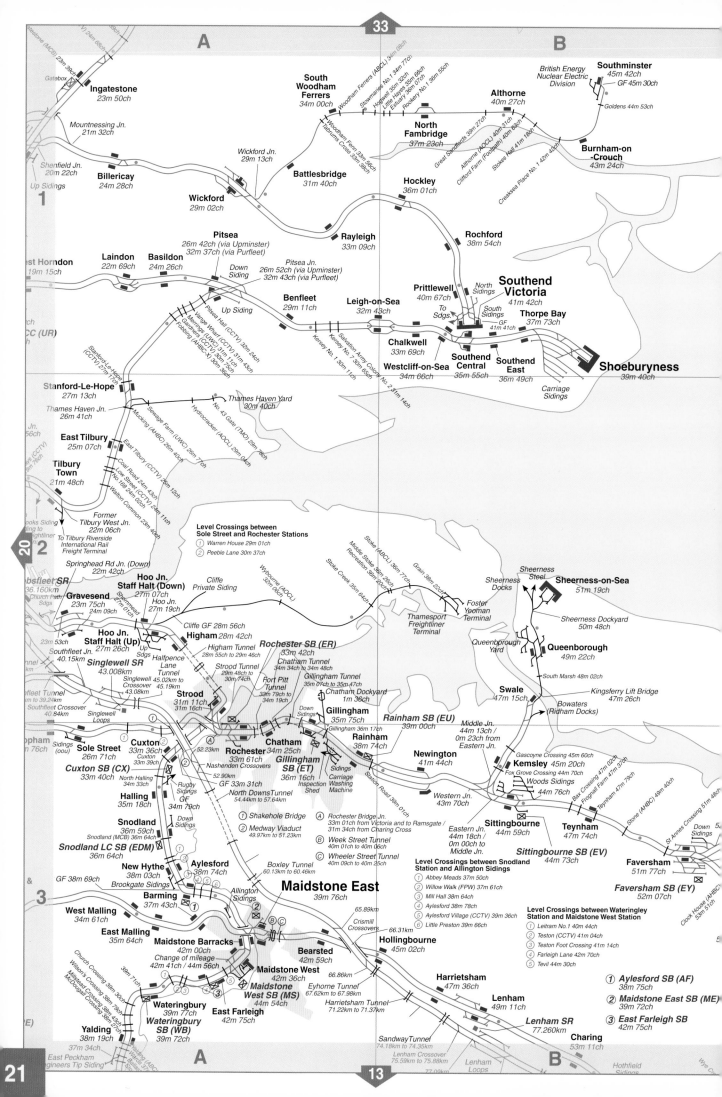

Ingatestone
23m 50ch

Gatebox
Mountnessing Jn.
21m 32ch

Shenfield Jn.
20m 22ch

Up Sidings

1

Billericay
24m 28ch

Wickford
29m 02ch

Wickford Jn.
29m 13ch

South Woodham Ferrers
34m 00ch

Woodham Ferrers (ABCL) 34m 07ch
Stowmaries No.1 34m 77ch
Woodham Fenn 35m 56ch
Hogwell 35m 32ch
Trabums Cross 35m 35ch
Little Hayes 35m 66ch
Estuary 36m 07ch
Rookery No.1 36m 55ch

Althorne
40m 27ch

British Energy Nuclear Electric Division

Southminster
45m 42ch
GF 45m 30ch

Goldens 44m 53ch

North Fambridge
37m 23ch

Great Sandfords 39m 27ch
Althorne (AOCL) 40m 31ch
Clifford Farm (Footpath) 40m 63ch
Stokes Hall 41m 18ch

Burnham-on-Crouch
43m 24ch

Creeksea Place No.1 42m 42ch

Battlesbridge
31m 40ch

Rayleigh
33m 09ch

Hockley
36m 01ch

Rochford
38m 54ch

Pitsea
26m 42ch (via Upminster)
32m 37ch (via Purfleet)

Down Siding

Laindon
22m 69ch

Basildon
24m 26ch

Pitsea Jn.
26m 52ch (via Upminster)
32m 43ch (via Purfleet)

West Horndon
19m 15ch

Benfleet
29m 11ch

Leigh-on-Sea
32m 43ch

Prittlewell
40m 67ch

North Sidings

Southend Victoria
41m 42ch

To Sdgs.
South Sidings
GF 41m 41ch

Thorpe Bay
37m 73ch

Up Siding

CC (UR)

Pitsea Hall (CCTV) 32m 24ch
Vange Wharf (UWC) 31m 43ch
Merrings (UWC) 30m 11ch
Gardner (CCTV) 30m 08ch
Fobbing (AHBC-X) 30m 36ch

Salvation Army Colony No.2 31m 14ch
Kersey No.1 30m 11ch
Kersey No.1 30m 65ch

Chalkwell
33m 69ch

Westcliff-on-Sea
34m 66ch

Southend Central
34m 55ch

Southend East
36m 49ch

GF

Shoeburyness
39m 40ch

Carriage Sidings

Stanford-Le-Hope
27m 13ch

Stanford-Le-Hope (CCTV) 27m 13ch

Thames Haven Jn.
26m 41ch

Thames Haven Yard
30m 40ch

East Tilbury
25m 07ch

Sewage Farm (UWC) 26m 41ch
Muckling
No. 43 Gate (TMO) 29m 04ch
Hydrocracker (AOCL) 29m 04ch

East Tilbury (CCTV) 26m 40ch

Tilbury Town
21m 48ch

Coal Road 24m 43ch
Cow Street (CCTV) 24m 11ch
No. 168 24m 00ch
Walton Common 23m 40ch

20

2

Former Tilbury West Jn.
22m 06ch

To Tilbury Riverside International Rail Freight Terminal

Springhead Rd Jn. (Down)
22m 42ch

ooks Siding
ding to
ghtliner

bsfleet SR
36.160km
Church Path
Sdgs

Gravesend
23m 75ch

Hoo Jn.
Staff Halt (Down)
27m 07ch

Shornmead 27m 01ch
Hoo Jn.
24m 09ch
Hoo Jn.
27m 19ch

Cliffe Private Siding

Wybourne (AOCL)
3m 06ch

Level Crossings between Sole Street and Rochester Stations
① Warren House 29m 01ch
② Peeble Lane 30m 37ch

Stoke (ABCL) 36m 77ch
Middle Stoke 36m 20ch
Recreation 36m 20ch
Stoke Creek 35m 64ch
Grain 39m 22ch

Sheerness Steel

Sheerness Docks

Sheerness-on-Sea
51m 19ch

Sheerness Dockyard
50m 48ch

Foster Yeoman Terminal

Thamesport Freightliner Terminal

Queenbrough Yard

Queenborough
49m 22ch

South Marsh 48m 02ch

Swale
47m 15ch

Kingsferry Lift Bridge
47m 26ch

Bowaters (Ridham Docks)

Cliffe GF 28m 56ch

Higham
28m 42ch

Rochester SB (ER)
33m 42ch

Higham Tunnel
28m 55ch to 29m 46ch

Chatham Tunnel
34m 34ch to 34m 48ch

Gillingham Tunnel
35m 07ch to 35m 47ch

Chatham Dockyard
1m 36ch

Hoo Jn.
Staff Halt (Up)
27m 26ch

Singlewell SR
43.008km

Singlewell 45.02km to 45.19km
Crossover 43.08km

Singlewell Loops

Strood Tunnel
29m 34ch to 30m 74ch

Fort Pitt Tunnel
33m 79ch to 34m 19ch

Strood
31m 11ch
31m 16ch

Down Sidings

Gillingham
35m 75ch

Rainham SB (EU)
39m 00ch

Gillingham 36m 17ch

Southfleet Jn.
40.15km

nfleet Tunnel
m to 39.24km
Southfleet Crossover
40.84km

23m 53ch

Southfleet Jn.

Halfpence Lane Tunnel

Higham

Chatham
34m 25ch

Rochester
33m 61ch

Cuxton 33m 39ch

Nashenden Crossovers
52.23km
52.90km

Gillingham SB (ET)
36m 16ch

Sidings
Carriage Washing Machine

Rainham
38m 74ch

Newington
41m 44ch

Station Road 39m 01ch

Middle Jn.
44m 13ch /
0m 23ch from Eastern Jn.

Gascoyne Crossing 45m 60ch

Kemsley
45m 20ch

Fox Grove Crossing 44m 70ch
Woods Sidings
44m 76ch

Bax Crossing 47m 02ch
Frognall Farm 47m 37ch
Teynham 47m 79ch

Middle Jn.

ph am
SR

pham
76ch

Sole Street
26m 71ch

Sidings (oou)

Cuxton
33m 36ch

Cuxton SB (CX)
33m 40ch

North Halling 34m 33ch

Halling
35m 18ch

GF 34m 79ch

Rugby Sidings 35.19km

Rochester Bridge Jn.
33m 01ch from Victoria and to Ramsgate / 31m 34ch from Charing Cross

① Shakehole Bridge
② Medway Viaduct
49.97km to 51.23km

Ⓐ Rochester Bridge Jn.
Ⓑ Week Street Tunnel
40m 01ch to 40m 06ch
Ⓒ Wheeler Street Tunnel
40m 09ch to 40m 25ch

North Downs Tunnel
54.44km to 57.64km

Western Jn.
43m 70ch

Eastern Jn.
44m 18ch /
0m 00ch to Middle Jn.

Sittingbourne
44m 59ch

Sittingbourne SB (EV)
44m 73ch

Teynham
47m 74ch

Stone (AHBC) 49m 40ch

St Annes Crossing 51m 48ch

Down Sidings

Snodland
36m 59ch

Snodland (MCB) 36m 64ch

Snodland LC SB (EDM)
36m 64ch

Down Sidings

New Hythe
38m 03ch

Brookgate Sidings

GF 38m 69ch

Aylesford
38m 74ch

Boxley Tunnel
60.13km to 60.46km

Maidstone East
39m 76ch

Allington Sidings

Level Crossings between Snodland Station and Allington Sidings
① Abbey Meads 37m 50ch
② Willow Walk (FPW) 37m 61ch
③ Mill Hall 38m 64ch
④ Aylesford 38m 78ch
⑤ Aylesford Village (CCTV) 39m 36ch
⑥ Little Preston 39m 66ch

Faversham
51m 77ch

Faversham SB (EY)
52m 07ch

Clock House (AHBC)
53m

Barming
37m 43ch

West Malling
34m 61ch

East Malling
35m 64ch

Maidstone Barracks
42m 00ch

Change of mileage
42m 41ch / 44m 56ch

Maidstone West
42m 36ch

Crismill Crossovers
66.31km
65.89km

Bearsted
42m 59ch

Hollingbourne
45m 02ch

Eyhorne Tunnel
67.62km to 67.98km

Harrietsham
47m 36ch

Harrietsham Tunnel
71.22km to 71.37km

Level Crossings between Wateringley Station and Maidstone West Station
① Leitram No.1 40m 44ch
② Teston (CCTV) 41m 04ch
③ Teston Foot Crossing 41m 14ch
④ Farleigh Lane 42m 70ch
⑤ Tevil 44m 30ch

Church Crossing 39m 30ch
Wilson's Crossing 38m 79ch
Milstead Crossing 38m 49ch
McDougall Crossing 38m 22ch

39m 71ch

Maidstone West SB (MS)
44m 54ch

Lenham
49m 11ch

Lenham SR
77.260km

Sandway Tunnel
74.18km to 74.35km

Lenham Crossover
75.59km to 75.88km

Lenham Loops

Charing
53m 11ch

Hothfield Sidings

① **Aylesford SB (AF)**
38m 75ch

② **Maidstone East SB (ME)**
39m 72ch

③ **East Farleigh SB**
42m 75ch

Wateringbury
38m 34ch

Wateringbury SB (WB)
39m 72ch

East Farleigh
42m 75ch

Yalding
37m 34ch

East Peckham
gineers Tip Siding

E)

21

1

2

Margate SB (GE)
73m 53ch

Westgate-on-Sea
72m 35ch

Down Siding (ooU)

Margate
73m 69ch

74m 01ch

Birchington
70m 56ch

Ramsgate SB (HE)
85m 61ch

EMU Depot

West Yard

Broadstairs
77m 09ch

Dumpton Park
78m 26ch

Herne Bay
62m 58ch

Minster West SB (EBE)
81m 74ch

Minster East Jn.
82m 17ch /
0m 00ch to
Minster South Jn.

Rough Crossing 85m 35ch

Sevenscore (AHBC) 83m 01ch

Sidings

Whitstable
59m 06ch

Grove Ferry (AHBC) 71m 36ch

Cater Crossing 77m 62ch

Sarre Bridge 78m 37ch

Mile Drove 78m 06ch

Monkton Court 79m 36ch

Wall End 77m 28ch

Port Farm 76m 06ch

Minster
81m 64ch

Cliffsend (AHBC) 84m 04ch

Ramsgate
79m 21ch from
Victoria via Herne Bay
85m 67ch from
Charing Cross via Wye

Chestfield & Swalecliffe
60m 45ch

Hoplands Farm 74m 51ch

Sturry
72m 57ch

72m 56ch

River Stour

Walters Hall 80m 44ch

Sheriffs Court 80m 60ch

Minster (R/G) 81m 58ch

Minster South Jn.
82m 21ch /
0m 32ch from
Minster East Jn.

Broad Oak (AHBC) 71m 77ch

Folly Farm (UWC) 71m 36ch

St Stephen's (CCTV) 70m 56ch

Canterbury West SB (EDH)
70m 37ch

Sturry SB (ST)
72m 58ch

Graveney (AHBC) 54m 77ch

Austin Crossing 53m 74ch

Canterbury West
70m 27ch

St Dunstan's (CCTV) 70m 15ch

Canterbury / Wye ACC (EBT) 70m 36ch

Canterbury East SB (CB) 61m 67ch

Richborough Castle 84m 48ch

Long Salts 85m 07ch

Richborough (AHBC) 85m 24ch

Ash Road (AHBC) 86m 12ch

Woodnesborough (CCTV) 85m 60ch

Sandwich SB (SW)
86m 43ch

Sandwich
86m 46ch

Chartham Hatch (AHBC) 58m 65ch

Chartham
67m 14ch

Bekesbourne
64m 58ch

Whitehall (R/G) 61m 65ch

Canterbury East

Horton (UWC) 67m 10ch

Deanery Crossing 66m 17ch

Shalmsford Street (UWC) 66m 50ch

Adisham
67m 60ch

Sandwich 86m 37ch

Sin Green (UWC) 87m 19ch

Laslett (UWC) 87m 42ch

Blue Pigeon 87m 46ch

Gore Top 87m 69ch

Northwall (R/G) 90m 09ch

Middle 90m 42ch

Chilham
65m 09ch

Chilham Mill (CCTV) 64m 76ch

Chilham Road (CCTV) 65m 40ch

Aylesham
68m 66ch

Soles Farm 70m 56ch

Deal SB (EBZ)
90m 43ch

Deal
90m 56ch

Tunnel to 56m 52ch

Blackwell Bri

Snowdown
69m 60ch

Walmer
92m 27ch

Former connection to East Kent Light Rly

Shepherds Well SB (SH)
71m 51ch

Down Sidings

Cold Blow

3

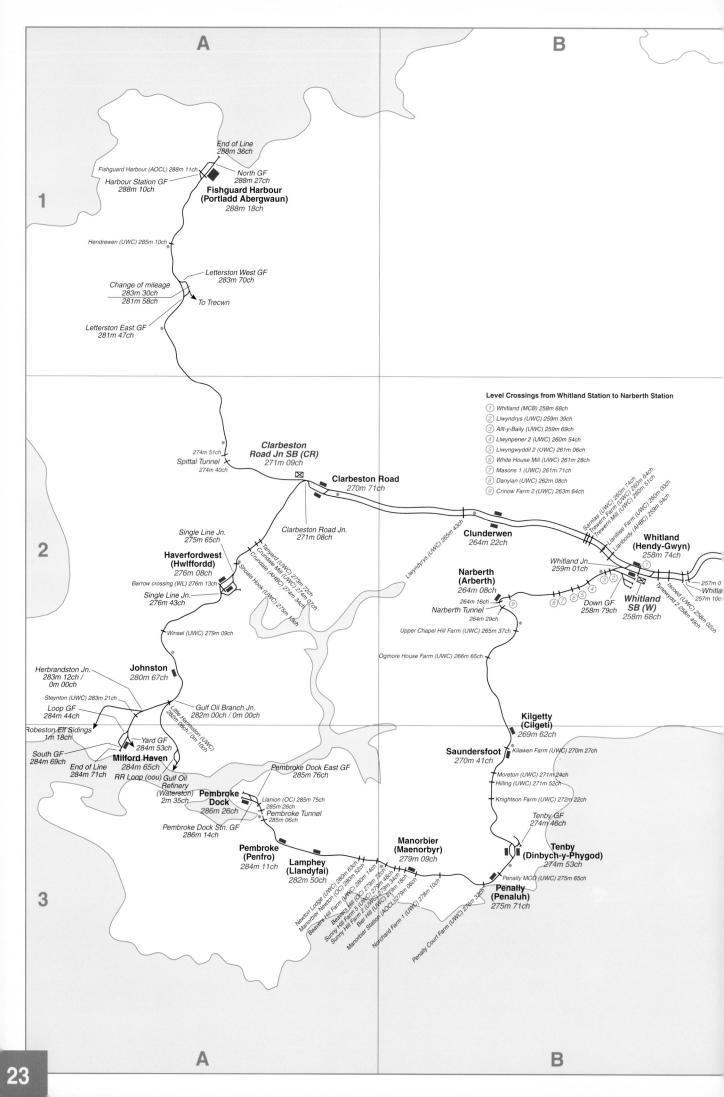

A

B

1

End of Line
288m 36ch

Fishguard Harbour (AOCL) 288m 11ch

North GF
288m 27ch

Harbour Station GF
288m 10ch

**Fishguard Harbour
(Portladd Abergwaun)**
288m 18ch

Hendrewen (UWC) 285m 10ch

Change of mileage
283m 30ch
281m 58ch

Letterston West GF
283m 70ch

To Trecwn

Letterston East GF
281m 47ch

2

Level Crossings from Whitland Station to Narberth Station

① Whitland (MCB) 258m 68ch
② Llwyndrys (UWC) 259m 39ch
③ Allt-y-Baily (UWC) 259m 69ch
④ Llwynpener 2 (UWC) 260m 54ch
⑤ Llwyngwyddil 2 (UWC) 261m 06ch
⑥ White House Mill (UWC) 261m 28ch
⑦ Masons 1 (UWC) 261m 71ch
⑧ Danylan (UWC) 262m 08ch
⑨ Crinow Farm 2 (UWC) 263m 64ch

274m 51ch
Spittal Tunnel
274m 40ch

*Clarbeston
Road Jn SB (CR)*
271m 09ch

Clarbeston Road
270m 71ch

Clarbeston Road Jn.
271m 08ch

Single Line Jn.
275m 65ch

Sarnlas (UWC) 260m 74ch
Trewern Farm (UWC) 260m 64ch
Trewern Mill (UWC) 260m 51ch
Llanlliwe Farm (UWC) 260m 00ch
Llanboidy (AHBC) 259m 54ch

Clunderwen
264m 22ch

**Whitland
(Hendy-Gwyn)**
258m 74ch

**Haverfordwest
(Hwlffordd)**
276m 08ch

Tanyard (UWC) 273m 72ch
Crundale Mill (UWC) 274m 07ch
Crundale (AHBC) 274m 34ch
Shoals Hook (UWC) 275m 13ch

Barrow crossing (WL) 276m 13ch

Single Line Jn.
276m 43ch

Llwyndyrys (UWC) 265m 43ch

**Narberth
(Arberth)**
264m 08ch

Whitland Jn.
259m 01ch

Iscoed (UWC) 259m 02ch
Whitla

257m 0
Whitla
257m 10c

Winsel (UWC) 279m 09ch

264m 16ch

Narberth Tunnel
264m 29ch

Down GF
258m 79ch

**Whitland
SB (W)**
258m 68ch

Tynewydd 2 258m 49ch

Upper Chapel Hill Farm (UWC) 265m 37ch

Ogmore House Farm (UWC) 266m 65ch

Herbrandston Jn.
283m 12ch /
0m 00ch

Johnston
280m 67ch

Steynton (UWC) 283m 21ch

Loop GF
284m 44ch

Gulf Oil Branch Jn.
282m 00ch / 0m 00ch

Little Harmiston (UWC)
282m 06ch 0m 10ch

**Kilgetty
(Cilgeti)**
269m 62ch

Robeston Elf Sidings
1m 18ch

Yard GF
284m 53ch

Saundersfoot
270m 41ch

Kilawen Farm (UWC) 270m 27ch

South GF
284m 69ch

Milford Haven
284m 65ch

End of Line
284m 71ch

RR Loop (oou) Gulf Oil
Refinery
(Waterston)
2m 35ch

Pembroke Dock East GF
285m 76ch

Moreton (UWC) 271m 24ch
Hilling (UWC) 271m 52ch

Knightson Farm (UWC) 272m 22ch

Tenby GF
274m 46ch

**Pembroke
Dock**
286m 26ch

Llanion (OC) 285m 75ch
285m 26ch
Pembroke Tunnel
285m 06ch

**Tenby
(Dinbych-y-Phygod)**
274m 53ch

Pembroke Dock Stn. GF
286m 14ch

3

**Pembroke
(Penfro)**
284m 11ch

**Lamphey
(Llandyfai)**
282m 50ch

Newton Lodge (UWC) 280m 63ch
Manorbier Newton (OC) 280m 52ch
Beavers Hill Farm (UWC) 280m 14ch
Beavers Mill (OC) 279m 70ch
Sunny Hill Farm 5 (UWC) 279m 48ch
Sunny Hill Farm 2 (UWC) 279m 34ch
Bier Hill (UWC) 279m 18ch
Manorbier Station (AOCL) 279m 06ch

**Manorbier
(Maenorbyr)**
279m 09ch

Penally MOD (UWC) 275m 65ch

**Penally
(Penaluh)**
275m 71ch

Norchard Farm 1 (UWC) 278m 10ch

Penally Court Farm (UWC) 276m 32ch

A

B

23

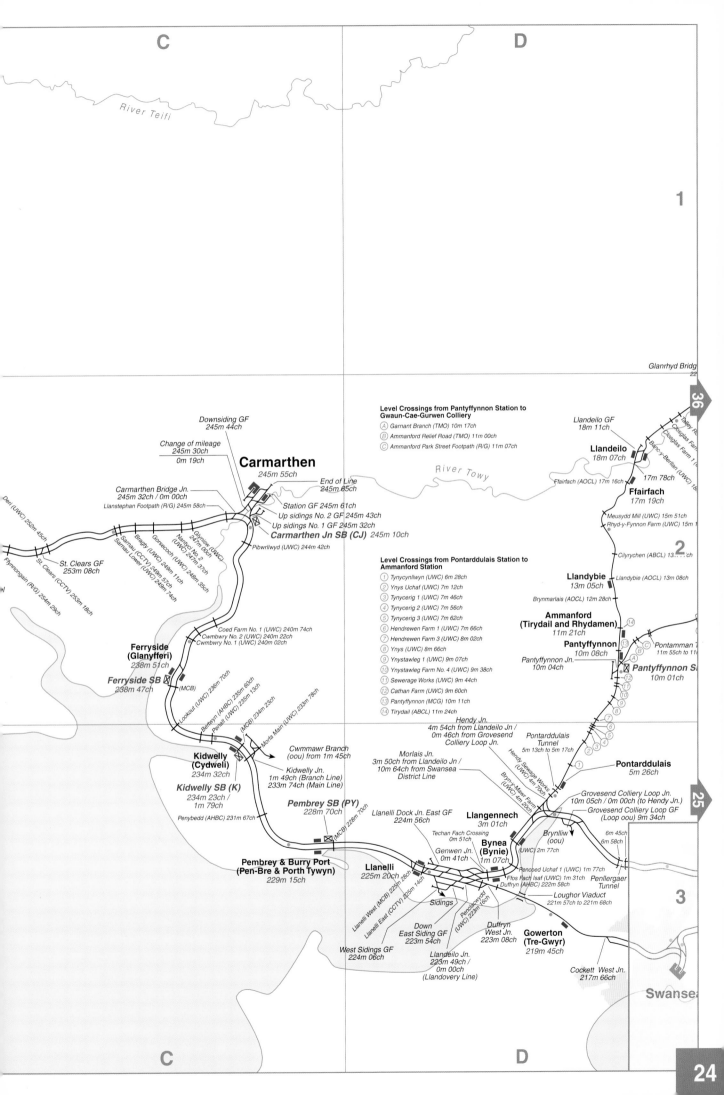

C   D

1

River Teifi

Glanrhyd Bridg...
22...

36

Downsiding GF
245m 44ch

Change of mileage
245m 30ch
0m 19ch

Carmarthen
245m 55ch

End of Line
245m 65ch

Carmarthen Bridge Jn.
245m 32ch / 0m 00ch

Llanstephan Footpath (R/G) 245m 58ch

Station GF 245m 61ch

Up sidings No. 2 GF 245m 43ch

Up sidings No. 1 GF 245m 32ch

Carmarthen Jn SB (CJ) 245m 10ch

Pibwrllwyd (UWC) 244m 42ch

River Towy

**Level Crossings from Pantyffynnon Station to
Gwaun-Cae-Gurwen Colliery**
Ⓐ Garnant Branch (TMO) 10m 17ch
Ⓑ Ammanford Relief Road (TMO) 11m 00ch
Ⓒ Ammanford Park Street Footpath (R/G) 11m 07ch

Llandeilo GF
18m 11ch

Llandeilo
18m 07ch

Talley R...
Closglas Farm 1...
Banc-y-Berllan (UWC) 18...

17m 78ch

Ffairfach
17m 19ch

Ffairfach (AOCL) 17m 16ch

Meusydd Mill (UWC) 15m 51ch
Rhyd-y-Fynnon Farm (UWC) 15m 1...

Deri (UWC) 252m 45ch

St. Clears GF
253m 08ch

Sarnau (UWC) 249m 57ch
Sarnau Lower (UWC) 249m 74ch
Gorsecoch (UWC) 248m 35ch
Bragdy (UWC) 248m 11ch
Nantyci No. 2
(UWC) 247m 37ch
Glynisw (UWC)
247m 00ch

Ffynnongain (R/G) 254m 29ch

St. Clears (CCTV) 253m 18ch

Cilyrychen (ABCL) 13... ch

2

Llandybie
13m 05ch

Llandybie (AOCL) 13m 08ch

Brynmarlais (AOCL) 12m 28ch

Ammanford
(Tirydail and Rhydamen)
11m 21ch

Pantyffynnon
10m 08ch

Pontamman T...
11m 55ch to 11...

**Level Crossings from Pontarddulais Station to
Ammanford Station**
① Tynycynllwyn (UWC) 6m 28ch
② Ynys Uchaf (UWC) 7m 12ch
③ Tynycerig 1 (UWC) 7m 46ch
④ Tynycerig 2 (UWC) 7m 56ch
⑤ Tynycerig 3 (UWC) 7m 62ch
⑥ Hendrewen Farm 1 (UWC) 7m 66ch
⑦ Hendrewen Farm 3 (UWC) 8m 02ch
⑧ Ynys (UWC) 8m 66ch
⑨ Ynystawleg 1 (UWC) 9m 07ch
⑩ Ynystawleg Farm No. 4 (UWC) 9m 38ch
⑪ Sewerage Works (UWC) 9m 44ch
⑫ Cathan Farm (UWC) 9m 60ch
⑬ Pantyffynnon (MCG) 10m 11ch
⑭ Tirydail (ABCL) 11m 24ch

Coed Farm No. 1 (UWC) 240m 74ch
Cwmbwry No. 2 (UWC) 240m 22ch
Cwmbwry No. 1 (UWC) 240m 02ch

Ferryside
(Glanyfferi)
238m 51ch

Ferryside SB ⊠
238m 47ch

(MCB)

Pantyffynnon Jn.
10m 04ch

⑭

⑬ ⑫ Ⓒ
Ⓐ
Ⓑ

⊠ *Pantyffynnon S...*
10m 01ch

Lookout (UWC) 235m 70ch
Benkyn (AHBC) 235m 60ch
Penalt (UWC) 235m 13ch
(MCB) 234m 23ch
Morfa Main (UWC) 233m 78ch

Kidwelly
(Cydweli)
234m 32ch

Kidwelly SB (K)
234m 23ch /
1m 79ch

Penybedd (AHBC) 231m 67ch

Cwmmawr Branch
(oou) from 1m 45ch

Kidwelly Jn.
1m 49ch (Branch Line)
233m 74ch (Main Line)

Hendy Jn.
4m 54ch from Llandeilo Jn /
0m 46ch from Grovesend
Colliery Loop Jn.

Pontarddulais Tunnel
5m 13ch to 5m 17ch

Pontarddulais
5m 26ch

Morlais Jn.
3m 50ch from Llandeilo Jn /
10m 64ch from Swansea
District Line

Hendy Sewage Works (UWC) 4m 70ch

Bryn-y-Mawr Farm (UWC) 4m 20ch

Pembrey SB (PY)
228m 70ch

(MCB) 228m 70ch

⊠

Llanelli Dock Jn. East GF
224m 56ch

Llangennech
3m 01ch

Techan Fach Crossing
0m 51ch

Genwen Jn.
0m 41ch

Bynea
(Bynie)
1m 07ch

Brynlliw
(oou)

(UWC) 2m 77ch

Grovesend Colliery Loop Jn.
10m 05ch / 0m 00ch (to Hendy Jn.)

Grovesend Colliery Loop GF
(Loop oou) 9m 34ch

25

6m 45ch
6m 58ch

Pembrey & Burry Port
(Pen-Bre & Porth Tywyn)
229m 15ch

Llanelli
225m 20ch

Lanelli West (MCB) 225m 28ch
Llanelli East (CCTV) 225m 14ch

Sidings

West Sidings GF
224m 06ch

Down
East Siding GF
223m 54ch

Penplacwydd
(UWC) 223m 14ch

Llandeilo Jn.
223m 49ch /
0m 00ch
(Llandovery Line)

Duffryn
West Jn.
223m 08ch

Pencoed Uchaf 1 (UWC) 1m 77ch
Ffos Fach Isaf (UWC) 1m 31ch
Duffryn (AHBC) 222m 58ch

Loughor Viaduct
221m 57ch to 221m 68ch

Penllergaer
Tunnel

3

Gowerton
(Tre-Gwyr)
219m 45ch

Cockett West Jn.
217m 66ch

Swansea

C   D

24

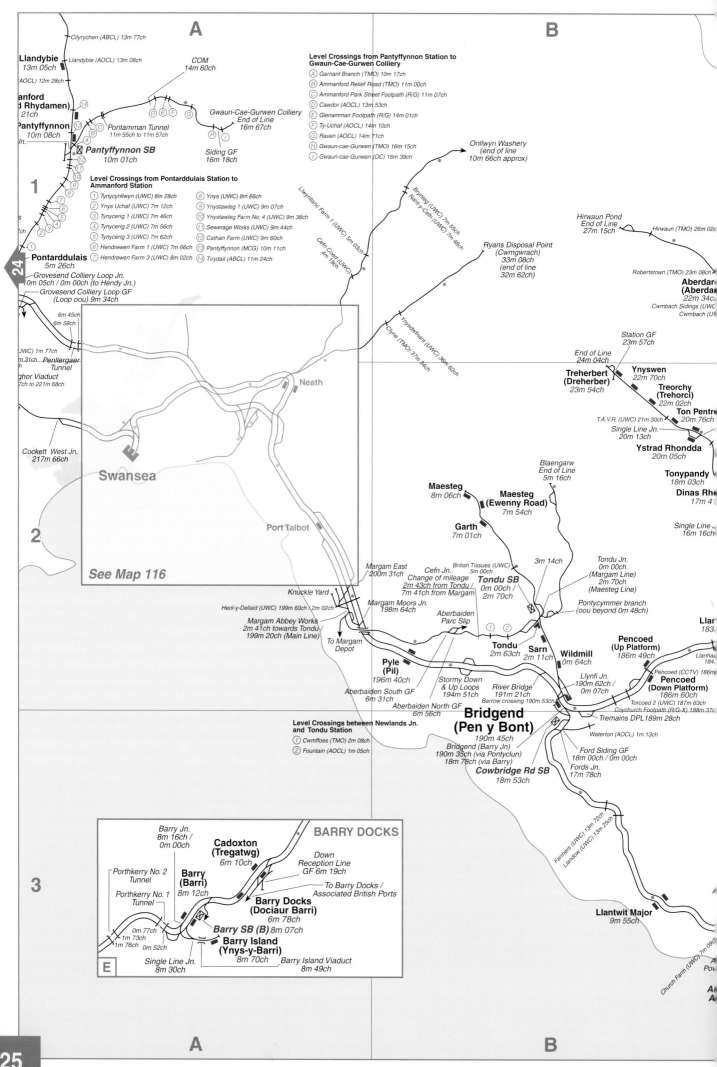

Cilyrychen (ABCL) 13m 77ch

Llandybie
13m 05ch
Llandybie (AOCL) 13m 08ch

COM
14m 60ch

(AOCL) 12m 28ch

anford
d Rhydamen)
21ch

Gwaun-Cae-Gurwen Colliery
End of Line
16m 67ch

Pantyffynnon
10m 08ch

Pontamman Tunnel
11m 55ch to 11m 57ch

Jn.

Pantyffynnon SB
10m 01ch

Siding GF
16m 18ch

**Level Crossings from Pantyffynnon Station to
Gwaun-Cae-Gurwen Colliery**

Ⓐ Garnant Branch (TMO) 10m 17ch
Ⓑ Ammanford Relief Road (TMO) 11m 00ch
Ⓒ Ammanford Park Street Footpath (R/G) 11m 07ch
Ⓓ Cawdor (AOCL) 13m 53ch
Ⓔ Glenamman Footpath (R/G) 14m 01ch
Ⓕ Ty-Uchaf (AOCL) 14m 10ch
Ⓖ Raven (AOCL) 14m 71ch
Ⓗ Gwaun-cae-Gurwen (TMO) 16m 15ch
Ⓘ Gwaun-cae-Gurwen (OC) 16m 39ch

Onllwyn Washery
(end of line
10m 66ch approx)

Brynteg (UWC) 7m 55ch
Nant-y-Cefn (UWC) 7m 48ch

Hirwaun Pond
End of Line
27m 15ch

Hirwaun (TMO) 26m 02c

**Level Crossings from Pontarddulais Station to
Ammanford Station**

① Tynycynllwyn (UWC) 6m 28ch
② Ynys Uchaf (UWC) 7m 12ch
③ Tynycerig 1 (UWC) 7m 46ch
④ Tynycerig 2 (UWC) 7m 56ch
⑤ Tynycerig 3 (UWC) 7m 62ch
⑥ Hendrewen Farm 1 (UWC) 7m 66ch
⑦ Hendrewen Farm 3 (UWC) 8m 02ch
⑧ Ynys (UWC) 8m 66ch
⑨ Ynystawleg 1 (UWC) 9m 07ch
⑩ Ynystawleg Farm No. 4 (UWC) 9m 38ch
⑪ Sewerage Works (UWC) 9m 44ch
⑫ Cathan Farm (UWC) 9m 60ch
⑬ Pantyffynnon (MCG) 10m 11ch
⑭ Tirydail (ABCL) 11m 24ch

Llwynllanc Farm 1 (UWC) 5m 03ch

Cefn Coed (UWC)
4m 19ch

Ryans Disposal Point
(Cwmgwrach)
33m 08ch
(end of line
32m 62ch)

Robertstown (TMO) 23m 08ch

Aberdar
(Aberda
22m 34c

Cwmbach Sidings (UWC
Cwmbach (U

Pontarddulais
5m 26ch

Grovesend Colliery Loop Jn.
0m 05ch / 0m 00ch (to Hendy Jn.)
Grovesend Colliery Loop GF
(Loop oou) 9m 34ch

Ynysdwrhant (UWC) 36m 34ch
Clyne (TMO) 37m 34ch

Station GF
23m 57ch

End of Line
24m 04ch

Treherbert
(Dreherber)
23m 54ch

Ynyswen
22m 70ch

Treorchy
(Trehorci)
22m 02ch

6m 45ch
6m 58ch

Ton Pentr
20m 76ch

(UWC) 1m 77ch
m 31ch
Penllergaer
Tunnel

T.A.V.R. (UWC) 21m 30ch

Single Line Jn.
20m 13ch

ghor Viaduct
7ch to 221m 68ch

Ystrad Rhondda
20m 05ch

Neath

Tonypandy
18m 03ch

Cockett West Jn.
217m 66ch

Dinas Rh
17m

Swansea

Single Line J
16m 16c

2

Blaengarw
End of Line
5m 16ch

Maesteg
8m 06ch

Maesteg
(Ewenny Road)
7m 54ch

Port Talbot

Garth
7m 01ch

3m 14ch

Tondu Jn.
0m 00ch (Margam Line)
2m 70ch (Maesteg Line)

See Map 116

Margam East
200m 31ch

British Tissues (UWC)
5m 00ch

Cefn Jn.
Change of mileage
2m 43ch from Tondu /
7m 41ch from Margam

Tondu SB
0m 00ch /
2m 70ch

Pontycymmer branch
(oou beyond 0m 48ch)

Knuckle Yard

Heol-y-Deliaid (UWC) 199m 60ch \2m 02ch

Margam Moors Jn.
198m 64ch

Aberbaiden
Parc Slip

Margam Abbey Works
2m 41ch towards Tondu
199m 20ch (Main Line)

① ②

Llar
183

To Margam
Depot

Tondu
2m 63ch

Sarn
2m 11ch

Wildmill
0m 64ch

Pencoed
(Up Platform)
186m 49ch

Pyle
(Pil)
196m 40ch

Stormy Down
& Up Loops
194m 51ch

River Bridge
191m 21ch

Llynfi Jn.
190m 62ch /
0m 07ch

Llanha
184

Pencoed (CCTV) 186m

Aberbaiden South GF
6m 31ch

Barrow crossing 190m 53ch

Pencoed
(Down Platform)
186m 60ch

Aberbaiden North GF
6m 56ch

Bridgend
(Pen y Bont)
190m 45ch

Torcoed 2 (UWC) 187m 63ch
Coychurch Footpath (R/G-X) 188m 37c

Tremains DPL 189m 28ch

**Level Crossings between Newlands Jn.
and Tondu Station**

① Cwmffoes (TMO) 2m 08ch
② Fountain (AOCL) 1m 05ch

Bridgend (Barry Jn)
190m 35ch (via Pontyclun)
18m 78ch (via Barry)

Cowbridge Rd SB
18m 53ch

Waterton (AOCL) 1m 13ch

Ford Siding GF
18m 00ch / 0m 00ch

Fords Jn.
17m 78ch

Farmers (UWC) 13m 72ch
Llandow (UWC) 13m 25ch

Barry Jn.
8m 16ch /
0m 00ch

BARRY DOCKS

Cadoxton
(Tregatwg)
6m 10ch

Down
Reception Line
GF 6m 19ch

Llantwit Major
9m 55ch

Porthkerry No. 2
Tunnel

Barry
(Barri)
8m 12ch

To Barry Docks /
Associated British Ports

3

Porthkerry No. 1
Tunnel

Barry Docks
(Dociaur Barri)
6m 78ch

Barry SB (B) 8m 07ch

0m 77ch
1m 73ch
1m 76ch   0m 52ch

Barry Island
(Ynys-y-Barri)
8m 70ch

Church Farm (UWC) 7m 00ch

A
A

Single Line Jn.
8m 30ch

Barry Island Viaduct
8m 49ch

E

24

25

A   B

A   B

① Change of mileage
15m 01ch from Cardiff /
12m 41ch towards
Cwmbargoed

② Ystrad Mynach South Jn.
13m 41ch

**Abergavenny
(Y Fenni)**
22m 63ch

Up Goods
Loop

⊠ **Abergavenny SB**
22m 75ch

Penny Farm (UWC) 19m 02ch

Penpergwm (UWC) 25m 41ch

North GF
23m 72ch

**Rhymney
(Rhymni)**
23m 64ch

*End of Line
24m 00ch*

Reads GF
23m 31ch
(Temporary oou)

*End of Line
18m 45ch*

**Ebbw Vale
Parkway**
18m 35ch

South GF
23m 51ch

Pontlottyn
22m 65ch

*End of Line
20m 75ch*

Cwmbargoed
(TMO)
20m 37ch

Loop
20m 41ch

Private Boundary
19m 59ch

Merthyr Tydfil
24m 44ch

**Little Mill Jn
SB (LM)**
30m 52ch

⊠

Little Mill Jn.
30m 55ch

Craig Rhymney (UWC) 20m 72ch

Tir-Phil
20m 40ch

*(Change of ELR)
Former Aberbeeg Jn.
14m 23ch*

37ch

Change of mileage
22m 23ch from Cardiff /
m 68ch towards Aberdare

Pentre-Bach
23m 03ch

Troed-Y-Rhiw
South Jn.
21m 52ch

Brithdir
19m 31ch

*Bargoed SB
18m 07ch*
⊠

former
Glascoed branch
oou from 29m 15ch

Troed-y-Rhiw
21m 69ch

Abercwmboi Loop
21m 22ch

Single Line Jn
18m 09ch

Bargoed
18m 03ch

Llanhilleth
13m 29ch

**Pontypool & New Inn
(Pont-y-Pwl)**
32m 19ch

ch

**Merthyr
Vale**
19m 77ch

Bargoed South Jn.
17m 54ch

**Gilfach
Fargoed**
17m 35ch

Panteg
Steelworks

Pilkington Glass
Siding

Fernhill
20m 79ch

Single Line Jn.
20m 16ch /
0m 38ch

Blacklion Jn.
19m 62ch

**Quakers Yard
(Mynwent y
Crynwr)**
17m 73ch

Pengam
16m 30ch

Up Goods
Siding

Chapel Lane GF
34m 22ch

Mountain Ash
20m 02ch

Single Line Jn.
19m 60ch /
0m 00ch

Change of ELR
13m 53ch

Gibbons (UWC) 15m 40ch

Newbridge
10m 45ch

Cwmbran
35m 13ch

Penrhiwceiber
18m 75ch

Abercynon Jn.
16m 20ch

Llancaiach Isaf
(UWC) 13m 26ch

①

Hengoed
14m 55ch

e Jn.
ch
C) 19m 63ch

Abercynon
16m 26ch

⊠ **Abercynon SB**
16m 25ch

②

Ystrad Mynach
*13m 63ch (Up) /
13m 57ch (Down)*

Crosskeys Jn.
7m 18ch

pia

Former
Stormstown Jn.
15m 40ch

⊠ **Ysyrad
Mynach SB (YM)**
13m 33ch

Crosskeys
7m 05ch

Ponthir (UWC) 38m 03ch

Trehafod
14m 72ch

Llanbradach
*10m 74ch (Up) /
10m 68ch (Down)*

Newport

Porth
6m 09ch

Pontypridd
12m 72ch

Pontypridd Jn.
13m 04ch

Trefforest
12m 00ch

**Caerphilly
(Caerffili)**
8m 21ch

Engineer's
Siding

Pontypridd South Jn.
12m 47ch

Aber
8m 70ch

7m 14ch

*Bishton
152m 30ch*

Bishton (MCG)
153m 01ch

2

Trefforest Estate
9m 53ch

Caerphilly Tunnel

6m 06ch

To Exchange
Sidings

Mag
151m

Llantrisant West GF
181m 77ch

**Kisvane &
Thornhill
(Llys-Faen)**
5m 45ch

West GF

Llanwern Works
East Connection
153m 05ch

**Taffs Well
(Ffynnon Taf)**
7m 24ch

Pontyclun
181m 40ch

Llanishen
4m 61ch

Llanwern Works
West Connection
156m 03ch

See Map 117

nt West
181m 76ch

179m 52ch

Up / Down
Goods Loop

179m 02ch

**Cardiff
Queen Street**

Mandy Bach (UWC) 178m 65ch

Pontsarn (A4BC) 178m 39ch

Gywn-y-Gaer (UWC) 177m 75ch

Morlanga (UWC) 176m 07ch

St. George's (CCTV) 175m 61ch

St. George's Church (UWC) 175m 40ch

**Cardiff
Central**

See Map 117

3

15

Cement GF
36ch

See Left

Cement
Works

Barry

*Yatton GF
130m 41ch*

Ya
130

(CCTV)

Yatton
Loops

n

Rhoose
3m 22ch

Hulsh (CCTV) 13

wan /
v SB

*Single Line
137m 14ch*

Worle
134m 42ch

Weston-S-M Up GF
137m 22ch

Weston Milton
136m 12ch

Puxton & Worle (MCB) 13

Weston-super-Mare
137m 33ch

Worle Jn.
135m 1

River Usk

1

27

r Taff

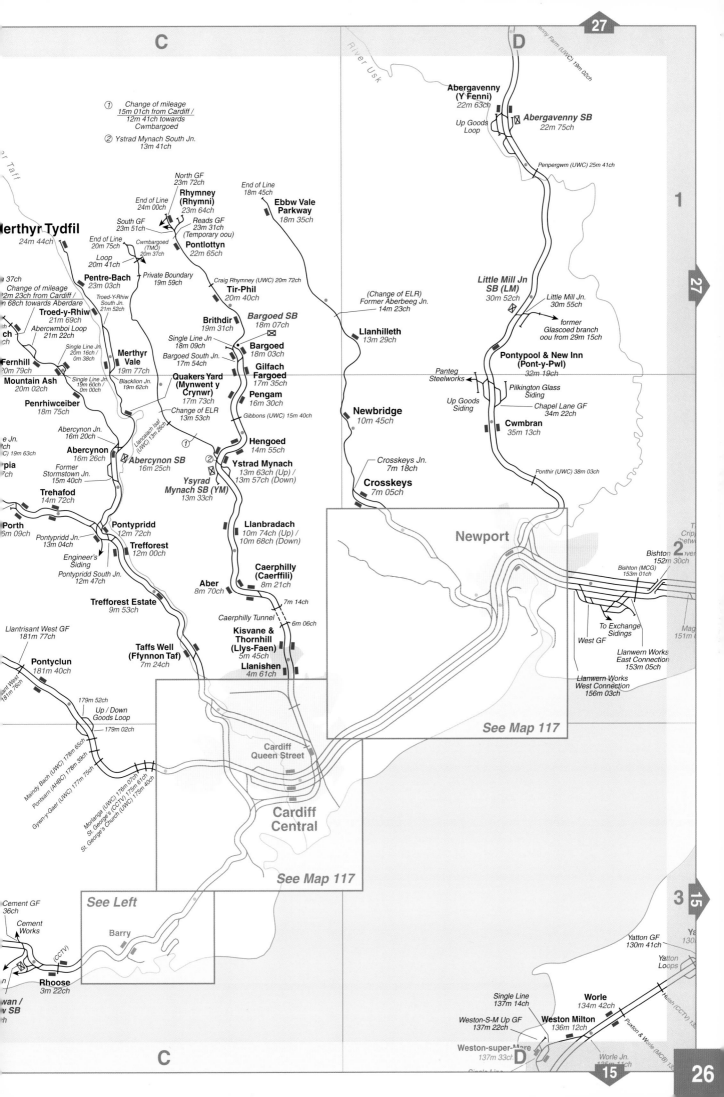

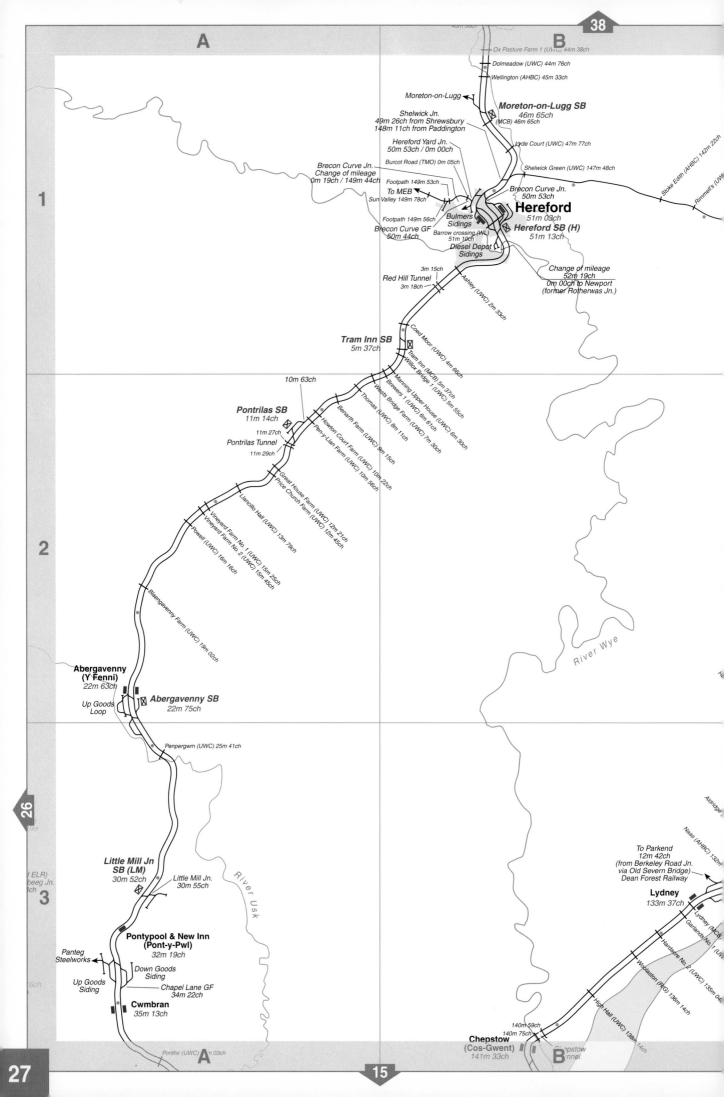

Ox Pasture Farm 1 (UWC) 44m 38ch
Dolmeadow (UWC) 44m 76ch
Wellington (AHBC) 45m 33ch

Moreton-on-Lugg ◄

Moreton-on-Lugg SB
(MCB) 46m 65ch
46m 65ch

Shelwick Jn.
49m 26ch from Shrewsbury
148m 11ch from Paddington

Lyde Court (UWC) 47m 77ch

Hereford Yard Jn.
50m 53ch / 0m 00ch

Burcot Road (TMO) 0m 05ch

Shelwick Green (UWC) 147m 48ch

Brecon Curve Jn.
Change of mileage
0m 19ch / 149m 44ch

Footpath 149m 53ch

Stoke Edith (AHBC) 142m 22ch

Rimmell's (U...

To MEB ◄

Sun Valley 149m 78ch

Brecon Curve Jn.
50m 53ch

Hereford
51m 03ch

Footpath 149m 56ch

Bulmers
Sidings

Barrow crossing (WL)
51m 10ch

Brecon Curve GF
50m 44ch

Hereford SB (H)
51m 13ch

Diesel Depot
Sidings

Change of mileage
52m 19ch
0m 00ch to Newport
(former Rotherwas Jn.)

3m 15ch

Red Hill Tunnel
3m 18ch

Ashley (UWC) 2m 33ch

Tram Inn SB
5m 37ch

Coed Moor (UWC) 4m 66ch

Tram Inn (MCB) 5m 37ch

Willox Bridge 1 (UWC) 5m 55ch

10m 63ch

Manning Upper House (UWC) 6m 30ch

Brewers 1 (UWC) 6m 61ch

Wests Bridge Farm (UWC) 7m 30ch

Thomas (UWC) 8m 11ch

Pontrilas SB
11m 14ch

Howton Court Farm (UWC) 9m 15ch

Benarth Farm (UWC) 9m 61ch

11m 27ch

Pen-y-Llan Farm (UWC) 10m 22ch

Pontrilas Tunnel
11m 29ch

Great House Farm (UWC) 10m 56ch

Price Church Farm (UWC) 12m 45ch

Llancillo Hall (UWC) 13m 79ch

Great House Farm (UWC) 12m 21ch

Vineyard Farm No.1 (UWC) 15m 25ch

Vineyard Farm No.2 (UWC) 15m 45ch

Powell (UWC) 16m 16ch

Blaengaventy Farm (UWC) 19m 02ch

River Wye

**Abergavenny
(Y Fenni)**
22m 63ch

Up Goods
Loop

Abergavenny SB
22m 75ch

Penpergwm (UWC) 25m 41ch

River Usk

26

Use

*(Y ELR)
beeg Jn.
...ch*

Aldridge

Naas (AHBC) 132m...

To Parkend
12m 42ch
(from Berkeley Road Jn.
via Old Severn Bridge)
Dean Forest Railway

Lydney
133m 37ch

Lydney (MCB)...

Garlands No.1...

**Little Mill Jn
SB (LM)**
30m 52ch

Little Mill Jn.
30m 55ch

Hardwire No.2 (UWC) 135m 04ch

Woolaston (R/G) 136m 14ch

High Hall (UWC) 138m 14ch

**Pontypool & New Inn
(Pont-y-Pwl)**
32m 19ch

Panteg
Steelworks ◄

Down Goods
Siding

Up Goods
Siding

Chapel Lane GF
34m 22ch

Cwmbran
35m 13ch

140m 59ch

140m 75ch

**Chepstow
(Cas-Gwent)**
141m 33ch

Chepstow
Tunnel

6ch

Ponthir (UWC) ...m 03ch

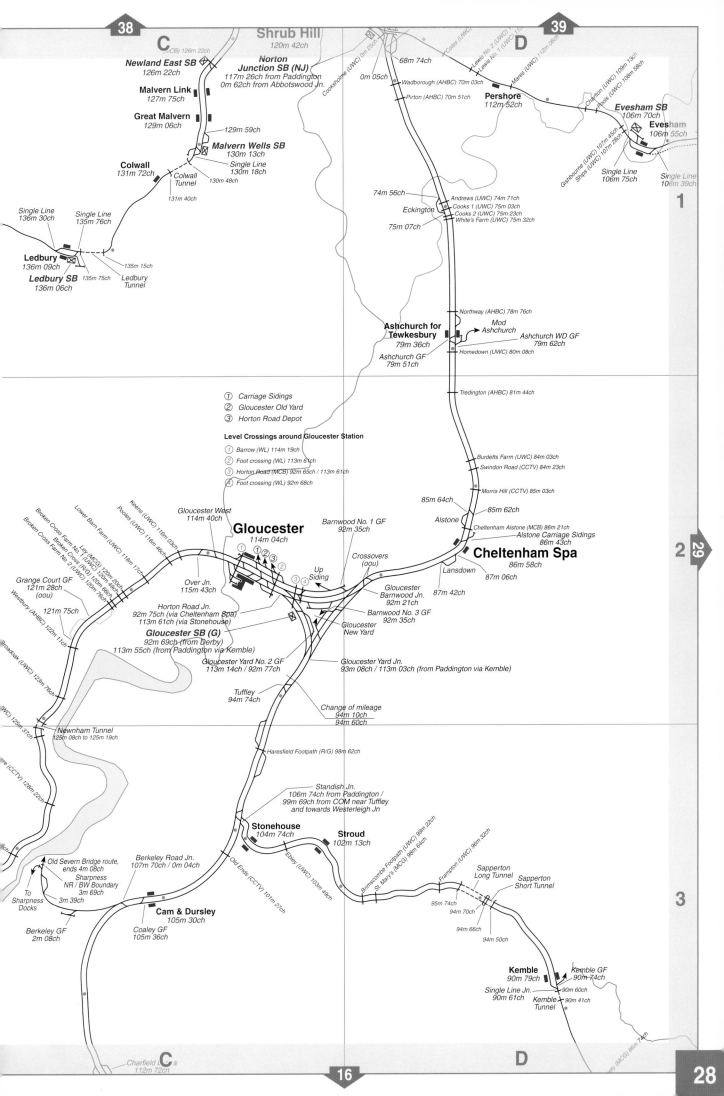

Shrub Hill
120m 42ch

(MCB) 126m 22ch
Newland East SB
126m 22ch

Norton
Junction SB (NJ)
117m 26ch from Paddington
0m 62ch from Abbotswood Jn.

Malvern Link
127m 75ch

Great Malvern
129m 06ch

129m 59ch

Malvern Wells SB
130m 13ch

Colwall
131m 72ch

Single Line
130m 18ch

130m 48ch

Colwall
Tunnel
131m 40ch

Single Line
136m 30ch

Single Line
135m 76ch

135m 15ch

Ledbury
136m 09ch

Ledbury SB
136m 06ch

135m 75ch

Ledbury
Tunnel

Cooksholme (UWC) 0m 25ch

68m 74ch

0m 05ch

Wadborough (AHBC) 70m 03ch

Pirton (AHBC) 70m 51ch

Coles (UWC)

Lewis No. 2 (UWC)
Lewis No. 1 (UWC)

Mares (UWC) 112m 06ch

Chilton (UWC) 109m 13ch

Cools (UWC) 108m 58ch

Pershore
112m 52ch

Evesham SB
106m 70ch

Evesham
106m 55ch

Gishbourne (UWC) 107m 45ch

Ships (UWC) 107m 26ch

Single Line
106m 75ch

Single Line
106m 39ch

74m 56ch

Andrews (UWC) 74m 71ch
Cooks 1 (UWC) 75m 03ch
Cooks 2 (UWC) 75m 23ch
White's Farm (UWC) 75m 32ch

Eckington

75m 07ch

Northway (AHBC) 78m 76ch

Mod
Ashchurch

Ashchurch for
Tewkesbury
79m 36ch

Ashchurch GF
79m 51ch

Ashchurch WD GF
79m 62ch

Homedown (UWC) 80m 08ch

Tredington (AHBC) 81m 44ch

① Carriage Sidings
② Gloucester Old Yard
③ Horton Road Depot

Level Crossings around Gloucester Station

① Barrow (WL) 114m 19ch
② Foot crossing (WL) 113m 61ch
③ Horton Road (MCB) 92m 65ch / 113m 61ch
④ Foot crossing (WL) 92m 68ch

Burdetts Farm (UWC) 84m 03ch
Swindon Road (CCTV) 84m 23ch

Morris Hill (CCTV) 85m 03ch

85m 64ch

85m 62ch

Alstone

Cheltenham Alstone (MCB) 86m 21ch

Alstone Carriage Sidings
86m 43ch

Cheltenham Spa
86m 58ch

87m 06ch

Lansdown

87m 42ch

Broken Cross Farm No. 1 (UWC) 120m 48ch
Broken Cross Farm (FG) 120m 46ch
Broken Cross Farm No. 2 (UWC) 120m 86ch

Lower Barn Farm (UWC) 118m 17ch

Ley (MCG) 120m 20ch

Keens (UWC) 116m 03ch

Pooles (UWC) 116m 46ch

Gloucester West
114m 40ch

Gloucester
114m 04ch

Barnwood No. 1 GF
92m 35ch

Crossovers
(oou)

Grange Court GF
121m 28ch
(oou)

121m 75ch

Westbury (AHBC) 122m 11ch

Over Jn.
115m 43ch

Up
Siding

Horton Road Jn.
92m 75ch (via Cheltenham Spa)
113m 61ch (via Stonehouse)

Gloucester
Barnwood Jn.
92m 21ch

Barnwood No. 3 GF
92m 35ch

Gloucester SB (G)
92m 69ch (from Derby)
113m 55ch (from Paddington via Kemble)

Gloucester
New Yard

Broadoak (UWC) 123m 76ch

Gloucester Yard No. 2 GF
113m 14ch / 92m 77ch

Gloucester Yard Jn.
93m 08ch / 113m 03ch (from Paddington via Kemble)

(UWC) 125m 37ch

Tuffley
94m 74ch

Change of mileage
94m 10ch
94m 60ch

Newnham Tunnel
125m 08ch to 125m 19ch

(CCTV) 128m 22ch

Haresfield Footpath (R/G) 98m 62ch

Standish Jn.
106m 74ch from Paddington /
99m 69ch from COM near Tuffley
and towards Westerleigh Jn

Stonehouse
104m 74ch

Stroud
102m 13ch

Brimscombe Footpath (UWC) 99m 22ch

St. Mary's (MCG) 98m 64ch

Frampton (UWC) 96m 32ch

Sapperton
Long Tunnel

Sapperton
Short Tunnel

Old Severn Bridge route,
ends 4m 08ch

Sharpness
NR / BW Boundary
3m 69ch

3m 39ch

To
Sharpness
Docks

Berkeley Road Jn.
107m 70ch / 0m 04ch

Ebley (UWC) 103m 49ch

Old Ends (CCTV) 101m 27ch

95m 74ch

94m 70ch

94m 66ch

94m 50ch

Cam & Dursley
105m 30ch

Berkeley GF
2m 08ch

Coaley GF
105m 36ch

Kemble
90m 79ch

Single Line Jn.
90m 61ch

Kemble GF
90m 74ch

90m 60ch

90m 41ch

Kemble
Tunnel

107m (MCG) 86m 41ch

Charfield LCs
112m 72ch

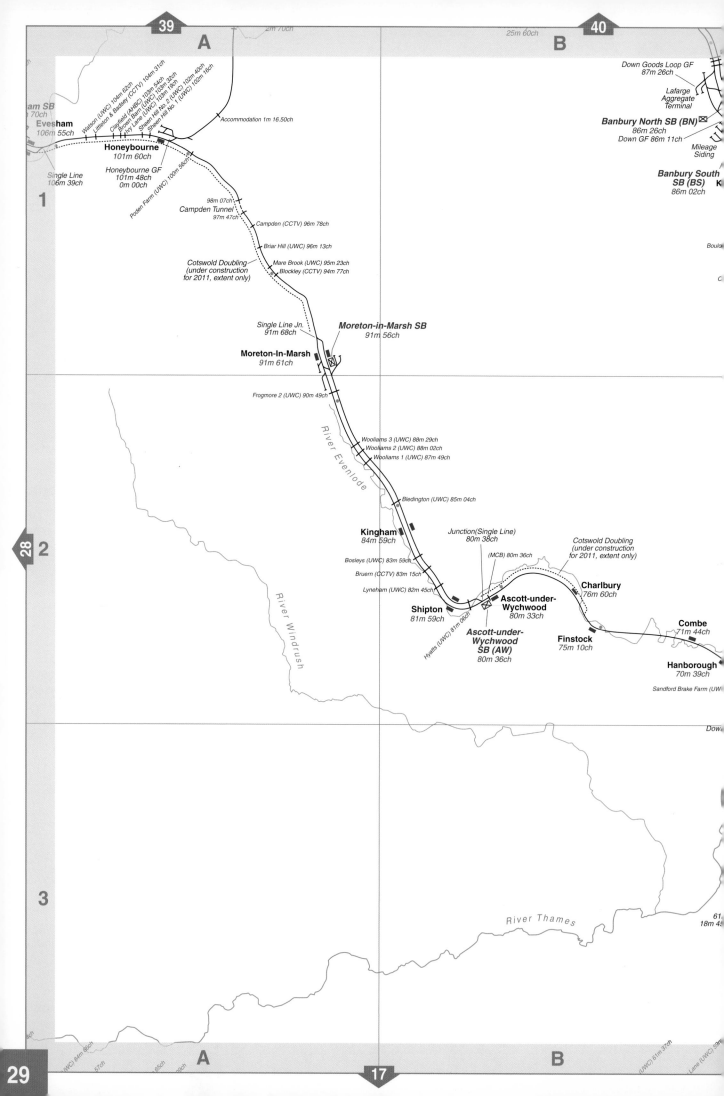

2m 70ch

25m 60ch

Down Goods Loop GF
87m 26ch

Lafarge
Aggregate
Terminal

Banbury North SB (BN) ⊠
86m 26ch
Down GF 86m 11ch

Mileage
Siding

Banbury South
SB (BS) K
86m 02ch

Boula

C

am SB
70ch
Evesham
106m 55ch

Watson (UWC) 104m 62ch
Littleton & Badsey (CCTV) 104m 31ch
Clayfield (AHBC) 103m 54ch
Brown Barn (UWC) 103m 32ch
Ivy Lane (UWC) 103m 19ch
Sheen Hill No 2 (UWC) 102m 40ch
Sheen Hill No 1 (UWC) 102m 16ch

Accommodation 1m 16.50ch

Honeybourne
101m 60ch

Honeybourne GF
101m 48ch
0m 00ch

Single Line
106m 39ch

Poden Farm (UWC) 100m 56ch

98m 07ch

Campden Tunnel
97m 47ch

Campden (CCTV) 96m 78ch

Briar Hill (UWC) 96m 13ch

Cotswold Doubling
(under construction
for 2011, extent only)

Mare Brook (UWC) 95m 23ch
Blockley (CCTV) 94m 77ch

Single Line Jn.
91m 68ch

Moreton-in-Marsh SB
91m 56ch

Moreton-In-Marsh
91m 61ch

Frogmore 2 (UWC) 90m 49ch

River Evenlode

Wooliams 3 (UWC) 88m 29ch
Wooliams 2 (UWC) 88m 02ch
Wooliams 1 (UWC) 87m 49ch

Bledington (UWC) 85m 04ch

Kingham
84m 59ch

Junction(Single Line)
80m 38ch

(MCB) 80m 36ch

Cotswold Doubling
(under construction
for 2011, extent only)

Bosleys (UWC) 83m 59ch

Bruern (CCTV) 83m 15ch

Lyneham (UWC) 82m 45ch

Charlbury
76m 60ch

River Windrush

Shipton
81m 59ch

Ascott-under-
Wychwood
80m 33ch

Combe
71m 44ch

Hyatts (UWC) 81m 06ch

Ascott-under-
Wychwood
SB (AW)
80m 36ch

Finstock
75m 10ch

Hanborough
70m 39ch

Sandford Brake Farm (UW

Dow

River Thames

61
18m 4

28
1
2
3

(WC) 84m 06ch
57ch
65ch

(UWC) 61m 37ch

Lane (UWC

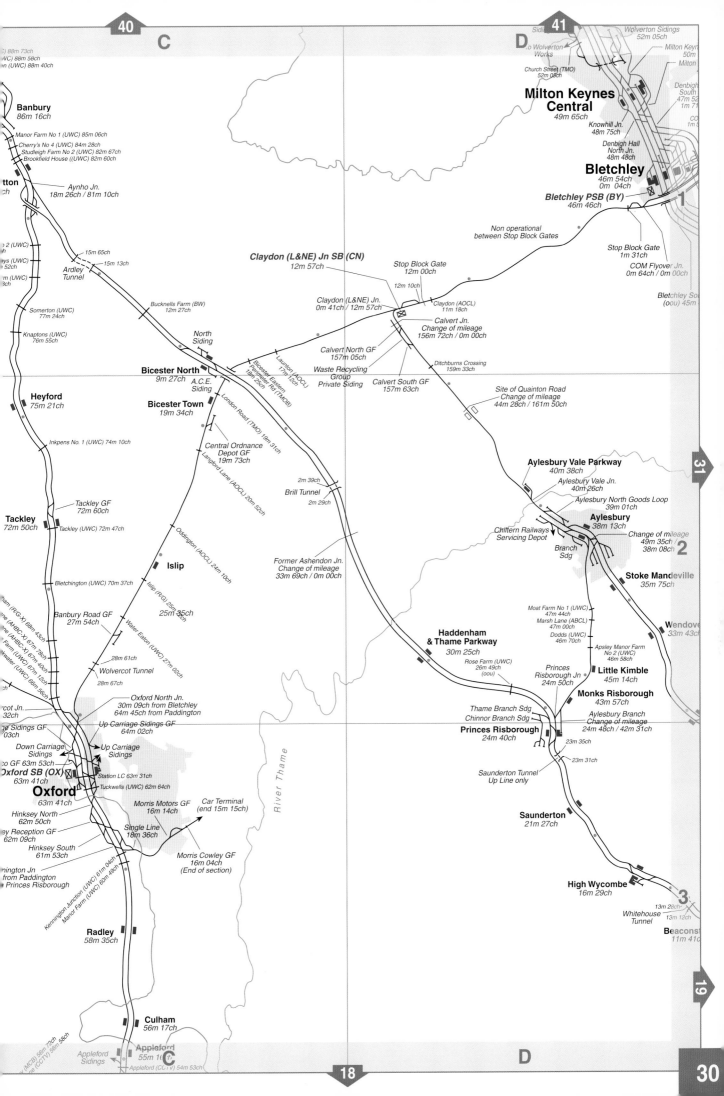

88m 73ch
WC) 88m 58ch
(UWC) 88m 40ch

Banbury
86m 16ch

Manor Farm No 1 (UWC) 85m 06ch
Cherry's No 4 (UWC) 84m 28ch
Studleigh Farm No 2 (UWC) 82m 67ch
Brookfield House ((UWC) 82m 60ch

tton

Aynho Jn.
18m 26ch / 81m 10ch

2 (UWC)
ys (UWC)
m (UWC)
ch

15m 65ch

15m 13ch

Ardley
Tunnel

Somerton (UWC)
77m 24ch

Knaptons (UWC)
76m 55ch

Heyford
75m 21ch

Inkpens No. 1 (UWC) 74m 10ch

Tackley GF
72m 60ch

Tackley
72m 50ch

Tackley (UWC) 72m 47ch

Bletchington (UWC) 70m 37ch

Banbury Road GF
27m 54ch

ham (R.G.X) 69m 43ch
ne (AHBC-X) 67m 78ch
ne (AHBC-X) 67m 76ch
Farm (UWC) 67m 12ch
water (UWC) 66m 56ch

Bucknells Farm (BW)
12m 27ch

North
Siding

Bicester North
9m 27ch

A.C.E.
Siding

Claydon (L&NE) Jn SB (CN)
12m 57ch

Stop Block Gate
12m 00ch

12m 10ch

Claydon (L&NE) Jn.
0m 41ch / 12m 57ch

Claydon (AOCL)
11m 18ch

Calvert Jn.
Change of mileage
156m 72ch / 0m 00ch

Calvert North GF
157m 05ch

Waste Recycling
Group
Private Siding

Calvert South GF
157m 63ch

Ditchburns Crossing
159m 33ch

Non operational
between Stop Block Gates

Milton Keynes
Central
49m 65ch

o Wolverton
Works

Wolverton Sidings
52m 05ch

Milton Keyn
50m

Milton

Church Street (TMO)
52m 08ch

Denbigh
South
47m 52ch
1m 71

CO
1m 5

Knowhill Jn.
48m 75ch

Denbigh Hall
North Jn.
48m 48ch

Bletchley
46m 54ch
0m 04ch

Bletchley PSB (BY)
46m 46ch

Stop Block Gate
1m 31ch

COM Flyover Jn.
0m 64ch / 0m 00ch

Bletchley So
(oou) 45m

Bicester Eastern
Perimeter Rd (TMOB)
18m 25ch

Launton (AOCL)
17m 12ch

Bicester Town
19m 34ch

London Road (TMO) 19m 31ch

Central Ordnance
Depot GF
19m 73ch

Langford Lane (AOCL) 20m 52ch

Oddington (AOCL) 24m 10ch

2m 39ch

Brill Tunnel
2m 29ch

Site of Quainton Road
Change of mileage
44m 28ch / 161m 50ch

Aylesbury Vale Parkway
40m 38ch

Aylesbury Vale Jn.
40m 26ch

Aylesbury North Goods Loop
39m 01ch

Aylesbury
38m 13ch

Chiltern Railways
Servicing Depot

Change of mileage
49m 35ch /
38m 08ch

Branch
Sdg

Stoke Mandeville
35m 75ch

Wendove
33m 43ch

Islip

Islip (R.(G) 25m 35ch

25m 35ch

Water Eaton (UWC) 27m 02ch

28m 61ch

Wolvercot Tunnel

28m 67ch

Former Ashendon Jn.
Change of mileage
33m 69ch / 0m 00ch

Haddenham
& Thame Parkway
30m 25ch

Rose Farm (UWC)
26m 49ch
(oou)

Moat Farm No 1 (UWC)
47m 44ch
Marsh Lane (ABCL)
47m 00ch
Dodds (UWC)
46m 70ch

Apsley Manor Farm
No 2 (UWC)
46m 58ch

Little Kimble
45m 14ch

Princes
Risborough Jn.
24m 50ch

Monks Risborough
43m 57ch

Oxford North Jn.
30m 09ch from Bletchley
64m 45ch from Paddington

Up Carriage Sidings GF
64m 02ch

Up Carriage
Sidings

rcot Jn.
32ch

ge Sidings GF
03ch

Down Carriage
Sidings

co GF 63m 53ch

Oxford SB (OX)
63m 41ch

Oxford
63m 41ch

Station LC 63m 31ch

Tuckwells (UWC) 63m 29ch

Hinksey North
62m 50ch

y Reception GF
62m 09ch

Hinksey South
61m 53ch

nington Jn
from Paddington
Princes Risborough

Kennington Junction (UWC) 61m 04ch/ 60m 49ch

Manor Farm (UWC) 60m 49ch

Morris Motors GF
16m 14ch

Car Terminal
(end 15m 15ch)

Single Line
18m 36ch

Morris Cowley GF
16m 04ch
(End of section)

River Thame

Thame Branch Sdg
Chinnor Branch Sdg

Princes Risborough
24m 40ch

Aylesbury Branch
Change of mileage
24m 48ch / 42m 31ch

23m 35ch

23m 31ch

Saunderton Tunnel
Up Line only

Saunderton
21m 27ch

High Wycombe
16m 29ch

Whitehouse
Tunnel

13m 28ch
13m 12ch

Beaconsf
11m 41

Radley
58m 35ch

Culham
56m 17ch

(MCB) 56m 72ch/ 56m 58ch
idge (CCTV) 56m 53ch

Appleford
55m 1

Appleford
Sidings

Appleford (CCTV) 54m 53ch

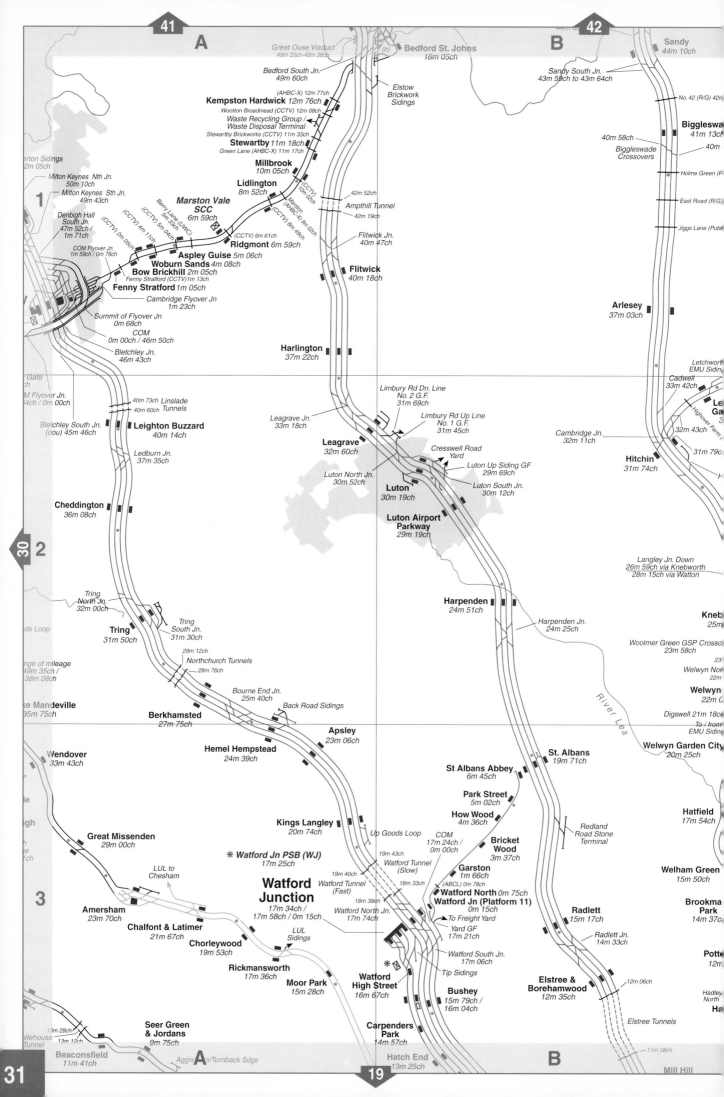

A

B

Sandy
44m 10ch

Great Ouse Viaduct
49m 33ch–49m 38ch

(b) Bedford St. Johns
16m 05ch

Bedford South Jn.
49m 60ch

Sandy South Jn.
43m 59ch to 43m 64ch

No. 42 (R/G) 42m

Elstow
Brickwork
Sidings

(AHBC-X) 12m 77ch

Kempston Hardwick 12m 76ch

Wootton Broadmead (CCTV) 12m 08ch

Bigglesw...
41m 13ch

40m 58ch

40m

Waste Recycling Group /
Waste Disposal Terminal

*Bigglesw...
Crossovers*

Stewartby Brickworks (CCTV) 11m 33ch

Stewartby 11m 18ch

Holme Green (F...

Green Lane (AHBC-X) 11m 17ch

Millbrook
10m 05ch

East Road (R/G...

(CCTV)
10m 02ch

Lidlington
8m 52ch

42m 52ch

Marston
(AHBC-X) 9m 02ch

Ampthill Tunnel
42m 19ch

Jiggs Lane (Pub...

Marston Vale
SCC
6m 59ch

*Berry Lane (UWC)
5m 33ch*

(CCTV)
5m 04ch

(CCTV) 8m 49ch

Flitwick Jn.
40m 47ch

(CCTV) 4m 11ch

(CCTV) 2m 05ch

(CCTV) 6m 61ch

Ridgmont 6m 59ch

Flitwick
40m 18ch

Arlesey
37m 03ch

Milton Keynes Nth Jn.
50m 10ch

Milton Keynes Sth Jn.
49m 43ch

Aspley Guise 5m 06ch

Woburn Sands 4m 08ch

Denbigh Hall
South Jn.
47m 52ch /
1m 71ch

Bow Brickhill 2m 05ch

Fenny Stratford (CCTV) 1m 13ch

Fenny Stratford 1m 05ch

COM Flyover Jn.
1m 59ch / 0m 76ch

Cambridge Flyover Jn.
1m 23ch

Harlington
37m 22ch

Letchwort...
EMU Sidin...

Summit of Flyover Jn.
0m 68ch

COM
0m 00ch / 46m 50ch

Limbury Rd Dn. Line
No. 2 G.F.
31m 69ch

Cadwell
33m 42ch

Bletchley Jn.
46m 43ch

Leagrave Jn.
33m 18ch

Limbury Rd Up Line
No. 1 G.F.
31m 45ch

Le...
Ga...

Leagrave
32m 60ch

Cresswell Road
Yard

32m 43ch

M Flyover Jn.
4ch / 0m 00ch

40m 73ch *Linslade*
40m 60ch *Tunnels*

31m 79c...

Bletchley South Jn.
(oou) 45m 46ch

Leighton Buzzard
40m 14ch

Luton North Jn.
30m 52ch

Luton Up Siding GF
29m 69ch

Cambridge Jn.
32m 11ch

Hitchin
31m 74ch

Ledburn Jn.
37m 35ch

Luton
30m 19ch

Luton South Jn.
30m 12ch

Cheddington
36m 08ch

Luton Airport
Parkway
29m 19ch

Langley Jn. Down
26m 59ch via Knebworth
28m 15ch via Watton

30

2

Tring
North Jn.
32m 00ch

Harpenden
24m 51ch

Kneb...
25m...

Tring
South Jn.
31m 30ch

Harpenden Jn.
24m 25ch

Woolmer Green GSP Cross...
23m 58ch

Tring
31m 50ch

Welwyn Nor...
22m...

ds Loop

29m 12ch
Northchurch Tunnels
28m 76ch

Welwyn
22m 0...

ge of mileage
49m 35ch /
38m 08ch

Bourne End Jn.
25m 40ch

Digswell 21m 18c...

Back Road Sidings

To / from
EMU Siding...

e Mandeville
35m 75ch

Berkhamsted
27m 75ch

Welwyn Garden City
20m 25ch

Apsley
23m 06ch

Wendover
33m 43ch

Hemel Hempstead
24m 39ch

St. Albans
19m 71ch

St Albans Abbey
6m 45ch

River Lea

Park Street
5m 02ch

Redland
Road Stone
Terminal

Hatfield
17m 54ch

Kings Langley
20m 74ch

Up Goods Loop

How Wood
4m 36ch

Great Missenden
29m 00ch

※ *Watford Jn PSB (WJ)*
17m 25ch

COM
17m 24ch /
0m 00ch

Bricket
Wood
3m 37ch

Welham Green
15m 50ch

19m 43ch

Watford Tunnel
(Slow)

Garston
1m 66ch

LUL to
Chesham

19m 40ch

Watford Tunnel
(Fast)

18m 33ch

(ABCL) 0m 78ch

Watford North 0m 75ch

Watford Jn (Platform 11)
0m 15ch

Brookma...
Park
14m 37c...

Watford
Junction
17m 34ch /
17m 58ch / 0m 15ch

18m 38ch

Watford North Jn.
17m 74ch

To Freight Yard

Yard GF
17m 21ch

Radlett
15m 17ch

Amersham
23m 70ch

LUL
Sidings

Watford South Jn.
17m 06ch

Radlett Jn.
14m 33ch

Pott...
12m...

Chalfont & Latimer
21m 67ch

Tip Sidings

Chorleywood
19m 53ch

※

Watford South Jn.

Watford
High Street
16m 67ch

Watford
12m 06ch

Elstree &
Borehamwood
12m 35ch

Rickmansworth
17m 36ch

Bushey
15m 79ch /
16m 04ch

Hadley
North
Ha...

Moor Park
15m 28ch

Elstree Tunnels

Seer Green
& Jordans
9m 75ch

Carpenders
Park
14m 57ch

13m 28ch
13m 12ch

hitehouse
Tunnel

Beaconsfield
11m 41ch

Aggreg...e/Turnback Sdgs

A

Hatch End
13m 25ch

B

11m 38ch

Mill Hill

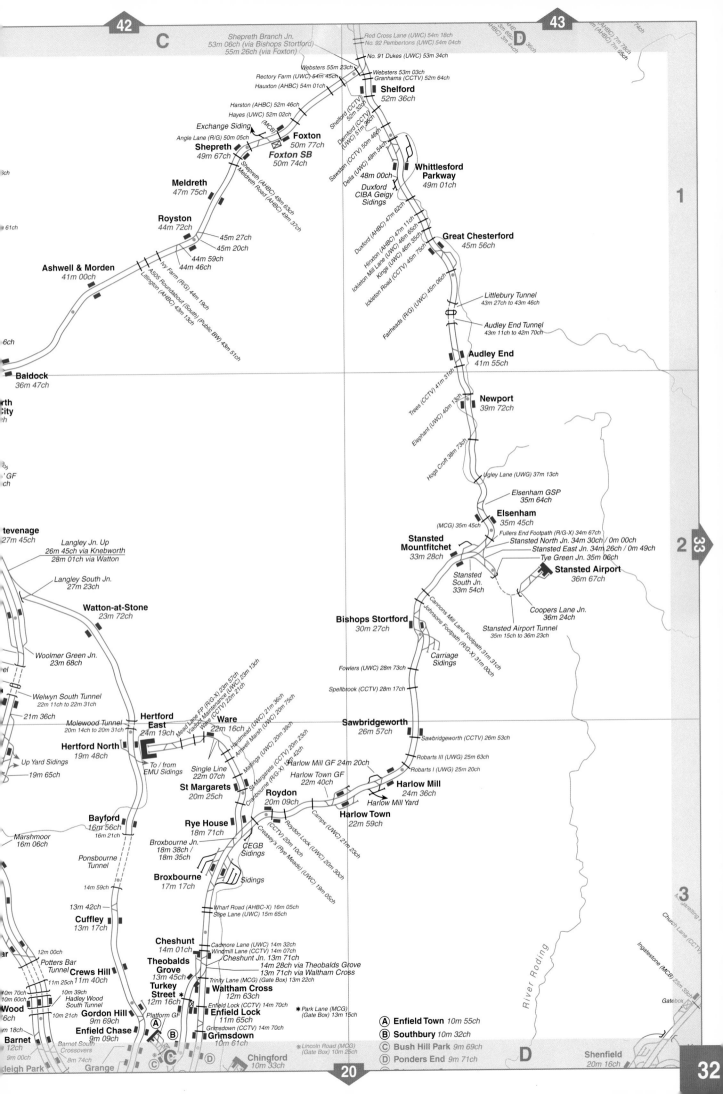

Shepreth Branch Jn.
53m 06ch (via Bishops Stortford)
55m 26ch (via Foxton)

Red Cross Lane (UWC) 54m 18ch
No. 92 Pembertons (UWC) 54m 04ch

No. 91 Dukes (UWC) 53m 34ch

Websters 55m 23ch
Rectory Farm (UWC) 54m 45ch
Hauxton (AHBC) 54m 01ch

Websters 53m 03ch
Granhams (CCTV) 52m 64ch

Shelford
52m 36ch

Harston (AHBC) 52m 46ch
Hayes (UWC) 52m 02ch

Shelford (CCTV)
52m 32ch

Dernford (CCTV)
(UWC) 51m 36ch

Sawston (UWC) 49m 54ch

Whittlesford Parkway
49m 01ch

Exchange Siding (MCB)

Angle Lane (R/G) 50m 05ch

Foxton
50m 77ch

Foxton SB
50m 74ch

Della 48m 00ch

Shepreth
49m 67ch

Duxford
CIBA Geigy
Sidings

Shepreth (AHBC) 49m 63ch
Meldreth Road (AHBC) 49m 37ch

Meldreth
47m 75ch

Duxford (AHBC) 47m 62ch

Hinxton (AHBC) 47m 11ch

Great Chesterford
45m 56ch

Royston
44m 72ch

Ickleton Mill Lane (UWC) 46m 65ch
Kings (UWC) 46m 35ch

45m 27ch
45m 20ch

Ickleton Road (CCTV) 45m 75ch

44m 59ch
44m 46ch

Fairheads (R/G) (UWC) 45m 06ch

Ashwell & Morden
41m 00ch

Ivy Farm (R/G) 44m 19ch

A505 Roundabout (South) (Public BW) 43m 51ch
Litlington (AHBC) 43m 13ch

Littlebury Tunnel
43m 27ch to 43m 46ch

Audley End Tunnel
43m 11ch to 42m 70ch

Baldock
36m 47ch

Audley End
41m 55ch

Trees (CCTV) 41m 31ch

Newport
39m 72ch

Elephant (UWC) 40m 13ch

Hogs Croft 38m 73ch

Ugley Lane (UWG) 37m 13ch

Elsenham GSP
35m 64ch

Elsenham
35m 45ch

tevenage
27m 45ch

Langley Jn. Up
26m 45ch via Knebworth
28m 01ch via Watton

(MCG) 35m 45ch

Fullers End Footpath (R/G-X) 34m 67ch

Stansted Mountfitchet
33m 28ch

Stansted North Jn. 34m 30ch / 0m 00ch
Stansted East Jn. 34m 26ch / 0m 49ch
Tye Green Jn. 35m 06ch

Langley South Jn.
27m 23ch

Stansted
South Jn.
33m 54ch

Stansted Airport
36m 67ch

Watton-at-Stone
23m 72ch

Coopers Lane Jn.
36m 24ch

Woolmer Green Jn.
23m 68ch

Cannons Mill Lane Footpath 31m 31ch

Stansted Airport Tunnel
35m 15ch to 36m 23ch

Johnsons Footpath (R/G-X) 31m 00ch

Bishops Stortford
30m 27ch

Welwyn South Tunnel
22m 11ch to 22m 31ch

Carriage
Sidings

21m 36ch

Fowlers (UWC) 28m 73ch

Molewood Tunnel
20m 14ch to 20m 31ch

Spellbrook (CCTV) 28m 17ch

Hertford East
24m 19ch

Mead Lane FP (R/G-X) 23m 57ch
Viaduct Maintenance (UWC) 23m 13ch
Ware (CCTV) 22m 21ch

Ware
22m 16ch

Sawbridgeworth
26m 57ch

Hertford North
19m 48ch

Hardmead (UWC) 21m 36ch
Amwell Marsh (UWC) 20m 75ch

Sawbridgeworth (CCTV) 26m 53ch

To / from
EMU Sidings

Maltings (UWC) 20m 39ch

Robarts III (UWG) 25m 63ch

Up Yard Sidings

Single Line
22m 07ch

Mallings (CCTV) 20m 23ch

Harlow Mill GF 24m 20ch

Robarts I (UWG) 25m 20ch

19m 65ch

St-Margarets (UWC) 20m 42ch

St Margarets
20m 25ch

Cripboxne (R/G) 20m 17ch

Harlow Town GF
22m 40ch

Harlow Mill
24m 36ch

Roydon
20m 09ch

Harlow Mill Yard

Bayford
16m 56ch

16m 21ch

Rye House
18m 71ch

Roydon Lock (UWC) 20m 10ch

Camps (UWC) 21m 23ch

Harlow Town
22m 59ch

Marshmoor
16m 06ch

Broxbourne Jn.
18m 38ch /
18m 35ch

(CCTV) 20m 10ch

Creassey's (Rye Meads) (UWC) 19m 05ch

CEGB
Sidings

Ponsbourne
Tunnel

Broxbourne
17m 17ch

Sidings

14m 59ch

Wharf Road (AHBC-X) 16m 05ch
Stipe Lane (UWC) 15m 65ch

13m 42ch

Cuffley
13m 17ch

Cheshunt
14m 01ch

Cadmore Lane (UWC) 14m 32ch
Windmill Lane (CCTV) 14m 07ch

Cheshunt Jn. 13m 71ch

12m 00ch

Potters Bar
Tunnel

Theobalds Grove
13m 45ch

14m 28ch via Theobalds Grove
13m 71ch via Waltham Cross

Crews Hill
11m 40ch

11m 25ch

Trinity Lane (MCG) (Gate Box) 13m 22ch

10m 70ch
10m 60ch

Hadley Wood
South Tunnel

Turkey Street
12m 16ch

Waltham Cross
12m 63ch

Wood

10m 39ch

10m 21ch

Gordon Hill
9m 69ch

Enfield Lock (CCTV) 14m 70ch

Park Lane (MCG)
(Gate Box) 13m 15ch

18ch

Platform GF

Enfield Lock
11m 65ch

(A) Enfield Town 10m 55ch

Barnet
12ch

Enfield Chase
9m 09ch

Grimsdown (CCTV) 14m 70ch

(B) Southbury 10m 32ch

00ch

Barnet South
Crossovers

Grimsdown
10m 61ch

(C) Bush Hill Park 9m 69ch

8m 74ch

(A)

(B)

Lincoln Road (MCG)
(Gate Box) 10m 25ch

(D) Ponders End 9m 71ch

leigh Park

Grange

(C)

(D)

Chingford
10m 33ch

Shenfield
20m 16ch

River Roding

Church Lane (CCTV)

Ingatestone (MCB) 23m 39ch

Gatebox

Dullingham SB (DH)
10m 54ch

32

2

3

IPSWICH

Westerfield Station (AHBC) 72m 16ch

Westerfield
72m 20ch

72m 00ch

Westerfield Jn.
72m 23ch

74m 30ch

East Suffolk Jn.
69m 41ch

Upper Yard

69m 60ch

Ranelagh Road (MCG) 0m 56ch

Ipswich Freight Terminal

Derby Road
74m 67ch

To / from Ipswich Docks

75m 12ch

Ipswich Goods Jn.
68m 72ch

68m 70ch
Siding

① ②
oou

Stoke Bridge 1m 23ch

Ipswich
68m 59ch

Siding
68m 47ch

Ipswich Tunnel
68m 31ch

Siding

Halifax Jn.
67m 72ch / 67m 67ch / 0m 00ch
to Griffin Wharf

To Griffin Wharf

Griffin Wharf Boundary
0m 47ch

To West Bank Terminal
0m 38ch

① Field Siding No. 1
② Field Siding No. 2

E

River Blackwater

Sudbury Ladysbridge (UWC) 58m 25ch
Cornard (ABCL) 57m 42ch
Shaffords (UWC) 56m 73ch
Sewage Works Lane (UWC) 56m 62ch

Sudbury
58m 32ch

River Stour

Mount Bures (ABCL) 52m 61ch

Bures
53m 45ch

Museum GF
50m 26ch

Chappel & Wakes Colne
50m 18ch

East Anglian Railway Museum

Church House Farm
47m 56ch

Chitts Hill (MCBI) 49m 41ch

Colchester SB (CO)
51m 37ch

Ardleigh (C

Carriage Sidings

Colchester
51m 52ch

Ardleigh G
56m 00c

Colchester Jn.
51m 65ch

Marks Tey Jn.
46m 56ch
46m 53ch

Colchester Town
53m 76ch
53m 63ch

Hythe
53m 49ch

Marks Tey GF
47m 43ch

Marks Tey
46m 49ch /
46m 59ch

Sidings

Colne Jn.
53m 30ch /0m 00ch

Wivenhoe
56m 00ch

Alres
57

Braintree
17m 71ch

Braintree Freeport
18m 54ch

Cousins No. 2 (UWC) 19m 18ch
Cressing (ABCL) 19m 75ch

Cressing
20m 00ch

Fairheads No. 39 (UWC) 20m 77ch

White Notley
21m 10ch

White Notley (ABCL) 21m 11ch
New House Farm No. 43 21m 65ch

Kelvedon
42m 21ch

Long Green FP (R/G-X) 45m 66ch

Church Street (AHBC-X) 41m 57ch

Cut Throat Lane (R/G) 24m 05ch

Witham Jn.
38m 55ch / 24m 15ch
(Braintree Line)

Motts Lane FP (R/G-X) 39m 02ch

Witham
38m 47ch

River Chelmer

Hatfield Peverel
35m 74ch

Brick House Crossovers
33m 24ch

Siding

Chelmsford
29m 60ch

Arbour Lane Crossovers
30m 30ch

Margaretting FP (R/G) 25m 39ch

Church Lane (CCTV) 24m 68ch

atestone (MCB) 23m 39ch

atebox

South
Woodham

(ABCL) 34m 08ch
1 34m 77ch
1 32m 66ch
1 35m 07ch
1 35m 55ch

Briti **B** nergy
Nucl **B** Electric
Division

Southminster
45m 42ch

GF 45m 30ch

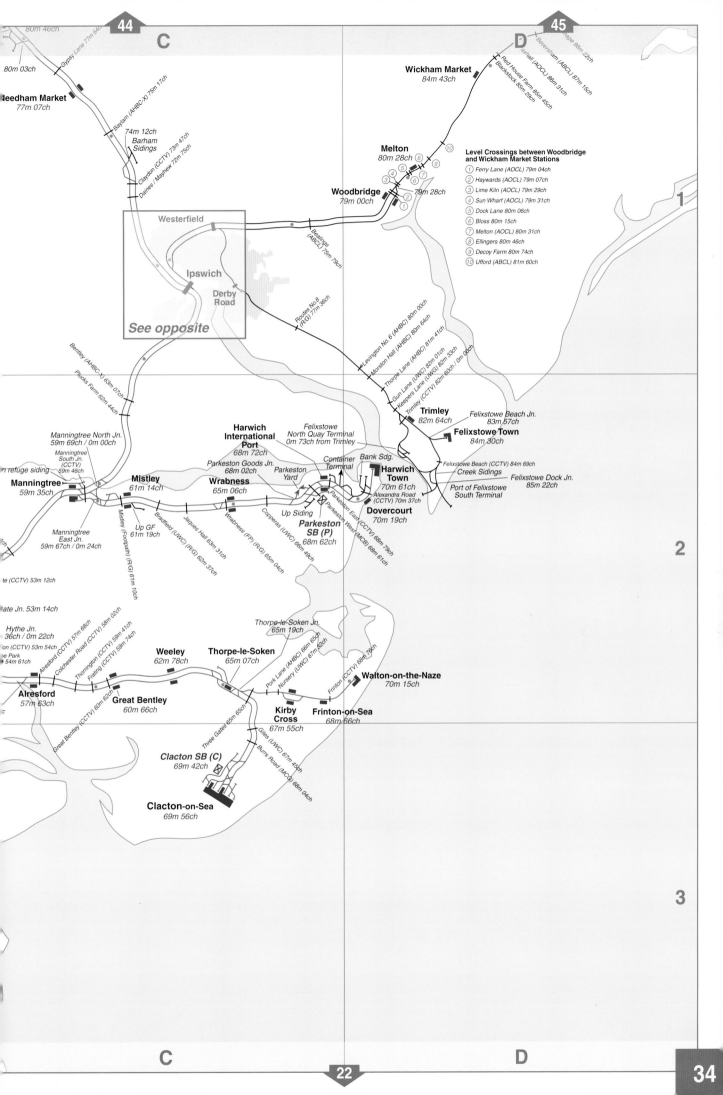

44 C

45 D

1

2

3

22 C — D

34

80m 46ch

80m 03ch

Gypsy Lane 77m 54ch

Needham Market
77m 07ch

Baylam (AHBC-X) 75m 17ch

74m 12ch
Barham
Sidings

Claydon (CCTV) 73m 47ch
Daines / Mayhew 72m 75ch

Wickham Market
84m 43ch

Foxhall (AOCL) (ABCL) 87m 15ch
Beversham (ABCL) 86m 22ch
Red House Farm 86m 31ch
Blackstock 85m 29ch / 45ch

**Level Crossings between Woodbridge
and Wickham Market Stations**
① Ferry Lane (AOCL) 79m 04ch
② Haywards (AOCL) 79m 07ch
③ Lime Kiln (AOCL) 79m 29ch
④ Sun Wharf (AOCL) 79m 31ch
⑤ Dock Lane 80m 06ch
⑥ Bloss 80m 15ch
⑦ Melton (AOCL) 80m 31ch
⑧ Ellingers 80m 46ch
⑨ Decoy Farm 80m 74ch
⑩ Ufford (ABCL) 81m 60ch

Melton
80m 28ch

79m 28ch

Woodbridge
79m 00ch

Westerfield

Ipswich

Derby
Road

See opposite

Bealings (ABCL) 75m 79ch

Routes No 8 (R/G) 77m 36ch

Levington No. 6 (AHBC) 80m 00ch
Morston Hall (AHBC) 80m 64ch
Thorpe Lane (AHBC) 81m 41ch
Gun Lane (UWC) 82m 01ch
Keepers Lane (UWG) 82m 33ch
Trimley (CCTV) 82m 60ch / 0m 00ch

Trimley
82m 64ch

Felixstowe Beach Jn.
83m 57ch

Felixstowe Town
84m 30ch

Felixstowe North Quay Terminal
0m 73ch from Trimley

Bank Sdg.

Felixstowe Beach (CCTV) 84m 69ch
Creek Sidings
Felixstowe Dock Jn.
85m 22ch

Port of Felixstowe
South Terminal

Harwich International
Port
68m 72ch

Parkeston Goods Jn.
68m 02ch

Container
Terminal

Parkeston
Yard

Harwich
Town
70m 61ch

Alexandra Road
(CCTV) 70m 37ch

Dovercourt
70m 19ch

Parkeston East (CCTV) 68m 79ch
Parkeston West (MCB) 68m 61ch

Bentley (AHBC-X) 63m 07ch
Pluc ks Farm 62m 44ch

Manningtree North Jn.
59m 69ch / 0m 00ch

Manningtree
South Jn.
(CCTV)
59m 46ch

n refuge siding

Manningtree
59m 35ch

Mistley
61m 14ch

Wrabness
65m 06ch

Parkeston
SB (P)
68m 62ch

Up Siding

Mistley (Footpath) (R/G) 61m 10ch

Up GF
61m 19ch

Manningtree
East Jn.
59m 67ch / 0m 24ch

Bradfield (UWC) (R/G) 62m 37ch

Jaques Hall 63m 31ch

Wrabness (FP) (R/G) 65m 04ch

Copperas (UWC) 66m 48ch

ate (CCTV) 53m 12ch
ate Jn. 53m 14ch

Hythe Jn.
36ch / 0m 22ch

on (CCTV) 53m 54ch
pe Park
54m 61ch

Alresford (CCTV) 57m 68ch
Colchester Road (CCTV) 58m 02ch
Thorrington (CCTV) 59m 41ch
Frating (CCTV) 59m 74ch

Weeley
62m 78ch

Thorpe-le-Soken
65m 07ch

Thorpe-le-Soken Jn.
65m 19ch

Pork Lane (AHBC) 66m 65ch
Nursery (UWC) 67m 92ch

Frinton (CCTV) 68m 76ch

Walton-on-the-Naze
70m 15ch

Alresford
57m 63ch

Great Bentley
60m 66ch

Great Bentley (CCTV) 60m 62ch

Kirby
Cross
67m 55ch

Frinton-on-Sea
68m 66ch

Three Gates 65m 65ch

Giles (UWC) 67m 45ch
Burrs Road (MCB) 68m 04ch

Clacton SB (C)
69m 42ch

Clacton-on-Sea
69m 56ch

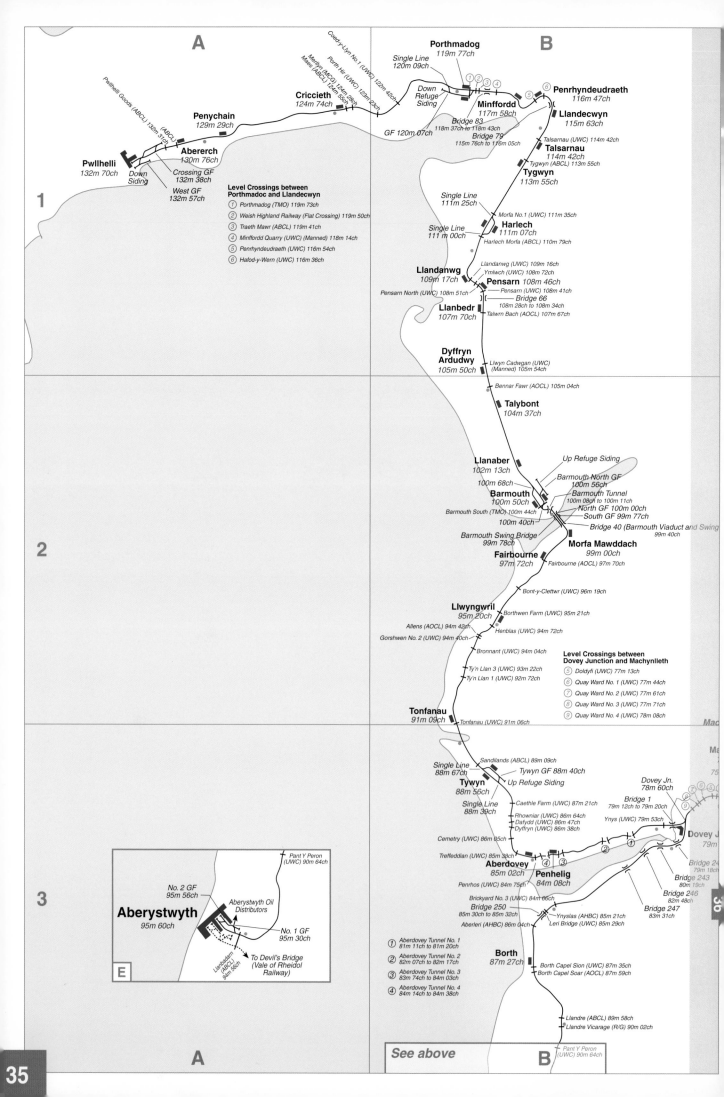

Pwllhelli 132m 70ch
Pwllhelli Goods (ABCL) 132m 31ch
(ABCL)
Down Siding
Abererch 130m 76ch
Crossing GF 132m 38ch
West GF 132m 57ch
Penychain 129m 29ch
Criccieth 124m 74ch
Coed-y-Llyn No.1 (UWC) 122m 26ch
Porth Hir (UWC) 123m 23ch
Merllyn (MCG) 124m 28ch
Mates (ABCL) 124m 55ch

Porthmadog 119m 77ch
Single Line 120m 09ch
Down Refuge Siding
GF 120m 07ch
Minffordd 117m 58ch
Bridge 83 118m 37ch to 118m 43ch
Bridge 79 115m 76ch to 116m 05ch
① ② ③ ④ ⑤ ⑥
Penrhyndeudraeth 116m 47ch
Llandecwyn 115m 63ch
Talsarnau (UWC) 114m 42ch
Talsarnau 114m 42ch
Tygwyn (ABCL) 113m 55ch
Tygwyn 113m 55ch
Single Line 111m 25ch
Morfa No.1 (UWC) 111m 35ch
Harlech 111m 07ch
Single Line 111m 00ch
Harlech Morfa (ABCL) 110m 79ch
Llandanwg 109m 17ch
Llandanwg (UWC) 109m 16ch
Ymlwch (UWC) 108m 72ch
Pensarn 108m 46ch
Pensarn North (UWC) 108m 51ch
Pensarn (UWC) 108m 41ch
Bridge 66 108m 28ch to 108m 34ch
Llanbedr 107m 70ch
Talwrn Bach (AOCL) 107m 67ch

Dyffryn Ardudwy 105m 50ch
Llwyn Cadwgan (UWC) (Manned) 105m 54ch
Bennar Fawr (AOCL) 105m 04ch
Talybont 104m 37ch

Llanaber 102m 13ch
Up Refuge Siding
Barmouth North GF 100m 56ch
100m 68ch
Barmouth Tunnel 100m 08ch to 100m 11ch
Barmouth 100m 50ch
North GF 100m 00ch
Barmouth South (TMO) 100m 44ch
South GF 99m 77ch
100m 40ch
Bridge 40 (Barmouth Viaduct and Swing... 99m 40ch
Barmouth Swing Bridge 99m 78ch
Morfa Mawddach 99m 00ch
Fairbourne 97m 72ch
Fairbourne (AOCL) 97m 70ch
Bont-y-Clettwr (UWC) 96m 19ch
Llwyngwril 95m 20ch
Borthwen Farm (UWC) 95m 21ch
Allens (AOCL) 94m 42ch
Henblas (UWC) 94m 72ch
Gorshwen No.2 (UWC) 94m 40ch
Bronnant (UWC) 94m 04ch
Ty'n Llan 3 (UWC) 93m 22ch
Ty'n Llan 1 (UWC) 92m 72ch
Tonfanau 91m 09ch
Tonfanau (UWC) 91m 06ch

Level Crossings between Porthmadoc and Llandecwyn
① Porthmadog (TMO) 119m 73ch
② Welsh Highland Railway (Flat Crossing) 119m 50ch
③ Traeth Mawr (ABCL) 119m 41ch
④ Minffordd Quarry (UWC) (Manned) 118m 14ch
⑤ Penrhyndeudraeth (UWC) 116m 54ch
⑥ Hafod-y-Wern (UWC) 116m 36ch

Level Crossings between Dovey Junction and Machynlleth
⑤ Doldyfi (UWC) 77m 13ch
⑥ Quay Ward No.1 (UWC) 77m 44ch
⑦ Quay Ward No.2 (UWC) 77m 61ch
⑧ Quay Ward No.3 (UWC) 77m 71ch
⑨ Quay Ward No.4 (UWC) 78m 08ch

Single Line 88m 67ch
Sandilands (ABCL) 89m 09ch
Tywyn GF 88m 40ch
Up Refuge Siding
Tywyn 88m 56ch
Single Line 88m 39ch
Caethle Farm (UWC) 87m 21ch
Rhowniar (UWC) 86m 64ch
Dafydd (UWC) 86m 47ch
Dyffryn (UWC) 86m 38ch
Cemetry (UWC) 86m 05ch
Treffeddian (UWC) 85m 38ch
Dovey Jn. 78m 60ch
Bridge 1 79m 12ch to 79m 20ch
Ynys (UWC) 79m 53ch
Dovey J... 79m...
Aberdovey 85m 02ch
Penhelig 84m 08ch
Penrhos (UWC) 84m 75ch
Brickyard No.3 (UWC) 84m 66ch
Bridge 250 85m 30ch to 85m 32ch
Ynyslas (AHBC) 85m 21ch
Leri Bridge (UWC) 85m 29ch
Aberleri (AHBC) 86m 04ch
Bridge 24... 79m 18ch
Bridge 243 80m 19ch
Bridge 246 82m 48ch
Bridge 247 83m 31ch

① Aberdovey Tunnel No.1 81m 11ch to 81m 20ch
② Aberdovey Tunnel No.2 82m 07ch to 82m 17ch
③ Aberdovey Tunnel No.3 83m 74ch to 84m 03ch
④ Aberdovey Tunnel No.4 84m 14ch to 84m 38ch

Borth 87m 27ch
Borth Capel Sion (UWC) 87m 35ch
Borth Capel Soar (AOCL) 87m 59ch

Llandre (ABCL) 89m 58ch
Llandre Vicarage (R/G) 90m 02ch
Pant Y Peron (UWC) 90m 64ch

Pant Y Peron (UWC) 90m 64ch
No.2 GF 95m 56ch
Aberystwyth Oil Distributors
Aberystwyth 95m 60ch
No.1 GF 95m 30ch
Llanbadarn (ABCL) 94m 56ch
To Devil's Bridge (Vale of Rheidol Railway)
E

See above
Pant Y Peron (UWC) 90m 64ch

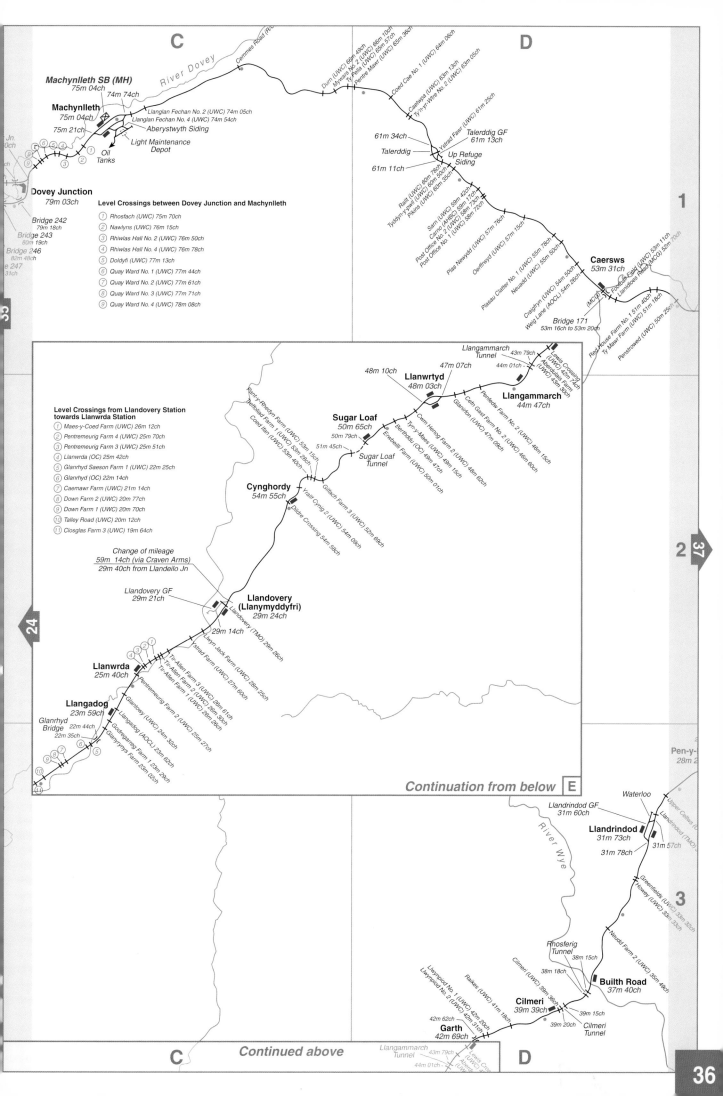

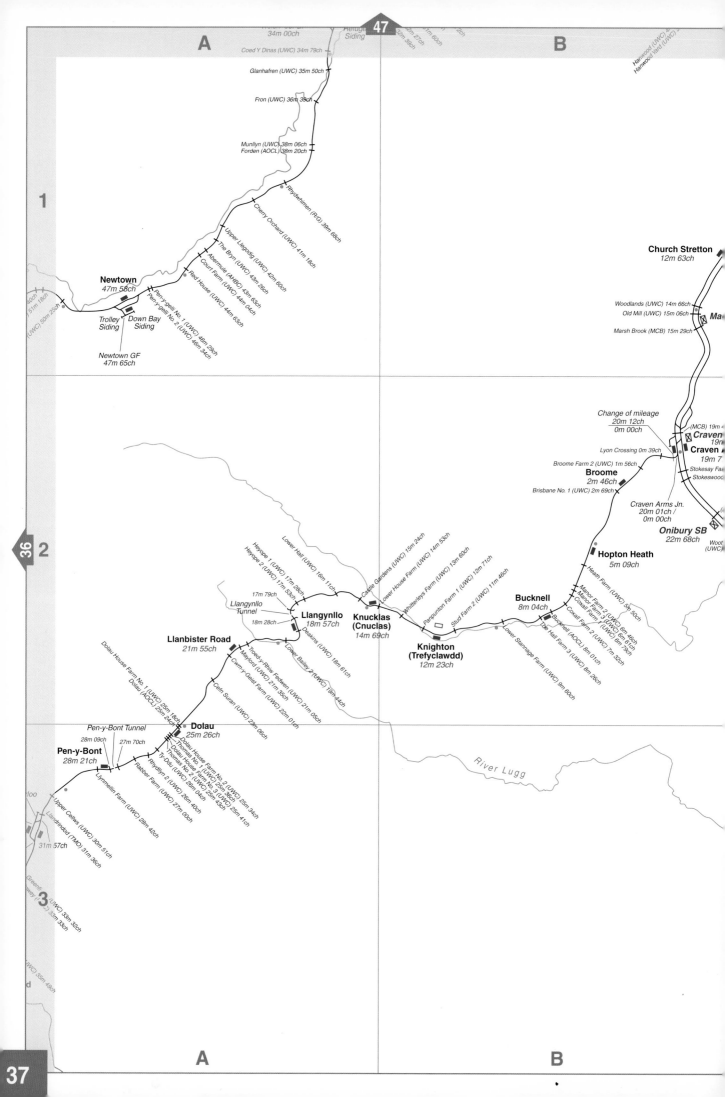

34m 00ch
Heluge
Siding

Coed Y Dinas (UWC) 34m 79ch

Glanhafren (UWC) 35m 50ch

Fron (UWC) 36m 39ch

Munllyn (UWC) 38m 06ch
Forden (AOCL) 38m 20ch

Rhydwhimen (R/G) 39m 68ch

Cherry Orchard (UWC) 41m 18ch

Upper Llegodig (UWC) 42m 60ch

The Bryn (UWC) 43m 26ch

Abermule (AHBC) 43m 63ch

Court Farm (UWC) 44m 04ch

Red House (UWC) 44m 63ch

Newtown
47m 58ch

Perry-y-geilli No. 1 (UWC) 46m 29ch
Perry-y-geilli No. 2 (UWC) 46m 34ch

**Trolley
Siding** **Down Bay
Siding**

**Newtown GF
47m 65ch**

51m 18ch
40ch
(UWC) 50m 25ch

Church Stretton
12m 63ch

Woodlands (UWC) 14m 66ch
Old Mill (UWC) 15m 06ch **Ma**

Marsh Brook (MCB) 15m 29ch

Change of mileage
20m 12ch
0m 00ch

(MCB) 19m

Craven
19m

Lyon Crossing 0m 39ch **Craven**
19m 7

Broome Farm 2 (UWC) 1m 56ch

Stokesay Fa

Broome
2m 46ch Stokeswood

Brisbane No. 1 (UWC) 2m 69ch

Craven Arms Jn.
20m 01ch /
0m 00ch

Onibury SB
22m 68ch   Woot
(UWC)

Lower Hall (UWC) 16m 11ch

Heyope 1 (UWC) 17m 26ch

Heyope 2 (UWC) 17m 53ch

Castle Gardens (UWC) 15m 24ch

Lower House Farm (UWC) 14m 53ch

Whitterleys Farm (UWC) 13m 60ch

Panpunton Farm 1 (UWC) 12m 71ch

Stud Farm 2 (UWC) 11m 46ch

Hopton Heath
5m 09ch

Heath Farm (UWC) 5m 50ch

Manor Farm 2 (UWC) 6m 46ch
Manor Farm 3 (UWC) 6m 67ch
Manor Farm 1 (UWC) 6m 79ch

Coxall Farm 2 (UWC) 7m 32ch

Bucknell
8m 04ch

Bucknell (AOCL) 8m 01ch

The Hall Farm 3 (UWC) 8m 26ch

Lower Stermage Farm (UWC) 9m 60ch

17m 79ch

*Llangynllo
Tunnel*

18m 28ch **Llangynllo**
18m 57ch

Deakins (UWC) 18m 61ch

**Knucklas
(Cnuclas)**
14m 69ch

**Knighton
(Trefyclawdd)**
12m 23ch

Llanbister Road
21m 55ch

Troed-y-Rhiw Fedwen (UWC) 21m 53ch

Lower Bailey 2 (UWC) 19m 44ch

Maylord (UWC) 21m 35ch

Cwm-y-Geist Farm (UWC) 22m 01ch

Dolau House Farm No. 1 (UWC) 25m 18ch
Dolau (AOCL) 25m 24ch

Cefn Suran (UWC) 23m 06ch

Pen-y-Bont Tunnel **Dolau**
25m 26ch

Dolau House Farm No. 2 (UWC) 25m 34ch

28m 09ch Thomas No. 1 (UWC) 25m 36ch
Thomas House Farm No. 3 (UWC) 25m 41ch

27m 70ch Thomas No. 2 (UWC) 25m 42ch

Ty-Dau (UWC) 26m 04ch

Pen-y-Bont
28m 21ch   Rhyddyn 2 (UWC) 26m 40ch

Rabber Farm (UWC) 27m 00ch

Llynmellin Farm (UWC) 28m 42ch

loo

Upper Cellws (UWC) 28m 51ch

Llandrindod (TMO) 31m 36ch

31m 57ch

(UWC) 33m 32ch

(UWC) 35m 49ch

d

River Lugg

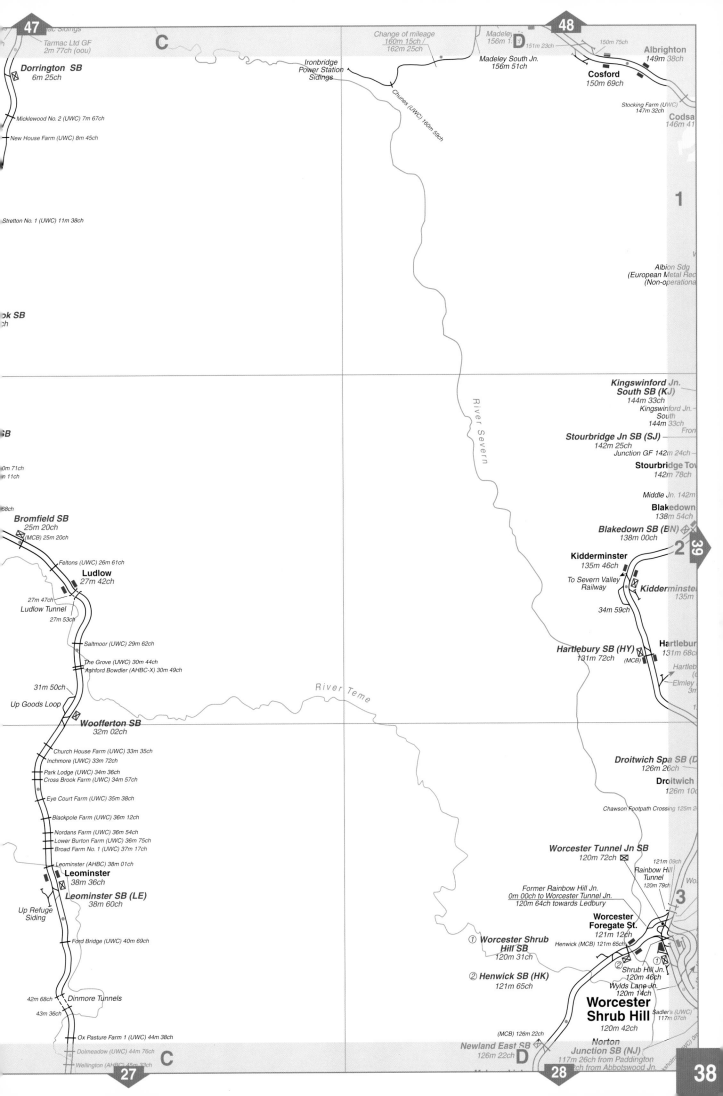

C

Tarmac Sidings

Tarmac Ltd GF
2m 77ch (oou)

Dorrington SB
6m 25ch

Micklewood No. 2 (UWC) 7m 67ch

New House Farm (UWC) 8m 45ch

Stretton No. 1 (UWC) 11m 38ch

ok SB
ch

SB

0m 71ch
n 11ch

68ch

Bromfield SB
25m 20ch
(MCB) 25m 20ch

Feltons (UWC) 26m 61ch

Ludlow
27m 42ch

27m 47ch
Ludlow Tunnel
27m 53ch

Saltmoor (UWC) 29m 62ch

The Grove (UWC) 30m 44ch
Ashford Bowdler (AHBC-X) 30m 49ch

31m 50ch

Up Goods Loop

Woofferton SB
32m 02ch

Church House Farm (UWC) 33m 35ch
Inchmore (UWC) 33m 72ch
Park Lodge (UWC) 34m 36ch
Cross Brook Farm (UWC) 34m 57ch

Eye Court Farm (UWC) 35m 38ch

Blackpole Farm (UWC) 36m 12ch

Nordans Farm (UWC) 36m 54ch
Lower Burton Farm (UWC) 36m 75ch
Broad Farm No. 1 (UWC) 37m 17ch

Leominster (AHBC) 38m 01ch
Leominster
38m 36ch

Leominster SB (LE)
38m 60ch

Up Refuge
Siding

Ford Bridge (UWC) 40m 69ch

42m 68ch
Dinmore Tunnels
43m 36ch

Ox Pasture Farm 1 (UWC) 44m 38ch

Dolmeadow (UWC) 44m 76ch
Wellington (AHBC) 45m 33ch

Change of mileage
160m 15ch /
162m 25ch

Ironbridge
Power Station
Sidings

Chunes (UWC) 160m 59ch

Madeley
156m 1
Madeley South Jn.
156m 51ch

D
151m 23ch

150m 75ch

Albrighton
149m 38ch

Cosford
150m 69ch

Stocking Farm (UWC)
147m 32ch

Codsa
146m 41

1

River Severn

**Kingswinford Jn.
South SB (KJ)**
144m 33ch
Kingswinford Jn.
South
144m 33ch

Fron

Stourbridge Jn SB (SJ)
142m 25ch
Junction GF 142m 24ch

Stourbridge Tov
142m 78ch

Middle Jn. 142m

Blakedown
138m 54ch

Blakedown SB (BN)
138m 00ch

Kidderminster
135m 46ch

To Severn Valley
Railway

Kidderminste
135m

34m 59ch

Hartlebury SB (HY)
131m 72ch
(MCB)

Hartlebu
131m 68c

Hartleb
Elmley
3m

2

River Teme

Droitwich Spa SB (D
126m 26ch

Droitwich
126m 10

Chawson Footpath Crossing 125m 2

Worcester Tunnel Jn SB
120m 72ch

121m 09ch
Rainbow Hill
Tunnel
120m 79ch

Former Rainbow Hill Jn.
0m 00ch to Worcester Tunnel Jn.
120m 64ch towards Ledbury

**Worcester
Foregate St.**
121m 12ch

Henwick (MCB) 121m 65ch

Wo

3

① **Worcester Shrub
Hill SB**
120m 31ch

② **Henwick SB (HK)**
121m 65ch

② Shrub Hill Jn.
120m 46ch
Wylds Lane Jn.
120m 14ch

Sadler's (UWC)
117m 07ch

**Worcester
Shrub Hill**
120m 42ch

(MCB) 126m 22ch

Newland East SB
126m 22ch

**Norton
Junction SB (NJ)**
117m 26ch from Paddington
ch from Abbotswood Jn.

Albion Sdg
(European Metal Rec
(Non-operationa

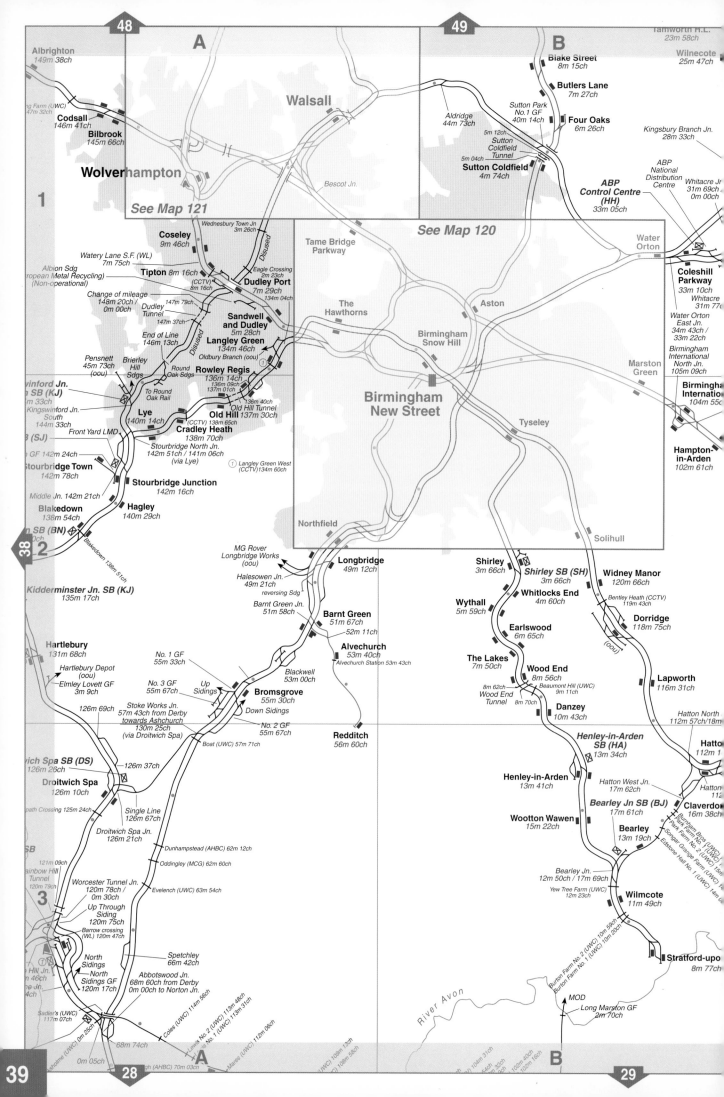

48 | A | **49** | B

Tamworth H.L. 23m 58ch

Wilnecote 25m 47ch

Albrighton 149m 38ch

Long Farm (UWC) 147m 32ch

Codsall 146m 41ch

Bilbrook 145m 66ch

Blake Street 8m 15ch

Butlers Lane 7m 27ch

Aldridge 44m 73ch

Sutton Park No.1 GF 40m 14ch

Four Oaks 6m 26ch

Kingsbury Branch Jn. 28m 33ch

Wolverhampton

See Map 121

Bescot Jn.

5m 12ch Sutton Coldfield Tunnel

5m 04ch Sutton Coldfield 4m 74ch

ABP National Distribution Centre

ABP Control Centre (HH) 33m 05ch

Whitacre Jr 31m 69ch / 0m 00ch

Walsall

See Map 120

Tame Bridge Parkway

Water Orton

Coleshill Parkway 33m 10ch

Coseley 9m 46ch

Wednesbury Town Jn 3m 26ch

Eagle Crossing 2m 23ch

Aston

Whitacre 31m 77

Water Orton East Jn. 34m 43ch / 33m 22ch

Watery Lane S.F. (WL) 7m 75ch

Albion Sdg European Metal Recycling) (Non-operational)

Tipton 8m 16ch

(CCTV) 8m 16ch

Dudley Port 7m 29ch / 134m 04ch

The Hawthorns

Birmingham Snow Hill

Birmingham International North Jn. 105m 09ch

Change of mileage 148m 20ch / 0m 00ch

147m 79ch Dudley Tunnel 147m 37ch

Sandwell and Dudley 5m 28ch

End of Line 146m 13ch

Langley Green 134m 46ch

Oldbury Branch (oou)

Marston Green

Birmingham Internation 104m 55c

Pensnett 45m 73ch (oou)

Brierley Hill Sdgs

To Round Oak Rail

Round Oak Sdgs

Rowley Regis 136m 14ch / 136m 09ch / 137m 01ch

Birmingham New Street

winford Jn. n SB (KJ) m 33ch

Kingswinford Jn. South 144m 33ch

Lye 140m 14ch

136m 40ch

Old Hill 137m 30ch

Old Hill Tunnel (CCTV) 138m 65ch

Tyseley

B (SJ)

Front Yard LMD

Cradley Heath 138m 70ch

Hampton-in-Arden 102m 61ch

GF 142m 24ch

Stourbridge North Jn. 142m 51ch / 141m 06ch (via Lye)

① Langley Green West (CCTV) 134m 60ch

Stourbridge Town 142m 78ch

Stourbridge Junction 142m 16ch

Middle Jn. 142m 21ch

Blakedown 138m 54ch

Hagley 140m 29ch

MG Rover Longbridge Works (oou)

Longbridge 49m 12ch

Northfield

Solihull

Shirley 3m 66ch

Shirley SB (SH) 3m 66ch

Widney Manor 120m 66ch

n SB (BN) Blakedown 139m 51ch

Halesowen Jn. 49m 21ch reversing Sdg

Wythall 5m 59ch

Whitlocks End 4m 60ch

Bentley Heath (CCTV) 119m 43ch

Kidderminster Jn. SB (KJ) 135m 17ch

Barnt Green Jn. 51m 58ch

Barnt Green 51m 67ch

52m 11ch

Earlswood 6m 65ch

Dorridge 118m 75ch

Hartlebury 131m 68ch

No. 1 GF 55m 33ch

Alvechurch 53m 40ch

Alvechurch Station 53m 43ch

The Lakes 7m 50ch

Wood End 8m 56ch

Beaumont Hill (UWC) 9m 11ch

Lapworth 116m 31ch

Hartlebury Depot (oou) Elmley Lovett GF 3m 9ch

No. 3 GF 55m 67ch

Up Sidings

Blackwell 53m 00ch

8m 62ch Wood End Tunnel 8m 70ch

126m 69ch

Bromsgrove 55m 30ch

Down Sidings

Danzey 10m 43ch

Hatton North 112m 57ch / 18m

Stoke Works Jn. 57m 43ch from Derby towards Ashchurch 130m 25ch (via Droitwich Spa)

No. 2 GF 55m 67ch

Redditch 56m 60ch

Henley-in-Arden SB (HA) 13m 34ch

Hatto 112m

wich Spa SB (DS) 126m 26ch

126m 37ch

Boat (UWC) 57m 71ch

Henley-in-Arden 13m 41ch

Hatton West Jn. 17m 62ch

Hatton 112

Droitwich Spa 126m 10ch

Single Line 126m 67ch

Bearley Jn SB (BJ) 17m 61ch

Claverdo 16m 38ch

path Crossing 125m 24ch

Droitwich Spa Jn. 126m 21ch

Dunhampstead (AHBC) 62m 12ch

Oddingley (MCG) 62m 60ch

Evelench (UWC) 63m 54ch

Wootton Wawen 15m 22ch

Bearley 13m 19ch

Burnham Spa (UWC) Park Farm No.1 (UWC)

Park Farm No. 2 (UWC) 15m

Songar Grange Farm (UWC) 14m

Edstone Hall No. 1 (UWC) 14m 0c

SB

121m 09ch

inbow Hill Tunnel 120m 79ch

Worcester Tunnel Jn. 120m 78ch / 0m 30ch

Up Through Siding 120m 75ch

Barrow crossing (WL) 120m 47ch

Bearley Jn. 12m 50ch / 17m 69ch

Yew Tree Farm (UWC) 12m 23ch

Wilmcote 11m 49ch

Hill Jn. m 46ch ne Jn. 4ch

3

North Sidings

North Sidings GF 120m 17ch

Spetchley 66m 42ch

Abbotswood Jn. 68m 60ch from Derby 0m 00ch to Norton Jn.

River Avon

Burton Farm No. 2 (UWC) 10m 59ch Burton Farm No. 1 (UWC) 10m 20ch

Stratford-upo 8m 77ch

Sadler's (UWC) 117m 07ch

68m 74ch

Coles (UWC) 114m 56ch Lewis No.2 (UWC) 113m 48ch Lewis No. 1 (UWC) 113m 31ch

(UWC) 112m 06ch

Mares (UWC) 112m 12ch

MOD Long Marston GF 2m 70ch

39 | 0m 05ch | **28** | A | sholme (UWC) 0m 25ch | gh (AHBC) 70m 03ch | (UWC) 108m 58ch | (UWC) 109m 13ch | (UWC) 104m 51ch | 40ch | 102m 16ch | **B** | **29**

See Map 121

1

38

2

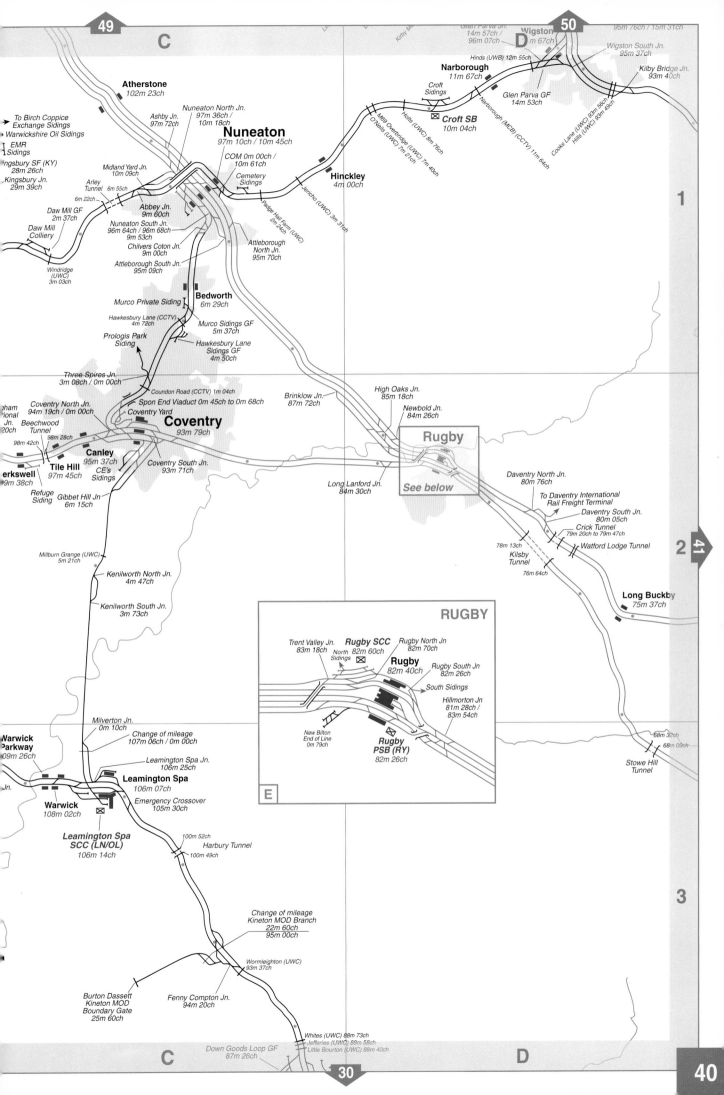

Glen Parva Jn.
14m 57ch /
96m 07ch

Wigston
m 67ch

95m 76ch / 15m 31ch

Kirby M

Narborough
11m 67ch

Hinds (UWB) 12m 55ch

Wigston South Jn.
95m 37ch

Croft
Sidings

Glen Parva GF
14m 53ch

Kilby Bridge Jn.
93m 40ch

Atherstone
102m 23ch

Ashby Jn.
97m 72ch

Nuneaton North Jn.
97m 36ch /
10m 18ch

Croft SB
10m 04ch

Holts (UWC) 8m 76ch

Narborough (MCB) (CCTV) 11m 64ch

Cooks Lane (UWC) 93m 56ch
Hills (UWC) 93m 49ch

→ To Birch Coppice
Exchange Sidings
■ Warwickshire Oil Sidings
┤ EMR
Sidings

ngsbury SF (KY)
28m 26ch
Kingsbury Jn.
29m 39ch

Midland Yard Jn.
10m 09ch

Nuneaton
97m 10ch / 10m 45ch

COM 0m 00ch /
10m 61ch

M69 Overbridge (UWC) 8m 76ch
O'Neils (UWC) 7m 21ch

Arley
Tunnel
6m 55ch
6m 22ch

Daw Mill GF
2m 37ch

Abbey Jn.
9m 60ch

Cemetery
Sidings

Hinckley
4m 00ch

Daw Mill
Colliery

Nuneaton South Jn.
96m 64ch / 96m 68ch
9m 53ch

Chilvers Coton Jn.
9m 00ch

Padge Hall Farm (UWC)
2m 24ch

Jericho (UWC) 3m 31ch

Windridge
(UWC)
3m 03ch

Attleborough South Jn.
95m 09ch

Attleborough
North Jn.
95m 70ch

Bedworth
6m 29ch

Murco Private Siding

Hawkesbury Lane (CCTV)
4m 72ch

Murco Sidings GF
5m 37ch

Prologis Park
Siding

Hawkesbury Lane
Sidings GF
4m 50ch

Three Spires Jn.
3m 08ch / 0m 00ch

Coundon Road (CCTV) 1m 04ch

Spon End Viaduct 0m 45ch to 0m 68ch

Brinklow Jn.
87m 72ch

High Oaks Jn.
85m 18ch

gham
ional
20ch

Coventry North Jn.
94m 19ch / 0m 00ch

Beechwood
Tunnel
98m 42ch 98m 28ch

Coventry Yard

Coventry
93m 79ch

Newbold Jn.
84m 26ch

Rugby

See below

Daventry North Jn.
80m 76ch

→ To Daventry International
Rail Freight Terminal

Canley
95m 37ch
CE's
Sidings

Coventry South Jn.
93m 71ch

Long Lanford Jn.
84m 30ch

Daventry South Jn.
80m 05ch

Crick Tunnel
79m 20ch to 79m 47ch

erkswell
9m 38ch

Tile Hill
97m 45ch

78m 13ch

Watford Lodge Tunnel

Refuge
Siding

Gibbet Hill Jn
6m 15ch

Kilsby
Tunnel

76m 64ch

Millburn Grange (UWC)
5m 21ch

Kenilworth North Jn.
4m 47ch

Long Buckby
75m 37ch

Kenilworth South Jn.
3m 73ch

RUGBY

Trent Valley Jn.
83m 18ch

Rugby SCC
82m 60ch

North
Sidings

Rugby North Jn
82m 70ch

Rugby
82m 40ch

Rugby South Jn
82m 26ch

South Sidings

Hillmorton Jn
81m 28ch /
83m 54ch

New Bilton
End of Line
0m 79ch

*Rugby
PSB (RY)*
82m 26ch

E

Milverton Jn.
0m 10ch

Change of mileage
107m 06ch / 0m 00ch

68m 32ch
68m 09ch

Warwick
Parkway
09m 26ch

Leamington Spa Jn.
106m 25ch

Jn.

Leamington Spa
106m 07ch

Stowe Hill
Tunnel

Warwick
108m 02ch

Emergency Crossover
105m 30ch

*Leamington Spa
SCC (LN/OL)*
106m 14ch

100m 52ch

Harbury Tunnel

100m 49ch

Change of mileage
Kineton MOD Branch
22m 60ch /
95m 00ch

Wormleighton (UWC)
93m 37ch

Burton Dassett
Kineton MOD
Boundary Gate
25m 60ch

Fenny Compton Jn.
94m 20ch

Whites (UWC) 88m 73ch
Jefferies (UWC) 88m 58ch
Little Bourton (UWC) 88m 40ch

Down Goods Loop GF
87m 26ch

1

2   41

3

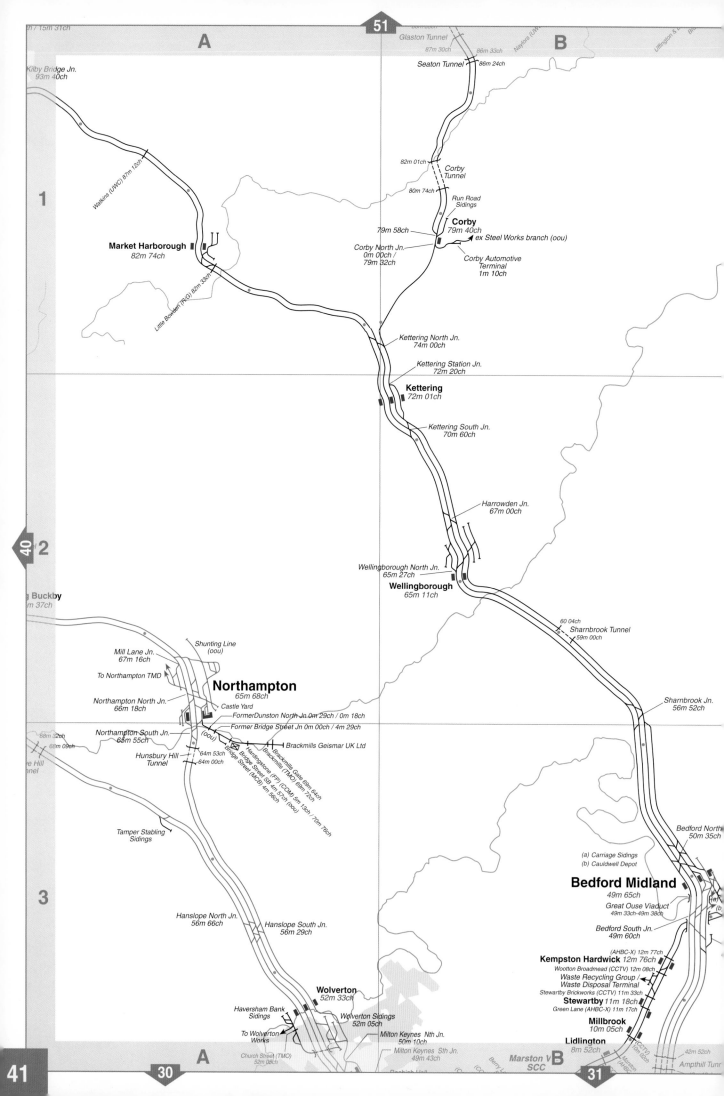

Kilby Bridge Jn.
93m 40ch

Watkins (UWC) 87m 12ch

Market Harborough
82m 74ch

Little Bowden (R/G) 82m 33ch

Glaston Tunnel
87m 30ch

Seaton Tunnel
86m 24ch

86m 33ch

Naylors (UWC)

82m 01ch

Corby
Tunnel

80m 74ch

Run Road
Sidings

Corby
79m 40ch

79m 58ch

ex Steel Works branch (oou)

Corby North Jn.
0m 00ch /
79m 32ch

Corby Automotive
Terminal
1m 10ch

Kettering North Jn.
74m 00ch

Kettering Station Jn.
72m 20ch

Kettering
72m 01ch

Kettering South Jn.
70m 60ch

Harrowden Jn.
67m 00ch

Wellingborough North Jn.
65m 27ch

Wellingborough
65m 11ch

60m 04ch

Sharnbrook Tunnel
59m 00ch

Sharnbrook Jn.
56m 52ch

Long Buckby
?m 37ch

Mill Lane Jn.
67m 16ch

Shunting Line
(oou)

To Northampton TMD

Northampton North Jn.
66m 18ch

Northampton
65m 68ch

Castle Yard

Former Dunston North Jn 0m 29ch / 0m 18ch

Former Bridge Street Jn 0m 00ch / 4m 29ch

Brackmills Geismar UK Ltd

Northampton South Jn.
65m 55ch

(oou)

Brackmills Gate 69m 64ch

Hardingstone (FP) (COM) 5m 13ch / 70m 76ch

Bridge Street SB 4m 57ch (oou)

Bridge Street (MCB) 4m 56ch

68m 32ch

68m 09ch

?re Hill
?nnel

Hunsbury Hill
Tunnel

64m 53ch

64m 00ch

Tamper Stabling
Sidings

Hanslope North Jn.
56m 66ch

Hanslope South Jn.
56m 29ch

Bedford North
50m 35ch

(a) Carriage Sidings
(b) Cauldwell Depot

Bedford Midland
49m 65ch

Great Ouse Viaduct
49m 33ch-49m 38ch

(a)
(b)

Bedford South Jn.
49m 60ch

(AHBC-X) 12m 77ch

Kempston Hardwick 12m 76ch

Wootton Broadmead (CCTV) 12m 08ch

Waste Recycling Group
Waste Disposal Terminal

Stewartby Brickworks (CCTV) 11m 33ch

Stewartby 11m 18ch

Green Lane (AHBC-X) 11m 17ch

Millbrook
10m 05ch

Wolverton
52m 33ch

Haversham Bank
Sidings

Wolverton Sidings
52m 05ch

To Wolverton
Works

Milton Keynes Nth Jn.
50m 10ch

Milton Keynes Sth Jn.
49m 43ch

Church Street (TMO)
52m 06ch

**Marston V
SCC**

Lidlington
8m 52ch

(CCTV) 10m 02ch

42m 52ch

Ampthill Tunn?

40/2

1

2

3

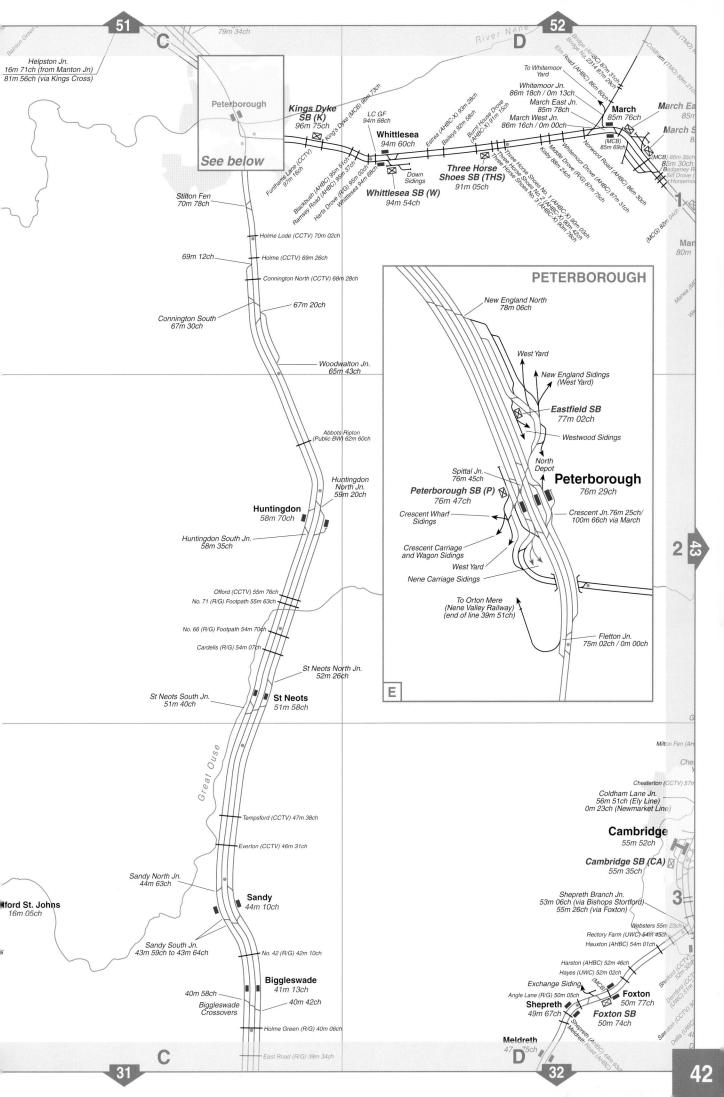

51 C — 79m 34ch — River Nene — D **52**

Helpston Jn.
16m 71ch (from Manton Jn)
81m 56ch (via Kings Cross)

Peterborough

See below

Kings Dyke SB (K)
96m 75ch

LC GF
94m 68ch

Whittlesea
94m 60ch

Kings Dyke (MCB) 96m 73ch

Funthams Lane (CCTV) 97m 16ch

Blackbush (AHBC) 95m 51ch
Ramsey Road (AHBC) 95m 37ch
Harts Drove (RG) 95m 02ch
Whittlesea 94m 68ch

Down Sidings

Whittlesea SB (W)
94m 54ch

Three Horse Shoes SB (THS)
91m 05ch

Estrea (AHBC-X) 93m 28ch
Baileys 92m 58ch
Burnt House Drove (AHBC-X) 91m 15ch

Three Horse Shoes No. 1 (AHBC-X) 90m 03ch
Three Horse Shoes No. 2 (AHBC-X) 90m 42ch
Three Horse Shoes No. 3 (AHBC-X) 90m 76ch

To Whitemoor Yard

Whitemoor Jn.
86m 18ch / 0m 13ch
March East Jn.
85m 78ch
March West Jn.
86m 16ch / 0m 00ch

Whitemoor Drove (AHBC-X) 87m 31ch
Norwood Road (AHBC) 86m 30ch
Elm Road (AHBC) 86m 60ch
Bridge No. 231E 87m 23ch
Bridge A (I-IBC) 87m 77ch

Coldham (TMO) 89m 21ch
Fosea (TMO) 89m...

March
85m 76ch

March East
85m...

March S...

(MCB) 85m 69ch
(MCB) 85m 35ch
85m 30ch
Badgeney R...
Silt Drove...
Horsemo...

Middle Drove (RG) 87m 75ch
Kisby 88m 24ch

(MCG) 82m 04ch

Man...
80m

Man... (M...)
Manea (M...)
We...

Stilton Fen
70m 78ch

Holme Lode (CCTV) 70m 02ch
Holme (CCTV) 69m 26ch
69m 12ch
Connington North (CCTV) 68m 28ch
67m 20ch
Connington South
67m 30ch

Woodwalton Jn.
65m 43ch

Abbots Ripton
(Public BW) 62m 60ch

Huntingdon North Jn.
59m 20ch

Huntingdon
58m 70ch

Huntingdon South Jn.
58m 35ch

Offord (CCTV) 55m 76ch
No. 71 (R/G) Footpath 55m 63ch
No. 66 (R/G) Footpath 54m 70ch
Cardells (R/G) 54m 07ch

St Neots North Jn.
52m 26ch

St Neots South Jn.
51m 40ch

St Neots
51m 58ch

PETERBOROUGH

New England North
78m 06ch

West Yard

New England Sidings
(West Yard)

Eastfield SB
77m 02ch

Westwood Sidings

North Depot

Spittal Jn.
76m 45ch

Peterborough SB (P)
76m 47ch

Crescent Wharf Sidings

Crescent Carriage and Wagon Sidings

West Yard

Nene Carriage Sidings

Peterborough
76m 29ch

Crescent Jn. 76m 25ch /
100m 66ch via March

To Orton Mere
(Nene Valley Railway)
(end of line 39m 51ch)

Fletton Jn.
75m 02ch / 0m 00ch

E

2 **43**

Milton Fen (AH...

Che...
Y...

Chesterton (CCTV) 57m...

Coldham Lane Jn.
56m 51ch (Ely Line)
0m 23ch (Newmarket Line)

Cambridge
55m 52ch

Cambridge SB (CA)
55m 35ch

Shepreth Branch Jn.
53m 06ch (via Bishops Stortford)
55m 26ch (via Foxton)

Websters 55m 23ch
Rectory Farm (UWC) 54m 45ch
Hauxton (AHBC) 54m 01ch

Harston (AHBC) 52m 46ch
Hayes (UWC) 52m 02ch

Exchange Siding
Angle Lane (R/G) 50m 05ch

Foxton
50m 77ch

Foxton SB
50m 74ch

Shepreth
49m 67ch

Shepreth (AHBC) 49m 63ch
Meldreth Road (AHBC)...

Meldreth
47m 75ch

3

Great Ouse

Tempsford (CCTV) 47m 38ch

Everton (CCTV) 46m 31ch

Sandy North Jn.
44m 63ch

Sandy
44m 10ch

...ford St. Johns
16m 05ch

Sandy South Jn.
43m 59ch to 43m 64ch

No. 42 (R/G) 42m 10ch

40m 58ch

Biggleswade
41m 13ch

Biggleswade Crossovers

40m 42ch

Holme Green (R/G) 40m 06ch

C — East Road (R/G) 39m 34ch — D

31 **32** **42**

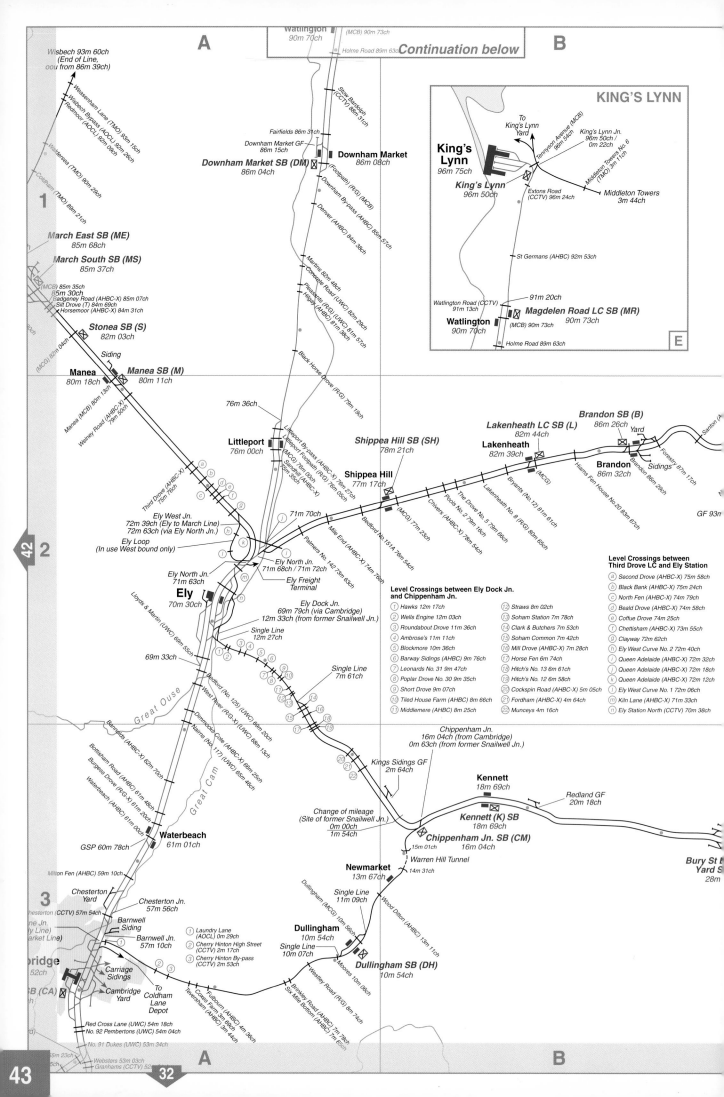

A / **B**

Watlington 90m 70ch

(MCB) 90m 73ch

Continuation below

Holme Road 89m 63ch

KING'S LYNN

To King's Lynn Yard

Tennyson Avenue (MCB) 96m 54ch

King's Lynn Jn. 96m 50ch / 0m 22ch

King's Lynn 96m 75ch

Middleton Towers No. 6 (TMO) 3m 11ch

King's Lynn 96m 50ch

Extons Road (CCTV) 96m 24ch

Middleton Towers 3m 44ch

St Germans (AHBC) 92m 53ch

Watlington Road (CCTV) 91m 13ch

91m 20ch

Magdelen Road LC SB (MR) 90m 73ch

Watlington 90m 70ch (MCB) 90m 73ch

Holme Road 89m 63ch

E

Wisbech 93m 60ch (End of Line, oou from 86m 39ch)

Weasenham Lane (TMO) 93m 15ch
Wisbech Bypass (AOCL) 92m 26ch
Redmoor (AOCL) 92m 09ch
Waldersea (TMO)
Coldham (TMO) 90m 29ch

Stow Bardolph (CCTV) 88m 31ch

Fairfields 86m 31ch
Downham Market GF 86m 15ch
Downham Market 86m 08ch
Downham Market SB (DM) 86m 04ch
(Footpath) (R/G) (MCB)

Denver (AHBC) 84m 38ch
Downham Bypass (MCB) 85m 57ch

1

March East SB (ME) 85m 68ch

March South SB (MS) 85m 37ch

(MCB) 85m 35ch
85m 30ch
Badgeney Road (AHBC-X) 85m 07ch
Silt Drove (T) 84m 69ch
Horsemoor (AHBC-X) 84m 31ch

(MCG) 82m 04ch

Stonea SB (S) 82m 03ch

Siding

Manea 80m 18ch
Manea SB (M) 80m 11ch

Manea (MCB) 80m 13ch
Welney Road (AHBC-X) 79m 50ch

Martins 82m 48ch
Comegate Road (UWC) 82m 29ch
Pleasants (R/G) (UWC) 81m 57ch
Hilgay (AHBC) 81m 38ch

Black Horse Drove (R/G) 79m 19ch

76m 36ch

Littleport 76m 00ch

Littleport Bypass (AHBC-X) 76m 27ch
Littleport Footpath (R/G) 76m 09ch
(MCG) 76m 00ch
Sandhill (AHBC-X) 75m 35ch

Shippea Hill SB (SH) 78m 21ch

Shippea Hill 77m 17ch

Lakenheath LC SB (L) 82m 44ch

Lakenheath 82m 39ch

Brandon SB (B) 86m 26ch

Yard

Forestry 87m 17ch
Santon (A)

Brandon 86m 32ch
Brandon 86m 29ch
Sidings

Hiams Fen House No.20 83m 67ch

GF 93m

Bedford No.151A 76m 54ch
The Drove No. 5 79m 16ch
Pools No. 2 79m 16ch
Chivers (AHBC-X) 78m 54ch
Lakenheath No. 8 (R/G) 80m 65ch
Bryants (No.12) 81m 61ch
(MCG) 77m 23ch
(MCG)

Ely West Jn. 72m 39ch (Ely to March Line) 72m 63ch (via Ely North Jn.)

Ely Loop (In use West bound only)

71m 70ch

Mile End (AHBC-X) 74m 78ch
Palmers No. 142 73m 63ch

Ely North Jn. 71m 63ch

Ely North Jn. 71m 68ch / 71m 72ch

Ely 70m 30ch

Ely Freight Terminal

Ely Dock Jn. 69m 79ch (via Cambridge) 12m 33ch (from former Snailwell Jn.)

69m 33ch

Single Line 12m 27ch

Single Line 7m 61ch

Level Crossings between Ely Dock Jn. and Chippenham Jn.
1 Hawks 12m 17ch
2 Wells Engine 12m 03ch
3 Roundabout Drove 11m 36ch
4 Ambrose's 11m 11ch
5 Blockmore 10m 36ch
6 Barway Sidings (AHBC) 9m 76ch
7 Leonards No. 31 9m 47ch
8 Poplar Drove No. 30 9m 35ch
9 Short Drove 9m 07ch
10 Tiled House Farm (AHBC) 8m 66ch
11 Middlemere (AHBC) 8m 25ch
12 Straws 8m 02ch
13 Soham Station 7m 78ch
14 Clark & Butchers 7m 53ch
15 Soham Common 7m 42ch
16 Mill Drove (AHBC-X) 7m 28ch
17 Horse Fen 6m 74ch
18 Hitch's No. 13 6m 61ch
19 Hitch's No. 12 6m 58ch
20 Cockspin Road (AHBC-X) 5m 05ch
21 Fordham (AHBC-X) 4m 64ch
22 Munceys 4m 16ch

Level Crossings between Third Drove LC and Ely Station
a Second Drove (AHBC-X) 75m 58ch
b Black Bank (AHBC-X) 75m 24ch
c North Fen (AHBC-X) 74m 79ch
d Beald Drove (AHBC-X) 74m 58ch
e Coffue Drove 74m 25ch
f Chettisham (AHBC-X) 73m 55ch
g Clayway 72m 62ch
h Ely West Curve No. 2 72m 40ch
i Queen Adelaide (AHBC-X) 72m 32ch
j Queen Adelaide (AHBC-X) 72m 18ch
k Queen Adelaide (AHBC-X) 72m 12ch
l Ely West Curve No. 1 72m 06ch
m Kiln Lane (AHBC-X) 71m 33ch
n Ely Station North (CCTV) 70m 38ch

Third Drove (AHBC-X) 75m 76ch

2 / 42

Lloyds & Martin (UWC) 69m 55ch

Bedford (No.125) (UWC) 69m 20ch
West River (R/G-X) (UWC) 68m 13ch
Dimmocks Cote (AHBC-X) 66m 25ch
Nairns (No.117) (UWC) 65m 46ch

Chippenham Jn. 16m 04ch (from Cambridge) 0m 63ch (from former Snailwell Jn.)

Kings Sidings GF 2m 64ch

Kennett 18m 69ch

Redland GF 20m 18ch

Kennett (K) SB 18m 69ch

Chippenham Jn. SB (CM) 16m 04ch

15m 01ch

Warren Hill Tunnel

14m 31ch

Newmarket 13m 67ch

Wood Ditton (AHBC) 13m 11ch

Change of mileage (Site of former Snailwell Jn.) 0m 00ch 1m 54ch

Single Line 11m 09ch

Dullingham (MCG) 10m 56ch

Dullingham 10m 54ch

Single Line 10m 07ch

Moores 10m 06ch

Dullingham SB (DH) 10m 54ch

Westley Road 10m 06ch

Brinkley Road (R/G) 8m 74ch
Six Mile Bottom (AHBC) 7m 65ch

Fulbourn (AHBC) 4m 36ch
Coxes Farm 3m 69ch
Teversham (AHBC) 3m 44ch

Great Ouse

Great Cam

Barnlees (AHBC-X) 62m 70ch
Bottisham Road (AHBC) 61m 48ch
Burgess Drove (R/G-X) 61m 20ch
Waterbeach (AHBC) 61m 00ch

GSP 60m 78ch

Waterbeach 61m 01ch

Milton Fen (AHBC) 59m 10ch

3

Chesterton Yard

Chesterton Jn. 57m 56ch

Barnwell Siding

Chesterton (CCTV) 57m 54ch
...n Jn. (...y Line)

Barnwell Jn. 57m 10ch

1 Laundry Lane (AOCL) 0m 29ch
2 Cherry Hinton High Street (CCTV) 2m 17ch
3 Cherry Hinton By-pass (CCTV) 2m 53ch

Carriage Sidings

...bridge 52ch

Cambridge SB (CA)

To Coldham Lane Depot

Cambridge Yard

Red Cross Lane (UWC) 54m 18ch
No. 92 Pembertons (UWC) 54m 04ch
No. 91 Dukes (UWC) 53m 34ch

...m 23ch
5ch
Websters 53m 03ch
Granhams (CCTV) 52...

43 / **32**

A / **B**

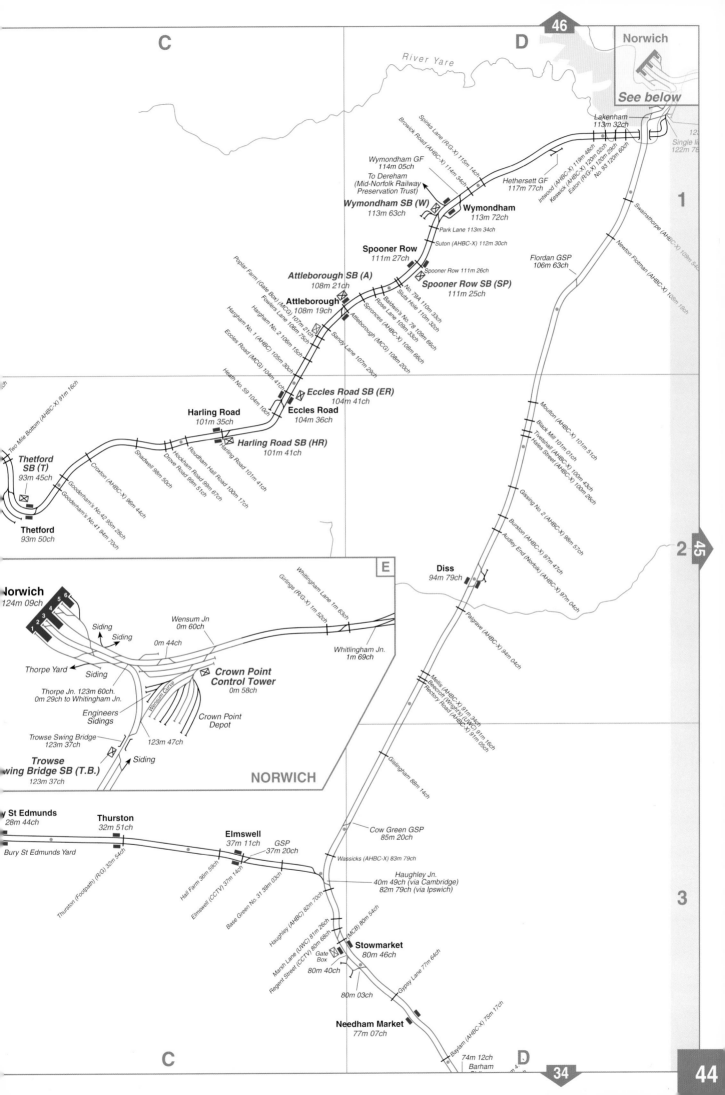

C

D

Norwich

River Yare

See below

Lakenham
113m 32ch

Single li
122m 78

Spinks Lane (R/G-X) 115m 14ch

Browick Road (AHBC-X) 114m 34ch

Wymondham GF
114m 05ch

To Dereham
(Mid-Norfolk Railway
Preservation Trust)

Hethersett GF
117m 77ch

Intwood (AHBC-X) 119m 48ch

Keswick (AHBC-X) 120m 02ch

Eaton (R/G-X) 120m 29ch

No. 93 120m 60ch

Swainsthorpe (AHBC-X) 108m 54

Newton Flotman (AHBC-X) 109m 18c

Wymondham SB (W)
113m 63ch

Wymondham
113m 72ch

Park Lane 113m 34ch

Suton (AHBC-X) 112m 30ch

Spooner Row
111m 27ch

Spooner Row 111m 26ch

Spooner Row SB (SP)
111m 25ch

Flordan GSP
106m 63ch

1

Attleborough SB (A)
108m 21ch

Poplar Farm (Gate Box) (MCG) 107m 21ch

No. 79A 110m 33ch

Sluts Hole 110m 32ch

Baldwin's No. 78 109m 66ch

Rose Lane 109m 35ch

Spronces (AHBC-X) 108m 66ch

Attleborough
108m 19ch

Fowlers Lane 108m 75ch

Hargham No. 1 (AHBC) 106m 15ch

Hargham No. 2 106m 75ch

Eccles Road (MCG) 104m 30ch

Sandy Lane 107m 29ch

Attleborough (MCG) 108m 20ch

Heath No. 59 104m 10ch

Two Mile Bottom (AHBC-X) 91m 16ch

Eccles Road SB (ER)
104m 41ch

Eccles Road
104m 36ch

Moulton (AHBC-X) 101m 01ch

Black Mill (AHBC-X) 100m 43ch

Tivetshall (AHBC-X) 100m 26ch

Hales Street (AHBC-X) 100m 26ch

Harling Road
101m 35ch

Harling Road SB (HR)
101m 41ch

Roudham Hall Road 100m 17ch

Hockham Road 99m 67ch

Drove Road 99m 51ch

Harling Road 101m 41ch

Shadwell 98m 50ch

Croxton (AHBC-X) 96m 44ch

Gissing No. 2 (AHBC-X) 98m 57ch

Burston (AHBC-X) 97m 47ch

Audley End (Norfolk) (AHBC-X) 97m 04ch

**Thetford
SB (T)**
93m 45ch

Gooderham's No. 42 95m 28ch

Gooderham's No. 41 94m 70ch

Thetford
93m 50ch

2

45

E

Whitlingham Lane 1m 63ch

Girlings (R/G-X) 1m 52ch

Diss
94m 79ch

Palgrave (AHBC-X) 94m 04ch

Norwich
124m 09ch

5 6
4 3
2
1

Siding

Siding

Wensum Jn
0m 60ch

0m 44ch

Wensum Curve

Whitlingham Jn.
1m 69ch

Thorpe Yard

Siding

**Crown Point
Control Tower**
0m 58ch

Mellis (AHBC-X) 91m 34ch

Bacons (Wright's) (UWC) 91m 16ch

Rectory Road (AHBC-X) 91m 05ch

Thorpe Jn. 123m 60ch.
0m 29ch to Whitingham Jn.

Engineers
Sidings

Crown Point
Depot

Trowse Swing Bridge
123m 37ch

123m 47ch

**Trowse
wing Bridge SB (T.B.)**
123m 37ch

Siding

NORWICH

Gislingham 88m 14ch

y St Edmunds
28m 44ch

Thurston
32m 51ch

Elmswell
37m 11ch

GSP
37m 20ch

Cow Green GSP
85m 20ch

Bury St Edmunds Yard

Thurston (Footpath) (R/G) 32m 54ch

Hall Farm 36m 59ch

Elmswell (CCTV) 37m 14ch

Base Green No. 31 39m 03ch

Wassicks (AHBC-X) 83m 79ch

Haughley Jn.
40m 49ch (via Cambridge)
82m 79ch (via Ipswich)

3

Haughley (AHBC) 82m 70ch

Marsh Lane (UWC) 81m 26ch

Regent Street (CCTV) 80m 68ch

Gate
Box
80m 40ch

(MCB) 80m 54ch

Stowmarket
80m 46ch

80m 03ch

Gypsy Lane 77m 64ch

Baylam (AHBC-X) 75m 17ch

Needham Market
77m 07ch

74m 12ch
Barham

C

D

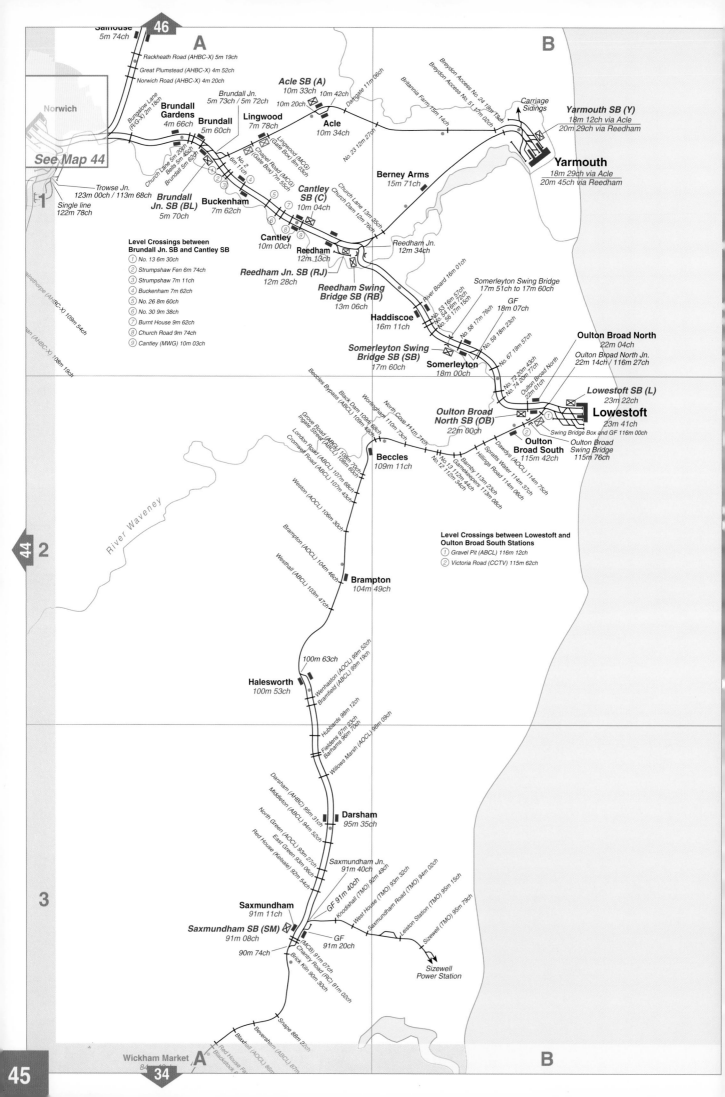

Salhouse
5m 74ch

A

B

Rackheath Road (AHBC-X) 5m 19ch

Great Plumstead (AHBC-X) 4m 52ch

Norwich Road (AHBC-X) 4m 20ch

Bungalow Lane (R/G-X) 2m 18ch

Brundall Jn.
5m 73ch / 5m 72ch

Acle SB (A)
10m 33ch   10m 42ch

Brundall
Gardens
4m 66ch

Brundall
5m 60ch

Lingwood
7m 78ch

Acle
10m 34ch

Breydon Access No. 24 19m 13ch
Breydon Access No. 51 17m 02ch

Britannia Farm 15m 14ch

Darfgate 11m 06ch

Carriage
Sidings

Yarmouth SB (Y)
18m 12ch via Acle
20m 29ch via Reedham

Norwich

See Map 44

Church Lane 5m 20ch
Bells 5m 45ch
Brundall 5m 62ch

No. 2
6m 11ch

Chapel Road (MCG)
Lingwood (MCG)
(Gate Box) 8m 03ch

No. 23 12m 27ch

Church Lane 13m 35ch
Church Dam 12m 76ch

Berney Arms
15m 71ch

Yarmouth
18m 29ch via Acle
20m 45ch via Reedham

Trowse Jn.
123m 00ch / 113m 68ch

Single line
122m 78ch

Brundall
Jn. SB (BL)
5m 70ch

Buckenham
7m 62ch

Cantley
SB (C)
10m 04ch

Reedham Jn.
12m 34ch

River Board 16m 01ch

Somerleyton Swing Bridge
17m 51ch to 17m 60ch

No. 53 16m 57ch
No. 54 16m 72ch
No. 56 17m 15ch

GF
18m 07ch

Oulton Broad North
22m 04ch

Level Crossings between
Brundall Jn. SB and Cantley SB
① No. 13 6m 30ch
② Strumpshaw Fen 6m 74ch
③ Strumpshaw 7m 11ch
④ Buckenham 7m 62ch
⑤ No. 26 8m 60ch
⑥ No. 30 9m 38ch
⑦ Burnt House 9m 62ch
⑧ Church Road 9m 74ch
⑨ Cantley (MWG) 10m 03ch

Cantley
10m 00ch

Reedham
12m 13ch

Reedham Jn. SB (RJ)
12m 28ch

Reedham Swing
Bridge SB (RB)
13m 06ch

Haddiscoe
16m 11ch

No. 58 17m 76ch
No. 59 18m 23ch

No. 67 19m 57ch

Oulton Broad North Jn.
22m 14ch / 116m 27ch

Lowestoft SB (L)
23m 22ch

Somerleyton Swing
Bridge SB (SB)
17m 60ch

Somerleyton
18m 00ch

No. 72 20m 43ch
No. 74 20m 57ch

Oulton Broad North
22m 01ch

Lowestoft
23m 41ch

Swing Bridge Box and GF 116m 00ch

Beccles Bypass (ABCL) 109m 44ch

Black Dam 109m 16ch

Worlingham 110m 73ch

North Cove +14m 71ch

Oulton Broad
North SB (OB)
22m 00ch

Oulton
Broad South
115m 42ch

Oulton Broad
Swing Bridge
115m 76ch

Grove Road (ABCL) 108m 79ch
Ingate Street (ABCL) 108m 66ch

London Road (ABCL) 107m 68ch

Cromwell Road (ABCL) 107m 43ch

Beccles
109m 11ch

No. 12 112m 24ch
No. 13 112m 34ch
Gamekeepers 113m 08ch

Barnby 113m 23ch
Hillings Road 114m 37ch

Spratts Water 114m 75ch

Dawdys 114m 06ch

Weston (AOCL) 106m 30ch

Level Crossings between Lowestoft and
Oulton Broad South Stations
① Gravel Pit (ABCL) 116m 12ch
② Victoria Road (CCTV) 115m 62ch

Brampton (AOCL) 104m 46ch

Westhall (ABCL) 103m 47ch

Brampton
104m 49ch

River Waveney

44

2

100m 63ch

Wenhaston (AOCL) 99m 52ch
Bramfield (ABCL) 99m 19ch

Halesworth
100m 53ch

Hubbards 98m 23ch

Fielders 97m 23ch
Bathans 96m 70ch

Willows Marsh (AOCL) 96m 09ch

Darsham (AHBC) 95m 31ch
Middleton (ABCL) 94m 90ch

North Green (AOCL) 93m 52ch
East Green 93m 27ch

Red House (Kelsale) 92m 54ch

Darsham
95m 35ch

Saxmundham Jn.
91m 40ch

GF 91m 40ch

Knodishall (TMO) 92m 49ch

West House (TMO) 93m 32ch

Saxmundham Road (TMO) 94m 02ch

Leiston Station (TMO) 95m 15ch

Sizewell (TMO) 95m 79ch

3

Saxmundham
91m 11ch

Saxmundham SB (SM)
91m 08ch

90m 74ch

GF
91m 20ch

Charity Road (MCB) 91m 07ch

Brick Kiln 90m 30ch

Sizewell
Power Station

Snape 88m 22ch

Beversham 87m

Blaxhall (AOCL) 86m

Red House Fm

Blackstock Fm

Wickham Market
84m

A

34

B

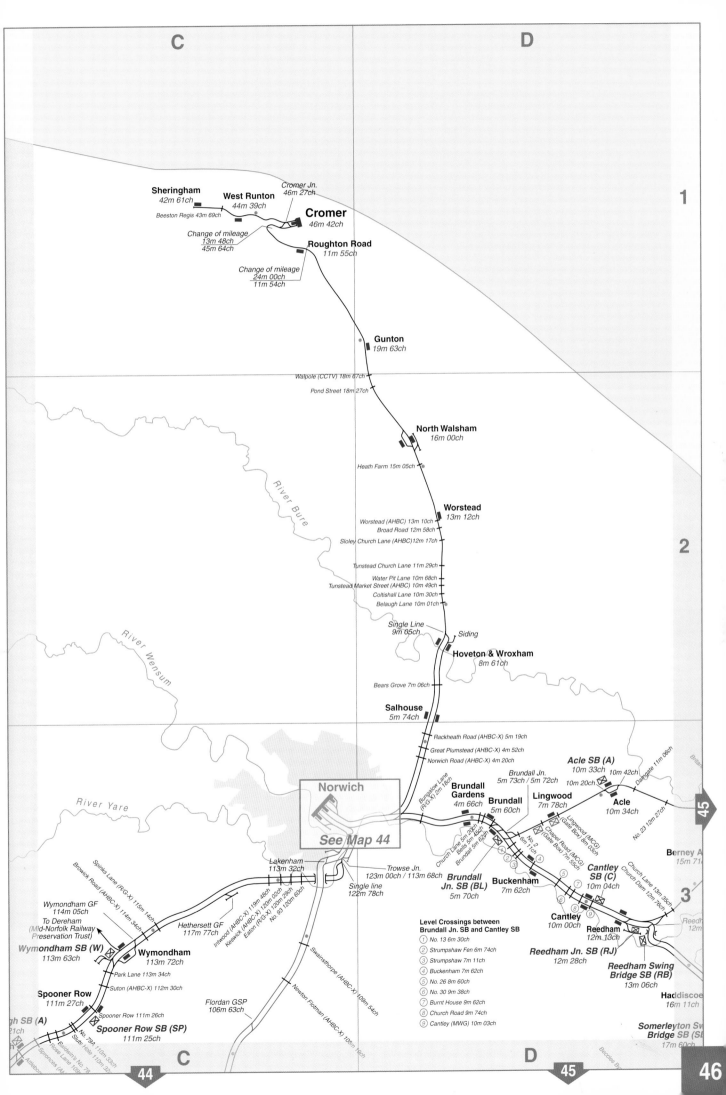

C | **D**

1

Sheringham
42m 61ch

West Runton
44m 39ch

Cromer Jn.
46m 27ch

Cromer
46m 42ch

Beeston Regis 43m 69ch

Change of mileage
13m 48ch
45m 64ch

Roughton Road
11m 55ch

Change of mileage
24m 00ch
11m 54ch

Gunton
19m 63ch

Walpole (CCTV) 18m 67ch
Pond Street 18m 27ch

North Walsham
16m 00ch

Heath Farm 15m 05ch

2

Worstead
13m 12ch

Worstead (AHBC) 13m 10ch
Broad Road 12m 58ch
Sloley Church Lane (AHBC)12m 17ch

Tunstead Church Lane 11m 29ch
Water Pit Lane 10m 68ch
Tunstead Market Street (AHBC) 10m 49ch
Coltishall Lane 10m 30ch
Belaugh Lane 10m 01ch

Single Line
9m 05ch

Siding

Hoveton & Wroxham
8m 61ch

River Bure

Bears Grove 7m 06ch

River Wensum

Salhouse
5m 74ch

Rackheath Road (AHBC-X) 5m 19ch
Great Plumstead (AHBC-X) 4m 52ch
Norwich Road (AHBC-X) 4m 20ch

Acle SB (A)
10m 33ch | *10m 42ch*
10m 20ch

Dangate 11m 06ch

Brundall Jn.
5m 73ch / 5m 72ch

Brundall
Gardens
4m 66ch

Brundall
5m 60ch

Lingwood
7m 78ch

Lingwood (MCG)
(Gate Box) 8m 03ch

Norwich

See Map 44

Bungalow Lane (R/G-X) 2m 18ch

Church Lane 5m 20ch
Bells 5m 45ch
Brundall 5m 62ch

No. 2
6m 11ch

Chapel Road (MCG)
(Gate Box) 7m 55ch

Acle
10m 34ch

No. 23 12m 27ch

45

Berney A

Lakenham
113m 32ch

Trowse Jn.
123m 00ch / 113m 68ch

Single line
122m 78ch

Brundall
Jn. SB (BL)
5m 70ch

Buckenham
7m 62ch

Cantley
SB (C)
10m 04ch

3

River Yare

Spinks Lane 116m 14ch
Browick Road (AHBC-X) 115m 14ch

Wymondham GF 114m 05ch

To Dereham
(Mid-Norfolk Railway
Preservation Trust)

Wymondham SB (W)
113m 63ch

Hethersett GF
117m 77ch

Intwood (AHBC-X) 119m 48ch
Keswick (AHBC-X) 120m 02ch
Eaton (R/G-X) 120m 29ch
No. 93 120m 60ch

Church Dam 13m 35ch
Church Lane 13m 36ch

Reedh
12m

Wymondham
113m 72ch

Park Lane 113m 34ch
Suton (AHBC-X) 112m 30ch

Flordan GSP
106m 63ch

Swainsthorpe (AHBC-X) 109m 54ch

Level Crossings between
Brundall Jn. SB and Cantley SB

① No. 13 6m 30ch
② Strumpshaw Fen 6m 74ch
③ Strumpshaw 7m 11ch
④ Buckenham 7m 62ch
⑤ No. 26 8m 60ch
⑥ No. 30 9m 38ch
⑦ Burnt House 9m 62ch
⑧ Church Road 9m 74ch
⑨ Cantley (MWG) 10m 03ch

Cantley
10m 00ch

Reedham
12m 13ch

Reedham Jn. SB (RJ)
12m 28ch

Reedh

Spooner Row
111m 27ch

Spooner Row 111m 26ch

Reedham Swing
Bridge SB (RB)
13m 06ch

Haddiscoe
16m 11ch

gh SB (A)
21ch

Newton Flotman (AHBC-X) 106m 14ch

Spooner Row SB (SP)
111m 25ch

No. 79A 110m 33ch
Stuts Hole 110m 32ch
Bridgeham's No. 76
Rose Lane 109m

Somerleyton Sw
Bridge SB (S
17m 60ch

Attleborough (At
Spoonches

44 | **C** | **D** | **45** | **46**

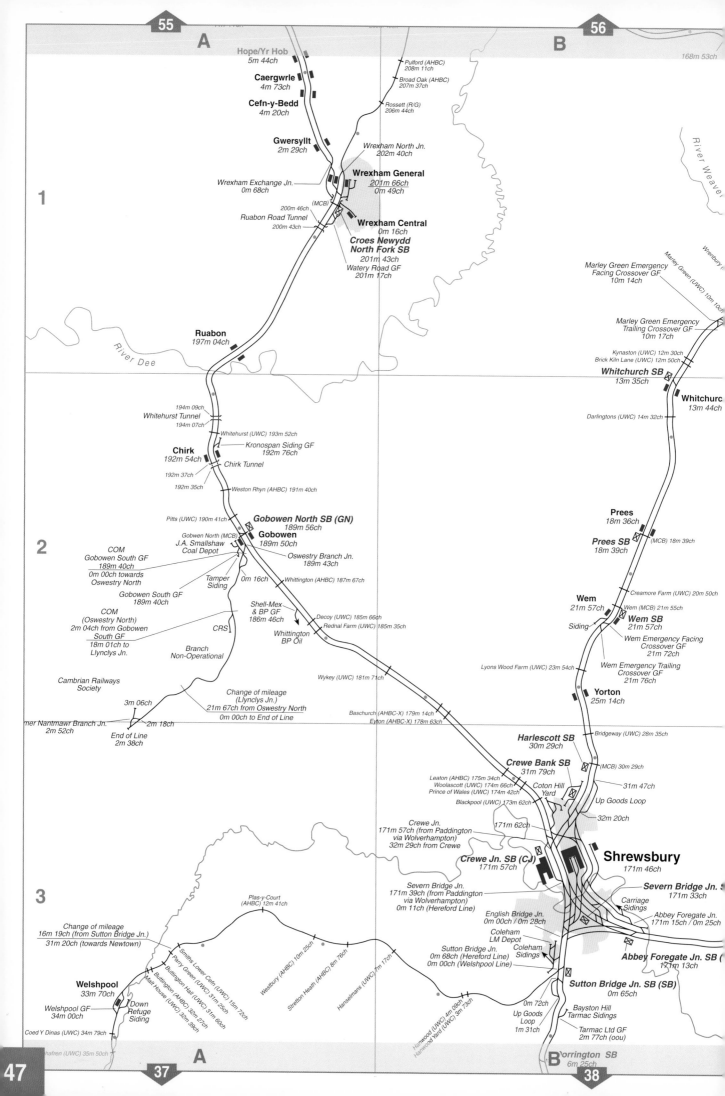

Hope/Yr Hob
5m 44ch

168m 53ch

Caergwrle
4m 73ch

Pulford (AHBC)
208m 11ch

Broad Oak (AHBC)
207m 37ch

Cefn-y-Bedd
4m 20ch

Rossett (R/G)
206m 44ch

River Weaver

1

Gwersyllt
2m 29ch

Wrexham North Jn.
202m 40ch

Wrexham Exchange Jn.
0m 68ch

Wrexham General
201m 66ch
0m 49ch

(MCB)

200m 46ch
Ruabon Road Tunnel
200m 43ch

Wrexham Central
0m 16ch

**Croes Newydd
North Fork SB**
201m 43ch

Marley Green Emergency
Facing Crossover GF
10m 14ch

Marley Green (UWC) 10m 10ch

Wrenbury

Watery Road GF
201m 17ch

Marley Green Emergency
Trailing Crossover GF
10m 17ch

Kynaston (UWC) 12m 30ch
Brick Kiln Lane (UWC) 12m 50ch

Ruabon
197m 04ch

River Dee

Whitchurch SB
13m 35ch

194m 09ch
Whitehurst Tunnel
194m 07ch

Whitehurst (UWC) 193m 52ch

Whitchurc
13m 44ch

Darlingtons (UWC) 14m 32ch

Kronospan Siding GF
192m 76ch

Chirk
192m 54ch

192m 37ch
Chirk Tunnel
192m 35ch

Weston Rhyn (AHBC) 191m 40ch

Pitts (UWC) 190m 41ch

Gobowen North SB (GN)
189m 56ch

Prees
18m 36ch

2

Gobowen North (MCB)

Gobowen
189m 50ch

Prees SB
18m 39ch

(MCB) 18m 39ch

J.A. Smallshaw
Coal Depot

**COM
Gobowen South GF
189m 40ch**
0m 00ch towards
Oswestry North

Oswestry Branch Jn.
189m 43ch

Tamper
Siding

0m 16ch

Whittington (AHBC) 187m 67ch

Creamore Farm (UWC) 20m 50ch

Wem
21m 57ch

Wem (MCB) 21m 55ch

Gobowen South GF
189m 40ch

Shell-Mex
& BP GF
186m 46ch

Decoy (UWC) 185m 66ch

Wem SB
21m 57ch

**COM
(Oswestry North)
2m 04ch from Gobowen
South GF**
18m 01ch to Llynclys Jn.

CRS

Whittington
BP Oil

Rednal Farm (UWC) 185m 35ch

Siding

Wem Emergency Facing
Crossover GF
21m 72ch

Branch
Non-Operational

**Cambrian Railways
Society**

Wem Emergency Trailing
Crossover GF
21m 76ch

Lyons Wood Farm (UWC) 23m 54ch

Wykey (UWC) 181m 71ch

Yorton
25m 14ch

3m 06ch

**Change of mileage
(Llynclys Jn.)
21m 67ch from Oswestry North**
0m 00ch to End of Line

mer Nantmawr Branch Jn.
2m 52ch

2m 18ch

Baschurch (AHBC-X) 179m 14ch
Eyton (AHBC-X) 178m 63ch

Bridgeway (UWC) 28m 35ch

End of Line
2m 38ch

Harlescott SB
30m 29ch

Crewe Bank SB
31m 79ch

(MCB) 30m 29ch

Leaton (AHBC) 175m 34ch
Woolascott (UWC) 174m 66ch
Prince of Wales (UWC) 174m 42ch

31m 47ch

**Coton Hill
Yard**

Blackpool (UWC) 173m 62ch

32m 20ch

171m 62ch

Up Goods Loop

**Crewe Jn.
171m 57ch (from Paddington
via Wolverhampton)
32m 29ch from Crewe**

Shrewsbury
171m 46ch

3

Plas-y-Court
(AHBC) 12m 41ch

Crewe Jn. SB (CJ)
171m 57ch

Severn Bridge Jn. S
171m 33ch

**Change of mileage
16m 19ch (from Sutton Bridge Jn.)
31m 20ch (towards Newtown)**

Severn Bridge Jn.
171m 39ch (from Paddington
via Wolverhampton)
0m 11ch (Hereford Line)

Carriage
Sidings

English Bridge Jn.
0m 00ch / 0m 28ch

Abbey Foregate Jn.
171m 15ch / 0m 25ch

Smiths Lower Cefn (UWC) 15m 72ch
Parry Green (UWC) 31m 25ch
Buttington (AHBC) 31m 60ch
Buttington Hall (UWC) 32m 27ch

Westbury (AHBC) 10m 25ch
Stretton Heath (AHBC) 8m 76ch

Hanselmans (UWC) 7m 17ch

**Coleham
LM Depot**

Welshpool
33m 70ch

Malt House (UWC) 32m 39ch

Coleham
Sidings

Sutton Bridge Jn.
0m 68ch (Hereford Line)
0m 00ch (Welshpool Line)

Abbey Foregate Jn. SB (
171m 13ch

Welshpool GF
34m 00ch

Down
Refuge
Siding

Hanwood (UWC) 4m 09ch
Hanwood Yard (UWC) 3m 73ch

Sutton Bridge Jn. SB (SB)
0m 65ch

Coed Y Dinas (UWC) 34m 79ch

0m 72ch
Up Goods
Loop
1m 31ch

Bayston Hill
Tarmac Sidings

Tarmac Ltd GF
2m 77ch (oou)

hafren (UWC) 35m 50ch

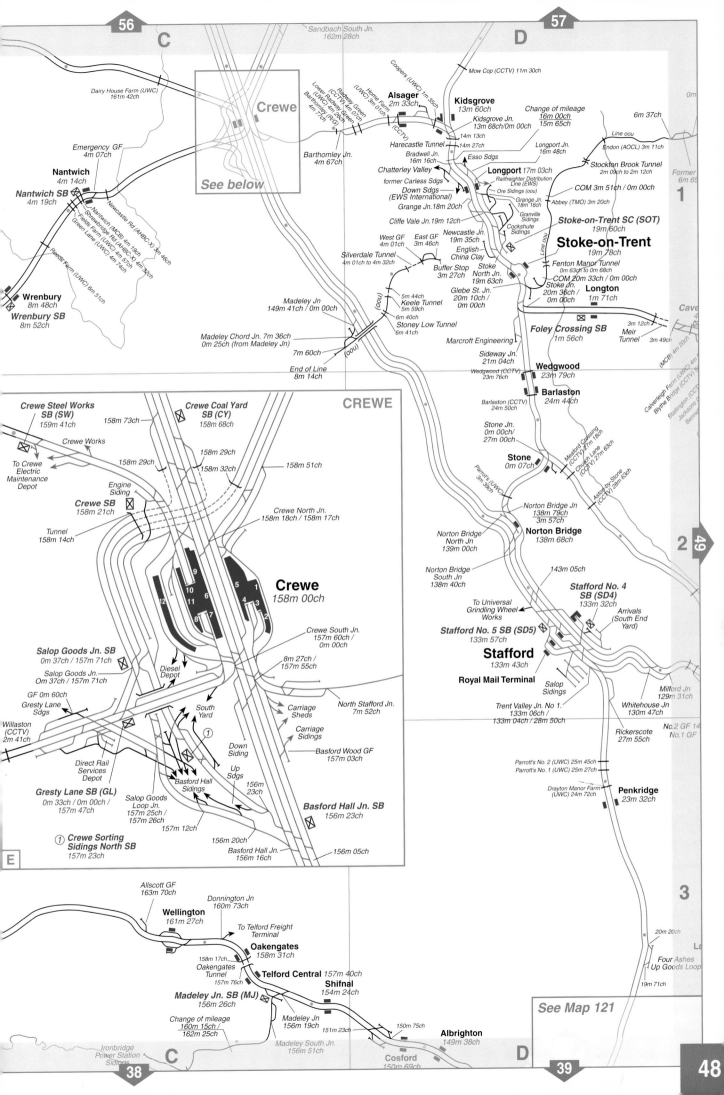

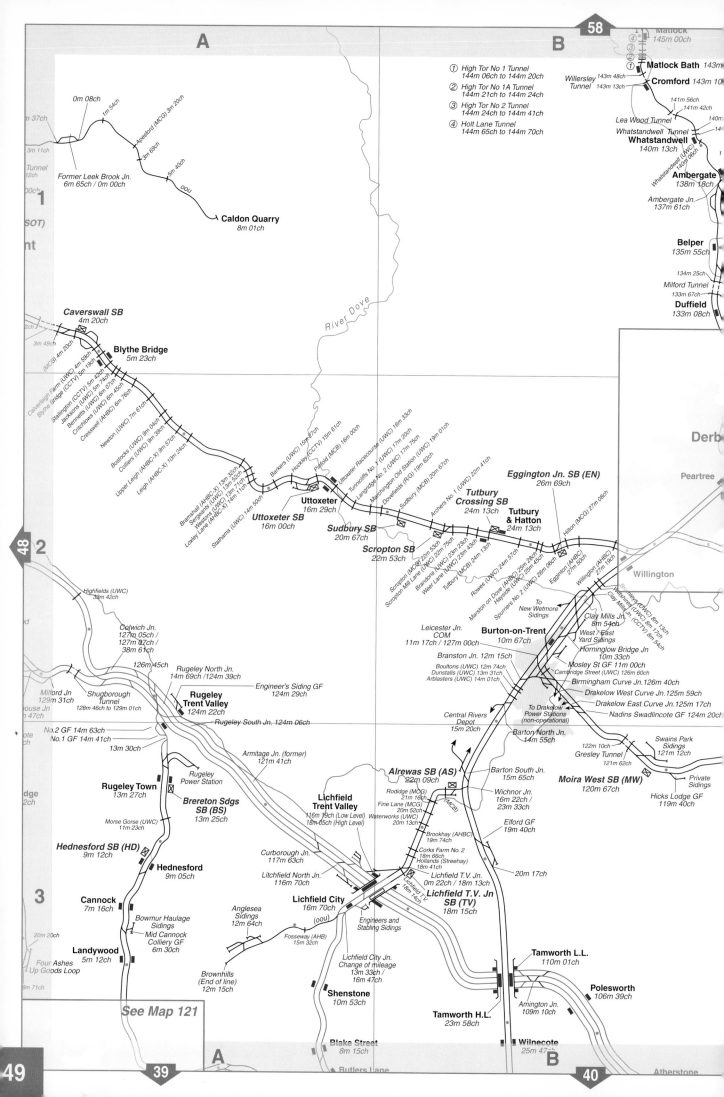

Matlock *145m 00ch*

① High Tor No 1 Tunnel
144m 06ch to 144m 20ch

② High Tor No 1A Tunnel
144m 21ch to 144m 24ch

③ High Tor No 2 Tunnel
144m 24ch to 144m 41ch

④ Holt Lane Tunnel
144m 65ch to 144m 70ch

Matlock Bath *143m*

Willersley Tunnel *143m 48ch*
Cromford *143m 10*

141m 56ch
141m 42ch

Lea Wood Tunnel

Whatstandwell Tunnel *143m 13ch*
Whatstandwell
140m 13ch

Whatstandwell Tunnel (UWC) *140m 06ch*

Ambergate *138m 18ch*

Ambergate Jn.
137m 61ch

Belper *135m 55ch*

134m 25ch

Milford Tunnel
133m 67ch

Duffield *133m 08ch*

0m 08ch

1m 54ch

Apesford (MCG) *3m 20ch*

3m 69ch

5m 40ch

oou

Former Leek Brook Jn.
6m 65ch / 0m 00ch

Caldon Quarry *8m 01ch*

0m 37ch

3m 11ch

Tunnel *12ch*

00ch

River Dove

Derb

Peartree

3m 49ch

Caverswall SB *4m 20ch*

2ch

(MCG) 4m 20ch

Blythe Bridge *5m 23ch*

Caverleigh Farm (UWC) *4m 59ch*
Blythe Bridge (CCTV) *5m 19ch*
Stallington (UWC) *5m 42ch*
Jacksons (UWC) *5m 74ch*
Bennetts (UWC) *6m 07ch*
Critchlows (UWC) *6m 45ch*
Cresswell (AHBC) *6m 76ch*

Newton (UWC) *7m 61ch*

Bostocks (UWC) *9m 04ch*
Colliers (UWC) *9m 39ch*

Upper Leigh (AHBC-X) *9m 57ch*
Leigh (AHBC-X) *10m 24ch*

Bramshall (AHBC-X) *13m 32ch*
Sergeants (UWC) *13m 52ch*
Westons (UWC) *13m 71ch*
Loxley Lane (AHBC-X) *14m 11ch*
Stathams (UWC) *14m 50ch*

Barkers (UWC) *15m 27ch*
Hockley (CCTV) *15m 61ch*
Diefold (MCB) *16m 00ch*

Uttoxeter Racecourse (UWC) *16m 33ch*
Tunnicliffs No. 1 (UWC) *17m 20ch*
Langradge No. 2 (UWC) *17m 75ch*
Marchington Old Station (UWC) *19m 01ch*
Dovefields (P/G) *19m 62ch*
Sudbury (MCB) *20m 67ch*

Uttoxeter *16m 29ch*

Uttoxeter SB *16m 00ch*

Sudbury SB *20m 67ch*

Scropton SB *22m 53ch*

Scropton (MCG) *22m 53ch*
Scropton Mill Lane (UWC) *22m 75ch*
Brandons (UWC) *23m 23ch*
Weer Lane (UWC) *23m 45ch*
Tutbury (MCB) *24m 13ch*

Archers No. 1 (UWC) *22m 41ch*

Tutbury Crossing SB *24m 13ch*

Tutbury & Hatton *24m 13ch*

Hilton (MCG) *27m 08ch*

Eggington Jn. SB (EN) *26m 69ch*

Rowes (AHBC) *25m 28ch*
Marston on Dove (UWC) *25m 45ch*
Hayside (UWC) *25m 06ch*
Spurriers No. 2 (UWC) *27m 19ch*

Eggington (AHBC) *27m 50ch*

Willington (AHBC)

Spurriers (UWC) *8m 13ch*
Finishing (UWC) *8m 17ch*
Clay Mills (CCTV) *8m 54ch*

Willington

To New Wetmore Sidings

Clay Mills Jn. *8m 54ch*

West / East Yard Sidings

Horninglow Bridge Jn
10m 33ch

Burton-on-Trent *10m 67ch*

**Leicester Jn.
COM** *11m 17ch / 127m 00ch*

Mosley St GF *11m 00ch*

Cambridge Street (UWC) *126m 60ch*

Birmingham Curve Jn. *126m 40ch*

Branston Jn. *12m 15ch*

Boultons (UWC) *12m 74ch*
Dunstalls (UWC) *13m 31ch*
Arblasters (UWC) *14m 01ch*

Drakelow West Curve Jn. *125m 59ch*

Drakelow East Curve Jn. *125m 17ch*

Nadins Swadlincote GF *124m 20ct*

To Drakelow Power Stations (non-operational)

Highfields (UWC) *38m 42ch*

Colwich Jn.
*127m 05ch /
127m 07ch /
38m 61ch*

126m 45ch

Milford Jn *129m 31ch*

Shugborough Tunnel
128m 46ch to 129m 01ch

Rugeley North Jn.
14m 69ch /124m 39ch

Engineer's Siding GF
124m 29ch

Rugeley Trent Valley *124m 22ch*

Rugeley South Jn. *124m 06ch*

13m 30ch

No.2 GF *14m 63ch*
No.1 GF *14m 41ch*

Armitage Jn. (former)
121m 41ch

Rugeley Power Station

Central Rivers Depot *15m 20ch*

Barton North Jn.
14m 55ch

Moira West SB (MW) *120m 67ch*

122m 10ch

Swains Park Sidings *121m 12ch*

Gresley Tunnel *121m 62ch*

Private Sidings

Hicks Lodge GF *119m 40ch*

Rugeley Town *13m 27ch*

Brereton Sdgs SB (BS) *13m 25ch*

Morse Gorse (UWC) *11m 23ch*

Hednesford SB (HD) *9m 12ch*

Hednesford *9m 05ch*

Barton South Jn.
15m 65ch

Alrewas SB (AS) *22m 09ch*

Rodidge (MCG) *21m 16ch*
Fine Lane (MCG) *20m 52ch*
Waterworks (UWC) *20m 13ch*

Wichnor Jn.
*16m 22ch /
23m 33ch*

Lichfield Trent Valley
*116m 19ch (Low Level) /
18m 05ch (High Level)*

Brookhay (AHBC) *19m 74ch*

Elford GF *19m 40ch*

Corks Farm No. 2 *18m 66ch*
Hollands (Streehay) *18m 41ch*

Curborough Jn.
117m 63ch

Litchfield North Jn.
116m 70ch

Lichfield T.V. Jn.
0m 22ch / 18m 13ch

Lichfield T.V. Jn SB (TV) *18m 15ch*

20m 17ch

Litchfield T.V.
18m 14ch

(MCB)

Cannock *7m 16ch*

Bowmur Haulage Sidings
Mid Cannock Colliery GF *6m 30ch*

Anglesea Sidings *12m 64ch*

Lichfield City *16m 70ch*

(oou)

Fosseway (AHB) *15m 32ch*

Engineers and Stabling Sidings

Tamworth L.L. *110m 01ch*

Polesworth *106m 39ch*

Landywood *5m 12ch*

20m 20ch

Four Ashes Up Goods Loop

9m 71ch

Brownhills (End of line) *12m 15ch*

Lichfield City Jn.
Change of mileage *13m 33ch / 16m 47ch*

Shenstone *10m 53ch*

Amington Jn. *109m 10ch*

Tamworth H.L. *23m 58ch*

Wilnecote *25m 47ch*

Blake Street *8m 15ch*

Butlers Lane

Atherstone

See Map 121

(SOT)

nt

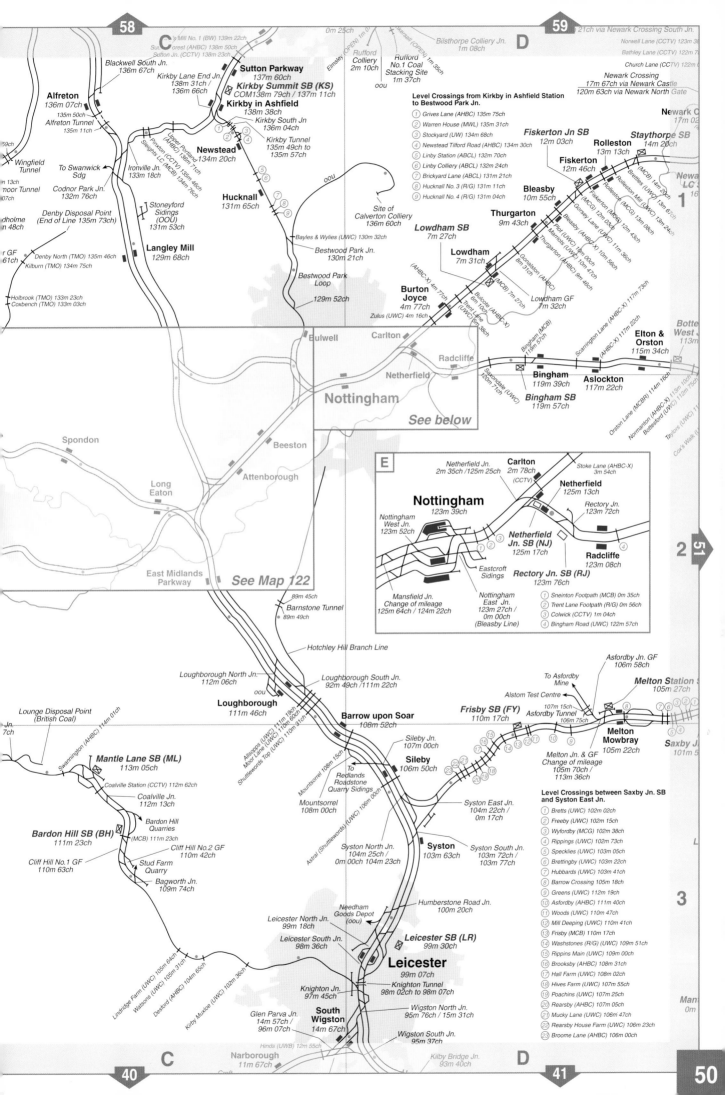

Sutton's Mill No. 1 (BW) 139m 22ch
Sutton Forest (AHBC) 138m 50ch
Sutton Jn. (CCTV) 138m 23ch
0m 25ch
Annesley (OPEN) 1m 0ch
Bilsthorpe Colliery Jn. 1m 08ch
21ch via Newark Crossing South Jn.
Norwell Lane (CCTV) 123m 36
Bathley Lane (CCTV) 122m 74
Church Lane (CCTV) 122m

Blackwell South Jn. 136m 67ch
Sutton Parkway 137m 60ch
Kirkby Lane End Jn. 138m 31ch / 136m 66ch
Kirkby Summit SB (KS) COM138m 79ch / 137m 11ch
Rufford Colliery 2m 10ch
Rufford No.1 Coal Stacking Site 1m 37ch
oou

Alfreton 136m 07ch
135m 50ch
Alfreton Tunnel 135m 11ch
Kirkby in Ashfield 138m 38ch
Kirkby South Jn 136m 04ch
Kirkby Tunnel 135m 49ch to 135m 57ch

Newark Crossing 17m 67ch via Newark Castle
120m 63ch via Newark North Gate

Newark C 17m 02
Newa LC'S

Level Crossings from Kirkby in Ashfield Station to Bestwood Park Jn.
① Grives Lane (AHBC) 135m 75ch
② Warren House (MWL) 135m 31ch
③ Stockyard (UW) 134m 68ch
④ Newstead Tilford Road (AHBC) 134m 30ch
⑤ Linby Station (ABCL) 132m 70ch
⑥ Linby Colliery (ABCL) 132m 24ch
⑦ Brickyard Lane (ABCL) 131m 21ch
⑧ Hucknall No. 3 (R/G) 131m 11ch
⑨ Hucknall No. 4 (R/G) 131m 00ch

Wingfield Tunnel
Codnor Park Jn. 132m 76ch
Upper Portland (AHBC) 136m 71ch / 135m 46ch
Pinxton (CCTV) 135m 34ch / 134m 76ch
Sleights LC (MCB) 134m 76ch
Ironville Jn. 133m 18ch
Newstead 136m 20ch

Fiskerton Jn SB 12m 03ch
Rolleston 13m 13ch
Staythorpe SB 14m 20ch
Brettes (MCB) 14m 29ch
Rolleston Mill (UWC) 13m 67ch

Denby Disposal Point (End of Line 135m 73ch)
Stoneyford Sidings (OOU) 131m 53ch
Fiskerton 12m 46ch
Fiskerton (MCG) 12m 03ch
Rolleston (MCG) 13m 24ch

Bleasby 10m 55ch
Bleasby (AHBC) 11m 03ch
Gorsey Lane (UWC) 11m 36ch
Plot (UWC) 10m 00ch
Marriots (UWC) 10m 56ch

Thurgarton 9m 43ch
Thurgarton (UWC) 10m 47ch
Gonalston (AHBC) 9m 00ch

Denby North (TMO) 135m 46ch
Kilburn (TMO) 134m 75ch
Holbrook (TMO) 133m 23ch
Coxbench (TMO) 133m 03ch

Langley Mill 129m 68ch

Site of Calverton Colliery 136m 60ch
Bayles & Wylies (UWC) 130m 32ch
Bestwood Park Jn. 130m 21ch
Bestwood Park Loop 129m 52ch

Lowdham SB 7m 27ch
Lowdham 7m 31ch
Lowdham (MCB) 7m 27ch
Bulcote (AHBC-X) 6m 10ch
Trent Lane (UWC) 6m 36ch
Lowdham GF 7m 32ch

Burton Joyce 4m 77ch
(AHBC-X) 4m 77ch
Zulus (UWC) 4m 16ch

Bingham (MCB) 119m 57ch
Saxondale (UWC) 120m 71ch
Scarrington Lane (AHBC-X) 117m 22ch
Elton & Orston 115m 34ch
Botte West 113m

Bulwell
Carlton
Radcliffe
Netherfield
Nottingham
See below

Bingham 119m 39ch
Bingham SB 119m 57ch
Aslockton 117m 22ch
Orston Lane (MCBR) 114m 16ch / 113m 10ch / 112m 75ch
Normanton (AHBC-X) 117m 16ch
Bottesford (UWC) 112m 11ch
Taylors (UWC) 112m 71ch
Cox's Walk

Spondon
Beeston
Attenborough
Long Eaton

East Midlands Parkway
See Map 122

E
Netherfield Jn. 2m 35ch /125m 25ch
Carlton 2m 78ch (CCTV)
Stoke Lane (AHBC-X) 3m 54ch
Netherfield 125m 13ch
Rectory Jn. 123m 72ch

Nottingham 123m 39ch
Nottingham West Jn. 123m 52ch
Netherfield Jn. SB (NJ) 125m 17ch
Eastcroft Sidings
Radcliffe 123m 08ch
Rectory Jn. SB (RJ) 123m 76ch

Mansfield Jn. Change of mileage 125m 64ch / 124m 22ch
Nottingham East Jn. 123m 27ch / 0m 00ch (Bleasby Line)

① Sneinton Footpath (MCB) 0m 35ch
② Trent Lane Footpath (R/G) 0m 56ch
③ Colwick (CCTV) 1m 04ch
④ Bingham Road (UWC) 122m 57ch

51 2

89m 45ch
Barnstone Tunnel
89m 49ch
Hotchley Hill Branch Line

Loughborough North Jn. 112m 06ch
Loughborough South Jn. 92m 49ch /111m 22ch
oou
Loughborough 111m 46ch

Barrow upon Soar 108m 52ch

Frisby SB (FY) 110m 17ch

Asfordby Jn. GF 106m 58ch
To Asfordby Mine
Alstom Test Centre
Melton Station S 105m 27ch
Asfordby Tunnel 106m 75ch

Lounge Disposal Point (British Coal)
Jn. 7ch
Swannington (AHBC) 114m 01ch

Mantle Lane SB (ML) 113m 05ch
Coalville Station (CCTV) 112m 62ch
Allsopps (UWC) 111m 19ch
Moor Lane (UWC) 110m 60ch
Shuttleworths Top (UWC) 110m 31ch

Sileby Jn. 107m 00ch
Sileby 106m 50ch

To Redlands Roadstone Quarry Sidings
Mountsorrel (UWC) 108m 15ch
Mountsorrel 108m 00ch
Astral (Shuttleworths) (UWC) 106m 00ch

Syston East Jn. 104m 22ch / 0m 17ch
Melton Mowbray 105m 22ch
Melton Jn. & GF Change of mileage 105m 70ch / 113m 36ch
Saxby J 101m 5

Coalville Jn. 112m 13ch
Bardon Hill SB (BH) 111m 23ch
Bardon Hill Quarries
(MCB) 111m 23ch
Cliff Hill No.2 GF 110m 42ch
Cliff Hill No.1 GF 110m 63ch
Stud Farm Quarry
Bagworth Jn. 109m 74ch

Syston North Jn. 104m 25ch / 0m 00ch 104m 23ch
Syston 103m 63ch
Syston South Jn. 103m 72ch / 103m 77ch

Level Crossings between Saxby Jn. SB and Syston East Jn.
① Bretts (UWC) 102m 02ch
② Freeby (UWC) 102m 15ch
③ Wyfordby (MCG) 102m 38ch
④ Rippings (UWC) 102m 73ch
⑤ Specklies (UWC) 103m 05ch
⑥ Brettingby (UWC) 103m 22ch
⑦ Hubbards (UWC) 103m 41ch
⑧ Barrow Crossing 105m 18ch
⑨ Greens (UWC) 112m 19ch
⑩ Asfordby (AHBC) 111m 40ch
⑪ Woods (UWC) 110m 47ch
⑫ Mill Deeping (UWC) 110m 41ch
⑬ Frisby (MCB) 110m 17ch
⑭ Washstones (R/G) (UWC) 109m 51ch
⑮ Rippins Main (UWC) 109m 00ch
⑯ Brooksby (AHBC) 108m 31ch
⑰ Hall Farm (UWC) 108m 02ch
⑱ Hives Farm (UWC) 107m 45ch
⑲ Poachins (UWC) 107m 25ch
⑳ Rearsby (AHBC) 107m 05ch
㉑ Mucky Lane (UWC) 106m 47ch
㉒ Rearsby House Farm (UWC) 106m 23ch
㉓ Broome Lane (AHBC) 106m 00ch

Humberstone Road Jn. 100m 20ch
Needham Goods Depot (oou)
Leicester North Jn. 99m 18ch
Leicester South Jn. 98m 36ch
Leicester SB (LR) 99m 30ch
Leicester 99m 07ch

Lindridge Farm (UWC) 105m 64ch
Watsons (UWC) 105m 31ch
Destford (AHBC) 104m 65ch
Kirby Muxloe (UWC) 102m 36ch

Knighton Jn. 97m 45ch
Knighton Tunnel 98m 02ch to 98m 07ch
Glen Parva Jn. 14m 57ch / 96m 07ch
South Wigston 14m 67ch
Wigston North Jn. 95m 76ch / 15m 31ch
Wigston South Jn. 95m 37ch

Narborough 11m 67ch
Hinds (UWB) 12m 55ch
Kilby Bridge Jn. 93m 40ch
Man 0m

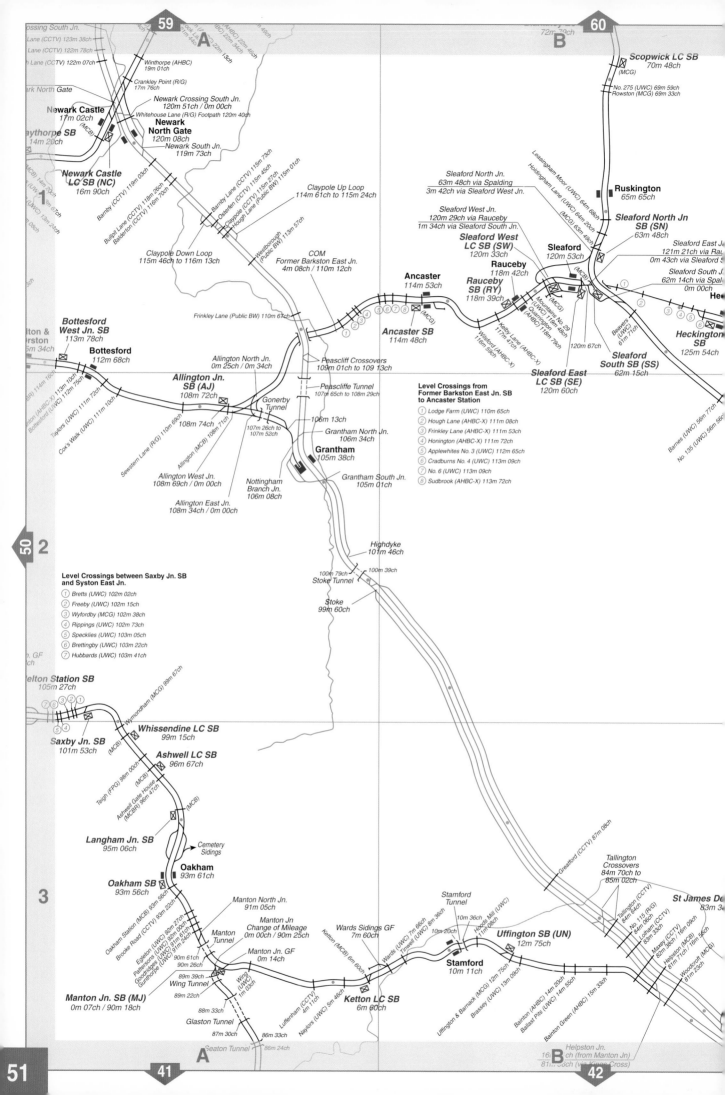

Crossing South Jn.
Lane (CCTV) 123m 38ch
Lane (CCTV) 122m 78ch
Lane (CCTV) 122m 07ch

Scopwick LC SB
70m 48ch
(MCG)

No. 275 (UWC) 69m 59ch
Rowston (MCG) 69m 33ch

Winthorpe (AHBC)
19m 01ch

Crankley Point (R/G)
17m 76ch

Newark Castle
17m 02ch
(MCB)

ark North Gate

aythorpe SB
14m 20ch

Newark Crossing South Jn.
120m 51ch / 0m 00ch
Whitehouse Lane (R/G) Footpath 120m 40ch

Newark
North Gate
120m 08ch

Newark South Jn.
119m 73ch

Newark Castle
LC SB (NC)
16m 90ch

Leasingham Moor (UWC) 64m 68ch
Holdingham Lane (UWC) 64m 20ch
(MCG) 63m 49ch

Ruskington
65m 65ch

Barnby (CCTV) 119m 03ch
Bullpit Lane (CCTV) 118m 26ch
Balderton (CCTV) 116m 70ch

Barnby Lane (CCTV) 115m 73ch
Osterfen (CCTV) 115m 45ch
Claypole (CCTV) 115m 27ch
Hough Lane (Public BW) 115m 01ch

Claypole Up Loop
114m 61ch to 115m 24ch

Sleaford North Jn.
63m 48ch via Spalding
3m 42ch via Sleaford West Jn.

Sleaford West Jn.
120m 29ch via Rauceby
1m 34ch via Sleaford South Jn.

Sleaford North Jn
SB (SN)
63m 48ch

Sleaford East Jn.
121m 21ch via Rau
0m 43ch via Sleaford S

Claypole Down Loop
115m 46ch to 116m 13ch

Westborough
(Public BW) 113m 57ch

COM
Former Barkston East Jn.
4m 08ch / 110m 12ch

Sleaford West
LC SB (SW)
120m 33ch

Sleaford
120m 53ch
(MCB)

Sleaford South J.
62m 14ch via Spal
0m 00ch

Frinkley Lane (Public BW) 110m 67ch

Ancaster
114m 53ch

Rauceby
Rauceby
SB (RY)
118m 39ch

Rauceby
118m 42ch

Sleaford South SB (SS)
62m 15ch

He

Mountains No. 29
(MCG) 119m 48ch
Quarrington
(UWC) 118m 79ch

Beavers
(UWC)
61m 71ch

Heckington
SB

Bottesford
West Jn. SB
113m 78ch

Ancaster SB
114m 48ch

① ② ③ ④ ⑤ ⑥ ⑦ ⑧
(MCG)

Kelby Lane (AHBC) 118m 07ch
Wilsford (AHBC-X) 116m 58ch

Heckington
SB
125m 54ch

Bottesford
112m 68ch
(MCB)

elton &
rston
m 34ch

Allington North Jn.
0m 25ch / 0m 34ch

Peascliff Crossovers
109m 01ch to 109 13ch

Level Crossings from
Former Barkston East Jn. SB
to Ancaster Station

Sleaford East
LC SB (SE)
120m 60ch

120m 67ch

Barnes (UWC) 56m 77ch

No. 135 (UWC) 56m 56ch

Allington Jn.
SB (AJ)
108m 72ch

108m 74ch

Peascliffe Tunnel
107m 65ch to 108m 29ch

Gonerby
Tunnel

① Lodge Farm (UWC) 110m 65ch
② Hough Lane (AHBC-X) 111m 08ch
③ Frinkley Lane (AHBC-X) 111m 53ch
④ Honington (AHBC-X) 111m 72ch
⑤ Applewhites No. 3 (UWC) 112m 65ch
⑥ Cradburns No. 4 (UWC) 113m 09ch
⑦ No. 6 (UWC) 113m 09ch
⑧ Sudbrook (AHBC-X) 113m 72ch

Taylors (UWC) 111m 10ch
Cox's Walk (UWC) 111m 10ch
(AHBC-X) 113m 10ch
ottesford (UWC) 112m 75ch

108m 71ch

107m 26ch to
107m 52ch

106m 13ch

Grantham North Jn.
106m 34ch

Sewstern Lane (R/G) 110m 69ch

Allington (MCB) 108m 77ch

Allington West Jn.
108m 69ch / 0m 00ch

Nottingham
Branch Jn.
106m 08ch

Grantham
105m 38ch

Grantham South Jn.
105m 01ch

Allington East Jn.
108m 34ch / 0m 00ch

50 2

Highdyke
101m 46ch

Level Crossings between Saxby Jn. SB
and Syston East Jn.

① Bretts (UWC) 102m 02ch
② Freeby (UWC) 102m 15ch
③ Wyfordby (MCG) 102m 38ch
④ Rippings (UWC) 102m 73ch
⑤ Specklies (UWC) 103m 05ch
⑥ Brettingby (UWC) 103m 22ch
⑦ Hubbards (UWC) 103m 41ch

100m 79ch   100m 39ch
Stoke Tunnel

Stoke
99m 60ch

elton Station SB
105m 27ch

⑦⑥⑤ ③②①
⑤④

Greatford (CCTV) 87m 08ch

Whissendine LC SB
99m 15ch

Saxby Jn. SB
101m 53ch
(MCB)

Ashwell LC SB
96m 67ch

Teigh (FPG) 98m 00ch
Ashwell Gate House
(MCBR) 96m 47ch
(MCB)

Tallington
Crossovers
84m 70ch to
85m 02ch

Tallington (CCTV)
84m 64ch
No. 115 (R/G)
84m 06ch

St James De
83m 3

Langham Jn. SB
95m 06ch

Cemetery
Sidings

Stamford
Tunnel

Lotham (CCTV)
83m 30ch

Oakham SB
93m 56ch

Oakham
93m 61ch

10m 36ch
10m 20ch

Woods Mill (UWC)
11m 06ch

Uffington SB (UN)
12m 75ch

Maxey (CCTV)
82m 38ch / 16m 09ch

Helpston (MCB)
81m 71ch / 16m 49ch
Woodcroft (MCG)

3

Oakham Station (MCB) 93m 56ch
Brooke Road (CCTV) 93m 22ch

Manton North Jn.
91m 05ch

Manton Jn
Change of Mileage
0m 00ch / 90m 25ch

Wards Sidings GF
7m 60ch

Stamford
Tunnel

Stamford
10m 11ch

Egleton (UWC) 92m 27ch
Pattersons (UWC) 92m 00ch
Goodridges (UWC) 91m 61ch
Gunthorpe (UWC) 91m 24ch

90m 61ch
90m 26ch

Manton
Tunnel

Manton Jn. GF
0m 14ch

Ketton (MCB) 6m 00ch

Uffington & Barnack (MCG) 12m 75ch

Bainton (AHBC) 14m 20ch
Ballast Pits (UWC) 14m 55ch
Bainton Green (AHBC) 15m 33ch

Manton Jn. SB (MJ)
0m 07ch / 90m 18ch

89m 39ch
Wing Tunnel

89m 22ch

Wing
(UWC)
1m 03ch

Luffenham (CCTV)
4m 11ch

Ketton LC SB
6m 60ch

Wards (UWC) 7m 66ch
Tinwell (UWC) 8m 36ch

Naylors (UWC) 5m 46ch

Glaston Tunnel

88m 33ch   86m 33ch
87m 30ch   86m 24ch

Seaton Tunnel

51

Helpston Jn.
ch (from Manton Jn)
ch (via Kings Cross)

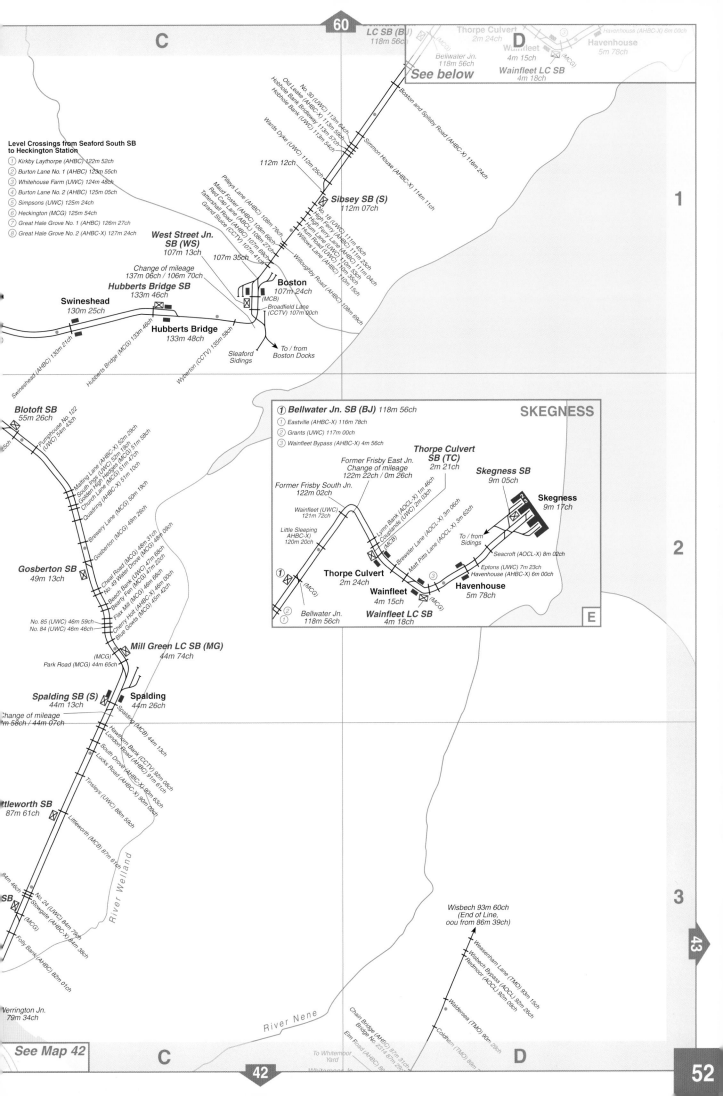

C

D

Wainfleet
LC SB (BJ)
118m 56ch

Thorpe Culvert
2m 24ch

Havenhouse (AHBC-X) 6m 00ch

Havenhouse
5m 78ch

Wainfleet
4m 15ch

Bellwater Jn.
118m 56ch

See below

Wainfleet LC SB
4m 18ch

Boston and Spilsby Road (AHBC-X) 116m 24ch

No. 30 (UWC) 113m 06ch
Hobhole Bank Bridleway 113m 59ch
Hobhole Bank (UWC) 113m 57ch

Simmon House (AHBC-X) 114m 11ch

1

Wards Dyke (UWC) 112m 25ch

112m 12ch

**Level Crossings from Seaford South SB
to Heckington Station**
① Kirkby Laythorpe (AHBC) 122m 52ch
② Burton Lane No. 1 (AHBC) 123m 55ch
③ Whitehouse Farm (UWC) 124m 48ch
④ Burton Lane No. 2 (AHBC) 125m 05ch
⑤ Simpsons (UWC) 125m 24ch
⑥ Heckington (MCG) 125m 54ch
⑦ Great Hale Grove No. 1 (AHBC) 126m 27ch
⑧ Great Hale Grove No. 2 (AHBC-X) 127m 24ch

No. 18 (UWC) 111m 45ch
High Ferry (AHBC) 111m 23ch
High Lane (AHBC) 111m 04ch
Hurn Lane (UWC) 110m 53ch
Hurn Road (UWC) 110m 35ch
Willows Lane (AHBC) 110m 15ch

Sibsey SB (S)
112m 07ch

Pilleys Lane (AHBC) 108m 76ch
Maud Foster (AHBC) 108m 27ch
Red Cap Lane (ABCL) 108m 68ch
Tattershall Road (AHBC) 107m 69ch
Grand Sluice (CCTV) 107m 41ch

Willoughby Road (AHBC) 108m 69ch

**West Street Jn.
SB (WS)**
107m 13ch

107m 35ch

Boston
107m 24ch
(MCB)

Broadfield Lane
(CCTV) 107m 00ch

**Change of mileage
137m 06ch / 106m 70ch**

Hubberts Bridge SB
133m 46ch

Swineshead
130m 25ch

Swineshead (AHBC) 130m 21ch

Hubberts Bridge (MCG) 133m 46ch

Hubberts Bridge
133m 48ch

Wyberton (CCTV) 135m 58ch

Sleaford
Sidings

To / from
Boston Docks

① **Bellwater Jn. SB (BJ)** 118m 56ch

① Eastville (AHBC-X) 116m 78ch
② Grants (UWC) 117m 00ch
③ Wainfleet Bypass (AHBC-X) 4m 56ch

SKEGNESS

Blotoft SB
55m 26ch

55m 26ch

Pumphouse No. 122
(UWC) 54m 43ch

Malting Lane (AHBC-X) 52m 29ch
South Ings (UWC) 52m 19ch
Golden High Hedges (MCG) 51m 58ch
Church Lane (MCG) 51m 47ch

Brewery Lane (MCG) 50m 07ch

Gosberton (MCG) 49m 26ch

Gosberton SB
49m 13ch

Cheal Road (MCG) 48m 31ch
No. 49 Water Drove (MCG) 48m 09ch
Beech Bank (UWC) 47m 68ch
Beery Fen (MCG) 47m 22ch
Flax Mill (MCG) 46m 66ch
Cherry Holt (AHBC-X) 46m 00ch
Blue Gowts (MCG) 45m 42ch

No. 85 (UWC) 46m 59ch
No. 84 (UWC) 46m 46ch

(MCG)

Mill Green LC SB (MG)
44m 74ch

Park Road (MCG) 44m 65ch

**Former Frisby East Jn.
Change of mileage
122m 22ch / 0m 26ch**

**Thorpe Culvert
SB (TC)**
2m 21ch

Skegness SB
9m 05ch

Former Frisby South Jn.
122m 02ch

Lymn Bank (AOCL-X) 1m 46ch
Couplands (UWC) 2m 03ch
(MCB)

Skegness
9m 17ch

Wainfleet (UWC)
121m 72ch

Brewster Lane (AOCL-X) 3m 06ch
Matt Pitts Lane (AOCL-X) 3m 62ch

To / from
Sidings

Little Sleeping
AHBC-X)
120m 20ch

Seacroft (AOCL-X) 8m 02ch

Thorpe Culvert
2m 24ch

Eptons (UWC) 7m 23ch
Havenhouse (AHBC-X) 6m 00ch

Wainfleet
4m 15ch

Havenhouse
5m 78ch

① Bellwater Jn.
118m 56ch

Wainfleet LC SB
4m 18ch

(MCG)

E

2

Spalding SB (S)
44m 13ch

Spalding
44m 26ch

Change of mileage
m 58ch / 44m 07ch

Spalding (MCG) 44m 13ch

Hawthorn Bank (CCTV) 92m 08ch
London Road (AHBC) 91m 61ch
South Drove (AHBC) 90m 63ch
Lucks Road (AHBC-X) 90m 06ch
Tinsleys (UWC) 88m 59ch

ttleworth SB
87m 61ch

Littleworth (MCB) 87m 61ch

River Welland

84m 46ch

No. 24 (UWC) 84m 79ch
Stowgate (AHBC-X) 84m 38ch

SB

(MCG)

Folly Bank (AHBC) 82m 01ch

Werrington Jn.
79m 34ch

Wisbech 93m 60ch
(End of Line,
oou from 86m 39ch)

3

Weasenham Lane (TMO) 93m 31ch
Wisbech Bypass (AOCL) 93m 26ch
Redmoor (AOCL) 92m 09ch

Waldersea (TMO) 90m 28ch

Chain Bridge (AHBC) 87m 31ch
Bridge No. 2214 87m 29ch

Coldham (TMO) 89m

Elm Road (AHBC) 86m

See Map 42

C

River Nene

To Whitemoor
Yard

Whitemoor Jn.

D

43

52

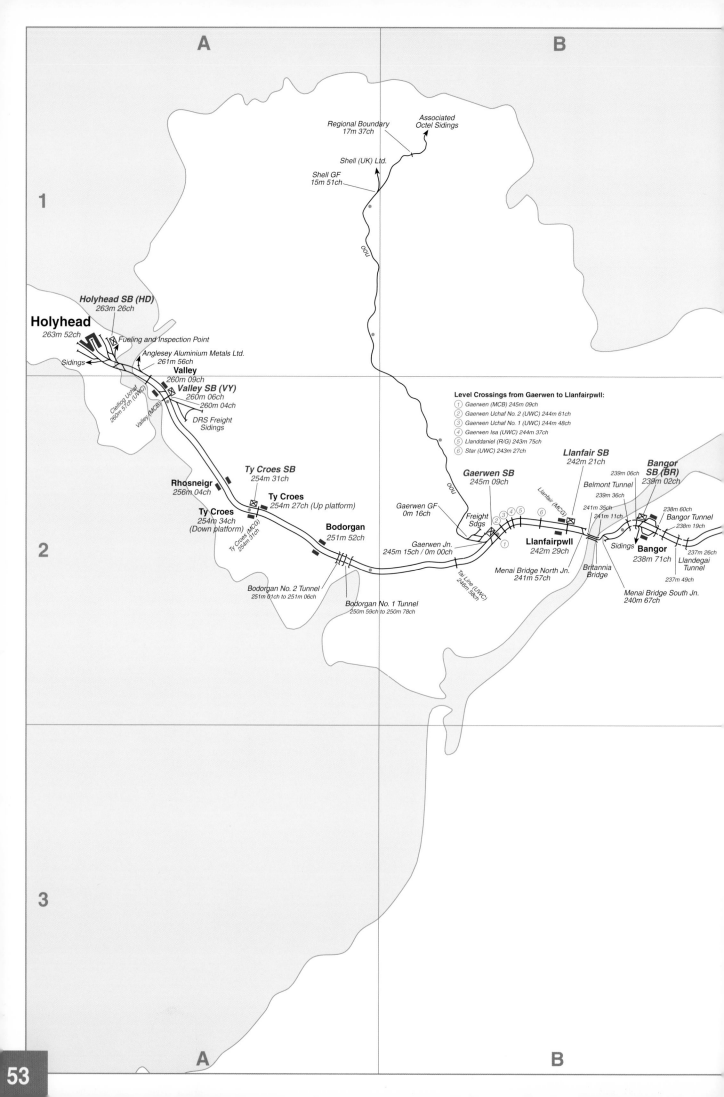

Regional Boundary
17m 37ch

Associated
Octel Sidings

Shell (UK) Ltd.

Shell GF
15m 51ch

OOU

Holyhead SB (HD)
263m 26ch

Holyhead
263m 52ch

Fueling and Inspection Point

Anglesey Aluminium Metals Ltd.
261m 56ch

Sidings

Valley
260m 09ch

Cleifiog Uchaf
260m 57ch (UWC)

Valley SB (VY)
260m 06ch
260m 04ch

Valley (MCB)

DRS Freight
Sidings

Level Crossings from Gaerwen to Llanfairpwll:
① Gaerwen (MCB) 245m 09ch
② Gaerwen Uchaf No. 2 (UWC) 244m 61ch
③ Gaerwen Uchaf No. 1 (UWC) 244m 48ch
④ Gaerwen Isa (UWC) 244m 37ch
⑤ Llanddaniel (R/G) 243m 75ch
⑥ Star (UWC) 243m 27ch

Ty Croes SB
254m 31ch

Rhosneigr
256m 04ch

Gaerwen SB
245m 09ch

Llanfair SB
242m 21ch

239m 06ch

**Bangor
SB (BR)**
239m 02ch

Ty Croes
254m 27ch (Up platform)

Belmont Tunnel
239m 36ch

Ty Croes
254m 34ch
(Down platform)

Ty Croes (MCG)
254m 31ch

Gaerwen GF
0m 16ch

Bodorgan
251m 52ch

Freight
Sdgs

Llanfair (MCG)

241m 35ch
241m 11ch

238m 60ch

Bangor Tunnel
238m 19ch

Sidings

Bangor
238m 71ch

Gaerwen Jn.
245m 15ch / 0m 00ch

③④⑤

⑥

Llanfairpwll
242m 29ch

237m 26ch
Llandegai
Tunnel
237m 49ch

②

①

Bodorgan No. 2 Tunnel
251m 01ch to 251m 06ch

Bodorgan No. 1 Tunnel
250m 59ch to 250m 78ch

Tai Line (UWC)
246m 58ch

Menai Bridge North Jn.
241m 57ch

Britannia
Bridge

Menai Bridge South Jn.
240m 67ch

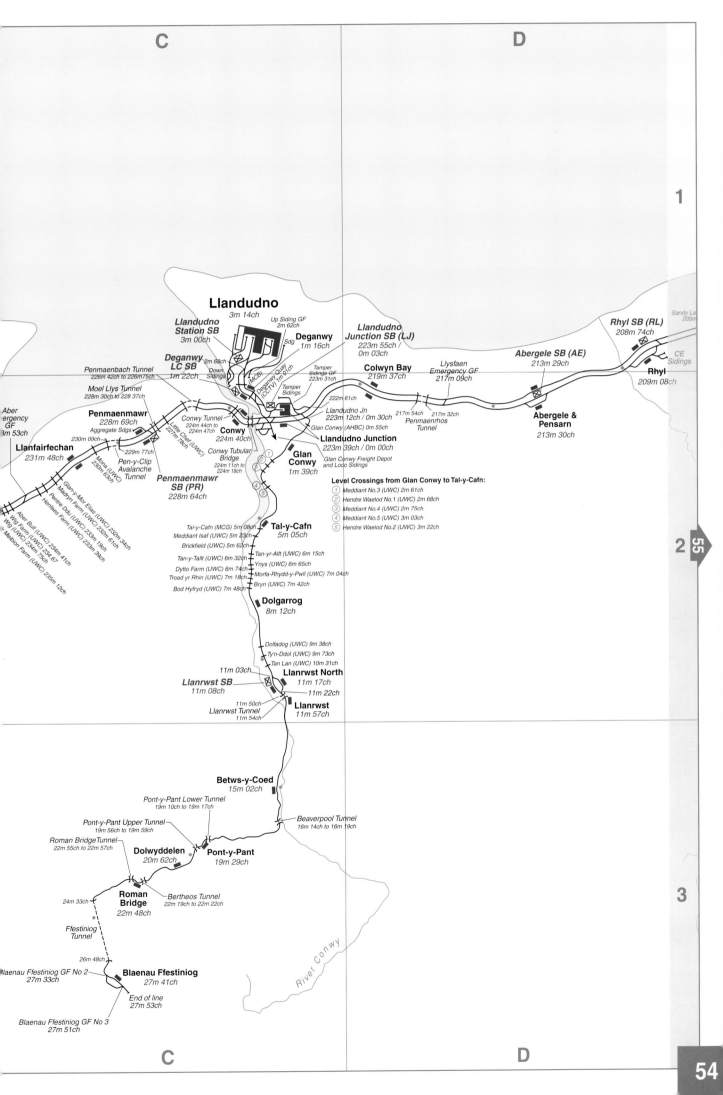

Llandudno
3m 14ch

Llandudno Station SB
3m 00ch

Up Siding GF
2m 62ch

Sdg

Deganwy
1m 16ch

Llandudno Junction SB (LJ)
223m 55ch / 0m 03ch

Rhyl SB (RL)
208m 74ch

Sandy La
205m

CE Sidings

Deganwy LC SB
1m 22ch

2m 68ch

Down Sidings

(MCB)

Deganwy Quay (CCTV) *1m 01ch*

Tamper Sidings GF
223m 31ch

Colwyn Bay
219m 37ch

Llysfaen Emergency GF
217m 09ch

Abergele SB (AE)
213m 29ch

Rhyl
209m 08ch

Penmaenbach Tunnel
226m 42ch to 226m 75ch

Tamper Sidings

Moel Llys Tunnel
228m 30ch to 228 37ch

Conwy Tunnel
224m 44ch to 224m 47ch

Conwy
224m 40ch

Llandudno Jn
223m 12ch / 0m 30ch

222m 61ch

Glan Conwy (AHBC) *0m 55ch*

217m 54ch *217m 32ch*

Penmaenrhos Tunnel

Abergele & Pensarn
213m 30ch

Penmaenmawr
228m 69ch

Little Chef (UWC)
227m 76ch

Llandudno Junction
223m 39ch / 0m 00ch

Aggregate Sdgs.

230m 09ch

Pen-y-Clip Avalanche Tunnel

Conwy Tubular Bridge
224m 11ch to 224m 18ch

Glan Conwy Freight Depot and Loco Sidings

Aber Emergency GF
3m 53ch

Llanfairfechan
231m 48ch

Mona (UWC)
230m 63ch

229m 77ch

Penmaenmawr SB (PR)
228m 64ch

Glan Conwy
1m 39ch

Level Crossings from Glan Conwy to Tal-y-Cafn:
① Meddiant No.3 (UWC) *2m 61ch*
② Hendre Waelod No.1 (UWC) *2m 68ch*
③ Meddiant No.4 (UWC) *2m 75ch*
④ Meddiant No.5 (UWC) *3m 03ch*
⑤ Hendre Waelod No.2 (UWC) *3m 22ch*

Glan-y-Mor Elias (UWC) *232m 09ch*
Madryn Farm (UWC) *232m 63ch*
Pentre Ddu (UWC) *233m 19ch*
Henflas Farm (UWC) *233m 39ch*
Aber Bull (UWC) *234m 41ch*
Wig Farm (UWC) *234m 67ch*
Wig (UWC) *234m 75ch*
Melibon Farm (UWC) *235m 12ch*

Tal-y-Cafn (MCG) *5m 08ch*
Meddiant Isaf (UWC) *5m 23ch*
Brickfield (UWC) *5m 62ch*
Tan-y-Tallt (UWC) *6m 32ch*
Dytto Farm (UWC) *6m 74ch*
Troad yr Rhin (UWC) *7m 18ch*
Bod Hyfryd (UWC) *7m 48ch*

Tal-y-Cafn
5m 05ch

Tan-yr-Allt (UWC) *6m 15ch*
Ynys (UWC) *6m 65ch*
Morfa-Rhydd-y-Pwll (UWC) *7m 04ch*
Bryn (UWC) *7m 42ch*

Dolgarrog
8m 12ch

Dolfadog (UWC) *9m 38ch*
Ty'n-Ddol (UWC) *9m 73ch*
Tan Lan (UWC) *10m 31ch*

11m 03ch

Llanrwst North
11m 17ch

Llanrwst SB
11m 08ch

11m 22ch

11m 50ch
Llanrwst Tunnel
11m 54ch

Llanrwst
11m 57ch

Betws-y-Coed
15m 02ch

Pont-y-Pant Lower Tunnel
19m 10ch to 19m 17ch

Beaverpool Tunnel
16m 14ch to 16m 19ch

Pont-y-Pant Upper Tunnel
19m 56ch to 19m 59ch

Roman Bridge Tunnel
22m 55ch to 22m 57ch

Dolwyddelen
20m 62ch

Pont-y-Pant
19m 29ch

Roman Bridge
22m 48ch

Bertheos Tunnel
22m 19ch to 22m 22ch

24m 33ch

Ffestiniog Tunnel

26m 48ch

Blaenau Ffestiniog GF No 2
27m 33ch

Blaenau Ffestiniog
27m 41ch

End of line
27m 53ch

Blaenau Ffestiniog GF No 3
27m 51ch

River Conwy

55

2

54

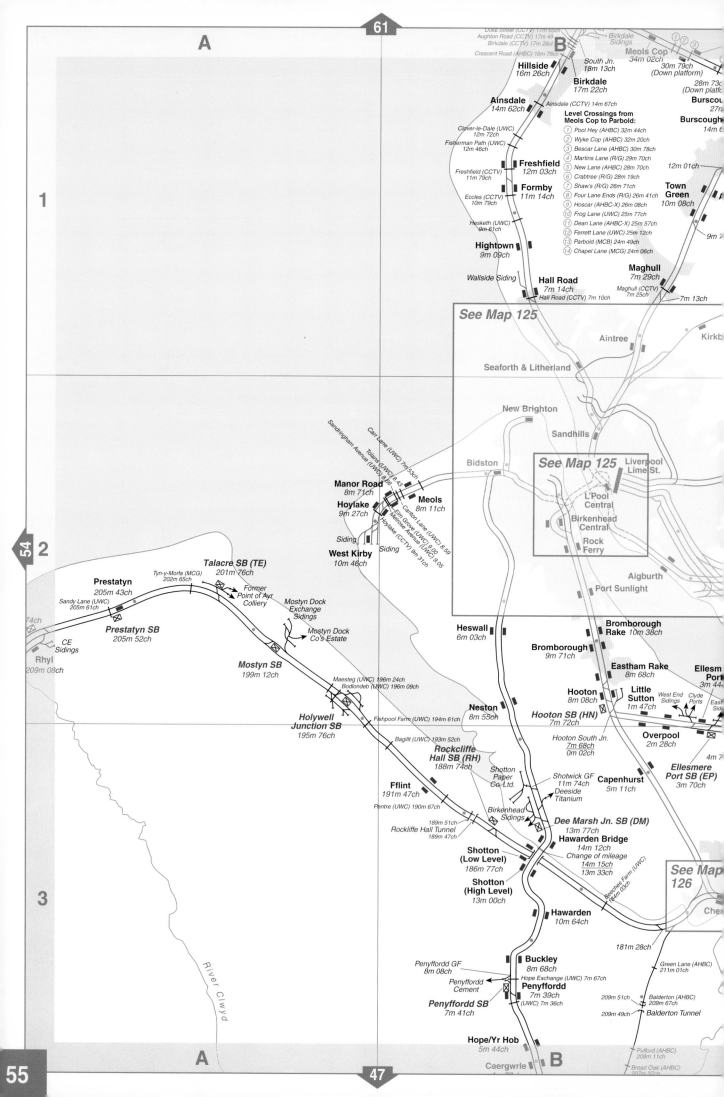

Duke Street (CCTV) 17m 65ch
Aughton Road (CCTV) 17m 49
Birkdale (CCTV) 17m 26ch
Crescent Road (AHBC) 16m 76ch

Birkdale Sidings

Meols Cop
34m 02ch

South Jn.
18m 13ch

30m 79ch
(Down platform)

Hillside
16m 26ch

Birkdale
17m 22ch

28m 73c
(Down platfo

Ainsdale
14m 62ch

Ainsdale (CCTV) 14m 67ch

Burscou
27m

**Level Crossings from:
Meols Cop to Parbold:**

Burscough
14m 6

Clover-le-Dale (UWC)
12m 72ch

① Pool Hey (AHBC) 32m 44ch
② Wyke Cop (AHBC) 32m 20ch
③ Bescar Lane (AHBC) 30m 78ch
④ Martins Lane (R/G) 29m 70ch
⑤ New Lane (AHBC) 28m 70ch
⑥ Crabtree (R/G) 28m 19ch
⑦ Shaw's (R/G) 26m 71ch
⑧ Four Lane Ends (R/G) 26m 41ch
⑨ Hoscar (AHBC-X) 26m 08ch
⑩ Frog Lane (UWC) 25m 77ch
⑪ Dean Lane (AHBC-X) 25m 57ch
⑫ Ferrett Lane (UWC) 25m 12ch
⑬ Parbold (MCB) 24m 49ch
⑭ Chapel Lane (MCG) 24m 06ch

Fisherman Path (UWC)
12m 46ch

Freshfield
12m 03ch

Freshfield (CCTV)
11m 79ch

12m 01ch

Formby
11m 14ch

**Town
Green**
10m 08ch

Eccles (CCTV)
10m 79ch

Hesketh (UWC)
9m 61ch

9m 7

Hightown
9m 09ch

Maghull
7m 29ch

Wallside Siding

Hall Road
7m 14ch

Maghull (CCTV)
7m 25ch

7m 13ch

Hall Road (CCTV) 7m 10ch

See Map 125

Aintree

Kirkb

Seaforth & Litherland

New Brighton

Sandhills

See Map 125

Liverpool
Lime St.

Bidston

Carr Lane (UWC) 7m 50ch
Tolans (UWC) 8.43
Sandringham Avenue (UWC) 8.66

L'Pool
Central

Manor Road
8m 71ch

Carlton Lane (UWC) 8.59
Elm Grove (UWC) 9.00
Melrose Avenue (UWC) 9.31
Hoylake (CCTV) 9m 05ch

Meols
8m 11ch

Birkenhead
Central

Hoylake
9m 27ch

Rock
Ferry

Siding

West Kirby
10m 46ch

Siding

Aigburth

Port Sunlight

Heswall
6m 03ch

**Bromborough
Rake** 10m 38ch

Talacre SB (TE)
201m 76ch

Bromborough
9m 71ch

Prestatyn
205m 43ch

Tyn-y-Morfa (MCG)
202m 65ch

Former
Point of Ayr
Colliery

Eastham Rake
8m 68ch

**Ellesm
Port**
3m 44

Sandy Lane (UWC)
205m 61ch

Mostyn Dock
Exchange
Sidings

Prestatyn SB
205m 52ch

Hooton
8m 08ch

**Little
Sutton**
1m 47ch

West End
Sidings

Clyde
Ports

74ch

Mostyn Dock
Co's Estate

Hooton SB (HN)
7m 72ch

Eas

CE
Sidings

Overpool
2m 28ch

Rhyl
209m 08ch

Mostyn SB
199m 12ch

Maesteg (UWC) 196m 24ch
Bodlondeb (UWC) 196m 09ch

Hooton South Jn.
7m 68ch
0m 02ch

4m 7

**Ellesmere
Port SB (EP)**
3m 70ch

Fishpool Farm (UWC) 194m 61ch

Neston
8m 55ch

**Holywell
Junction SB**
195m 76ch

Bagillt (UWC) 193m 52ch

**Rockcliffe
Hall SB (RH)**
188m 74ch

Shotton
Paper
Co. Ltd.

Shotwick GF
11m 74ch

Capenhurst
5m 11ch

Deeside
Titanium

Fflint
191m 47ch

Pentre (UWC) 190m 67ch

Birkenhead
Sidings

Dee Marsh Jn. SB (DM)
13m 77ch

189m 51ch
189m 47ch

Rockliffe Hall Tunnel

Hawarden Bridge
14m 12ch
Change of mileage
14m 15ch
13m 33ch

**See Map
126**

**Shotton
(Low Level)**
186m 77ch

Beeches Farm (UWC)
184m 03ch

Ch

**Shotton
(High Level)**
13m 00ch

181m 28ch

Hawarden
10m 64ch

Penyffordd GF
8m 08ch

Buckley
8m 68ch

Green Lane (AHBC)
211m 01ch

Hope Exchange (UWC) 7m 67ch

Penyffordd
7m 39ch

Penyffordd
Cement

209m 51ch

Balderton (AHBC)
209m 67ch

Penyffordd SB
7m 41ch

(UWC) 7m 36ch

209m 49ch

Balderton Tunnel

Hope/Yr Hob
5m 44ch

Caergwrle

Pulford (AHBC)
208m 11ch

Broad Oak (AHBC)
207m 37ch

River Clwyd

54

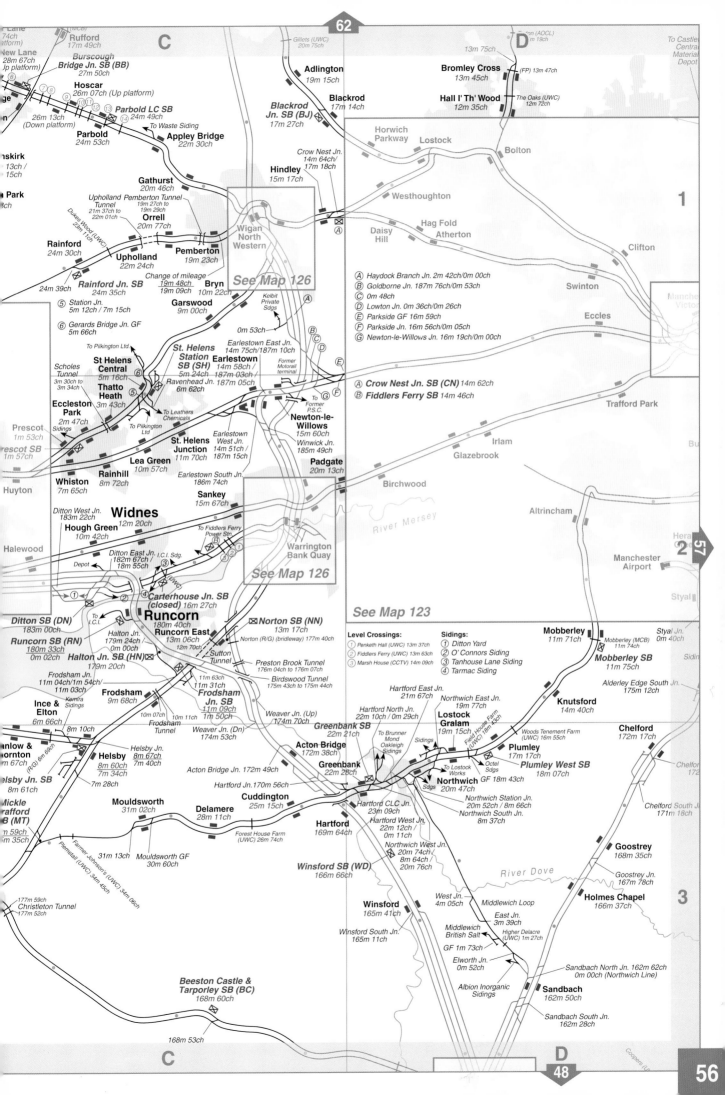

Rufford
17m 49ch

New Lane
28m 67ch
(Up platform)

Burscough
Bridge Jn. SB (BB)
27m 50ch

Hoscar
26m 07ch (Up platform)

Parbold LC SB
24m 49ch

Parbold
24m 53ch

Appley Bridge
22m 30ch

Gathurst
20m 46ch

Upholland Tunnel
21m 37ch to
22m 01ch

Pemberton Tunnel
19m 27ch to
19m 29ch

Orrell
20m 77ch

Rainford
24m 30ch

Upholland
22m 24ch

Pemberton
19m 23ch

Dukes Wood (UWC)
23m 11ch

Rainford Jn. SB
24m 35ch

Change of mileage
19m 48ch
19m 09ch

Bryn
19m 22ch

Garswood
9m 00ch

⑤ Station Jn.
5m 12ch / 7m 15ch

⑥ Gerards Bridge Jn. GF
5m 66ch

To Pilkington Ltd.

Scholes Tunnel
3m 30ch to
3m 34ch

St. Helens
Station
SB (SH)
5m 24ch

St Helens
Central
5m 16ch

Thatto
Heath
3m 43ch

Ravenhead Jn.
6m 62ch

Earlestown
14m 58ch /
187m 03ch /
187m 05ch

Eccleston
Park
2m 47ch

Prescot
1m 53ch

Prescot SB
1m 57ch

St. Helens
Junction
11m 70ch

Earlestown
West Jn.
14m 51ch /
187m 15ch

Lea Green
10m 57ch

Rainhill
8m 72ch

Whiston
7m 65ch

Earlestown South Jn.
186m 74ch

Sankey
15m 67ch

Huyton

Widnes
12m 20ch

Hough Green
10m 42ch

Ditton West Jn.
183m 22ch

To Fiddlers Ferry
Power Stn.

Warrington
Bank Quay

Halewood

Ditton East Jn.
182m 67ch /
18m 55ch

I.C.I. Sdg.

Depot

Carterhouse Jn. SB
(closed) 16m 27ch

Ditton SB (DN)
183m 00ch

To
I.C.I.

Runcorn

Norton SB (NN)
13m 17ch

Runcorn SB (RN)
180m 33ch
0m 02ch

Runcorn East
13m 06ch
12m 70ch

Norton (R/G) (bridleway) 177m 40ch

Halton Jn. SB (HN)
179m 20ch

Halton Jn.
179m 24ch /
0m 00ch

Sutton
Tunnel

Preston Brook Tunnel
176m 04ch to 176m 07ch

Birdswood Tunnel
175m 43ch to 175m 44ch

Frodsham
11m 04ch/1m 54ch/
11m 03ch

Ince &
Elton
6m 66ch

Kemira
Sidings

Frodsham
9m 68ch

Frodsham
Jn. SB
11m 09ch
11m 50ch

11m 63ch
11m 31ch

Weaver Jn. (Up)
174m 70ch

Weaver Jn. (Dn)
174m 53ch

Greenbank SB
22m 21ch

Acton Bridge
172m 38ch

Greenbank
22m 28ch

10m 07ch
10m 11ch

Frodsham
Tunnel

Acton Bridge Jn. 172m 49ch

Hartford Jn. 170m 56ch

Helsby
8m 67ch
8m 60ch
7m 40ch
7m 34ch
7m 28ch

Hanlow &
Thornton
6m 67ch

Helsby Jn. SB
8m 61ch

Mickle
Trafford
SB (MT)
8m 59ch
8m 35ch

Mouldsworth
31m 02ch

Delamere
28m 11ch

Cuddington
25m 15ch

Hartford
169m 64ch

Forest House Farm
(UWC) 26m 74ch

31m 13ch
Mouldsworth GF
30m 60ch

Farmer Johnson's (UWC) 34m 06ch

Plemstall (UWC) 34m 45ch

177m 59ch
Christleton Tunnel
177m 52ch

Beeston Castle &
Tarporley SB (BC)
168m 60ch

168m 53ch

Adlington
19m 15ch

Blackrod
17m 14ch

Blackrod
Jn. SB (BJ)
17m 27ch

Hindley
15m 17ch

Crow Nest Jn.
14m 64ch/
17m 18ch

Gillets (UWC)
20m 75ch

Bromley Cross
(FP) 13m 47ch
13m 45ch

13m 75ch

Hall I' Th' Wood
12m 35ch

The Oaks (UWC)
12m 72ch

Horwich
Parkway

Lostock

Bolton

Westhoughton

Daisy
Hill

Hag Fold
Atherton

Wigan
North
Western

See Map 126

Kelbit
Private
Sdgs

Earlestown East Jn.
14m 75ch/187m 10ch

Former
Motorail
terminal

Winwick Jn.
185m 49ch

To
Former
P.S.C.

Newton-le-
Willows
15m 60ch

Padgate
20m 13ch

Birchwood

River Mersey

See Map 126

See Map 123

Mobberley
11m 71ch

Clifton

Swinton

Eccles

Trafford Park

Irlam

Glazebrook

Altrincham

Manchester
Airport

Styal

Manchester
Victoria

Hera

Styal Jn.
0m 40ch

Mobberley (MCB)
11m 74ch

Mobberley SB
11m 75ch

Alderley Edge South Jn.
175m 12ch

Knutsford
14m 40ch

Chelford
172m 17ch

(A) Haydock Branch Jn. 2m 42ch/0m 00ch
(B) Goldborne Jn. 187m 76ch/0m 53ch
(C) 0m 48ch
(D) Lowton Jn. 0m 36ch/0m 26ch
(E) Parkside GF 16m 59ch
(F) Parkside Jn. 16m 56ch/0m 05ch
(G) Newton-le-Willows Jn. 16m 19ch/0m 00ch

(A) Crow Nest Jn. SB (CN) 14m 62ch
(B) Fiddlers Ferry SB 14m 46ch

Hartford East Jn.
21m 67ch

Northwich East Jn.
19m 77ch

Hartford North Jn.
22m 10ch / 0m 29ch

Lostock
Gralam
19m 15ch

Field House Farm
(UWC) 18m 43ch

Plumley
17m 17ch

Plumley West SB
18m 07ch

Woods Tenement Farm
(UWC) 16m 55ch

Octel
Sdgs

To Brunner
Mond
Oakleigh
Sidings

Sidings

To Lostock
Works

Northwich
20m 47ch

GF 18m 43ch

Sdgs

Northwich Station Jn.
20m 52ch / 8m 66ch

Northwich South Jn.
8m 37ch

Hartford CLC Jn.
23m 09ch

Hartford West Jn.
22m 12ch /
0m 11ch

Northwich West Jn.
20m 74ch /
8m 64ch /
20m 76ch

Winsford SB (WD)
166m 66ch

West Jn.
4m 05ch

Middlewich Loop

East Jn.
3m 39ch

Winsford
165m 41ch

Winsford South Jn.
165m 11ch

Middlewich
British Salt

GF 1m 73ch

Higher Delacre
(UWC) 1m 27ch

Elworth Jn.
0m 52ch

Albion Inorganic
Sidings

Chelford South Jn.
171m 18ch

Chelford
172m

Goostrey
168m 35ch

Goostrey Jn.
167m 78ch

Holmes Chapel
166m 37ch

River Dove

Sandbach North Jn. 162m 62ch
0m 00ch (Northwich Line)

Sandbach
162m 50ch

Sandbach South Jn.
162m 28ch

Level Crossings:
① Penketh Hall (UWC) 13m 37ch
② Fiddlers Ferry (UWC) 13m 63ch
③ Marsh House (CCTV) 14m 09ch

Sidings:
① Ditton Yard
② O'Connors Siding
③ Tanhouse Lane Siding
④ Tarmac Siding

1

57

2

3

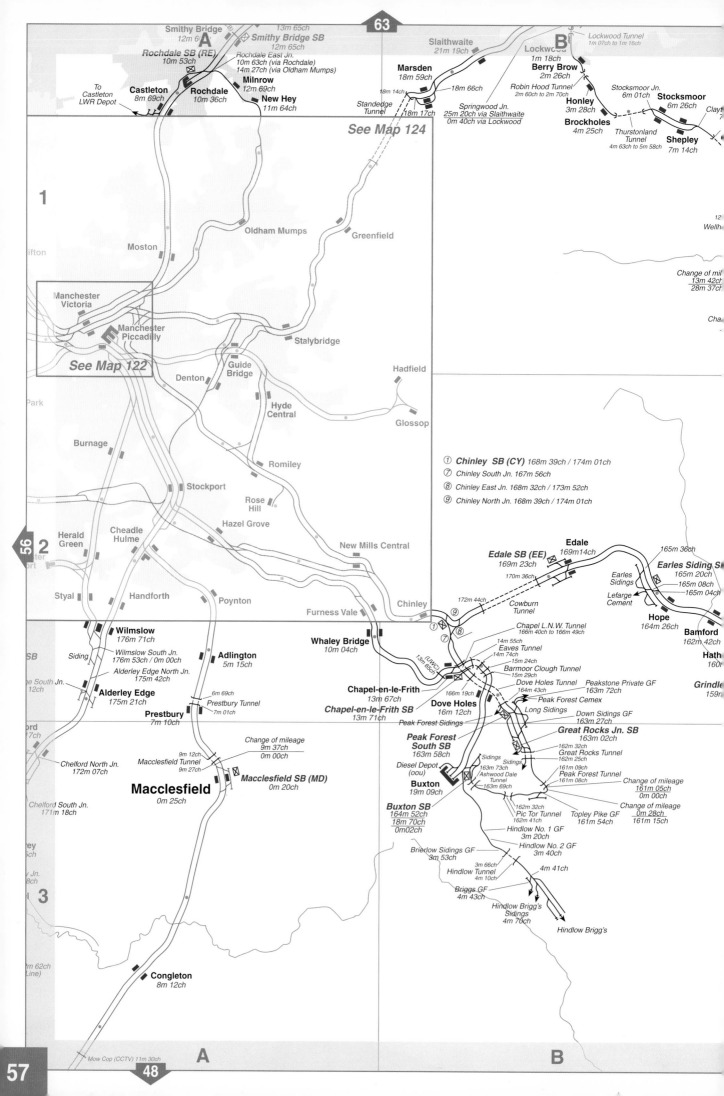

Smithy Bridge
12m 65ch
A
Smithy Bridge SB
12m 65ch
Rochdale SB (RE)
10m 53ch
Rochdale East Jn.
10m 63ch (via Rochdale)
14m 27ch (via Oldham Mumps)
Milnrow
12m 69ch
Castleton
8m 69ch
To Castleton
LWR Depot
Rochdale
10m 36ch
New Hey
11m 64ch

Slaithwaite
21m 19ch
Lockwood Tunnel
1m 07ch to 1m 16ch
B
Lockwood
1m 18ch
Marsden
18m 59ch
Berry Brow
2m 26ch
Robin Hood Tunnel
2m 60ch to 2m 70ch
Stocksmoor Jn.
6m 01ch
Stocksmoor
6m 26ch
18m 14ch
18m 66ch
Standedge Tunnel
18m 17ch
Springwood Jn.
25m 20ch via Slaithwaite
0m 40ch via Lockwood
Honley
3m 28ch
Brockholes
4m 25ch
Thurstonland Tunnel
4m 63ch to 5m 58ch
Shepley
7m 14ch
Clay
See Map 124

1

12
Wellh

Oldham Mumps
Greenfield
Moston

Change of mil
13m 42ch
28m 37ch

Cha

Manchester Victoria
Manchester Piccadilly
See Map 122
Denton
Guide Bridge
Stalybridge
Hadfield
Hyde Central
Glossop

Burnage
Romiley

Stockport
Rose Hill

① Chinley SB (CY) 168m 39ch / 174m 01ch
⑦ Chinley South Jn. 167m 56ch
⑧ Chinley East Jn. 168m 32ch / 173m 52ch
⑨ Chinley North Jn. 168m 39ch / 174m 01ch

56
2
Herald Green
Cheadle Hulme
Hazel Grove
New Mills Central
Edale SB (EE)
169m 23ch
Edale
169m 14ch
165m 36ch
Earles Siding S
165m 20ch
Earles Sidings
165m 08ch
165m 04ch
Lefarge Cement
170m 36ch
172m 44ch
Cowburn Tunnel
Hope
164m 26ch
Chinley
Bamford
162m 42ch
Styal
Handforth
Poynton
Furness Vale
Whaley Bridge
10m 04ch
⑨
Chapel L.N.W. Tunnel
166m 40ch to 166m 49ch
Hath
160
SB
Siding
Wilmslow
176m 71ch
Wilmslow South Jn.
176m 53ch / 0m 00ch
Alderley Edge North Jn.
175m 42ch
Adlington
5m 15ch
①
⑦
(UWC)
13m 65ch
⑧
14m 55ch
Eaves Tunnel
14m 74ch
15m 24ch
Barmoor Clough Tunnel
15m 29ch
Dove Holes Tunnel
164m 43ch
Peakstone Private GF
163m 72ch
Peak Forest Cemex
Grindle
159
Chapel-en-le-Frith
13m 67ch
Dove Holes
16m 12ch
Long Sidings
Down Sidings GF
163m 27ch
Alderley Edge
175m 21ch
6m 69ch
Prestbury Tunnel
7m 01ch
Chapel-en-le-Frith SB
13m 71ch
166m 19ch
Peak Forest Sidings
Great Rocks Jn. SB
163m 02ch
Prestbury
7m 10ch
e South Jn.
12ch
Chelford North Jn.
172m 07ch
Change of mileage
9m 37ch
0m 00ch
9m 12ch
Macclesfield Tunnel
9m 27ch
Macclesfield SB (MD)
0m 20ch
Peak Forest South SB
163m 58ch
162m 32ch
Great Rocks Tunnel
162m 25ch
Sidings
Sidings
161m 09ch
Peak Forest Tunnel
161m 08ch
ord
17ch
Chelford South Jn.
171m 18ch
Macclesfield
0m 25ch
Diesel Depot
(oou)
Buxton
19m 09ch
163m 73ch
Ashwood Dale Tunnel
163m 69ch
Change of mileage
161m 05ch
0m 00ch
ey Jn.
5ch
Buxton SB
164m 52ch
18m 70ch
0m 02ch
162m 32ch
Pic Tor Tunnel
162m 41ch
Topley Pike GF
161m 54ch
Change of mileage
0m 28ch
161m 15ch
Hindlow No. 1 GF
3m 20ch
Hindlow No. 2 GF
3m 40ch
Brierlow Sidings GF
3m 53ch
3m 66ch
Hindlow Tunnel
4m 10ch
4m 41ch
Briggs GF
4m 43ch
Hindlow Brigg's Sidings
4m 70ch
Hindlow Brigg's
Congleton
8m 12ch
m 62ch
Line)
Mow Cop (CCTV) 11m 30ch

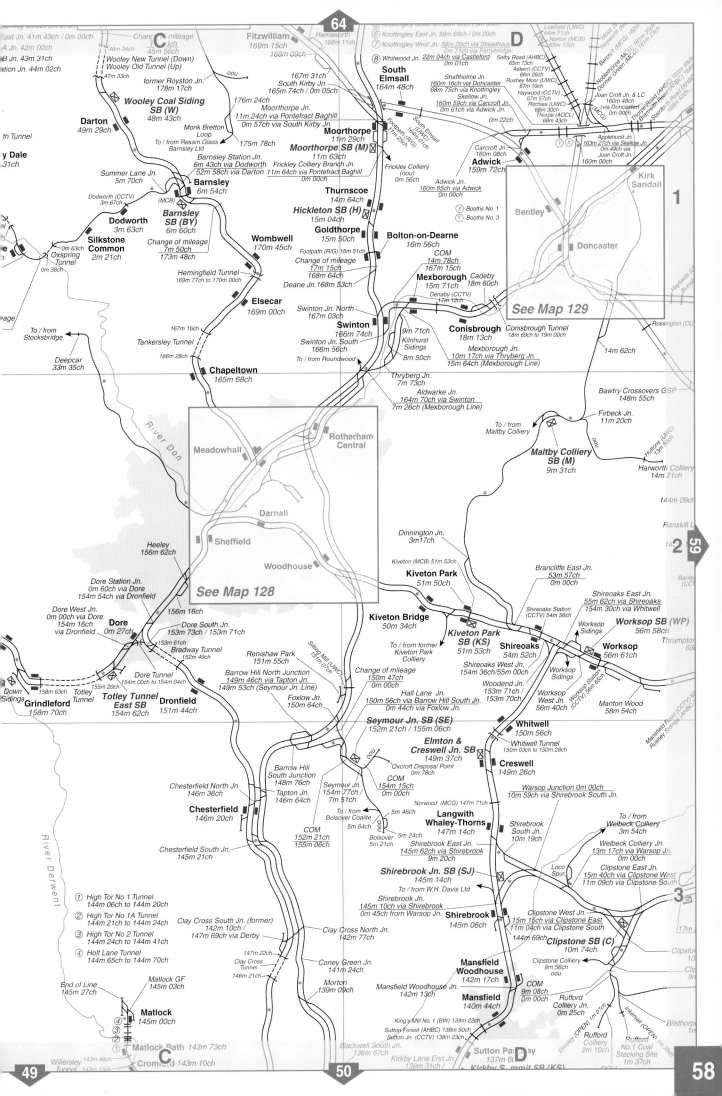

C

D

Barnley Street on or on
East Jn. 41m 43ch / 0m 00ch
A Jn. 42m 00ch
B Jn. 43m 31ch
ation Jn. 44m 02ch

Change of mileage
46m 34ch / 45m 56ch

Wooley New Tunnel (Down) Wooley Old Tunnel (Up)
47m 33ch

former Royston Jn.
178m 17ch

Wooley Coal Siding SB (W)
48m 43ch

Monk Bretton Loop
To / from Rexam Glass Barnsley Ltd

176m 24ch
Moorthorpe Jn.
11m 24ch via Pontefract Baghill
0m 57ch via South Kirby Jn
175m 78ch

Darton
49m 29ch

th Tunnel
31ch

Summer Lane Jn.
5m 70ch

Barnsley
6m 54ch

Barnsley Station Jn.
6m 43ch via Dodworth
52m 19ch via Darton

Barnsley SB (BY)
6m 60ch

(MCB)

Dodworth (CCTV)
3m 67ch

Dodworth
3m 63ch

Silkstone Common
2m 21ch

0m 63ch
Oxspring Tunnel
0m 38ch

y Dale

Change of mileage
7m 50ch / 173m 48ch

Wombwell
170m 45ch

Hemingfield Tunnel
169m 77ch to 170m 00ch

Elsecar
169m 00ch

167m 16ch

Tankersley Tunnel
166m 28ch

To / from Stocksbridge

Deepcar
33m 35ch

Chapeltown
165m 68ch

Fitzwilliam

Hemsworth
168m 11ch

South Kirby Jn.
165m 74ch / 0m 05ch

167m 31ch
168m 09ch

South Elmsall
164m 48ch

oou

Moorthorpe
11m 29ch

Moorthorpe SB (M)
11m 63ch

Frickley Colliery Branch Jn.
11m 64ch via Pontefract Baghill
0m 00ch

Footpath (R/G)
16m 01ch
11m 25ch

Footpath (R/G)

Frickley Colliery
(oou)
0m 56ch

Thurnscoe
14m 64ch

Hickleton SB (H)
15m 04ch

Goldthorpe
15m 50ch

Bolton-on-Dearne
16m 56ch

Footpath (R/G) 16m 51ch

Change of mileage
17m 15ch / 168m 64ch

Deane Jn. 168m 53ch

COM
14m 78ch
167m 15ch

Mexborough
15m 71ch

Cadeby
18m 60ch

Denaby (CCTV)
17m 12ch

Swinton Jn. North
167m 03ch

Swinton
166m 74ch

Swinton Jn. South
166m 56ch

To / from Roundwood

9m 71ch
Kilnhurst Sidings
8m 50ch

Thryberg Jn.
7m 73ch

Aldwarke Jn.
164m 70ch via Swinton
7m 26ch (Mexborough Line)

Mexborough Jn.
10m 17ch via Thryberg Jn.
15m 64ch (Mexborough Line)

Conisbrough
18m 13ch

Conisbrough Tunnel
18m 69ch to 19m 00ch

See Map 129

8

South Elmsall

Shaftholme Jn.
160m 16ch via Doncaster
68m 75ch via Knottingley
160m 59ch via Carcroft Jn.
0m 61ch via Adwick Jn.

Selby Road (AHBC)
65m 73ch
Askern (CCTV)
67m 10ch
Haywood (CCTV)
67m 57ch
Ritchies (UWC)
68m 30ch
Thorpe (AOCL)
68m 43ch

Noblemorne (MCG) 161m 35ch
Dormer Green (MCG) 161m 23ch

Barcroft (MCG) 164m 03ch

Joan Croft Jn. & LC
160m 48ch
(via Doncaster)

Thorpe Road (AHBC) 164m 60ch
Bramwith Reed (AHBC) 162m 53ch
Stainforth Road (AHBC) 165m 54ch

Lowfield (UWC)
Norton (MCB) 165m 12ch

Moss (Mxx)
Heyworth (Mxx)

22m 04ch via Castleford
0m 01ch

Whitwood Jn.

Knottingley South Jn. 56m 66ch / 0m 06ch
Knottingley East Jn. 58m 69ch / 0m 20ch
Knottingley West Jn. 58m 20ch via Streethous
2m 71ch via Ferrybridge

Adwick
159m 72ch

Carcroft Jn.
160m 08ch

Adwick Jn.
160m 65ch via Adwick
0m 00ch

Applehurst Jn.
163m 27ch via Skellow Jn.
0m 49ch via Joan Croft Jn.
160m 00ch

X Booths No. 1
Y Booths No. 3

0m 22ch

Kirk Sandall

Bentley

Doncaster

1

Rossington (CC

14m 62ch

Bawtry Crossovers GSP
148m 55ch

Firbeck Jn.
11m 20ch

To / from Maltby Colliery

Maltby Colliery SB (M)
9m 31ch

Huttons (UWC)
13m 50ch

Harworth Colliery
14m 21ch

144m 09ch

Ranskill L

14

2

59

Dinnington Jn.
3m 17ch

Kiveton (MCB) 51m 53ch

Kiveton Park
51m 50ch

Brancliffe East Jn.
53m 57ch
0m 00ch

Shireoaks East Jn.
55m 62ch via Shireoaks
154m 30ch via Whitwell

Shireoaks Station (CCTV) 54m 56ch

Worksop Sidings

Worksop SB (WP)
56m 58ch

Thrupptor
63

Kiveton Bridge
50m 34ch

Kiveton Park SB (KS)
51m 53ch

To / from former Kiveton Park Colliery

Change of mileage
150m 47ch / 0m 00ch

Hall Lane Jn.
150m 56ch via Barrow Hill South Jn.
0m 44ch via Foxlow Jn.

Shireoaks
54m 52ch

Shireoaks West Jn.
154m 36ch / 55m 00ch

Woodend Jn.
153m 71ch / 153m 70ch

Worksop West Jn.
56m 40ch

Worksop Sidings

Worksop
56m 61ch

Worksop Station (CCTV) 56m 65ch

Manton Wood
58m 54ch

Mansfield Road (CCTV) 6
Rushey Sidings (AHBC)

River Don

Meadowhall

Rotherham Central

Darnall

Sheffield

Woodhouse

See Map 128

Heeley
156m 62ch

Dore Station Jn.
0m 60ch via Dore
154m 54ch via Dronfield

156m 16ch

Dore West Jn.
0m 00ch via Dore
154m 16ch via Dronfield

Dore
0m 27ch

Dore South Jn.
153m 73ch / 153m 71ch

Bradway Tunnel
152m 49ch

153m 61ch

Dore Tunnel
154m 00ch to 154m 04ch

Renishaw Park
151m 55ch

Sitting Mill (UWC) 151m 07ch

Barrow Hill North Junction
149m 46ch via Tapton Jn.
149m 53ch (Seymour Jn. Line)

Change of mileage
150m 47ch / 0m 00ch

Foxlow Jn.
150m 64ch

Seymour Jn. SB (SE)
152m 21ch / 155m 06ch

oou

Oxcroft Disposal Point
0m 78ch

COM
154m 15ch
0m 00ch

Elmton & Creswell Jn. SB
149m 37ch

Creswell
149m 26ch

Whitwell
150m 56ch

Whitwell Tunnel
150m 03ch to 150m 28ch

Down Sidings

158m 63ch

Totley Tunnel

Totley Tunnel East SB
155m 20ch

Grindleford
158m 70ch

Dronfield
151m 44ch

Chesterfield North Jn.
146m 36ch

Tapton Jn.
146m 64ch

Seymour Jn.
154m 77ch / 7m 51ch

Barrow Hill South Junction
148m 76ch

To / from Bolsover Coalite

5m 46ch

5m 64ch

Bolsover 5m 24ch

Chesterfield
146m 20ch

COM
152m 21ch / 155m 06ch

Chesterfield South Jn.
145m 21ch

Norwood (MCG) 147m 71ch

Langwith Whaley-Thorns
147m 14ch

Shirebrook South Jn.
10m 19ch

Shirebrook East Jn.
145m 62ch via Shirebrook
9m 20ch

Shirebrook Jn. SB (SJ)
145m 14ch

To / from W.H. Davis Ltd

Shirebrook Jn.
145m 10ch via Shirebrook
0m 45ch from Warsop Jn.

Shirebrook
145m 06ch

Warsop Junction 0m 00ch
10m 59ch via Shirebrook South Jn.

To / from Welbeck Colliery
3m 54ch

Welbeck Colliery Jn.
13m 17ch via Warsop Jn.
0m 00ch

Clipstone East Jn.
15m 40ch via Clipstone West
11m 09ch via Clipstone South

Loco Spur

Clipstone West Jn.
15m 15ch via Clipstone East
11m 04ch via Clipstone South
144m 69ch

Clipstone SB (C)
10m 74ch

Clipstone Colliery
9m 56ch
oou

Clipstone
10
9

3

17m

River Derwent

① High Tor No 1 Tunnel
144m 06ch to 144m 20ch
② High Tor No 1A Tunnel
144m 21ch to 144m 24ch
③ High Tor No 2 Tunnel
144m 24ch to 144m 41ch
④ Holt Lane Tunnel
144m 65ch to 144m 70ch

Clay Cross South Jn. (former)
142m 10ch / 147m 69ch via Derby

Clay Cross North Jn.
142m 77ch

147m 22ch

Clay Cross Tunnel
146m 21ch

Coney Green Jn.
144m 24ch

Morton
139m 09ch

Mansfield Woodhouse Jn.
142m 13ch

Mansfield Woodhouse
142m 17ch

COM
9m 08ch
0m 00ch

Rufford Colliery Jn.
0m 25ch

Inkersall (OPEN) 1m 07ch

Bilsthorpe 1m

End of Line
145m 27ch

Matlock GF
145m 03ch

Matlock
145m 00ch

Mansfield
140m 44ch

King's Mill No. 1 (BW) 139m 22ch
Sutton Forest (AHBC) 138m 50ch
Sutton Jn. (CCTV) 138m 23ch

Sutton Parkway
137m 60ch

Rufford Colliery
2m 10ch

Rufford No.1 Coal Stacking Site
1m 37ch

Emsley (OPEN) 1m 00ch
Rufford (OPEN) 1m 39ch
1m

④③②①

Matlock Bath 143m 73ch

C

Willersley Tunnel 143m 13ch

Cromford 143m 10ch

Blackwell South Jn.
136m 67ch

Kirkby Lane End Jn.
138m 31ch

Kirkby Summit SB (KS)

D

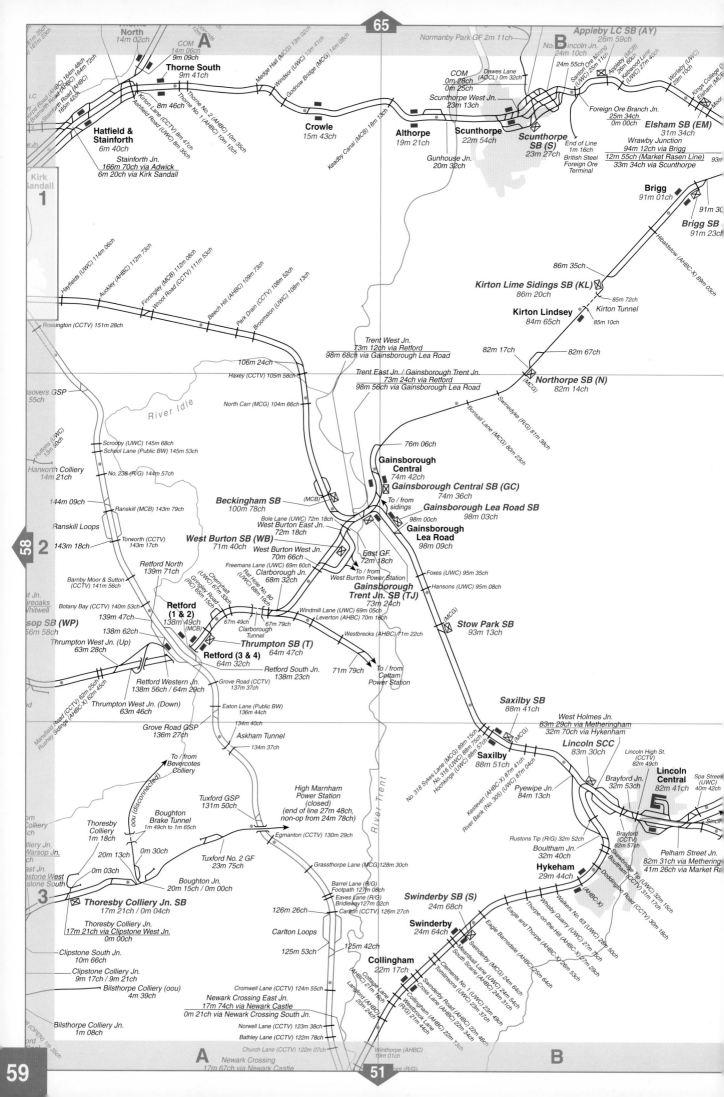

Thorne North 14m 02ch

COM A 14m 06ch
9m 09ch

Normanby Park GF 2m 11ch

Appleby LC SB (AY) 26m 59ch B

No. Lincoln LC 24m 10ch

Thorne South 9m 41ch

Medge Hall (MCG) 13m 41ch

Windsor (UWC) 13m 49ch
Godnow Bridge (MCG) 14m 08ch

24m 55ch Santon Ore Mining (UWC) 25m 11ch

Appleby (MCB) 26m 00ch

Kewood Lane (UWC) 27m 40ch

Worlaby (UWC) 29m 10ch

Kings College Elsham (UWC) 29m 16ch

Thorne No. 2 (AHBC) 10m 03ch
8m 46ch Thorne No. 1 (AHBC) 10m 12ch

COM 0m 28ch
0m 25ch

Dawes Lane (AOCL) 0m 32ch

Scunthorpe West Jn. 23m 13ch

Foreign Ore Branch Jn. 25m 34ch 0m 00ch

Elsham SB (EM) 31m 34ch

Kirton Road (AHBC) 164m 49ch
Kirton Road (AHBC) 164m 72ch

Brammith Stainforth Road (AHBC) 165m 42ch

Kirton Lane (CCTV) 8m 47ch
Astfield Road (UWC) 8m 35ch

Crowle 15m 43ch

Althorpe 19m 21ch

Scunthorpe 22m 54ch

Scunthorpe SB (S) 23m 27ch

End of Line 1m 16ch British Steel Foreign Ore Terminal

Wrawby Junction 94m 12ch via Brigg
12m 55ch (Market Rasen Line)
33m 34ch via Scunthorpe

Hatfield & Stainforth 6m 40ch

Stainforth Jn. 166m 70ch via Adwick 6m 20ch via Kirk Sandall

Gunhouse Jn. 20m 32ch

Keadby Canal (MCB) 18m 13ch

Brigg 91m 01ch

Brigg SB 91m 23ch

Kirk Sandall 1

Hibaldstow (AHBC-X) 89m 03ch

86m 35ch

Kirton Lime Sidings SB (KL) 86m 20ch

85m 72ch

Kirton Tunnel

Kirton Lindsey 84m 65ch

85m 10ch

Hayfields (UWC) 114m 06ch
Auckley (AHBC) 112m 73ch
Finningley (MCB) 112m 08ch
Wroot Road (CCTV) 111m 53ch
Beech Hill (AHBC) 109m 73ch
Park Drain (CCTV) 108m 52ch
Broomston (UWC) 108m 13ch

82m 17ch
82m 67ch

Northorpe SB (N) 82m 14ch

Rossington (CCTV) 151m 28ch

106m 24ch
Haxey (CCTV) 105m 58ch

Trent West Jn. 73m 12ch via Retford 98m 68ch via Gainsborough Lea Road

Trent East Jn. / Gainsborough Trent Jn. 73m 24ch via Retford 98m 56ch via Gainsborough Lea Road

Swinedyke (R/G) 81m 38ch

Bonsall Lane (MCG) 80m 23ch

River Idle

North Carr (MCG) 104m 66ch

76m 06ch

Gainsborough Central 74m 42ch

Gainsborough Central SB (GC) 74m 36ch

Scrooby (UWC) 145m 68ch
School Lane (Public BW) 145m 53ch

No. 238 (R/G) 144m 57ch

144m 09ch

Harworth Colliery 14m 21ch

Ranskill (MCB) 143m 79ch

Beckingham SB 100m 78ch

(MCB)

Bole Lane (UWC) 72m 18ch
West Burton East Jn. 72m 18ch

To / from sidings

98m 00ch

Gainsborough Lea Road SB 98m 03ch

Gainsborough Lea Road 98m 09ch

Ranskill Loops 143m 18ch

Torworth (CCTV) 143m 17ch

West Burton SB (WB) 71m 40ch

West Burton West Jn. 70m 66ch

East GF.

To / from West Burton Power Station

Retford North 139m 71ch

Freemans Lane (UWC) 69m 60ch

Barnby Moor & Sutton (CCTV) 141m 56ch

Cheryhalt (UWC) 67m 33ch
Gringley Road (HC) 65m 15ch

Pratt Hole No. 80 (UWC) 68m 19ch

Clarborough Jn. 68m 32ch

Gainsborough Trent Jn. SB (TJ) 73m 24ch

Foxes (UWC) 95m 35ch
Hansons (UWC) 95m 08ch

Botany Bay (CCTV) 140m 53ch

139m 47ch

Retford (1 & 2) 138m 49ch

67m 49ch (MCB)
Clarborough Tunnel

67m 79ch

Windmill Lane (UWC) 69m 05ch
Leverton (AHBC) 70m 16ch

(MCG)

Stow Park SB 93m 13ch

Worksop SB (WP) 56m 58ch

138m 62ch

Thrumpton West Jn. (Up) 63m 28ch

Thrumpton SB (T) 64m 47ch

Retford (3 & 4) 64m 32ch

Westbrecks (AHBC) 71m 22ch

71m 79ch

To / from Cottam Power Station

Mansfield Road (CCTV) 62m 25ch / 62m 45ch
Rushey Sidings (AHBC-X) 62m 45ch

Retford Western Jn. 138m 56ch / 64m 20ch

Grove Road (CCTV) 137m 37ch

Retford South Jn. 138m 23ch

Saxilby SB 88m 41ch

West Holmes Jn. 83m 29ch via Metheringham 32m 70ch via Hykeham

Thrumpton West Jn. (Down) 63m 46ch

Eaton Lane (Public BW) 136m 44ch

Lincoln SCC 83m 30ch

Lincoln High St. (CCTV) 82m 49ch

Grove Road GSP 136m 27ch

134m 40ch

Askham Tunnel

134m 37ch

No. 318 Sykes Lane (MCG) 89m 15ch
No. 316 (UWC) 88m 75ch
Hochkings (UWC) 88m 19ch

Saxilby 88m 51ch

(MCG)

Brayford Jn. 32m 53ch

Lincoln Central 82m 41ch

Spa Street (UWC) 40m 42ch

To / from Bevercotes Colliery

Tuxford GSP 131m 50ch

High Marnham Power Station (closed) (end of line 27m 48ch, non-op from 24m 78ch)

Kesteven (AHBC-X) 87m 41ch
River Bank (No. 305) 87m 04ch

Pyewipe Jn. 84m 13ch

Brayford (CCTV) 82m 57ch

Pelham Street Jn. 82m 31ch via Metheringham 41m 26ch via Market Rasen

Boughton Brake Tunnel 1m 49ch to 1m 65ch

Thoresby Colliery 1m 18ch

Egmanton (CCTV) 130m 29ch

Rustons Tip (R/G) 32m 52ch

Boultham Jn. 32m 40ch

Sincil

20m 13ch

Tuxford No. 2 GF 23m 75ch

Grassthorpe Lane (MCG) 128m 30ch

Boultham Jn. 32m 40ch

0m 30ch

Boughton Jn. 20m 15ch / 0m 00ch

Barrel Lane (R/G)
Footpath 127m 08ch
Eaves Lane (R/G)
Bridleway 127m 02ch
Carlton (CCTV) 126m 27ch

Hykeham 29m 44ch

0m 03ch

Clipstone South Jn. 10m 66ch

Thoresby Colliery Jn. SB 17m 21ch / 0m 04ch

Thoresby Colliery Jn. 17m 21ch via Clipstone West Jn.

Swinderby SB (S) 24m 68ch

Walkers No. 63 (UWC) 28m 50ch
Whisby Quarry (UWC) 28m 50ch
Thorpe-on-the-Hill (AHBC-X) 27m 20ch
Eagle and Thorpe (AHBC-X) 26m 03ch

Doddington Road (CCTV) 30m 19ch

Westbrook Lane (UWC) 32m 15ch

126m 26ch

Swinderby 24m 64ch

Clipstone Colliery Jn. 9m 17ch / 9m 21ch

Bilsthorpe Colliery (oou) 4m 39ch

Cromwell Lane (CCTV) 124m 55ch

125m 53ch

125m 42ch

Collingham 22m 17ch

Eagle Barnsdale (MCG) 24m 64ch

Swinderby (MCG) 24m 54ch
South Scarle (AHBC) 24m 31ch
Clements No. 1 (UWC) 24m 00ch

Bilsthorpe Colliery Jn. 1m 08ch

Newark Crossing East Jn. 17m 74ch via Newark Castle 0m 21ch via Newark Crossing South Jn.

Norwell Lane (CCTV) 123m 38ch
Bathley Lane (CCTV) 122m 78ch

Cottage Lane (AHBC) 21m 16ch
Langford (AHBC) 20m 24ch

Tomlinsons (UWC) 23m 31ch
Swinderby Road (UWC) 23m 49ch
Cross Lane (UWC) 23m 07ch
Westbrook Lane (AHBC) 22m 34ch
Langford (R/G) 21m 44ch

Carlton Loops

Church Lane (CCTV) 122m 07ch

Newark Crossing 17m 67ch via Newark Castle

Winthorpe (AHBC) 19m 01ch

(R/G)

A

51 B

Ulceby North Jn. 100m 44ch
Ulceby South Jn. 100m 31ch via Barnetby
1m 45ch via Habrough

Ulceby Jn. (MCB) 100m 32ch
Ulceby Jn. SB (UJ) 100m 32ch
Rye Hill Farm (UWC) 1m 12ch

Brocklesbury Jn. SB (B) 99m 31ch

Barnetby 94m 56ch

wby tion WJ) 2ch

Brocklesbury East Jn. 99m 39ch
Brocklesbury West Jn. 99m 20ch

New Barnetby (MCG) 95m 78ch

Barnetby East SB (BE) 94m 64ch

Habrough 101m 13ch
Habrough Jn. 100m 55ch / 0m 32ch

Roxton Sidings SB 102m 55ch

Stallingborough SB (ST) 104m 73ch

Stalling-borough 104m 72ch

Healing 105m 75ch

COM 0m 00ch 106m 50ch

To / from Eastern Jetty Sidings
Tioxide Sidings

To / from Freight Terminal Sidings

To / from Reception Sidings

Change of mileage 108m 73ch 4m 79ch

To / from Union Dock

(MCG) 4m 19ch

Fish Dock Road (CCTV) 110m 31ch

Great Coates 107m 19ch

Marsh West Jn. 107m 69ch

Lilifield Lane (CCTV) 108m 73ch
Friargate (CCTV) 109m 03ch
Wellowgate (CCTV) 109m 14ch

Grimsby Town 109m 20ch

Garden Street (CCTV) 109m 29ch

Grimsby Docks 110m 11ch

New Clee 110m 78ch

Sdgs.

Cleethorpes 112m 40ch

D

1

Howsham (AHBC-X) 16m 17ch

Folly Lane (UWC) 17m 52ch
North Kelsey (AHBC-X) 18m 03ch
Smithfield Road (AHBC-X) 18m 25ch

Moortown (AHBC-X) 19m 34ch

Holton Gatehouse (AHBC-X) 20m 43ch

Holton-le-Moor SB (H) 21m 11ch

(MCB)

Claxby Gatehouse (No. 24) (AHBC-X) 22m 07ch

Claxby & Usselby (AHBC-X) 23m 69ch

Walesby (AHBC-X) 24m 46ch

Hamiltons (UWC) 25m 34ch
Maypole Rasen (UWC) 25m 58ch

Market Rasen 26m 54ch

Market Rasen Footpath (R/G) 26m 52ch

Buslingthorpe (AHBC-X) 29m 00ch
Lissingley (AHBC-X) 29m 20ch

Wickenby SB (W) 30m 53ch

Wickenby (MCG) 30m 53ch

Thornally No. 47 (UWC) 31m 51ch
Thornally No. 48 (UWC) 31m 63ch
Snelland (AHBC-X) 35m 15ch

Reasby Manor (UWC) 32m 79ch

Stainton (AHBC-X) 33m 60ch

Scothearn (AHBC-X) 34m 51ch

Langworth (MCB) 35m 25ch

Langworth SB (L) 35m 25ch

Welton Crossover 35m 74ch

Manor Farm (UWC) 36m 25ch
Reepham (CCTV) 36m 61ch
Stonefield Farm (No. 65) (UWC) 37m 04ch
Stonefield Farm (No. 66) (UWC) 37m 16ch
Cherry Willingham (AHBC-X) 37m 55ch

Oil

m s

No. 68 (UWC) 38m 18ch

n Terrace Sidings

TV) 82m 19ch

Branston & Washingborough Cross Roads Tunnel 79m 44ch to 79m 47ch

Howards (UWC) 75m 70ch

Ox Pasture Lane (Public BW) 73m 62ch
Robinsons (UWC) 73m 43ch

Metheringham 73m 03ch

(MCG)

Blankney Estates (UWC) 72m 44ch
Marth Road (UWC) 72m 09ch

Blankney SB 72m 79ch

River Witham

Scopwick LC SB 70m 48ch

(MCG)

C

D

2

Level Crossings from Brocklesbury East Jn. to Marsh West Jn.

① Gorwood's (No. 9) (UWC) LC 99m 60ch
② Old Junction (UWC) LC 100m 38ch
③ Habrough (AHBC) 101m 13ch
④ Roxton Sidings (MCG) 102m 55ch
⑤ Little London (AHBC) 103m 56ch
⑥ Stallingborough (MCB) 104m 72ch
⑦ Healing (UWC) 105m 74ch
⑧ No. 29 (UWC) 106m 29ch
⑨ Great Coates (AHBC) 107m 19ch

② **Pyewipe Road SB (P)** 4m 20ch
③ **Great Coates No.1 SB** 108m 34ch
④ **Marsh Junction SB (M)** 107m 77ch
⑤ **Pasture Street SB (P)** 109m 48ch
⑦ **Immingham Reception Sidings SB (IR)** 104m 30ch
⑧ **Immingham East Jn SB (I)** 106m 34ch

A Barrow-in-Furness SB (BF)
29m 05ch

29m 28ch

Abbey
25m 44ch

Park House Farm (R/G) 26m 08ch

B

Carriage
sidings

Barrow-in-Furness
28m 76ch

Roose
27m 13ch

To Port of Barrow

Salthouse Jn. GF
27m 57ch

Salthouse Jn.
27m 59ch

Moreca
2m 10
Buffer
2m 1

1

Morecambe Jn. GF
1m 71ch /0m 00ch

Port of Heysham
(UWC) 3m 69ch

Heysham Port
4m 01ch

Heysham Powe
Station Sidings (
3m 53ch

2

Oil Sidings GF
17m 73ch

End of Line
18m 08ch

Hillhouse No.4 GF
17m 61ch

Hillhouse No.5 GF
17m 45ch

Burn Naze
ICI Power Station

Hillhouse No.3 GF
17m 44ch

oou

To Burn Naze Hillhouse VCM Siding

Poulton SB (PT)
14m 44ch

Hilly Laid (TMO) 16m 43ch
Thorton (TMO) 16m 10ch
Tarn Gate (UWC) 15m 58ch

To Blackpool Carriage
Sidings Depot

Layton
16m 32ch

Poulton Jn. 14m 40ch

Poulton-le-Fylde
14m 31ch

Blackpool North No.2
SB (BN2)
17m 30ch

(MCB)

Carleton
Crossing
(CN) SB
15m 44ch

Kirkham SB (KM
8m 29ch

Blackpool North

17m 49ch

Blackpool North No.1
SB (BN)
17m 00ch
(Switched out)
(UFN)

Kirkh
North
8m 2

8m 42ch

Kirkham Tip
Sidings

Blackpool Pleasure
Beach
19m 18ch

Blackpool
South
20m 00ch

Tarnbrick (UWC)
8m 54ch

Sidings

Squires Gate
18m 34ch

Moss Side
11m 14ch

Moss Side (ABCL)
11m 09ch

St Annes-on-the-Sea
16m 51ch

Ansdell &
Fairhaven
14m 75ch

Lytham
13m 56ch

3

Level Crossings from Meols Cop to Parbold:
① Pool Hey (AHBC) 32m 44ch
② Wyke Cop (AHBC) 32m 20ch
③ Bescar Lane (AHBC) 30m 78ch
④ Martins Lane (R/G) 29m 70ch

Southport
35m 27ch
18m 35ch

North Jn. 35m 08ch
Bradford Sidings
Stabling Sidings
To former Steamport (oou)
Goods Yard GF
34m 58ch

Carriage Sidings

Portland Street (CCTV) 18m 00ch
Duke Street (CCTV) 17m 65ch
Aughton Road (CCTV) 17m 49ch
Birkdale (CCTV) 17m 26ch
Crescent Road (AHBC) 16m 76ch

Birkdale
Sidings

Meols Cop
34m 02ch

Hillside
16m 26ch

South Jn.
18m 13ch

30m 79ch
(Down platform)

A

B

Birkdale

28m 73ch

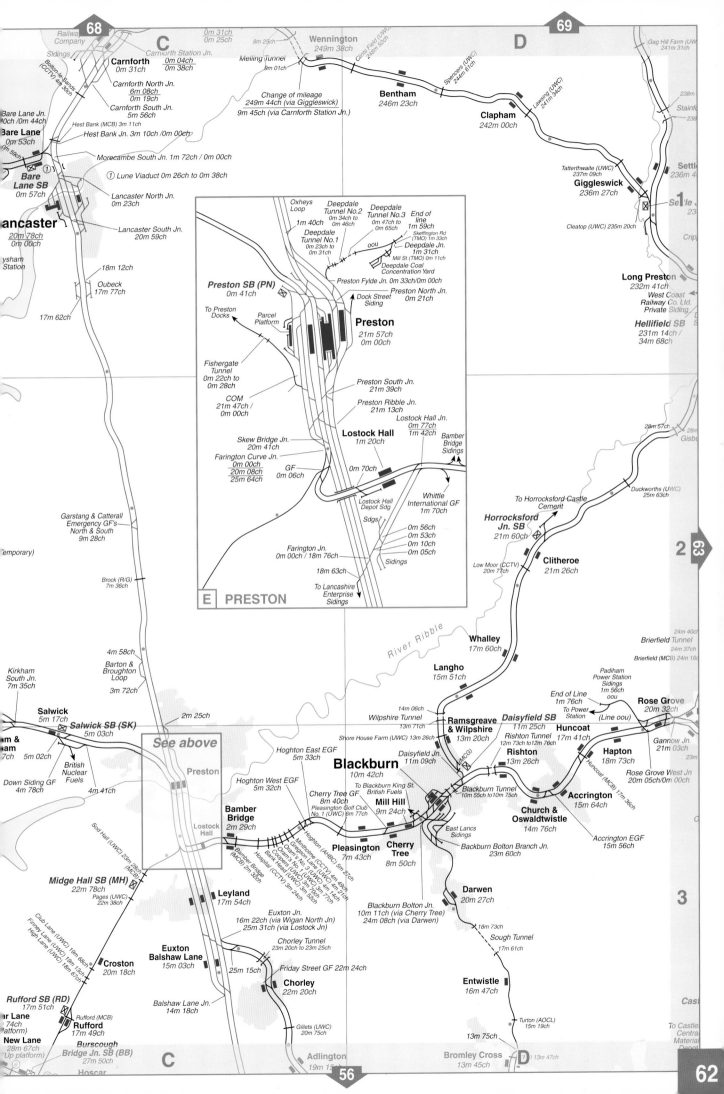

Railway
Company
Sidings
Bolton-le-Sands
(CCTV) 4m 30ch

Carnforth
0m 31ch

0m 04ch
0m 38ch

Carnforth Station Jn.

0m 31ch
0m 25ch

Wennington
249m 38ch

8m 25ch

Meiling Tunnel
9m 01ch

Clints Field (UWC)
249m 52ch

Spencers (UWC)
244m 61ch

Gag Hill Farm (UW
241m 31ch

Carnforth North Jn.
6m 08ch
0m 19ch

Carnforth South Jn.
5m 56ch

Bentham
246m 23ch

Lawsing (UWC)
241m 34ch

238m

Clapham
242m 00ch

Hest Bank (MCB) 3m 11ch

Change of mileage
249m 44ch (via Giggleswick)
9m 45ch (via Carnforth Station Jn.)

Bare Lane Jn.
0ch /0m 44ch

Bare Lane
0m 53ch

Hest Bank Jn. 3m 10ch /0m 00ch

Morecambe South Jn. 1m 72ch / 0m 00ch

Tatterthwaite (UWC)
237m 09ch

Stainfo
238

Bare
Lane SB
0m 57ch

① Lune Viaduct 0m 26ch to 0m 38ch

Giggleswick
236m 27ch

Se'le J
23

ancaster

Lancaster North Jn.
0m 23ch

Cleatop (UWC) 235m 20ch

Crip

20m 78ch
0m 00ch

Lancaster South Jn.
20m 59ch

Long Preston
232m 41ch

West Coast
Railway Co. Ltd.
Private Siding

ysham
Station

18m 12ch

Oubeck
17m 77ch

17m 62ch

Oxheys
Loop
1m 40ch

Deepdale
Tunnel No.2
0m 34ch to
0m 46ch

Deepdale
Tunnel No.3
0m 47ch to
0m 65ch

End of
line
1m 59ch

Skeffington Rd
(TMO) 1m 33ch

Hellifield SB
231m 14ch /
34m 68ch

Deepdale
Tunnel No.1
0m 23ch to
0m 31ch

oou

Deepdale Jn.
1m 31ch
Mill St (TMO) 0m 11ch

Preston SB (PN)
0m 41ch

Preston Fylde Jn. 0m 33ch/0m 00ch

Deepdale Coal
Concentration Yard

To Preston
Docks

Parcel
Platform

Preston North Jn.
0m 21ch

Dock Street
Siding

Preston
21m 57ch
0m 00ch

Fishergate
Tunnel
0m 22ch to
0m 28ch

Preston South Jn.
21m 39ch

COM
21m 47ch /
0m 00ch

Preston Ribble Jn.
21m 13ch

Lostock Hall Jn.
0m 77ch
1m 42ch

Bamber
Bridge
Sidings

Skew Bridge Jn.
20m 41ch

Lostock Hall
1m 20ch

Faringdon Curve Jn.
0m 00ch
20m 08ch
25m 64ch

GF
0m 06ch

0m 70ch

Whittle
International GF
1m 70ch

Lostock Hall
Depot Sdg

Sdgs

0m 56ch
0m 53ch
0m 10ch
0m 05ch

Farington Jn.
0m 00ch / 18m 76ch

Sidings

18m 63ch

To Lancashire
Enterprise
Sidings

E PRESTON

Horrocksford
Jn. SB
21m 60ch

To Horrocksford Castle
Cement

Duckworths (UWC)
25m 63ch

28m 57ch

28

Gisb

Garstang & Catterall
Emergency GF's
North & South
9m 28ch

Low Moor (CCTV)
20m 77ch

Clitheroe
21m 26ch

emporary)

Brock (R/G)
7m 36ch

Brierfield Tunnel
24m 37ch

Brierfield (MCB) 24m 16

24m 40ch

2
63

River Ribble

Whalley
17m 60ch

4m 58ch

Barton &
Broughton
Loop
3m 72ch

Langho
15m 51ch

Kirkham
South Jn.
7m 35ch

2m 25ch

14m 06ch

Padiham
Power Station
Sidings
1m 56ch
oou

Rose Grove
20m 32ch

Salwick
5m 17ch

Salwick SB (SK)
5m 03ch

Wilpshire Tunnel

13m 71ch

Ramsgreave
& Wilpshire
13m 20ch

Daisyfield SB
11m 25ch

End of Line
1m 76ch

To Power
Station
(Line oou)

Huncoat
17m 41ch

Gannow Jn.
21m 03ch

m &
am
ch

5m 02ch

Shore House Farm (UWC) 13m 26ch

Rishton Tunnel
12m 73ch to12m 76ch

Hapton
18m 73ch

23

British
Nuclear
Fuels

Daisyfield Jn.
11m 09ch

(MCG)

Rishton
13m 26ch

Huncoat (MCB) 17m 36ch

Rose Grove West Jn
20m 05ch/0m 00ch

Down Siding GF
4m 78ch

4m 41ch

See above

Preston

Hoghton East EGF
5m 33ch

Blackburn
10m 42ch

To Blackburn King St.
British Fuels

Blackburn Tunnel
10m 55ch to10m 75ch

Accrington
15m 64ch

Hoghton West EGF
5m 32ch

Mill Hill
9m 24ch

Church &
Oswaldtwistle
14m 76ch

Accrington EGF
15m 56ch

Lostock
Hall

Cherry Tree GF
8m 40ch
Pleasington Golf Club
No.1 (UWC) 6m 77ch

East Lancs
Sidings

Bamber
Bridge
2m 29ch

Mintholme (CCTV) 4m 27ch

Hoghton (A14BO) 4m 49ch

Gregson Lane (UWC) 4m 21ch

 Collier's No.1 (UWC) 3m 77ch

Cooper's No.3 (UWC) 3m 73ch

Cooper's No.1 (UWC) 3m 72ch

Bank Head (UWC) 3m 24ch

Bamber Bridge Hospital (MCB) 2m 32ch

Pleasington
7m 43ch

Cherry
Tree
8m 50ch

Blackburn Bolton Branch Jn.
23m 60ch

Backburn Bolton Jn.
10m 11ch (via Cherry Tree)
24m 08ch (via Darwen)

Midge Hall SB (MH)
22m 78ch

Pages (UWC)
22m 38ch

Leyland
17m 54ch

Euxton Jn.
16m 22ch (via Wigan North Jn)
25m 31ch (via Lostock Jn)

Darwen
20m 27ch

18m 73ch

3

Club Lane (UWC) 19m 68ch
Finney Lane (UWC) 19m 13ch
High Lane (UWC) 19m 67ch

Croston
20m 18ch

Euxton
Balshaw Lane
15m 03ch

Chorley Tunnel
23m 20ch to 23m 25ch

25m 15ch

Friday Street GF 22m 24ch

Sough Tunnel
17m 61ch

Rufford SB (RD)
17m 51ch

Rufford (MCB)

Chorley
22m 20ch

Entwistle
16m 47ch

r Lane
74ch
atform)

Rufford
17m 49ch

Balshaw Lane Jn.
14m 18ch

New Lane
28m 67ch
Up platform)

Burscough
Bridge Jn. SB (BB)
27m 50ch

Gillets (UWC)
20m 75ch

Turton (AOCL)
15m 19ch

13m 75ch

Cas

To Castle
Centra
Materia
Dep

Hoscar

Adlington
19m 15

Bromley Cross
13m 45ch

13m 47ch

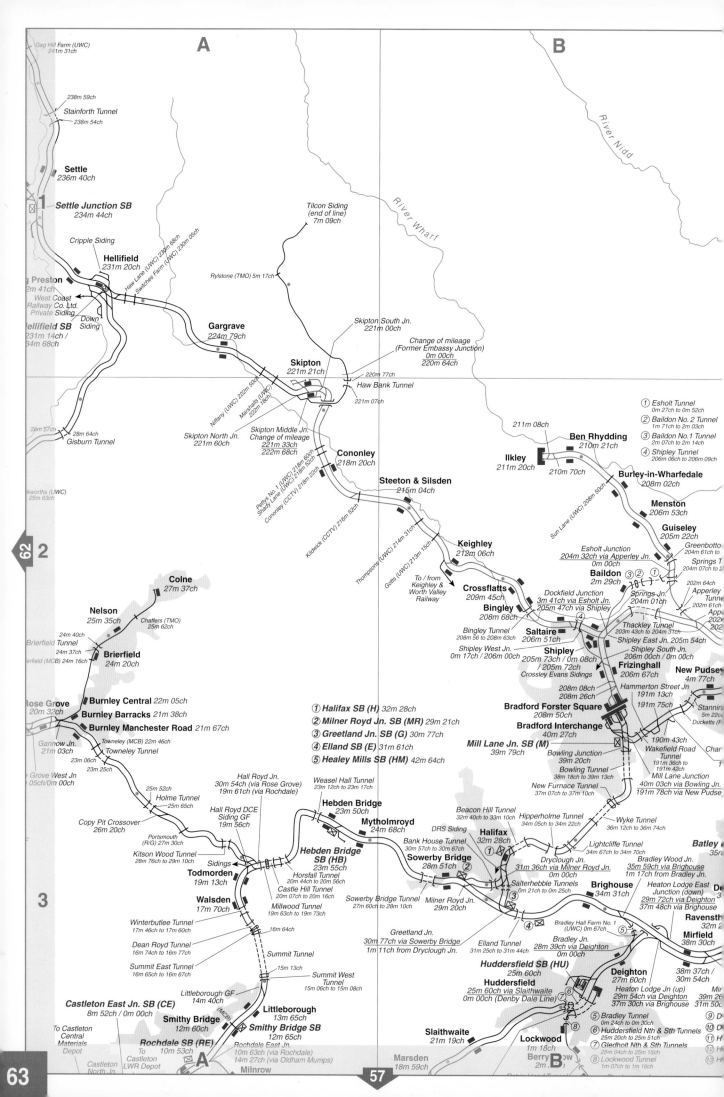

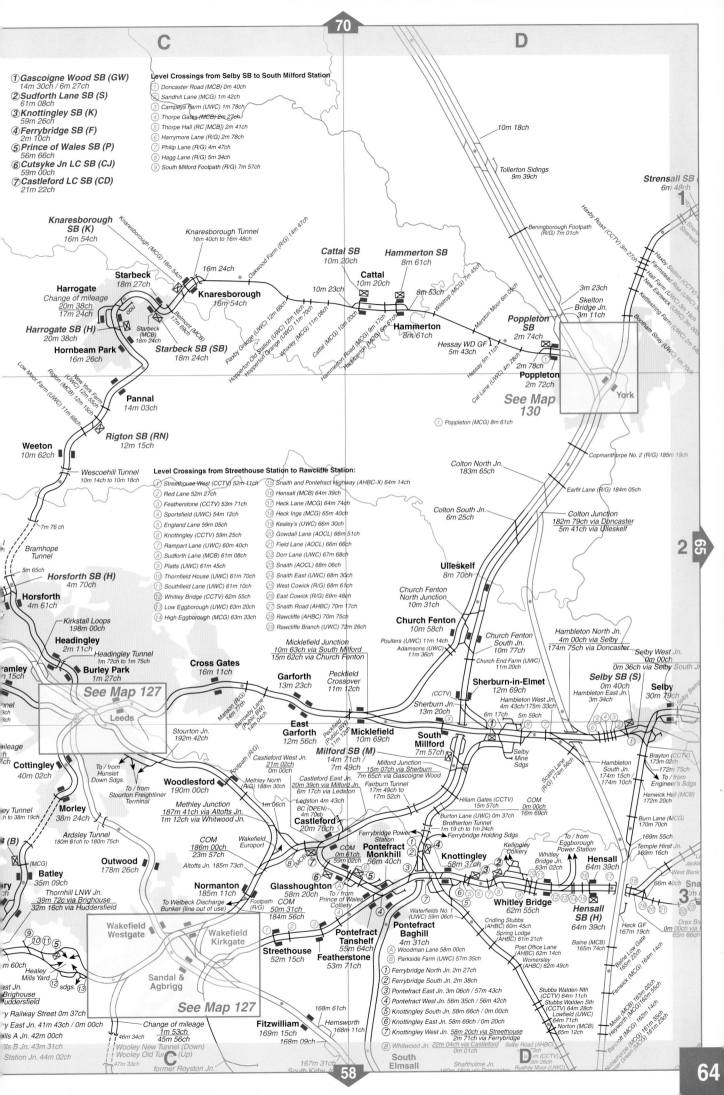

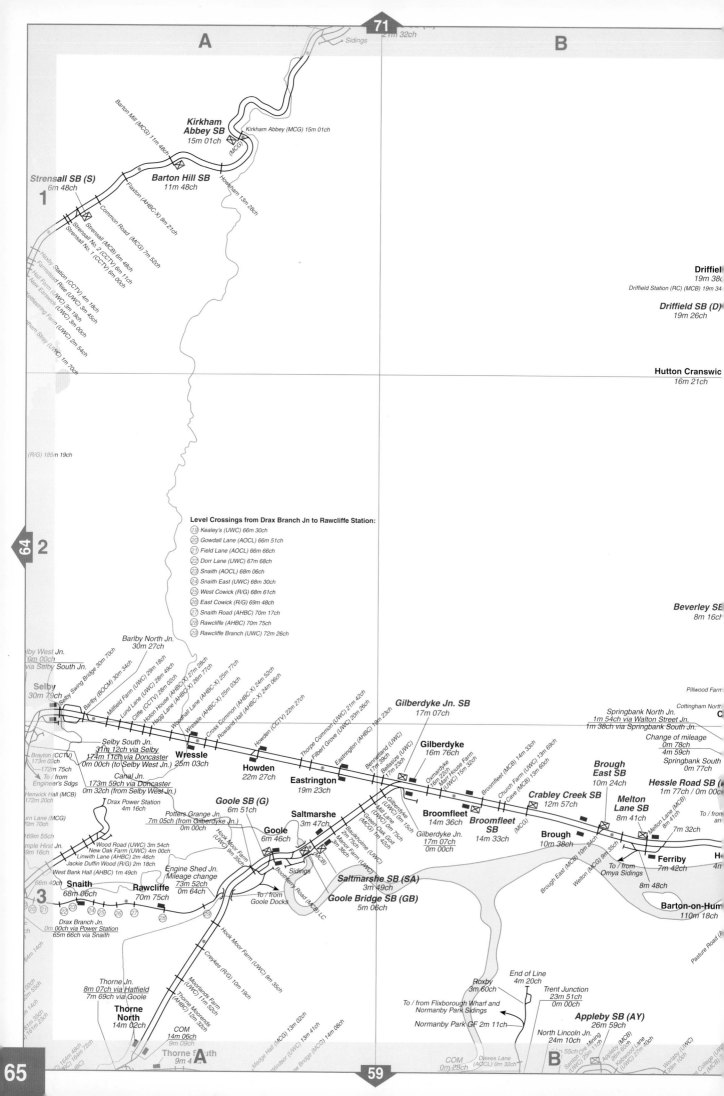

A

B

Sidings

Kirkham Abbey SB
15m 01ch

Kirkham Abbey (MCG) 15m 01ch

Barton Mill (MCG) 11m 48ch

(MCG)

Strensall SB (S)
6m 48ch

1

Barton Hill SB
11m 48ch

Howsham 13m 28ch

Flaxton (AHBC-X) 9m 21ch

Common Road (MCG) 7m 52ch

Strensall (MCB) 6m 48ch
Strensall No. 2 (CCTV) 6m 11ch
Strensall No. 1 (CCTV) 6m 00ch

Haxby Station (CCTV) 4m 18ch
Farmstead Rise (UWC) 3m 45ch
Hall Farm (UWC) 3m 18ch
New Earswick (UWC) 3m 00ch
Nestlestring Farm (UWC) 2m 54ch
Huntingham Stray (UWC) 1m 70ch

Driffiel
19m 38c

Driffield Station (RC) (MCB) 19m 34

Driffield SB (D)
19m 26ch

Hutton Cranswic
16m 21ch

(R/G) 185m 19ch

64
2

Level Crossings from Drax Branch Jn to Rawcliffe Station:
19 Kealey's (UWC) 66m 30ch
20 Gowdall Lane (AOCL) 66m 51ch
21 Field Lane (AOCL) 66m 66ch
22 Dorr Lane (UWC) 67m 68ch
23 Snaith (AOCL) 68m 06ch
24 Snaith East (UWC) 68m 30ch
25 West Cowick (R/G) 68m 61ch
26 East Cowick (R/G) 69m 48ch
27 Snaith Road (AHBC) 70m 17ch
28 Rawcliffe (AHBC) 70m 75ch
29 Rawcliffe Branch (UWC) 72m 26ch

Beverley SB
8m 16ch

Barlby North Jn.
30m 27ch

Selby West Jn.
0m 00ch
via Selby South Jn.

Pillwood Farm

Cottingham North

Selby
30m 79ch

Barlby Swing Bridge 30m 00ch
Barlby (BOCM) 30m 34ch
Millfield Farm (UWC) 29m 18ch
Lund Lane (UWC) 28m 49ch
Cliffe (CCTV) 28m 02ch
Hoton House (AHBC-X) 27m 28ch
Hagg Lane (AHBC-X) 26m 77ch
Woodhall Lane (AHBC-X) 25m 77ch
Wressle (AHBC-X) 25m 03ch
Cross Common (AHBC-X) 24m 52ch
Rowland Hall (AHBC-X) 24m 06ch

Howden (CCTV) 22m 27ch

Thorpe Common (UWC) 21m 42ch
Filber Grove (UWC) 20m 26ch

Eastrington (AHBC) 19m 23ch

Gilberdyke Jn. SB
17m 07ch

Springbank North Jn.
1m 54ch via Walton Street Jn.
1m 38ch via Springbank South Jn.

Bennetland (UWC)
17m 39ch
Bellasize (UWC)
17m 23ch

Gilberdyke
16m 76ch

Change of mileage
0m 78ch
4m 59ch

Springbank South Jn.
0m 77ch

Selby South Jn.
31m 12ch via Selby
174m 11ch via Doncaster
0m 00ch (to Selby West Jn.)

Wressle
25m 03ch

Howden
22m 27ch

Eastrington
19m 23ch

Oxmardyke (UWC)
16m 22ch
Marr House Farm
(UWC) 15m 30ch

Broomfleet (MCB) 14m 33ch
Church Farm (UWC) 13m 69ch
Cave (MCB) 13m 60ch

*Brough
East SB*
10m 24ch

Hessle Road SB
1m 77ch / 0m 00c

Brayton (CCTV)
173m 02ch
172m 75ch
To / from
Engineer's Sdgs

Canal Jn.
173m 59ch via Doncaster
0m 32ch (from Selby West Jn.)

Goole SB (G)
6m 51ch

Drax Power Station
4m 16ch

Potters Grange Jn.
7m 05ch (from Gilberdyke Jn.)
0m 00ch

Saltmarshe
3m 47ch

Gilberdyke
(UWC) 0m 15ch
Mill Lane (UWC) 0m 75ch
Green Oak Golf
(UWC) 1m 42ch

Broomfleet
14m 36ch

*Broomfleet
SB*
14m 33ch

Crabley Creek SB
12m 57ch

*Melton
Lane SB*
8m 41ch

To / from
an

Melton Lane (MCB)
8m 41ch

Henwick Hall (MCB)
172m 20ch

um Lane (MCG)
70m 70ch

Goole
6m 46ch

Hook Moor Farm
(UWC) 9m 35ch

Baulkholme (UWC)
2m 50ch
Manor Farm (UWC)
1m 75ch

Gilberdyke Jn.
17m 07ch
0m 00ch

Brough
10m 38ch

Welton (MCG) 9m 35ch

7m 32ch

ple Hirst Jn.
9m 16ch

Wood Road (UWC) 3m 54ch
New Oak Farm (UWC) 4m 00ch
Linwith Lane (AHBC) 2m 46ch
Jackie Duffin Wood (R/G) 2m 18ch
West Bank Hall (AHBC) 1m 49ch

Engine Shed Jn.
Mileage change
73m 52ch
0m 64ch

Saltmarshe SB (SA)
3m 49ch

Boothferry Road (MCB) LC

Green Oak Golf (MCG) 1m 42ch

Ferriby
7m 42ch

4m

66m 40ch

Snaith
68m 06ch

Rawcliffe
70m 75ch

Sidings

To / from
Goole Docks

Goole Bridge SB (GB)
5m 06ch

Brough East (MCB) 10m 24ch

8m 48ch

3

19 20 21 22 23 24 25 26 27 28 29

Drax Branch Jn.
0m 00ch via Power Station
65m 66ch via Snaith

To / from
Omya Sidings

Barton-on-Hum
110m 18ch

6m 14ch

Hook Moor Farm (UWC) 9m 35ch

Creykes (R/G) 10m 19ch

Pasture Road (M

0m
55ch

Thorne Jn.
8m 07ch via Hatfield
7m 69ch via Goole

Moorlands Farm
(UWC) 11m 50ch
Thorne Moorends
(AHBC) 12m 32ch

Roxby
3m 60ch

End of Line
4m 20ch

Trent Junction
23m 51ch
0m 00ch

Sinton Ore Mining

Appleby (MCB) 25m 11ch

4m
14ch

**Thorne
North**
14m 02ch

COM
14m 06ch
9m 09ch

Medge Hall (MCG) 13m 02ch
Windsor (UWC) 13m 41ch

Thorne Bridge (MCG) 14m 08ch

To / from Flixborough Wharf and
Normanby Park Sidings

Normanby Park GF 2m 11ch

North Lincoln Jn.
24m 10ch

Appleby SB (AY)
26m 59ch

Appleby Lane
(UWC) 27m 40ch

Katwood Lane
(UWC) 29m 11ch

Worlaby (UWC)
29m 10ch

4m 35ch
4m 23ch

Thorne South
9m 4

B

COM
0m 28ch

Dawes Lane
(AOCL) 0m 32ch

Barf Farm
Speeton (...)
C **D**

Bempton Sands (UWC) 39m 63ch
Flamborough (AHBC) 33m 31ch
Buckton Lane (AHBC) 35m ...
Bempton (AHBC) 34m 43ch
Sewerby (AHBC) 32m 35ch
31m 00ch
Bridlington Quay (CCTV) 31m 06ch
Bridlington SB (BN) 30m 58ch
Bridlington 30m 72ch
To / from Carriage Sidings
Carnaby (AHBC-X) 28m 52ch

1

Nafferton 21m 44ch
Burton Agnes (AHBC-X) 25m 45ch
Lowthorpe (AHBC-X) 23m 64ch
Nether Lane (AHBC-X) 21m 58ch
Wansford Road (...CTV) 19m 54ch
(AHBC-X)
...utton (AHBC-X) 16m 73ch
...ranswick (AHBC-X) 16m 18ch
...tton (AHBC-X) 14m 44ch
...wick (AHBC-X) 14m 01ch
...wick (AHBC-X) 13m 53ch
...ckington (AHBC-X) 12m 74ch
...corborough (AHBC-X) 12m 24ch
(AHBC-X)
Arram 11m 16ch
Beverley North (CCTV) 8m 62ch
Cherry Tree (CCTV) 8m 39ch
Beverley 8m 20ch
Beverley (MCB) 8m 16ch
Flemingate (RC) 8m 02ch
England Springs (UWC) 7m 57ch
Ashworths (UWC) 7m 01ch
Beverley Parks (AHBC-X) 6m 51ch

...m 00ch
West Parade North Jn. 0m 24ch / 0m 72ch
...m 17ch
...ham
...aite Gates ...) 3m 63ch
Walton Street Jn. 1m 29ch
Dock Security Gates 6m 73ch
Eastern Access (AOCL) 7m 69ch
Kingston Terminal Jn. 7m 72ch
Saltend and BP Chemicals 8m 56ch
(b) (c) (d) (e)
(a)
0m 25ch
Hull 0m 00ch
7 6 5 4 3 2 1
...m 06ch
...ight Yard ...oats
Station Sidings
Anlaby Road Jn. 0m 73ch / 0m 00ch
Hessel East Jn. 3m 20ch

Hall and Immingham Areas
(a) To Botanic Gardens Depot
(b) To / from B Quay
(c) To / from Hedon Road Sidings
(d) To / from King George Dock
(e) To / from Kingston Coal Terminal

1. Walton Street (CCTV) LC 1m 25ch
2. St Georges Road (CCTV) LC 1m 24ch
3. Chalk Lane (CCTV) LC 1m 49ch
4. Yorkshire Tar (TMO) LC 2m 44ch
5. Shell Mex (OPEN) LC 2m 34ch
6. New Inn (OPEN) LC 2m 19ch
7. Marsh Farm (OPEN) LC 0m 49ch
8. Western Entrance (CCTV) LC 104m 55ch
9. Ambulance (UWC) LC 104m 39ch
10. Kiln Lane (AOCL) LC 0m 51ch
11. Marsh Lane (AHBC) LC 1m 25ch
12. Wood Lane (AHBC) LC 3m 36ch
13. Gorwood's (No. 9) (UWC) LC 99m 60ch
14. Old Junction (UWC) LC 100m 38ch

1. *Hull Paragon SB (HP)* 0m 18ch
2. *Pyewipe Road LC SB (P)* 4m 20ch
6. *Immingham West Jn. SB (IW)* 105m 06ch
7. *Immingham Reception Sidings SB (IR)* 104m 30ch
8. *Immingham East Jn SB (I)* 106m 34ch

2

To / from New Holland Bulk Terminal
New Holland 106m 52ch (MCG)
Killingholme End of Line 2m 70ch
To / from Admiralty Sidings
Oxmarsh Crossing SB (OM) 106m 38ch
Barrow Road (MCG) 106m 57ch
To / from Coal Pad lines and Ore Terminal line
Goxhill SB 104m 51ch (MCG)
...63ch
Barrow Road (OPEN) 108m 07ch
Barrow Haven 108m 05ch
Goxhill 104m 55ch
To / from NCB Terminal Humber Road Jn. 104m 05ch
Change of mileage 0m 00ch / 105m 10ch
Butterswood (ABCL-X) 103m 48ch
To / from Lindsey Refinery
0m 11ch
Barton Road (MCG) 103m 12ch
Ulceby 100m 36ch
Robinsons (UWC) 101m 40ch
Humber International Terminal
Thornton Abbey 103m 04ch
Bystable 102m 10ch
Meadow Croft Farm (UWC) 101m 40ch
Garola House (UWC) 101m 39ch
To / from Humber Refinery
Grain Store Sidings
Loco Depot
Immingham East Jn 106m 31ch
Ulceby North Jn. 100m 44ch
Ulceby Jn. SB (UJ) 100m 32ch
Ulceby Jn. (MCB) 100m 32ch
Ulceby South Jn. 100m 31ch via Barnetby 1m 45ch via Habrough Jn.
Rye Hill Farm (UWC) 1m 12ch
To / from Eastern Jetty Sidings / Tioxide Sidings
Change of mileage 108m 73ch 4m 79ch
Brocklesbury Jn. SB (B) 99m 31ch
COM 0m 00ch 106m 50ch
To / from Freight Terminal Sidings
To / from Union Dock

3

C **D**

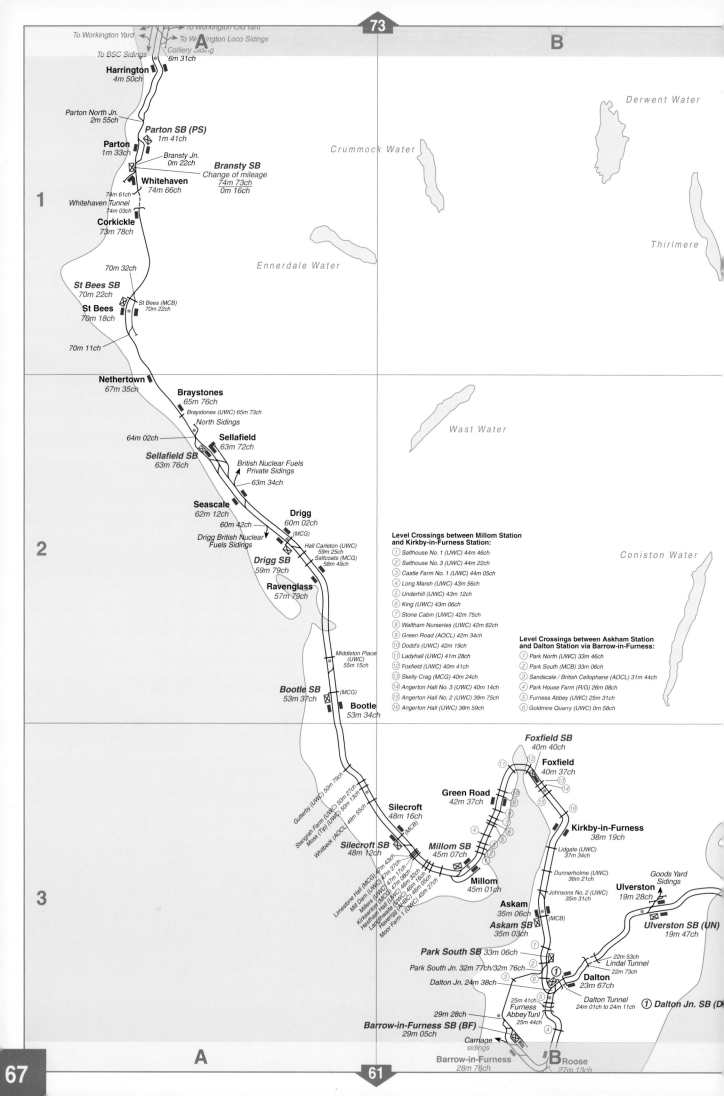

To Workington Old Yard
To Workington Yard
To Workington Loco Sidings
Colliery Siding
6m 31ch

A

B

Derwent Water

Harrington
4m 50ch

Parton North Jn.
2m 55ch

Crummock Water

Parton SB (PS)
1m 41ch

Parton
1m 33ch

Bransty Jn.
0m 22ch

Bransty SB
Change of mileage
74m 73ch
0m 16ch

Whitehaven
74m 66ch

Thirlmere

74m 61ch

Whitehaven Tunnel
74m 03ch

1

Corkickle
73m 78ch

70m 32ch

Ennerdale Water

St Bees SB
70m 22ch

St Bees (MCB)
70m 22ch

St Bees
70m 18ch

70m 11ch

Nethertown
67m 35ch

Braystones
65m 76ch

Wast Water

Braystones (UWC) 65m 73ch
North Sidings

64m 02ch

Sellafield
63m 72ch

Sellafield SB
63m 76ch

*British Nuclear Fuels
Private Sidings*
63m 34ch

Seascale
62m 12ch

Drigg
60m 02ch

60m 42ch

(MCG)

*Drigg British Nuclear
Fuels Sidings*

Hall Carleton (UWC)
59m 25ch
Saltcoats (MCG)
58m 49ch

**Level Crossings between Millom Station
and Kirkby-in-Furness Station:**

① Salthouse No. 1 (UWC) 44m 46ch
② Salthouse No. 3 (UWC) 44m 22ch
③ Castle Farm No. 1 (UWC) 44m 05ch
④ Long Marsh (UWC) 43m 56ch
⑤ Underhill (UWC) 43m 12ch
⑥ King (UWC) 43m 06ch
⑦ Stone Cabin (UWC) 42m 75ch
⑧ Waltham Nurseries (UWC) 42m 62ch
⑨ Green Road (AOCL) 42m 34ch
⑩ Dodd's (UWC) 42m 19ch
⑪ Ladyhall (UWC) 41m 28ch
⑫ Foxfield (UWC) 40m 41ch
⑬ Skelly Crag (MCG) 40m 24ch
⑭ Angerton Hall No. 3 (UWC) 40m 14ch
⑮ Angerton Hall No. 2 (UWC) 39m 75ch
⑯ Angerton Hall (UWC) 38m 59ch

Coniston Water

**Level Crossings between Askham Station
and Dalton Station via Barrow-in-Furness:**

① Park North (UWC) 33m 46ch
② Park South (MCB) 33m 06ch
③ Sandscale / British Cellophane (AOCL) 31m 44ch
④ Park House Farm (R/G) 26m 08ch
⑤ Furness Abbey (UWC) 25m 31ch
⑥ Goldmire Quarry (UWC) 0m 58ch

Drigg SB
59m 79ch

2

Ravenglass
57m 79ch

Middleton Place
(UWC)
55m 15ch

Bootle SB
53m 37ch

(MCG)

Bootle
53m 34ch

Foxfield SB
40m 40ch

Foxfield
40m 37ch

Gutterby (UWC) 50m 79ch
Stangrah Farm (UWC) 50m 27ch
Moss (Tip) (UWC) 50m 13ch
Whitbeck (AOCL) 49m 55ch

Green Road
42m 37ch

Silecroft
48m 16ch

Kirkby-in-Furness
38m 19ch

Limestone Hall (MCG) 47m 43ch
Mill Dam (UWC) 47m 27ch
Millers (UWC) 47m 17ch
Kirksanton (MCG) 47m 08ch
Heathland (UWC) 46m 32ch
Kirksanton (UWC) 46m 16ch
Langthwaite (UWC) 46m 05ch
Haverigg (AHBC) 45m 27ch
Moor Farm 1 (UWC) 45m 24ch

Silecroft SB
48m 12ch

(MCB)

Millom SB
45m 07ch

Lidgate (UWC)
37m 34ch

Dunnerholme (UWC)
36m 21ch

*Goods Yard
Sidings*

Ulverston
19m 28ch

3

Millom
45m 01ch

Johnsons No. 2 (UWC)
35m 31ch

Askam
35m 06ch

(MCB)

Ulverston SB (UN)
19m 47ch

Askam SB
35m 03ch

①

22m 53ch
Lindal Tunnel
22m 73ch

Park South SB 33m 06ch

②

Dalton
23m 67ch

Park South Jn. 32m 77ch/32m 76ch

③

⑥

Dalton Tunnel
24m 01ch to 24m 11ch

① **Dalton Jn. SB (D**

Dalton Jn. 24m 38ch

25m 41ch

⑤

④

**Furness
Abbey Tunl**
25m 44ch

Barrow-in-Furness SB (BF)
29m 05ch

29m 28ch

*Carriage
sidings*

Barrow-in-Furness
28m 76ch

B Roose
27m 13ch

A

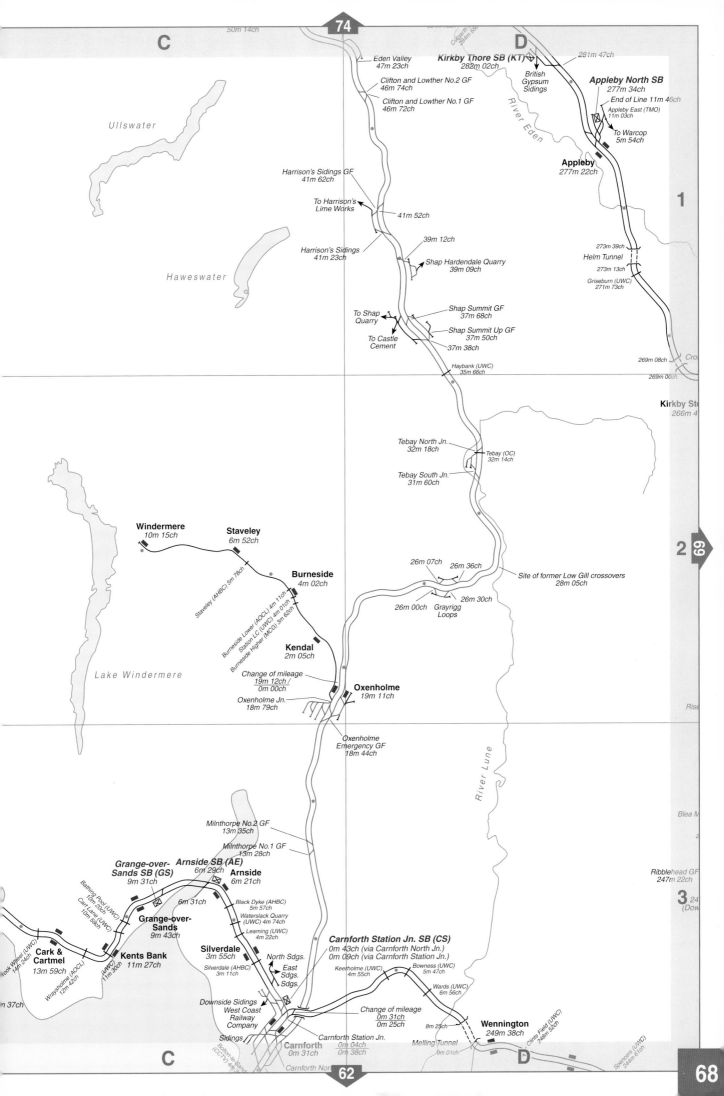

C

D

Ullswater

Eden Valley
47m 23ch

Clifton and Lowther No.2 GF
46m 74ch

Clifton and Lowther No.1 GF
46m 72ch

Kirkby Thore SB (KT)
282m 02ch

British Gypsum Sidings

281m 47ch

Appleby North SB
277m 34ch

End of Line 11m 46ch
Appleby East (TMO)
11m 03ch

To Warcop
5m 54ch

Appleby
277m 22ch

1

Harrison's Sidings GF
41m 62ch

To Harrison's
Lime Works

41m 52ch

Haweswater

Harrison's Sidings
41m 23ch

39m 12ch

Shap Hardendale Quarry
39m 09ch

273m 39ch

Helm Tunnel

273m 13ch

Griseburn (UWC)
271m 73ch

To Shap
Quarry

Shap Summit GF
37m 68ch

To Castle
Cement

Shap Summit Up GF
37m 50ch
37m 38ch

Haybank (UWC)
35m 66ch

269m 08ch

Cro

269m 00ch

Kirkby St
266m 4

Tebay North Jn.
32m 18ch

Tebay (OC)
32m 14ch

Tebay South Jn.
31m 60ch

Windermere
10m 15ch

Staveley
6m 52ch

2

26m 07ch

26m 36ch

Site of former Low Gill crossovers
28m 05ch

Staveley (AHBC) 5m 78ch

Burneside
4m 02ch

26m 00ch

26m 30ch

Grayrigg
Loops

Burneside Lower (AOCL) 4m 11ch
Station LC (UWC) 4m 01ch
Burneside Higher (MCG) 3m 62ch

Kendal
2m 05ch

Lake Windermere

Change of mileage
19m 12ch /
0m 00ch

Oxenholme
19m 11ch

Oxenholme Jn.
18m 79ch

River Lune

Oxenholme
Emergency GF
18m 44ch

Rise

Milnthorpe No.2 GF
13m 35ch

Milnthorpe No.1 GF
13m 28ch

Blea M

Grange-over-Sands SB (GS)
9m 31ch

Arnside SB (AE)
6m 29ch

Arnside
6m 21ch

Bathing Pool (UWC)
10m 20ch
Carr Lane (UWC)
10m 56ch

6m 31ch

Black Dyke (AHBC)
5m 57ch

Waterslack Quarry
(UWC) 4m 74ch

Leaming
4m 22ch

Ribblehead GF
247m 22ch

3

24
(Dow

Grange-over-Sands
9m 43ch

Silverdale
3m 55ch

North Sdgs.

Silverdale (AHBC)
3m 11ch

Carnforth Station Jn. SB (CS)
0m 43ch (via Carnforth North Jn.)
0m 09ch (via Carnforth Station Jn.)

Keerholme (UWC)
4m 55ch

Bowness (UWC)
5m 47ch

Wards (UWC)
6m 56ch

Clints Field (UWC)
248m 52ch

Spencers (UWC)
244m 61ch

Cark & Cartmel
13m 59ch

Brook Wheel (UWC)
14m 24ch

Wraysholme (AOCL)
12m 42ch

Kents Bank
11m 27ch

Kents Bank
11m 30ch (UWC)

East
Sdgs.
Sdgs.

Downside Sidings
West Coast
Railway
Company

Change of mileage
0m 31ch /
0m 25ch

8m 25ch

Wennington
249m 38ch

Sidings

Carnforth Station Jn.

Melling Tunnel

9m 01ch

Bolton-le-Sands (CCTV) 4m 3

Carnforth
0m 31ch
0m 04ch
0m 38ch

C

Carnforth North

D

69

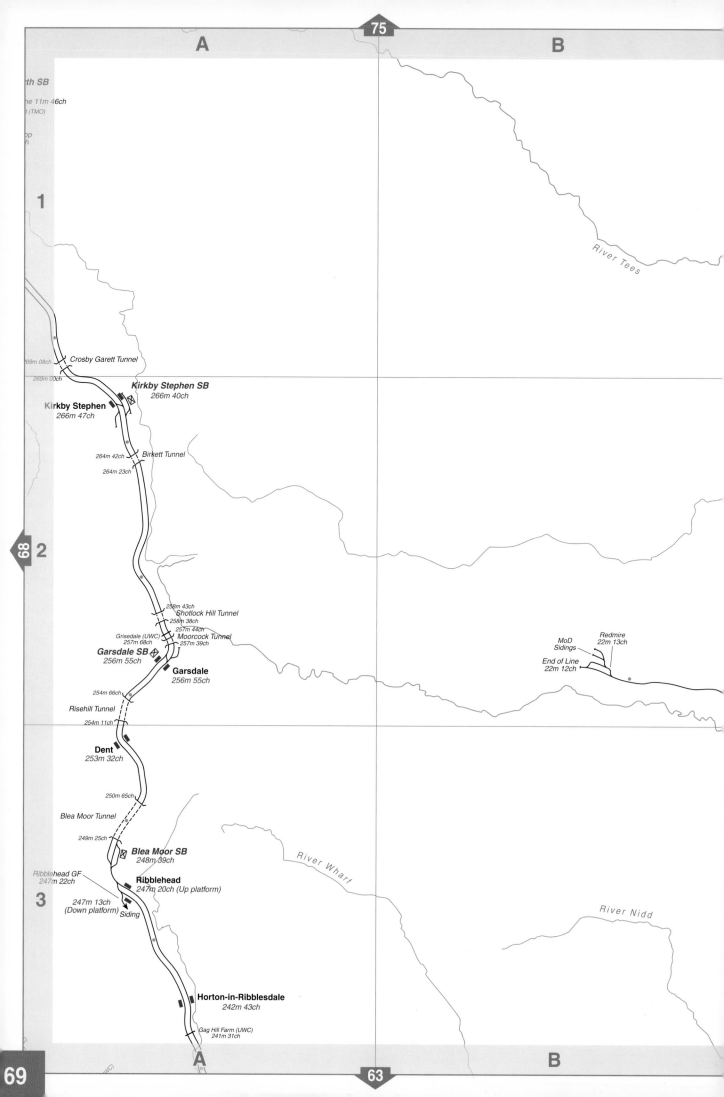

1

River Tees

th SB

ne 11m 46ch
t (TMO)

op
h

68

2

69m 08ch
Crosby Garett Tunnel

269m 00ch

Kirkby Stephen SB
266m 40ch

Kirkby Stephen
266m 47ch

264m 42ch *Birkett Tunnel*

264m 23ch

258m 43ch
Shotlock Hill Tunnel
258m 38ch
257m 44ch
Griesdale (UWC) *Moorcock Tunnel*
257m 68ch *257m 39ch*

Garsdale SB
256m 55ch

Garsdale
256m 55ch

254m 66ch

Risehill Tunnel

254m 11ch

Dent
253m 32ch

250m 65ch

Blea Moor Tunnel

249m 25ch

Blea Moor SB
248m 39ch

Ribblehead GF
247m 22ch

Ribblehead
247m 20ch (Up platform)

3

247m 13ch
(Down platform) *Siding*

River Wharf

MoD
Sidings

Redmire
22m 13ch

End of Line
22m 12ch

River Nidd

Horton-in-Ribblesdale
242m 43ch

Gag Hill Farm (UWC)
241m 31ch

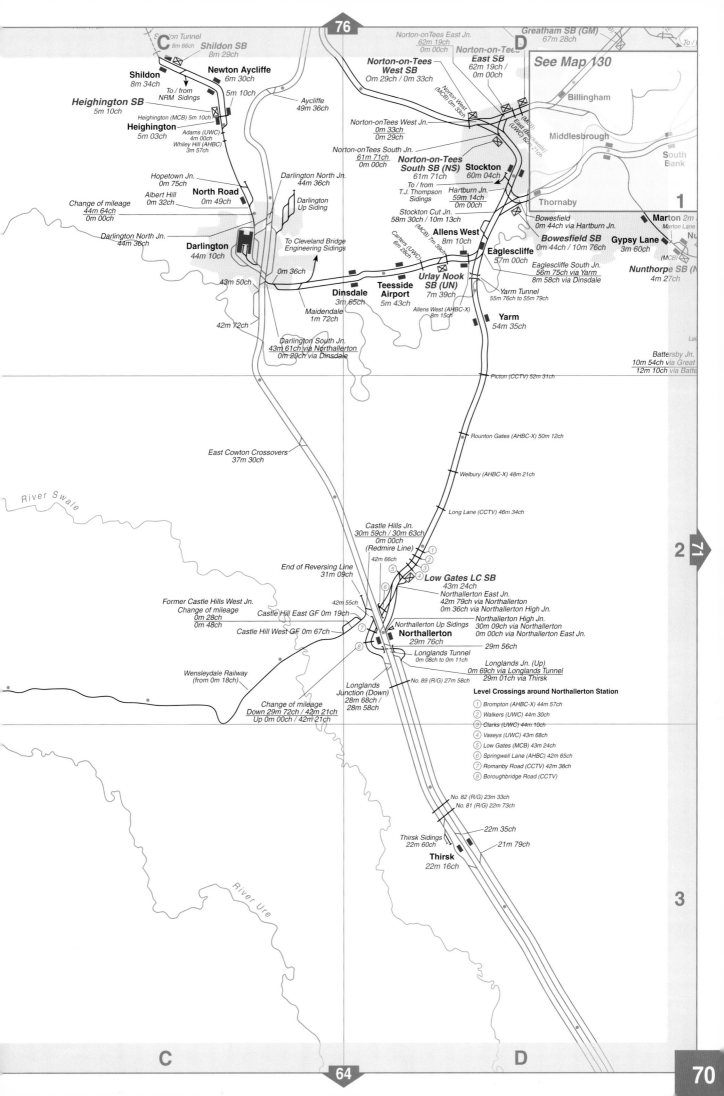

C

Shildon Tunnel 8m 66ch

Shildon SB 8m 29ch

Shildon 8m 34ch

Newton Aycliffe 6m 30ch

5m 10ch

To / from NRM Sidings

Heighington SB 5m 10ch

Heighington 5m 03ch

Heighington (MCB) 5m 10ch

Adams (UWC) 4m 00ch
Whiley Hill (AHBC) 3m 57ch

Aycliffe 49m 36ch

Hopetown Jn. 0m 75ch

Albert Hill 0m 32ch

Change of mileage 44m 64ch / 0m 00ch

Darlington North Jn. 44m 36ch

North Road 0m 49ch

Darlington North Jn. 44m 36ch

Darlington Up Siding

Darlington 44m 10ch

To Cleveland Bridge Engineering Sidings

0m 36ch

43m 50ch

42m 72ch

Dinsdale 3m 65ch

Teesside Airport 5m 43ch

Maidendale 1m 72ch

Darlington South Jn. 43m 61ch via Northallerton 0m 29ch via Dinsdale

Norton-onTees East Jn. 62m 19ch 0m 00ch

Norton-on-Tees West SB 0m 29ch / 0m 33ch

Norton-on-Tees East SB 62m 19ch / 0m 00ch

Norton West (MCB) 0m 33ch

East (Backwells) (UWC) 62m 21ch

Norton-onTees West Jn. 0m 33ch 0m 29ch

Norton-onTees South Jn. 61m 71ch 0m 00ch

Norton-on-Tees South SB (NS) 61m 71ch

Stockton 60m 04ch

To / from T.J. Thompson Sidings

Hartburn Jn. 59m 14ch 0m 00ch

Stockton Cut Jn. 58m 30ch / 10m 13ch

Allens West 8m 10ch

Carters (UWC) 6m 26ch

(MCB) 7m 39ch

Urlay Nook SB (UN) 7m 39ch

Allens West (AHBC-X) 8m 15ch

Eaglescliffe 57m 00ch

Bowesfield 0m 44ch via Hartburn Jn.

Bowesfield SB 0m 44ch / 10m 76ch

Eaglescliffe South Jn. 56m 75ch via Yarm 8m 58ch via Dinsdale

Yarm Tunnel 55m 76ch to 55m 79ch

Yarm 54m 35ch

Marton 2m
Marton Lane

Gypsy Lane 3m 60ch
(MCB)

Nunthorpe SB (N 4m 27ch

See Map 130

Billingham

Middlesbrough

South Bank

Thornaby

1

Battersby Jn. 10m 54ch via Great 12m 10ch via Batte

Picton (CCTV) 52m 31ch

Rounton Gates (AHBC-X) 50m 12ch

Welbury (AHBC-X) 48m 21ch

Long Lane (CCTV) 46m 34ch

East Cowton Crossovers 37m 30ch

River Swale

Castle Hills Jn. 30m 59ch / 30m 63ch 0m 00ch (Redmire Line)

42m 66ch

End of Reversing Line 31m 09ch

① ② ⑤ ③ ④ ⑥

Low Gates LC SB 43m 24ch

Northallerton East Jn. 42m 79ch via Northallerton 0m 36ch via Northallerton High Jn.

Northallerton High Jn. 30m 09ch via Northallerton 0m 00ch via Northallerton East Jn.

Former Castle Hills West Jn. Change of mileage 0m 28ch 0m 48ch

42m 55ch

Castle Hill East GF 0m 19ch

Castle Hill West GF 0m 67ch

⑦

⑧

Northallerton Up Sidings

Northallerton 29m 76ch

29m 56ch

Longlands Tunnel 0m 08ch to 0m 11ch

No. 89 (R/G) 27m 58ch

Longlands Jn. (Up) 0m 69ch via Longlands Tunnel 29m 01ch via Thirsk

Wensleydale Railway (from 0m 18ch)

Longlands Junction (Down) 28m 68ch / 28m 58ch

Change of mileage Down 29m 72ch / 42m 21ch Up 0m 00ch / 42m 21ch

Level Crossings around Northallerton Station

① *Brompton (AHBC-X) 44m 57ch*
② *Walkers (UWC) 44m 30ch*
③ *Clarks (UWC) 44m 10ch*
④ *Vaseys (UWC) 43m 68ch*
⑤ *Low Gates (MCB) 43m 24ch*
⑥ *Springwell Lane (AHBC) 42m 65ch*
⑦ *Romanby Road (CCTV) 42m 38ch*
⑧ *Boroughbridge Road (CCTV)*

River Ure

No. 82 (R/G) 23m 33ch

No. 81 (R/G) 22m 73ch

22m 35ch

Thirsk Sidings 22m 60ch

21m 79ch

Thirsk 22m 16ch

3

2

71

C

D

Greatham SB (GM) 67m 28ch

To I

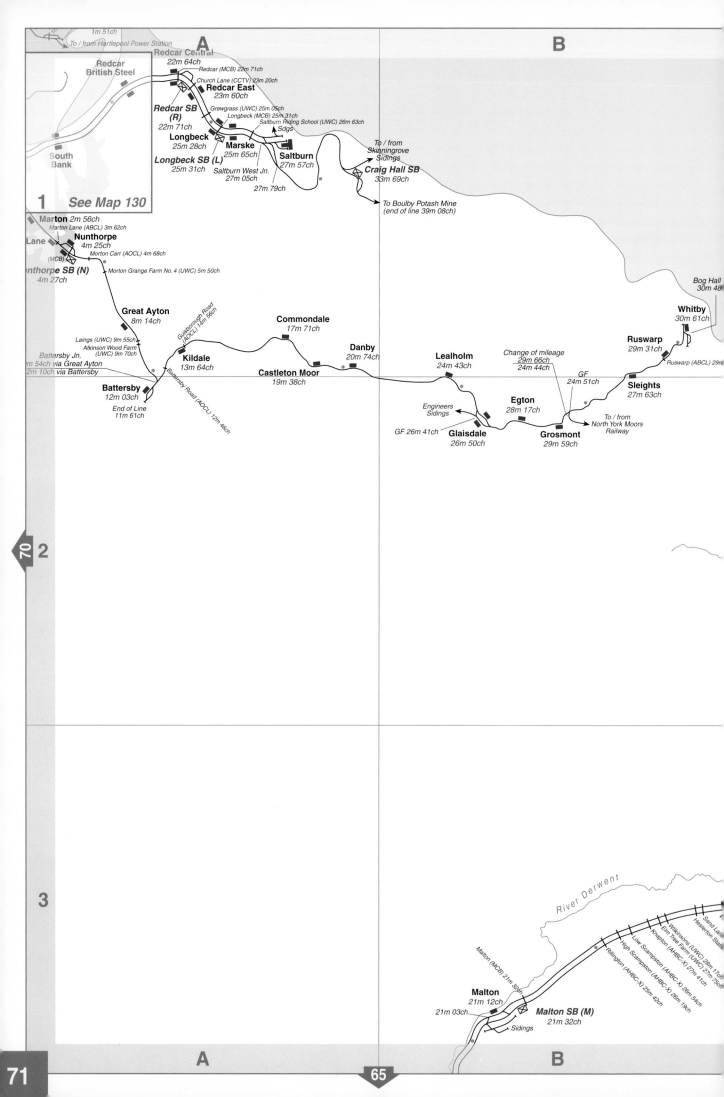

1m 51ch
To / from Hartlepool Power Station

Redcar
British Steel

Redcar Central
22m 64ch

Redcar (MCB) 22m 71ch

Church Lane (CCTV) 23m 20ch

Redcar East
23m 60ch

Redcar SB (R)
22m 71ch

Grewgrass (UWC) 25m 05ch
Longbeck (MCB) 25m 31ch
Saltburn Riding School (UWC) 26m 63ch
Sdgs

Longbeck
25m 28ch

Marske
25m 65ch

Longbeck SB (L)
25m 31ch

Saltburn
27m 57ch

Saltburn West Jn.
27m 05ch

27m 79ch

To / from
Skinningrove
Sidings

Craig Hall SB
33m 69ch

To Boulby Potash Mine
(end of line 39m 08ch)

South
Bank

1 **See Map 130**

Marton *2m 56ch*
Marton Lane (ABCL) 3m 62ch

Lane

Nunthorpe
4m 25ch

(MCB)

Morton Carr (AOCL) 4m 68ch

nthorpe SB (N)
4m 27ch

Morton Grange Farm No. 4 (UWC) 5m 50ch

Bog Hall
30m 48

Whitby
30m 61ch

Great Ayton
8m 14ch

Guisborough Road
(AOCL) 14m 56ch

Commondale
17m 71ch

Danby
20m 74ch

Lealholm
24m 43ch

Change of mileage
29m 66ch
24m 44ch

Ruswarp
29m 31ch

Ruswarp (ABCL) 29m

Laings (UWC) 9m 55ch
Atkinson Wood Farm
(UWC) 9m 70ch

Kildale
13m 64ch

Castleton Moor
19m 38ch

GF
24m 51ch

Sleights
27m 63ch

Battersby Jn.
m 54ch via Great Ayton
2m 10ch via Battersby

Battersby Road (AOCL) 12m 46ch

Egton
28m 17ch

To / from
North York Moors
Railway

Battersby
12m 03ch

End of Line
11m 61ch

Engineers
Sidings

GF 26m 41ch

Glaisdale
26m 50ch

Grosmont
29m 59ch

3

River Derwent

Wilkinsons (UWC) 28m 17ch
Hesterton Stati
Sand Lan
Elm Tree Farm (UWC) 27m 41ch
Knapton (AHBC-X) 26m 54ch
Low Scampston (AHBC-X) 26m 18ch
High Scampston (AHBC-X) 25m 42ch
Rillington (AHBC-X) 25m 42ch

Malton (MCB) 21m 32ch

Malton
21m 12ch

21m 03ch

Malton SB (M)
21m 32ch

Sidings

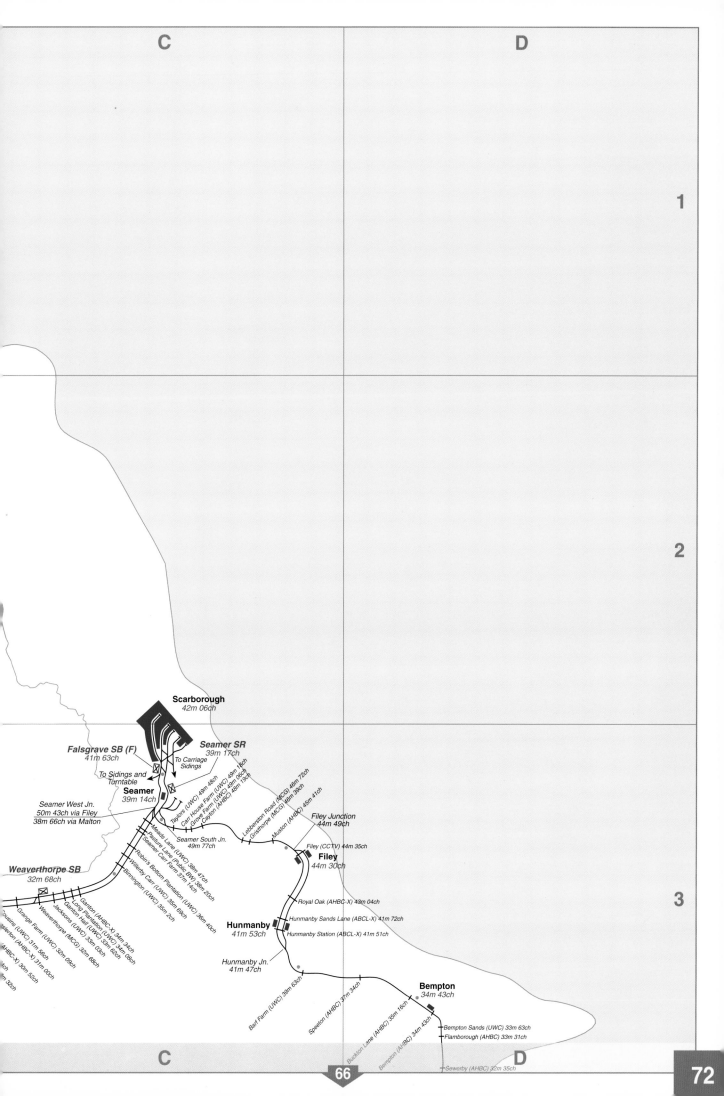

Scarborough
42m 06ch

Falsgrave SB (F)
41m 63ch

Seamer SR
39m 17ch

To Carriage Sidings

To Sidings and Turntable

Seamer
39m 14ch

Seamer West Jn.
50m 43ch via Filey
38m 66ch via Malton

Taylors (UWC) 39m 48ch

Carr House Farm (UWC) 49m 18ch
Grove Farm (UWC) 49m 06ch
Cayton (AHBC) 48m 19ch

Lebberston Road (MCG) 46m 72ch
Gristhorpe (MCG) 46m 39ch
Muston (AHBC) 45m 41ch

Filey Junction
44m 49ch

Meads Lane (UWC) 39m 47ch
Pasture Lane (Public BW) 38m 20ch
Seamer Carr Farm 37m 14ch

Seamer South Jn.
49m 77ch

Filey (CCTV) 44m 35ch

Filey
44m 30ch

Robin's Bottom Plantation (UWC) 36m 40ch
Willerby Carr (UWC) 35m 46ch
Binnington (UWC) 35m 2ch

Weaverthorpe SB
32m 68ch

Royal Oak (AHBC-X) 43m 04ch

Ganton (AHBC-X) 34m 34ch
Long Plantation (UWC) 33m 62ch
Ganton Hall (UWC) 33m 03ch
Jacksons (MCG) 32m 68ch
Weaverthorpe (UWC) 32m 08ch
Grange Farm (UWC) 31m 56ch
Cousins (UWC) 31m 56ch
...erton (AHBC-X) 30m 52ch
...(AHBC-X) 31m 00ch
...m 32ch

Hunmanby Sands Lane (ABCL-X) 41m 72ch

Hunmanby
41m 53ch

Hunmanby Station (ABCL-X) 41m 51ch

Hunmanby Jn.
41m 47ch

Bempton
34m 43ch

Barf Farm (UWC) 39m 63ch

Speeton (AHBC) 37m 34ch

Buckton Lane (AHBC) 35m 16ch

Bempton (AHBC) 34m 43ch

Bempton Sands (UWC) 33m 63ch
Flamborough (AHBC) 33m 31ch

Sewerby (AHBC) 32m 35ch

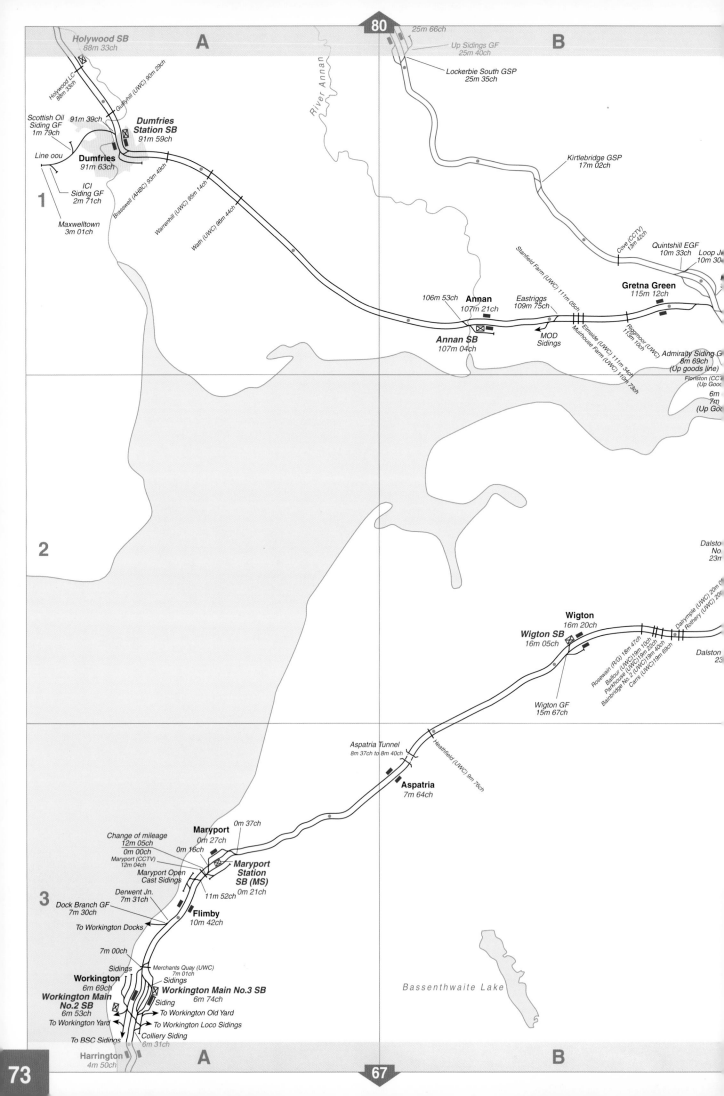

Holywood SB
88m 33ch

River Annan

25m 66ch

Up Sidings GF
25m 40ch

Lockerbie South GSP
25m 35ch

Holywood LC
88m 33ch

Gullyhill (UWC) 90m 29ch

Scottish Oil
Siding GF
1m 79ch

91m 39ch

Dumfries
Station SB
91m 59ch

Dumfries
91m 63ch

Line oou

Brasswell (AHBC) 93m 49ch

Warrenhill (UWC) 95m 14ch

Wath (UWC) 96m 44ch

Kirtlebridge GSP
17m 02ch

ICI
Siding GF
2m 71ch

Maxwelltown
3m 01ch

1

Cove (CCTV)
13m 10ch

Quintshill EGF
10m 33ch

Loop J
10m 30

106m 53ch

Annan
107m 21ch

Stanfield Farm (UWC) 111m 05ch

Eastriggs
109m 75ch

Gretna Green
115m 12ch

Annan SB
107m 04ch

MOD
Sidings

Elmside (UWC) 111m 34ch

Muirhouse Farm (UWC) 110m 73ch

Riggmoor (UWC)
113m 10ch

Admiralty Siding G
8m 69ch
(Up goods line)

Floriston (CC
(Up Good

6m
7m
(Up Goo

2

Dalsto
No.
23n

Wigton
16m 20ch

Wigton SB
16m 05ch

Rosewain (R/G) 18m 47ch

Balfour (UWC)19m 10ch

Parkhouse (UWC)19m 22ch

Bainbridge No. 2 (UWC)19m 40ch

Carrs (UWC)19m 69ch

Dalrymple (UWC) 20m 0

Rothery (UWC) 20m 0

Dalston
23

Wigton GF
15m 67ch

Aspatria Tunnel
8m 37ch to 8m 40ch

Heathfield (UWC) 9m 76ch

Aspatria
7m 64ch

0m 37ch

Maryport
0m 27ch

Change of mileage
12m 05ch
0m 00ch

0m 16ch

Maryport (CCTV)
12m 04ch

Maryport Open
Cast Sidings

**Maryport
Station
SB (MS)**
0m 21ch

Derwent Jn.
7m 31ch

11m 52ch

3

Dock Branch GF
7m 30ch

Flimby
10m 42ch

To Workington Docks

7m 00ch

Sidings

Merchants Quay (UWC)
7m 01ch

Sidings

Workington
6m 69ch

Workington Main No.3 SB
6m 74ch

**Workington Main
No.2 SB**
6m 53ch

Siding

To Workington Old Yard

To Workington Yard

To Workington Loco Sidings

Colliery Siding
6m 31ch

To BSC Sidings

Bassenthwaite Lake

Harrington
4m 50ch

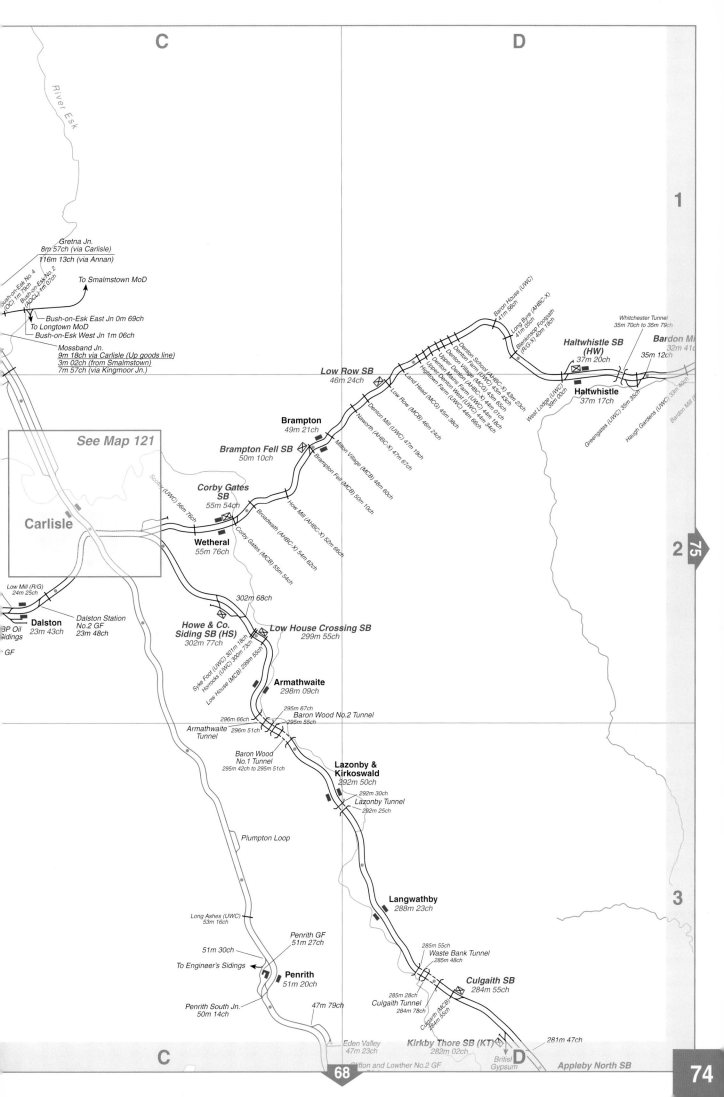

River Esk

Gretna Jn.
8m 57ch (via Carlisle)
116m 13ch (via Annan)

Bush-on-Esk No. 4
(OC) 1m 79ch
Bush-on-Esk No. 2
(AOCL) 1m 07ch

To Smalmstown MoD

Bush-on-Esk East Jn 0m 69ch
To Longtown MoD
Bush-on-Esk West Jn 1m 06ch

Mossband Jn.
9m 18ch via Carlisle (Up goods line)
3m 02ch (from Smalmstown)
7m 57ch (via Kingmoor Jn.)

Low Row SB
46m 24ch

Baron House (UWC)
41m 96ch
Long Byre (AHBC-X)
41m 05ch
Blenkinsop Footpath
(R/G-X) 40m 19ch

Whitchester Tunnel
35m 70ch to 35m 79ch

Haltwhistle SB
(HW)
37m 20ch

Bardon Mi
32m 41c

Denton School (AHBC-X) 43m 23ch
Denton Farm (UWC) 43m 43ch
Denton Village (MCG) 43m 65ch
Upper Denton (AHBC-X) 44m 01ch
Denton Mains (UWC) 44m 18ch
Upper Denton West (UWC) 44m 34ch
Hightown Farm (UWC) 44m 66ch

Land Head (MCG) 46m 24ch

Low Row (MCB) 46m 24ch

West Lodge (UWC)
39m 00ch

Haltwhistle
37m 17ch

Bardon Mill (
33m 40ch

Greengates (UWC) 35m 35ch
Haugh Gardens (UWC) 33m 44ch

Brampton
49m 21ch

Naworth (AHBC-X) 47m 19ch

Denton Mill (UWC) 47m 19ch

Brampton Fell SB
50m 10ch

Milton Village (MCB) 47m 67ch

Brampton Fell (MCB) 50m 10ch

Corby Gates
SB
55m 54ch

How Mill (AHBC-X) 52m 66ch

Scotby (UWC) 56m 76ch

Broadwath (AHBC-X) 54m 62ch

Corby Gates (MCB) 55m 54ch

Wetheral
55m 76ch

Carlisle

See Map 121

Low Mill (R/G)
24m 25ch

302m 68ch

Dalston
23m 43ch
BP Oil
Sidings
GF

Dalston Station
No.2 GF
23m 48ch

Howe & Co.
Siding SB (HS)
302m 77ch

Low House Crossing SB
299m 55ch

Syke Foot (UWC) 301m 18ch
Horrocks (UWC) 300m 73ch
Low House (MCB) 299m 55ch

Armathwaite
298m 09ch

295m 67ch
Baron Wood No.2 Tunnel
295m 55ch

296m 66ch

Armathwaite
Tunnel
296m 51ch

Baron Wood
No.1 Tunnel
295m 42ch to 295m 51ch

Lazonby &
Kirkoswald
292m 50ch

292m 30ch
Lazonby Tunnel
292m 25ch

Plumpton Loop

Langwathby
288m 23ch

Long Ashes (UWC)
53m 16ch

Penrith GF
51m 27ch

51m 30ch

To Engineer's Sidings

Penrith
51m 20ch

Penrith South Jn.
50m 14ch

47m 79ch

285m 55ch
Waste Bank Tunnel
285m 48ch

Culgaith SB
284m 55ch

285m 28ch
Culgaith Tunnel
284m 78ch

Culgaith (MCB)
284m 55ch

Kirkby Thore SB (KT)
282m 02ch

281m 47ch

Eden Valley
47m 23ch

British
Gypsum

Appleby North SB

Clifton and Lowther No.2 GF

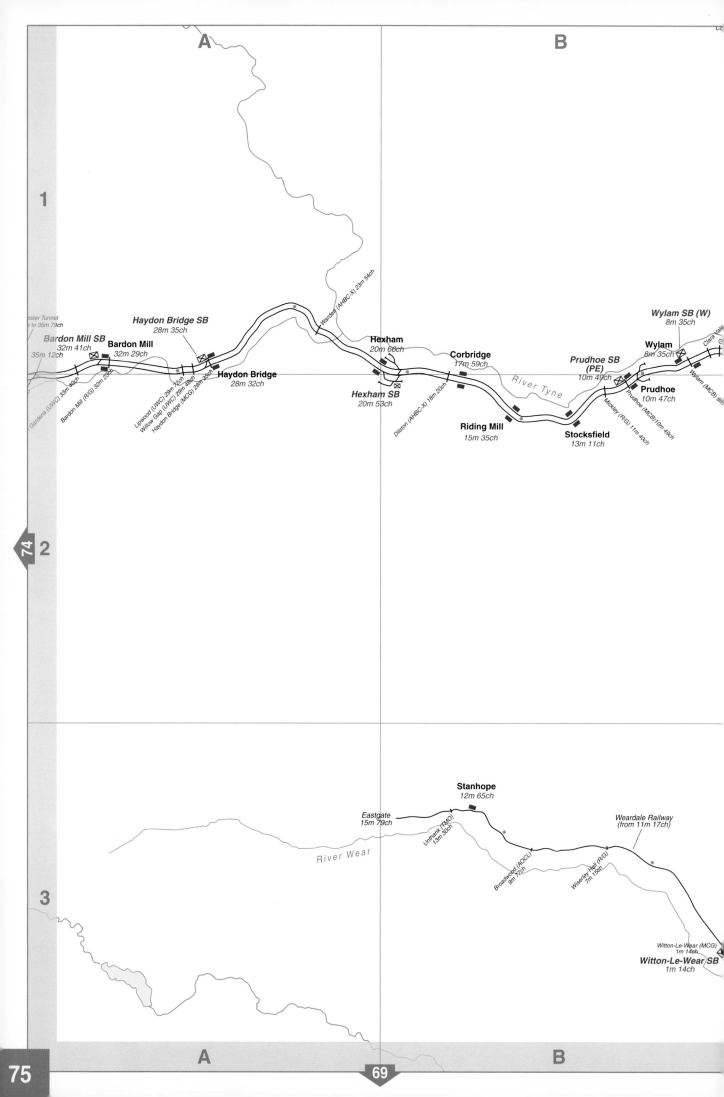

1

ester Tunnel
to 35m 79ch

Warden (AHBC-X) 23m 54ch

Wylam SB (W)
8m 35ch

Bardon Mill SB
32m 41ch
35m 12ch

Bardon Mill
32m 29ch

Haydon Bridge SB
28m 35ch

Hexham
20m 66ch

Corbridge
17m 59ch

Wylam
8m 35ch

Prudhoe SB
(PE)
10m 49ch

Haydon Bridge
28m 32ch

Prudhoe
10m 47ch

Gardens (UWC) 33m 40ch

Bardon Mill (R/G) 32m 23ch

Lipwood (UWC) 29m 42ch

Willow Gap (UWC) 29m 18ch

Haydon Bridge (MCG) 28m 36ch

Hexham SB
20m 53ch

Dilston (AHBC-X) 18m 20ch

Riding Mill
15m 35ch

Stocksfield
13m 11ch

River Tyne

Clara Vale

Mickley (R/G) 11m 40ch

Prudhoe (MCB)10m 49ch

Wylam (MCB) 8

74 **2**

3

Stanhope
12m 65ch

Eastgate
15m 79ch

Unthank (TMO)
13m 30ch

Weardale Railway
(from 11m 17ch)

River Wear

Broadwood (AOCL)
9m 12ch

Wiserley Hall (R/G)
7m 15ch

Witton-Le-Wear (MCG)
1m 14ch

Witton-Le-Wear SB
1m 14ch

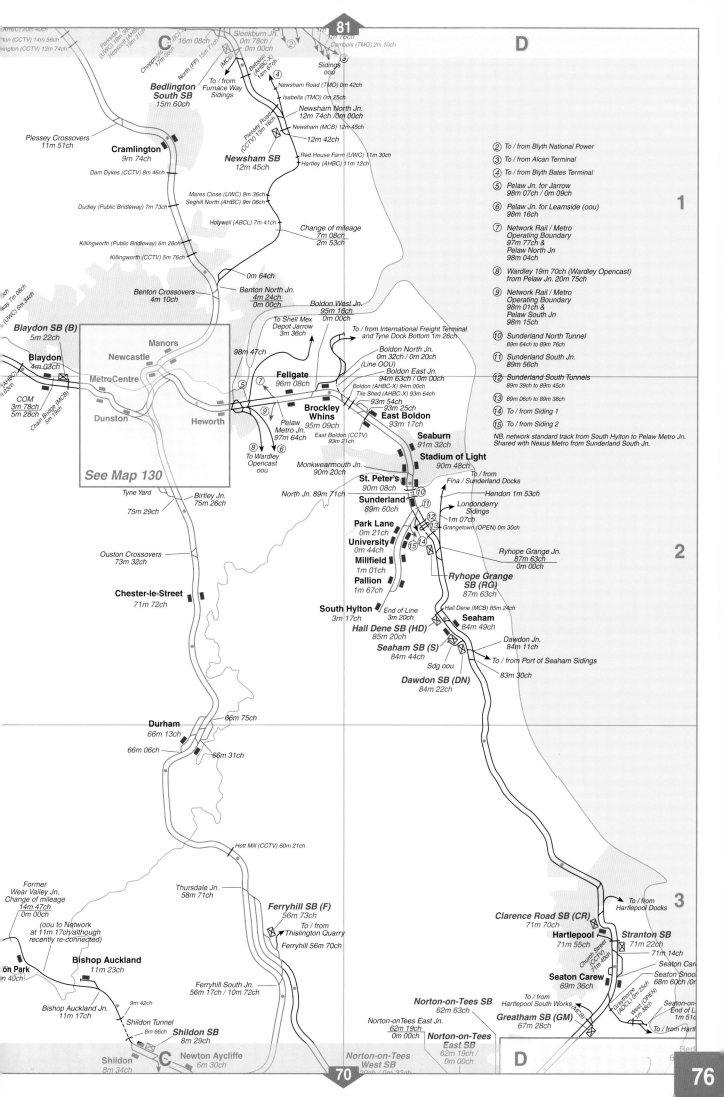

D

ARBC) 20m 40ch
-ton (CCTV) 14m 56ch
-ington (CCTV) 13m 74ch

Parkside (UWC) 19m 38ch
Hepscott (AHBC) 18m 21ch

Choppington 17m 00ch

16m 08ch

Sleekburn Jn.
0m 78ch /
0m 00ch

(2)

(MCB)

North (FP) 15m 1ch

1m 76ch
Cambois (TMO) 2m 10ch

(3)

Bedlington
South SB
15m 60ch

(C)

(MCB) 15m 01ch

To / from
Furnace Way
Sidings

Bebside
(AHBC-X)
14m 67ch

(4)

Sidings
oou

Plessey Crossovers
11m 51ch

Cramlington
9m 74ch

Newsham SB
12m 45ch

Plessey Road
(CCTV) 13m 16ch

Newsham Road (TMO) 0m 42ch

Isabella (TMO) 0m 25ch

Newsham North Jn.
12m 74ch / 0m 00ch

Newsham (MCB) 12m 45ch

12m 42ch

Dam Dykes (CCTV) 8m 46ch

Red House Farm (UWC) 11m 30ch
Hartley (AHBC) 11m 12ch

Dudley (Public Bridleway) 7m 73ch

Mares Close (UWC) 9m 36ch
Seghill North (AHBC) 9m 06ch

Holywell (ABCL) 7m 41ch

Change of mileage
7m 08ch
2m 53ch

Killingworth (Public Bridleway) 6m 28ch

Killingworth (CCTV) 5m 76ch

0m 64ch

(2) *To / from Blyth National Power*

(3) *To / from Alcan Terminal*

(4) *To / from Blyth Bates Terminal*

(5) *Pelaw Jn. for Jarrow*
98m 07ch / 0m 09ch

(6) *Pelaw Jn. for Leamside (oou)*
98m 16ch

(7) *Network Rail / Metro*
Operating Boundary
97m 77ch &
Pelaw North Jn
98m 04ch

(8) *Wardley 19m 70ch (Wardley Opencast)*
from Pelaw Jn. 20m 75ch

(9) *Network Rail / Metro*
Operating Boundary
98m 01ch &
Pelaw South Jn
98m 15ch

(10) *Sunderland North Tunnel*
89m 64ch to 89m 76ch

(11) *Sunderland South Jn.*
89m 56ch

(12) *Sunderland South Tunnels*
89m 39ch to 89m 45ch

(13) *89m 06ch to 89m 38ch*

(14) *To / from Siding 1*

(15) *To / from Siding 2*

NB. network standard track from South Hylton to Pelaw Metro Jn.
Shared with Nexus Metro from Sunderland South Jn.

Benton Crossovers
4m 10ch

Benton North Jn.
4m 24ch
0m 00ch

Boldon West Jn.
95m 16ch
0m 00ch

To Shell Mex
Depot Jarrow
3m 36ch

To / from International Freight Terminal
and Tyne Dock Bottom 1m 26ch

Blaydon SB (B)
5m 22ch

Blaydon
4m 03ch

Manors

Newcastle

MetroCentre

COM
3m 78ch
5m 28ch

Chain Bridge (MCB)
5m 19ch

Dunston

Heworth

98m 47ch

Fellgate
96m 08ch

Brockley
Whins
95m 25ch

(5)

(7)

(9)

Boldon North Jn.
0m 32ch / 0m 20ch
(Line OOU)

Boldon East Jn.
94m 63ch / 0m 00ch

Boldon (AHBC-X) 94m 00ch
Tile Shed (AHBC-X) 93m 64ch

93m 54ch

East Boldon
93m 17ch

See Map 130

Pelaw
Metro Jn.
97m 64ch

(8)

(6)

To Wardley
Opencast
oou

East Boldon (CCTV)
93m 21ch

Seaburn
91m 32ch

Stadium of Light
90m 48ch

Tyne Yard

Birtley Jn.
75m 26ch

75m 29ch

Monkwearmouth Jn.
90m 20ch

St. Peter's
90m 08ch

North Jn. 89m 71ch

Sunderland
89m 60ch

(10)

(11)

To / from
Fina / Sunderland Docks

Hendon 1m 53ch

Londonderry
Sidings
1m 07ch

Grangetown (OPEN) 0m 30ch

Ouston Crossovers
73m 32ch

Park Lane
0m 21ch

University
0m 44ch

Millfield
1m 01ch

Pallion
1m 67ch

(12)

(13)

(14)

(15)

Ryhope Grange Jn.
87m 63ch
0m 00ch

Chester-le-Street
71m 72ch

South Hylton
3m 17ch

End of Line
3m 20ch

Ryhope Grange
SB (RG)
87m 63ch

Hall Dene (MCB) 85m 24ch

Seaham
84m 49ch

Hall Dene SB (HD)
85m 20ch

Dawdon Jn.
84m 11ch

66m 75ch

Durham
66m 13ch

Seaham SB (S)
84m 44ch

To / from Port of Seaham Sidings

66m 06ch

66m 31ch

Sdg oou

83m 30ch

Dawdon SB (DN)
84m 22ch

Hett Mill (CCTV) 60m 21ch

Former
Wear Valley Jn.
Change of mileage
14m 47ch
0m 00ch

(oou to Network
at 11m 17ch although
recently re-connected)

Thursdale Jn.
58m 71ch

Ferryhill SB (F)
56m 73ch

To / from
Thislington Quarry

Ferryhill 56m 70ch

To / from
Hartlepool Docks

(3)

Clarence Road SB (CR)
71m 70ch

Stranton SB
71m 22ch

Hartlepool
71m 55ch

71m 14ch

Bishop Auckland
11m 23ch

Church Street
(CCTV) 71m 40ch

Seaton Car

Ferryhill South Jn.
56m 17ch / 10m 72ch

Seaton Carew
69m 36ch

Seaton Snoo
68m 60ch / 0r

Norton-on-Tees SB
62m 63ch

To / from
Hartlepool South Works

Grathorpe
(AOCL) 0m 25ch
West (OPEN)
1m 36ch

Seaton-on
End of Li
1m 51

-on Park

Bishop Auckland Jn.
11m 17ch

9m 42ch

Shildon Tunnel
8m 66ch

Shildon SB
8m 29ch

Norton-on Tees East Jn.
62m 19ch /
0m 00ch

Norton-on-Tees
East SB
62m 19ch /
0m 00ch

Greatham SB (GM)
67m 28ch

(MCB)

To / from Hart

Shildon
8m 34ch

(C)

Newton Aycliffe
6m 30ch

Norton-on-Tees
West SB
62m 19ch / 0m 00ch

(D)

Red

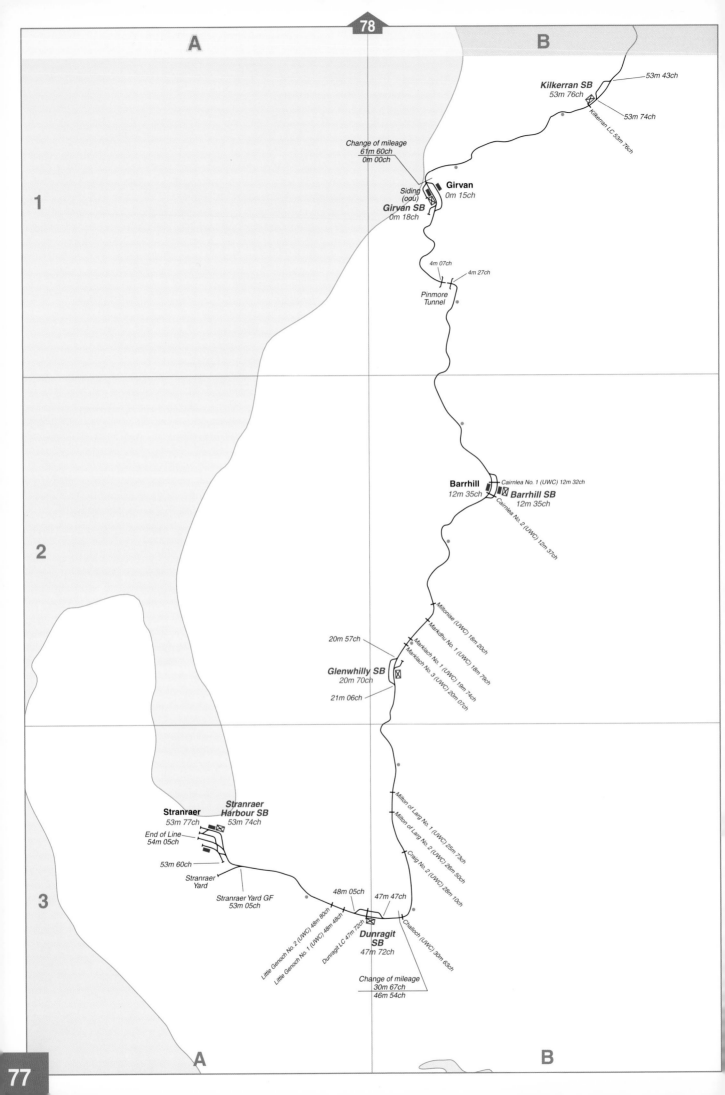

A

B

Kilkerran SB
53m 76ch

53m 43ch

53m 74ch

Kilkerran LC 53m 76ch

Change of mileage
61m 60ch
0m 00ch

Siding
(oou)
Girvan SB
0m 18ch

Girvan
0m 15ch

4m 07ch

4m 27ch

Pinmore
Tunnel

1

Barrhill
12m 35ch

Cairnlea No. 1 (UWC) 12m 32ch

Barrhill SB
12m 35ch

Cairnlea No. 2 (UWC) 12m 37ch

2

Miltonise (UWC) 18m 20ch

Markdhu No. 1 (UWC) 18m 79ch

20m 57ch

Marklach No. 1 (UWC) 19m 74ch

Marklach No. 3 (UWC) 20m 07ch

Glenwhilly SB
20m 70ch

21m 06ch

Milton of Larg No. 1 (UWC) 25m 73ch

Milton of Larg No. 2 (UWC) 26m 50ch

Craig No. 2 (UWC) 28m 10ch

Stranraer
53m 77ch

**Stranraer
Harbour SB**
53m 74ch

End of Line
54m 05ch

53m 60ch

Stranraer
Yard

Stranraer Yard GF
53m 05ch

Little Genoch No. 2 (UWC) 48m 80ch

Little Genoch No. 1 (UWC) 48m 48ch

Dunragit LC 47m 72ch

48m 05ch

47m 47ch

**Dunragit
SB**
47m 72ch

Challoch (UWC) 30m 63ch

Change of mileage
30m 67ch
46m 54ch

3

A

B

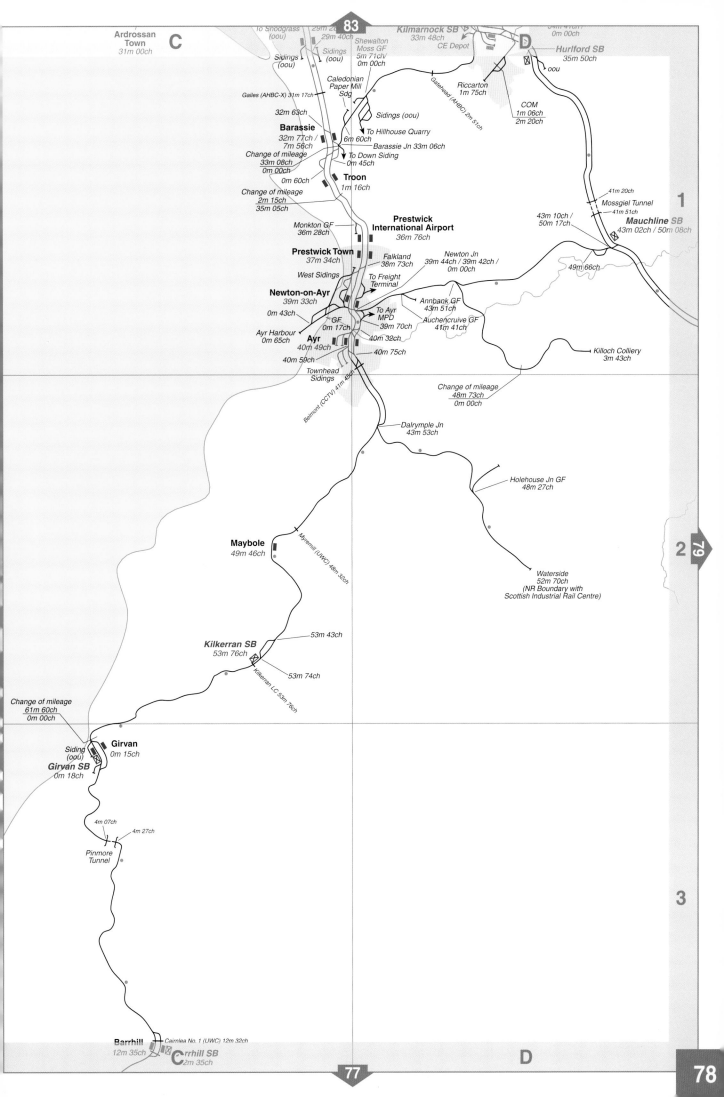

Ardrossan
Town
31m 00ch C

To Snodgrass
(oou)

29m 20ch
29m 40ch

Sidings
(oou)

Sidings
(oou)

Shewalton
Moss GF
5m 71ch/
0m 00ch

Kilmarnock SB
33m 48ch

CE Depot

D

Hurlford SB
35m 50ch

Gailes (AHBC-X) 31m 17ch

Caledonian
Paper Mill
Sdg

Gatehead (AHBC) 2m 51ch

Riccarton
1m 75ch

oou

32m 63ch

Barassie
32m 77ch /
7m 56ch

Change of mileage
33m 08ch
0m 00ch

6m 60ch

Sidings *(oou)*

To Hillhouse Quarry

Barassie Jn 33m 06ch

To Down Siding
0m 45ch

COM
1m 06ch
2m 20ch

0m 60ch **Troon**
1m 16ch

Change of mileage
2m 15ch
35m 05ch

41m 20ch

Mossgiel Tunnel
41m 51ch

43m 10ch /
50m 17ch

Mauchline *SB*
43m 02ch / 50m 08ch

Monkton GF
36m 28ch

**Prestwick
International Airport**
36m 76ch

Prestwick Town
37m 34ch

Falkland
38m 73ch

Newton Jn
39m 44ch / 39m 42ch /
0m 00ch

49m 66ch

West Sidings

To Freight
Terminal

Newton-on-Ayr
39m 33ch

Annbank GF
43m 51ch

0m 43ch

GF
0m 17ch

To Ayr
MPD

Auchencruive GF
41m 41ch

Ayr Harbour
0m 65ch **Ayr**
40m 49ch

39m 70ch

40m 32ch

Killoch Colliery
3m 43ch

40m 59ch

40m 75ch

Townhead
Sidings

Change of mileage
48m 73ch
0m 00ch

Belmont (CCTV) 41m 45ch

Dalrymple Jn
43m 53ch

Holehouse Jn GF
48m 27ch

Maybole
49m 46ch

Myremill (UWC) 48m 32ch

Waterside
52m 70ch
*(NR Boundary with
Scottish Industrial Rail Centre)*

53m 43ch

Kilkerran SB
53m 76ch

53m 74ch

Kilkerran LC 53m 76ch

Change of mileage
61m 60ch
0m 00ch

Siding
(oou)

Girvan
0m 15ch

Girvan SB
0m 18ch

4m 07ch

4m 27ch

Pinmore
Tunnel

Barrhill
12m 35ch

Cairnlea No. 1 (UWC) 12m 32ch

Barrhill SB
12m 35ch

D

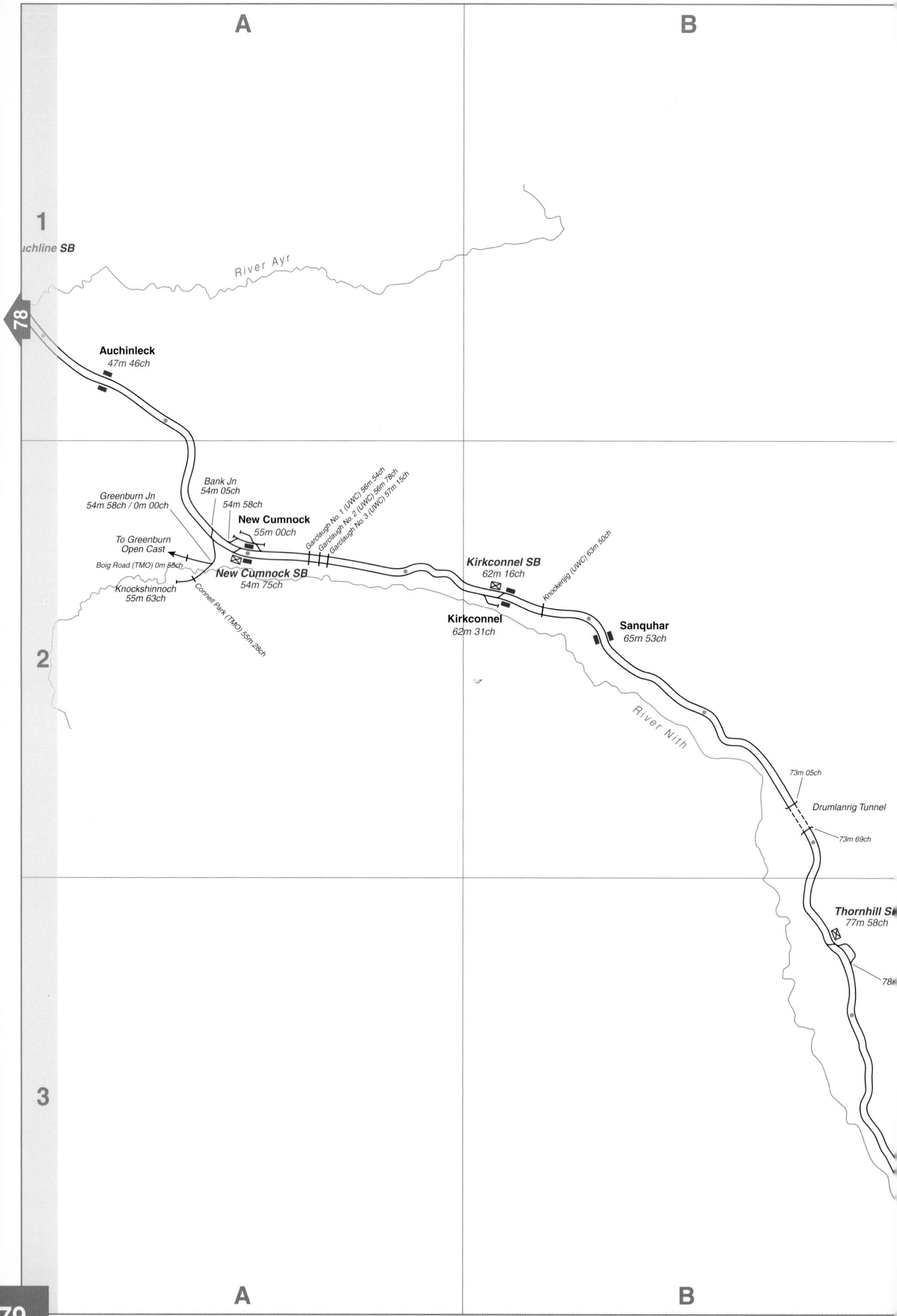

1

uchline SB

River Ayr

78

Auchinleck
47m 46ch

Greenburn Jn
54m 58ch / 0m 00ch

Bank Jn
54m 05ch
54m 58ch

New Cumnock
55m 00ch

Garclaugh No. 1 (UWC) 56m 54ch
Garclaugh No. 2 (UWC) 56m 78ch
Garclaugh No. 3 (UWC) 57m 15ch

To Greenburn
Open Cast

Boig Road (TMO) 0m 55ch

New Cumnock SB
54m 75ch

Knockshinnoch
55m 63ch

Connell Park (TMO) 55m 28ch

Kirkconnel SB
62m 16ch

Knockenjig (UWC) 63m 50ch

Kirkconnel
62m 31ch

Sanquhar
65m 53ch

River Nith

2

73m 05ch

Drumlanrig Tunnel

73m 69ch

Thornhill S
77m 58ch

78

3

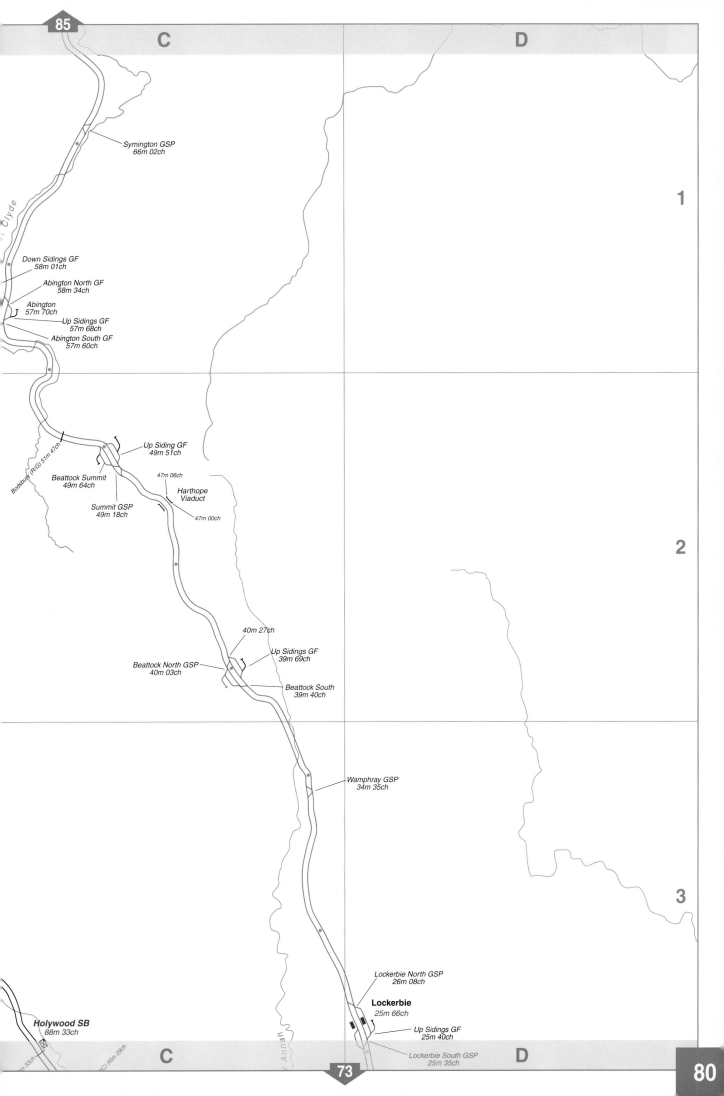

C

1

Symington GSP
66m 02ch

R. Clyde

Down Sidings GF
58m 01ch

Abington North GF
58m 34ch

Abington
57m 70ch

Up Sidings GF
57m 68ch

Abington South GF
57m 60ch

Bodsbury (R/G) 51m 47ch

Up Siding GF
49m 51ch

Beattock Summit
49m 64ch

47m 06ch

Harthope
Viaduct

Summit GSP
49m 18ch

47m 00ch

2

40m 27ch

Up Sidings GF
39m 69ch

Beattock North GSP
40m 03ch

Beattock South
39m 40ch

Wamphray GSP
34m 35ch

3

Lockerbie North GSP
26m 08ch

Lockerbie
25m 66ch

Holywood SB
88m 33ch

R. Annan

Up Sidings GF
25m 40ch

Lockerbie South GSP
25m 35ch

88m 33ch

(C) 90m 23ch

C

D

Easington (Public FP) 51m 72ch
Belford Burn (Public FP) 51m 64ch
51m 55ch

Belford (CCTV) 51m 45ch

51m 54ch

No. 174 (R/G) 50m 37ch

d Crossovers
m 39ch

Lucker (CCTV) 49m 17ch

No. 170 (Private Bridleway) 48m 63ch

No. 169 (Private Bridleway) 48m 18ch

No. 167 (Private Bridleway) 47m 57ch

Newham (CCTV) 47m 09ch

Chathill
46m 01ch

Chathill (CCTV) 45m 78ch

Chathill Crossovers
45m 67ch

No. 163 (Private Bridleway) 45m 10ch

No. 162 (Private Bridleway) 43m 65ch

Fallodon (CCTV) 43m 45ch

Christon Bank (CCTV) 43m 00ch

No. 161 (Private Bridleway) 42m 46ch

No. 158A (Private Bridleway) 40m 71ch

Stamford (CCTV) 40m 39ch

Little Mill Crossovers
39m 30ch

Little Mill (CCTV) 39m 34ch

1

No. 155A (Private Bridleway) 35m 74ch

Alnmouth SB (A)
34m 76ch

Alnmouth
34m 69ch

Alnmouth (R/G) 34m 63ch

No. 155 (Private Bridleway) 34m 38ch

34m 62ch

Wooden Gate 33m 71ch

33m 72ch

Wooden Gate Crossovers
33m 65ch

Warkworth (CCTV) 31m 67ch

No. 152 (Private Bridleway) 31m 42ch

No. 150 (Private Bridleway) 29m 51ch

Acklington
28m 43ch

2

Chevington North Crossovers
26m 55ch

26m 37ch

Chevington (CCTV) 25m 49ch

25m 55ch

To / from Widdrington Sidings

Felton Lane (CCTV) 25m 16ch

24m 63ch

Widdrington (CCTV) 23m 23ch

Widdrington Sidings Crossover
24m 60ch

Widdrington
23m 20ch

Ulgham Grange (CCTV) 22m 24ch

To / from
Butterwell
Opencast

Hirst Lane (MCG)
3m 21ch

Morpeth North Jn.
17m 26ch via Cramlington
20m 46ch via Bedlington North

Butterwell Jn.
20m 63ch

Ulgham Lane (CCTV) 20m 52ch

Longhirst (CCTV) 20m 17ch

Ashington SB
3m 02ch

① Ashington Jn. 3m 03ch

Green Lane (AHBC) 2m 43ch

① To / from Alcan Smelter Siding / Alcan Power Station / Lynemouth Alcan SB

② To / from Blyth National Power

③ To / from Alcan Terminal

④ To / from Blyth Bates Terminal

Morpeth
Electrification
Depot

Pegswood
18m 44ch

Morpeth North (CCTV) 16m 78ch

North Seaton (MCB) 1m 76ch

⊠ **Marchey's House SB** 1m 41ch

Morpeth SB (M)
16m 63ch

Marchey's House Jn.
1m 35ch / 0m 00ch

Marchey's House (MCB) 1m 41ch

Morpeth Jn.
16m 56ch via Cramlington
20m 47ch via Bedlington North

20m 07ch

North (MCB)
15m 71ch / 0m 00ch

Winning Jn. 0m 32ch / 0m 31ch

Winning SB 0m 36ch

Hepscott Jn.
19m 44ch

**Bedlington
North SB (BN)**
15m 71ch / 0m 00ch

(MCB)

(MCB)

⊠ **Freemans SB (F)**
1m 31ch

3

Morpeth
16m 50ch

20m 04ch

Parkside Farm
(UWC) 19m 38ch

West
Sleekburn Jn.
0m 78ch /
0m 00ch

1m 63ch

1m 76ch

Coopies Lane (AHBC) 20m 40ch

Hepscott (AHBC)
19m 21ch

16m 08ch

Cambois (TMO) 2m 10ch

Clifton (CCTV) 14m 56ch

Choppington (AHBC)
17m 06ch

②

Stannington (CCTV) 13m 74ch

North (FP) 15m 71ch

To / from
Furnace Way
Sidings

③

Sidings
ooII

Beside
(AHBC-X)
14m 6ch

④

**Bedlington
South SB**
15m 60ch

Newsham Road (TMO) 0m 42ch

Isabella (TMO) 0m 25ch

Newsham North Jn.
12m 74ch / 0m 00ch

Plessey Crossovers
11m 51ch

Plessey Road
(CCTV) 13m 16ch

Newsham (MCB) 12m 45ch

12m 42ch

Cramlington
9m 74ch

Red House Farm (UWC) 11m 30ch

Hartley (AHBC) 11m 12ch

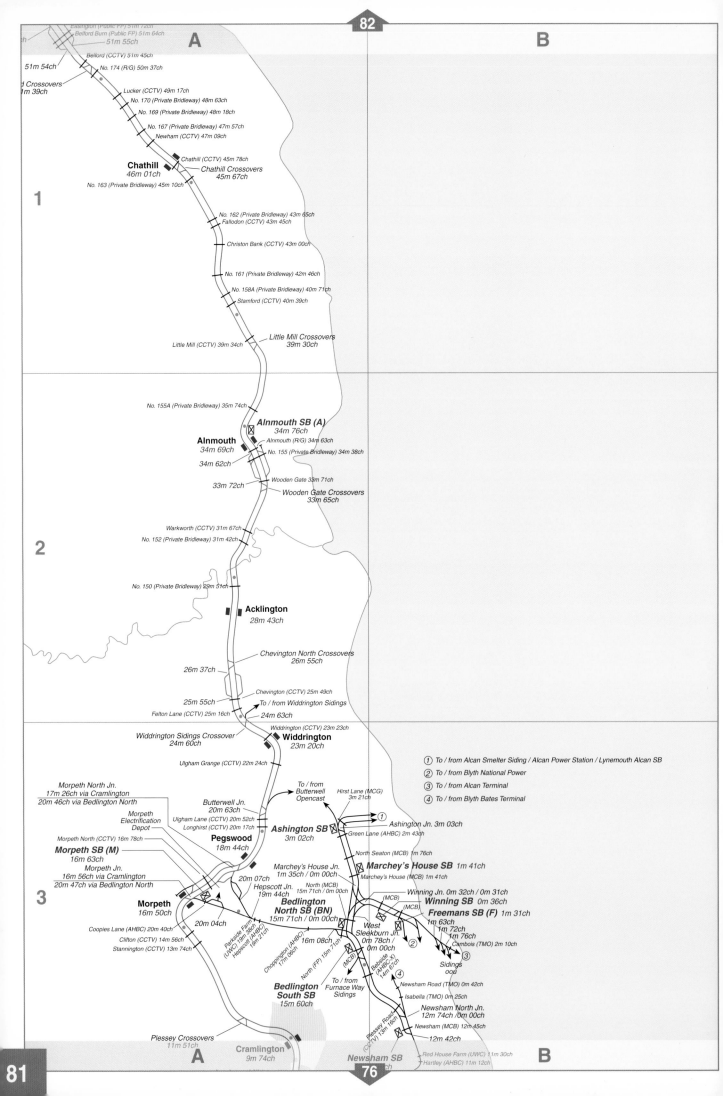

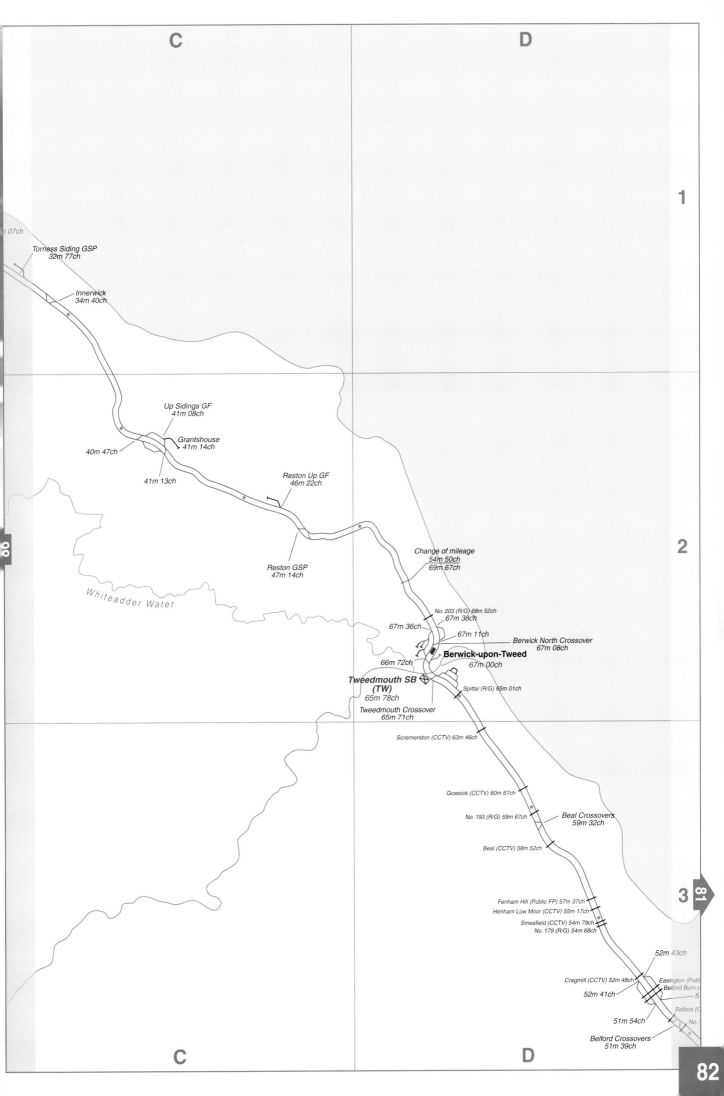

C

D

1

Torness Siding GSP
32m 77ch

n 07ch

Innerwick
34m 40ch

Up Sidings GF
41m 08ch

Grantshouse
41m 14ch

40m 47ch

41m 13ch

Reston Up GF
46m 22ch

2

Change of mileage
54m 50ch
69m 67ch

Reston GSP
47m 14ch

Whiteadder Water

No. 203 (R/G) 68m 52ch
67m 38ch

67m 36ch

67m 11ch

Berwick North Crossover
67m 08ch

66m 72ch

Berwick-upon-Tweed
67m 00ch

Tweedmouth SB
(TW)
65m 78ch

Spittal (R/G) 65m 01ch

Tweedmouth Crossover
65m 71ch

Scremerston (CCTV) 63m 46ch

Goswick (CCTV) 60m 67ch

No. 193 (R/G) 59m 67ch

Beal Crossovers
59m 32ch

Beal (CCTV) 58m 52ch

Fenham Hill (Public FP) 57m 37ch
Henham Low Moor (CCTV) 55m 17ch
Smeafield (CCTV) 54m 79ch
No. 179 (R/G) 54m 68ch

3

81

52m 43ch

Cragmill (CCTV) 52m 48ch

Easington (Publ
Belford Burn (

52m 41ch

5

Belford (C

51m 54ch

No.

Belford Crossovers
51m 39ch

C

D

82

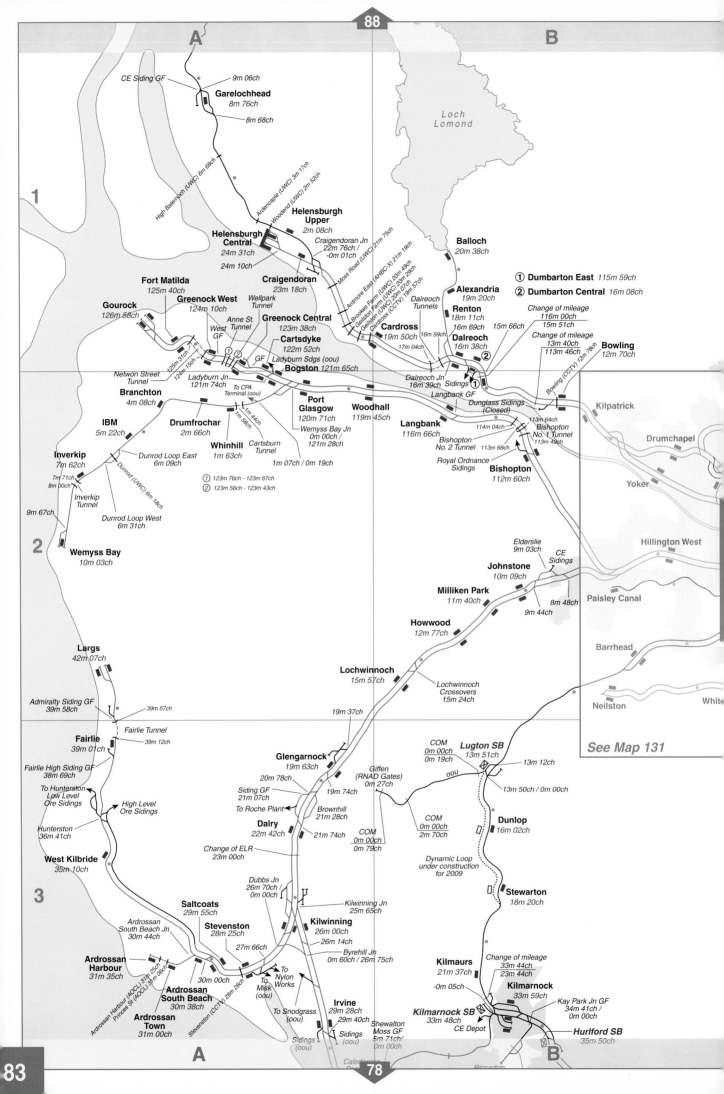

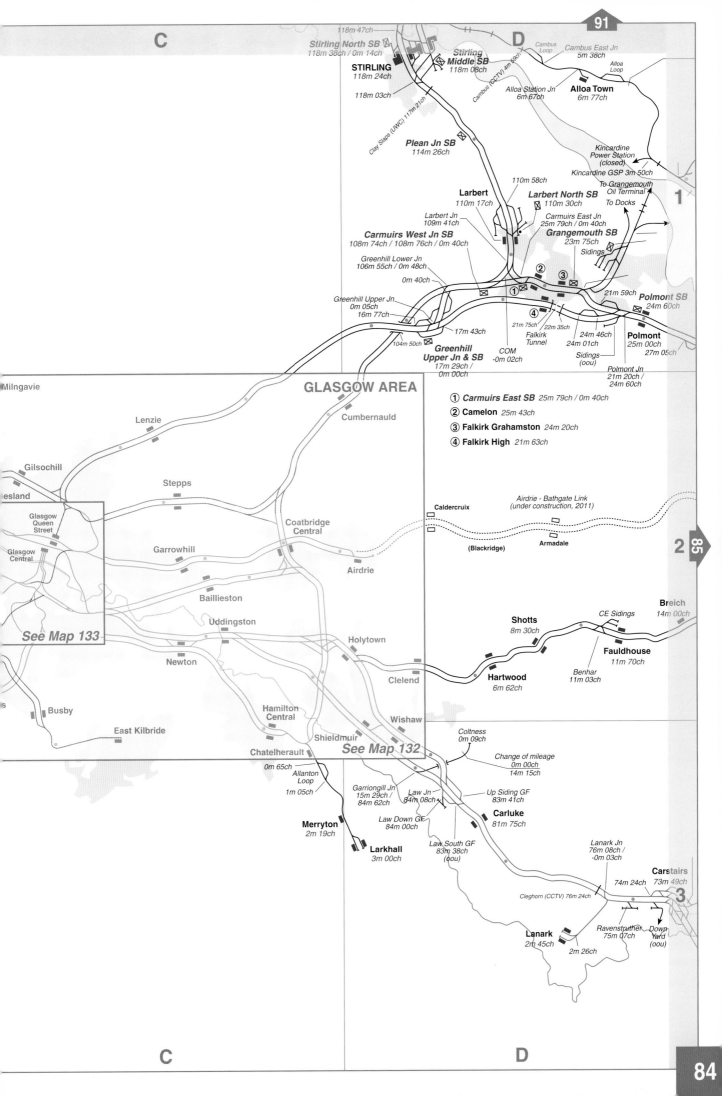

118m 47ch
Stirling North SB
118m 38ch / 0m 14ch

Cambus Loop   Cambus East Jn
5m 38ch

Stirling Middle SB
118m 08ch

Alloa Loop

STIRLING
118m 24ch

Cambus (CCTV) 4m 50ch   Alloa Station Jn
6m 67ch   **Alloa Town**
6m 77ch

118m 03ch

Clay Slaps (UWC) 117m 21ch

Plean Jn SB
114m 26ch

Kincardine Power Station (closed)
Kincardine GSP 3m 50ch

110m 58ch

To Grangemouth Oil Terminal
To Docks

1

Larbert
110m 17ch

Larbert North SB
110m 30ch

Larbert Jn
109m 41ch

Carmuirs East Jn
25m 79ch / 0m 40ch

Carmuirs West Jn SB
108m 74ch / 108m 76ch / 0m 40ch

Grangemouth SB
23m 75ch

Sidings

Greenhill Lower Jn
106m 55ch / 0m 48ch

② ③

0m 40ch

①

21m 59ch   **Polmont SB**
24m 60ch

Greenhill Upper Jn
0m 05ch
16m 77ch

④

21m 75ch   *22m 35ch*

24m 46ch
24m 01ch

Polmont
25m 00ch
27m 05ch

17m 43ch

Falkirk Tunnel

104m 50ch   **Greenhill Upper Jn & SB**
17m 29ch / 0m 00ch

COM -0m 02ch

Sidings (oou)

Polmont Jn
21m 20ch / 24m 60ch

GLASGOW AREA

① **Carmuirs East SB** *25m 79ch / 0m 40ch*
② **Camelon** *25m 43ch*
③ **Falkirk Grahamston** *24m 20ch*
④ **Falkirk High** *21m 63ch*

Milngavie

Lenzie

Cumbernauld

Gilsochill

Stepps

...esland

Glasgow Queen Street

Coatbridge Central

Caldercruix

Airdrie - Bathgate Link
(under construction, 2011)

Glasgow Central

Garrowhill

Airdrie

Armadale

(Blackridge)

Baillieston

Breich
14m 00ch

CE Sidings

Uddingston

Holytown

Shotts
8m 30ch

Fauldhouse
11m 70ch

See Map 133

Newton

Clelend

Benhar
11m 03ch

Busby

Hamilton Central

Wishaw

Hartwood
6m 62ch

East Kilbride

Shieldmuir

Coltness
0m 09ch

Chatelherault

See Map 132

Change of mileage
0m 00ch
14m 15ch

0m 65ch   *Allanton Loop*

1m 05ch

Garriongill Jn
15m 29ch / 84m 62ch   *Law Jn*
84m 08ch   *Up Siding GF*
83m 41ch

Law Down GF
84m 00ch

Carluke
81m 75ch

Merryton
2m 19ch

Law South GF
83m 38ch
(oou)

Larkhall
3m 00ch

Lanark Jn
76m 08ch / -0m 03ch

Carstairs
73m 49ch

74m 24ch

Cleghorn (CCTV) 76m 24ch

Ravenstruther
75m 07ch   *Down Yard*
(oou)

Lanark
2m 45ch

2m 26ch

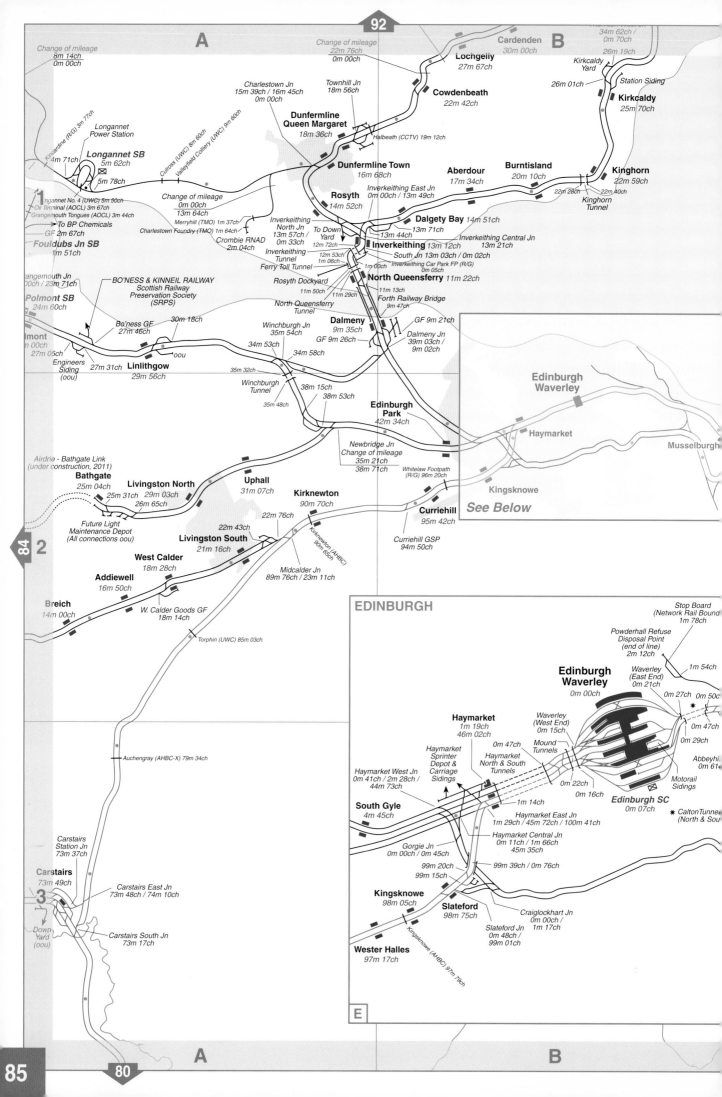

Change of mileage
8m 14ch
0m 00ch

Change of mileage
22m 76ch
0m 00ch

Cardenden
30m 00ch

34m 62ch /
0m 70ch

26m 19ch

Lochgelly
27m 67ch

Kirkcaldy
Yard

26m 01ch

Station Siding

Kirkcaldy
25m 70ch

Townhill Jn
18m 56ch

Charlestown Jn
15m 39ch / 16m 45ch
0m 00ch

Cowdenbeath
22m 42ch

Longannet
Power Station

Kincardine (R/G) 3m 77ch

Longannet SB
5m 62ch

4m 71ch

**Dunfermline
Queen Margaret**
18m 36ch

Halbeath (CCTV) 19m 12ch

Aberdour
17m 34ch

Burntisland
20m 10ch

Kinghorn
22m 59ch

Culross (UWC) 8m 60ch
Valleyfield Colliery (UWC) 9m 60ch

22m 28ch

22m 40ch

Kinghorn
Tunnel

5m 78ch

Dunfermline Town
16m 68ch

Longannet No. 4 (UWC) 5m 50ch
Oil Terminal (AOCL) 3m 67ch
Grangemouth Tongues (AOCL) 3m 44ch

Rosyth
14m 52ch

Dalgety Bay 14m 51ch

Inverkeithing East Jn
0m 00ch / 13m 49ch

13m 71ch

→ To BP Chemicals

GF 2m 67ch

Change of mileage
0m 00ch
13m 64ch

13m 44ch

Inverkeithing Central Jn
13m 21ch

Foudubs Jn SB
1m 51ch

Merryhill (TMO) 1m 37ch
Charlestown Foundry (TMO) 1m 64ch

Crombie RNAD
2m 04ch

Inverkeithing
North Jn
13m 57ch /
0m 33ch

South Jn 13m 03ch / 0m 02ch

Inverkeithing 13m 12ch

Grangemouth Jn
00ch / 23m 71ch

12m 72ch

12m 53ch
1m 06ch

Inverkeithing
Tunnel

To Down
Yard

Polmont SB
24m 60ch

Ferry Toll Tunnel

1m 00ch

Inverkeithing Car Park FP (R/G)
0m 05ch

Rosyth Dockyard

North Queensferry 11m 22ch

BO'NESS & KINNEIL RAILWAY
Scottish Railway
Preservation Society
(SRPS)

North Queensferry
Tunnel

11m 50ch

11m 29ch

11m 13ch

Forth Railway Bridge
9m 47ch

Polmont
00ch /
27m 05ch

Bo'ness GF
27m 46ch

30m 18ch

Dalmeny
9m 35ch

GF 9m 21ch

Engineers
Siding
(oou)

27m 31ch **Linlithgow**
29m 56ch

oou

GF 9m 26ch

Dalmeny Jn
39m 03ch /
9m 02ch

Winchburgh Jn
35m 54ch

34m 53ch

35m 32ch

34m 58ch

**Edinburgh
Waverley**

Winchburgh
Tunnel

38m 15ch

35m 48ch

38m 53ch

**Edinburgh
Park**
42m 34ch

Haymarket

Musselburgh

Airdrie - Bathgate Link
(under construction, 2011)

Newbridge Jn
Change of mileage
35m 21ch
38m 71ch

Whitelaw Footpath
(R/G) 96m 20ch

Kingsknowe

Bathgate
25m 04ch

Livingston North
29m 03ch

Uphall
31m 07ch

Kirknewton
90m 70ch

Curriehill
95m 42ch

See Below

25m 31ch

26m 65ch

22m 76ch

Future Light
Maintenance Depot
(All connections oou)

Livingston South
21m 16ch

22m 43ch

Kirknewton (AHBC)
90m 65ch

Curriehill GSP
94m 50ch

West Calder
18m 28ch

Midcalder Jn
89m 76ch / 23m 11ch

Addiewell
16m 50ch

Breich
14m 00ch

W. Calder Goods GF
18m 14ch

Torphin (UWC) 85m 03ch

EDINBURGH

Stop Board
(Network Rail Bound)
1m 78ch

Powderhall Refuse
Disposal Point
(end of line)
2m 12ch

1m 54ch

**Edinburgh
Waverley**
0m 00ch

Waverley
(East End)
0m 21ch

0m 27ch

0m 50c

Auchengray (AHBC-X) 79m 34ch

Haymarket
1m 19ch
46m 02ch

Waverley
(West End)
0m 15ch

0m 47ch

0m 47ch

0m 29ch

0m 47ch

Mound
Tunnels

Haymarket
Sprinter
Depot &
Carriage
Sidings

Haymarket
North & South
Tunnels

Abbeyhi
0m 61

Haymarket West Jn
0m 41ch / 2m 28ch /
44m 73ch

0m 22ch

1m 14ch

Edinburgh SC
0m 07ch

Motorail
Sidings

South Gyle
4m 45ch

Haymarket East Jn
1m 29ch / 45m 72ch / 100m 41ch

0m 16ch

Calton Tunne
(North & Sou

Gorgie Jn
0m 00ch / 0m 45ch

Haymarket Central Jn
0m 11ch / 1m 66ch
45m 35ch

**Carstairs
Station Jn**
73m 37ch

99m 20ch

99m 39ch / 0m 76ch

Carstairs
73m 49ch

99m 15ch

Carstairs East Jn
73m 48ch / 74m 10ch

Kingsknowe
98m 05ch

Craiglockhart Jn
0m 00ch /
1m 17ch

Slateford
98m 75ch

Down
Yard
(oou)

Carstairs South Jn
73m 17ch

Slateford Jn
0m 48ch /
99m 01ch

Kingsknowe (AHBC 97m 78ch

Wester Halles
97m 17ch

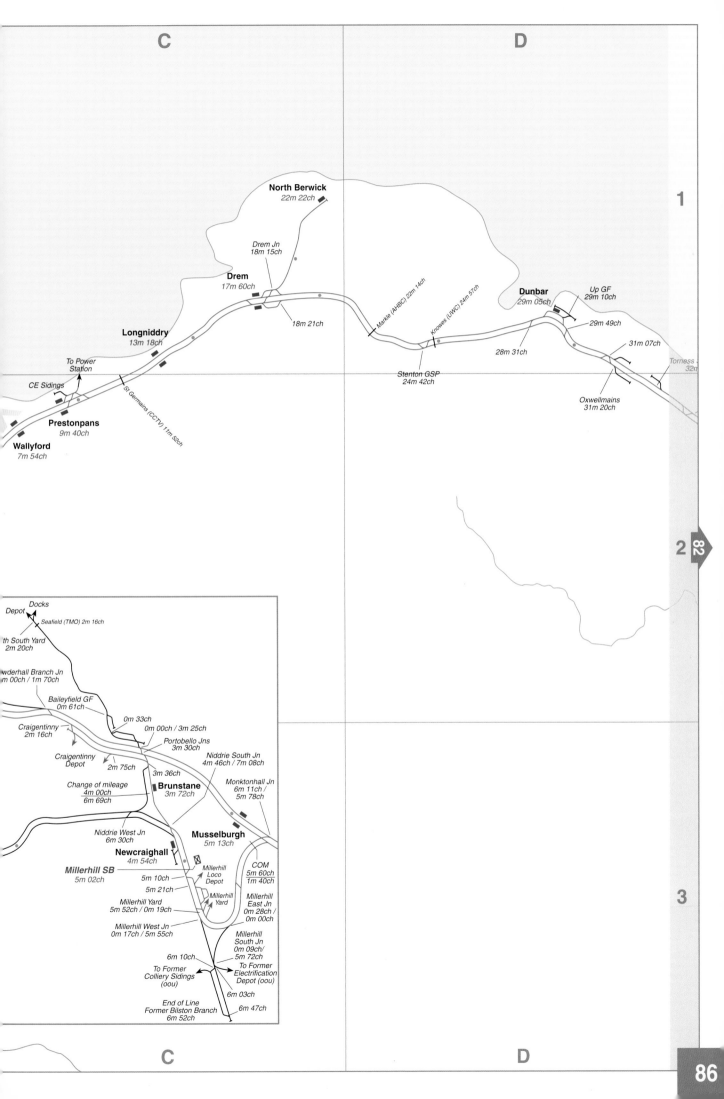

North Berwick
22m 22ch

Drem Jn
18m 15ch

Drem
17m 60ch

18m 21ch

Longniddry
13m 18ch

To Power Station

CE Sidings

St Germains (CCTV) 11m 52ch

Prestonpans
9m 40ch

Wallyford
7m 54ch

Markle (AHBC) 22m 14ch

Knowes (UWC) 24m 57ch

Dunbar
29m 05ch

Up GF
29m 10ch

29m 49ch

31m 07ch

Torness
32m

28m 31ch

Stenton GSP
24m 42ch

Oxwellmains
31m 20ch

Docks

Depot

Seafield (TMO) 2m 16ch

...th South Yard
2m 20ch

...wderhall Branch Jn
...m 00ch / 1m 70ch

Baileyfield GF
0m 61ch

0m 33ch

0m 00ch / 3m 25ch

Craigentinny
2m 16ch

Portobello Jns
3m 30ch

Craigentinny Depot

2m 75ch

3m 36ch

Niddrie South Jn
4m 46ch / 7m 08ch

Change of mileage
4m 00ch
6m 69ch

Brunstane
3m 72ch

Monktonhall Jn
6m 11ch /
5m 78ch

Niddrie West Jn
6m 30ch

Musselburgh
5m 13ch

Newcraighall
4m 54ch

Millerhill SB
5m 02ch

Millerhill Loco Depot

5m 10ch

5m 21ch

COM
5m 60ch
1m 40ch

Millerhill Yard

Millerhill Yard
5m 52ch / 0m 19ch

Millerhill East Jn
0m 28ch /
0m 00ch

Millerhill West Jn
0m 17ch / 5m 55ch

Millerhill South Jn
0m 09ch/
5m 72ch

6m 10ch

To Former Colliery Sidings
(oou)

To Former Electrification Depot (oou)

6m 03ch

End of Line Former Bilston Branch
6m 52ch

6m 47ch

A

B

1

2

3

Achaleven (UWC) 65m 00ch

Culnadalloch No. 1 (UWC) 63m 20ch
Culnadalloch No. 2 (UWC) 63m 12ch
Achnadoich No. 1 (UWC) 62m 71ch

Parkhill (UWC) 59m 75ch
Airds (UWC) 58m 78ch

58m 67ch
58m 47ch

*Oil
Sidings*

Connel Ferry
65m 30ch

Station GF

*Siding GF
71m 10ch*

Oban
71m 44ch

*To
Oil
Depot*

*East Siding GF
65m 10ch*

*West Siding GF
65m 23ch*

*Down Sidings
GF*

(Connection oou)

71m 22ch

Siding GF

*CE
Sidings*

Taynuilt
58m 55ch

Falls of Cruachan
52m 69ch

Loch
49m

Loch Awe

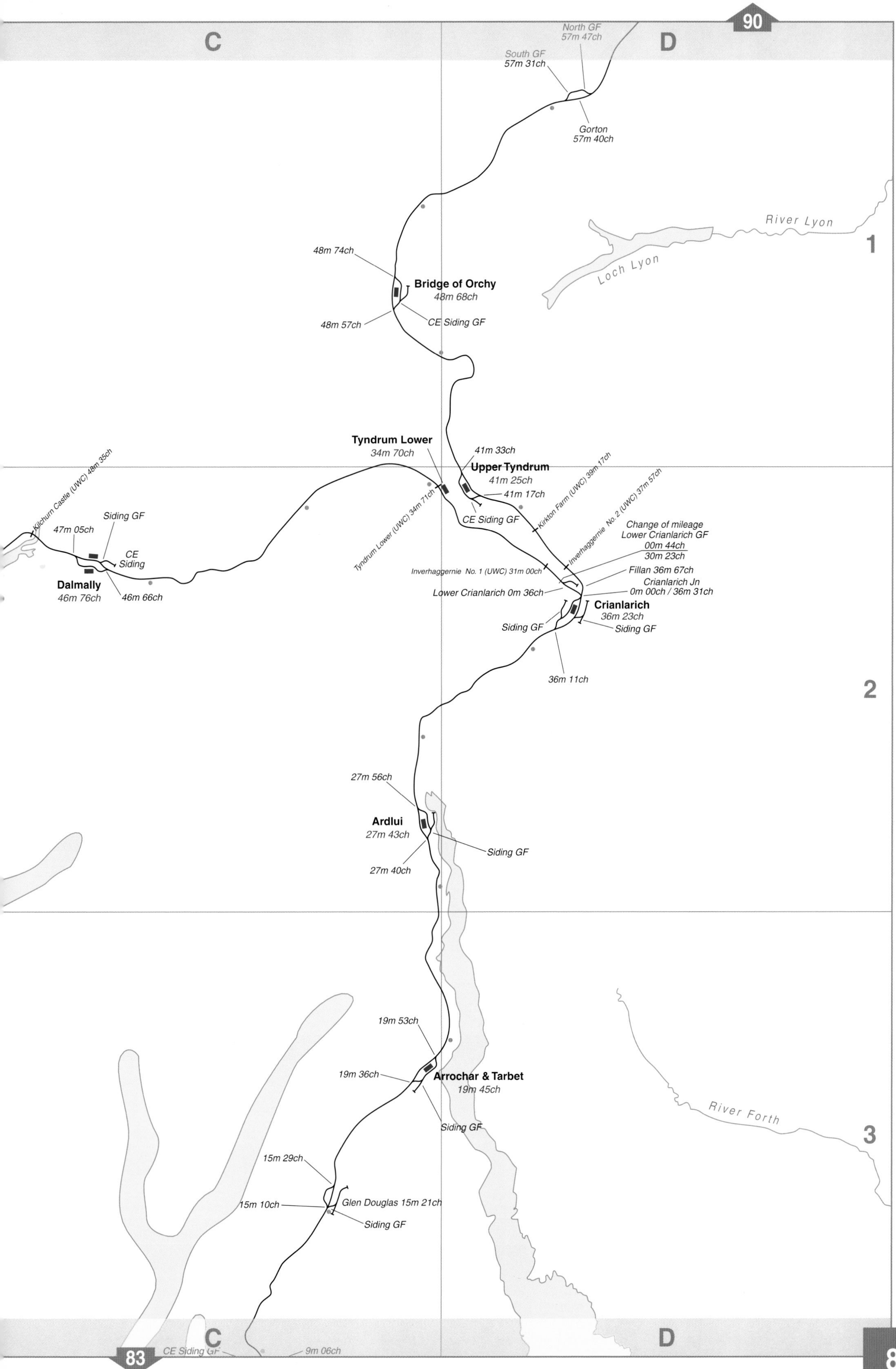

C | D

North GF
57m 47ch

South GF
57m 31ch

Gorton
57m 40ch

River Lyon

1

Loch Lyon

48m 74ch

Bridge of Orchy
48m 68ch

48m 57ch

CE Siding GF

Kilchurn Castle (UWC) 48m 35ch

Tyndrum Lower
34m 70ch

41m 33ch

Upper Tyndrum
41m 25ch

41m 17ch

Kirkton Farm (UWC) 39m 17ch

Inverhaggernie No. 2 (UWC) 37m 57ch

Siding GF

CE Siding GF

Change of mileage
Lower Crianlarich GF
00m 44ch
30m 23ch

CE
Siding

Tyndrum Lower (UWC) 34m 71ch

Inverhaggernie No. 1 (UWC) 31m 00ch

Fillan 36m 67ch

47m 05ch

Dalmally
46m 76ch

46m 66ch

Lower Crianlarich 0m 36ch

Crianlarich Jn
0m 00ch / 36m 31ch

Crianlarich
36m 23ch

Siding GF

Siding GF

36m 11ch

2

27m 56ch

Ardlui
27m 43ch

Siding GF

27m 40ch

19m 53ch

19m 36ch

Arrochar & Tarbet
19m 45ch

River Forth

3

Siding GF

15m 29ch

15m 10ch

Glen Douglas 15m 21ch

Siding GF

CE Siding GF

9m 06ch

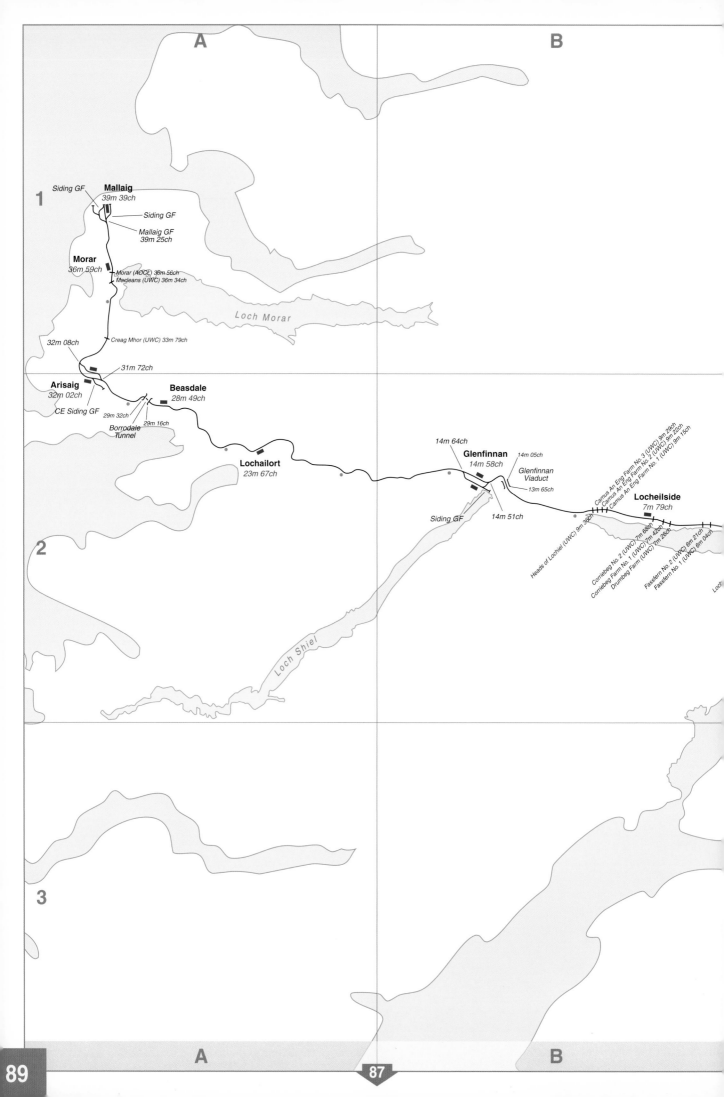

A

B

1

Mallaig
39m 39ch

Siding GF

Siding GF

Mallaig GF
39m 25ch

Morar
36m 59ch

Morar (AOCL) 36m 56ch
Macleans (UWC) 36m 34ch

Loch Morar

Creag Mhor (UWC) 33m 79ch

32m 08ch

31m 72ch

Arisaig
32m 02ch

Beasdale
28m 49ch

CE Siding GF

29m 32ch

29m 16ch

Borrodale
Tunnel

Lochailort
23m 67ch

14m 64ch

14m 05ch

Glenfinnan
14m 58ch

Glenfinnan
Viaduct

13m 65ch

Camus An Eirig Farm No. 3 (UWC) 9m 29ch
Camus An Eirig Farm No. 2 (UWC) 9m 22ch
Camus An Eirig Farm No. 1 (UWC) 9m 15ch

Locheilside
7m 79ch

Siding GF

14m 51ch

Heads of Lochiel (UWC) 9m 36ch

Corriebeg No. 2 (UWC) 7m 68ch
Corriebeg Farm No. 1 (UWC) 7m 42ch
Drumbeg Farm (UWC) 7m 26ch

Fassfern No. 2 (UWC) 6m 21ch
Fassfern No. 1 (UWC) 6m 04ch

2

Loch Shiel

3

A

B

C

D

1

Loch Lochy

Spean Bridge
90m 56ch

CE Siding GF

Kerrisys (UWC) 88m 49ch
Millens (UWC) 88m 27ch
Keppoch No. 1 (UWC) 87m 50ch

CE Siding GF

Tulloch
81m 59ch

Loop points South
90m 46ch

Roy Bridge
87m 35ch

81m 73ch

81m 55ch

Loop points North
90m 68ch

Banavie SC
0m 26ch

Canal
Swing Bridge
0m 27ch

Change of mileage
00m 00ch
1m 27ch

Loch Eil
utward Bound
4m 20ch

Banavie
0m 22ch

Corpach
1m 30ch

Siding GF
98m 33ch

79m 02ch

Fersit Tunnel

2

78m 75ch

m 19ch

o Pulp Mill
Sidings
2m 28ch

Annal West (R/C) 2m 22ch
Annal East 2m 14ch
Corpach (AOC) 1m 67ch
Canal (UWC) 1m 61ch
Stepps Cottage (UWC) 1m 33ch
Banavie (R/C) 1m 46ch
0m 18ch

Inverlochy Farm (UWC) 97m 65ch

To British Alcan

★ *Freight Terminal*
Loop Sidings

Oil Terminal
Sidings

0m 30ch

Fort William Jn SB
98m 65ch / 0m 05ch

Pollock (UWC) 71m 59ch

North GF
71m 63ch

CE Sidings

South GF

Corrour
71m 54ch

71m 45ch

Station GF

Fort William
99m 37ch

66m 00ch

Cruach
Snow Shed

65m 71ch

Siding GF

Rannoch
64m 36ch

3

64m 29ch

North GF
57m 47ch

South GF
57m 31ch

C

D

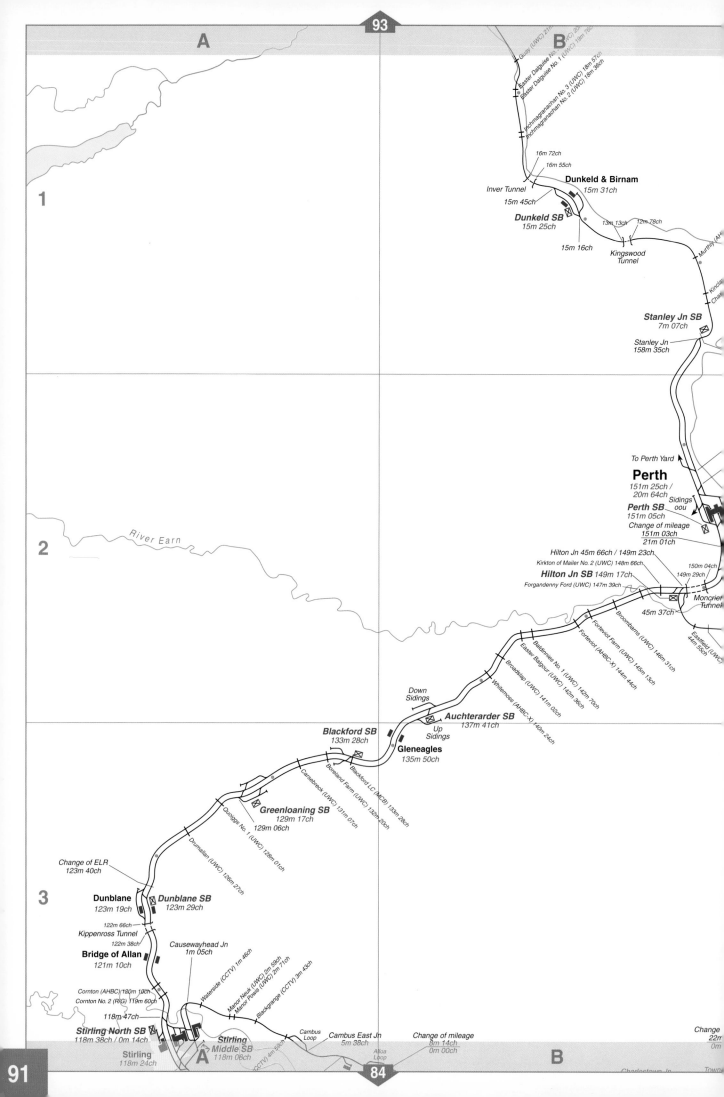

A

B

Quay (UWC) 21m

Easter Dalguise No. 2 (UWC) 20m

Easter Dalguise No. 1 (UWC) 19m 78ch

Inchmagranachan No. 3 (UWC) 18m 57ch

Inchmagranachan No. 2 (UWC) 18m 36ch

1

16m 72ch

16m 55ch

Dunkeld & Birnam
15m 31ch

Inver Tunnel
15m 45ch

Dunkeld SB
15m 25ch

13m 13ch

12m 78ch

Murthly (AH

15m 16ch

Kingswood Tunnel

Stanley Jn SB
7m 07ch

Kinclav
Chap

Stanley Jn
158m 35ch

To Perth Yard

Perth

151m 25ch /
20m 64ch

Sidings
oou

Perth SB
151m 05ch

Change of mileage
151m 03ch
21m 01ch

River Earn

2

Hilton Jn 45m 66ch / 149m 23ch

Kirkton of Mailer No. 2 (UWC) 148m 66ch

150m 04ch

149m 29ch

Hilton Jn SB *149m 17ch*

Forgandenny Ford (UWC) 147m 39ch

Moncrief Tunnel

45m 37ch

Eastfield
44m 55ch

44m

Broombarns (UWC) 146m 31ch

Fortoviot Farm (UWC) 145m 23ch

Fortoviot (AHBC-X) 144m 44ch

Baldinnies No. 1 (UWC) 142m 70ch

Easter Balgour (UWC) 142m 36ch

Down Sidings

Broadslap (UWC) 141m 02ch

Whitemoss (AHBC-X) 140m 24ch

Auchterarder SB
137m 41ch

Blackford SB
133m 28ch

Up Sidings

Gleneagles
135m 50ch

Borelend Farm (UWC) 132m 20ch

Blackford LC (MCB) 133m 28ch

Carsebreck (UWC) 131m 07ch

Greenloaning SB
129m 17ch
129m 06ch

Quoiggs No. 1 (UWC) 128m 01ch

Drumallan (UWC) 126m 27ch

Change of ELR
123m 40ch

3

Dunblane
123m 19ch

Dunblane SB
123m 29ch

122m 66ch

Kippenross Tunnel
122m 38ch

Bridge of Allan
121m 10ch

Causewayhead Jn
1m 05ch

Waterside (CCTV) 1m 46ch

Manor Neuk (UWC) 2m 59ch

Manor Powis (UWC) 2m 71ch

Blackgrange (CCTV) 3m 43ch

Cornton (AHBC) 120m 10ch

Cornton No. 2 (R/G) 119m 60ch

118m 47ch

Cambus Loop

Cambus East Jn
5m 38ch

Change of mileage
8m 14ch
0m 00ch

Change
22m

0m

Stirling North SB
118m 38ch / 0m 14ch

Stirling
118m 24ch

Stirling Middle SB
118m 08ch

(CCTV) 4m 59ch

Alloa Loop

Charlestown Jn

Town

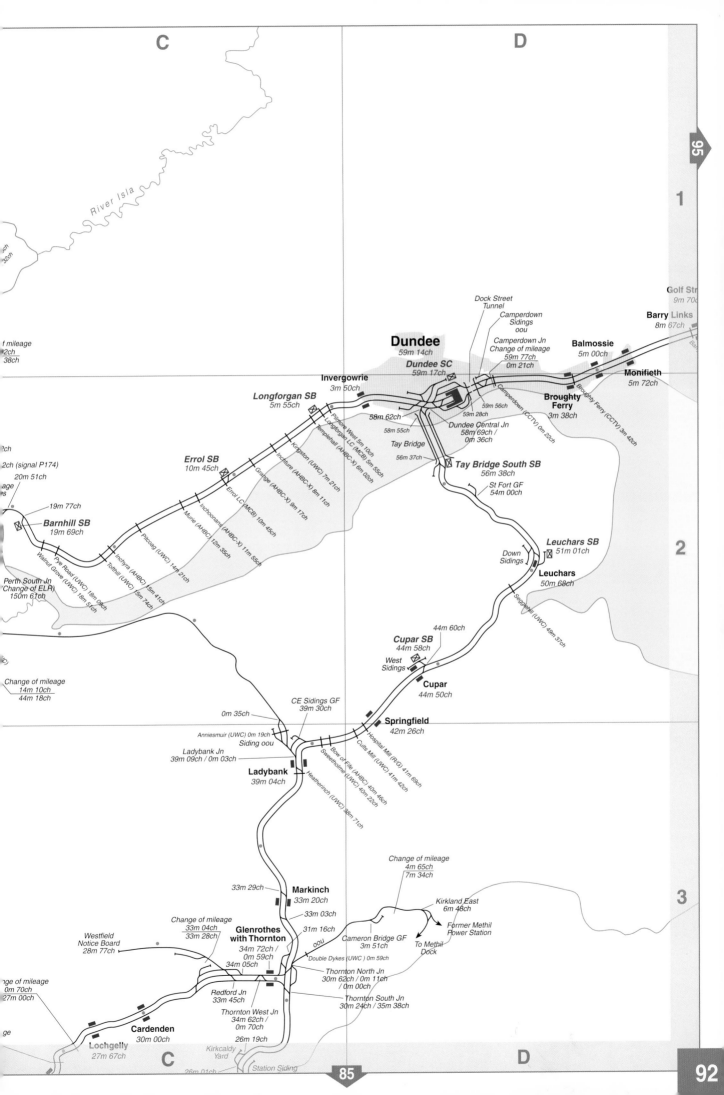

River Isla

1

f mileage
2ch
38ch

Dock Street
Tunnel

Camperdown
Sidings
oou

Dundee
59m 14ch

Camperdown Jn
Change of mileage
59m 77ch
0m 21ch

Balmossie
5m 00ch

Golf Str
9m 70c

Barry Links
8m 67ch

Dundee SC
59m 17ch

Monifieth
5m 72ch

Invergowrie
3m 50ch

Longforgan SB
5m 55ch

Pinmore West 5m 10ch

Longforgan LC (MCB) 5m 55ch

Templehall (AHBC-X) 6m 02ch

59m 56ch

Camperdown (CCTV) 0m 22ch

**Broughty
Ferry**
3m 38ch

Broughty Ferry (CCTV) 3m 42ch

58m 62ch

58m 55ch

Tay Bridge

59m 28ch

Dundee Central Jn
58m 69ch /
0m 36ch

Errol SB
10m 45ch

Kingston (UWC) 7m 21ch

Inchture (AHBC-X) 7m 21ch

Grange (AHBC-X) 9m 17ch

Errol LC (MCB) 10m 45ch

56m 37ch

Tay Bridge South SB
56m 38ch

St Fort GF
54m 00ch

2ch (signal P174)
20m 51ch

age
s

19m 77ch

Barnhill SB
19m 69ch

Pye Road (UWC) 18m 05ch

Walnut Grove (UWC) 18m 51ch

Murie (AHBC) 12m 35ch

Inchcoonans (AHBC-X) 11m 55ch

Pitcalg (UWC) 14m 21ch

Inchyra (AHBC) 15m 41ch

Toffhill (UWC) 15m 74ch

Perth South Jn
(Change of ELR)
150m 61ch

Down
Sidings

Leuchars SB
51m 01ch

Leuchars
50m 68ch

Seggiehill (UWC) 49m 37ch

Change of mileage
14m 10ch
44m 18ch

44m 60ch

Cupar SB
44m 58ch

West
Sidings

Cupar
44m 50ch

0m 35ch

CE Sidings GF
39m 30ch

Springfield
42m 26ch

Hospital Mill (R/G) 41m 69ch

Cults Mill (UWC) 41m 42ch

Anniesmuir (UWC) 0m 19ch
Siding oou

Ladybank Jn
39m 09ch / 0m 03ch

Bow of Fife (AHBC) 40m 46ch

Sweetholme (UWC) 40m 22ch

Ladybank
39m 04ch

Heatherinch (UWC) 38m 7ch

Change of mileage
4m 65ch
7m 34ch

3

Kirkland East
6m 48ch

33m 29ch

Markinch
33m 20ch

Former Methil
Power Station

33m 03ch

To Methil
Dock

Change of mileage
33m 04ch
33m 28ch

**Glenrothes
with Thornton**
34m 72ch /
0m 59ch
34m 05ch

31m 16ch

Cameron Bridge GF
3m 51ch

*Westfield
Notice Board*
28m 77ch

oou

Double Dykes (UWC) 0m 59ch

Thornton North Jn
30m 62ch / 0m 11ch
/ 0m 00ch

nge of mileage
0m 70ch
27m 00ch

Redford Jn
33m 45ch

Thornton South Jn
30m 24ch / 35m 38ch

Cardenden
30m 00ch

Thornton West Jn
34m 62ch /
0m 70ch

26m 19ch

ge

Lochgelly
27m 67ch

*Kirkcaldy
Yard*

Station Siding

26m 01ch

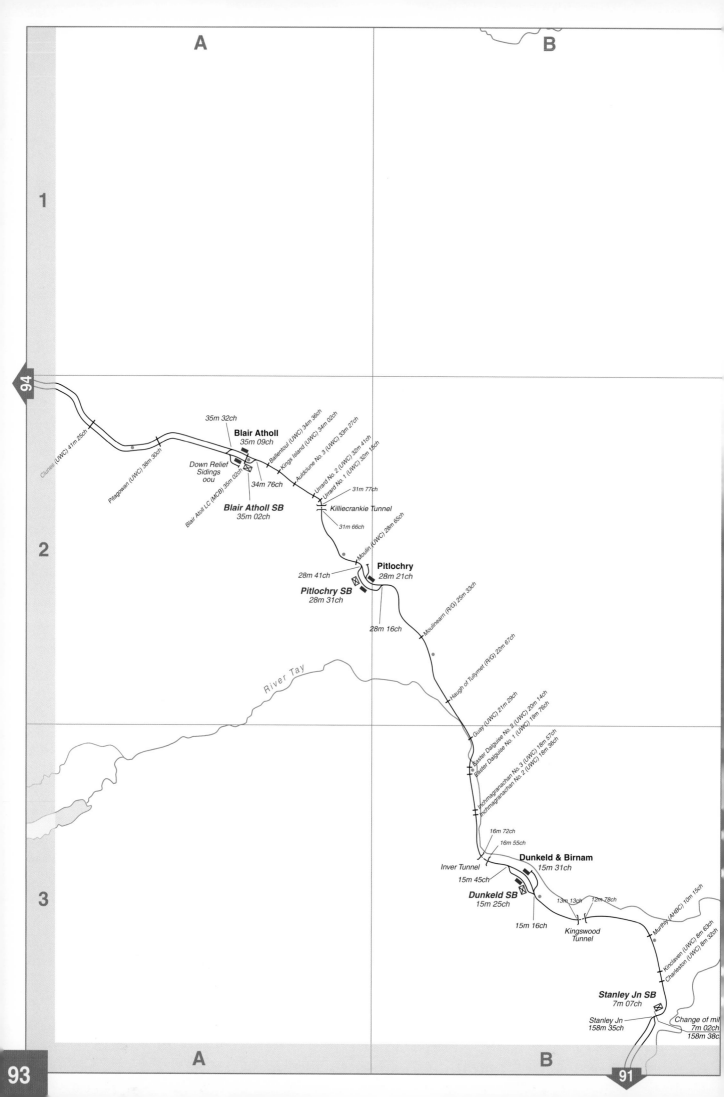

94

Clunes (UWC) 41m 25ch

Pitagowan (UWC) 38m 30ch

35m 32ch

Blair Atholl
35m 09ch

Ballentoul (UWC) 34m 36ch
Kings Island (UWC) 34m 02ch
Auldclune No 3 (UWC) 33m 27ch

*Down Relief
Sidings
oou*

34m 76ch

Blair Atholl LC (MCB) 35m 02ch

Blair Atholl SB
35m 02ch

Urrard No 2 (UWC) 32m 41ch
Urrard No 1 (UWC) 32m 15ch

31m 77ch

Killiecrankie Tunnel

31m 66ch

Moulin (UWC) 28m 65ch

Pitlochry

28m 41ch

28m 21ch

Pitlochry SB
28m 31ch

28m 16ch

Moulinearn (R/G) 25m 33ch

Haugh of Tullymet (R/G) 22m 67ch

River Tay

Guay (UWC) 21m 29ch

Easter Dalguise No 2 (UWC) 20m 14ch
Easter Dalguise No 1 (UWC) 19m 76ch

Inchmagranachan No 3 (UWC) 18m 57ch
Inchmagranachan No 2 (UWC) 18m 36ch

16m 72ch
16m 55ch

Dunkeld & Birnam
15m 31ch

Inver Tunnel

15m 45ch

Dunkeld SB
15m 25ch

15m 16ch

13m 13ch   12m 78ch

*Kingswood
Tunnel*

Murthly (AHBC) 10m 15ch

Kinclaven (UWC) 8m 63ch
Charleston (UWC) 8m 32ch

Stanley Jn SB
7m 07ch

Stanley Jn
158m 35ch

Change of mil
7m 02ch
158m 38c

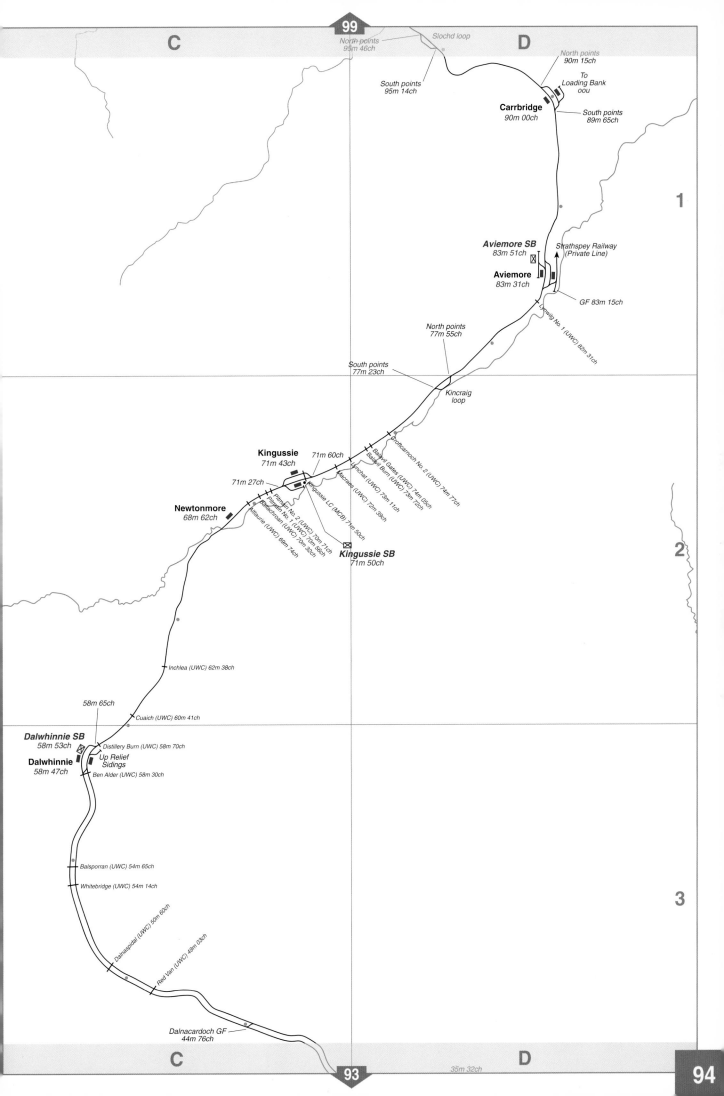

Siochd loop

North points
95m 46ch

North points
90m 15ch

South points
95m 14ch

To
Loading Bank
oou

Carrbridge
90m 00ch

South points
89m 65ch

1

Aviemore SB
83m 51ch

Strathspey Railway
(Private Line)

Aviemore
83m 31ch

GF 83m 15ch

Lxywilg No. 1 (UWC) 82m 31ch

North points
77m 55ch

South points
77m 23ch

Kincraig
loop

Croftcarnoch No. 2 (UWC) 74m 77ch

Balavil Gates (UWC) 74m 05ch

Balavil Burn (UWC) 73m 72ch

Kingussie
71m 43ch

71m 60ch

Unchat (UWC) 73m 11ch

71m 27ch

Macnaes (UWC) 72m 39ch

Kingussie LC (MCB) 71m 50ch

Newtonmore
68m 62ch

Pitmain No. 2 (UWC) 70m 71ch

Pitmain No. 1 (UWC) 70m 56ch

Ballachroan (UWC) 70m 32ch

Alltaurie (UWC) 69m 74ch

Kingussie SB
71m 50ch

2

Inchlea (UWC) 62m 38ch

58m 65ch

Cuaich (UWC) 60m 41ch

Dalwhinnie SB
58m 53ch

Distillery Burn (UWC) 58m 70ch

Up Relief
Sidings

Dalwhinnie
58m 47ch

Ben Alder (UWC) 58m 30ch

Balsporran (UWC) 54m 65ch

Whitebridge (UWC) 54m 14ch

3

Dalnaspidal (UWC) 50m 60ch

Red Van (UWC) 49m 03ch

Dalnacardoch GF
44m 76ch

35m 32ch

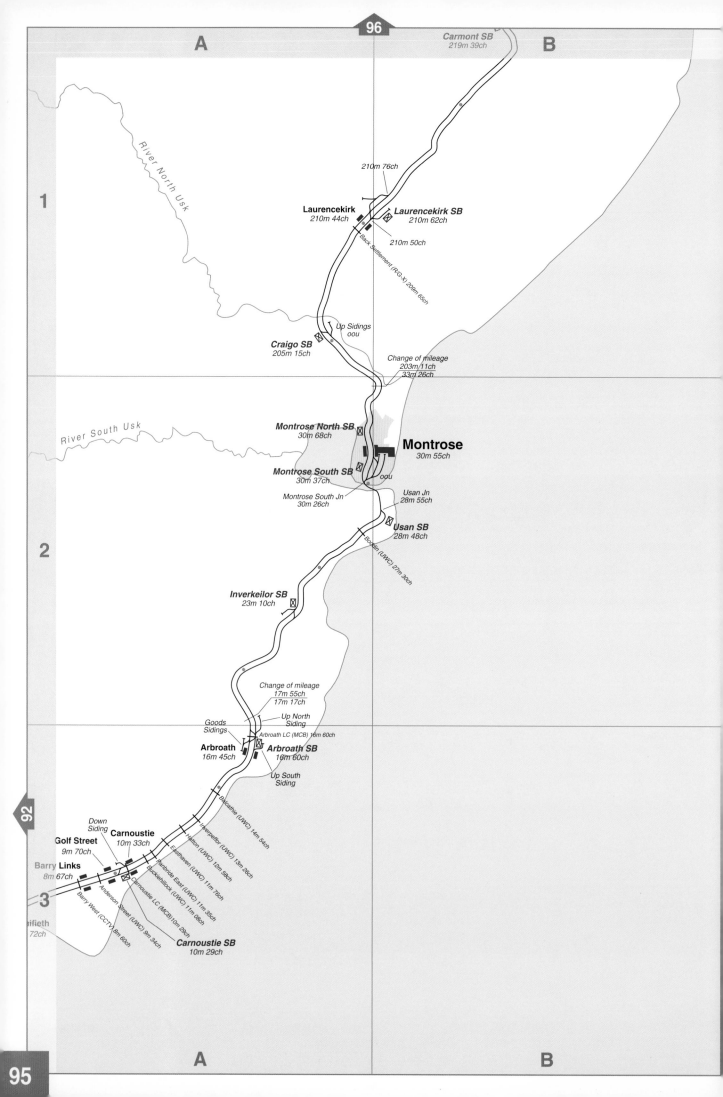

A

B

Carmont SB
219m 39ch

1

River North Usk

210m 76ch

Laurencekirk
210m 44ch

Laurencekirk SB
210m 62ch

210m 50ch

Back Settlement (R.G.X) 209m 65ch

Up Sidings
oou

Craigo SB
205m 15ch

Change of mileage
203m 11ch
33m 26ch

River South Usk

Montrose North SB
30m 68ch

Montrose
30m 55ch

Montrose South SB
30m 37ch

oou

Usan Jn
28m 55ch

Montrose South Jn
30m 26ch

Usan SB
28m 48ch

Bodtin (UWC) 27m 30ch

2

Inverkeilor SB
23m 10ch

Change of mileage
17m 55ch
17m 17ch

Up North
Siding

Goods
Sidings

Arbroath LC (MCB) 16m 60ch

Arbroath
16m 45ch

Arbroath SB
16m 60ch

Up South
Siding

Balcathie (UWC) 14m 54ch

Down
Siding

Carnoustie
10m 33ch

Inverpeffor (UWC) 13m 26ch

Golf Street
9m 70ch

Hatton (UWC) 12m 26ch

Easthaven (UWC) 11m 76ch

Barry Links
8m 67ch

Panbride East (UWC) 11m 35ch

Buckenhillock (UWC) 11m 08ch

Anderson Street

Carnoustie LC (MCB)10m 29ch

Barry West (CCTV) 8m 60ch

Carnoustie LC (UWC) 9m 34ch

3

Carnoustie SB
10m 29ch

nifieth
72ch

A

B

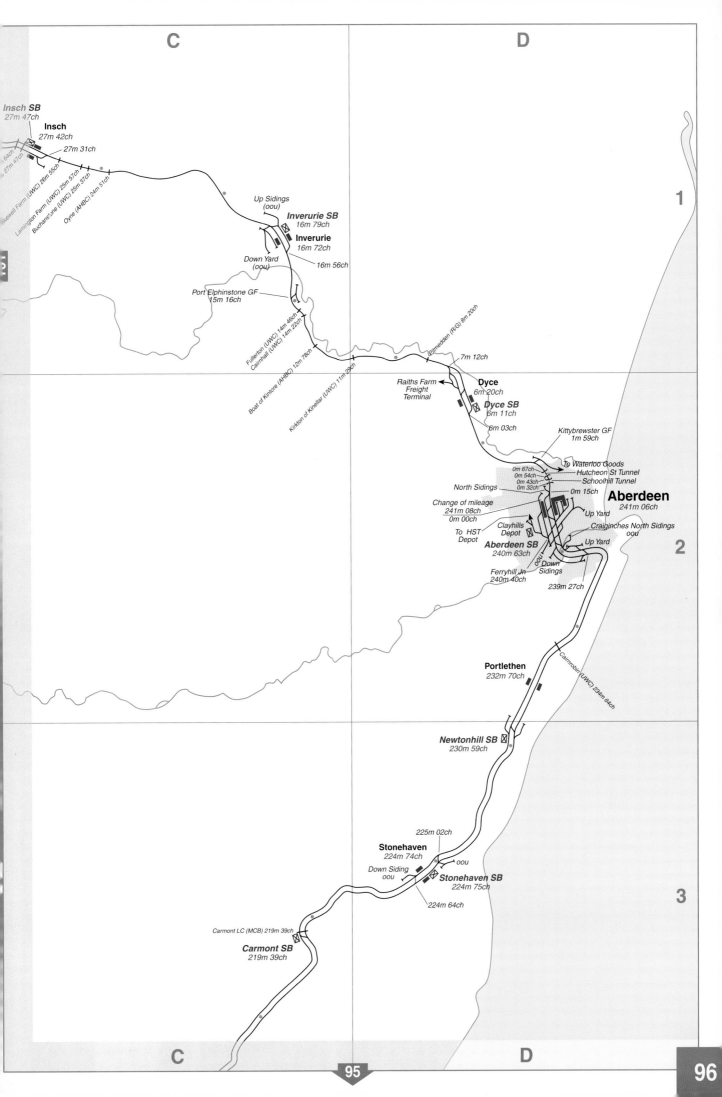

C

D

Insch SB
27m 47ch

Insch
27m 42ch

27m 31ch

m 64ch
27m 47ch

Likewell Farm (UWC) 26m 55ch
Lamington Farm (UWC) 25m 57ch
Buchanstone (UWC) 25m 37ch
Oyne (AHBC) 24m 51ch

Up Sidings
(oou)

Inverurie SB
16m 79ch

Inverurie
16m 72ch

Down Yard
(oou)

16m 56ch

Port Elphinstone GF
15m 16ch

Fullerton (UWC) 14m 46ch
Carnhill (UWC) 14m 22ch

Boat of Kintore (AHBC) 12m 78ch

Kirkton of Kinellar (UWC) 11m 29ch

Kintmedden (R/G) 8m 20ch

7m 12ch

Raiths Farm
Freight
Terminal

Dyce
6m 20ch

Dyce SB
6m 11ch

6m 03ch

Kittybrewster GF
1m 59ch

To Waterloo Goods
0m 67ch
0m 54ch — *Hutcheon St Tunnel*
0m 43ch — *Schoolhill Tunnel*
0m 32ch

North Sidings

0m 15ch

Change of mileage
241m 08ch
0m 00ch

Aberdeen
241m 06ch

Up Yard

To HST
Depot

Clayhills
Depot

Craiginches North Sidings
oou

Aberdeen SB
240m 63ch

Up Yard

Ferryhill Jn
240m 40ch

Down
Sidings

oou

239m 27ch

Cairnrobin (UWC) 234m 64ch

Portlethen
232m 70ch

Newtonhill SB
230m 59ch

225m 02ch

Stonehaven
224m 74ch

Down Siding
oou

oou

Stonehaven SB
224m 75ch

224m 64ch

Carmont LC (MCB) 219m 39ch

Carmont SB
219m 39ch

1

2

3

C

D

Achnashellach
40m 34ch

Craig (UWC) 38...

Achnashellach (UWC) 40m 37ch

Balnacra No. 2 (UWC) 42m 12ch
Balnacra (AOCL) 42m 58ch
Dalmartin (UWC) 43m 00ch
Coulags No. 1 (UWC) 43m 32ch
Coulags No. 3 (UWC) 44m 14ch
Blackwood No. 1 (UWC) 44m 35ch
Blackwood No. 2 (ABCL) 44m 67ch

Siding GF

Strathcarron
45m 74ch

*West End
Loop points
46m 01ch*

Strathcarron (AOCL) 45m 77ch
Auchintee (UWC) 46m 15ch

Attadale
48m 22ch

Stromeferry
53m 15ch

Plockton
58m 22ch

Duirinish
59m 58ch

Duncraig
57m 09ch

Duirinish Station (UWC) 59m 56ch

*East GF
63m 43ch*

GF

West Siding GF

Kyle of Lochalsh
63m 64ch

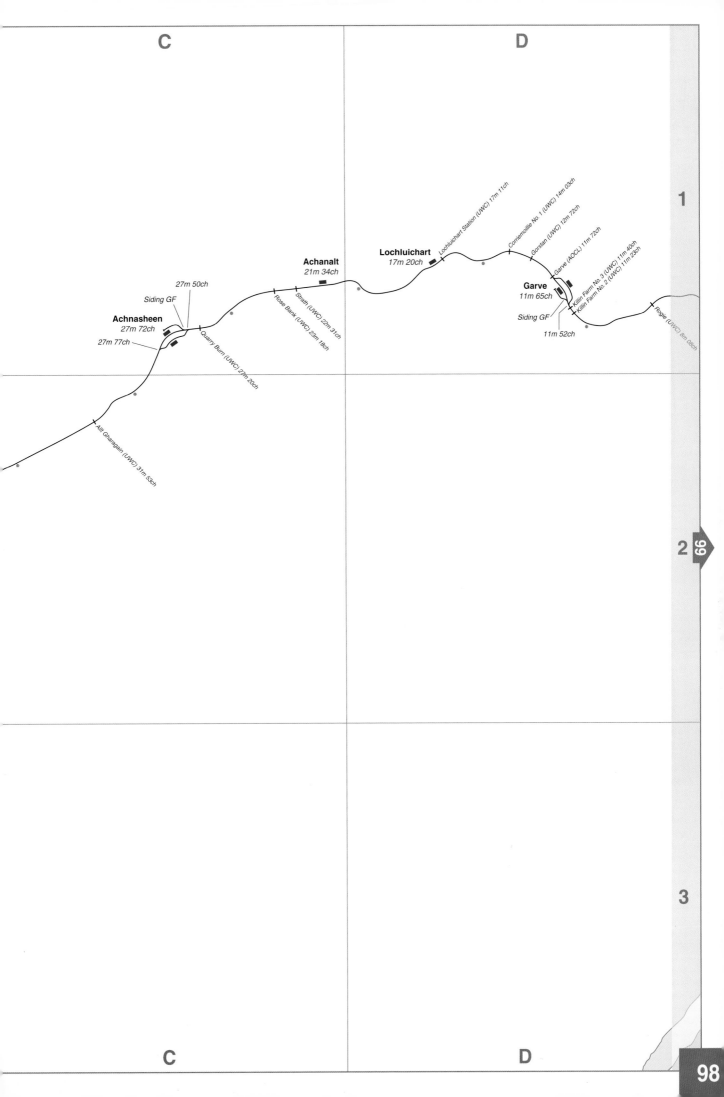

C

D

Lochluichart Station (UWC) 17m 11ch

Corriemollie No. 1 (UWC) 14m 03ch

Gorstan (UWC) 12m 72ch

Lochluichart
17m 20ch

Garve (AOCL) 11m 72ch

Achanalt
21m 34ch

Killin Farm No. 3 (UWC) 11m 40ch
Killin Farm No. 2 (UWC) 11m 23ch

27m 50ch

Siding GF

Garve
11m 65ch

Strath (UWC) 22m 31ch

Rose Bank (UWC) 23m 18ch

Siding GF

Achnasheen
27m 72ch

11m 52ch

Rogie (UWC) 8m 08ch

27m 77ch

Quarry Burn (UWC) 27m 20ch

Allt Gharagain (UWC) 31m 53ch

C

D

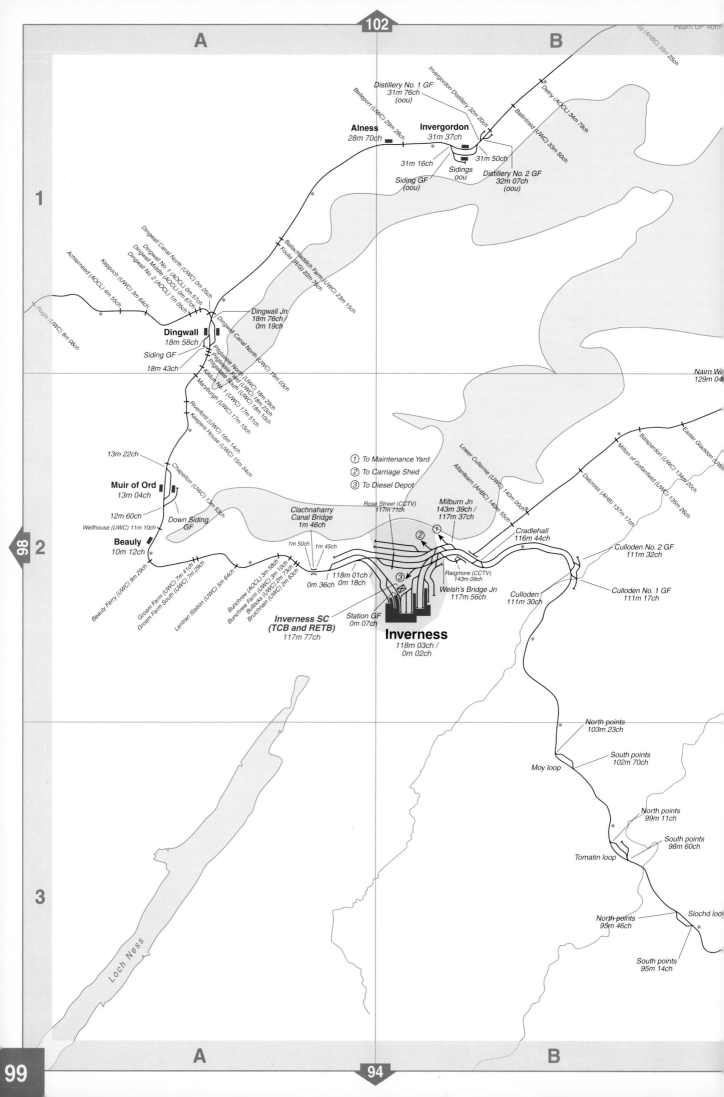

A | B

Fearn GF 40m

Invergordon Distillery 32m 20ch

Distillery No. 1 GF
31m 76ch
(oou)

Belleport (UWC) 29m 28ch

Delny (AOCL) 34m 79ch

Alness
28m 70ch

Invergordon
31m 37ch

Ballintrad (UWC) 33m 50ch

31m 16ch

31m 50ch

Siding GF
(oou)

Sidings
oou

Distillery No. 2 GF
32m 07ch
(oou)

1

Dingwall Canal North (UWC) 0m 25ch

Dingwall No. 1 (AOCL) 0m 57ch

Dingwall Middle (AOCL) 0m 67ch

Dingwall No. 2 (AOCL) 1m 05ch

Achterneed (AOCL) 4m 55ch

Kinnoch (UWC) 3m 64ch

Raigie (UWC) 8m 08ch

Ballachuidich Farm (UWC) 23m 15ch

Foulis (R/G) 22m 76ch

Dingwall Jn
18m 76ch /
0m 19ch

Dingwall
18m 58ch

Dingwall Canal North (UWC) 19m 03ch

Siding GF
18m 43ch

Nairn We
129m 04

Pitglassie North (UWC) 18m 29ch

Pitglassie Field (UWC) 18m 23ch

Pitglassie South (UWC) 18m 10ch

Kildun No. 1 (UWC) 17m 51ch

Maryburgh (UWC) 17m 15ch

Riverford (UWC) 16m 14ch

Keepers House (UWC) 15m 54ch

Lower Cullernie (UWC) 140m 00ch

Allanfearn (AHBC) 140m 55ch

Balgardon (UWC) 134m 20ch

Easter Glackton (UW

13m 22ch

Chapelton (UWC) 13m 53ch

Muir of Ord
13m 04ch

12m 60ch

Milton of Gollanfield (UWC) 135m 26ch

Dalcross (AHB) 137m 17ch

① To Maintenance Yard
② To Carriage Shed
③ To Diesel Depot

**Down Siding
GF**

Wellhouse (UWC) 11m 10ch

Clachnaharry
Canal Bridge
1m 46ch

Rose Street (CCTV)
117m 71ch

Milburn Jn
143m 39ch /
117m 37ch

Cradlehall
116m 44ch

Culloden No. 2 GF
111m 32ch

98

2

Beauly
10m 12ch

1m 50ch   1m 45ch

① 118m 01ch /
0m 18ch

③

Raigmore (CCTV)
143m 09ch

Welsh's Bridge Jn
117m 56ch

Culloden
111m 30ch

Culloden No. 1 GF
111m 17ch

Beauly Ferry (UWC) 9m 29ch

Groam Farm (UWC) 7m 41ch

Groam Farm South (UWC) 7m 29ch

Lentran Station (UWC) 5m 64ch

Bunchrew (AOCL) 3m 58ch

Bunchrew Farm (UWC) 3m 10ch

Bullocks (UWC) 2m 73ch

Bruichnain (UWC) 2m 63ch

**Inverness SC
(TCB and RETB)**
117m 77ch

Station GF
0m 07ch

0m 36ch

Inverness
118m 03ch /
0m 02ch

North points
103m 23ch

South points
102m 70ch

Moy loop

North points
99m 11ch

South points
98m 60ch

Tomatin loop

3

North points
95m 46ch

Slochd loo

South points
95m 14ch

Loch Ness

A | B

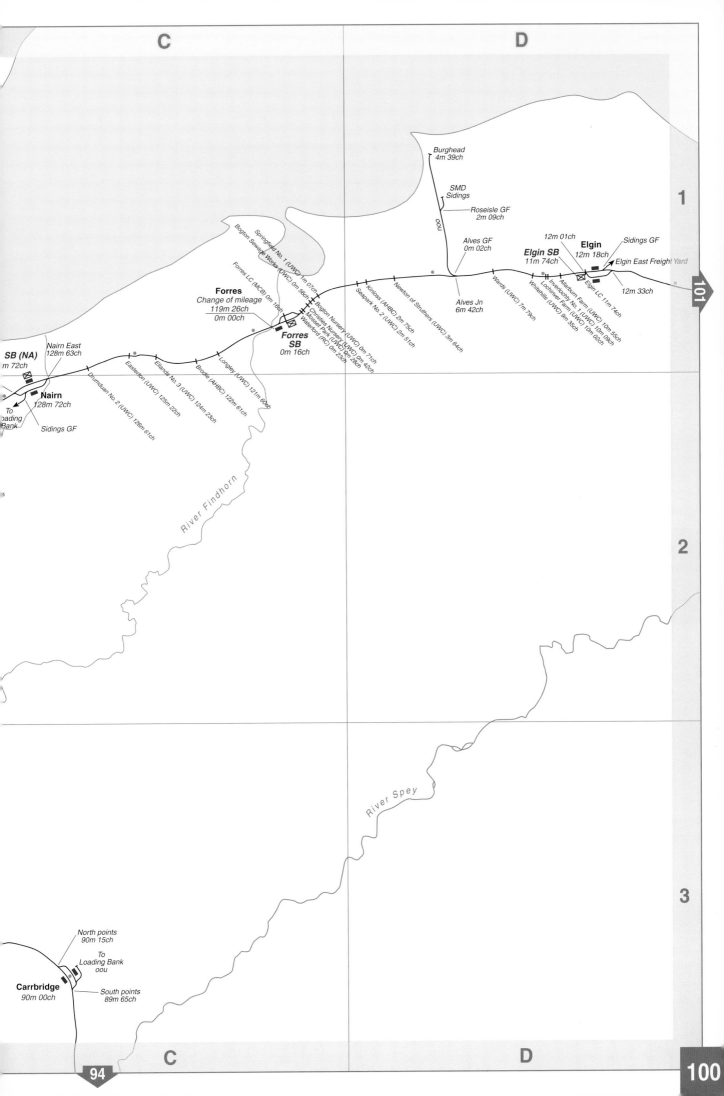

Burghead
4m 39ch

SMD
Sidings

Roseisle GF
2m 09ch

oou

Alves GF
0m 02ch

12m 01ch

Elgin
12m 18ch

Sidings GF

Elgin SB
11m 74ch

Elgin East Freight Yard

Bogton Sewage Works (UWC) 0m 56ch

Springfield No. 1 (UWC) 1m 07ch

Forres LC (MCB) 0m 16ch

Forres
Change of mileage
119m 26ch
0m 00ch

Bogton Nursery (UWC) 0m 42ch

Christies Nursery (UWC) 0m 26ch

Mosset Park (UWC) 0m 28ch

Waterford (RC) 0m 23ch

**Forres
SB**
0m 16ch

Kinloss (AHBC) 2m 75ch

Seapark No. 2 (UWC) 2m 51ch

Newton of Struthers (UWC) 3m 64ch

Alves Jn
6m 42ch

Wards (UWC) 7m 78ch

Inverlochty No. 1 (UWC) 10m 02ch

Lochinver Farm (UWC) 9m 35ch

Whitehills (UWC) 9m 35ch

Allarburn Farm (UWC) 10m 55ch

Elgin LC 11m 74ch

12m 33ch

SB (NA)
m 72ch

Nairn East
128m 63ch

Nairn
128m 72ch

To
Loading
Bank

Sidings GF

Drumduan No. 2 (UWC) 126m 61ch

Easterton (UWC) 125m 22ch

Eilands No. 3 (UWC) 124m 23ch

Brodie (AHBC) 122m 61ch

Longley (UWC) 121m 60ch

River Findhorn

River Spey

2

3

North points
90m 15ch

To
Loading Bank
oou

Carrbridge
90m 00ch

South points
89m 65ch

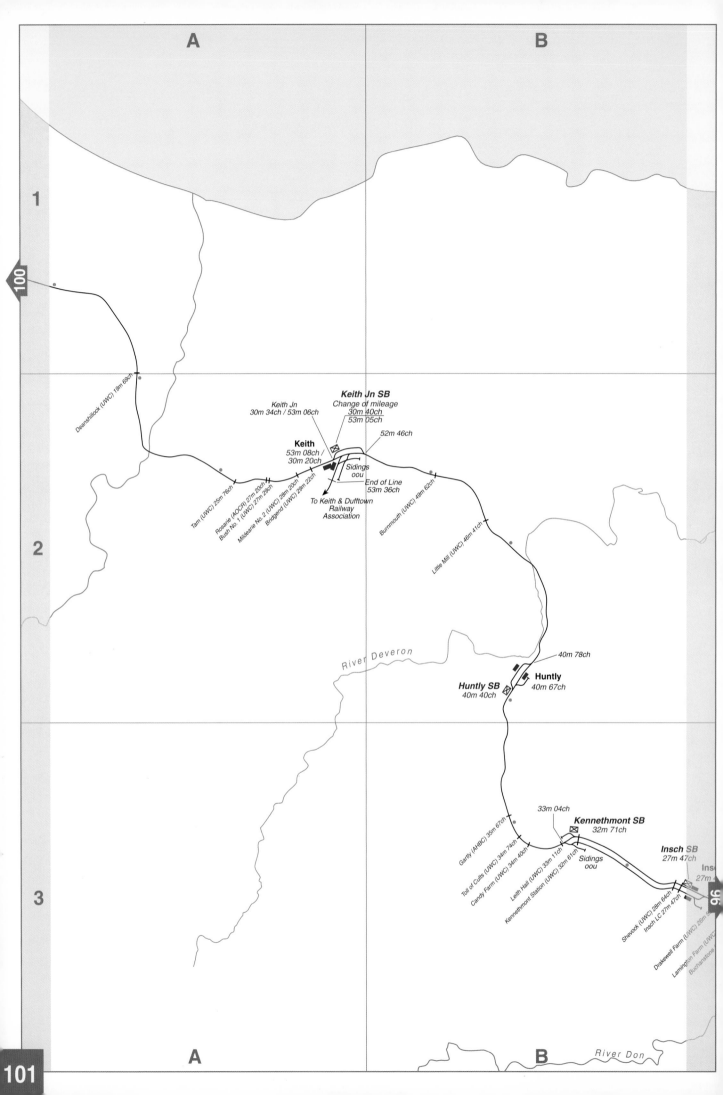

1

100

Keith Jn SB
Change of mileage
30m 40ch
53m 05ch

Keith Jn
30m 34ch / 53m 06ch

Deanshillock (UWC) 19m 69ch

52m 46ch

Keith
53m 08ch /
30m 20ch

Sidings
oou

End of Line
53m 36ch

To Keith & Dufftown
Railway
Association

Tarn (UWC) 25m 76ch

Rosarie (AOCR) 27m 20ch

Bush No. 1 (UWC) 27m 29ch

Mildearie No. 2 (UWC) 28m 20ch

Bridgend (UWC) 29m 22ch

Burnmouth (UWC) 49m 62ch

Little Mill (UWC) 46m 41ch

2

River Deveron

40m 78ch

Huntly
40m 67ch

Huntly SB
40m 40ch

33m 04ch

Kennethmont SB
32m 71ch

Insch SB
27m 47ch

Insc
27m

Gartly (AHBC) 35m 67ch

Toll of Cults (UWC) 34m 74ch

Candy Farm (UWC) 34m 40ch

Leith Hall (UWC) 33m 11ch

Kennethmont Station (UWC) 32m 61ch

Sidings
oou

Shevock (UWC) 28m 64ch

Insch Lc 27m 47ch

96

Drakewell Farm (UWC) 26m

Lamington Farm (UWC)

Buchanstone

3

River Don

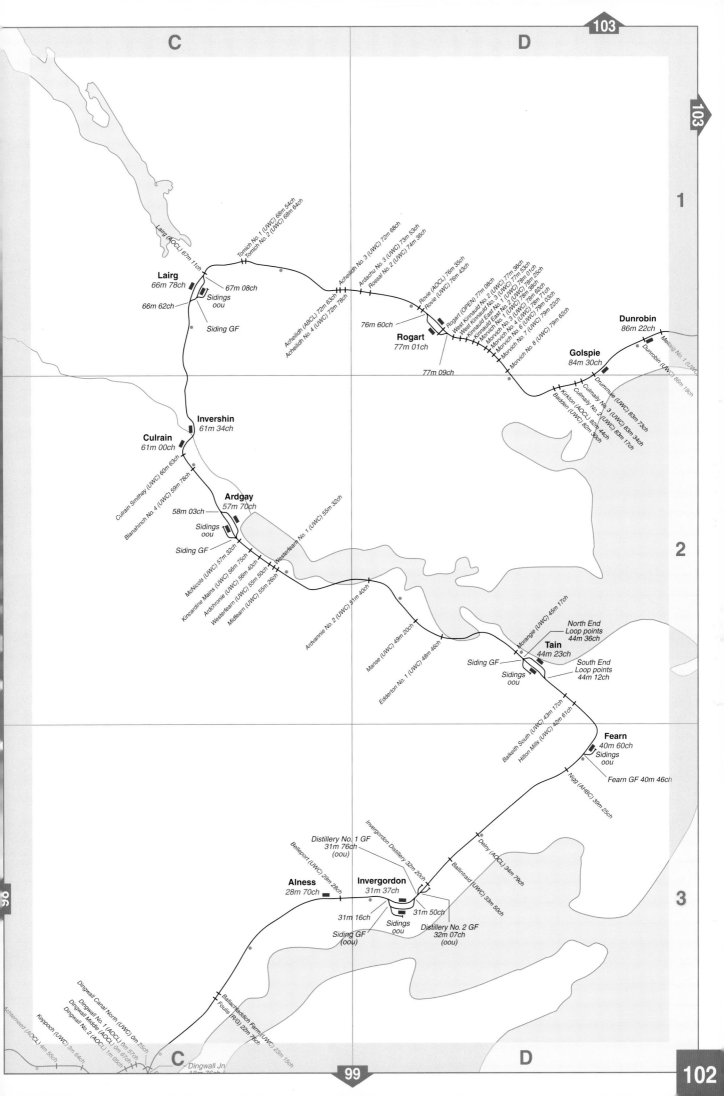

C

D

1

Tornich No. 1 (UWC) 68m 54ch
Tornich No. 2 (UWC) 68m 64ch

Lairg
66m 78ch

67m 08ch

66m 62ch

*Sidings
oou*

Siding GF

Acheilidh No. 3 (UWC) 72m 68ch
Acheilidh (ABCL) 72m 63ch
Acheilidh No. 4 (UWC) 72m 78ch

Ardachu No. 3 (UWC) 73m 53ch
Rossal No. 2 (UWC) 74m 36ch

76m 60ch

Rovie (AOCL) 76m 35ch
Rovie (UWC) 76m 43ch

Rogart
77m 01ch

77m 09ch

Rogart (OPEN) 77m 08ch
West Kinnauld No. 2 (UWC) 77m 36ch
West Kinnauld No. 3 (UWC) 77m 53ch
Kinnauld No. 1 (UWC) 78m 01ch
Kinnauld East No. 1 (UWC) 78m 25ch
Morvich No. 2 (UWC) 78m 36ch
Morvich No. 3 (UWC) 78m 62ch
Morvich No. 4 (UWC) 78m 71ch
Morvich No. 6 (UWC) 79m 03ch
Morvich No. 7 (UWC) 79m 22ch
Morvich No. 8 (UWC) 79m 62ch

Dunrobin
86m 22ch

Mellieg No. 1 (UWC)

Dunrobin (UWC) 86m 18ch

Golspie
84m 30ch

Drummuie (UWC) 83m 73ch
Culmaily No. 2 (UWC) 83m 34ch
Culmaily No. 3 (UWC) 83m 44ch
Kirkton (AOCL) 82m 44ch
Badden (UWC) 82m 30ch

Invershin
61m 34ch

Culrain
61m 00ch

Culrain Smithey (UWC) 60m 63ch

Blairahinch No. 4 (UWC) 59m 78ch

Ardgay
57m 70ch

58m 03ch

*Sidings
oou*

Siding GF

McNicols (UWC) 57m 32ch
Kincardine Mains (UWC) 56m 75ch
Ardchronie (UWC) 56m 40ch
Westerfearn (UWC) 55m 50ch
Midfearn (UWC) 55m 26ch

Westerfearn No. 1 (UWC) 55m 32ch

Ardvannie No. 2 (UWC) 51m 40ch

Manse (UWC) 49m 20ch

Edderton No. 1 (UWC) 48m 46ch

Morangie (UWC) 45m 17ch

**North End
Loop points
44m 36ch**

Tain
44m 23ch

Siding GF

*Sidings
oou*

**South End
Loop points
44m 12ch**

Balkeith South (UWC) 43m 17ch
Hilton Mills (UWC) 42m 61ch

Fearn
40m 60ch

*Sidings
oou*

Fearn GF 40m 46ch

Nigg (AHBC) 39m 25ch

Delny (AOCL) 34m 78ch

Ballintraid (UWC) 33m 50ch

2

*Distillery No. 1 GF
31m 76ch
(oou)*

Invergordon Distillery 32m 20ch

Belleport (UWC) 29m 28ch

Alness
28m 70ch

Invergordon
31m 37ch

31m 16ch

31m 50ch

*Sidings
oou*

*Siding GF
(oou)*

*Distillery No. 2 GF
32m 07ch
(oou)*

96

3

Dingwall Canal North (UWC) 0m 25ch
Dingwall No. 1 (AOCL) 0m 57ch
Dingwall Middle (UWC) 0m 67ch
Dingwall No. 2 (AOCL) 1m 08ch

Achterneed (AOCL) 4m 55ch

Kegpoch (UWC) 3m 64ch

Ballachladich Farm (UWC) 23m 16ch
Foulis (RG) 22m 76ch

Dingwall Jn
18m 76ch

C

D

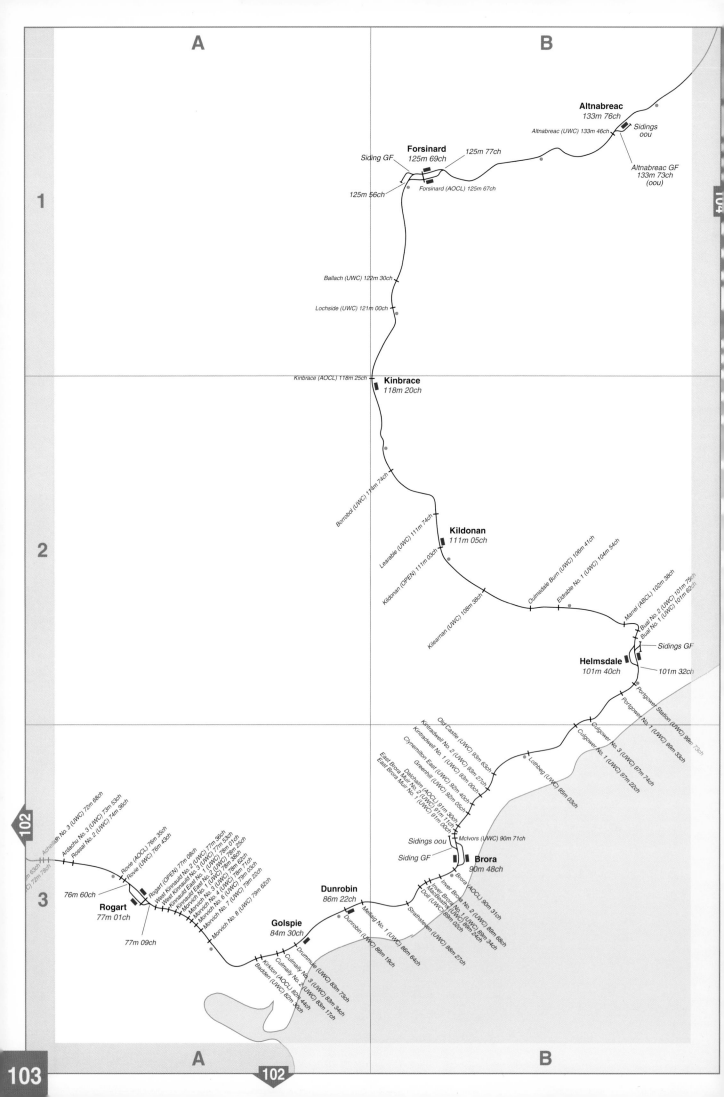

Altnabreac
133m 76ch

Altnabreac (UWC) 133m 46ch

Sidings
oou

*Altnabreac GF
133m 73ch
(oou)*

Forsinard
125m 69ch

125m 77ch

Siding GF

125m 56ch

Forsinard (AOCL) 125m 67ch

1

Ballach (UWC) 122m 30ch

Lochside (UWC) 121m 00ch

Kinbrace (AOCL) 118m 25ch

Kinbrace
118m 20ch

Borrobol (UWC) 114m 74ch

2

Learable (UWC) 111m 03ch

Kildonan
111m 05ch

Kildonan (OPEN) 111m 03ch

Quilmsdale Burn (UWC) 106m 41ch

Eldrable No. 1 (UWC) 104m 54ch

Marrel (ABCL) 102m 38ch

Kilearnan (UWC) 108m 38ch

Bual No. 2 (UWC) 101m 75ch
Bual No. 1 (UWC) 101m 62ch

Sidings GF

Helmsdale
101m 40ch

101m 32ch

Portgower Station (UWC) 99m 73ch

Portgower No. 1 (UWC) 99m 33ch

Old Castle (UWC) 93m 63ch

Kintradwell No. 2 (UWC) 93m 27ch

Kintradwell No. 1 (UWC) 93m 00ch

Culgower No. 3 (UWC) 97m 74ch

Culgower No. 1 (UWC) 97m 22ch

Lothbeg (UWC) 95m 03ch

Clynemilton East (UWC) 92m 40ch

Dalchalm (AOCL) 91m 30ch

Greenhill (UWC) 92m 11ch

East Brora Muir No. 2 (UWC) 91m 11ch
East Brora Muir No. 1 (UWC) 91m 00ch

McIvors (UWC) 90m 71ch

Sidings oou

Siding GF

Brora
90m 48ch

Brora (AOCL) 90m 31ch

Inver Brora No. 2 (UWC) 89m 68ch
Inver Brora No. 1 (UWC) 89m 34ch
Macdonalds (UWC) 89m 24ch
Doll (UWC) 89m 02ch

Strathsteven (UWC) 89m 27ch

Achelidh No. 3 (UWC) 72m 68ch

Ardachu No. 3 (UWC) 73m 53ch

Rossal No. 2 (UWC) 74m 36ch

C) 72m 78ch
n 63ch

Rovie (AOCL) 76m 35ch
Rovie (UWC) 76m 43ch

76m 60ch

Rogart
77m 01ch

77m 09ch

Rogart (OPEN) 77m 08ch
West Kinnauld No. 2 (UWC) 77m 36ch
West Kinnauld No. 3 (UWC) 77m 03ch
Kinnauld East No. 1 (UWC) 78m 01ch
Kinnauld East No. 2 (UWC) 78m 25ch
Morvich No. 1 (UWC) 78m 38ch
Morvich No. 3 (UWC) 78m 62ch
Morvich No. 4 (UWC) 78m 11ch
Morvich No. 7 (UWC) 79m 03ch
Morvich No. 8 (UWC) 79m 62ch

Dunrobin
86m 22ch

Dunrobin (UWC) 86m 19ch

Golspie
84m 30ch

Drummuie (UWC) 83m 75ch

Culmaily No. 3 (UWC) 83m 34ch

Kirkton (AOCL) 83m 44ch

Culmaily No. 2 (UWC) 83m 17ch

Badden (UWC) 82m 30ch

Meltaig No. 1 (UWC) 86m 64ch

3

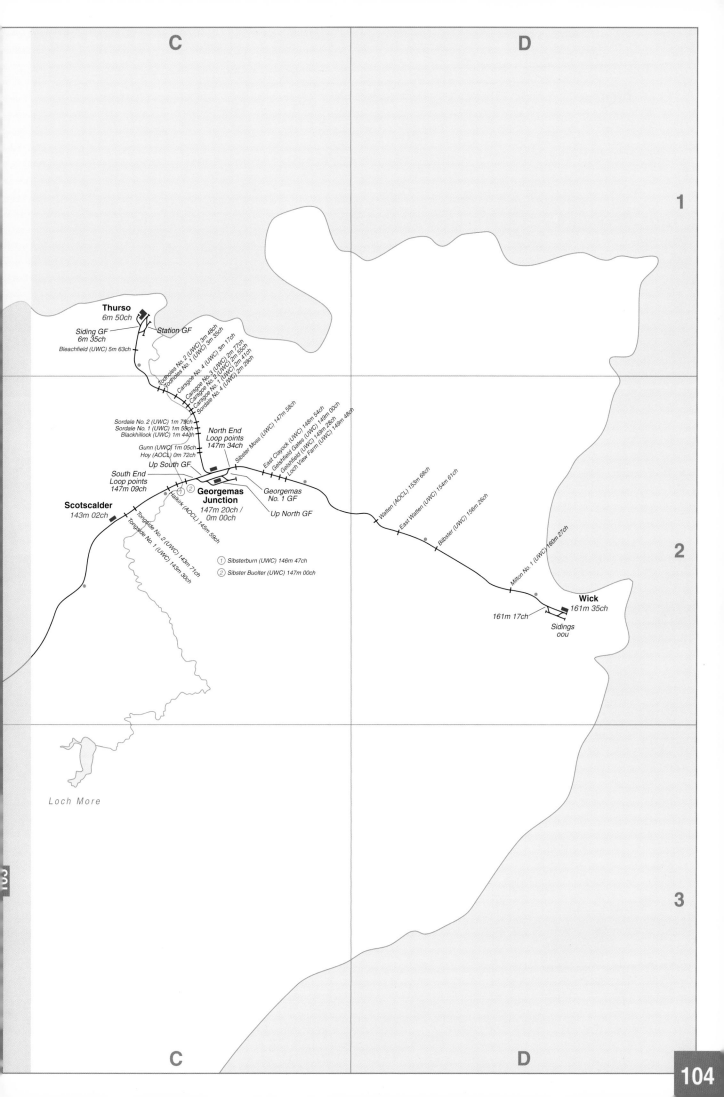

Thurso
6m 50ch

Siding GF
6m 35ch

Station GF

Bleachfield (UWC) *5m 63ch*

Todholes No. 2 (UWC) *3m 48ch*
Todholes No. 1 (UWC) *3m 35ch*
Carsgoe No. 4 (UWC) *3m 17ch*
Carsgoe No. 3 (UWC) *2m 77ch*
Carsgoe No. 2 (UWC) *2m 55ch*
Carsgoe No. 1 (UWC) *2m 41ch*
Sordale No. 4 (UWC) *2m 29ch*

Sordale No. 2 (UWC) *1m 79ch*
Sordale No. 1 (UWC) *1m 59ch*
Blackhillock (UWC) *1m 44ch*

Gunn (UWC) *1m 05ch*
Hoy (AOCL) *0m 72ch*

**North End
Loop points**
147m 34ch

Up South GF

Sibster Moss (UWC) *147m 58ch*
East Clayock (UWC) *148m 54ch*
Gelshfield Gates (UWC) *149m 00ch*
Gelshfield (UWC) *149m 28ch*
Loch View Farm (UWC) *149m 48ch*

**South End
Loop points**
147m 09ch

① ②

Halkirk (AOCL) *145m 59ch*

**Georgemas
Junction**
*147m 20ch /
0m 00ch*

Georgemas
No. 1 GF

Up North GF

Scotscalder
143m 02ch

Tongside No. 2 (UWC) *143m 71ch*
Tongside No. 1 (UWC) *143m 30ch*

① Sibsterburn (UWC) *146m 47ch*
② Sibster Buolter (UWC) *147m 00ch*

Watten (AOCL) *153m 68ch*
East Watten (UWC) *154m 61ch*
Bilbster (UWC) *156m 26ch*
Milton No. 1 (UWC) *160m 27ch*

Wick
161m 35ch

161m 17ch

Sidings
oou

Loch More

Notes

Contents: Area and Inset Maps

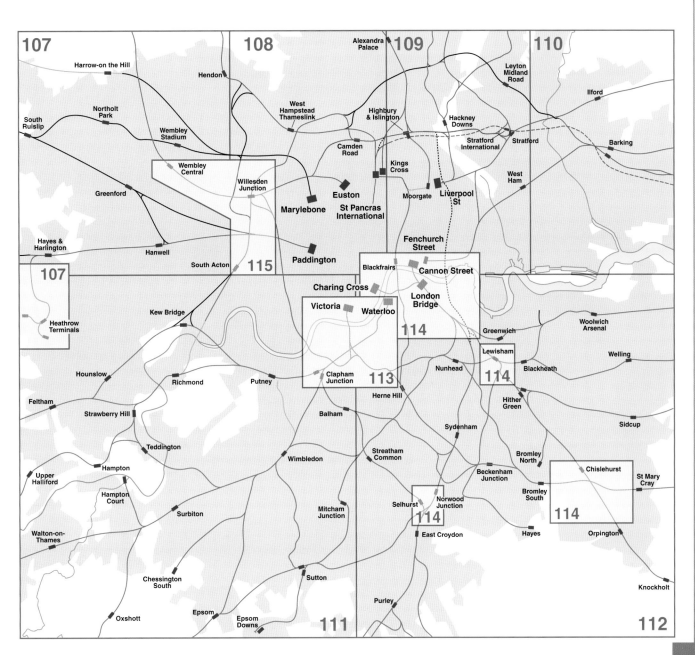

A

B

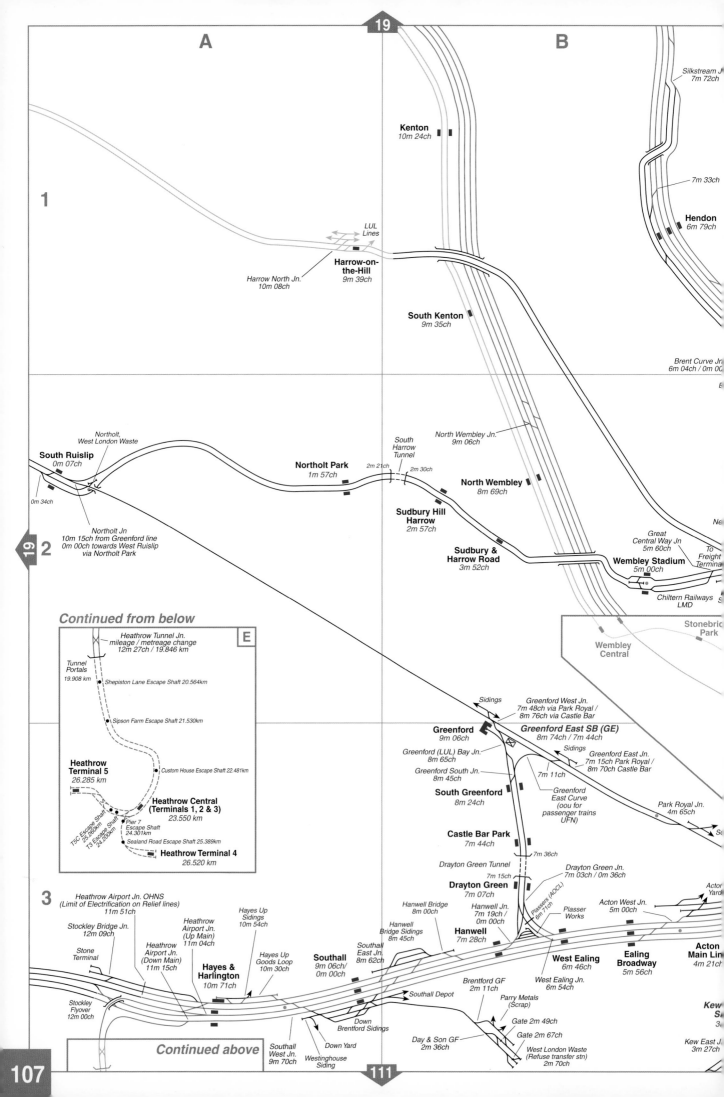

Kenton
10m 24ch

Silkstream J
7m 72ch

1

7m 33ch

Hendon
6m 79ch

*LUL
Lines*

**Harrow-on-
the-Hill**
9m 39ch

*Harrow North Jn.
10m 08ch*

South Kenton
9m 35ch

*Brent Curve Jr
6m 04ch / 0m 00*

E

*North Wembley Jn.
9m 06ch*

South Ruislip
0m 07ch

*Northolt,
West London Waste*

*South
Harrow
Tunnel*

Northolt Park
1m 57ch

2m 21ch   *2m 30ch*

North Wembley
8m 69ch

0m 34ch

*Northolt Jn
10m 15ch from Greenford line
0m 00ch towards West Ruislip
via Northolt Park*

**Sudbury Hill
Harrow**
2m 57ch

*Great
Central Way Jn*

Ne

2

**Sudbury &
Harrow Road**
3m 52ch

Wembley Stadium
5m 00ch

5m 60ch

*To
Freight
Termina*

*Chiltern Railways
LMD*

S

Continued from below

*Heathrow Tunnel Jn.
mileage / metreage change
12m 27ch / 19.846 km*

E

*Stonebri
Park*

*Wembley
Central*

*Tunnel Portals
19.908 km*

● Shepiston Lane Escape Shaft 20.564km

● Sipson Farm Escape Shaft 21.530km

**Heathrow
Terminal 5**
26.285 km

● Custom House Escape Shaft 22.481km

**Heathrow Central
(Terminals 1, 2 & 3)**
23.550 km

Sidings

*Greenford West Jn.
7m 48ch via Park Royal /
8m 76ch via Castle Bar*

Greenford
9m 06ch

Greenford East SB (GE)
8m 74ch / 7m 44ch

*Greenford (LUL) Bay Jn.
8m 65ch*

Sidings

*Greenford East Jn.
7m 15ch Park Royal /
8m 70ch Castle Bar*

T5C Escape Shaft 25.260km
T3 Escape Shaft 24.200km
*Pier 7
Escape Shaft
24.301km*

*Greenford South Jn.
8m 45ch*

7m 11ch

*Greenford
East Curve
(oou for
passenger trains
UFN)*

*Park Royal Jn.
4m 65ch*

● Sealand Road Escape Shaft 25.389km

Heathrow Terminal 4
26.520 km

South Greenford
8m 24ch

S

Castle Bar Park
7m 44ch

7m 36ch

Drayton Green Tunnel

7m 15ch

*Drayton Green Jn.
7m 03ch / 0m 36ch*

*Acto
Yard*

3

*Heathrow Airport Jn. OHNS
(Limit of Electrification on Relief lines)
11m 51ch*

*Hayes Up
Sidings
10m 54ch*

*Hanwell Bridge
8m 00ch*

Drayton Green
7m 07ch

*Hanwell Jn.
7m 19ch /
0m 00ch*

*Plassers (AOCL)
6m 71ch*

*Plasser
Works*

*Acton West Jn.
5m 00ch*

*Stockley Bridge Jn.
12m 09ch*

**Heathrow
Airport Jn.
(Up Main)**
11m 04ch

*Hanwell
Bridge Sidings
8m 45ch*

Hanwell
7m 28ch

**Acton
Main Lin**
4m 21ch

*Stone
Terminal*

*Heathrow
Airport Jn.
(Down Main)
11m 15ch*

**Hayes &
Harlington**
10m 71ch

*Hayes Up
Goods Loop
10m 30ch*

Southall
*9m 06ch/
0m 00ch*

*Southall
East Jn.
8m 62ch*

West Ealing
6m 46ch

**Ealing
Broadway**
5m 56ch

Kew
S
3

*Stockley
Flyover
12m 00ch*

Continued above

*Southall
West Jn.
9m 70ch*

*Down
Brentford Sidings*

*Westinghouse
Siding*

Down Yard

Southall Depot

*Brentford GF
2m 11ch*

*Parry Metals
(Scrap)*

*Day & Son GF
2m 36ch*

Gate 2m 49ch

Gate 2m 67ch

*West London Waste
(Refuse transfer stn)
2m 70ch*

*West Ealing Jn.
6m 54ch*

*Kew East J
3m 27ch*

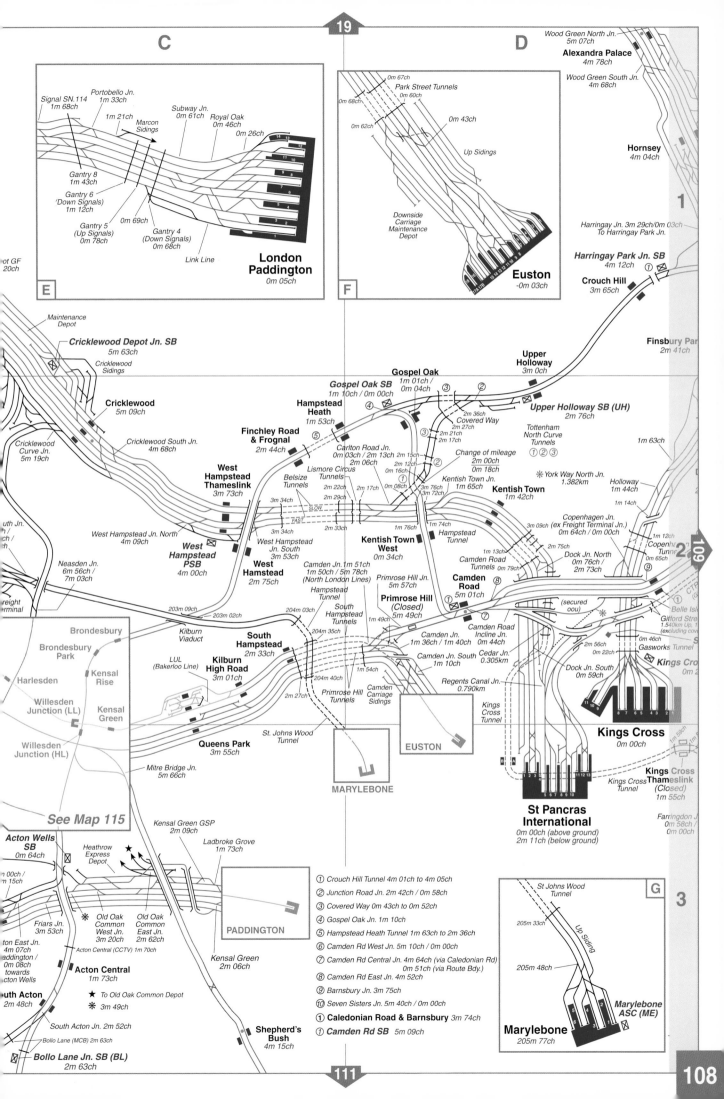

C

Signal SN.114
1m 68ch

Portobello Jn.
1m 33ch

1m 21ch

Subway Jn.
0m 61ch

Royal Oak
0m 46ch

Marcon
Sidings

0m 26ch

14 13
12
11 10
9
8
7
6
5 4
3 2
1

Gantry 8
1m 43ch

Gantry 6
('Down Signals)
1m 12ch

0m 69ch

Gantry 5
(Up Signals)
0m 78ch

Gantry 4
(Down Signals)
0m 68ch

Link Line

**London
Paddington**
0m 05ch

ot GF
20ch

E

D

Wood Green North Jn.
5m 07ch

Alexandra Palace
4m 78ch

Wood Green South Jn.
4m 68ch

Hornsey
4m 04ch

1

Harringay Jn. 3m 29ch/0m 03ch
To Harringay Park Jn.

Harringay Park Jn. SB
4m 12ch ①

Crouch Hill
3m 65ch

0m 67ch

Park Street Tunnels
0m 60ch

0m 68ch

0m 62ch

0m 43ch

Up Sidings

Downside
Carriage
Maintenance
Depot

Euston
-0m 03ch

F

Finsbury Par
2m 41ch

Maintenance
Depot

Cricklewood Depot Jn. SB
5m 63ch

Cricklewood
Sidings

Cricklewood
5m 09ch

Cricklewood South Jn.
4m 68ch

Cricklewood
Curve Jn.
5m 19ch

Gospel Oak

Gospel Oak SB
1m 10ch / 0m 00ch

**Upper
Holloway**
3m 0ch

④

Upper Holloway SB (UH)
2m 76ch

**Hampstead
Heath**
1m 53ch

⑤

2m 36ch
Covered Way
2m 27ch

③

②

2m 21ch
2m 17ch

Tottenham
North Curve
Tunnels
① ② ③

1m 63ch

**Finchley Road
& Frognal**
2m 44ch

Carlton Road Jn.
0m 03ch / 2m 13ch
2m 06ch

2m 15ch

③

②

0m 12ch

Change of mileage
2m 00ch
0m 18ch

❋ York Way North Jn.
1.382km

Holloway
1m 44ch

Lismore Circus
Tunnels

0m 16ch

Kentish Town
1m 42ch

1m 14ch

**West
Hampstead
Thameslink**
3m 73ch

Belsize
Tunnels
2m 22ch 2m 17ch

2m 29ch

0m 08ch

3m 76ch
3m 72ch

Kentish Town Jn.
1m 65ch

Copenhagen Jn.
(ex Freight Terminal Jn.)
3m 09ch 0m 64ch / 0m 00ch

1m 12ch
Copenh
Tunne
0m 65ch

3m 34ch SLOW

FAST

2m 33ch

1m 76ch

1m 74ch

**Kentish Town
West**
0m 34ch

Hampstead
Tunnel

Dock Jn. North
0m 76ch /
2m 73ch

2

West Hampstead Jn. North
4m 09ch

3m 34ch

West Hampstead
Jn. South
3m 53ch

1m 13ch

Camden Road
Tunnels 0m 79ch

⑨

*West
Hampstead
PSB*

⊠

**West
Hamstead**
2m 75ch

**Kentish Town
West**
0m 34ch

Camden Jn.1m 51ch
1m 50ch / 5m 78ch
(North London Lines)

Primrose Hill Jn.
5m 57ch

**Camden
Road**
5m 01ch

⑧

(secured
oou)

Belle Isl

Gifford Stre
1.540km Up. 1
(excluding cove

Neasden Jn.
6m 56ch /
7m 03ch

Hampstead
Tunnel

Primrose Hill
(Closed)
5m 49ch

⑦

❋

2m 56ch
0m 22ch

0m 46ch
Gasworks Tunnel

203m 09ch

203m 02ch

204m 03ch

South
Hampstead
Tunnels

Camden Jn.
1m 36ch / 1m 40ch
0m 44ch

Camden Road
Incline Jn.
0m 44ch

Dock Jn. South
0m 59ch

Kings Cro
0m 2

reight
erminal

Brondesbury

Brondesbury
Park

Kilburn
Viaduct

**South
Hampstead**
2m 33ch

204m 35ch

Cedar Jn.
0.305km

11 10 9

8 7 6 5 4 3 2 1

Kings Cross
0m 00ch

Harlesden

Kensal
Rise

LUL
(Bakerloo Line)

**Kilburn
High Road**
3m 01ch

1m 49ch

Camden Jn. South
1m 10ch

Camden
Carriage
Sidings

Regents Canal Jn.
0.790km

Kings
Cross
Tunnel

**Willesden
Junction (LL)**

Kensal
Green

204m 40ch

1m 54ch

Primrose Hill
Tunnels

EUSTON

**Willesden
Junction (HL)**

2m 27ch

St. Johns Wood
Tunnel

Queens Park
3m 55ch

**St Pancras
International**
0m 00ch (above ground)
2m 11ch (below ground)

Kings Cross
Tunnel

Kings Cross
Thameslink
(Closed)
1m 55ch

Farringdon J
0m 58ch /
0m 00ch

Mitre Bridge Jn.
5m 66ch

MARYLEBONE

See Map 115

Kensal Green GSP
2m 09ch

Heathrow
Express
Depot

Ladbroke Grove
1m 73ch

*Acton Wells
SB*
0m 64ch

St Johns Wood
Tunnel

G

00ch /
15ch

⊠

PADDINGTON

205m 33ch

Up Siding

3

❋

Friars Jn.
3m 53ch

Old Oak
Common
West Jn.
3m 20ch

Old Oak
Common
East Jn.
2m 62ch

205m 48ch

ton East Jn.
4m 07ch
addington /
0m 08ch
towards
cton Wells

Acton Central (CCTV) 1m 70ch

Acton Central
1m 73ch

Kensal Green
2m 06ch

① Crouch Hill Tunnel 4m 01ch to 4m 05ch
② Junction Road Jn. 2m 42ch / 0m 58ch
③ Covered Way 0m 43ch to 0m 52ch
④ Gospel Oak Jn. 1m 10ch
⑤ Hampstead Heath Tunnel 1m 63ch to 2m 36ch
⑥ Camden Rd West Jn. 5m 10ch / 0m 00ch
⑦ Camden Rd Central Jn. 4m 64ch (via Caledonian Rd)
   0m 51ch (via Route Bdy.)
⑧ Camden Rd East Jn. 4m 52ch
⑨ Barnsbury Jn. 3m 75ch
⑩ Seven Sisters Jn. 5m 40ch / 0m 00ch

⑪ **Caledonian Road & Barnsbury** 3m 74ch

⑫ *Camden Rd SB* 5m 09ch

⊠

Marylebone
205m 77ch

*Marylebone
ASC (ME)*

⊠

★ To Old Oak Common Depot
❋ 3m 49ch

uth Acton
2m 48ch

South Acton Jn. 2m 52ch

Bollo Lane (MCB) 2m 63ch

Bollo Lane Jn. SB (BL)
2m 63ch

**Shepherd's
Bush**
4m 15ch

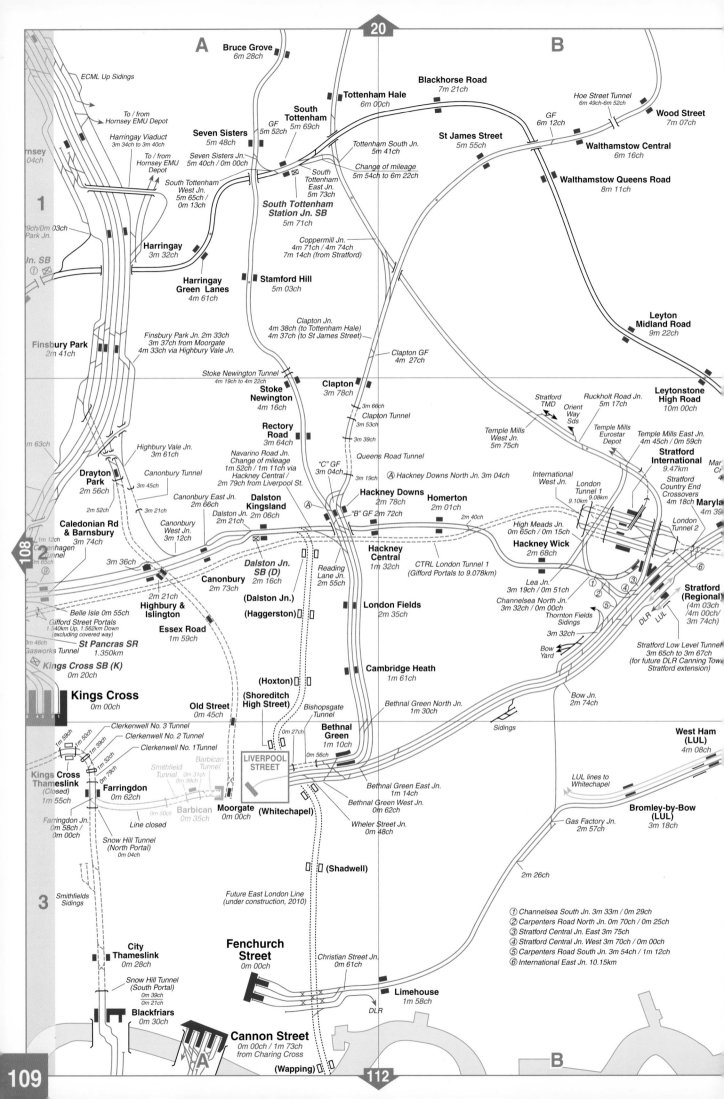

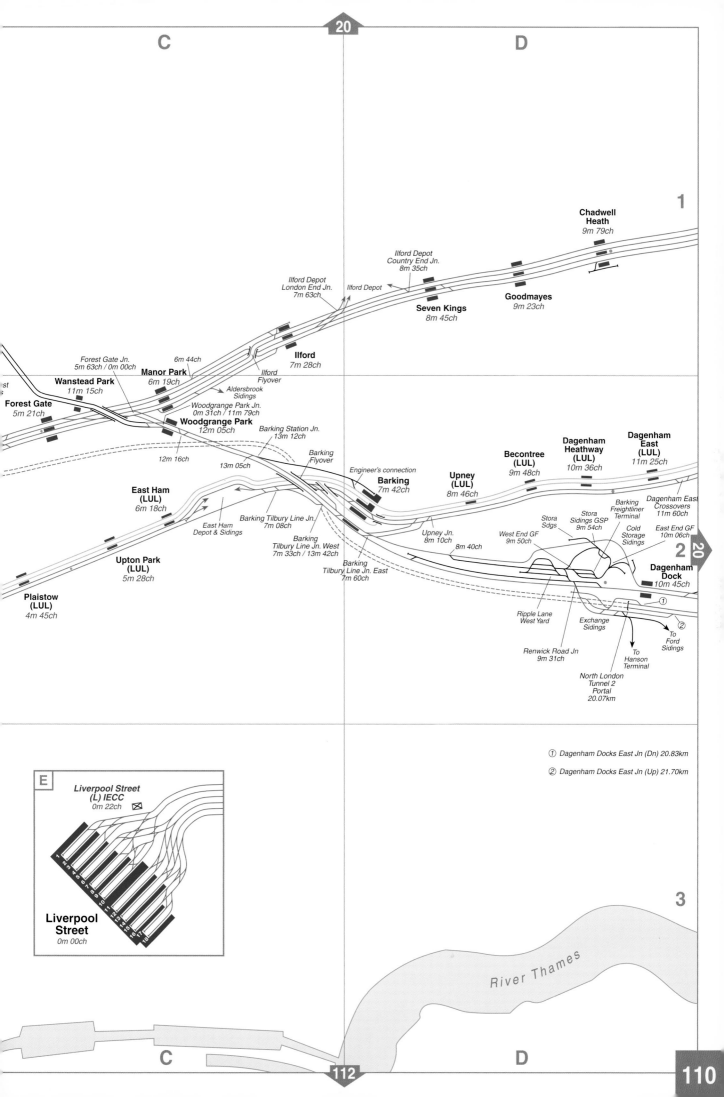

C

D

1

Chadwell
Heath
9m 79ch

*Ilford Depot
Country End Jn.
8m 35ch*

Goodmayes
9m 23ch

*Ilford Depot
London End Jn.
7m 63ch*

Ilford Depot

Seven Kings
8m 45ch

*Forest Gate Jn.
5m 63ch / 0m 00ch*

6m 44ch

Manor Park
6m 19ch

Ilford
7m 28ch

*Ilford
Flyover*

Wanstead Park
11m 15ch

Forest Gate
5m 21ch

*Aldersbrook
Sidings*

Woodgrange Park
12m 05ch

*Woodgrange Park Jn.
0m 31ch / 11m 79ch*

*Barking Station Jn.
13m 12ch*

12m 16ch

*Barking
Flyover*

13m 05ch

Engineer's connection

Barking
7m 42ch

Upney
(LUL)
8m 46ch

Becontree
(LUL)
9m 48ch

Dagenham
Heathway
(LUL)
10m 36ch

Dagenham
East
(LUL)
11m 25ch

East Ham
(LUL)
6m 18ch

*East Ham
Depot & Sidings*

*Barking Tilbury Line Jn.
7m 08ch*

*Barking
Tilbury Line Jn. West
7m 33ch / 13m 42ch*

*Barking
Tilbury Line Jn. East
7m 60ch*

*Upney Jn.
8m 10ch*

8m 40ch

*Stora
Sdgs*

*Stora
Sidings GSP
9m 54ch*

*Barking
Freightliner
Terminal*

*Dagenham East
Crossovers
11m 60ch*

*Cold
Storage
Sidings*

*West End GF
9m 50ch*

*East End GF
10m 06ch*

Dagenham
Dock
10m 45ch

Upton Park
(LUL)
5m 28ch

Plaistow
(LUL)
4m 45ch

*Ripple Lane
West Yard*

*Exchange
Sidings*

①

*Renwick Road Jn
9m 31ch*

*To
Hanson
Terminal*

②

*To
Ford
Sidings*

*North London
Tunnel 2
Portal
20.07km*

2

① *Dagenham Docks East Jn (Dn) 20.83km*

② *Dagenham Docks East Jn (Up) 21.70km*

E

*Liverpool Street
(L) IECC
0m 22ch*

Liverpool
Street
0m 00ch

3

River Thames

C

D

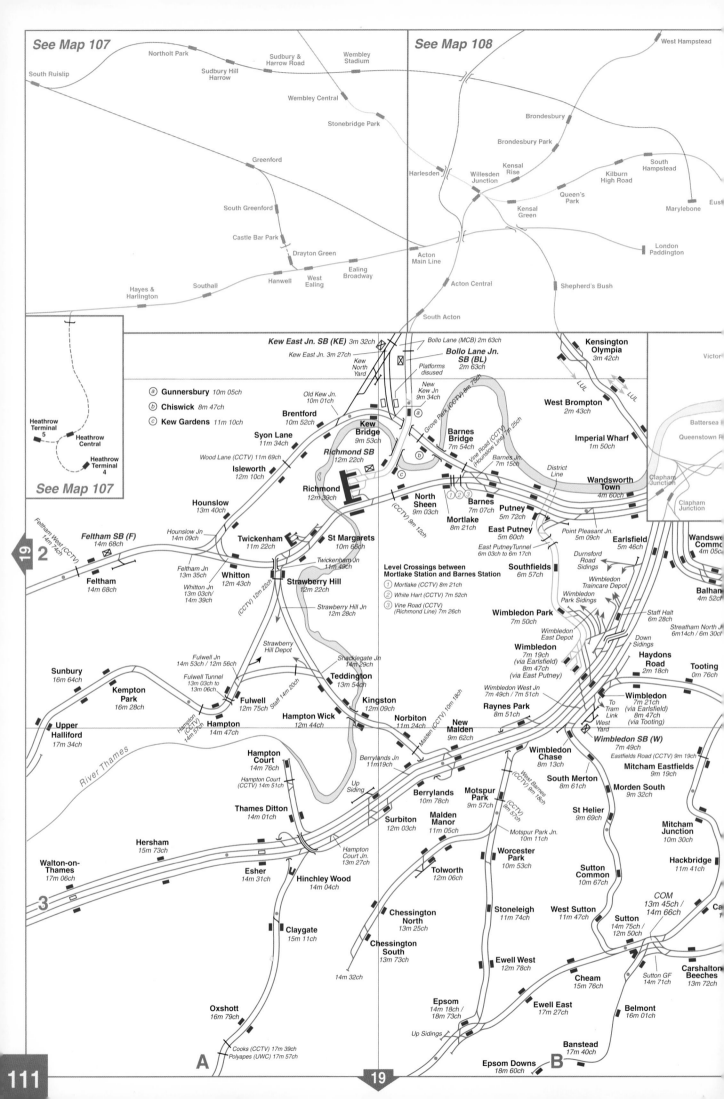

South Ruislip

Northolt Park

Sudbury Hill Harrow

Sudbury & Harrow Road

Wembley Stadium

Wembley Central

Stonebridge Park

West Hampstead

Brondesbury

Brondesbury Park

Greenford

Harlesden

Willesden Junction

Kensal Rise

Kensal Green

South Hampstead

Kilburn High Road

Queen's Park

Marylebone

Eus

South Greenford

Castle Bar Park

Drayton Green

Acton Main Line

London Paddington

Southall

Hanwell

West Ealing

Ealing Broadway

Acton Central

Shepherd's Bush

Hayes & Harlington

South Acton

Kew East Jn. SB (KE) 3m 32ch

Kew East Jn. 3m 27ch

Bollo Lane (MCB) 2m 63ch

Bollo Lane Jn. SB (BL) 2m 63ch

Kew North Yard

Platforms disused

Kensington Olympia 3m 42ch

Victor

ⓐ **Gunnersbury** 10m 05ch
ⓑ **Chiswick** 8m 47ch
ⓒ **Kew Gardens** 11m 10ch

Old Kew Jn. 10m 01ch

New Kew Jn 9m 34ch

ⓐ

Grove Park (CCTV) 8m 75ch

West Brompton 2m 43ch

LUL

LUL

Brentford 10m 52ch

Syon Lane 11m 34ch

Kew Bridge 9m 53ch

Barnes Bridge 7m 54ch

Vine Road (CCTV) (Hounslow Line) 7m 25ch

ⓑ

Battersea

Imperial Wharf 1m 50ch

Queenstown Ri

Wood Lane (CCTV) 11m 69ch

Richmond SB 12m 22ch

Isleworth 12m 10ch

Richmond 12m 39ch

North Sheen 9m 03ch

ⓒ

Barnes Jn. 7m 15ch

District Line

Wandsworth Town 4m 60ch

Clapham

Clapham Junction

Heathrow Terminal 5

Heathrow Central

Heathrow Terminal 4

See Map 107

Hounslow 13m 40ch

①②③

Barnes 7m 07ch

Mortlake 8m 21ch

Putney 5m 72ch

East Putney 5m 09ch

Point Pleasant Jn. 5m 60ch

(CCTV) 9m 12ch

Earlsfield 5m 46ch

Wandswo Commo 4m 05c

Feltham West (CCTV) 14m 74ch

Feltham SB (F) 14m 68ch

Twickenham 11m 22ch

St Margarets 10m 66ch

East Putney Tunnel 6m 03ch to 6m 17ch

Southfields 6m 57ch

Durnsford Road Sidings

Wimbledon Traincare Depot

Staff Halt 6m 28ch

Balham 4m 52ch

Hounslow Jn. 14m 09ch

Twickenham Jn 11m 49ch

Streatham North J 6m14ch / 6m 30ch

2

Feltham Jn 13m 35ch

Whitton 12m 43ch

Strawberry Hill 12m 22ch

Wimbledon Park Sidings

Feltham 14m 68ch

Whitton Jn 13m 03ch / 14m 39ch

Level Crossings between Mortlake Station and Barnes Station

Wimbledon Park 7m 50ch

Wimbledon East Depot

Down Sidings

Haydons Road 2m 18ch

Tooting 0m 76ch

(CCTV) 12m 22ch

Strawberry Hill Jn 12m 28ch

① Mortlake (CCTV) 8m 21ch
② White Hart (CCTV) 7m 52ch
③ Vine Road (CCTV) (Richmond Line) 7m 26ch

Wimbledon 7m 19ch (via Earlsfield) 8m 47ch (via East Putney)

Sunbury 16m 64ch

Fulwell Jn 14m 53ch / 12m 56ch

Strawberry Hill Depot

Shacklegate Jn 14m 29ch

Wimbledon West Jn 7m 49ch / 7m 51ch

Wimbledon 7m 21ch (via Earlsfield) 8m 47ch (via Tooting)

Kempton Park 16m 28ch

Fulwell Tunnel 13m 03ch to 13m 06ch

Teddington 13m 54ch

Raynes Park 8m 51ch

To Tram Link

West Yard

Fulwell 12m 75ch

Staff 14m 20ch

Kingston 12m 09ch

Wimbledon SB (W) 7m 49ch

Upper Halliford 17m 34ch

Hampton (CCTV) 14m 57ch

Hampton 14m 47ch

Hampton Wick 12m 44ch

Norbiton 11m 24ch

Malden (CCTV) 10m 18ch

New Malden 9m 62ch

Eastlands Road (CCTV) 9m 19ch

Wimbledon Chase 8m 13ch

Mitcham Eastfields 9m 19ch

Hampton Court 14m 76ch

Hampton Court (CCTV) 14m 51ch

Berrylands Jn 11m19ch

Up Siding

West Barnes (CCTV) 9m 18ch

(CCTV) 9m 57ch

South Merton 8m 61ch

Morden South 9m 32ch

River Thames

Thames Ditton 14m 01ch

Berrylands 10m 78ch

Motspur Park 9m 57ch

Motspur Park Jn. 10m 11ch

St Helier 9m 69ch

Mitcham Junction 10m 30ch

Hersham 15m 73ch

Surbiton 12m 03ch

Malden Manor 11m 05ch

Worcester Park 10m 53ch

Sutton Common 10m 67ch

Hackbridge 11m 41ch

Walton-on-Thames 17m 06ch

Esher 14m 31ch

Hampton Court Jn. 13m 27ch

Hinchley Wood 14m 04ch

Tolworth 12m 06ch

COM 13m 45ch / 14m 66ch

3

Claygate 15m 11ch

Chessington North 13m 25ch

Stoneleigh 11m 74ch

West Sutton 11m 47ch

Sutton 12m 75ch / 12m 50ch

Ca

Chessington South 13m 73ch

Ewell West 12m 78ch

Cheam 15m 76ch

Sutton GF 14m 71ch

Carshalton Beeches 13m 72ch

14m 32ch

Oxshott 16m 79ch

Epsom 14m 18ch / 18m 73ch

Ewell East 17m 27ch

Belmont 16m 01ch

Up Sidings

Banstead 17m 40ch

Cooks (CCTV) 17m 39ch
Polyapes (UWC) 17m 57ch

A

B

19

Epsom Downs 18m 60ch

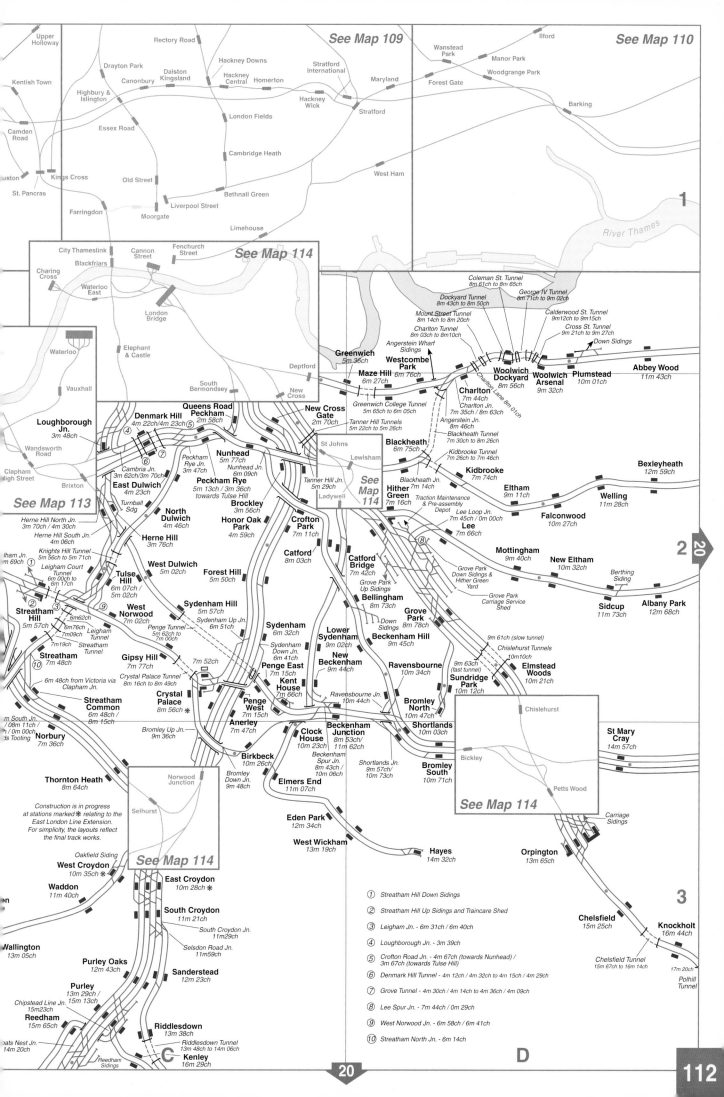

See Map 114
See Map 113
See Map 114
See Map 114

Upper Holloway
Rectory Road
Ilford
Wanstead Park
Manor Park
Woodgrange Park
Drayton Park
Hackney Downs
Kentish Town
Canonbury
Dalston Kingsland
Hackney Central
Homerton
Stratford International
Maryland
Forest Gate
Highbury & Islington
Hackney Wick
Barking
Essex Road
London Fields
Stratford
Camden Road
Cambridge Heath
West Ham
uston
Kings Cross
Old Street
St. Pancras
Farringdon
Moorgate
Bethnal Green
West Ham
Liverpool Street
Limehouse

River Thames

1

City Thameslink
Cannon Street
Fenchurch Street
Blackfriars
Charing Cross
Waterloo East
London Bridge

Coleman St. Tunnel
8m 61ch to 8m 65ch
George IV Tunnel
8m 71ch to 9m 02ch
Dockyard Tunnel
8m 43ch to 8m 50ch
Calderwood St. Tunnel
9m12ch to 9m15ch
Mount Street Tunnel
8m 14ch to 8m 20ch
Cross St. Tunnel
9m 21ch to 9m 27ch
Charlton Tunnel
8m 03ch to 8m10ch
Down Sidings
Angerstein Wharf Sidings

Waterloo
Elephant & Castle
Deptford
South Bermondsey
New Cross
Greenwich
5m 36ch
Westcombe Park
Maze Hill
6m 27ch
6m 76ch
Woolwich Dockyard
8m 56ch
Woolwich Arsenal
9m 32ch
Plumstead
10m 01ch
Abbey Wood
11m 43ch
Charlton Lane 8m 01ch
Charlton
7m 44ch
Charlton Jn.
7m 63ch
Greenwich College Tunnel
5m 65ch to 6m 05ch
Angerstein Jn.
8m 46ch

Vauxhall
Wandsworth Road
South Bermondsey
Queens Road Peckham
2m 58ch
New Cross Gate
2m 70ch
St Johns
Tanner Hill Tunnels
5m 22ch to 5m 26ch
Blackwall Jn.
7m 30ch to 8m 26ch
Blackheath Tunnel
Loughborough Jn.
3m 48ch
Denmark Hill
4m 22ch/4m 23ch
Peckham Rye Jn.
3m 47ch
Nunhead
5m 77ch
Nunhead Jn.
6m 09ch
Lewisham
Blackheath
6m 75ch
Kidbrooke Tunnel
7m 26ch to 7m 46ch
Bexleyheath
12m 59ch

Clapham High Street
Cambria Jn.
3m 62ch/3m 70ch
Peckham Rye
5m 13ch / 3m 36ch towards Tulse Hill
Brockley
3m 56ch
Tanner Hill Jn.
5m 29ch
See Map 114
Hither Green
7m 16ch
Kidbrooke
7m 74ch
Eltham
9m 11ch
Blackheath Jn.
7m 14ch
Welling
11m 28ch

Brixton
East Dulwich
4m 23ch
Turnball Sdg
North Dulwich
4m 46ch
Honor Oak Park
4m 59ch
Crofton Park
7m 11ch
Ladywell
Traction Maintenance & Pre-assembly Depot
Lee Loop Jn.
7m 45ch / 0m 00ch
Falconwood
10m 27ch

Herne Hill North Jn.
3m 70ch / 4m 30ch
Herne Hill South Jn.
4m 06ch
Herne Hill
3m 76ch
Catford
8m 03ch
Catford Bridge
7m 42ch
Lee
7m 66ch

2 **20**

ham Jn.
69ch
Knights Hill Tunnel
5m 56ch to 5m 71ch
Leigham Court Tunnel
6m 00ch to 6m 17ch
West Dulwich
5m 02ch
Forest Hill
5m 50ch
Grove Park Up Sidings
Grove Park Down Sidings & Hither Green Yard
Mottingham
9m 40ch
New Eltham
10m 32ch
Berthing Siding

Tulse Hill
6m 07ch / 5m 02ch
Streatham Hill
5m 57ch
West Norwood
7m 02ch
Sydenham Hill
5m 57ch
Sydenham Up Jn.
6m 51ch
Sydenham
6m 32ch
Lower Sydenham
9m 17ch
Bellingham
8m 73ch
Grove Park
8m 78ch
Grove Park Carriage Service Shed
Sidcup
11m 73ch
Albany Park
12m 68ch

6m62ch
6m76ch
7m09ch
7m19ch
Leigham Tunnel
Streatham Tunnel
Penge Tunnel
5m 62ch to 7m 00ch
Sydenham Down Jn.
6m 41ch
Beckenham Hill
9m 45ch
9m 61ch (slow tunnel)
Chislehurst Tunnels
10m10ch
Elmstead Woods
10m 21ch

Streatham
7m 48ch
Gipsy Hill
7m 77ch
Crystal Palace Tunnel
8m 16ch to 8m 49ch
Penge East
7m 15ch
Kent House
7m 66ch
New Beckenham
9m 44ch
Ravensbourne
10m 34ch
9m 63ch (fast tunnel)
Sundridge Park
10m 12ch
Chislehurst

6m 48ch from Victoria via Clapham Jn.
Streatham Common
6m 48ch / 8m 15ch
Crystal Palace
8m 56ch ✳
Penge West
7m 15ch
Anerley
7m 47ch
Ravensbourne Jn.
10m 44ch
Bromley North
10m 47ch
Shortlands
10m 03ch
St Mary Cray
14m 57ch

m South Jn.
/ 08m 11ch /
/ 0m 00ch
s Tooting
Norbury
7m 36ch
Bromley Up Jn.
9m 36ch
Clock House
10m 23ch
Beckenham Junction
8m 53ch / 11m 62ch
Beckenham Spur Jn.
8m 43ch / 10m 06ch
Shortlands Jn.
9m 57ch / 10m 73ch
Bromley South
10m 71ch
Bickley
Petts Wood

Thornton Heath
8m 64ch
Norwood Junction
Birkbeck
10m 26ch
Bromley Down Jn.
9m 48ch
Elmers End
11m 07ch
See Map 114
Carriage Sidings

Construction is in progress at stations marked ✳ relating to the East London Line Extension. For simplicity, the layouts reflect the final track works.

Selhurst
Eden Park
12m 34ch
West Wickham
13m 19ch
Hayes
14m 32ch
Orpington
13m 65ch

Oakfield Siding
West Croydon
10m 35ch ✳
Waddon
11m 40ch
East Croydon
10m 28ch ✳
See Map 114

3

① Streatham Hill Down Sidings
② Streatham Hill Up Sidings and Traincare Shed
③ Leigham Jn. - 6m 31ch / 6m 40ch
④ Loughborough Jn. - 3m 39ch
⑤ Crofton Road Jn. - 4m 67ch (towards Nunhead) / 3m 67ch (towards Tulse Hill)
⑥ Denmark Hill Tunnel - 4m 12ch / 4m 32ch to 4m 15ch / 4m 29ch
⑦ Grove Tunnel - 4m 30ch / 4m 14ch to 4m 36ch / 4m 09ch
⑧ Lee Spur Jn. - 7m 44ch / 0m 29ch
⑨ West Norwood Jn. - 6m 58ch / 6m 41ch
⑩ Streatham North Jn. - 6m 14ch

Wallington
13m 05ch
South Croydon
11m 21ch
Chelsfield
15m 25ch
Knockholt
16m 44ch

Purley Oaks
12m 43ch
South Croydon Jn.
11m29ch
Selsdon Road Jn.
11m59ch
Sanderstead
12m 23ch
Chelsfield Tunnel
15m 67ch to 16m 14ch
17m 20ch

Purley
13m 29ch / 15m 13ch
Chipstead Line Jn.
15m23ch
Riddlesdown
13m 38ch
Polhill Tunnel

Reedham
15m 65ch
Riddlesdown Tunnel
13m 48ch to 14m 06ch

ats Nest Jn.
m 20ch
Reedham Sidings
Kenley
16m 29ch

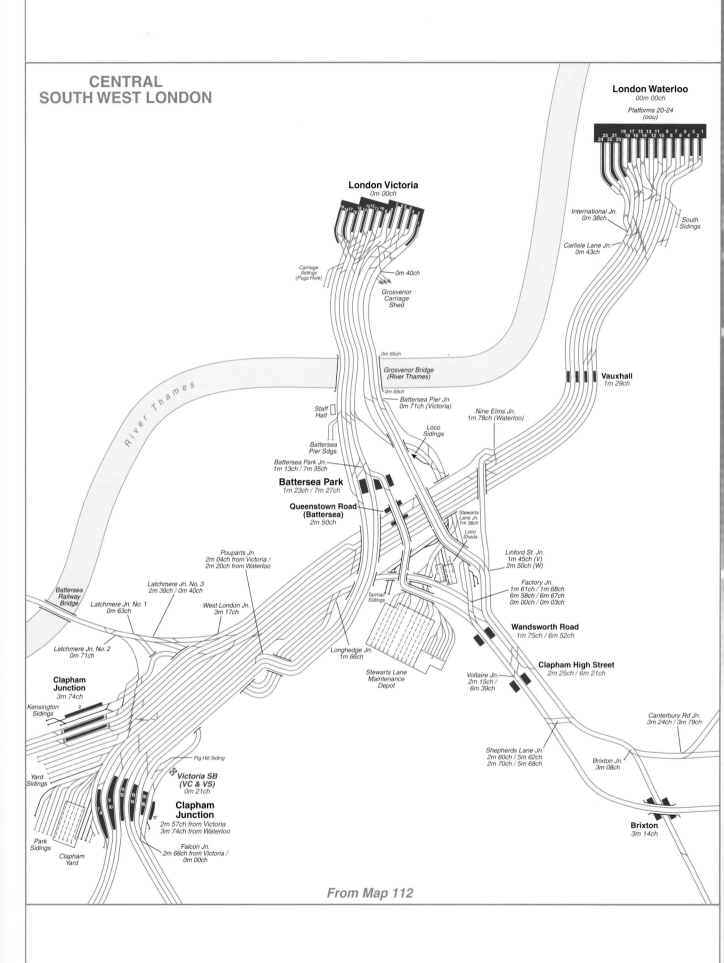

London Victoria
0m 00ch

London Waterloo
00m 00ch

*Platforms 20-24
(oou)*

*International Jn.
0m 38ch*

*South
Sidings*

*Carlisle Lane Jn.
0m 43ch*

*Carriage
Sidings
(Pugs Hole)*

0m 40ch

*Grosvenor
Carriage
Shed*

0m 65ch

*Grosvenor Bridge
(River Thames)*

Vauxhall
1m 29ch

0m 69ch

*Battersea Pier Jn.
0m 71ch (Victoria)*

*Nine Elms Jn.
1m 78ch (Waterloo)*

River Thames

*Staff
Halt*

*Loco
Sidings*

*Battersea
Pier Sdgs.*

*Battersea Park Jn.
1m 13ch / 7m 35ch*

Battersea Park
1m 23ch / 7m 27ch

**Queenstown Road
(Battersea)**
2m 50ch

*Stewarts
Lane Jn.
1m 36ch*

*Loco
Sheds*

*Pouparts Jn.
2m 04ch from Victoria /
2m 20ch from Waterloo*

*Linford St. Jn.
1m 45ch (V)
2m 50ch (W)*

*Battersea
Railway
Bridge*

*Latchmere Jn. No. 3
2m 39ch / 0m 40ch*

*Latchmere Jn. No. 1
0m 63ch*

*West London Jn.
3m 17ch*

*Tarmac
Sidings*

*Factory Jn.
1m 61ch / 1m 68ch
6m 58ch / 6m 67ch
0m 00ch / 0m 03ch*

*Latchmere Jn. No. 2
0m 71ch*

*Longhedge Jn.
1m 66ch*

Wandsworth Road
1m 75ch / 6m 52ch

**Clapham
Junction**
3m 74ch

*Kensington
Sidings*

*Stewarts Lane
Maintenance
Depot*

*Voltaire Jn.
2m 15ch /
6m 39ch*

Clapham High Street
2m 25ch / 6m 21ch

*Canterbury Rd Jn.
3m 24ch / 3m 79ch*

*Yard
Sidings*

Pig Hill Siding

*Shepherds Lane Jn.
2m 60ch / 5m 62ch
2m 70ch / 5m 68ch*

*Brixton Jn.
3m 08ch*

**Victoria SB
(VC & VS)**
0m 21ch

**Clapham
Junction**
*2m 57ch from Victoria
3m 74ch from Waterloo*

*Park
Sidings*

*Clapham
Yard*

*Falcon Jn.
2m 66ch from Victoria /
0m 00ch*

Brixton
3m 14ch

From Map 112

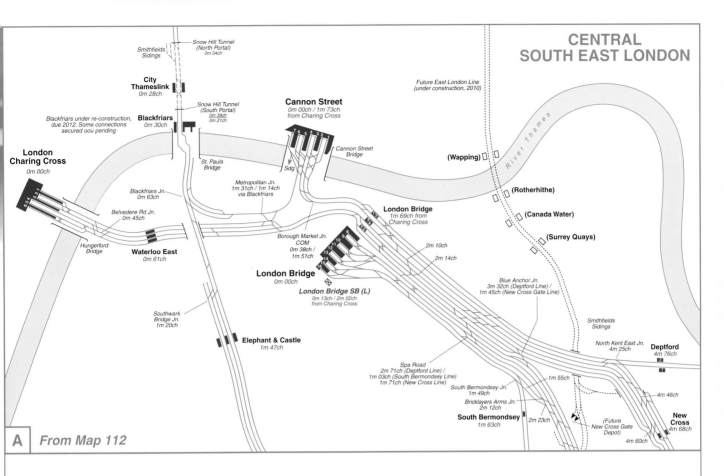

Snow Hill Tunnel
(North Portal)
0m 04ch

Smithfields
Sidings

City Thameslink
0m 28ch

Blackfriars under re-construction,
due 2012. Some connections
secured oou pending

Snow Hill Tunnel
(South Portal)
0m 39ch
0m 21ch

Blackfriars
0m 30ch

St. Pauls
Bridge

Cannon Street
0m 00ch / 1m 73ch
from Charing Cross

6 5 4 3 2 1

Cannon Street
Bridge

Sdg

Future East London Line
(under construction, 2010)

River Thames

(Wapping)

(Rotherhithe)

(Canada Water)

(Surrey Quays)

**London
Charing Cross**
0m 00ch

6 5 4 3 2 1

Blackfriars Jn.
0m 63ch

Metropolitan Jn.
1m 31ch / 1m 14ch
via Blackfriars

London Bridge
1m 69ch from
Charing Cross

2m 10ch

2m 14ch

Belvedere Rd Jn.
0m 45ch

Hungerford
Bridge

Waterloo East
0m 61ch

Borough Market Jn.
COM
0m 38ch /
1m 51ch

9
10 11
12
13
14
15

London Bridge
0m 00ch

London Bridge SB (L)
0m 13ch / 2m 02ch
from Charing Cross

Blue Anchor Jn.
3m 32ch (Deptford Line) /
1m 45ch (New Cross Gate Line)

Smithfields
Sidings

North Kent East Jn.
4m 25ch

Deptford
4m 76ch

Southwark
Bridge Jn.
1m 20ch

Elephant & Castle
1m 47ch

Spa Road
2m 71ch (Deptford Line) /
1m 03ch (South Bermondsey Line)
1m 71ch (New Cross Line)

South Bermondsey Jn.
1m 49ch

Bricklayers Arms Jn.
2m 12ch

1m 55ch

(Future
New Cross Gate
Depot)

**New
Cross**
4m 68ch

4m 46ch

South Bermondsey
1m 63ch

2m 23ch

4m 60ch

A *From Map 112*

SELHURST

**Norwood
Junction**
8m 55ch

Siding
oou

Selhurst
9m 31ch

Selhurst
Depot SB

Selhurst
Depot

9m 37ch

Selhurst Jn.
9m 43ch
9m 46ch

Field
Sidings
(oou)

Norwood Fork Jn.
9m 33ch

MPV Depot

Gloucester Road Jn.
9m 49ch (L. Br.) /
9m 66ch (Vic.)

Cottage Jn.
9m 64ch (Vic.) /
9m 52ch (L. Br.)

Windmill Bridge Jn.
10m 12ch (Vic.) /
9m 69ch (L. Br.)

From Map 112 **B**

LEWISHAM   *From Map 112*

Lewisham Vale Jn.
7m 37ch via Nunhead.
5m 57ch via New Cross.

St Johns
5m 47ch

5m 54ch

5m 79ch

Lewisham
7m 61ch via Nunhead.
6m 04ch via St. Johns.

5m 75ch

Courthill Loop
North Jn.
6m 21ch

Parks Bridge Jn
6m 14ch

Ladywell Jn
6m 29ch
via St. Johns
6m 41ch
via Lewisham

Courthill Loop
South Jn.
6m 43ch / 6m 21ch

C

Ladywell
6m 62ch

REDHILL

No.1 Up
Siding

Down
Siding

Snow Plough
Siding

No.2
Up Siding

Post
Office
Dock

Redhill
22m 40ch

20m 62ch

Change of mileage
23m 16ch /
21m 37ch

Redhill
Tunnel

23m 40ch

21m 12ch

Earlswood
21m 50ch

D

*From
Map 20*

CHISLEHURST

Chislehurst
11m 19ch

Chislehurst Jn.
11m 33ch

St Mary Cray Down Jn.
12m 79ch (Victoria) /
11m 71ch (Charing Cross)

Bickley Jn.
12m 38ch

St Mary Cray Up Jn.
13m 17ch

13m 46ch

Bickley
11m 76ch

Hawkwood Jn.
12m 74ch (Victoria) /
11m 68ch (Charing Cross)

Petts Wood Jn. Slow Loop
12m 27ch (Charing Cross) /
13m 35ch (Victoria)

Petts Wood Jn.
Fast Loop
12m 24ch (Charing Cross) /
13m 29ch (Victoria)

Petts Wood
12m 53ch

E *From Map 112*

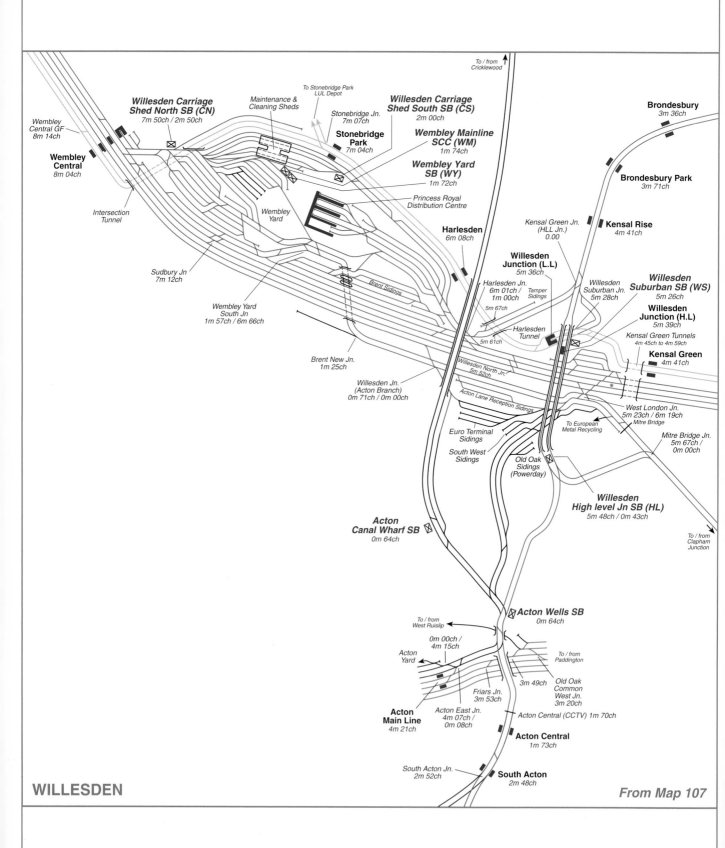

Wembley Central GF
8m 14ch

Wembley Central
8m 04ch

Intersection Tunnel

Willesden Carriage Shed North SB (CN)
7m 50ch / 2m 50ch

Maintenance & Cleaning Sheds

To Stonebridge Park LUL Depot

Stonebridge Jn. 7m 07ch

Stonebridge Park
7m 04ch

Willesden Carriage Shed South SB (CS)
2m 00ch

Wembley Mainline SCC (WM)
1m 74ch

Wembley Yard SB (WY)
1m 72ch

Princess Royal Distribution Centre

Harlesden
6m 08ch

To / from Cricklewood

Brondesbury
3m 36ch

Brondesbury Park
3m 71ch

Kensal Green Jn. (HLL Jn.) 0.00

Kensal Rise
4m 41ch

Willesden Junction (L.L)
5m 36ch

Harlesden Jn. 6m 01ch / 1m 00ch

Tamper Sidings

5m 67ch

Willesden Suburban Jn. 5m 28ch

Willesden Suburban SB (WS)
5m 26ch

Willesden Junction (H.L)
5m 39ch

Kensal Green Tunnels 4m 45ch to 4m 59ch

Kensal Green
4m 41ch

Wembley Yard

Sudbury Jn 7m 12ch

Wembley Yard South Jn 1m 57ch / 6m 66ch

Brent Sidings

Harlesden Tunnel

5m 61ch

Brent New Jn. 1m 25ch

Willesden Jn. (Acton Branch) 0m 71ch / 0m 00ch

Willesden North Jn. 5m 52ch

Acton Lane Reception Sidings

West London Jn. 5m 23ch / 6m 19ch

Mitre Bridge

Mitre Bridge Jn. 5m 67ch / 0m 00ch

To European Metal Recycling

Euro Terminal Sidings

South West Sidings

Old Oak Sidings (Powerday)

Willesden High level Jn SB (HL)
5m 48ch / 0m 43ch

To / from Clapham Junction

Acton Canal Wharf SB
0m 64ch

To / from West Ruislip

0m 00ch / 4m 15ch

Acton Yard

Acton Wells SB
0m 64ch

To / from Paddington

3m 49ch

Old Oak Common West Jn. 3m 20ch

Friars Jn. 3m 53ch

Acton East Jn. 4m 07ch / 0m 08ch

Acton Central (CCTV) 1m 70ch

Acton Main Line
4m 21ch

Acton Central
1m 73ch

South Acton Jn. 2m 52ch

South Acton
2m 48ch

WILLESDEN

From Map 107

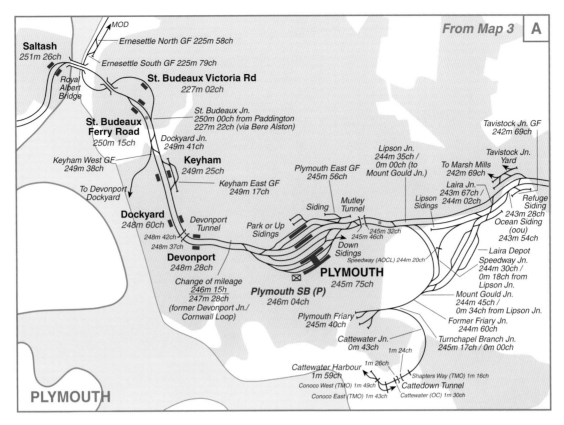

From Map 3 — A

PLYMOUTH

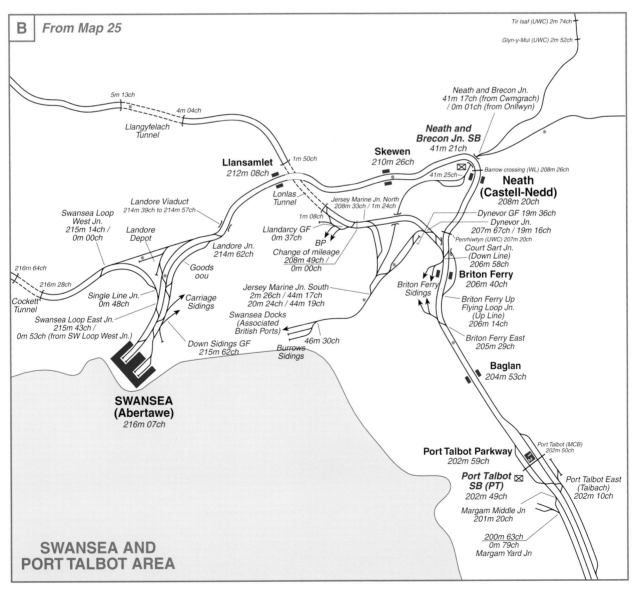

B — From Map 25

SWANSEA AND PORT TALBOT AREA

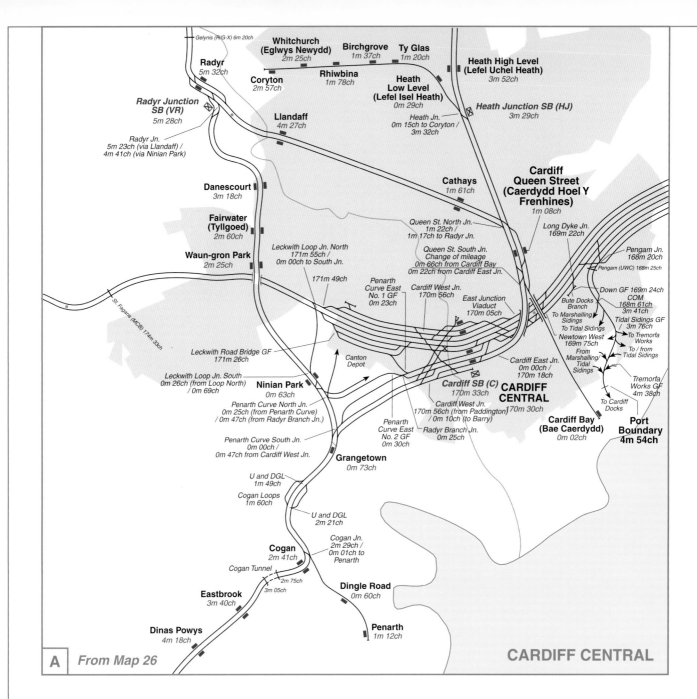

A *From Map 26*

Gelynis (R/G-X) 6m 20ch

Radyr
5m 32ch

Whitchurch (Eglwys Newydd)
2m 25ch

Birchgrove
1m 37ch

Ty Glas
1m 20ch

Heath High Level (Lefel Uchel Heath)
3m 52ch

Coryton
2m 57ch

Rhiwbina
1m 78ch

Heath Low Level (Lefel Isel Heath)
0m 29ch

Radyr Junction SB (VR)
5m 28ch

Heath Junction SB (HJ)
3m 29ch

Heath Jn.
0m 15ch to Coryton /
3m 32ch

Radyr Jn.
5m 23ch (via Llandaff) /
4m 41ch (via Ninian Park)

Llandaff
4m 27ch

Cardiff Queen Street (Caerdydd Hoel Y Frenhines)
1m 08ch

Danescourt
3m 18ch

Cathays
1m 61ch

Queen St. North Jn.
1m 22ch /
1m 17ch to Radyr Jn.

Long Dyke Jn.
169m 22ch

Fairwater (Tyllgoed)
2m 60ch

Queen St. South Jn.
Change of mileage
0m 66ch from Cardiff Bay
0m 22ch from Cardiff East Jn.

Pengam Jn.
168m 20ch

Waun-gron Park
2m 25ch

Leckwith Loop Jn. North
171m 55ch /
0m 00ch to South Jn.

Cardiff West Jn.
170m 56ch

East Junction Viaduct
170m 05ch

Pengam (UWC) 168m 25ch

Down GF 169m 24ch
COM
168m 61ch
3m 41ch

Bute Docks Branch

171m 49ch

Penarth Curve East No. 1 GF
0m 23ch

To Marshalling Sidings

Tidal Sidings GF /
3m 76ch

To Tidal Sidings

To Tremorfa Works

Leckwith Road Bridge GF
171m 26ch

Canton Depot

Newtown West
169m 75ch

To / from Tidal Sidings

St. Fagans (MCB) 174m 33ch

Cardiff East Jn.
0m 00ch /
170m 18ch

From Marshalling/ Tidal Sidings

Leckwith Loop Jn. South
0m 26ch (from Loop North) /
0m 69ch

Ninian Park
0m 63ch

Cardiff SB (C)
170m 33ch

CARDIFF CENTRAL

Tremorfa Works GF
4m 38ch

Penarth Curve North Jn.
0m 25ch (from Penarth Curve)
/ 0m 47ch (from Radyr Branch Jn.)

Cardiff West Jn.
170m 56ch (from Paddington) /
0m 10ch (to Barry)

To Cardiff Docks

Port Boundary
4m 54ch

Penarth Curve South Jn.
0m 00ch /
0m 47ch from Cardiff West Jn.

Penarth Curve East No. 2 GF
0m 30ch

Radyr Branch Jn.
0m 25ch

Cardiff Bay (Bae Caerdydd)
0m 02ch

Grangetown
0m 73ch

U and DGL
1m 49ch

Cogan Loops
1m 60ch

U and DGL
2m 21ch

Cogan Jn.
2m 29ch /
0m 01ch to Penarth

Cogan
2m 41ch

Cogan Tunnel

Dingle Road
0m 60ch

2m 75ch
3m 05ch

Eastbrook
3m 40ch

Dinas Powys
4m 18ch

Penarth
1m 12ch

CARDIFF CENTRAL

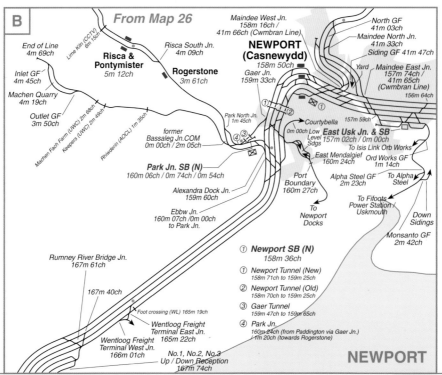

B *From Map 26*

Lime Kiln (CCTV) 6m 15ch

Maindee West Jn.
158m 16ch /
41m 66ch (Cwmbran Line)

North GF
41m 03ch

End of Line
4m 69ch

Risca & Pontymister
5m 12ch

Risca South Jn.
4m 09ch

NEWPORT (Casnewydd)
158m 50ch

Maindee North Jn.
41m 33ch

Siding GF 41m 47ch

Inlet GF
4m 45ch

Rogerstone
3m 61ch

Gaer Jn.
159m 33ch

Yard

Maindee East Jn.
157m 74ch /
41m 65ch (Cwmbran Line)

Machen Quarry
4m 19ch

156m 64ch

Outlet GF
3m 50ch

Park North Jn.
1m 45ch

① ①

157m 59ch

Machen Fach Farm (UWC) 2m 68ch

Keepers (UWC) 2m 49ch

Rhiwderin (AOCL) 1m 35ch

former Bassaleg Jn.COM
0m 00ch / 2m 05ch

② ②

Courtybella

0m 00ch Low Level Sdgs

East Usk Jn. & SB
157m 02ch / 0m 00ch

To Isis Link Orb Works

④ ③

East Mendalgief
160m 24ch

Ord Works GF
1m 14ch

Park Jn. SB (N)
160m 06ch / 0m 74ch / 0m 54ch

Alpha Steel GF
2m 23ch

To Alpha Steel

Alexandra Dock Jn.
159m 60ch

Port Boundary
160m 27ch

Ebbw Jn.
160m 07ch /0m 00ch
to Park Jn.

To Newport Docks

To Fifoots Power Station / Uskmouth

Down Sidings

Rumney River Bridge Jn.
167m 61ch

① **Newport SB (N)**
158m 36ch

Monsanto GF
2m 42ch

167m 40ch

① *Newport Tunnel (New)*
158m 71ch to 159m 25ch

② *Newport Tunnel (Old)*
158m 70ch to 159m 25ch

Foot crossing (WL) 165m 19ch

③ *Gaer Tunnel*
159m 47ch to 159m 65ch

Wentloog Freight Terminal East Jn.
165m 22ch

④ *Park Jn.*
160m 24ch (from Paddington via Gaer Jn.)
1m 20ch (towards Rogerstone)

Wentloog Freight Terminal West Jn.
166m 01ch

No.1, No.2, No.3
Up / Down Reception
167m 74ch

NEWPORT

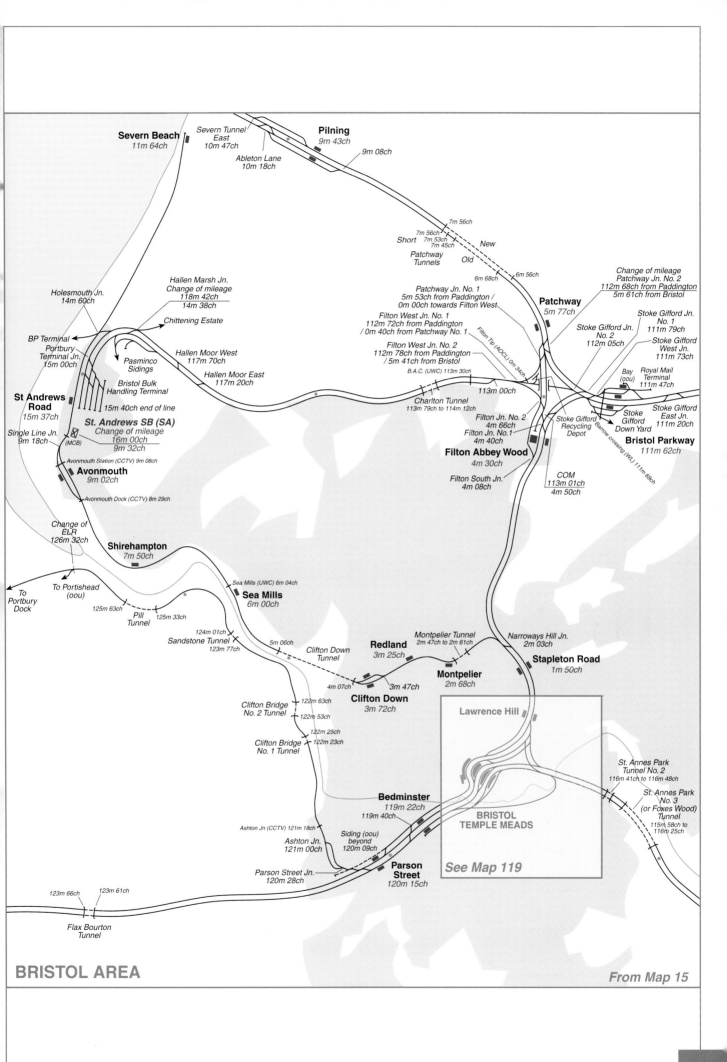

Severn Beach
11m 64ch

Severn Tunnel East 10m 47ch

Ableton Lane 10m 18ch

Pilning
9m 43ch

9m 08ch

7m 56ch

7m 56ch
7m 53ch
7m 45ch

Short
New

Patchway Tunnels
Old

6m 68ch
6m 56ch

Change of mileage Patchway Jn. No. 2 112m 68ch from Paddington 5m 61ch from Bristol

Patchway Jn. No. 1 5m 53ch from Paddington / 0m 00ch towards Filton West

Patchway
5m 77ch

Stoke Gifford Jn. No. 1 111m 79ch

Stoke Gifford Jn. No. 2 112m 05ch

Stoke Gifford West Jn. 111m 73ch

Hallen Marsh Jn. Change of mileage 118m 42ch 14m 38ch

Holesmouth Jn. 14m 60ch

Filton West Jn. No. 1 112m 72ch from Paddington / 0m 40ch from Patchway No. 1

Filton West Jn. No. 2 112m 78ch from Paddington / 5m 41ch from Bristol

Filton Tip (AOCL) 0m 34ch

Chittening Estate

BP Terminal

Portbury Terminal Jn. 15m 00ch

Pasminco Sidings

Hallen Moor West 117m 70ch

Bristol Bulk Handling Terminal

Hallen Moor East 117m 20ch

B.A.C. (UWC) 113m 30ch

113m 00ch

Bay (oou)

Royal Mail Terminal 111m 47ch

Stoke Gifford East Jn. 111m 20ch

St Andrews Road
15m 37ch

15m 40ch end of line

Charlton Tunnel 113m 79ch to 114m 12ch

Stoke Gifford Down Yard

Bristol Parkway
111m 62ch

St. Andrews SB (SA) Change of mileage 16m 00ch 9m 32ch

Filton Jn. No. 2 4m 66ch

Filton Jn. No. 1 4m 40ch

Stoke Gifford Recycling Depot

Barrow crossing (WL) 111m 69ch

Single Line Jn. 9m 18ch

(MCB)

Avonmouth Station (CCTV) 9m 08ch

Filton Abbey Wood
4m 30ch

Avonmouth
9m 02ch

Filton South Jn. 4m 08ch

COM 113m 01ch 4m 50ch

Avonmouth Dock (CCTV) 8m 29ch

Change of ELR 126m 32ch

Shirehampton
7m 50ch

Sea Mills (UWC) 6m 04ch

Sea Mills
6m 00ch

To Portishead (oou)

To Portbury Dock

125m 63ch

Pill Tunnel

125m 33ch

124m 01ch

Sandstone Tunnel 123m 77ch

5m 06ch

Clifton Down Tunnel

Redland
3m 25ch

Montpelier Tunnel 2m 47ch to 2m 61ch

Narroways Hill Jn. 2m 03ch

Stapleton Road
1m 50ch

Clifton Down
3m 72ch

4m 07ch

3m 47ch

Montpelier
2m 68ch

Clifton Bridge No. 2 Tunnel

122m 63ch

122m 53ch

122m 25ch

122m 23ch

Clifton Bridge No. 1 Tunnel

Lawrence Hill

St. Annes Park Tunnel No. 2 116m 41ch to 116m 48ch

St. Annes Park No. 3 (or Foxes Wood) Tunnel 115m 58ch to 116m 25ch

Bedminster
119m 22ch

119m 40ch

BRISTOL TEMPLE MEADS

See Map 119

Ashton Jn (CCTV) 121m 18ch

Siding (oou) beyond 120m 09ch

Ashton Jn. 121m 00ch

Parson Street
120m 15ch

Parson Street Jn. 120m 28ch

123m 66ch

123m 61ch

Flax Bourton Tunnel

BRISTOL AREA

From Map 15

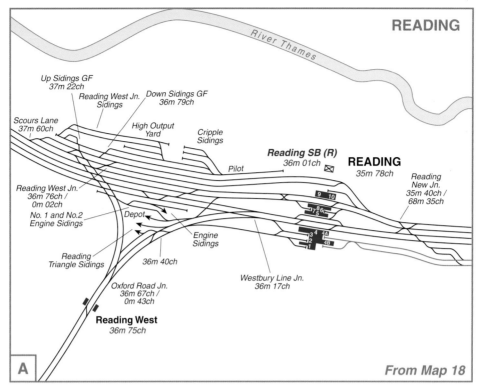

READING

River Thames

Up Sidings GF
37m 22ch

Reading West Jn.
Sidings

Down Sidings GF
36m 79ch

Scours Lane
37m 60ch

High Output
Yard

Cripple
Sidings

Pilot

Reading SB (R)
36m 01ch

READING
35m 78ch

Reading New Jn.
35m 40ch /
68m 35ch

Reading West Jn.
36m 76ch /
0m 02ch

No. 1 and No.2
Engine Sidings

Depot

Engine
Sidings

Reading
Triangle Sidings

36m 40ch

Westbury Line Jn.
36m 17ch

Oxford Road Jn.
36m 67ch /
0m 43ch

Reading West
36m 75ch

9 10

17 8 6
5

3 4 4A
2
1 4B

From Map 18

A

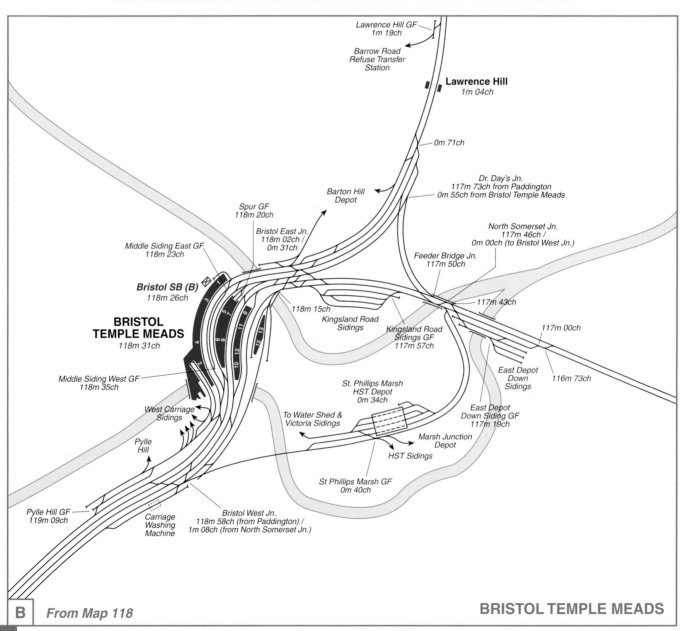

Lawrence Hill GF
1m 19ch

Barrow Road
Refuse Transfer
Station

Lawrence Hill
1m 04ch

0m 71ch

Dr. Day's Jn.
117m 73ch from Paddington
0m 55ch from Bristol Temple Meads

Spur GF
118m 20ch

Barton Hill
Depot

Bristol East Jn.
118m 02ch /
0m 31ch

North Somerset Jn.
117m 46ch /
0m 00ch (to Bristol West Jn.)

Middle Siding East GF
118m 23ch

Feeder Bridge Jn.
117m 50ch

Bristol SB (B)
118m 26ch

**BRISTOL
TEMPLE MEADS**
118m 31ch

118m 15ch

117m 43ch

Kingsland Road
Sidings

Kingsland Road
Sidings GF
117m 57ch

117m 00ch

116m 73ch

Middle Siding West GF
118m 35ch

East Depot
Down
Sidings

West Carriage
Sidings

To Water Shed &
Victoria Sidings

St. Phillips Marsh
HST Depot
0m 34ch

East Depot
Down Siding GF
117m 19ch

Pylle
Hill

Marsh Junction
Depot

HST Sidings

Pylle Hill GF
119m 09ch

Carriage
Washing
Machine

Bristol West Jn.
118m 58ch (from Paddington) /
1m 08ch (from North Somerset Jn.)

St Phillips Marsh GF
0m 40ch

B *From Map 118*

BRISTOL TEMPLE MEADS

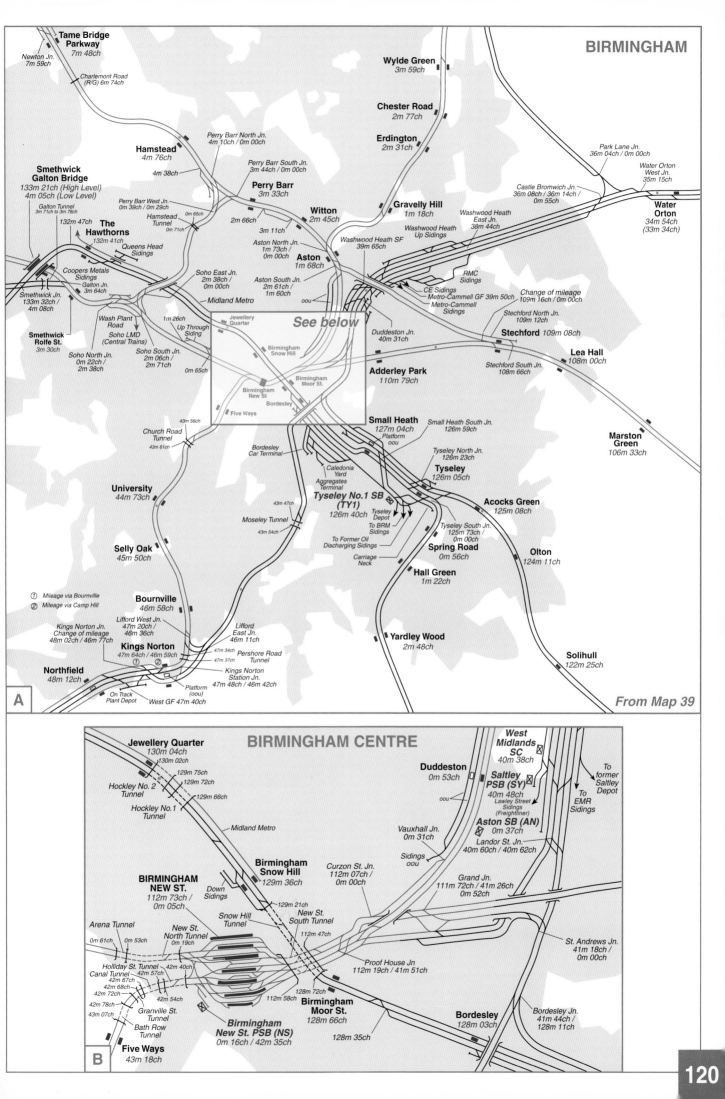

Tame Bridge Parkway 7m 48ch

Newton Jn. 7m 59ch

Charlemont Road (R/G) 6m 74ch

Wylde Green 3m 59ch

Chester Road 2m 77ch

Erdington 2m 31ch

Hamstead 4m 76ch

Perry Barr North Jn. 4m 10ch / 0m 00ch

4m 38ch

Perry Barr South Jn. 3m 44ch / 0m 00ch

Perry Barr 3m 33ch

Park Lane Jn. 36m 04ch / 0m 00ch

Water Orton West Jn. 35m 15ch

Smethwick Galton Bridge 133m 21ch (High Level) 4m 05ch (Low Level)

Galton Tunnel 3m 71ch to 3m 78ch

132m 47ch

The Hawthorns 132m 41ch

Queens Head Sidings

Perry Barr West Jn. 0m 39ch / 0m 29ch

Hamstead Tunnel 0m 71ch

0m 65ch

2m 66ch

3m 11ch

Witton 2m 45ch

Gravelly Hill 1m 18ch

Washwood Heath East Jn. 38m 44ch

Water Orton 34m 54ch (33m 34ch)

Castle Bromwich Jn. 36m 08ch / 36m 14ch / 0m 55ch

Coopers Metals Sidings

Galton Jn. 3m 64ch

Aston North Jn. 1m 73ch / 0m 00ch

Aston 1m 68ch

Washwood Heath SF 39m 65ch

Washwood Heath Up Sidings

Smethwick Jn. 133m 32ch / 4m 08ch

Soho East Jn. 2m 38ch / 0m 00ch

Aston South Jn. 2m 61ch / 1m 60ch

oou

RMC Sidings

Change of mileage 109m 16ch / 0m 00ch

Smethwick Rolfe St. 3m 30ch

Wash Plant Road

Soho LMD (Central Trains)

1m 26ch

Up Through Siding

Jewellery Quarter

See below

CE Sidings

Metro-Cammell GF 39m 50ch

Metro-Cammell Sidings

Stechford North Jn. 109m 12ch

Stechford 109m 08ch

Soho North Jn. 0m 22ch / 2m 38ch

Soho South Jn. 2m 06ch / 2m 71ch

Midland Metro

0m 65ch

Birmingham Snow Hill

Birmingham Moor St.

Duddeston Jn. 40m 31ch

Adderley Park 110m 79ch

Stechford South Jn. 108m 66ch

Lea Hall 108m 00ch

Birmingham New St

Bordesley

Five Ways

University 44m 73ch

43m 56ch

Church Road Tunnel

43m 61ch

Bordesley Car Terminal

Small Heath 127m 04ch

Platform oou

Small Heath South Jn. 126m 59ch

Tyseley North Jn. 126m 23ch

Marston Green 106m 33ch

Caledonia Yard Aggregates Terminal

Tyseley 126m 05ch

Tyseley No.1 SB (TY1) 126m 40ch

43m 47ch

Moseley Tunnel

43m 54ch

Tyseley Depot

To BRM Sidings

Acocks Green 125m 08ch

Selly Oak 45m 50ch

To Former Oil Discharging Sidings

Tyseley South Jn. 125m 73ch / 0m 00ch

Spring Road 0m 56ch

Olton 124m 11ch

Carriage Neck

Hall Green 1m 22ch

① Mileage via Bournville
② Mileage via Camp Hill

Bournville 46m 58ch

Lifford West Jn. 47m 20ch / 46m 36ch

Lifford East Jn. 46m 11ch

Yardley Wood 2m 48ch

Kings Norton Jn. Change of mileage 48m 02ch / 46m 77ch

Kings Norton 47m 64ch / 46m 59ch

① ②

47m 34ch

47m 37ch

Pershore Road Tunnel

Kings Norton Station Jn. 47m 48ch / 46m 42ch

Solihull 122m 25ch

Northfield 48m 12ch

On Track Plant Depot

Platform (oou)

West GF 47m 40ch

From Map 39

A

BIRMINGHAM CENTRE

Jewellery Quarter 130m 04ch

130m 02ch

129m 75ch

Hockley No. 2 Tunnel

129m 72ch

129m 66ch

Hockley No. 1 Tunnel

Midland Metro

Duddeston 0m 53ch

West Midlands SC 40m 38ch

Saltley PSB (SY) 40m 48ch

Lawley Street Sidings (Freightliner)

To former Saltley Depot

To EMR Sidings

oou

Vauxhall Jn. 0m 31ch

Aston SB (AN) 0m 37ch

Landor St. Jn. 40m 60ch / 40m 62ch

BIRMINGHAM SNOW HILL 129m 36ch

Sidings oou

BIRMINGHAM NEW ST. 112m 73ch / 0m 05ch

Down Sidings

Curzon St. Jn. 112m 07ch / 0m 00ch

Snow Hill Tunnel

129m 21ch

New St. South Tunnel

Grand Jn. 111m 72ch / 41m 26ch 0m 52ch

Arena Tunnel

0m 61ch

0m 53ch

New St. North Tunnel 0m 19ch

112m 47ch

St. Andrews Jn. 41m 18ch / 0m 00ch

Holliday St. Tunnel

Canal Tunnel

42m 40ch

42m 57ch

42m 67ch

42m 68ch

42m 72ch

42m 78ch

42m 54ch

Proof House Jn 112m 19ch / 41m 51ch

Granville St. Tunnel

43m 07ch

Bath Row Tunnel

112m 58ch

128m 72ch

Birmingham Moor St. 128m 66ch

Birmingham New St. PSB (NS) 0m 16ch / 42m 35ch

128m 35ch

Bordesley 128m 03ch

Bordesley Jn. 41m 44ch / 128m 11ch

Five Ways 43m 18ch

B

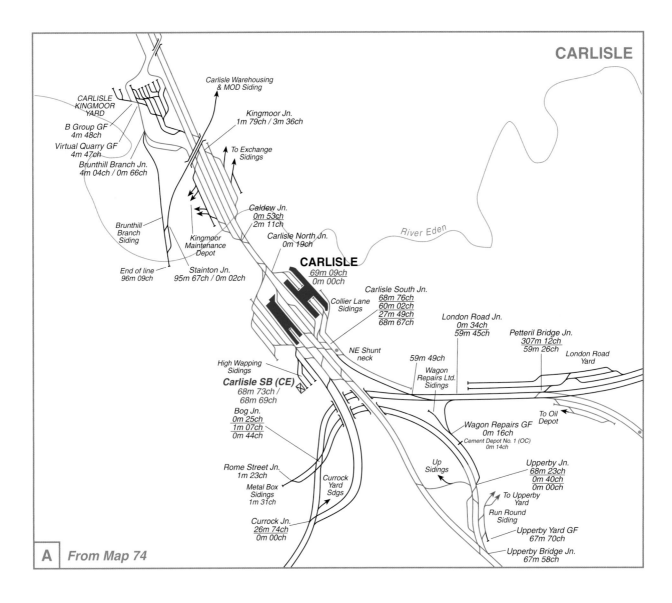

CARLISLE

Carlisle Warehousing & MOD Siding

CARLISLE KINGMOOR YARD

B Group GF
4m 48ch

Virtual Quarry GF
4m 47ch

Brunthill Branch Jn.
4m 04ch / 0m 66ch

Kingmoor Jn.
1m 79ch / 3m 36ch

To Exchange Sidings

Brunthill Branch Siding

Kingmoor Maintenance Depot

End of line
96m 09ch

Stainton Jn.
95m 67ch / 0m 02ch

Caldew Jn.
0m 53ch
2m 11ch

Carlisle North Jn.
0m 19ch

River Eden

CARLISLE
69m 09ch
0m 00ch

Collier Lane Sidings

Carlisle South Jn.
68m 76ch
60m 02ch
27m 49ch
68m 67ch

London Road Jn.
0m 34ch
59m 45ch

Petteril Bridge Jn.
307m 12ch
59m 26ch

London Road Yard

NE Shunt neck

59m 49ch

Wagon Repairs Ltd. Sidings

High Wapping Sidings

Carlisle SB (CE)
68m 73ch /
68m 69ch

To Oil Depot

Bog Jn.
0m 25ch
1m 07ch
0m 44ch

Wagon Repairs GF
0m 16ch

Cement Depot No. 1 (OC)
0m 14ch

Rome Street Jn.
1m 23ch

Up Sidings

Upperby Jn.
68m 23ch
0m 40ch
0m 00ch

Metal Box Sidings
1m 31ch

Currock Yard Sdgs

To Upperby Yard

Run Round Siding

Currock Jn.
26m 74ch
0m 00ch

Upperby Yard GF
67m 70ch

Upperby Bridge Jn.
67m 58ch

A *From Map 74*

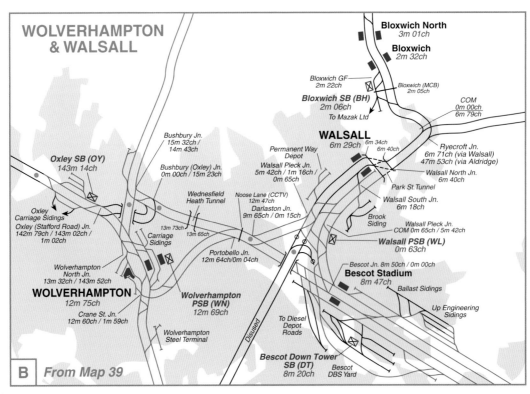

WOLVERHAMPTON & WALSALL

Bloxwich North
3m 01ch

Bloxwich
2m 32ch

Bloxwich GF
2m 22ch

Bloxwich (MCB)
2m 05ch

Bloxwich SB (BH)
2m 06ch

To Mazak Ltd

COM
0m 00ch
6m 79ch

Oxley SB (OY)
143m 14ch

Bushbury Jn.
15m 32ch /
14m 43ch

WALSALL
6m 29ch

6m 34ch
6m 40ch

Ryecroft Jn.
6m 71ch (via Walsall)
47m 53ch (via Aldridge)

Permanent Way Depot

Walsall North Jn.
6m 40ch

Bushbury (Oxley) Jn.
0m 00ch / 15m 23ch

Walsall Pleck Jn.
5m 42ch / 1m 16ch /
0m 65ch

Park St. Tunnel

Walsall South Jn.
6m 18ch

Oxley Carriage Sidings

Oxley (Stafford Road) Jn.
142m 79ch / 143m 02ch /
1m 02ch

Wednesfield Heath Tunnel

Noose Lane (CCTV)
12m 47ch

Darlaston Jn.
9m 65ch / 0m 15ch

Brook Siding

Walsall Pleck Jn.
COM 0m 65ch / 5m 42ch

13m 73ch
13m 65ch

Carriage Sidings

Walsall PSB (WL)
0m 63ch

Wolverhampton North Jn.
13m 32ch / 143m 52ch

Portobello Jn.
12m 64ch / 0m 04ch

Bescot Jn. 8m 50ch / 0m 00ch

WOLVERHAMPTON
12m 75ch

Bescot Stadium
8m 47ch

Ballast Sidings

Crane St. Jn.
12m 60ch / 1m 59ch

Wolverhampton PSB (WN)
12m 69ch

To Diesel Depot Roads

Up Engineering Sidings

Disused

Wolverhampton Steel Terminal

Bescot Down Tower SB (DT)
8m 20ch

Bescot DBS Yard

B *From Map 39*

DERBY

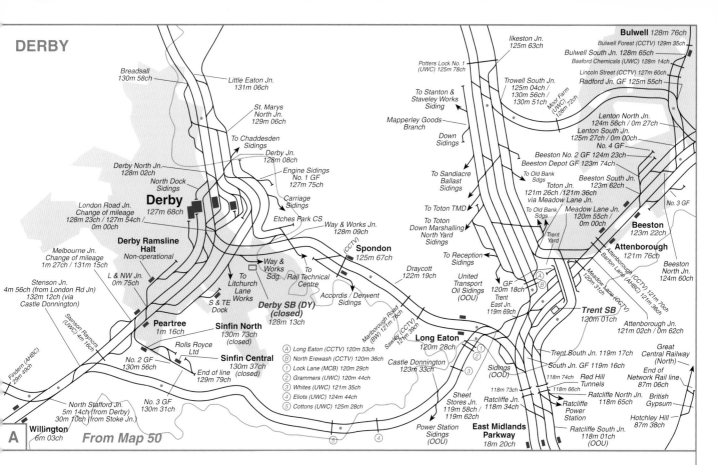

Breadsall
130m 58ch

Little Eaton Jn.
131m 06ch

St. Marys
North Jn.
129m 06ch

To Chaddesden
Sidings

Derby Jn.
128m 08ch

Derby North Jn.
128m 02ch

North Dock
Sidings

Engine Sidings
No. 1 GF
127m 75ch

Carriage
Sidings

Derby
127m 68ch

London Road Jn.
Change of mileage
128m 23ch / 127m 54ch /
0m 00ch

Etches Park CS

Way & Works Jn.
128m 09ch

Melbourne Jn.
Change of mileage
1m 27ch / 131m 15ch

**Derby Ramsline
Halt**
Non-operational

L & NW Jn.
0m 75ch

Way &
Works
Sdg.

To
Litchurch
Lane
Works

(CCTV)

Spondon
125m 67ch

Stenson Jn.
4m 56ch (from London Rd Jn)
132m 12ch (via
Castle Donington)

S & TE
Dock

To
Rail Technical
Centre

**Derby SB (DY)
(closed)**
128m 13ch

Accordis / Derwent
Sidings

Draycott
122m 19ch

Stenson Raynors
(UWC) 4m 16ch

Peartree
1m 16ch

Rolls Royce
Ltd

Sinfin North
130m 73ch
(closed)

Marlborough Road
(BW) 121m 76ch

Sawley (CCTV)
121m 39ch

Long Eaton
120m 28ch

Findern (AHBC)
2m 43ch

No. 2 GF
130m 56ch

Sinfin Central
130m 37ch
(closed)

End of line
129m 79ch

(A) Long Eaton (CCTV) 120m 53ch
(B) North Erewash (CCTV) 120m 36ch
(1) Lock Lane (MCB) 120m 29ch
(2) Grammers (UWC) 120m 44ch
(3) Whites (UWC) 121m 35ch
(4) Eliots (UWC) 124m 44ch
(5) Cottons (UWC) 125m 28ch

Castle Donington
123m 33ch

North Stafford Jn.
5m 14ch (from Derby)
30m 10ch (from Stoke Jn.)

No. 3 GF
130m 31ch

Sheet
Stores Jn.
119m 58ch /
119m 62ch

Willington
6m 03ch

From Map 50

Power Station
Sidings
(OOU)

**East Midlands
Parkway**
18m 20ch

Ilkeston Jn.
125m 63ch

Potters Lock No. 1
(UWC) 125m 78ch

Bulwell 128m 76ch
Bulwell Forest (CCTV) 129m 35ch
Bulwell South Jn. 128m 65ch
Basford Chemicals (UWC) 128m 14ch
Lincoln Street (CCTV) 127m 60ch
Radford Jn. GF 125m 55ch

Trowell South Jn.
125m 04ch /
130m 56ch /
130m 51ch

To Stanton &
Staveley Works
Siding

Mapperley Goods
Branch

Down
Sidings

Moor Farm
(UWC)
128m 72ch

Lenton North Jn.
124m 56ch / 0m 27ch

Lenton South Jn.
125m 27ch / 0m 00ch

No. 4 GF

To Sandiacre
Ballast
Sidings

To Old Bank
Sdgs

Beeston No. 2 GF 124m 23ch

Beeston Depot GF 123m 74ch

Beeston South Jn.
123m 62ch

To Toton TMD

To Toton
Down Marshalling
North Yard
Sidings

Toton Jn.
121m 26ch /121m 36ch
via Meadow Lane

To Old Bank
Sdgs

Meadow Lane Jn.
120m 55ch /
0m 00ch

No. 3 GF

Beeston
123m 22ch

Attenborough
121m 76ch

Beeston
North Jn.
124m 60ch

To Reception
Sidings

United
Transport
Oil Sidings
(OOU)

GF
120m 18ch
Trent
East Jn.
119m 69ch

Trent
Yard

(A)
(B)

Attenborough (CCTV) 121m 70ch

Barton Lane (AHBC)

Meadow Lane (CCTV) 121m 36ch

Trent SB
120m 01ch

Attenborough Jn.
121m 02ch / 0m 62ch

Trent South Jn. 119m 17ch

South Jn. GF 119m 16ch

118m 74ch
118m 66ch

Red Hill
Tunnels

Ratcliffe North Jn.
118m 65ch

**Great
Central Railway
(North)**

End of
Network Rail line
87m 06ch

British
Gypsum

Sidings
(OOU)

118m 73ch

Ratcliffe Jn.
118m 34ch

Ratcliffe
Power
Station

Ratcliffe South Jn.
118m 01ch
(OOU)

Hotchley Hill
87m 38ch

CENTRAL MANCHESTER

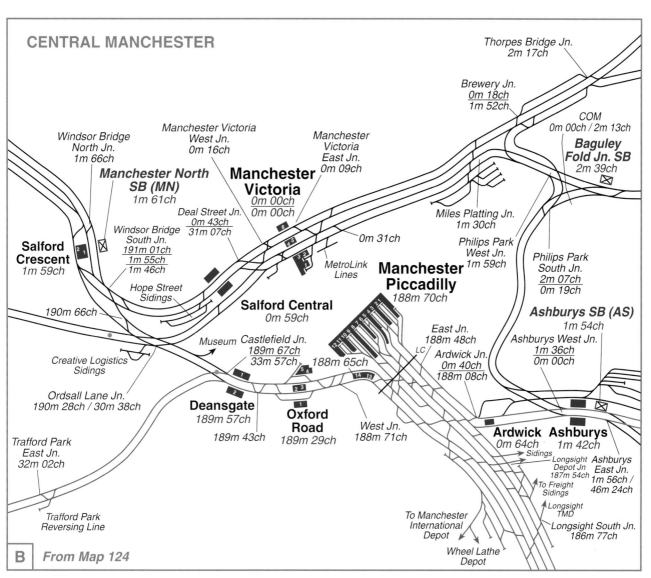

Thorpes Bridge Jn.
2m 17ch

Brewery Jn.
0m 18ch
1m 52ch

COM
0m 00ch / 2m 13ch

**Baguley
Fold Jn. SB**
2m 39ch

Windsor Bridge
North Jn.
1m 66ch

Manchester Victoria
West Jn.
0m 16ch

Manchester
Victoria
East Jn.
0m 09ch

**Manchester
North
SB (MN)**
1m 61ch

**Manchester
Victoria**
0m 00ch
0m 00ch

Deal Street Jn.
0m 43ch
31m 07ch

Miles Platting Jn.
1m 30ch

Philips Park
West Jn.
1m 59ch

Philips Park
South Jn.
2m 07ch
0m 19ch

**Salford
Crescent**
1m 59ch

Windsor Bridge
South Jn.
191m 01ch
1m 55ch
1m 46ch

0m 31ch

MetroLink
Lines

**Manchester
Piccadilly**
188m 70ch

Ashburys SB (AS)
1m 54ch

Hope Street
Sidings

Ashburys West Jn.
1m 36ch
0m 00ch

190m 66ch

Salford Central
0m 59ch

East Jn.
188m 48ch

Creative Logistics
Sidings

Museum

Castlefield Jn.
189m 67ch
33m 57ch

LC

Ardwick Jn.
0m 40ch
188m 08ch

Ordsall Lane Jn.
190m 28ch / 30m 38ch

188m 65ch

14 13

West Jn.
188m 71ch

Ardwick
0m 64ch

Ashburys
1m 42ch

Deansgate
189m 57ch

189m 43ch

**Oxford
Road**
189m 29ch

Sidings

Ashburys
East Jn.
1m 56ch /
46m 24ch

**Trafford Park
East Jn.**
32m 02ch

Longsight
Depot Jn
187m 54ch

To Freight
Sidings

Longsight
TMD

Longsight South Jn.
186m 77ch

**Trafford Park
Reversing Line**

To Manchester
International
Depot

Wheel Lathe
Depot

From Map 124

122

A

B

Astley Bridge Jn.
11m 66ch

Lostock Jn.
13m 39ch

10m 72ch Bradshawgate Tunnel
11m 01ch 10m 68ch

Lostock
13m 52ch

11m 05ch

Bolton West Jn. 10m 55ch
10m 50ch

Moor Lane
Tunnels

Bolton

Bolton East Jn. 10m 31ch

**Horwich
Parkway**
15m 50ch

Burnden Jn.
Sidings

Sidings

Burnden Jn. 10m 04ch

Moses Gate Jn. 9m 28ch

Moses Gate 9m 06ch

Westhoughton
15m 25ch

1

Metal Box Co.

Crossover oou

9m 31ch

Farnworth 8m 31ch

8m 24ch

Kearsley 7m 57ch

Farnworth Tunnels
8m 10ch

Daisy Hill
12m 57ch

Hag Fold
11m 59ch

Clifton
4m 57ch

Atherton
11m 01ch

Atherton Goods Yard
SB (AN)
11m 18ch

Walkden
7m 42ch

Moorside
5m 61ch

To Eurofreight
Terminal

Agecroft North Jn
3m 33ch

Walkden SB (WN)
7m 33ch

Swinton
5m 04ch

Up Sidings (Tarmac)

Pendlebury Tunnel
4m 34ch to 4m 43ch

Pendleton Tunnel
2m 25ch to 2m 27ch

Patricroft
26m 46ch

Eccles
27m 46ch

To Weaste
Network Rail / MSC
Boundary
0m 54ch

Eccles Station Jn.
27m 51ch

Eccles SB (ES)
27m 59ch / 0m 03ch

Culcheth Farm
(UWC) 19m 39ch

(UWC)

United F.C. Halt
31m 70ch

2

Astley SB (AY)
22m 54ch

To Trafford Park Siding
31m 35ch

Trafford Park
30m 68ch

Trafford Park West Jn.
31m 66ch

Chassen Road
28m 40ch

Humphrey Park
30m 17ch

*Glazebrook
East Jn. SB (GE)*
24m 60ch

Irlam
25m 51ch

Urmston
29m 02ch

Glazebrook
24m 37ch

25m 12ch

Flixton
27m 65ch

To Glazebrook
(MSC) (oou)

24m 53ch 24m 62ch

Shell
Chemicals
(U.K.)

Timperley
6m 55ch

Deansgate Jn.
0m 33ch
7m 05ch

Northenden Jn. SB (NN)
33m 49ch

Birchwood
21m 44ch

30m 12ch
0m 00ch

Skelton Jn. 30m 14ch

River Mersey

Deansgate Jn (MCB) 7m 06ch

30m 39ch

Navigation Road
7m 25ch

Navigation Road (CCTV) 7m 30ch

*Deansgate Jn. SB
(DJ)*
7m 06ch

Northenden GF
33m 28ch

Aggrega
Siding

Altrincham
7m 74ch

G.M.C.
Private Sidir

3

Hale
8m 31ch

Hale (CCTV) 8m 36ch

Heald Green W. Jn.
1m 10ch

Hea

Manchester Airport
0m 00ch

Ashley
10m 05ch

Mercer's (UWC)11m 37ch

A

B

From Map 5

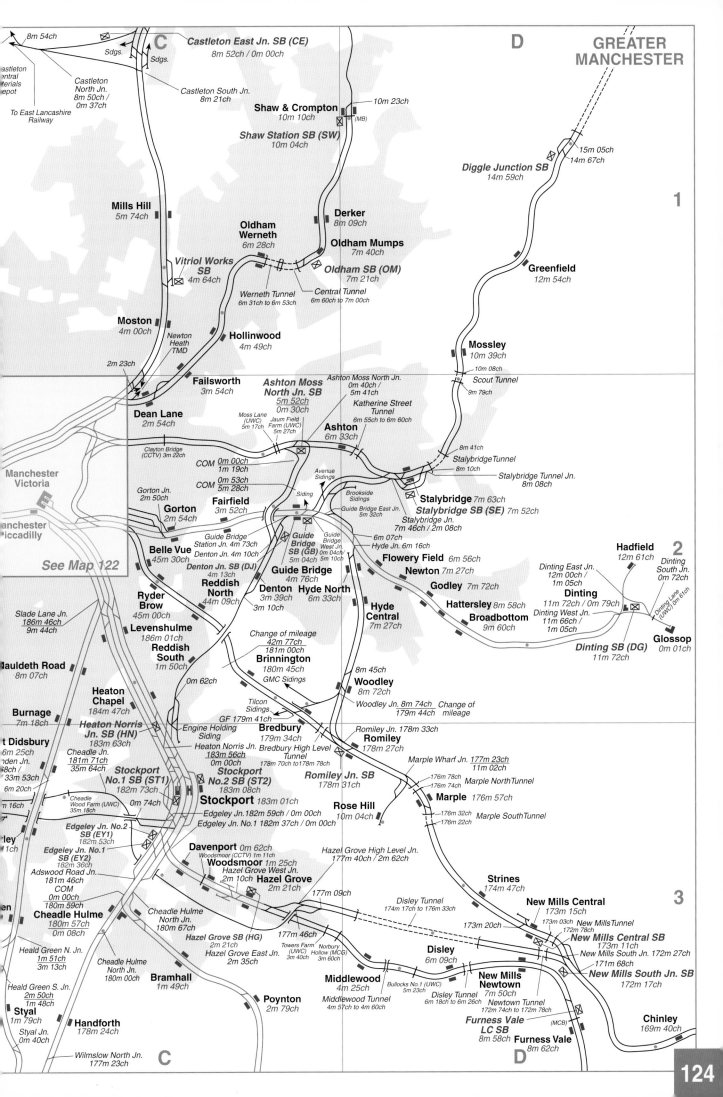

8m 54ch

C Castleton East Jn. SB (CE)
8m 52ch / 0m 00ch

Sdgs.   Sdgs.

Castleton Central Materials Depot

Castleton North Jn.
8m 50ch / 0m 37ch

Castleton South Jn.
8m 21ch

To East Lancashire Railway

D GREATER MANCHESTER

Shaw & Crompton   10m 23ch
10m 10ch   (MB)

Shaw Station SB (SW)
10m 04ch

Diggle Junction SB
14m 59ch

15m 05ch
14m 67ch

1

Mills Hill
5m 74ch

Derker
8m 09ch

Oldham Werneth
6m 28ch

Oldham Mumps
7m 40ch

Greenfield
12m 54ch

Vitriol Works SB
4m 64ch

Oldham SB (OM)
7m 21ch

Central Tunnel
6m 60ch to 7m 00ch

Werneth Tunnel
6m 31ch to 6m 53ch

Moston
4m 00ch

Newton Heath TMD

Hollinwood
4m 49ch

Mossley
10m 39ch

10m 08ch

Scout Tunnel

9m 79ch

2m 23ch

Failsworth
3m 54ch

Ashton Moss North Jn. SB
5m 52ch / 0m 30ch

Ashton Moss North Jn.
0m 40ch / 5m 41ch

Katherine Street Tunnel
6m 55ch to 6m 60ch

8m 41ch

Dean Lane
2m 54ch

Moss Lane (UWC)
5m 17ch

Jaum Field Farm (UWC)
5m 27ch

Ashton
6m 33ch

Stalybridge Tunnel

8m 10ch

Stalybridge Tunnel Jn.
8m 08ch

Manchester Victoria

Clayton Bridge (CCTV) 3m 22ch

COM 0m 00ch
1m 19ch

Avenue Sidings

Brookside Sidings

Stalybridge 7m 63ch

Stalybridge SB (SE) 7m 52ch

Manchester Piccadilly

Gorton Jn.
2m 50ch

COM 0m 53ch
5m 28ch

Siding

Stalybridge Jn.
7m 46ch / 2m 08ch

Fairfield
3m 52ch

Gorton
2m 54ch

Guide Bridge East Jn.
5m 32ch

See Map 122

Guide Bridge Station Jn. 4m 73ch
Denton Jn. 4m 10ch

Guide Bridge SB (GB)
5m 04ch

Guide Bridge West Jn.
0m 04ch / 5m 10ch

6m 07ch

Hyde Jn. 6m 16ch

Flowery Field 6m 56ch

2

Hadfield
12m 61ch

Dinting South Jn.
0m 72ch

Belle Vue
45m 30ch

Denton SB (DJ)
4m 13ch

Guide Bridge
4m 76ch

Newton 7m 27ch

Godley 7m 72ch

Dinting East Jn.
12m 00ch / 1m 05ch

Dinting
11m 72ch / 0m 79ch

Dinting Lane (UWC) 0m 61ch

Reddish North
44m 09ch

Denton
3m 39ch

Hyde North
6m 33ch

Hattersley 8m 58ch

Broadbottom
9m 60ch

Dinting West Jn.
11m 66ch / 1m 05ch

Glossop
0m 01ch

Ryder Brow
45m 00ch

3m 10ch

Hyde Central
7m 27ch

Dinting SB (DG)
11m 72ch

Slade Lane Jn.
186m 46ch
9m 44ch

Levenshulme
186m 01ch

Change of mileage
42m 77ch
181m 00ch

Reddish South
1m 50ch

Brinnington
180m 45ch

GMC Sidings

8m 45ch

Woodley
8m 72ch

Mauldeth Road
8m 07ch

0m 62ch

Woodley Jn. 8m 74ch
179m 44ch

Change of mileage

Tilcon Sidings

Burnage
7m 18ch

Heaton Chapel
184m 47ch

GF 179m 41ch

Romiley Jn. 178m 33ch

Heaton Norris Jn. SB (HN)
183m 63ch

Engine Holding Siding

Bredbury
179m 34ch

Romiley
178m 27ch

t Didsbury
6m 25ch
nden Jn.
8ch /
33m 53ch

Heaton Norris Jn.
183m 56ch
0m 00ch

Bredbury High Level Tunnel
178m 70ch to 178m 78ch

Marple Wharf Jn. 177m 23ch
11m 02ch

6m 20ch

Cheadle Jn.
181m 71ch
35m 64ch

Stockport No.1 SB (ST1)
182m 73ch

Stockport No.2 SB (ST2)
183m 08ch

Romiley Jn. SB
178m 31ch

176m 78ch Marple North Tunnel
176m 74ch

m 16ch

Cheadle Wood Farm (UWC) 35m 18ch

0m 74ch

Stockport 183m 01ch

Rose Hill
10m 04ch

Marple 176m 57ch

ley
1ch

Edgeley Jn. No.2 SB (EY1)
182m 53ch

Edgeley Jn. 182m 59ch / 0m 00ch

Edgeley Jn. No.1 182m 37ch / 0m 00ch

176m 32ch Marple South Tunnel
176m 22ch

Edgeley Jn. No.1 SB (EY2)
182m 36ch

Davenport 0m 62ch

Adswood Road Jn.
181m 46ch

Woodsmoor (CCTV) 1m 11ch

Hazel Grove High Level Jn.
177m 40ch / 2m 62ch

COM 0m 00ch
180m 59ch

Woodsmoor 1m 25ch

Hazel Grove West Jn.
2m 10ch

Strines
174m 47ch

Cheadle Hulme
180m 57ch
0m 08ch

Hazel Grove
2m 21ch

177m 09ch

New Mills Central
173m 15ch

3

Cheadle Hulme North Jn.
180m 67ch

Disley Tunnel
174m 17ch to 176m 33ch

173m 20ch

173m 03ch

New Mills Tunnel
172m 78ch

Heald Green N. Jn.
1m 51ch
3m 13ch

Hazel Grove SB (HG)
2m 21ch

177m 46ch

New Mills Central SB
173m 11ch

Cheadle Hulme North Jn.
180m 00ch

Hazel Grove East Jn.
2m 35ch

Towers Farm (UWC)
3m 40ch

Norbury Hollow (MCG)
3m 60ch

Disley
6m 09ch

New Mills South Jn. 172m 27ch

171m 68ch

Bramhall
1m 49ch

Middlewood
4m 25ch

Bullocks No.1 (UWC)
5m 23ch

New Mills Newtown
7m 50ch

New Mills South Jn. SB
172m 17ch

Heald Green S. Jn.
2m 50ch
1m 48ch

Poynton
2m 79ch

Middlewood Tunnel
4m 57ch to 4m 60ch

Disley Tunnel
6m 18ch to 6m 26ch

Newtown Tunnel
172m 74ch to 172m 78ch

Styal
1m 79ch

Handforth
178m 24ch

Furness Vale LC SB
8m 58ch

(MCB)

Chinley
169m 40ch

Styal Jn.
0m 40ch

Furness Vale
8m 62ch

Wilmslow North Jn.
177m 23ch

C **D**

124

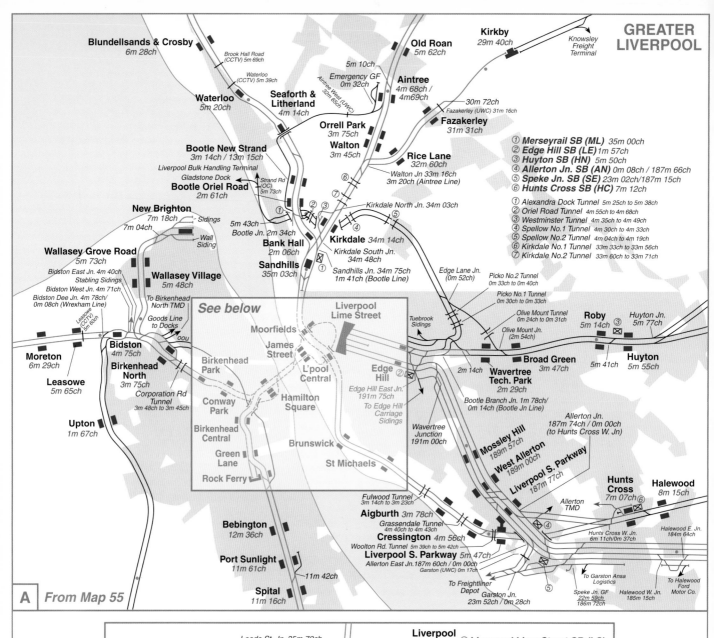

Blundellsands & Crosby
6m 28ch

Brook Hall Road
(CCTV) 5m 69ch

Waterloo
(CCTV) 5m 39ch

5m 10ch

Old Roan
5m 62ch

Kirkby
29m 40ch

Knowsley
Freight
Terminal

Emergency GF
0m 32ch

Aintree
4m 68ch /
4m 69ch

Waterloo
5m 20ch

Seaforth &
Litherland
4m 14ch

Aintree West (UWC)
32m 65ch

30m 72ch

Fazakerley (UWC) 31m 16ch

Fazakerley
31m 31ch

Orrell Park
3m 75ch

Walton
3m 45ch

Rice Lane
32m 60ch

Bootle New Strand
3m 14ch / 3m 15ch

Liverpool Bulk Handling Terminal
Gladstone Dock

Strand Rd
(OC)
5m 73ch

Walton Jn 33m 16ch
3m 20ch (Aintree Line)

Bootle Oriel Road
2m 61ch

Kirkdale North Jn. 34m 03ch

New Brighton
7m 18ch
7m 04ch

Sidings

Wall Siding

5m 43ch
Bootle Jn. 2m 34ch

Bank Hall
2m 06ch

Kirkdale 34m 14ch

Kirkdale South Jn.
34m 48ch

① Merseyrail SB (ML) 35m 00ch
② Edge Hill SB (LE) 1m 57ch
③ Huyton SB (HN) 5m 50ch
④ Allerton Jn. SB (AN) 0m 08ch / 187m 66ch
⑤ Speke Jn. SB (SE) 23m 02ch/187m 15ch
⑥ Hunts Cross SB (HC) 7m 12ch

Wallasey Grove Road
5m 73ch

Bidston East Jn. 4m 40ch
Stabling Sidings
Bidston West Jn. 4m 71ch
Bidston Dee Jn. 4m 78ch/
0m 08ch (Wrexham Line)

Wallasey Village
5m 48ch

Sandhills
35m 03ch

Sandhills Jn. 34m 75ch
1m 41ch (Bootle Line)

Edge Lane Jn.
(0m 52ch)

Picko No.2 Tunnel
0m 33ch to 0m 40ch

Picko No.1 Tunnel
0m 30ch to 0m 33ch

Olive Mount Tunnel
0m 24ch to 0m 31ch

Olive Mount Jn.
(2m 54ch)

Roby
5m 14ch

Huyton Jn.
5m 77ch

① Alexandra Dock Tunnel 5m 25ch to 5m 38ch
② Oriel Road Tunnel 4m 55ch to 4m 68ch
③ Westminster Tunnel 4m 35ch to 4m 49ch
④ Spellow No.1 Tunnel 4m 30ch to 4m 33ch
⑤ Spellow No.2 Tunnel 4m 04ch to 4m 19ch
⑥ Kirkdale No.1 Tunnel 33m 33ch to 33m 56ch
⑦ Kirkdale No.2 Tunnel 33m 60ch to 33m 71ch

Leasowe
(CCTV) 6m 60ch

Goods Line
to Docks

To Birkenhead
North TMD

See below

Liverpool
Lime Street

Tuebrook
Sidings

Huyton
5m 55ch

Moreton
6m 29ch

Bidston
4m 75ch

Moorfields

Birkenhead
Park

James
Street

L'pool
Central

Edge
Hill

Broad Green
3m 47ch

2m 14ch

Wavertree
Tech. Park
2m 29ch

Leasowe
5m 65ch

Birkenhead
North
3m 75ch

Corporation Rd
Tunnel
3m 48ch to 3m 45ch

Conway
Park

Hamilton
Square

Edge Hill East Jn.
191m 75ch

To Edge Hill
Carriage
Sidings

Wavertree
Junction
191m 00ch

Mossley Hill
189m 57ch

West Allerton
189m 00ch

Upton
1m 67ch

Birkenhead
Central

Brunswick

St Michaels

Liverpool S. Parkway
187m 77ch

Allerton Jn.
187m 74ch / 0m 00ch
(to Hunts Cross W. Jn)

Hunts
Cross
7m 07ch ⑥

Halewood
8m 15ch

Green
Lane

Rock Ferry

Allerton
TMD

Hunts Cross W. Jn.
6m 11ch/0m 37ch

Halewood E. Jn.
184m 64ch

Bebington
12m 36ch

Fulwood Tunnel
3m 14ch to 3m 23ch

Aigburth 3m 78ch

Grassendale Tunnel
4m 40ch to 4m 43ch

Cressington 4m 56ch

Woolton Rd. Tunnel 5m 39ch to 5m 42ch

④

⑤

To Garston Ansa
Logistics

Speke Jn. GF
22m 59ch
186m 72ch

Halewood W. Jn.
185m 15ch

To Halewood
Ford
Motor Co.

Port Sunlight
11m 61ch

Liverpool S. Parkway
5m 47ch

Allerton East Jn.187m 60ch / 0m 00ch
Garston (UWC) 0m 17ch

To Freightliner
Depot

Garston Jn.
23m 52ch / 0m 28ch

11m 42ch

Spital
11m 16ch

From Map 55

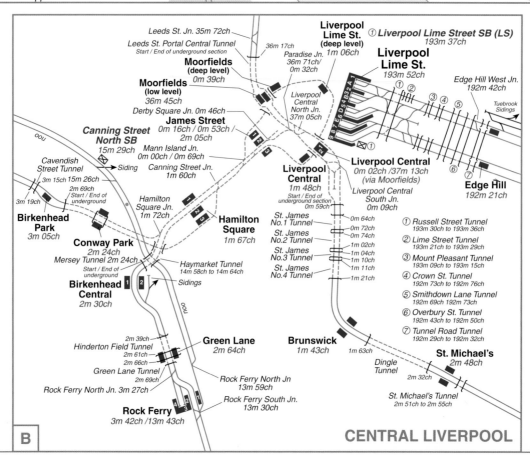

Leeds St. Jn. 35m 72ch

Leeds St. Portal Central Tunnel
Start / End of underground section

36m 17ch

Liverpool
Lime St.
(deep level)
1m 06ch

① Liverpool Lime Street SB (LS)
193m 37ch

Moorfields
(deep level)
0m 39ch

Paradise Jn.
36m 71ch/
0m 32ch

Liverpool
Lime St.
193m 52ch

Edge Hill West Jn.
192m 42ch

Moorfields
(low level)
36m 45ch

Derby Square 0m 46ch

Liverpool
Central North Jn.
37m 05ch

Tuebrook
Sidings

James Street
0m 16ch / 0m 53ch /
2m 05ch

Canning Street
North SB
15m 29ch

Mann Island Jn.
0m 00ch / 0m 69ch

Cavendish
Street Tunnel

Canning Street Jn.
1m 60ch

Siding

Liverpool Central
0m 02ch / 37m 13ch
(via Moorfields)

3m 15ch 15m 26ch

2m 69ch
Start / End of
underground

Hamilton
Square Jn.
1m 72ch

Liverpool
Central
1m 48ch

Start / End of
underground section
0m 59ch

Liverpool Central
South Jn.
0m 09ch

Edge Hill
192m 21ch

3m 19ch

Birkenhead
Park
3m 05ch

Hamilton
Square
1m 67ch

St. James
No.1 Tunnel

0m 64ch

① Russell Street Tunnel
193m 30ch to 193m 36ch

St. James
No.2 Tunnel

0m 72ch
0m 74ch

② Lime Street Tunnel
193m 21ch to 193m 29ch

Conway Park
2m 24ch

Mersey Tunnel 2m 24ch

St. James
No.3 Tunnel

1m 02ch
1m 04ch

③ Mount Pleasant Tunnel
193m 09ch to 193m 15ch

Start / End of
underground

Haymarket Tunnel
14m 58ch to 14m 64ch

St. James
No.4 Tunnel

1m 10ch
1m 11ch

④ Crown St. Tunnel
192m 73ch to 192m 76ch

Birkenhead
Central
2m 30ch

Sidings

1m 21ch

⑤ Smithdown Lane Tunnel
192m 69ch 192m 73ch

⑥ Overbury St. Tunnel
192m 43ch to 192m 50ch

Green Lane
2m 64ch

Brunswick
1m 43ch

1m 63ch

⑦ Tunnel Road Tunnel
192m 29ch to 192m 32ch

2m 39ch

Hinderton Field Tunnel
2m 61ch
2m 66ch

Green Lane Tunnel
2m 69ch

Rock Ferry North Jn
13m 59ch

Dingle
Tunnel

St. Michael's
2m 48ch

2m 32ch

Rock Ferry North Jn. 3m 27ch

St. Michael's Tunnel
2m 51ch to 2m 55ch

Rock Ferry
3m 42ch / 13m 43ch

Rock Ferry South Jn.
13m 30ch

CENTRAL LIVERPOOL

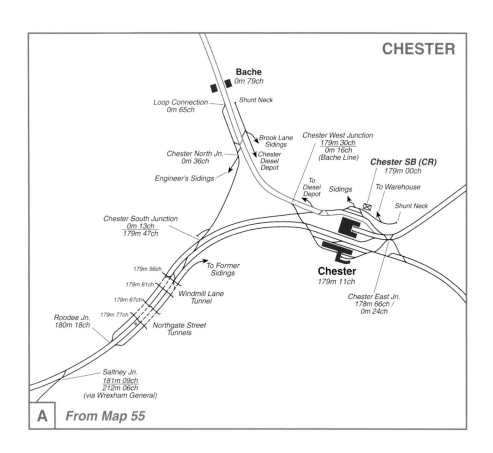

CHESTER

Bache
0m 79ch

Loop Connection
0m 65ch

Shunt Neck

Brook Lane
Sidings

Chester
Diesel
Depot

Chester North Jn.
0m 36ch

Engineer's Sidings

Chester West Junction
179m 30ch
0m 16ch
(Bache Line)

Chester SB (CR)
179m 00ch

To Diesel
Depot

Sidings

To Warehouse

Shunt Neck

Chester South Junction
0m 13ch
179m 47ch

179m 56ch

To Former
Sidings

179m 61ch

179m 67ch

Windmill Lane
Tunnel

Chester
179m 11ch

Chester East Jn.
178m 66ch /
0m 24ch

Roodee Jn.
180m 18ch

179m 77ch

Northgate Street
Tunnels

Saltney Jn.
181m 09ch
212m 06ch
(via Wrexham General)

A *From Map 55*

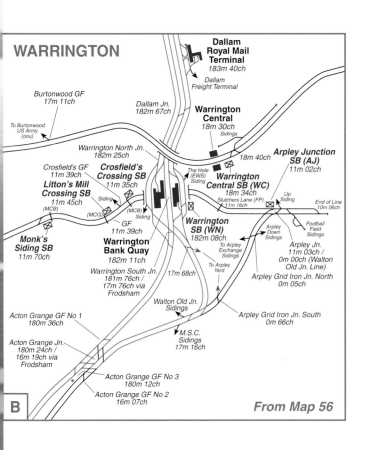

WARRINGTON

Burtonwood GF
17m 11ch

**Dallam
Royal Mail
Terminal**
183m 40ch

Dallam
Freight Terminal

Dallam Jn.
182m 67ch

To Burtonwood
US Army
(oou)

**Warrington
Central**
18m 30ch

Sidings

Warrington North Jn.
182m 25ch

18m 40ch

**Arpley Junction
SB (AJ)**
11m 02ch

Crosfield's GF
11m 39ch

**Crosfield's
Crossing SB**
11m 35ch

The Hole
(EWS)
Siding

**Warrington
Central SB (WC)**
18m 34ch

**Litton's Mill
Crossing SB**
11m 45ch
(MCB)

Siding

(MCG)

(MCB)
Siding

Slutchers Lane (FP)
11m 16ch

Up
Siding

End of Line
10m 06ch

**Monk's
Siding SB**
11m 70ch

GF
11m 39ch

**Warrington
SB (WN)**
182m 08ch

Football
Field
Sidings

**Warrington
Bank Quay**
182m 42ch

Arpley
Down
Sidings

Arpley Jn.
11m 03ch /
0m 00ch (Walton
Old Jn. Line)

To Arpley
Exchange
Sidings

Warrington South Jn.
181m 76ch /
17m 76ch via
Frodsham

17m 68ch

To Arpley
Yard

Walton Old Jn.
Sidings

Arpley Grid Iron Jn. North
0m 05ch

Acton Grange GF No 1
180m 36ch

M.S.C.
Sidings
17m 16ch

Arpley Grid Iron Jn. South
0m 66ch

Acton Grange Jn.
180m 24ch /
16m 19ch via
Frodsham

Acton Grange GF No 3
180m 12ch

Acton Grange GF No 2
16m 07ch

B *From Map 56*

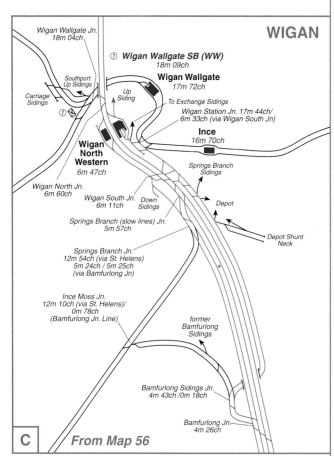

WIGAN

Wigan Wallgate Jn.
18m 04ch

① **Wigan Wallgate SB (WW)**
18m 09ch

Southport
Up Sidings

Wigan Wallgate
17m 72ch

Carriage
Sidings

Up
Siding

To Exchange Sidings

①

Wigan Station Jn. 17m 44ch/
6m 33ch (via Wigan South Jn)

Ince
16m 70ch

**Wigan
North
Western**
6m 47ch

Springs Branch
Sidings

Wigan North Jn.
6m 60ch

Wigan South Jn.
6m 11ch

Down
Sidings

Depot

Springs Branch (slow lines) Jn.
5m 57ch

Depot Shunt
Neck

Springs Branch Jn.
12m 54ch (via St. Helens)
5m 24ch / 5m 25ch
(via Bamfurlong Jn)

Ince Moss Jn.
12m 10ch (via St. Helens)/
0m 78ch
(Bamfurlong Jn. Line)

former
Bamfurlong
Sidings

Bamfurlong Sidings Jn.
4m 43ch /0m 18ch

Bamfurlong Jn.
4m 26ch

C *From Map 56*

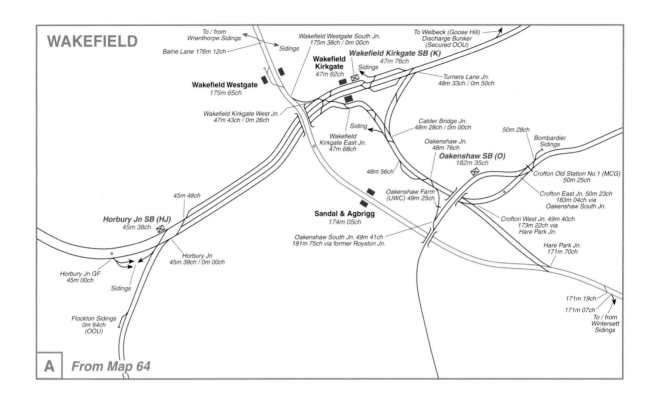

WAKEFIELD

To / from Wrenthorpe Sidings

Balne Lane 176m 12ch

Sidings

Wakefield Westgate South Jn. 175m 38ch / 0m 00ch

Wakefield Kirkgate 47m 62ch

Wakefield Kirkgate SB (K) 47m 76ch

To Welbeck (Goose Hill) Discharge Bunker (Secured OOU)

Sidings

Turners Lane Jn. 48m 33ch / 0m 50ch

Wakefield Westgate 175m 65ch

Wakefield Kirkgate West Jn. 47m 43ch / 0m 26ch

Siding

Wakefield Kirkgate East Jn. 47m 68ch

Calder Bridge Jn. 48m 28ch / 0m 00ch

Oakenshaw Jn. 48m 76ch

50m 28ch

Bombardier Sidings

Oakenshaw SB (O) 182m 35ch

Crofton Old Station No.1 (MCG) 50m 25ch

48m 56ch

45m 48ch

Oakenshaw Farm (UWC) 49m 25ch

Crofton East Jn. 50m 23ch 183m 04ch via Oakenshaw South Jn.

Crofton West Jn. 49m 40ch 173m 22ch via Hare Park Jn.

Horbury Jn SB (HJ) 45m 38ch

Sandal & Agbrigg 174m 05ch

Hare Park Jn. 171m 70ch

Horbury Jn 45m 39ch / 0m 00ch

Oakenshaw South Jn. 49m 41ch 181m 75ch via former Royston Jn.

Horbury Jn GF 45m 00ch

Sidings

171m 19ch

171m 07ch

Flockton Sidings 0m 64ch (OOU)

To / from Wintersett Sidings

A | *From Map 64*

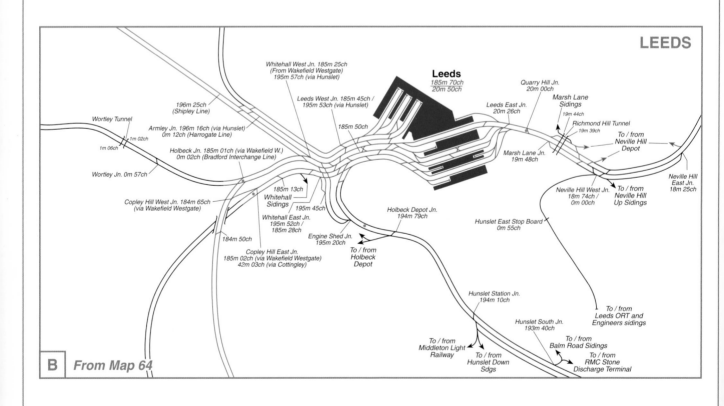

LEEDS

Whitehall West Jn. 185m 25ch (From Wakefield Westgate) 195m 57ch (via Hunslet)

Leeds 185m 70ch 20m 50ch

Quarry Hill Jn. 20m 00ch

Marsh Lane Sidings

196m 25ch (Shipley Line)

Leeds West Jn. 185m 45ch / 195m 53ch (via Hunslet)

Leeds East Jn. 20m 26ch

19m 44ch

Wortley Tunnel

Armley Jn. 196m 16ch (via Hunslet) 0m 12ch (Harrogate Line)

185m 50ch

Richmond Hill Tunnel 19m 39ch

To / from Neville Hill Depot

1m 02ch

1m 06ch

Holbeck Jn. 185m 01ch (via Wakefield W.) 0m 02ch (Bradford Interchange Line)

Marsh Lane Jn. 19m 48ch

Neville Hill East Jn. 18m 25ch

Wortley Jn. 0m 57ch

185m 13ch

Whitehall Sidings

195m 45ch

Neville Hill West Jn. 18m 74ch / 0m 00ch

To / from Neville Hill Up Sidings

Copley Hill West Jn. 184m 65ch (via Wakefield Westgate)

Whitehall East Jn. 195m 52ch / 185m 28ch

Holbeck Depot Jn. 194m 79ch

Hunslet East Stop Board 0m 55ch

184m 50ch

Engine Shed Jn. 195m 20ch

To / from Holbeck Depot

Copley Hill East Jn. 185m 02ch (via Wakefield Westgate) 42m 03ch (via Cottingley)

Hunslet Station Jn. 194m 10ch

To / from Leeds ORT and Engineers sidings

Hunslet South Jn. 193m 40ch

To / from Balm Road Sidings

To / from Middleton Light Railway

To / from Hunslet Down Sdgs

To / from RMC Stone Discharge Terminal

B | *From Map 64*

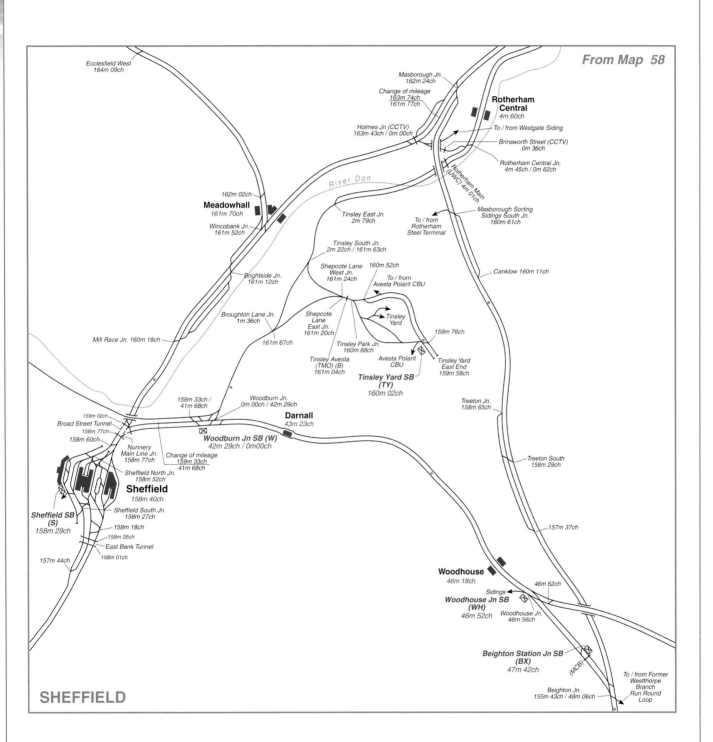

Ecclesfield West
164m 09ch

Masborough Jn.
162m 24ch

Change of mileage
163m 74ch
161m 77ch

Rotherham Central
4m 60ch

Holmes Jn (CCTV)
163m 43ch / 0m 00ch

To / from Westgate Siding

Brinsworth Street (CCTV)
0m 36ch

Rotherham Central Jn.
4m 45ch / 0m 62ch

River Don

162m 02ch

Meadowhall
161m 70ch

Rotherham Main
(UWC) 4m 01ch

Wincobank Jn.
161m 52ch

Tinsley East Jn.
2m 79ch

To / from
Rotherham
Steel Terminal

Masborough Sorting
Sidings South Jn.
160m 61ch

Tinsley South Jn.
2m 22ch / 161m 63ch

Canklow 160m 11ch

Shepcote Lane
West Jn.
161m 24ch

160m 52ch

To / from
Avesta Polarit CBU

Brightside Jn.
161m 12ch

Broughton Lane Jn.
1m 36ch

Shepcote
Lane
East Jn.
161m 20ch

Tinsley
Yard

159m 76ch

Mill Race Jn. 160m 18ch

161m 67ch

Tinsley Park Jn.
161m 68ch

Tinsley Avesta
(TMO) (B)
161m 04ch

Avesta Polarit
CBU

Tinsley Yard
East End
159m 58ch

**Tinsley Yard SB
(TY)**
160m 02ch

Treeton Jn.
158m 65ch

159m 33ch /
41m 68ch

Woodburn Jn.
0m 00ch / 42m 29ch

159m 02ch

Darnall
43m 23ch

Broad Street Tunnel
158m 77ch

158m 60ch

Nunnery
Main Line Jn.
158m 77ch

Woodburn Jn SB (W)
42m 29ch / 0m00ch

Change of mileage
159m 33ch
41m 68ch

Sheffield North Jn.
158m 52ch

Treeton South
158m 29ch

Sheffield
158m 40ch

Sheffield South Jn.
158m 27ch

**Sheffield SB
(S)**
158m 29ch

158m 18ch

158m 05ch

East Bank Tunnel

157m 44ch

158m 01ch

157m 37ch

Woodhouse
46m 18ch

46m 62ch

Sidings

**Woodhouse Jn SB
(WH)**
46m 52ch

Woodhouse Jn.
46m 56ch

**Beighton Station Jn SB
(BX)**
47m 42ch

(MCB)

To / from Former
Westthorpe
Branch
Run Round
Loop

Beighton Jn.
155m 43ch / 48m 06ch

SHEFFIELD

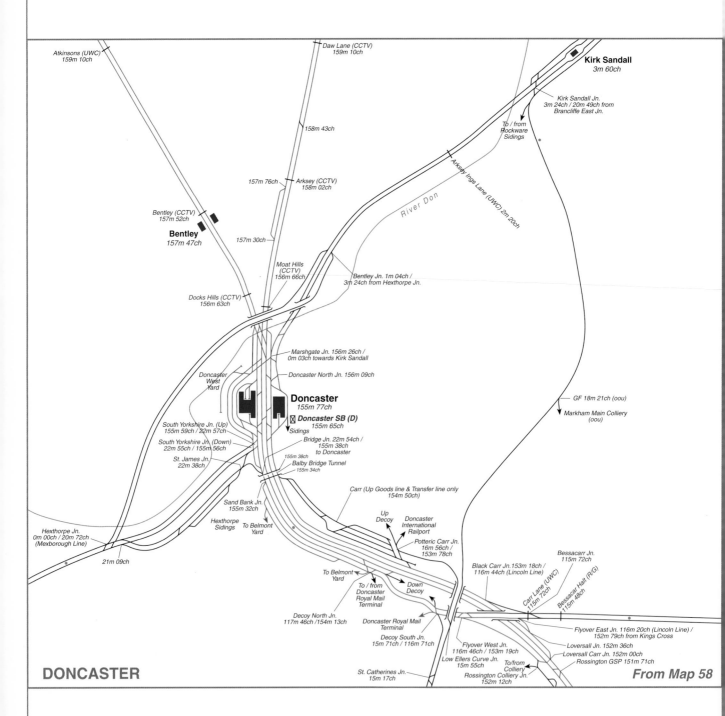

Atkinsons (UWC)
159m 10ch

Daw Lane (CCTV)
159m 10ch

Kirk Sandall
3m 60ch

Kirk Sandall Jn.
3m 24ch / 20m 49ch from
Brancliffe East Jn.

158m 43ch

To / from
Rockware
Sidings

157m 76ch

Arksey (CCTV)
158m 02ch

River Don

Arksey Ings Lane (UWC) 2m 20ch

Bentley (CCTV)
157m 52ch

Bentley
157m 47ch

157m 30ch

Moat Hills
(CCTV)
156m 66ch

Bentley Jn. 1m 04ch /
3m 24ch from Hexthorpe Jn.

Docks Hills (CCTV)
156m 63ch

Marshgate Jn. 156m 26ch /
0m 03ch towards Kirk Sandall

Doncaster
West
Yard

Doncaster North Jn. 156m 09ch

GF 18m 21ch (oou)

Doncaster
155m 77ch

Markham Main Colliery
(oou)

⊠ *Doncaster SB (D)*
155m 65ch

South Yorkshire Jn. (Up)
155m 59ch / 22m 57ch

Sidings

Bridge Jn. 22m 54ch /
155m 38ch /
to Doncaster

South Yorkshire Jn (Down)
22m 55ch / 155m 56ch

St. James Jn.
22m 38ch

155m 38ch

Balby Bridge Tunnel
155m 34ch

Sand Bank Jn.
155m 32ch

Carr (Up Goods line & Transfer line only
154m 50ch)

Hexthorpe Jn.
0m 00ch / 20m 72ch
(Mexborough Line)

Hexthorpe
Sidings

To Belmont
Yard

Up
Decoy

Doncaster
International
Railport

Potteric Carr Jn.
16m 56ch /
153m 78ch

Bessacarr Jn.
115m 72ch

21m 09ch

To Belmont
Yard

Down
Decoy

Black Carr Jn.153m 18ch /
116m 44ch (Lincoln Line)

Carr Lane (UWC)
115m 72ch

Bessacar Halt (R/G)
115m 48ch

To / from
Doncaster
Royal Mail
Terminal

Decoy North Jn.
117m 46ch /154m 13ch

Doncaster Royal Mail
Terminal

Decoy South Jn.
15m 71ch / 116m 71ch

Flyover West Jn.
116m 46ch / 153m 19ch

Low Ellers Curve Jn.
15m 55ch

Flyover East Jn. 116m 20ch (Lincoln Line) /
152m 79ch from Kings Cross

Loversall Jn. 152m 36ch

Loversall Carr Jn. 152m 00ch

Rossington GSP 151m 71ch

To/from
Colliery

St. Catherines Jn.
15m 17ch

Rossington Colliery Jn.
152m 12ch

DONCASTER

From Map 58

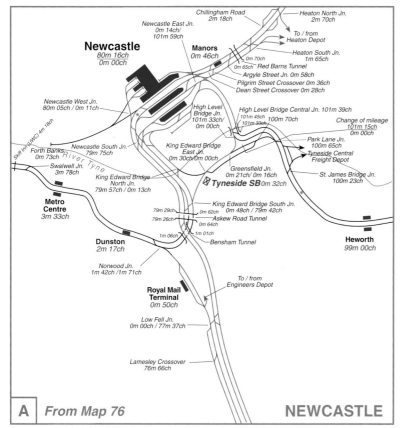

A — From Map 76 — NEWCASTLE

Chillingham Road 2m 18ch
Heaton North Jn. 2m 70ch
Newcastle East Jn. 0m 14ch/ 101m 59ch
To / from Heaton Depot
Newcastle 80m 16ch / 0m 00ch
Manors 0m 46ch
Heaton South Jn. 1m 65ch
0m 70ch
0m 65ch — Red Barns Tunnel
Argyle Street Jn. 0m 58ch
Pilgrim Street Crossover 0m 36ch
Dean Street Crossover 0m 28ch
Newcastle West Jn. 80m 05ch / 0m 11ch
High Level Bridge Jn. 101m 33ch/ 0m 00ch
High Level Bridge Central Jn. 101m 39ch
101m 45ch
100m 70ch
101m 33ch
Change of mileage 101m 15ch / 0m 00ch
Park Lane Jn. 100m 65ch
Tyneside Central Freight Depot
Skiff Inn (UWC) 4m 18ch
Forth Banks 0m 73ch
Newcastle South Jn. 79m 75ch
King Edward Bridge East Jn. 0m 30ch/0m 00ch
Greensfield Jn. 0m 21ch/ 0m 16ch
St. James Bridge Jn. 100m 23ch
River Tyne
Swalwell Jn. 3m 78ch
King Edward Bridge North Jn. 79m 57ch / 0m 13ch
Tyneside SB 0m 32ch
Metro Centre 3m 33ch
79m 29ch
79m 26ch
King Edward Bridge South Jn. 0m 48ch / 79m 42ch
0m 62ch
0m 64ch
Askew Road Tunnel
1m 06ch
1m 01ch
Bensham Tunnel
Heworth 99m 00ch
Dunston 2m 17ch
Norwood Jn. 1m 42ch /1m 71ch
To / from Engineers Depot
Royal Mail Terminal 0m 50ch
Low Fell Jn. 0m 00ch / 77m 37ch
Lamesley Crossover 76m 66ch

B — From Map 64 — YORK

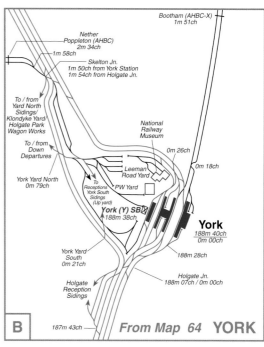

Bootham (AHBC-X) 1m 51ch
Nether Poppleton (AHBC) 2m 34ch
1m 58ch
Skelton Jn. 1m 50ch from York Station 1m 54ch from Holgate Jn.
To / from Yard North Sidings/ Klondyke Yard/ Holgate Park Wagon Works
National Railway Museum
To / from Down Departures
0m 26ch
0m 18ch
York Yard North 0m 79ch
Leeman Road Yard
To Receptions York South Sidings (Up yard)
PW Yard
York (Y) SB 188m 38ch
York 188m 40ch / 0m 00ch
York Yard South 0m 21ch
188m 28ch
Holgate Reception Sidings
Holgate Jn. 188m 07ch / 0m 00ch
187m 43ch

C — From Map 70 — TEESIDE

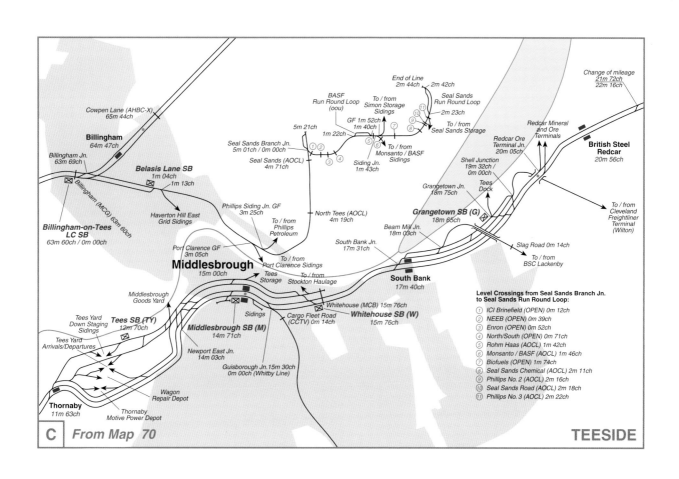

Cowpen Lane (AHBC-X) 65m 44ch
End of Line 2m 44ch
2m 42ch
Change of mileage 21m 72ch / 22m 16ch
BASF Run Round Loop (oou)
Seal Sands Run Round Loop 2m 23ch
To / from Simon Storage Sidings
Billingham 64m 47ch
GF 1m 52ch 1m 40ch
To / from Seal Sands Storage
Redcar Mineral and Ore Terminals
5m 21ch
1m 22ch
Billingham Jn. 63m 69ch
Belasis Lane SB 1m 04ch
1m 13ch
Seal Sands Branch Jn. 5m 01ch / 0m 00ch
To / from Monsanto / BASF Sidings
Redcar Ore Terminal Jn. 20m 05ch
British Steel Redcar 20m 56ch
Billingham (MCG) 63m 60ch
Seal Sands (AOCL) 4m 71ch
Siding Jn. 1m 43ch
Shell Junction 19m 32ch / 0m 00ch
Billingham-on-Tees LC SB 63m 60ch / 0m 00ch
Haverton Hill East Grid Sidings
Phillips Siding Jn. GF 3m 25ch
North Tees (AOCL) 4m 19ch
Grangetown Jn. 18m 75ch
Tees Dock
To / from Phillips Petroleum
Port Clarence GF 3m 05ch
Grangetown SB (G) 18m 65ch
To / from Cleveland Freightliner Terminal (Wilton)
Middlesbrough 15m 00ch
Beam Mill Jn. 18m 03ch
To / from Port Clarence Sidings
South Bank Jn. 17m 31ch
Middlesbrough Goods Yard
Tees Storage
To / from Stockton Haulage
Slag Road 0m 14ch
Whitehouse (MCB) 15m 76ch
South Bank 17m 40ch
To / from BSC Lackenby
Tees SB (TY) 12m 70ch
Tees Yard Down Staging Sidings
Sidings
Cargo Fleet Road (CCTV) 0m 14ch
Whitehouse SB (W) 15m 76ch
Tees Yard Arrivals/Departures
Middlesbrough SB (M) 14m 71ch
Newport East Jn. 14m 03ch
Guisborough Jn. 15m 30ch 0m 00ch (Whitby Line)
Thornaby 11m 63ch
Wagon Repair Depot
Thornaby Motive Power Depot

Level Crossings from Seal Sands Branch Jn. to Seal Sands Run Round Loop:
1. ICI Brinefield (OPEN) 0m 12ch
2. NEEB (OPEN) 0m 39ch
3. Enron (OPEN) 0m 52ch
4. North/South (OPEN) 0m 71ch
5. Rohm Haas (AOCL) 1m 42ch
6. Monsanto / BASF (AOCL) 1m 46ch
7. Biofuels (OPEN) 1m 74ch
8. Seal Sands Chemical (AOCL) 2m 11ch
9. Phillips No. 2 (AOCL) 2m 16ch
10. Seal Sands Road (AOCL) 2m 18ch
11. Phillips No. 3 (AOCL) 2m 22ch

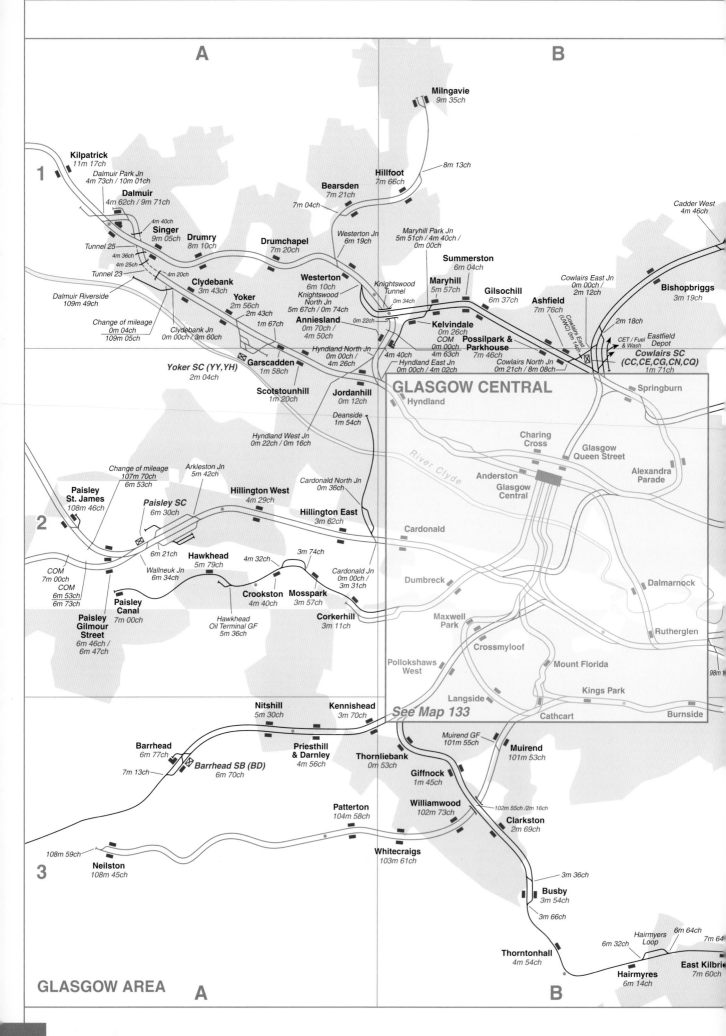

Milngavie
9m 35ch

Kilpatrick
11m 17ch

Dalmuir Park Jn
4m 73ch / 10m 01ch

8m 13ch

Hillfoot
7m 66ch

Dalmuir
4m 62ch / 9m 71ch

Bearsden
7m 21ch

4m 40ch
Singer
9m 05ch

Drumry
8m 10ch

7m 04ch

Cadder West
4m 46ch

Tunnel 25

Drumchapel
7m 20ch

Westerton Jn
6m 19ch

Maryhill Park Jn
5m 51ch / 4m 40ch /
0m 00ch

Summerston
6m 04ch

4m 36ch
4m 25ch
Tunnel 23

Clydebank
3m 43ch

Westerton
6m 10ch
Knightswood
North Jn
5m 67ch / 0m 74ch

Knightswood
Tunnel
0m 34ch

Maryhill
5m 57ch

Gilsochill
6m 37ch

Cowlairs East Jn
0m 00ch /
2m 12ch

Bishopbriggs
3m 19ch

4m 20ch

Dalmuir Riverside
109m 49ch

Ashfield
7m 76ch

Change of mileage
0m 04ch
109m 05ch

Yoker
2m 56ch
2m 43ch

Clydebank Jn
0m 00ch / 3m 60ch

Anniesland
0m 70ch /
4m 50ch

Hyndland North Jn
0m 00ch /
4m 26ch

0m 22ch

Kelvindale
0m 26ch
COM
0m 00ch

4m 40ch

Possilpark &
Parkhouse
7m 46ch

Cowlairs North Jn
0m 21ch / 8m 08ch

2m 18ch

Cowlairs East
(UWC) 0m 14ch

CET / Fuel
& Wash

Eastfield
Depot

Cowlairs SC
(CC,CE,CG,CN,CQ)
1m 71ch

Garscadden
1m 58ch

1m 67ch

Hyndland East Jn
0m 00ch / 4m 02ch

4m 63ch

Yoker SC (YY,YH)
2m 04ch

Scotstounhill
1m 20ch

Jordanhill
0m 12ch

GLASGOW CENTRAL

Hyndland

Springburn

Deanside
1m 54ch

Hyndland West Jn
0m 22ch / 0m 16ch

Charing
Cross

Glasgow
Queen Street

Alexandra
Parade

Change of mileage
107m 70ch
6m 53ch

Arkleston Jn
5m 42ch

Cardonald North Jn
0m 36ch

River Clyde

Paisley
St. James
108m 46ch

Hillington West
4m 29ch

Paisley SC
6m 30ch

Anderston

Cardonald

Hillington East
3m 62ch

Glasgow
Central

6m 21ch

Hawkhead
5m 79ch

4m 32ch

3m 74ch

Cardonald Jn
0m 00ch /
3m 31ch

Dumbreck

Dalmarnock

COM
7m 00ch
COM
6m 53ch
6m 73ch

Wallneuk Jn
6m 34ch

Crookston
4m 40ch

Mosspark
3m 57ch

Maxwell
Park

Rutherglen

Paisley
Canal
7m 00ch

Corkerhill
3m 11ch

Crossmyloof

Paisley
Gilmour
Street
6m 46ch /
6m 47ch

Hawkhead
Oil Terminal GF
5m 36ch

Pollokshaws
West

Mount Florida

Kings Park

Burnside

Langside

98m

Cathcart

Nitshill
5m 30ch

Kennishead
3m 70ch

See Map 133

Barrhead
6m 77ch

Priesthill
& Darnley
4m 56ch

Thornliebank
0m 53ch

Muirend GF
101m 55ch

Muirend
101m 53ch

7m 13ch

Barrhead SB (BD)
6m 70ch

Giffnock
1m 45ch

102m 55ch /2m 16ch

Williamwood
102m 73ch

Patterton
104m 58ch

Clarkston
2m 69ch

108m 59ch

Whitecraigs
103m 61ch

3m 36ch

Neilston
108m 45ch

Busby
3m 54ch

6m 64ch

3m 66ch

Hairmyres
Loop

7m 64

6m 32ch

Thorntonhall
4m 54ch

East Kilbri
7m 60ch

Hairmyres
6m 14ch

Gartshore
Emergency GF
10m 46ch

Croy
11m 40ch

10m 03ch

Gartshore
10m 25ch

10m 14ch

Down Relief
Sidings

Greenfaulds
100m 43ch

Cumbernauld
101m 18ch

Cadder East
5m 34ch

Lenzie
6m 20ch

Cadder
Down Yard

Greenfoot (CCTV) 97m 60ch

97m 16ch

Garnqueen North Jn
97m 05ch / 1m 33ch

Stepps
99m 64ch

Heathfield (UWC) 98m 31ch

Sidings
oou

Gartcosh GF

Airdrie - Bathgate Link
(under construction, 2011)

Russell's Siding GF
98m 06ch

Gartcosh
97m 31ch

Heatherbell (CCTV) 96m 17ch

Gartsherrie South Jn
95m 64ch

Change of ELR
97m 09ch

Gartcosh Jn
97m 06ch / 0m 00ch

95m 16ch

To Gunnie Yard 8m 41ch (oou)

Sunnyside Jn 8m 43ch

Coatbridge
Freightliner
Terminal

Coatbridge Sunnyside
8m 51ch

Blairhill
7m 75ch

Coatdyke
9m 50ch

Airdrie
10m 38ch

Drumgelloch
11m 65ch

Easterhouse
5m 30ch

Coatbridge
Central
94m 63ch

Signals M243/245 9m 14ch
9m 27ch

GF 9m 45ch

arntyne
2m 36ch

Shettleston
3m 17ch

Garrowhill
4m 30ch

Whifflet North Jn
0m 00ch / 94m 05ch
(COM)

Coatbridge Jn
94m 49ch / 7m 03ch

9m 60ch

Whifflet South Jn
93m 65ch / 9m 63ch

3m 08ch
3m 22ch

Shettleston
Workshops

3m 67ch

Kirkwood
6m 04ch

Whifflet
94m 02ch

Bargeddie
5m 02ch

Langloan Jn
6m 34ch

COM
6m 59ch /
0m 34ch
92m 47ch

Baillieston
3m 29ch

Mount Vernon
2m 48ch

Burnhouse
92m 12ch

Carmyle
1m 42ch

To
Down
Sidings

Mossend
Yard

Mossend North Jn
91m 42ch / -0m 06ch

Newton West Jn
96m 34ch

Newton East Jn
95m 14ch

Uddingston
93m 71ch

Bellshill
2m 30ch

Mossend East Jn
3m 63ch / 0m 40ch
/ 0m 31ch

Cambuslang
97m 24ch

Mossend South Jn
91m 12ch / 0m 00ch
/ 91m 08ch

Mossend West Jn
91m 50ch / 3m 04ch

Newton, Hamilton Jn
95m 47ch / 0m 07ch

Holytown Jn
1m 27ch / 89m 66ch

Bellside GF
3m 60ch

Kirkhill
97m 15ch

Newton
95m 57ch

95m 52ch /
0m 01ch

Uddingston Jn
93m 58ch /
-0m 03ch

91m 08ch

Ravenscraig
Sdg

CE Siding
oou

96m 74ch

96m 61ch

Kirkhill
Tunnel

Newton, Kirkhill Jn
95m 77ch

Holytown
1m 10ch

Carfin
1m 69ch

Cleland
3m 52ch

To Maintenance
Depot
89m 63ch

90m 17ch

Findlay's Sidings

Braidhurst Loops

Findlay's GF

Blantyre
2m 29ch

Logan's Road (CCTV)
89m 77ch

Lesmahagow Jn
89m 51ch / 89m 50ch /
-0m 01ch

River Clyde

3m 62ch

3m 71ch

Motherwell
89m 38ch /
0m 00ch

89m 12ch

Dalzall
Plate
Works

Wishaw
Central Jn
86m 63ch

To Earnock
Sidings

Hamilton West
4m 12ch

Airbles
0m 61ch

0m 27ch

Motherwell
SC
88m 77ch

88m 19ch

3

5m 15ch

Change of mileage
1m 44ch

6m 61ch

Shieldmuir
87m 59ch

Wishaw
86m 31ch

Barncluith
Tunnel

87m 46ch

5m 62ch

5m 79ch

6m 22ch

Shieldmuir North Jn
87m 41ch /
87m 43ch

Shieldmuir
Royal Mail Terminal
87m 26ch

Hamilton Central
5m 03ch

Haughhead Jn
0m 00ch / 6m 18ch

Chatelherault
0m 52ch

Shieldmuir South Jn
87m 07ch

84

2

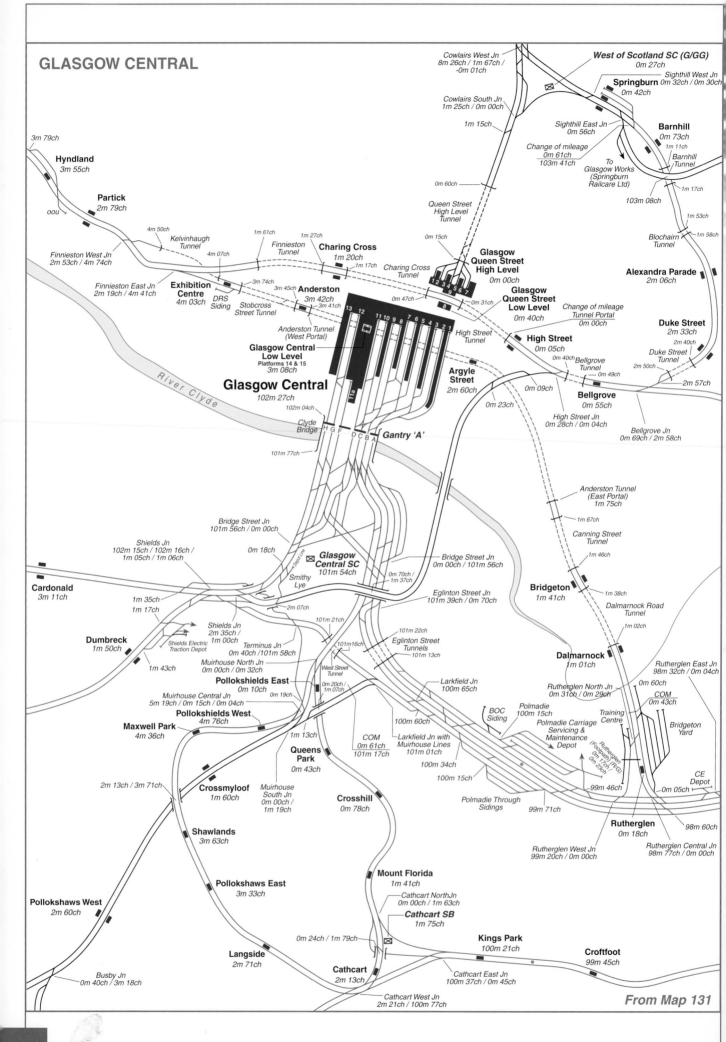

GLASGOW CENTRAL

3m 79ch

Hyndland
3m 55ch

Partick
2m 79ch

oou

Kelvinhaugh
Tunnel
4m 50ch

Finnieston West Jn
2m 53ch / 4m 74ch

Finnieston East Jn
2m 19ch / 4m 41ch

**Exhibition
Centre**
4m 03ch

DRS
Siding

Stobcross
Street Tunnel

Finnieston
Tunnel
1m 61ch

1m 27ch

Charing Cross
1m 20ch

1m 17ch

Charing Cross
Tunnel

0m 47ch

4m 07ch

3m 74ch

3m 45ch

Anderston
3m 42ch

3m 41ch

Anderston Tunnel
(West Portal)

**Glasgow Central
Low Level**
Platforms 14 & 15
3m 08ch

Glasgow Central
102m 27ch

102m 04ch

Clyde
Bridge

H G F   D C B A

Gantry 'A'

101m 77ch

13 12   11 10 9 8   7 6 5 4 3 2 1

Cowlairs West Jn
8m 26ch / 1m 67ch /
-0m 01ch

West of Scotland SC (G/GG)
0m 27ch

Sighthill West Jn
0m 32ch / 0m 30ch

Springburn
0m 42ch

Cowlairs South Jn
1m 25ch / 0m 00ch

1m 15ch

Sighthill East Jn
0m 56ch

Change of mileage
0m 61ch
103m 41ch

To
Glasgow Works
(Springburn
Railcare Ltd)

0m 60ch

Queen Street
High Level
Tunnel

0m 15ch

**Glasgow
Queen Street
High Level**
0m 00ch

1 2 3 4 5 6 7

6

0m 31ch

**Glasgow
Queen Street
Low Level**
0m 40ch

Change of mileage
Tunnel Portal
0m 00ch

Barnhill
0m 73ch

1m 11ch

Barnhill
Tunnel

103m 08ch

1m 17ch

1m 53ch

Blochairn
Tunnel

1m 58ch

Alexandra Parade
2m 06ch

Duke Street
2m 33ch

2m 40ch

Duke Street
Tunnel

2m 50ch

2m 57ch

High Street
Tunnel

High Street
0m 05ch

0m 40ch

0m 49ch

Bellgrove
Tunnel

**Argyle
Street**
2m 60ch

0m 09ch

0m 23ch

Bellgrove
0m 55ch

High Street Jn
0m 28ch / 0m 04ch

Bellgrove Jn
0m 69ch / 2m 58ch

River Clyde

Anderston Tunnel
(East Portal)
1m 75ch

1m 67ch

Canning Street
Tunnel

1m 46ch

Bridge Street Jn
101m 56ch / 0m 00ch

0m 18ch

✉ **Glasgow
Central SC**
101m 54ch

Smithy
Lye

Shields Jn
102m 15ch / 102m 16ch /
1m 05ch / 1m 06ch

Cardonald
3m 11ch

1m 35ch
1m 17ch

2m 07ch

Shields Jn
2m 35ch /
1m 00ch

Shields Electric
Traction Depot

Terminus Jn
0m 40ch / 101m 58ch

Muirhouse North Jn
0m 00ch / 0m 32ch

Bridge Street Jn
0m 00ch / 101m 56ch

0m 70ch
1m 37ch

Eglinton Street Jn
101m 39ch / 0m 70ch

101m 21ch

101m 16ch

101m 22ch

Eglinton Street
Tunnels
101m 13ch

West Street
Tunnel

Pollokshields East
0m 10ch

0m 19ch

0m 20ch
1m 07ch

Bridgeton
1m 41ch

1m 38ch

Dalmarnock Road
Tunnel

1m 02ch

Dalmarnock
1m 01ch

Rutherglen East Jn
98m 32ch / 0m 04ch

0m 60ch

Rutherglen North Jn
0m 31ch / 0m 29ch

COM
0m 43ch

Training
Centre

Dumbreck
1m 50ch

1m 43ch

Muirhouse Central Jn
5m 19ch / 0m 15ch / 0m 04ch

Pollokshields West
4m 76ch

Maxwell Park
4m 36ch

Muirhouse
South Jn
0m 00ch /
1m 19ch

1m 13ch

**Queens
Park**
0m 43ch

COM
0m 61ch

Larkfield Jn with
Muirhouse Lines
101m 17ch

Larkfield Jn
100m 65ch

100m 60ch

100m 34ch

100m 15ch

BOC
Siding

Polmadie
100m 15ch

Polmadie Carriage
Servicing &
Maintenance
Depot

Rutherglen
(Footpath) (R/G)
0m 11ch /
0m 23ch

99m 46ch

**Bridgeton
Yard**

**CE
Depot**

0m 05ch

98m 60ch

Crossmyloof
1m 60ch

2m 13ch / 3m 71ch

Shawlands
3m 63ch

Crosshill
0m 78ch

Polmadie Through
Sidings

99m 71ch

Rutherglen
0m 18ch

Rutherglen West Jn
99m 20ch / 0m 00ch

Rutherglen Central Jn
98m 77ch / 0m 00ch

Pollokshaws East
3m 33ch

Mount Florida
1m 41ch

Cathcart North Jn
0m 00ch / 1m 63ch

Cathcart SB
1m 75ch

Kings Park
100m 21ch

Croftfoot
99m 45ch

Pollokshaws West
2m 60ch

0m 24ch / 1m 79ch

Langside
2m 71ch

Busby Jn
0m 40ch / 3m 18ch

✉

Cathcart
2m 13ch

Cathcart East Jn
100m 37ch / 0m 45ch

Cathcart West Jn
2m 21ch / 100m 77ch

From Map 131

Index

Index

This Index lists the named locations that appear in the main map and inset map sections of the Atlas in alphabetical order. The reference which appears after each name gives the map number and the grid reference of the square in which the name or its related relevant symbol appears. Stations are shown in capital letters. To create an index of manageable size, the full list of names was subjected to reduction against a set of rules. Duplicates were removed and the editor selected the most appropriate reference for such duplicated items. Generally, level crossings, ground frames and sidings were subjected to a greater reduction in the number of entries than junctions and tunnels; sidings especially so. Where a location appears within an Area or Inset map, that reference is given in preference to the reference within the main body of maps.

Attleborough (MCG) 44 D1
Attleborough North Jn. 40 C1
Attleborough SB (A) 44 C1
Attleborough South Jn. 40 C1
Auchencruive GF 78 D1
Auchengray (AHBC-X) 85 A3
AUCHINLECK 79 A1
Auchintee (UWC) 97 B2
Auchterarder SB 91 B2
Auckley (AHBC) 59 A1
AUDLEY END 32 D1
Audley End (Norfolk) (AHBC-X) 44 D2
Audley End Tunnel 32 D1
AUGHTON PARK 55 B1
Aughton Road (CCTV) 61 B3
Auldclune No. 3 (UWC) 93 A2
Austin Crossing 22 C3
Aveley Viaduct 20 D1
AVIEMORE 94 D1
Aviemore SB 94 D1
Avon View Farm (UWC) 16 D2
AVONCLIFF 16 C2
AVONMOUTH 118
Avonmouth Dock (CCTV) 118
Avonmouth Station (CCTV) 118
Awre (CCTV) 28 C3
Axe (AHBC) 7 A2
AXMINSTER 7 A3
Axminster (CCTV) 7 A3
Aycliffe 70 C1
AYLESBURY 30 D2
Aylesbury North Goods Loop 30 D2
Aylesbury Vale Jn. 30 D2
AYLESBURY VALE PARKWAY 30 D2
AYLESFORD 21 A3
Aylesford 21 A3
Aylesford SB (AF) 21 A3
Aylesford Village (CCTV) 21 A3
AYLESHAM 22 C3
Aynho Jn. 30 C1
AYR 78 C1
Ayr Harbour 78 C1
Ayr MPD 78 D1

B

B Group GF 121 A
B.A.C. (UWC) 118
BACHE 126 A
Back Settlement (R/G-X) 95 A1
Backburn Bolton Branch Jn. 62 D3
Badcock's Middle (UWC) 6 C2
Badden (UWC) 102 D2
Badgeney Road (AHBC-X) 43 A1
Bagillt (UWC) 55 B3
BAGLAN 116 B
BAGSHOT 19 A3
Bagshot Tunnel 19 A3
Baguley Fold Jn. SB 122 B
Bagworth Jn. 50 C3
BAILDON 63 B2
Baildon Tunnels 63 B2
Baileyfield GF 86 E
Baileys 42 D1
BAILLIESTON 132 C2
Bainbridge No. 2 (UWC) 73 B2
Bainton (AHBC) 51 B3
Bainton Green (AHBC) 51 B3
Bakers (Accom) 13 B2
Baker's 11 B1
Balavil Burn (UWC) 94 D2
Balavil Gates (UWC) 94 D2
Balby Bridge Tunnel 129 A1
Balcathie (UWC) 95 A3
BALCOMBE 12 C1
Balcombe Tunnel 12 C1
Balcombe Tunnel Jn. 12 C1
Balderton (AHBC) 55 B3
Balderton (CCTV) 51 A1
Balderton Tunnel 55 B3
Baldinnies No. 1 (UWC) 91 B2
BALDOCK 32 C1
Baldwin's No. 78 44 D1
Balfour (UWC) 73 B2
BALHAM 111 B2
Balham Jn. 112 C2
Balkeith South (UWC) 102 D2
Ballach (UWC) 103 B1
Ballachladdich Farm (UWC) 99 A1
Ballachroan (UWC) 94 C2
Ballast Hole 13 A1
Ballentoul (UWC) 93 A2
Ballintraid (UWC) 99 B1
BALLOCH 83 B1
BALMOSSIE 92 D1
Balnacra (AOCL) 97 B2
Balnacra No. 2 (UWC) 97 B2
Balne (MCB) 64 D3
Balne Lane 127 A
Balne Low Gate 64 D3
Balshaw Lane Jn. 62 C3
Balspardon (UWC) 99 B2
Balsporran (UWC) 94 C3
Baltic Siding 10 C1
BAMBER BRIDGE 62 C3
Bamber Bridge (MCB) 62 C3
BAMFORD 57 B2
Bamfurlong Jn. 126 C
Bamfurlong Sidings Jn. 126 C
BANAVIE 90 C2
Banavie (R/C) 90 C2
Banavie SC 90 C2
BANBURY 30 C1
Banbury North SB (BN) 29 B1
Banbury Road GF 30 C2
Banbury South SB (BS) 29 B1
Banc-y-Berllan (UWC) 24 D2
BANGOR 53 B2
Bangor SB (BR) 53 B2
Bangor Tunnel 53 B2
BANK HALL 125 A
Bank Head (UWC) 62 C3
Bank House Tunnel 63 B3
Bank Jn. 79 A2
Banks Crossing 9 B2
Bannolds (AHBC-X) 43 A3
BANSTEAD 111 B3
BARASSIE 78 C1
Barassie Jn. 78 D1
BARBICAN 109 A3
Barbican Tunnel 109 A3
Barcroft (MCG) 58 D1
Bardon Hill Quarries 50 C3
Bardon Hill SB (BH) 50 C3
BARDON MILL 75 A1
Bardon Mill (R/G) 75 A2
Bardon Mill SB 75 A1
BARE LANE 62 C1
Bare Lane (MCB) 62 C1
Bare Lane Jn. 62 C1
Bare Lane SB 62 C1
Barf Farm (UWC) 72 C3
Barford Footpath Crossing (R/G) 8 D1
BARGEDDIE 132 C2
BARGOED 26 C1
Bargoed SB 26 C1
Bargoed South Jn. 26 C1
Barham Sidings 44 D3
Barhams 45 A3
Barkers (UWC) 49 A2
BARKING 110 D2
Barking Flyover 110 C2
Barking Freightliner Terminal 110 D2
Barking Station Jn. 110 C2
Barking Tilbury Line Jns. 110 C2
BARLASTON 48 D1
Barlaston (CCTV) 48 D1
Barlby (BOCM) 65 A2
Barlby North Jn. 65 A2
BARMING 21 A3
Barmoor Clough Tunnel 57 B2
BARMOUTH 35 B2
Barmouth North GF 35 B2
Barmouth South (TMO) 35 B2
Barmouth Swing Bridge 35 B2
Barmouth Tunnel 35 B2
Barnby (CCTV) 51 A1
Barnby 45 B2
Barnby Lane (CCTV) 51 A1
Barnby Moor & Sutton (CCTV) 59 A2
Barncluith Tunnel 132 D3
BARNEHURST 20 D2
BARNES 111 B2
Barnes (UWC) 51 B2
BARNES BRIDGE 111 B2
Barnes Jn. 111 B2
Barnet South Crossovers 32 C3
Barnet Tunnel 20 C1
BARNETBY 60 C1
Barnetby East SB (BE) 60 C1
BARNHAM 11 A3
Barnham SB (BH) 11 A3
BARNHILL 133
Barnhill SB 92 C2
Barnhill Tunnel 133
Barn's Green (AHBC) 11 B2
Barnsbury Jn. 108 D2
BARNSLEY 58 C1
Barnsley SB (BY) 58 C1
Barnsley Station Jn. 58 C1
BARNSTAPLE 5 A1
Barnstaple GF 5 A1
Barnstone Tunnel 50 C2
BARNT GREEN 39 A2
Barnt Green Jn. 39 A2
Barnwell Jn. 43 A3
Barnwell Siding 43 A3
Barnwood No. 1 GF 28 C2
Barnwood No. 3 GF 28 D2
Baron House (UWC) 74 D1
Baron Wood No.2 Tunnel 74 C2
Baron Wood No.1 Tunnel 74 C3
Barrel Lane (R/G) Footpath 59 A3
BARRHEAD 131 A3
Barrhead SB (BD) 131 A3
BARRHILL 77 B2
Barrhill SB 77 B2
BARROW HAVEN 66 C3
Barrow Haven (OPEN) 66 C3
Barrow Hill North Jn. 58 C2
Barrow Hill South Junction 58 C3
Barrow Road (MCG) 66 C3
Barrow Road Refuse Transfer Stn 119 A
BARROW UPON SOAR 50 C2
Barrowby Lane (Public BW) 64 C3
BARROW-IN-FURNESS 61 A1
Barrow-in-Furness SB (BF) 67 A3
BARRY 25 E
BARRY DOCKS 25 E
Barry Docks 25 E
BARRY ISLAND 25 E
Barry Island Viaduct 25 E
Barry Jn. 25 E
BARRY LINKS 95 A3
Barry SB (B) 25 E
Barry West (CCTV) 95 A3
Barthomley (R/G) 48 C1
Barthomley Jn. 48 C1
Barton & Broughton Loop 62 C2
Barton Hill Depot 119 B
Barton Hill SB 65 A1
Barton Lane (AHBC) 122 A
Barton Mill (MCG) 65 A1
Barton Mill Carriage Sidings 18 D3
Barton North Jn. 49 B3
Barton Road (MCG) 66 C3
Barton South Jn. 49 B3
Barts (Accom) 13 B2
Barway Sidings (AHBC) 43 A2
Baschurch (AHBC-X) 47 A2
Base Green No. 31 44 C3
Basford Chemicals (UWC) 122 A
Basford Hall Jn. 48 E
Basford Hall Jn. SB 48 E
Basford Hall Sidings 48 E
Basford Wood GF 48 E
BASILDON 21 A1
Basin Road (CCTV) 11 A3
BASINGSTOKE 18 D3
Basingstoke ASC (YW) (Basingstoke Old) 18 D3
Basingstoke SCC (BE) (Basingstoke New) 18 C3
BAT & BALL 20 D3
Bath Goods 16 C2
Bath Road Jn. 19 A2
Bath Row Tunnel 120 B
BATH SPA 16 C2
Bath West GF 16 C2
Bathampton Jn. 16 C2
BATHGATE 85 A2
Bathing Pool (UWC) 68 C3
Bathley Lane (CCTV) 59 A3
BATLEY 64 C3
Batley LC SB (B) 64 C3
BATTERSBY 71 A2
Battersby Jn. 71 A2
Battersby Road (AOCL) 71 A1
BATTERSEA PARK 113
Battersea Park Jn. 113
Battersea Pier Jn. 113
Battersea Railway Bridge 113
BATTLE 13 A2
Battle Road (AHBC) 13 A2
BATTLESBRIDGE 21 A1
Baulkholme (UWC) 65 A3
Bawtry Crossovers GSP 58 D2
Bax Crossing 21 B3
BAYFORD 32 C3
Baylam (AHBC-X) 44 D3
Bayles & Wylies (UWC) 50 C1
Beach Road (RC) 12 D3
Beacon Hill Tunnel 63 B3
BEACONSFIELD 31 A3
Beal (CCTV) 82 D3
Beal Crossovers 82 D3
Beald Drove (AHBC-X) 43 A2
Bealings (ABCL) 34 C1
Beam Mill Jn. 130 C
BEARLEY 39 B3
Bearley Jn. SB (BJ) 39 B3
Bearley Jn. 39 B3
Bears Grove 46 D2
BEARSDEN 131 A1
BEARSTED 21 A3
Bearty Fen (MCG) 52 C2
BEASDALE 89 A2
Beattock North GSP 80 C2
Beattock South 80 C2
Beattock Summit 80 C2
BEAULIEU ROAD 9 B2
BEAULY 99 A2
Beauly Ferry (UWC) 99 A2
Beaumont Hill (UWC) 39 B2
Beaverpool Tunnel 54 C3
Beavers (UWC) 51 B1
Beavers Hill (OC) 23 B3
Beavers Hill Farm (UWC) 23 A3
BEBINGTON 125 A
Bebside (AHBC-X) 76 C1
BECCLES 45 B2
Beccles Bypass (ABCL) 45 B2
BECKENHAM HILL 112 D2
BECKENHAM JUNCTION 112 C2
Beckenham Spur Jn. 112 C3
Becketts (AHBC) 13 B2
Beckingham SB 59 A2
BECONTREE(LUL) 110 D2
Beddingham (AHBC) 12 C3
Bedford (No. 125) (UWC) 43 A2
BEDFORD MIDLAND 41 B3
Bedford No.151A 43 A2
Bedford North Jn. 41 B3
Bedford South Jn. 41 B3
BEDFORD ST. JOHNS 31 B1
BEDHAMPTON 10 D2
Bedhampton (CCTV) 10 D2
Bedlam Tunnel 16 C3
Bedlington North SB (BN) 81 A3
Bedlington South SB 81 A3
Bedmill Farm No. 1 Crossing 7 B2
BEDMINSTER 118
BEDWORTH 40 C1
BEDWYN 17 B2
Beech Bank (UWC) 52 C2
Beech Drive (UWC) 17 B2
Beech Hill (AHBC) 59 A1
Beeches Farm (UWC) 55 B3
Beechgrove GF 16 D3
Beechwood Tunnel 40 C2
Beecroft (Wright's) (UWC) 44 D2
Beer Hackett Crossing 7 B2
BEESTON 122 A
Beeston Castle & Tarporley SB (BC) 56 C3
Beeston Depot GF 122 A
Beeston No. 2 GF 122 A
Beeston North Jn. 122 A
Beeston Regis 46 C1
Beeston South Jn. 122 A
Beighton Jn. 128 A1
Beighton Station Jn. SB (BX) 128 A1
Bejowan (UWC) 2 C1
BEKESBOURNE 22 C3
Belasis Lane SB 130 C
Belaugh Lane 46 D2
Belford (CCTV) 81 A1
Belford Burn (Public FP) 82 D3
Belford Crossovers 82 D3
Bellasize (UWC) 65 B3
Belle Isle 109 A2
BELLE VUE 124 C2
Belleport (UWC) 99 B1
BELLGROVE 133
Bellgrove Jn. 133
Bellgrove Tunnel 133
BELLINGHAM 112 D2
Bells 45 A1
BELLSHILL 132 D2
Bellside GF 132 D3
Bellwater Jn. 52 E
Bellwater Jn. SB (BJ) 52 E
BELMONT 111 B3
Belmont (CCTV) 78 D1
Belmont (MCB) 64 C1
Belmont Tunnel 53 B2
BELPER 49 B1
Belper GF 50 C1
Belsize Tunnels 108 C2
BELTRING 13 A1
Beltring (AHBC) 13 A1
BELVEDERE 20 D2
Belvedere Rd Jn. 114 A
BEMPTON 72 D3
Bempton (AHBC) 72 D3
Bempton Sands (UWC) 72 D3
Ben Alder (UWC) 94 C3
BEN RHYDDING 63 B2
Benarth Farm (UWC) 27 A2
BENFLEET 21 A1
Benhar 84 D2
Beningborough Footpath (R/G) 64 D1
Bennar Fawr (AOCL) 35 B2
Bennetland (UWC) 65 A3
Bennetts (UWC) 49 A2
Bensham Tunnel 130 A
BENTHAM 62 D1
BENTLEY (Hants.) 18 D3
BENTLEY (S. Yorks.) 129 A1
Bentley (AHBC-X) 34 C2
Bentley (CCTV) 129 A1
Bentley Heath (CCTV) 39 B2
Bentley Jn. 129 A1
Benton Crossovers 76 C1
Benton North Jn. 76 C1
BERE ALSTON 3 B1
Bere Alston Jn. / GF 3 A2
BERE FERRERS 3 B2
Berkeley GF 28 C3
Berkeley Road Jn. 28 C3
BERKHAMSTED 31 A2
BERKSWELL 40 C2
BERNEY ARMS 45 B1
BERRY BROW 57 B1
Berry Lane (UWC) 31 A1
BERRYLANDS 111 B3
Berrylands Jn. 111 A3
Berthddu (OC) 36 E
Bertheos Tunnel 54 C3
Bertwyn (AHBC) 24 C3
BERWICK 12 D3
Berwick 12 D3
Berwick North Crossover 82 D2
Berwick SB (BK) 12 D3
BERWICK-UPON-TWEED 82 D2
BESCAR LANE 61 B3

Carsgoe No. 1 (UWC)	104	C2
Carsgoe No. 2 (UWC)	104	C2
Carsgoe No. 3 (UWC)	104	C2
Carsgoe No. 4 (UWC)	104	C2
CARSHALTON	111	B3
CARSHALTON BEECHES	111	B3
CARSTAIRS	85	A3
Carstairs East Jn.	85	A3
Carstairs South Jn.	85	A3
Carstairs Station Jn.	85	A3
Cart Lane (UWC)	68	C3
Carterhouse Jn. SB (closed)	56	C2
Carters (UWC)	70	D1
Cartsburn Tunnel	83	A2
CARTSDYKE	83	A1
CASTLE BAR PARK	107	B3
Castle Bromwich Jn.	120	A
CASTLE CARY	7	B1
Castle Cary Jn.	7	B1
Castle Donnington	122	A
Castle Farm No. 1 (UWC)	67	B3
Castle Gardens (UWC)	37	A2
Castle Hill East GF	70	D2
Castle Hill Portal	14	D1
Castle Hill Tunnel	63	A3
Castle Hill West GF	70	D2
Castle Hills Jn.	70	D2
Castlefield Jn.	122	B
CASTLEFORD	64	C3
Castleford East Jn.	64	C3
Castleford LC SB (CD)	64	D3
Castleford West Jn.	64	C3
CASTLETON	57	A1
Castleton Central Materials Depot	56	D1
Castleton East Jn. SB (CE)	124	C1
Castleton Farm Crossing	8	C2
Castleton LWR Depot	57	A1
CASTLETON MOOR	71	A1
Castleton North Jn.	124	C1
Castleton South Jn.	124	C1
Cat Lane (UWC)	64	D2
Cater Crossing	22	D3
CATERHAM	20	C3
CATFORD	112	C2
CATFORD BRIDGE	112	D2
Cathan Farm (UWC)	24	D2
CATHAYS	117	A
CATHCART	133	
Cathcart East Jn.	133	
Cathcart North Jn.	133	
Cathcart SB	133	
Cathcart West Jn.	133	
CATTAL	64	D1
Cattal (MCG)	64	D1
Cattal SB	64	D1
Cattedown Tunnel	116	A
Cattewater (OC)	116	A
Cattewater Harbour	116	A
Cattewater Jn.	116	A
Cauldwell Depot	41	B3
CAUSELAND	3	A2
Causeway (MCB)	18	C1
Causewayhead Jn.	91	A3
Cave (MCB)	65	B3
Cavendish Street Tunnel	125	B
Caverswall (MCB)	49	A1
Caverswall SB	49	A1
Cawdor (AOCL)	25	A1
Cayton (AHBC)	72	C3
Cedar Jn.	108	D2
Cefn Coed (UWC)	25	A1
Cefn Gast Farm No. 2 (UWC)	36	E
Cefn Jn.	25	B2
Cefn Suran (UWC)	37	A2
CEFN-Y-BEDD	47	A1
Cement Depot No. 1 (OC)	121	A
Cement Works Sidings	16	D3
Cemetery Lane (UWC)	16	C2
Cemetry (UWC)	35	B3
Cemmes Road (R/G)	36	C1
Central Ordnance Depot GF	30	C2
Central Rivers Depot	49	B2
Central Treviscoe GF	2	C1
Central Tunnel	124	C1
CHADWELL HEATH	110	D1
Chaffers (TMO)	63	A2
CHAFFORD HUNDRED	20	D1
Chain Bridge (AHBC)	42	D1
Chain Bridge (MCB)	76	C2
CHALFONT & LATIMER	31	A3
Chalk Lane (CCTV) LC	66	C3
Chalk Tunnel	19	A3
CHALKWELL	21	B1
Challoch (UWC)	77	B3
Challow	17	B1
Chandlers Crossing	9	E
CHANDLERS FORD	9	B2
Chandlers Ford (UWC)	9	B2
Channelsea North Jn.	109	B2
Channelsea South Jn.	109	B2
Chantry (Footpath)	8	D1
Chantry Road (RC)	45	A3
Chapel (AOCL)	2	C1
Chapel Farm 1 (UWC)	2	C1
Chapel Farm 3 (UWC)	2	C1
Chapel L.N.W. Tunnel	57	B2
Chapel Lane (MCG)	56	C1
Chapel Lane GF	26	D2
Chapel Road (MCG)	45	A1
CHAPEL-EN-LE-FRITH	57	B2
Chapel-en-le-Frith SB	57	A2
Chapelton (UWC)	99	A2
CHAPELTOWN	58	C1
CHAPLETON	5	A1
Chapleton Station (UWC)	5	A1
CHAPPEL & WAKES COLNE	33	B2
Chard Jn.	7	A2
Chard Jn. Down Sidings GF	7	A2
Chard Jn. SB	7	A2
Charfield Hall Farm (UWC)	16	C1
Charfield Loops	16	C1
CHARING	21	B3
CHARING CROSS	133	
Charing Cross Tunnel	133	
CHARLBURY	29	B2
Charlemont Road (R/G)	120	A
Charleston (UWC)	91	B1
Charlestown Foundry (TMO)	85	A1
Charlestown Jn.	85	A1
CHARLTON	112	D2
Charlton (UWC)	28	D1
Charlton Jn.	112	D2
Charlton Lane	112	D1
Charlton Tunnel (Dover)	14	D1
Charlton Tunnel (Bristol)	118	
Charlton Tunnel (London)	112	D1
Chart Crossing	13	B1
Chart Leacon Repair Shop	13	B1
CHARTHAM	22	C3
Chartham	22	C3
Chartham Hatch (AHBC)	22	C3
CHASSEN ROAD	123	B2
CHATELHERAULT	132	D3
CHATHAM	21	A3
Chatham Dockyard	21	A2
Chatham Tunnel	21	A2
CHATHILL	81	A1
Chathill (CCTV)	81	A1
Chathill Crossovers	81	A1
Chatterley Valley	48	D1
Chawson Footpath Crossing	38	D3
CHEADLE HULME	124	C3
Cheadle Hulme North Jn.	124	C3
Cheadle Jn.	124	C3
Cheadle Wood Farm (UWC)	124	C3
Cheal Road (MCG)	52	C2
CHEAM	111	B3
CHEDDINGTON	31	A2
CHELFORD	56	D3
Chelford North Jn.	56	D3
Chelford South Jn.	56	D3
CHELMSFORD	33	A3
CHELSFIELD	112	D3
Chelsfield Tunnel	112	D3
Cheltenham Alstone (MCB)	28	D2
CHELTENHAM SPA	28	D2
Chenson No. 1 (UWC)	5	B2
Chenson No. 2 (UWC)	5	B2
Chenson No. 3 (UWC)	5	B2
CHEPSTOW	27	B3
Chepstow Tunnel	15	B1
Cheriton Jn.	14	D1
Cherry Hinton By-pass (CCTV)	43	A3
Cherry Hinton High Street (CCTV)	43	A3
Cherry Holt (AHBC-X)	52	C2
Cherry Orchard (UWC)	37	A1
CHERRY TREE	62	D3
Cherry Tree (CCTV)	66	C2
Cherry Tree GF	62	D3
Cherry Willingham (AHBC-X)	60	C3
Cherryhalt (UWC)	59	A2
Cherry's No. 4 (UWC)	30	C1
CHERTSEY	19	B2
CHESHUNT	32	C3
Cheshunt Jn.	32	C3
CHESSINGTON NORTH	111	B3
CHESSINGTON SOUTH	111	A3
CHESTER	126	A
Chester Diesel Depot	126	A
Chester East Jn.	126	A
Chester Line Jn.	18	E
Chester North Jn.	126	A
CHESTER ROAD	120	A
Chester SB (CR)	126	A
Chester South Jn.	126	A
Chester West Jn.	126	A
CHESTERFIELD	58	C3
Chesterfield North Jn.	58	C3
Chesterfield South Jn.	58	C3
CHESTER-LE-STREET	76	C2
Chesterton (CCTV)	43	A3
Chesterton Jn.	43	A3
Chesterton Yard	43	A3
CHESTFIELD & SWALECLIFFE	22	C3
CHETNOLE	7	B2
Chettisham (AHBC-X)	43	A2
Chevington (CCTV)	81	A2
Chevington North Crossovers	81	A2
CHICHESTER	11	A3
Chichester SB (CC)	10	D2
Chicks Farm Crossing	8	C3
Chicks Farm Foot (UWC)	8	C3
CHILHAM	22	C3
Chilham Mill (CCTV)	22	C3
Chilham Road (CCTV)	22	C3
Chillingham Road	130	A
Chiltern Railways LMD	107	B2
Chiltern Railways Servicing Depot	30	D2
Chilvers Coton Jn.	40	C1
CHILWORTH	19	A3
Chilworth (CCTV)	11	A1
CHINGFORD	20	C1
CHINLEY	124	D3
Chinley East Jn.	57	B2
Chinley North Jn.	57	B2
Chinley SB (CY)	57	B2
Chinley South Jn.	57	B2
Chinnor Branch Siding	30	D2
CHIPPENHAM	16	D2
Chippenham Jn.	43	B2
Chippenham Jn. SB (CM)	43	B3
Chipping Sodbury East GF	16	C1
Chipping Sodbury Tunnel	16	C1
CHIPSTEAD	20	C3
Chipstead Line Jn.	112	C3
CHIRK	47	A2
Chirk Tunnel	47	A2
CHISLEHURST	114	E
Chislehurst Jn.	114	E
Chislehurst Tunnels	112	D2
Chiswells Farm (UWC)	30	C1
CHISWICK	111	B2
Chitts Hill (MCB)	33	B2
Chivers (AHBC-X)	43	B2
CHOLSEY	18	C1
Choppington (AHBC)	76	C1
CHORLEY	62	C3
Chorley Tunnel	62	C3
CHORLEYWOOD	31	A3
CHRISTCHURCH	9	A3
Christian Street Jn.	109	A3
Christies Nursery (UWC)	100	C1
Christleton Tunnel	56	C3
Christon Bank (CCTV)	81	A1
CHRIST'S HOSPITAL	11	B1
CHURCH & OSWALDTWISTLE	62	D3
Church (Footpath)	13	A1
Church Crossing	21	A3
Church Dam	45	B1
Church End Farm (UWC)	64	D2
Church Farm (UWC) (Aberthaw)	25	B3
Church Farm (UWC) (Broomfleet)	65	B3
Church Farm No. 1 (UWC)	16	D2
Church Farm No. 2 (UWC)	16	D2
CHURCH FENTON	64	D2
Church Fenton North Jn.	64	D2
Church Fenton South Jn.	64	D2
Church House Farm (Marks Tey)	33	B2
Church House Farm (UWC) (Leominster)	38	C3
Church Lane (CCTV) (Chelmsford)	33	A1
Church Lane (CCTV) (Newark)	59	A3
Church Lane (CCTV) (Redcar)	71	D2
Church Lane (CCTV) (Stone)	48	A3
Church Lane (MCG) (Spalding)	52	C2
Church Lane (Reedham)	45	B1
Church Road	45	A1
Church Road Tunnel	120	A
Church Street (AHBC-X)	33	B3
Church Street (CCTV)	76	D3
Church Street (TMO)	41	A3
CHURCH STRETTON	37	B1
CILMERI	36	D3
Cilmeri (UWC)	36	D3
Cilmeri Tunnel	36	D3
Cilyrychen (ABCL)	24	D2
City Basin Jn.	6	C3
CITY THAMESLINK	109	A3
Clachnaharry Canal Bridge	99	A2
Clacton SB (C)	34	C3
CLACTON-ON-SEA	34	C3
CLANDON	19	B3
CLAPHAM	62	D1
CLAPHAM HIGH STREET	113	
Clapham Yard	113	
CLAPHAMJUNCTION	113	
CLAPTON	109	A2
Clapton GF	109	A1
Clapton Jn.	109	A1
Clapton Tunnel	109	A2
Clara Vale (AHBC-X)	75	B1
CLARBESTON ROAD	23	A2
Clarbeston Road Jn. SB (CR)	23	A2
Clarbeston Road Jn.	23	A2
Clarborough Jn.	59	A2
Clarborough Tunnel	59	A2
Clarence Road SB (CR)	76	D3
Clark & Butchers	43	A2
Clarks (UWC)	70	D2
CLARKSTON	131	B3
CLAVERDON	39	B3
Claverton (UWC)	16	C2
Claxby & Usselby (AHBC-X)	60	C2
Claxby Gatehouse (No. 24) (AHBC-X)	60	C1
Clay Cross North Jn.	58	C3
Clay Cross South Jn. (former)	58	C3
Clay Cross Tunnel	58	C3
Clay Lane (AHBC)	10	D2
Clay Mills Jn. (CCTV)	49	B2
Clay Mills Jn.	49	B2
Clay Slaps (UWC)	84	D1
Claydon (AOCL)	30	D1
Claydon (CCTV)	34	C1
Claydon (L&NE) Jn. SB (CN)	30	D1
Claydon (L&NE) Jn.	30	D1
Clayfield (AHBC)	29	A1
CLAYGATE	111	A3
Claypole (CCTV)	51	A1
Claypole Down Loop	51	A1
Claypole Up Loop	51	A1
Clayton (UWC)	91	B2
Clayton Bridge (CCTV)	124	C2
Clayton Tunnel	12	C2
Clayton West Jn.	57	B1
Clayway	43	A2
Cleatop (UWC)	62	D1
CLEETHORPES	60	D1
Cleghorn (CCTV)	84	D3
Cleifiog Uchaf (UWC)	53	A2
CLELAND	132	D3
Clements No. 1 (UWC)	59	B3
Clerkenwell No. 1Tunnel	109	A3
Clerkenwell No. 2 Tunnel	109	A3
Clerkenwell No. 3 Tunnel	109	A3
Clerks Tunnel	4	D1
Cleveland Freightliner Terminal (Wilton)	130	C
Cliff Hill No. 1 GF	50	C3
Cliff Hill No. 2 GF	50	C3
Cliffe (CCTV)	65	A2
Cliffe Vale Jn.	48	D1
Clifford Farm (Footpath)	21	B1
Cliffsend (AHBC)	22	D3
CLIFTON	123	B1
Clifton (CCTV)	81	A3
Clifton and Lowther No.1 GF	68	D1
Clifton and Lowther No.2 GF	68	D1
Clifton Bridge No. 1 Tunnel	118	
Clifton Bridge No. 2 Tunnel	118	
CLIFTON DOWN	118	
Clifton Down Tunnel	118	
Cliftonville Tunnel	14	E
Clink Road Jn.	16	C3
Clints Field (UWC)	62	D1
Clints Field (UWC)	68	D3
Clipstone Colliery	58	D3
Clipstone Colliery Jn.	58	D3
Clipstone East Jn.	58	D3
Clipstone SB (C)	58	D3
Clipstone South Jn.	58	D3
Clipstone West Jn.	58	D3
CLITHEROE	62	D2
CLOCK HOUSE	112	C3
Clock House (AHBC)	21	B3
Closglas Farm 1 (UWC)	24	D2
Closglas Farm 3 (UWC)	24	D2
Clover-le-Dale (UWC)	55	B1
Club Lane (UWC)	62	C3
CLUNDERWEN	23	B2
Clunes (UWC)	93	A2
Clyde Bridge	133	
CLYDEBANK	131	A1
Clydebank Jn.	131	A1
Clyne (TMO)	25	B1
Clynemilton East (UWC)	103	B3
Coal Road	21	A2
Coaley GF	28	C3
Coalville Jn.	50	C3
Coalville Station (CCTV)	50	C3
COATBRIDGE CENTRAL	132	D2
Coatbridge Freightliner Terminal	132	D2
Coatbridge Jn.	132	D2
COATBRIDGE SUNNYSIDE	132	D2
COATDYKE	132	D2
COBHAM & STOKE D'ABERNON	19	B3
Cockett Tunnel	116	B
Cockett West Jn.	24	D3
Cocklebury Sidings	17	A1
Cockshute Sidings	48	D1
Cockspin Road (AHBC-X)	43	B2
Codford (AHBC)	16	D3
Codnor Park Jn.	50	C1
CODSALL	39	A1
Coed Cae No. 1 (UWC)	36	D1
Coed Farm No. 1 (UWC)	24	C2
Coed Ifan (UWC)	36	E
Coed Moor (UWC)	27	B1
Coed Y Dinas (UWC)	47	A3
Coed-y-Llyn No.1 (UWC)	35	B1
Coffue Drove	43	A2
COGAN	117	A
Cogan Jn.	117	A
Cogan Loops	117	A
Cogan Tunnel	117	A
Cogload Jns	7	A1
COLCHESTER	33	B2
Colchester Jn.	33	B2
Colchester Road (CCTV)	34	C2
Colchester SB (CO)	33	B2
COLCHESTER TOWN	33	B2
Cold Blow (R/G)	14	D1
Coldham (TMO)	52	D3
Coldham Lane Depot	43	A3
Coldham Lane Jn.	42	D3
Coldharbour (OPEN)	13	B2
Coleham LM Depot	47	B3

Coleham Sidings 47 B3
Coleman St. Tunnel 112 D1
Colemans (UWC) 8 C3
Coles (UWC) 39 A3
COLESHILL PARKWAY 39 B1
Collaton Barton Farm 1 (UWC) 5 B2
Colliers (UWC) 49 A2
COLLINGHAM 59 B3
Collingham (AHBC) 59 B3
COLLINGTON 13 A3
Collins Farm (UWC) 3 B1
Colnbrook Oil Terminal 19 B2
COLNE 63 A2
Colne Jn. 33 B2
Colthrop (MCB) 18 C2
Coltishall Lane 46 D2
Coltness 84 D3
Colton Jn. 64 D2
Colton North Jn. 64 D2
Colton South Jn. 64 D2
COLWALL 28 C1
Colwall Tunnel 28 C1
Colwich Jn. 49 A2
Colwick (CCTV) 50 E
COLWYN BAY 54 D1
COMBE 29 B2
Combe Lane Crossing 19 B3
Common Moor 1 (UWC) 5 B3
Common Moor 2 (UWC) 5 B3
Common Road (MCG) 65 A1
COMMONDALE 71 A1
Compeday (UWC) 18 C2
Concrete Road (UWC) 43 A1
Coney Green Jn. 58 C3
CONGLETON 57 A3
CONISBROUGH 58 D1
Conisbrough Tunnel 58 D1
CONNEL FERRY 87 B1
Connell Park (TMO) 79 A2
Connington North (CCTV) 42 C1
Connington South 42 C1
Conoco East (TMO) 116 A
Conoco West (TMO) 116 A
CONONLEY 63 A2
Cononley (CCTV) 63 A2
CONWAY PARK 125 B
CONWY 54 C2
Conwy Tubular Bridge 54 C2
Conwy Tunnel 54 C2
COODEN BEACH 13 A3
Cookes (Accom) 13 B2
COOKHAM 19 A1
Cookham (ABCL) 19 A1
Cooks (CCTV) 111 A3
Cooks 1 (UWC) 28 D1
Cooks 2 (UWC) 28 D1
Cooks Lane (UWC) 40 D1
Cooks No. 1 (Accom) 13 B2
COOKSBRIDGE 12 C2
Cooksbridge (CCTV) 12 C2
Cooksholme (UWC) 28 D1
COOMBE 3 A2
Coombe (UWC) 3 A2
Coombe Jn. 2 D1
Coombe No 1 GF 2 D1
Coombe No 2 GF 2 D1
Coopers & Farmers (UWC) 13 B2
Coopers (UWC) 48 D1
Coopers (UWC) 62 C3
Coopers 13 B2
Coopers Lane Jn. 32 D2
Coopies Lane (AHBC) 81 A3
Copenhagen Jn. 108 D2
Copenhagen Tunnel 108 D2
Copley Hill East Jn. 127 B
Copley Hill West Jn. 127 B
Copmanthorpe No. 2 (R/G) 64 D2
Copperas (UWC) 34 C2
Coppermill Jn. 109 A1
COPPLESTONE 5 B2
Copy Pit Crossover 63 A3
Copyhold Jn. 12 C2
CORBRIDGE 75 B1
CORBY 41 B1
Corby Automotive Terminal 41 B1
Corby Gates (MCB) 74 C2
Corby Gates SB 74 C2
Corby North Jn. 41 B1
Corby Tunnel 41 B1
CORKERHILL 131 A2
CORKICKLE 67 A1
Corks Farm No. 2 49 B3
Cornard (ABCL) 33 B1
Cornton (AHBC) 91 A3
Cornton No. 2 (R/G) 91 A3
CORPACH 90 C2
Corpach (AOCL) 90 C2
Corporation Rd Tunnel 125 A
Corriebeg Farm No. 1 (UWC) 89 B2
Corriebeg No. 2 (UWC) 89 B2
Corriemoillie No. 1 (UWC) 98 D1
CORROUR 90 D3
Corscombe (UWC) 5 A3
Corton Steps Crossing 16 D3
CORYTON 117 A
Coryton Tunnel 4 D1
COSELEY 39 A1
COSFORD 38 D1
COSHAM 10 C2
Cosham Jn. 10 D2
Coswarth (AOCL) 2 C1
Coswarth 1 & 2 (UWC) 2 C1
Coswarth 3 & 4 (UWC) 2 C1
Coswarth Tunnel 2 C1
Coton Hill Yard 47 B3
Cottage Jn. 114 B
Cottage Lane (AHBC) 59 B3
Cottam Power Station 59 A2
COTTINGHAM 66 C2
Cottingham North (CCTV) 65 B2
COTTINGLEY 64 C3
Cottons (UWC) 122 A
Coulags No. 1 (UWC) 97 B2
Coulags No. 3 (UWC) 97 B2
COULSDON SOUTH 20 C3
Coundon Road (CCTV) 40 C2
Couplands (UWC) 52 E
Court Farm (UWC) 37 A1
Court Sart Jn. (Down Line) 116 B
Courthill Loop North Jn. 114 C
Courthill Loop South Jn. 114 C
Courtybella 117 B
Cousins (UWC) 72 C3
Cousins No. 2 (UWC) 33 A2
Couston Bottom Crossing 9 A1
Cove (CCTV) 73 B1
COVENTRY 40 C2
Coventry North Jn. 40 C2
Coventry South Jn. 40 C2
Coventry Yard 40 C2
Covered Way 108 D2
Cow Crossing 12 C3
Cow Green GSP 44 D3
Cow Lane 11 A3
Cowbridge Rd SB 25 B3
Cowburn Tunnel 57 B2
COWDEN 12 D1
COWDENBEATH 85 B1
Cowlairs East (UWC) 131 B1
Cowlairs East Jn. 131 B1
Cowlairs North Jn. 131 B2
Cowlairs SC (CC,CE,CG,CN,CQ) 131 B2
Cowlairs South Jn. 133
Cowlairs West Jn. 133
Cowley Bridge Jn. 6 C3
Cowpen Lane (AHBC-X) 130 C
Coxall Farm 1 (UWC) 37 B2
Coxall Farm 2 (UWC) 37 B2
Coxbench (TMO) 50 C1
Coxes Farm 43 A3
Coxmoor (UWC) 5 B3
Cox's Walk (UWC) 51 A2
Coychurch Footpath (R/G-X) 25 B2
Crabley Creek SB 65 B3
Crabtree (R/G) 56 C1
Cradburns No. 4 (UWC) 51 B1
Cradlehall 99 B2
CRADLEY HEATH 39 A2
Cradley Heath (CCTV) 39 A2
Cragmill (CCTV) 82 D3
Craig (UWC) 97 B2
Craig Hall SB 71 A1
Craig No. 2 (UWC) 77 B3
Craig Rhymney (UWC) 26 C1
CRAIGENDORAN 83 A1
Craigendoran Jn. 83 A1
Craigentinny 86 E
Craigentinny Depot 86 E
Craigfryn (UWC) 36 D1
Craiglockhart Jn. 85 E
Craigo SB 95 A1
CRAMLINGTON 76 C1
Crampmoor Crossing 9 B1
Cranbourne (R/G-X) 32 C3
Crane St. Jn. 121 B
Crankley Point (R/G) 51 A1
Cranmore Loop 13 A1
Crannaford (AHBC) 6 C3
Crannel's (UWC) 18 C2
Cranswick (AHBC-X) 66 C2
CRAVEN ARMS 37 B2
Craven Arms (MCB) 37 B2
Craven Arms Jn. 37 B2
Craven Arms SB 37 B2
Crawford (UWC) 9 B1
CRAWLEY 12 C1
Crawley High Street (CCTV) 12 C1
Crawley New Yard 12 C1
Cray Lane (AHBC) 11 B2
CRAYFORD 20 D2
Crayford Creek Jn. 20 D2
Crayford Spur 'A' Jn. 20 D2
Crayford Spur 'B' Jn. 20 D2
Creag Mhor (UWC) 89 A1
Creaksea Place No. 1 21 B1
Creamore Farm (UWC) 47 B2
Creasey's (Rye Meads) (UWC) 32 C3
CREDITON 5 B3
Crediton (MCB) 5 B3
Crediton SB (CN) 5 B3
Crescent Jn. 42 E
Crescent Road (AHBC) 61 B3
Crescent Wharf Sidings 42 E
CRESSING 33 A2
Cressing (ABCL) 33 A2
CRESSINGTON 125 A
Cresswell (AHBC) 49 A2
CRESWELL 58 D3
CREWE 48 C1
Crewe Bank SB 47 B3
Crewe Coal Yard SB (CY) 48 E
Crewe Electric Maintenance Depot 48 E
Crewe Jn. 47 B3
Crewe Jn. SB (CJ) 47 B3
Crewe North Jn. 48 E
Crewe SB 48 E
Crewe South Jn. 48 E
Crewe Steel Works SB (SW) 48 E
Crewe Works 48 E
CREWKERNE 7 B2
Crewkerne (AHBC) 7 B2
Crewkerne Tunnel 7 A2
CREWS HILL 32 C3
Creykes (R/G) 65 A3
CRIANLARICH 88 D2
Crianlarich Jn. 88 D2
CRICCIETH 35 A1
Crick Tunnel 40 D2
CRICKLEWOOD 108 C2
Cricklewood Curve Jn. 108 C2
Cricklewood Depot Jn. SB 108 C1
Cricklewood South Jn. 108 C2
Cridling Stubbs (AHBC) 64 D3
Crinow Farm 2 (UWC) 23 B2
Crismill Crossovers 21 A3
Critchlows (UWC) 49 A2
Crockway Crossing 7 B3
Croes Newydd North Fork SB 47 A1
Croft SB 40 D1
Croft Sidings 40 D1
Croftcarnoch No. 2 (UWC) 94 D2
CROFTFOOT 133
Crofton (R/G) 17 B2
Crofton East Jn. 127 A
Crofton Old Station No.1 (MCG) 127 A
CROFTON PARK 112 C2
Crofton Road Jn. 112 C2
Crofton West Jn. 127 A
Crombie RNAD 85 A1
CROMER 46 C1
Cromer Jn. 46 C1
CROMFORD 49 B1
Cromwell Lane (CCTV) 59 A3
Cromwell Road (ABCL) 45 A2
Crook Wheel (UWC) 68 C3
CROOKSTON 131 A2
Crosby Garett Tunnel 69 A1
Crosfield's Crossing SB 126 B
Crosfield's GF 126 B
Cross Brook Farm (UWC) 38 C3
Cross Common (AHBC-X) 65 A3
Cross Cottage (UWC) 16 C3
CROSS GATES 64 C2
Cross Lane (AHBC) 59 B3
Cross St. Tunnel 112 D1
CROSSFLATTS 63 B2
CROSSHILL 133
Crossing GF 35 A1
CROSSKEYS 26 D2
Crosskeys Jn. 26 D2
Crossley Evans Sidings 63 B2
CROSSMYLOOF 133
CROSTON 62 C3
CROUCH HILL 108 D1
Crouch Hill Tunnel 108 D1
Crow Nest Jn. 56 C1
Crow Nest Jn. SB (CN) 56 D2
CROWBOROUGH 12 D1
Crowborough Jn. 12 D1
Crowborough Tunnel 12 D1
CROWHURST 13 A2
Crowhurst Bridge (AHBC) 13 A2
CROWLE 59 A1
Crown Point Control Tower 44 E
Crown Point Depot 44 E
Crown St. Tunnel 125 B
CROWTHORNE 18 D2
Croxton (AHBC-X) 44 C2
CROY 132 D1
Cruach Snow Shed 90 D3
Crugwallins Siding 2 C2
Crundale (AHBC) 23 A2
Crundale Mill (UWC) 23 A2
CRYSTAL PALACE 112 C2
Crystal Palace Tunnel 112 C2
Cuaich (UWC) 94 C2
CUDDINGTON 56 C3
CUFFLEY 32 C3
Culcheth Farm (UWC) 123 A2
Culgaith SB 74 D3
Culgaith Tunnel 74 D3
Culgarth (MCB) 74 D3
Culgower No. 1 (UWC) 103 B3
Culgower No. 3 (UWC) 103 B2
CULHAM 30 C3
Culloden No. 1 GF 99 B2
Culloden No. 2 GF 99 B2
Culloden 99 B2
Culmaily No. 2 (UWC) 102 D2
Culmaily No. 3 (UWC) 102 D2
Culnadalloch No. 1 (UWC) 87 B1
Culnadalloch No. 2 (UWC) 87 B1
CULRAIN 102 C2
Culrain Smithey (UWC) 102 C2
Culross (UWC) 85 A1
Cults Mill (UWC) 92 D3
CUMBERNAULD 132 D1
Cumberworth Tunnel 57 B1
CUPAR 92 D2
Cupar SB 92 D2
Curb Hut (UWC) 15 B1
Curborough Jn. 49 A3
CURRIEHILL 85 B2
Curriehill GSP 85 B2
Currock Jn. 121 A
Curzon St. Jn. 120 B
Custom House Escape Shaft 107 E
Cut Throat Lane (R/G) 33 A3
Cutsyke Jn LC SB (CJ) 64 D3
Cutts Drove (UWC) 7 A1
CUXTON 21 A3
Cuxton SB (CX) 21 A3
Cuxton 21 A3
Cwm Henog Farm 2 (UWC) 36 E
CWMBACH 26 C1
Cwmbach (UWC) 26 C1
Cwmbach Sidings (UWC) 26 C1
Cwmbargoed (TMO) 26 C1
CWMBRAN 26 D2
Cwmbwry No. 1 (UWC) 24 C2
Cwmbwry No. 2 (UWC) 24 C2
Cwmffoes (TMO) 25 B2
Cwmmawr Branch 24 C3
Cwm-y-Geist Farm (UWC) 37 A2
CYNGHORDY 36 E

D

Dafydd (UWC) 35 B3
Dagenham Docks East Jn. 110 D2
Dagenham East Crossovers 110 D2
DAGENHAM DOCK 110 D2
DAGENHAM EAST (LUL) 110 D2
DAGENHAM HEATHWAY (LUL) 110 D2
Daines / Mayhew 34 C1
Dainton Tunnel 4 D1
Dairy House Farm (UWC) 48 C1
DAISY HILL 123 A1
Daisyfield Jn. 62 D2
Daisyfield SB 62 D2
Dalchalm (AOCL) 103 B3
Dalcross (AHB) 99 B2
DALGETY BAY 85 B1
Dallam Freight Terminal 126 B
Dallam Jn. 126 B
DALLAM ROYAL MAIL TERMINAL 126 B
DALMALLY 88 C2
DALMARNOCK 133
Dalmarnock Road Tunnel 133
Dalmartin (UWC) 97 B2
DALMENY 85 A1
Dalmeny Jn. 85 B1
DALMUIR 131 A1
Dalmuir Park Jn. 131 A1
Dalmuir Riverside 131 A1
Dalnacardoch GF 94 C3
Dalnaspidal (UWC) 94 C3
DALREOCH 83 B1
Dalreoch Jn. 83 B2
Dalreoch Tunnels 83 B1
DALRY 83 A3
Dalrymple (UWC) 73 B2
Dalrymple Jn. 78 D2
DALSTON 74 C2
DALSTON JN. 109 A2
Dalston Jn. 109 A2
Dalston Jn. SB (D) 109 A2
DALSTON KINGSLAND 109 A2
Dalston Oil Depot GF 74 C2
Dalston Station No. 1 GF 74 C2
Dalston Station No. 2 GF 74 C2
DALTON 67 B3
Dalton Jn. 67 B3
Dalton Jn. SB (DJ) 67 B3
Dalton Tunnel 67 B3
DALWHINNIE 94 C3
Dalwhinnie SB 94 C3
Dam Dykes (CCTV) 76 C1
Damgate 45 A1
DANBY 71 A1
Danes (UWC) 18 A2
DANESCOURT 117 A
Danylan (UWC) 23 B2
DANZEY 39 B2
Darkies (UWC) 8 C3
Darlaston Jn. 121 B
DARLINGTON 70 C1
Darlington North Jn. 70 C1
Darlington South Jn. 70 C1
Darlingtons (UWC) 47 B2
DARNALL 128 A1
DARSHAM 45 A3
Darsham (AHBC) 45 A3
DARTFORD 20 D2
Dartford Jn. 20 D3

DARTON	58	C1
DARWEN	62	D3
DATCHET	19	A2
Datchet (CCTV)	19	A2
DAVENPORT	124	C3
Daventry International Rail Freight Terminal	40	D2
Daventry North Jn.	40	D2
Daventry South Jn.	40	D2
Daw Lane (CCTV)	129	A1
Daw Mill Colliery	40	C1
Dawdon Jn.	76	D2
Dawdon SB (DN)	76	D2
Dawdys (AOCL)	45	B2
Dawes Lane (AOCL)	59	B1
DAWLISH	4	D1
DAWLISH WARREN	4	D1
Daws (UWC)	6	C3
Day & Son GF	107	B3
Deakins (UWC)	37	A2
DEAL	22	D3
Deal SB (EBZ)	22	D3
Deal Street Jn.	122	B
DEAN	9	B1
Dean (AHBC)	9	B1
Dean Hill (AHBC)	9	B1
DEAN LANE	124	C2
Dean Lane (AHBC-X)	56	C1
Dean Royd Tunnel	63	A3
Dean Street Crossover	130	A
Deane Jn.	58	C1
Deanery Crossing	22	C3
DEANSGATE	122	B
Deansgate Jn (MCB)	123	B3
Deansgate Jn.	123	B3
Deansgate Jn. SB (DJ)	123	B3
Deanshillock (UWC)	101	A2
Deanside	131	A2
Decoy (UWC)	47	A2
Decoy Crossing	11	A3
Decoy Farm	34	D1
Decoy North Jn.	129	A1
Decoy South Jn.	129	A1
Dee Marsh Jn. SB (DM)	55	B3
Deep Wharf	20	D2
Deepcar	58	C1
Deepdale Jn.	62	E
Deepdale Tunnel No. 1	62	E
Deepdale Tunnel No. 2	62	E
Deepdale Tunnel No. 3	62	E
DEGANWY	54	C1
Deganwy LC SB	54	C1
Deganwy Quay (CCTV)	54	C2
DEIGHTON	63	B3
DELAMERE	56	C3
Della (UWC)	32	D1
Delny (AOCL)	99	B1
Denaby (CCTV)	58	D1
Denbigh Hall North Jn.	30	D1
Denbigh Hall South Jn.	31	A1
DENBY DALE	58	C1
Denby North (TMO)	50	C1
DENHAM	19	A1
DENHAM GOLF CLUB	19	A1
DENMARK HILL	112	C2
Denmark Hill Tunnel	112	C2
Denning's (UWC)	16	C3
DENT	69	A3
DENTON	124	C2
Denton Farm (UWC)	74	D1
Denton Jn.	124	C2
Denton Jn. SB (DJ)	124	C2
Denton Mains Farm (UWC)	74	D1
Denton Mill (UWC)	74	D2
Denton School (AHBC-X)	74	D1
Denton Village (MCG)	74	D1
Denver (AHBC)	43	A1
DEPTFORD	114	A
DERBY	122	A
Derby Green (UWC)	18	D2
Derby Jn.	122	A
Derby North Jn.	122	A
DERBY RAMSLINE HALT	122	A
DERBY ROAD	33	E
Derby SB (DY) (closed)	122	A
Derby Square Jn.	125	B
Dereham	44	D1
Deri (UWC)	24	C2
DERKER	124	C1
Dernford (CCTV) (UWC)	32	D1
Derwent Jn.	73	A3
Desford (AHBC)	50	C3
DEVONPORT	116	A
Devonport Dockyard	116	A
Devonport Tunnel	116	A
DEWSBURY	64	C3
Dewsbury East Jn.	63	B3
Dewsbury Railway St. Jn.	63	B3
Didcot East	18	E
Didcot East Jn.	18	E
Didcot North Jn.	18	E
DIDCOT PARKWAY	18	E
Didcot Railway Centre	18	E
Didcot West Curve Jn.	18	E
Didcot Yard Sidings	18	E
DIGBY AND SOWTON	6	C3
Diggle Junction SB	124	D1
Digswell	31	B2
Dildre Crossing	36	E
Dilston (AHBC-X)	75	B2
DILTON MARSH	16	C3
Dimmocks Cote (AHBC-X)	43	A2
DINAS POWYS	117	B
DINAS RHONDDA	26	C2
DINGLE ROAD	117	A
Dingle Tunnel	125	B
DINGWALL	99	A1
Dingwall Canal North (UWC)	99	A1
Dingwall Jn.	99	A1
Dingwall Middle (AOCL)	99	A1
Dingwall No. 1 (AOCL)	99	A1
Dingwall No. 2 (AOCL)	99	A1
Dinmore Tunnels	38	C3
Dinnington Jn.	58	D2
DINSDALE	70	D1
DINTING	124	D2
Dinting East Jn.	124	D2
Dinting Lane (UWC)	124	D2
Dinting SB (DG)	124	D2
Dinting South Jn.	124	D2
Dinting West Jn.	124	D2
Dinton East	8	D1
Dinton Manor Farm Crossing	8	D1
Direct Rail Services Depot	48	E
DISLEY	124	D3
Disley Tunnel	124	D3
DISS	44	D2
Distillery Burn (UWC)	94	C3
Distillery No. 1 GF	99	B1
Distillery No. 2 GF	99	B1
Ditchburns Crossing	30	D1
Ditchling Road Tunnel	14	E
Ditton East Jn.	56	C2
Ditton SB (DN)	56	C2
Ditton West Jn.	56	C2
Dock Jn. North	108	D2
Dock Jn. South	108	D2
Dock Lane	34	D1
Dock Security Gates	66	C2
Dock Street Tunnel	92	D1
Dockfield Jn.	63	B2
Docks Hills (CCTV)	129	A1
DOCKYARD	116	A
Dockyard Jn.	116	A
Dockyard Tunnel	112	D1
Doddington Road (CCTV)	59	B3
Dodd's (UWC)	67	B3
Dodds (UWC)	30	D2
DODWORTH	58	C1
Dodworth (CCTV)	58	C1
DOLAU	37	A3
Dolau (AOCL)	37	A2
Dolau House Farm No. 1 (UWC)	37	A2
Dolau House Farm No. 2 (UWC)	37	A3
Dolau House Farm No. 3 (UWC)	37	A3
Dolcoath (AHBC)	1	B2
Doldyfi (UWC)	36	C1
DOLEHAM	13	A2
Doleham	13	B2
Dolfadog (UWC)	54	C2
DOLGARROG	54	C2
Doll (UWC)	103	B3
Dollands Moor West Jn.	14	C1
Dollands Moor Yard	14	C1
Dolmeadow (UWC)	27	B1
Dolphin Jn.	19	A2
DOLWYDDELEN	54	C3
DONCASTER	129	A1
Doncaster International Railport	129	A1
Doncaster North Jn.	129	A1
Doncaster Road (MCB)	64	D3
Doncaster Royal Mail Terminal	129	A1
Doncaster SB (D)	129	A1
Donnington Jn.	48	C3
Dorchester Jn.	8	C3
DORCHESTER SOUTH	8	C3
Dorchester South SB (DR)	8	C3
DORCHESTER WEST	8	C3
DORE	58	C2
Dore South Jn.	58	C2
Dore Station Jn.	58	C2
Dore Tunnel	58	C2
Dore West Jn.	58	C2
DORKING	19	B3
DORKING (DEEPDENE)	19	B3
Dorking SB (CBK)	19	B3
DORKING WEST	19	B3
DORMANS	12	C1
Dormer Green (MCG)	58	D1
Dorr Lane (UWC)	65	A3
DORRIDGE	39	B2
Dorrington SB	38	C1
Double Dykes (UWC)	92	C3
DOVE HOLES	57	B2
Dove Holes Tunnel	57	B2
Dovefields (R/G)	49	B2
Dover Harbour Tunnel	14	D1
DOVER PRIORY	14	D1
Dover Priory Tunnel	14	D1
DOVERCOURT	34	D2
Dovey Jn.	35	B3
DOVEY JUNCTION	35	B3
Down Farm 1 (UWC)	36	E
Down Farm 2 (UWC)	36	E
Down Yard	16	C3
Downham By-pass (AHBC)	43	A1
DOWNHAM MARKET	43	A1
Downham Market GF	43	A1
Downham Market SB (DM)	43	A1
Dr. Day's Jn.	119	B
Drakelow East Curve Jn.	49	B2
Drakelow Power Stations	49	B2
Drakelow West Curve Jn.	49	B2
Drakes No. 2 (UWC)	18	D2
Drakewell Farm (UWC)	101	B3
Drax Branch Jn.	65	A3
Drax Power Station	65	A3
Drayton (AHBC)	11	A3
DRAYTON GREEN	107	B3
Drayton Green Jn.	107	B3
Drayton Green Tunnel	107	B3
Drayton Manor Farm (UWC)	48	D2
DRAYTON PARK	109	A2
Drayton Up Sidings	11	A3
DREM	86	C1
Drem Jn.	86	C1
DRIFFIELD	65	B1
Driffield SB (D)	65	B1
Driffield Station (RC) (MCB)	65	B1
Drift Lane (AHBC)	10	D2
DRIGG	67	A2
Drigg (MCG)	67	A2
Drigg SB	67	A2
Drinkwater (UWC)	30	C2
Drinnick Mill	2	C1
DROITWICH SPA	39	A3
Droitwich Spa Jn.	39	A3
Droitwich Spa SB (DS)	39	A3
DRONFIELD	58	C2
Drove Road	44	C2
Drumallan (UWC)	91	A3
Drumbeg Farm (UWC)	89	B2
DRUMCHAPEL	131	A1
Drumduan No. 2 (UWC)	100	C1
DRUMFROCHAR	83	A2
DRUMGELLOCH	132	D2
Drumlanrig Tunnel	79	B2
Drummuie (UWC)	102	D1
DRUMRY	131	A1
Dryclough Jn.	63	B3
Dubbs Jn.	83	A3
Ducketts (R/G)	63	B2
Duckworths (UWC)	62	D2
DUDDESTON	120	B
Duddeston Jn.	120	A
Dudley (Public Bridleway)	76	C1
DUDLEY PORT	39	A1
Dudley Tunnel	39	A1
DUFFIELD	49	B1
Duffryn (AHBC)	24	D3
Duffryn West Jn.	24	D3
DUIRINISH	97	A3
Duirinish Station (UWC)	97	A3
DUKE STREET	133	
Duke Street (CCTV)	61	B3
Duke Street Tunnel	133	
Dukes	12	D3
Dukes Wood (UWC)	56	C1
DULLINGHAM	43	A3
Dullingham (MCG)	43	A3
Dullingham SB (DH)	43	A3
DUMBARTON CENTRAL	83	B1
DUMBARTON EAST	83	B2
DUMBRECK	133	
DUMFRIES	73	A1
Dumfries A392 Station SB	73	A1
DUMPTON PARK	22	D3
DUNBAR	86	D1
DUNBLANE	91	A3
Dunblane SB	91	A3
DUNBRIDGE	9	B1
Dunbridge (AHBC)	9	B1
Dunbridge Crossing	9	B1
DUNCRAIG	97	A3
DUNDEE	92	D1
Dundee Central Jn.	92	D2
Dundee SC	92	D1
DUNFERMLINE QUEEN MARGARET	85	A1
DUNFERMLINE TOWN	85	A1
Dungeness GF	14	A2
Dunhampstead (AHBC)	39	A3
DUNKELD & BIRNAM	91	B1
Dunkeld SB	91	B1
DUNLOP	83	B3
Dunnerholme (UWC)	67	B3
Dunragit LC	77	A3
Dunragit SB	77	A3
DUNROBIN	102	D1
Dunrobin (UWC)	102	D1
Dunrod (UWC)	83	A2
Dunrod Loop East	83	A2
Dunrod Loop West	83	A2
Dunstalls (UWC)	49	B2
DUNSTON	130	A
DUNTON GREEN	20	D3
DURHAM	76	C2
Durham Farm	12	C3
Durn (UWC)	36	C1
DURRINGTON-ON-SEA	11	B3
Duxford (AHBC)	32	D1
DYCE	96	D2
Dyce SB	96	D2
Dyffryn (UWC)	35	B3
DYFFRYN ARDUDWY	35	B1
Dynevor GF	116	B
Dynevor Jn.	116	B
Dytto Farm (UWC)	54	C2
E		
Eagle and Thorpe (AHBC-X)	59	B3
Eagle Barnsdale (AHBC)	59	B3
Eagle Crossing	39	A1
EAGLESCLIFFE	70	D1
Eaglescliffe South Jn.	70	D1
EALING BROADWAY	107	B3
Earfit Lane (R/G)	64	D2
Earles Siding SB	57	B2
EARLESTOWN	56	C1
Earlestown East Jn.	56	C1
Earlestown South Jn.	56	C2
Earlestown West Jn.	56	C2
EARLEY	18	D2
EARLSFIELD	111	B2
EARLSWOOD	114	D
Easington (Public FP)	82	D3
East (Blackwells) (UWC)	70	D1
East Anglian Railway Museum	33	B2
East Bank Tunnel	128	A1
EAST BOLDON	76	D2
East Boldon (CCTV)	76	C2
East Brora Muir No. 1 (UWC)	103	B3
East Brora Muir No. 2 (UWC)	103	B3
East Burton (CCTV)	8	C3
East Chiltington	12	C2
East Clayock (UWC)	104	C2
East Cowick (R/G)	65	A3
East Cowton Crossovers	70	C2
EAST CROYDON	112	C3
East Dean Crossing	9	B1
EAST DIDSBURY	124	C3
EAST DULWICH	112	C2
East End	13	B1
EAST FARLEIGH	21	A3
East Farleigh SB	21	A3
EAST GARFORTH	64	C2
East Gate (CCTV)	34	C2
East Gate Jn.	34	C2
East Green	45	A3
East Grimstead GF	9	A1
EAST GRINSTEAD	12	C1
East Guldeford (AHBC)	13	B2
East Ham Depot	110	C2
EAST HAM (LUL)	110	C2
East Heslerton (AHBC-X)	72	C3
East Junction Viaduct	117	A
EAST KILBRIDE	131	B3
EAST MALLING	21	A3
East Mendalgief	117	B
EAST MIDLANDS PARKWAY	122	A
East Peckham Engineers Tip Siding	13	A1
EAST PUTNEY	111	B2
East Putney Tunnel	111	B2
East Road (R/G)	31	B1
East Shalford Crossing	11	A1
East Somerset Jn.	16	C3
EAST STAFF HALT	14	D1
East Suffolk Jn.	33	E
EAST TILBURY	21	A2
East Tilbury (CCTV)	21	A2
East Usk Jn. & SB	117	B
East Watten (UWC)	104	D2
EAST WORTHING	11	B3
EASTBOURNE	12	D3
EASTBROOK	117	B
Easter Balgour (UWC)	91	B2
Easter Dalguise No. 1 (UWC)	91	B1
Easter Dalguise No. 2 (UWC)	91	B1
Easter Glackton (UWC)	99	B2
EASTERHOUSE	132	C2
Eastern Access (AOCL)	66	C3
Eastern Jn.	21	B3
Easterton (UWC)	100	C1
Eastfield (UWC)	91	B2
Eastfield Depot	131	B1
Eastfield SB	42	E
Eastfields Road (CCTV)	111	B3
Eastgate	75	B3
EASTHAM RAKE	55	B2
Easthaven (UWC)	95	A3
EASTLEIGH	10	E
Eastleigh SB (E)	10	E
Eastleigh South Jn.	10	E
Eastleigh Works	10	E
Eastriggs	73	B1
EASTRINGTON	65	A3
Eastrington (AHBC)	65	A3
Eastville (AHBC-X)	52	E
Eaton (R/G-X)	44	D1
Eaton Lane (Public BW)	59	A2
Eaves Lane (R/G) Bridleway	59	A3
Eaves Tunnel	57	B2
EBBSFLEET	20	D2
Ebbsfleet SR	20	D2
Ebbw Jn.	117	B

EBBW VALE PARKWAY	26	C1
Ebley (UWC)	28	C3
ECCLES	123	B2
Eccles (CCTV)	55	B1
ECCLES ROAD	44	C2
Eccles Road (MCG)	44	C1
Eccles Road SB (ER)	44	C2
Eccles SB (ES)	123	B2
Eccles Station Jn.	123	B2
Ecclesfield West	128	A1
ECCLESTON PARK	56	C2
Eckington	28	D1
ECML Up Sidings	109	A1
EDALE	57	B2
Edale SB (EE)	57	B2
Edderton No. 1 (UWC)	102	D2
EDEN PARK	112	C3
Eden Valley	68	D1
EDENBRIDGE	20	C3
EDENBRIDGE TOWN	12	C1
Edenbridge Tunnel	20	C3
EDGE HILL	125	B
Edge Hill East Jn.	125	A
Edge Hill SB (LE)	125	A
Edge Hill West Jn.	125	B
Edge Lane Jn.	125	A
Edgeley Jn. No. 1	124	C3
Edgeley Jn. No. 1 SB (EY2)	124	C3
Edgeley Jn. No. 2 SB (EY1)	124	C3
Edgeley Jn.	124	C3
EDINBURGH PARK	85	B2
Edinburgh SC	85	E
EDINBURGH WAVERLEY	85	E
EDMONTON GREEN	20	C1
Edstone Hall No. 1 (UWC)	39	B3
Effingham Jn.	19	B3
EFFINGHAM JUNCTION	19	B3
Eggborough Power Station	64	D3
EGGESFORD	5	B2
Eggesford (TMO)	5	B2
Eggington Jn. SB (EN)	49	B2
Egginton (AHBC)	49	B2
EGHAM	19	A2
Egham (CCTV)	19	A2
Egleton (UWC)	51	A3
Eglinton Street Jn.	133	
Eglinton Street Tunnels	133	
Egmanton (CCTV)	59	A3
EGTON	71	B2
Elderslie	83	B2
Eldrable No. 1 (UWC)	103	B2
ELEPHANT & CASTLE	114	A
Elephant (UWC)	32	D2
Elford GF	49	B3
ELGIN	100	D1
Elgin East Freight Yard	100	D1
Elgin LC	100	D1
Elgin SB	100	D1
Eliots (UWC)	122	A
Elland SB (E)	63	B3
Elland Tunnel	63	B3
Ellands No. 3 (UWC)	100	C1
ELLESMERE PORT	55	B2
Ellesmere Port SB (EP)	55	B3
Ellingers	34	D1
Elm Grove (UWC)	55	B2
ELM PARK (LUL)	20	D1
Elm Road (AHBC)	42	D1
Elm Tree Farm (UWC)	71	B3
ELMERS END	112	C3
Elmley Lovett GF	39	A2
Elmside (UWC)	73	B1
Elmsley (OPEN)	58	D3
ELMSTEAD WOODS	112	D2
ELMSWELL	44	C3
Elmswell (CCTV)	44	C3
Elmton & Creswell Jn. SB	58	D3
ELSECAR	58	C1
ELSENHAM	32	D2
Elsenham GSP	32	D2
Elsham (MCB)	60	C1
Elsham SB (EM)	59	B1
ELSTREE & BOREHAMWOOD	31	B3
Elstree Tunnels	31	B3
ELTHAM	112	D2
ELTON & ORSTON	50	D1
Elworth Jn.	56	D3
ELY	43	A2
Ely Dock Jn.	43	A2
Ely Freight Terminal	43	A2
Ely North Jn.	43	A2
Ely Station North	43	A2
Ely West Curve No. 1	43	A2
Ely West Curve No. 2	43	A2
Ely West Jn.	43	A2
EMERSON PARK	20	D1
EMSWORTH	10	D2
Endon (AOCL)	48	D1
ENFIELD CHASE	32	C3
ENFIELD LOCK	32	C3
Enfield Lock (CCTV)	32	C3
ENFIELD TOWN	32	D3
England Lane	64	D3
England Springs (UWC)	66	C2
Englemere	19	A2
English Bridge Jn.	47	B3
Enham (UWC)	17	B3
ENTWISTLE	62	D3
EPSOM	111	B3
EPSOM DOWNS	111	B3
Eptons (UWC)	52	E
ERDINGTON	120	A
ERIDGE	12	D1
ERITH	20	D2
Ernesettle North GF	116	A
Ernesettle South GF	116	A
Errol LC (MCB)	92	C2
Errol SB	92	C2
Erwbeilli Farm (UWC)	36	E
ESHER	111	A3
Esholt Jn.	63	B2
Esholt Tunnel	63	B2
Essex Portals	20	D2
ESSEX ROAD	109	A2
Esso (UWC)	20	D2
Estrea (AHBC-X)	42	D1
Estuary	21	B1
ETCHINGHAM	13	A2
Etchingham (CCTV)	13	A2
Eton College Road	8	D1
Euro Terminal (Swindon)	17	A1
Euro Terminal (Willesden)	115	
Eurofreight Terminal	123	B1
EUROTUNNEL TERMINAL	14	C1
EUSTON	108	F
EUXTON BALSHAW LANE	62	C3
Euxton Jn.	62	C3
Evelench (UWC)	39	A3
Evershot Tunnel	7	B2
Everton (CCTV)	42	C3
EVESHAM	28	D1
Evesham SB	28	D1
EWELL EAST	111	B3
EWELL WEST	111	B3
EXETER CENTRAL	6	C3
Exeter Central Goods Jn.	6	C3
Exeter SB (E)	5	B3
EXETER ST DAVIDS	5	B3
Exeter St Davids Jn.	5	B3
EXETER ST THOMAS	6	C3
EXHIBITION CENTRE	133	
EXMOUTH	4	D1
Exmouth Jn.	6	C3
Exmouth Jn. SB (EJ)	6	C3
EXTON	6	C3
Extons Road (CCTV)	43	B1
Eye Court Farm (UWC)	38	C3
Eyhorne Tunnel	21	A3
EYNSFORD	20	D2
Eynsford Tunnel	20	D2
Eyton (AHBC-X)	47	B2

F

Factory Jn.	113	
FAILSWORTH	124	C2
FAIRBOURNE	35	B2
Fairbourne (AOCL)	35	B2
Fairburn Tunnel	64	D3
FAIRFIELD	124	C2
Fairfield (UWC)	17	B2
Fairfields	43	A1
Fairheads (R/G) (UWC)	32	D1
Fairheads No. 39 (UWC)	33	A2
FAIRLIE	83	A3
Fairlie High Siding GF	83	A3
Fairlie Tunnel	83	A3
FAIRWATER (TYLLGOED)	117	A
Fairwood Jn.	16	C3
Falcon Jn.	113	
FALCONWOOD	112	D2
FALKIRK GRAHAMSTON	84	D1
FALKIRK HIGH	84	D1
Falkirk Tunnel	84	D1
Falkland	78	D1
Fallodon (CCTV)	81	A1
FALLS OF CRUACHAN	87	B2
FALMER	12	C3
Falmer Tunnel	12	C2
FALMOUTH	1	B3
FALMOUTH DOCKS	2	C3
Falmouth No. 1 GF	1	B3
Falmouth No. 2 GF	2	C3
FALMOUTH TOWN	1	B3
Falsgrave SB (F)	72	C3
Fancy (UWC)	2	C1
FAREHAM	10	C2
Fareham East Jn.	10	C2
Fareham No. 1 Tunnel	10	C2
Fareham No. 2 Tunnel	10	C2
Farington Curve Jn.	62	E
Farington Jn.	62	E
Farleigh Lane	21	A3
Farlington Jn.	10	D2
Farm (UWC)	40	C3
Farmer Johnson's (UWC)	56	C3
Farmers (UWC)	25	B3
Farmstead Rise (UWC)	64	D1
FARNBOROUGH	19	A3
FARNBOROUGH NORTH	19	A3
Farnborough North Footpath (R/G)	18	D3
FARNCOMBE	11	A1
Farncombe East (CCTV)	11	A1
Farnecombe SB (WZ)	11	A1
FARNHAM	11	A1
Farnham (CCTV)	18	D3
Farnham Depot	18	D3
Farnham Road	19	A1
Farnham SB (FN)	11	A1
FARNINGHAM ROAD	20	D2
FARNWORTH	123	B1
Farnworth Tunnels	123	B1
FARRINGDON	109	A3
Farringdon Jn.	109	A3
Fassfern No. 1 (UWC)	89	B2
Fassfern No. 2 (UWC)	89	B2
FAULDHOUSE	84	D2
FAVERSHAM	21	B3
Faversham SB (EY)	21	B3
Fawkham Jn.	20	D2
Fawley Oil Refinery	10	C2
FAYGATE	11	B1
FAZAKERLEY	125	A
Fazakerley (UWC)	125	A
FEARN	102	D3
Fearn GF	102	D3
FEATHERSTONE	64	C3
Featherstone (CCTV)	64	C3
Feeder Bridge Jn.	119	B
Felixstowe Beach (CCTV)	34	D2
Felixstowe Beach Jn.	34	D2
Felixstowe Dock Jn.	34	D2
Felixstowe North Quay Terminal	34	C2
FELIXSTOWE TOWN	34	D2
FELLGATE	76	C1
FELTHAM	111	A2
Feltham Jn.	111	A2
Feltham SB (F)	111	A2
Feltham West (CCTV)	111	A2
Felton Lane (CCTV)	81	A2
Feltons (UWC)	38	C2
FENCHURCH STREET	109	A3
Fenham Hill (Public FP)	82	D3
FENITON	6	D3
Feniton	6	D3
Fenny Compton Jn.	40	A3
FENNY STRATFORD	31	A1
Fenny Stratford (CCTV)	31	A1
Fenton Manor Tunnel	48	D1
Fenwick (MCG)	64	D3
FERNHILL	26	C1
Ferrett Lane (UWC)	56	C1
FERRIBY	65	B3
Ferring (CCTV)	11	B3
Ferry Lane (AOCL)	34	D1
Ferry Road (CCTV)	13	B2
Ferry Toll Tunnel	85	A1
Ferrybridge North Jn.	64	D3
Ferrybridge Power Station	64	D3
Ferrybridge SB (F)	64	D3
Ferrybridge South Jn.	64	D3
Ferryhill	76	C3
Ferryhill Jn.	96	D2
Ferryhill SB (F)	76	C3
Ferryhill South Jn.	76	C3
FERRYSIDE	24	C2
Ferryside (MCB)	24	C2
Ferryside SB	24	C2
Fersit Tunnel	90	D2
FFAIRFACH	24	D2
Ffairfach (AOCL)	24	D2
Ffestiniog Tunnel	54	C3
FFLINT	55	B3
Ffos Fach Isaf (UWC)	24	D3
Ffynnongain (R/G)	24	C2
Fiddlers Ferry (UWC)	56	C2
Fiddlers Ferry Power Stn.	56	C2
Fiddlers Ferry SB	56	C1
Field (UWC)	6	C3
Field House Farm (UWC)	56	D3
Field Lane (AOCL)	64	D3
Fieldens	45	A3
Fielders (OPEN)	13	B2
Fields Farm (UWC)	48	C1
Fifoots Power Station / Uskmouth	117	B
Filbert Grove (UWC)	65	A3
FILEY	72	C3
Filey (CCTV)	72	C3
Filey Junction	72	C3
Fillan	88	D2
FILTON ABBEY WOOD	118	
Filton Jn. No. 2	118	
Filton Jn. No. 1	118	
Filton South Jn.	118	
Filton Tip (AOCL)	118	
Filton West Jn. No. 1	118	
Filton West Jn. No. 2	118	
FINCHLEY ROAD & FROGNAL	108	C2
Findern (AHBC)	122	A
Findlay's GF	132	D3
Fine Lane (MCG)	49	B3
Finney Lane (UWC)	62	C3
Finnieston East Jn.	133	
Finnieston Tunnel	133	
Finnieston West Jn.	133	
Finningley (MCB)	59	A1
FINSBURY PARK	109	A1
Finsbury Park Jn.	109	A1
FINSTOCK	29	B2
Firbeck Jn.	58	D2
Firle	12	D3
Fish Dock Road (CCTV)	60	D1
FISHBOURNE	10	D2
Fishbourne Footpath (R/G)	10	D2
Fishergate Tunnel	62	E
Fisherman Path (UWC)	55	B1
Fishers (Footpath)	13	A1
Fisher's (UWC)	16	C2
FISHERSGATE	11	B3
Fisherton Tunnel	9	A1
FISHGUARD HARBOUR	23	A1
Fishguard Harbour (AOCL)	23	A1
Fishley (UWC)	5	A1
Fishpool Farm (UWC)	55	A2
FISKERTON	50	D1
Fiskerton (MCG)	50	D1
Fiskerton Jn SB	50	D1
FITZWILLIAM	64	C3
FIVE WAYS	120	B
Flamborough (AHBC)	72	D3
Flax Bourton Tunnel	118	
Flax Mill (MCG)	52	C2
Flaxby Grange (UWC)	64	C1
Flaxton (AHBC-X)	65	A1
FLEET	18	D3
Flemingate (RC)	66	C2
Fletton Jn.	42	E
FLIMBY	73	A3
FLITWICK	31	A1
Flitwick Jn.	31	A1
Flixborough Wharf	65	B3
FLIXTON	123	B2
Flockton Sidings	127	A
Flordan GSP	44	D1
FLOWERY FIELD	124	D2
Flyover East Jn.	129	A1
Flyover Jn.	31	A1
Flyover West Jn.	129	A1
Fobbing (AHBC-X)	21	A1
Foley Crossing SB	48	D1
FOLKESTONE	14	C1
FOLKESTONE CENTRAL	14	C1
Folkestone East SB (YE)	14	D1
FOLKESTONE HARBOUR	14	C1
Folkestone Harbour SB (EBB)	14	D1
FOLKESTONE WEST	14	C1
Folly Bank (AHBC)	52	C3
Folly Farm (UWC)	22	C3
Folly Lane (UWC)	60	C1
Folly Road (CCTV)	14	D1
Football Field (UWC)	36	D1
FORD	11	A3
Ford (CCTV)	11	A3
Ford Bridge (UWC)	38	C3
Ford Crossing	11	B1
Ford Jn.	11	A3
Ford River Bridge	11	A3
Ford Siding GF	25	B3
Forden (AOCL)	37	A1
Fordgate	7	A1
Fordham (AHBC-X)	43	A3
Fords Jn.	25	B3
Foreign Ore Branch Jn.	59	B1
FOREST GATE	110	C2
Forest Gate Jn.	110	C1
FOREST HILL	112	C2
Forest House Farm (UWC)	56	C3
Forestry	43	B2
Forestry (UWC)	16	C3
Forgandenny Ford (UWC)	91	B2
Forge Farm (R/G)	12	D1
FORMBY	55	B1
FORRES	100	C1
Forres LC (MCB)	100	C1
Forres SB	100	C1
FORSINARD	103	B1
Forsinard (AOCL)	103	B1
FORT MATILDA	83	A1
Fort Pitt Tunnel	21	A2
FORT WILLIAM	90	C2
Fort William Jn. SB	90	C2
Forteviot (AHBC-X)	91	B2
Forteviot Farm (UWC)	91	B2
Forth Banks	130	A
Forth Railway Bridge	85	A1
Forty Steps (F/P)	11	B2
Forty Steps (UWC)	18	C3
Fosseway (AHB)	49	A3
Foster Yeoman Sidings	17	A1
Foster Yeoman Terminal (Thamesport)	21	B2
Fouldubs Jn. SB	85	A1
Foulis (R/G)	99	A1
Fountain (AOCL)	25	B2
Four Ashes Up Goods Loop	48	D3
Four Lane Ends (R/G)	56	C1
FOUR OAKS	39	B1
Fowey Dock	2	D2
Fowlers (UWC)	32	C2
Fowlers Lane	44	C1
Fox Grove Crossing	21	B3
Foxes (UWC)	59	B2
FOXFIELD	67	B3
Foxfield (UWC)	67	B3
Foxfield SB	67	B3
Foxhall Jn.	18	E

Foxhills Tunnel	19	A3
Foxlow Jn.	58	C2
FOXTON	32	C1
Foxton (MCB)	42	D3
Foxton SB	32	C1
Frampton (UWC)	28	D3
FRANT	12	D1
Frating (CCTV)	34	C2
FRATTON	10	F
Fratton East	10	F
Fratton Traincare Depot	10	F
Freeby (UWC)	50	B2
Freemans Lane (UWC)	59	A2
Freemans SB (F)	81	B3
FRESHFIELD	55	B1
Freshfield (CCTV)	55	B1
FRESHFORD	16	C2
Freshford (UWC)	16	C2
Friargate (CCTV)	60	D1
Friars Jn.	108	C3
Frickley Colliery Branch Jn.	58	D1
Friday Street GF	62	C3
FRIMLEY	19	A3
Frimley Crossing	19	A3
Frinkley Lane (AHBC-X)	51	A1
Frinkley Lane (Public BW)	51	A1
Frinton (CCTV)	34	C2
FRINTON-ON-SEA	34	C2
Frisby (MCB)	50	B3
Frisby East Jn. (former)	52	E
Frisby SB (FY)	50	D2
FRIZINGHALL	63	B2
FRODSHAM	56	C2
Frodsham Jn.	56	C2
Frodsham Jn. SB	56	C2
Frodsham Tunnel	56	C2
Frog Lane (UWC)	56	C1
Frogmore 2 (UWC)	29	A2
Frognall Farm	21	B3
FROME	16	C3
Frome Avoiding Line	16	C3
Frome North Jn.	16	C3
Fron (UWC)	37	A1
Frost Lane (AHBC)	9	B2
Frying Pan Farm (UWC)	16	D2
Fulbourn (AHBC)	43	A3
Fullers End Footpath (R/G-X)	32	D2
Fullerton (UWC)	96	C1
FULWELL	111	A2
Fulwell Jn.	111	A2
Fulwell Tunnel	111	A2
Fulwood Tunnel	125	A
Funthams Lane (CCTV)	42	C1
Funtington (AHBC)	10	D2
Furness Abbey (UWC)	67	B3
Furness Abbey Tunnel	67	B3
FURNESS VALE	124	D3
Furness Vale LC SB	124	D3
FURZE PLATT	19	A1
Furze Platt (ABCL)	19	A2
Furzebrook	8	D3

G

Gaer Jn.	117	B
Gaer Tunnel	117	B
Gaerwen (MCB)	53	B2
Gaerwen GF	53	B2
Gaerwen Isa (UWC)	53	B2
Gaerwen Jn.	53	B2
Gaerwen SB	53	B2
Gaerwen Uchaf No. 1 (UWC)	53	B2
Gaerwen Uchaf No. 2 (UWC)	53	B2
Gag Hill Farm (UWC)	69	A3
Gailes (AHBC-X)	78	C1
GAINSBOROUGH CENTRAL	59	A2
Gainsborough Central SB (GC)	59	B2
GAINSBOROUGH LEA ROAD	59	B2
Gainsborough Lea Road SB	59	B2
Gainsborough Trent Jn. SB (TJ)	59	B2
Gallachers (UWC)	17	B3
Galton Jn.	120	A
Galton Tunnel	120	A
Gambols (UWC)	17	A1
Gamekeepers	45	B2
Gannow Jn.	62	D2
Ganton (AHBC-X)	72	C3
Ganton Hall (UWC)	72	C3
Gantry 'A'	133	
Garclaugh No. 1 (UWC)	79	A2
Garclaugh No. 2 (UWC)	79	A2
Garclaugh No. 3 (UWC)	79	A2
Garden Street (CCTV)	60	D1
Gardners (CCTV)	21	A1
GARELOCHHEAD	83	A1
GARFORTH	64	C2
GARGRAVE	63	A1
Garlands No. 1 (UWC)	27	B3
Garnant Branch (TMO)	24	D2
Garnqueen North Jn.	132	D1
Garola House (UWC)	66	C3
Garriongill Jn.	84	D3
GARROWHILL	132	C2
GARSCADDEN	131	A2
GARSDALE	69	A2
Garsdale SB	69	A2
Garstang & Catterall Emergency GFs	62	C2

GARSTON	31	B3
Garston (UWC)	125	A
Garston Jn.	125	A
GARSWOOD	56	C1
GARTCOSH	132	C2
Gartcosh GF	132	C2
Gartcosh Jn.	132	C2
GARTH (Maesteg)	25	B2
GARTH (Powys)	36	D3
Gartly (AHBC)	101	B3
Gartsherrie South Jn.	132	D2
Gartshore	132	C1
Gartshore Emergency GF	132	C1
GARVE	98	D1
Garve (AOCL)	98	D1
Gas Factory Jn.	109	B3
Gas House Lane (UWC)	15	A2
Gascoigne Wood SB (GW)	64	D3
Gascoyne Crossing	21	B3
Gasworks Tunnel	108	D2
Gatehead (AHBC)	78	D1
GATHURST	56	C1
GATLEY	124	C3
GATWICK AIRPORT	12	C1
Geilston (UWC)	83	A1
Geilston Farm (UWC)	83	A1
Gelshfield (UWC)	104	C2
Gelshfield Gates (UWC)	104	C2
Gelynis (R/G-X)	117	A
Genwen Jn.	24	D3
George IV Tunnel	112	D1
GEORGEMAS JUNCTION	104	C2
Georgemas No. 1 GF	104	C2
Gerards Bridge Jn. GF	56	C1
GERRARDS CROSS	19	A1
Gibbet Hill Jn.	40	A2
Gibbons (UWC)	26	C2
GIDEA PARK	20	D1
Giffen (RNAD Gates)	83	A3
GIFFNOCK	131	B3
Gifford Street Portals	109	A2
GIGGLESWICK	62	D1
GILBERDYKE	65	B3
Gilberdyke (UWC)	65	B3
Gilberdyke Jn.	65	B3
Gilberdyke Jn. SB	65	B2
Giles (UWC)	34	C3
GILFACH FARGOED	26	C1
Gilfach Farm 3 (UWC)	36	E
Gillets (UWC)	62	C3
Gillingham	21	A3
GILLINGHAM (Dorset)	8	C1
GILLINGHAM (Kent)	21	A2
Gillingham SB (ET)	21	A3
Gillingham SB (GM)	8	C1
Gillingham Tunnel (Dorset)	8	C1
Gillingham Tunnel (Kent)	21	A2
GILSOCHILL	131	B1
GIPSY HILL	112	C2
Girlings (R/G-X)	44	E
GIRVAN	77	B1
Girvan SB	77	B1
Gisburn Tunnel	63	A2
Gishbourne (UWC)	28	D1
Gislingham	44	D3
Gissing No. 2 (AHBC-X)	44	D2
Glackton (UWC)	100	C2
GLAISDALE	71	B2
GLAN CONWY	54	C2
Glan Conwy (AHBC)	54	C2
Glanhafren (UWC)	37	A1
Glanirfon (UWC)	36	E
Glanrhyd (OC)	36	E
Glanrhyd Bridge	36	E
Glanrhyd Saeson Farm 1 (UWC)	36	E
Glantowy (UWC)	36	E
Glan-y-Mor Elias (UWC)	54	C2
Glanyrynys Farm	36	E
GLASGOW CENTRAL	133	
GLASGOW CENTRAL LOW LEVEL	133	
Glasgow Central SC	133	
GLASGOW QUEEN ST. HIGH LEVEL	133	
GLASGOW QUEEN ST. LOW LEVEL	133	
GLASSHOUGHTON	64	C3
Glass's	16	C2
Glaston Tunnel	51	A3
GLAZEBROOK	123	A2
Glazebrook East Jn. SB (GE)	123	A2
Glebe St. Jn.	48	D1
Gledholt Nth & Sth Tunnels	63	B3
Glen Douglas	88	C3
Glen Parva GF	40	D1
Glen Parva Jn.	50	C3
Glenamman Footpath (R/G)	25	A1
GLENEAGLES	91	B3
GLENFINNAN	89	B2
Glenfinnan Viaduct	89	B2
GLENGARNOCK	83	A3
GLENROTHESWITH THORNTON	92	C3
Glenwhilly SB	77	B2
GLOSSOP	124	D2
GLOUCESTER	28	C2
Gloucester Foot crossing (WL)	28	C2
Gloucester New Yard	28	C2
Gloucester Road Jn.	114	B
Gloucester SB (G)	28	C2

Gloucester West	28	C2
Gloucester Yard Jn.	28	C2
Gloucester Yard No. 2 GF	28	C2
Gloucester Barnwood Jn.	28	D2
GLYNDE	12	D3
Glynisw (UWC)	24	C2
Glyn-y-Mul (UWC)	116	B
GOBOWEN	47	A2
Gobowen North SB (GN)	47	A2
Gobowen South GF	47	A2
Gobwen North (MCB)	47	A2
GODALMING	11	A1
GODLEY	124	D2
Godnow Bridge (MCG)	59	A1
Godregarreg Farm 1	36	E
GODSTONE	20	C3
Godstone Tip	12	C1
Golant (OC)	2	D2
Goldborne Jn.	56	C1
Golden High Hedges (MCG)	52	C2
Goldens	21	B1
Goldmire Quarry (UWC)	67	B3
GOLDTHORPE	58	C1
Golf Course Bridleway	75	B1
GOLF STREET	95	A3
GOLSPIE	102	D1
GOMSHALL	19	B3
Gonalston (AHBC)	50	D1
Gonerby Tunnel	51	A2
Gooderham's No. 41	44	C2
Gooderham's No. 42	44	C2
GOODMAYES	110	D1
Goodridges (UWC)	51	A3
Goodrington Yard Sidings	4	D2
Goods Yard Sidings	67	B3
GOOLE	65	A3
Goole Bridge SB (GB)	65	A3
Goole Docks	65	A3
Goole SB (G)	65	A3
Goonbarrow Jn. SB (G)	2	C1
GOOSTREY	56	D3
Goostrey Jn.	56	D3
GORDON HILL	32	C3
Gore Top	22	D3
Gorgie Jn.	85	E
GORING & STREATLEY	18	C1
GORING-BY-SEA	11	B3
Goring-by-Sea (CCTV)	11	B3
Gorsecoch (UWC)	24	C2
Gorsey Lane (UWC)	50	D1
Gorshwen No. 2 (UWC)	35	B2
Gorstan (UWC)	98	D1
Gorton	88	D1
GORTON	124	C2
Gorton Jn.	124	C2
Gorton North GF	88	D1
Gorton South GF	88	D1
Gorwood's (No. 9) (UWC)	60	C1
Gosberton (MCG)	52	C2
Gosberton SB	52	C2
GOSPEL OAK	108	D2
Gospel Oak Jn.	108	D2
Gospel Oak SB	108	D2
Goswick (CCTV)	82	D3
Gotts (UWC)	63	B2
GOUROCK	83	A1
Gowdall Lane (AOCL)	64	D3
GOWERTON	24	D3
GOXHILL	66	C3
Goxhill SB	66	C3
Grain	21	B2
Grammers (UWC)	122	A
Gramshaw Road Crossing	9	A1
Grand Jn.	120	B
Grand Sluice (CCTV)	52	C1
Grange (AHBC-X)	92	C2
Grange Court GF	28	C2
Grange Farm (UWC)	72	C3
Grange Jn.	48	D1
GRANGE PARK	20	C1
Grangemouth Jn	85	A1
Grangemouth Oil Terminal	84	D1
Grangemouth SB	84	D1
Grangemouth Tongues (AOCL)	85	A1
GRANGE-OVER- SANDS	68	C3
Grange-over- Sands SB (GS)	68	C3
GRANGETOWN	117	A
Grangetown (OPEN)	76	D2
Grangetown Jn.	130	C
Grangetown SB (G)	130	C
Granhams (CCTV)	32	D1
GRANTHAM	51	A2
Grantham North Jn.	51	A2
Grantham South Jn.	51	A2
Grants (UWC)	52	E
Grantshouse	82	C2
Granville Sidings	48	D1
Granville St. Tunnel	120	B
Grassendale Tunnel	125	A
Grassthorpe Lane (MCG)	59	A3
GRATELEY	17	B3
Gravel Pit (ABCL)	45	B2
GRAVELLY HILL	120	A
Graveney (AHBC)	22	C3
GRAVESEND	21	A2
Grayrigg Loops	68	D2

GRAYS	20	D2
Grays (CCTV)	20	D2
Graythorpe (AOCL)	76	D3
Grazeley Green (UWC)	18	D2
GREAT AYTON	71	A1
GREAT BENTLEY	34	C2
Great Bentley (CCTV)	34	C3
Great Central Way Jn.	107	B2
GREAT CHESTERFORD	32	D1
GREAT COATES	60	D1
Great Coates (AHBC)	60	C1
Great Coates No. 1 SB	60	D1
Great Elm Tunnel	16	C3
Great Fisherton Farm 1 (UWC)	5	A1
Great Fisherton Farm 2 (UWC)	5	A1
Great Hale Grove No. 1 (AHBC)	52	C1
Great Hale Grove No. 2 (AHBC-X)	52	C1
Great House Farm (UWC)	27	A2
GREAT MALVERN	28	C1
GREAT MISSENDEN	31	A3
Great Ouse Viaduct	41	B3
Great Park (UWC)	18	A2
Great Plumstead (AHBC-X)	45	A1
Great Rocks Jn. SB	57	B3
Great Rocks Tunnel	57	B3
Great Sandfords	21	B1
Greatford (CCTV)	51	B3
Greatham (MCB)	70	D1
Greatham SB (GM)	76	D3
GREEN LANE	125	B
Green Lane (AHBC) (Ashington Jn)	81	A3
Green Lane (AHBC) (Chester)	55	B3
Green Lane (AHBC-X) (Stewartby)	41	B3
Green Lane (UWC) (Nantwich)	48	C1
Green Lane Crossing	10	D2
Green Lane Tunnel	125	B
Green Oak Goit (MCG)	65	A3
GREEN ROAD	67	B3
Green Road (AOCL)	67	B3
GREENBANK	56	D3
Greenbank SB	56	D3
Greenbottom Tunnel	63	B2
Greenburn Jn.	79	A2
Greenburn Open Cast	79	A2
GREENFAULDS	132	D1
GREENFIELD	124	D1
Greenfields (UWC)	36	D3
Greenfoot (CCTV)	132	D1
GREENFORD	107	B3
Greenford (LUL) Bay Jn.	107	B3
Greenford East Jn.	107	B3
Greenford East SB (GE)	107	B3
Greenford South Jn.	107	B3
Greenford West Jn.	107	B2
Greengates (UWC)	74	D2
Greenhill (UWC)	103	B3
Greenhill Lower Jn.	84	D1
Greenhill Upper Jn. SB	84	D1
GREENHITHE FOR BLUEWATER	20	D2
Greenhithe Tunnel	20	D2
Greenhurst Jn.	12	D2
Greenland Mill (AHBC)	16	C2
Greenloaning SB	91	A3
GREENOCK CENTRAL	83	A1
GREENOCK WEST	83	A1
Greens (UWC)	50	B3
Greensfield Jn.	130	A
GREENWICH	112	C2
Greenwich College Tunnel	112	D2
Greetland Jn.	63	B3
Greetland Jn. SB (G)	63	B3
Gregson Lane (UWC)	62	C3
Gresley Tunnel	49	B3
Gresty Lane SB (GL)	48	E
GRETNA GREEN	73	B1
Gretna Jn.	74	C1
Grewgrass (UWC)	71	A1
Griffin Wharf (Ipswich)	33	E
Griggs (UWC)	2	C1
GRIMSBY DOCKS	60	D1
GRIMSBY TOWN	60	D1
GRIMSDOWN	32	C3
Grimsdown (CCTV)	32	C3
Grimston & Frampton Tunnel	7	B3
GRINDLEFORD	58	C2
Grindleford SB	58	C2
Gringley Road (RC)	59	A2
Griseburn (UWC)	68	D1
Grisedale (UWC)	69	A2
Gristhorpe (MCG)	72	C3
Grives Lane (AHBC)	50	D1
Groam Farm (UWC)	99	A2
Groam Farm South (UWC)	99	A2
GROSMONT	71	B2
Grosvenor Bridge (River Thames)	113	
Grosvenor Carriage Shed	113	
Grove (UWC)	17	B1
Grove Farm (UWC)	72	C3
Grove Farm No. 1 Crossing (UWC)	7	B2
Grove Farm No. 2 Crossing (UWC)	7	B2
Grove Ferry (AHBC)	22	C3
Grove Hill Tunnel	12	D1
Grove Jn.	12	D1
Grove Lane (OPEN)	13	B2
GROVE PARK	112	D2
Grove Park (CCTV)	111	B2

Grove Park Sidings	112	D2
Grove Road (ABCL)	45	A2
Grove Road (CCTV) (Retford)	59	A2
Grove Road (CCTV) (Rye)	13	B2
Grove Road GSP	59	A3
Grove Tunnel	112	C2
Grovesend Colliery Loop GF	24	D3
Grovesend Colliery Loop Jn.	24	D3
Gryphon Lodge (UWC)	16	D1
Guay (UWC)	91	B1
GUIDE BRIDGE	124	C2
Guide Bridge East Jn.	124	C2
Guide Bridge SB (GB)	124	C2
Guide Bridge Station Jn.	124	C2
Guide Bridge West Jn.	124	C2
GUILDFORD	19	A3
Guildford SB (GD)	19	A3
Guillyhill (UWC)	73	A1
Guisborough Jn.	130	C
Guisborough Road(AOCL)	71	A1
GUISELEY	63	B2
Gulf Oil Branch Jn.	23	A2
Gulf Oil Refinery (Waterston)	23	A3
Gun Lane (UWC)	34	D2
Gunhouse Jn.	59	B1
Gunn (UWC)	104	C2
GUNNERSBURY	111	B2
GUNNISLAKE	3	B1
Gunthorpe (UWC)	51	A3
GUNTON	46	D1
Guston Tunnel	14	D1
Gutterby (UWC)	67	A3
Gwaun-cae-Gurwen (OC)	25	A1
Gwaun-cae-Gurwen (TMO)	25	A1
Gwaun-Cae-Gurwen Colliery	25	A1
GWERSYLLT	47	A1
Gwinear Road (AHBC)	1	A2
GYPSY LANE	70	D1
Gypsy Lane	44	D3
Gywn-y-Gaer (UWC)	26	C3

H

HABROUGH	60	C1
Habrough (AHBC)	60	C1
Habrough Jn.	60	C1
HACKBRIDGE	111	B3
Hackhurst Lane Bridleway	19	B3
HACKNEY CENTRAL	109	A2
HACKNEY DOWNS	109	A2
Hackney Downs North Jn.	109	A2
Hackney Engineers Sidings	4	D1
HACKNEY WICK	109	B2
HADDENHAM & THAME PARKWAY	30	D2
HADDISCOE	45	A1
HADFIELD	124	D2
Hadfold No. 2 Crossing	11	B2
HADLEY WOOD	32	C3
Hadley Wood North Tunnel	32	C3
Hadley Wood South Tunnel	32	C3
Hafod-y-Wern (UWC)	35	B1
HAG FOLD	123	A1
Hagg Lane (AHBC-X)	65	A3
Hagg Lane (R/G)	64	D3
HAGGERSTON	109	A2
HAGLEY	39	A2
Hairmyers Loop	131	B3
HAIRMYRES	131	B3
Halbeath (CCTV)	85	A1
HALE	123	B3
Hale (CCTV)	123	B3
Hales Street (AHBC-X)	44	D2
Halesowen Jn.	39	A2
HALESWORTH	45	A2
HALEWOOD	125	A
Halewood E. Jn.	125	A
Halewood W. Jn.	125	A
Halfpence Lane Tunnel	21	A2
HALIFAX	63	B3
Halifax Jn.	33	E
Halifax SB (H)	63	B3
Halkirk (AOCL)	104	C2
Hall Carleton (UWC)	67	A2
Hall Dene (MCB)	76	D2
Hall Dene SB (HD)	76	D2
Hall Farm	44	C3
Hall Farm (UWC)	50	B3
Hall Farm (UWC)	64	D1
HALL GREEN	120	A
HALL I' TH' WOOD	56	D1
Hall Lane Jn.	58	D2
HALL ROAD	55	B1
Hall Road (CCTV)	55	B1
Hall Royd DCE Siding GF	63	A3
Hall Royd Jn.	63	A3
Hallen Marsh Jn.	118	
Hallen Moor East	118	
Hallen Moor West	118	
HALLING	21	A3
Halloon (AOCL)	2	C1
Halterworth (AHBC)	9	B1
Halton Jn.	56	C2
Halton Jn. SB (HN)	56	C2
HALTWHISTLE	74	D2
Haltwhistle SB(HW)	74	D1
HAM STREET	13	B1
HAMBLE	10	C2
Hamble Viaduct	10	C2
Hambleton East Jn.	64	D2
Hambleton North Jn.	64	D2
Hambleton South Jn.	64	D3
Hambleton West Jn.	64	D2
HAMILTON CENTRAL	132	D3
HAMILTON SQUARE	125	B
Hamilton Square Jn.	125	B
HAMILTON WEST	132	C3
Hamiltons (UWC)	60	C2
HAMMERTON	64	D1
Hammerton (MCG)	64	C1
Hammerton Road (MCG)	64	D1
Hammerton SB	64	D1
Hammerton Street Jn.	63	B2
HAMPDEN PARK	12	D3
Hampden Park SB (CDB)	12	D3
HAMPSTEAD HEATH	108	C2
Hampstead Heath Tunnel	108	C2
Hampstead Tunnel	108	C2
HAMPTON	111	A2
HAMPTON COURT	111	A3
Hampton Court (CCTV)	111	A3
HAMPTON WICK	111	A2
Hampton(CCTV)	111	A3
Hampton Court Jn.	111	A3
HAMPTON-IN-ARDEN	39	B2
Hamsey (AHBC)	12	C2
HAMSTEAD	120	A
Hamstead (CCTV)	17	B2
Hamstead Tunnel	120	A
HAMWORTHY	8	D3
Hamworthy SB (HW)	8	D3
HANBOROUGH	29	B2
HANDFORTH	124	C3
Hangman's Lane (UWC)	14	D1
Hanselmans (UWC)	47	B3
Hanslope North Jn.	41	A3
Hanslope South Jn.	41	A3
Hansons (UWC)	59	B2
HANWELL	107	B3
Hanwell Bridge	107	B3
Hanwell Jn.	107	B3
Hanwood (UWC)	47	B3
Hanwood Yard (UWC)	47	B3
Hapsford (UWC)	16	C3
HAPTON	62	D2
Harbury Tunnel	40	C3
Hardacre No. 2 (UWC)	27	B3
Hardham (AHBC)	11	B2
Hardingstone (FP)	41	A3
Hardley Siding GF	9	B2
Hardmead (UWC)	32	C3
Hare Park Jn.	127	A
Harecastle Tunnel	48	D1
Haresfield Footpath (R/G)	28	C3
Hargham No. 1 (AHBC)	44	C1
Hargham No. 2	44	C1
HARLECH	35	B1
Harlech Morfa	35	B1
Harlescott SB	47	B3
HARLESDEN	115	
Harlesden Jn.	115	
Harlesden Tunnel	115	
HARLING ROAD	44	C2
Harling Road	44	C2
Harling Road SB (HR)	44	C2
HARLINGTON	31	A1
HARLOW MILL	32	D3
Harlow Mill GF	32	D3
HARLOW TOWN	32	C3
Harlow Town GF	32	C3
HAROLD WOOD	20	D1
HARPENDEN	31	B2
Harpenden Jn.	31	B2
HARRIETSHAM	21	B3
Harrietsham Tunnel	21	B3
HARRINGAY	109	A1
HARRINGAY GREEN LANES	109	A1
Harringay Jn.	108	D1
Harringay Park Jn. SB	108	D1
Harringay Viaduct	109	A1
HARRINGTON	67	A1
Harris (UWC)	5	A1
Harrison's Sidings GF	68	D1
HARROGATE	64	C1
Harrogate SB (H)	64	C1
HARROW & WEALDSTONE	19	B1
Harrow North Jn.	107	A1
Harrowden Jn.	41	B2
HARROW-ON-THE-HILL	107	A1
Harrow-on-the-Hill North Jn.	19	A1
Harrymore Lane (R/G)	64	D3
Harston (AHBC)	42	D3
Hartburn Jn.	70	D1
HARTFORD	56	C3
Hartford CLC Jn.	56	D3
Hartford East Jn.	56	D2
Hartford Jn.	56	C3
Hartford North Jn.	56	D2
Hartford West Jn.	56	D3
Harthope Viaduct	80	C2
HARTLEBURY	39	A2
Hartlebury (MCB)	38	D2
Hartlebury Depot (oou)	39	A2
Hartlebury SB (HY)	38	D2
HARTLEPOOL	76	D3
Hartlepool Docks	76	D3
Hartlepool Power Station	76	D3
Hartley (AHBC)	76	C1
Harts Drove (R/G)	42	D1
HARTWOOD	84	D2
Harveys (UWC)	18	D2
Harwich Container Terminal	34	C2
HARWICH INTERNATIONAL PORT	34	C2
HARWICH TOWN	34	D2
Harworth Colliery	58	D2
HASLEMERE	11	A1
Haslemere SB (EW)	11	A1
HASSOCKS	12	C2
HASTINGS	13	A3
Hastings Line Jn.	13	B1
Hastings SB (EDL)	13	A2
Hastings Tunnel	13	A3
HATCH END	19	B1
Hatch Path	8	D1
HATFIELD	31	B3
HATFIELD & STAINFORTH	59	A1
HATFIELD PEVEREL	33	A3
HATHERSAGE	58	C2
HATTERSLEY	124	D2
HATTON	39	B3
Hatton (UWC)	95	A3
Hatton North Jn.	39	B2
Hatton Station Jn.	39	B3
Hatton West Jn.	39	B3
Haugh Gardens (UWC)	74	D2
Haugh of Tullymet (R/G)	93	B2
Haughhead Jn.	132	D3
Haughley (AHBC)	44	C3
Haughley Jn.	44	D3
Hauxton (AHBC)	32	C1
HAVANT	10	D2
Havant ASC (HT)	10	D2
Havant Jn.	10	D2
Havant New Lane (MCB)(CCTV)	10	D2
HAVENHOUSE	52	E
Havenhouse (AHBC-X)	52	E
Havensmouth	13	A3
HAVERFORDWEST	23	A2
Haverigg (AHBC)	67	B3
Haw Bank Tunnel	63	A2
Haw Lane (UWC)	63	A1
HAWARDEN	55	B3
HAWARDEN BRIDGE	55	B3
Hawkeridge Jn.	16	D2
Hawkes Point Foot Crossing	1	A2
Hawkesbury Lane (CCTV)	40	C1
Hawkesbury Lane Sidings GF	40	C1
HAWKHEAD	131	A2
Hawkhead Oil Terminal GF	131	A2
Hawks	43	A2
Hawkwood Jn.	114	E
Hawthorn Bank (CCTV)	52	C3
Haxby Road (CCTV)	64	D1
Haxby Station (CCTV)	64	D1
Haxey (CCTV)	59	A1
Hay Crossing	7	A2
Haybank (UWC)	68	D1
Haydock Branch Jn.	56	C1
HAYDON BRIDGE	75	A1
Haydon Bridge (MCG)	75	A2
Haydon Bridge SB	75	A1
HAYDONS ROAD	111	B2
HAYES	112	D3
HAYES & HARLINGTON	107	A3
Hayes (UWC)	42	D3
Hayes Up Goods Loop	107	A3
Hayfields (UWC)	59	A1
HAYLE	1	A2
Hayle Footpath (R/G)	1	A2
HAYMARKET	85	E
Haymarket Central Jn.	85	E
Haymarket East Jn.	85	E
Haymarket North & South Tunnels	85	E
Haymarket Sprinter Depot	85	E
Haymarket Tunnel	125	B
Haymarket West Jn.	85	E
Hayside (UWC)	49	B2
Haystacks	13	B2
Haywards (AOCL)	34	D1
HAYWARDS HEATH	12	C2
Haywards Heath Tunnel	12	C2
Haywood (CCTV)	58	D1
HAZEL GROVE	124	C3
Hazel Grove East Jn.	124	C3
Hazel Grove High Level Jn.	124	C3
Hazel Grove SB (HG)	124	C3
Hazel Grove West Jn.	124	C3
HEADCORN	13	A1
HEADINGLEY	64	C2
Headingley Tunnel	64	C2
Heads of Lochiel (UWC)	89	B2
HEADSTONE LANE	19	B1
HEALD GREEN	124	C3
Heald Green N. Jn.	124	C3
Heald Green S. Jn.	124	C3
Heald Green W. Jn.	123	B3
Healey Mills SB (HM)	64	C3
Healey Mills Yard	64	C3
HEALING	60	C1
Healing (UWC)	60	C1
Healy Mills A Jn.	63	B3
Healy Mills B Jn.	63	B3
Heath Farm	46	D2
Heath Farm (UWC)	37	B2
HEATH HIGH LEVEL	117	A
Heath Jn.	117	A
Heath Junction SB (HJ)	117	A
HEATH LOW LEVEL	117	A
Heath No. 59	44	C2
Heatherbell (CCTV)	132	D2
Heatherinch (UWC)	92	C3
Heathfield	4	D1
Heathfield (UWC) (Aspatria)	73	B3
Heathfield (UWC) (Gartcosh)	132	C2
Heathfield Branch Jn.	4	D1
Heathrow Airport Jn.	107	A3
HEATHROW CENTRAL (TERMINALS 1, 2 & 3)	107	E
Heathrow Express Depot	108	C3
HEATHROW TERMINAL 4	107	E
HEATHROW TERMINAL 5	107	E
Heathrow Tunnel Jn.	107	E
HEATON CHAPEL	124	C2
Heaton Depot	130	A
Heaton Lodge Jns.	63	B3
Heaton Norris Jn.	124	C3
Heaton Norris Jn. SB (HN)	124	C3
Heaton North Jn.	130	A
Heaton South Jn.	130	A
HEBDEN BRIDGE	63	A3
Hebden Bridge SB (HB)	63	A3
Heck GF	64	D3
Heck Ings (MCG)	64	D3
Heck Lane (MCG)	64	D3
HECKINGTON	52	C1
Heckington (MCG)	52	C1
Heckington SB	51	B1
HEDGE END	10	C2
HEDNESFORD	49	A3
Hednesford SB (HD)	49	A3
Heeley	58	C2
HEIGHINGTON	70	C1
Heighington (MCB)	70	C1
Heighington SB	70	C1
Hele & Bradninch	6	C2
HELENSBURGH CENTRAL	83	A1
HELENSBURGH UPPER	83	A1
HELLIFIELD	63	A1
Hellifield SB	62	D1
Helm Tunnel	68	D1
HELMSDALE	103	B2
Helpston (MCB)	51	B3
Helpston Jn.	51	B3
HELSBY	56	C3
Helsby Jn.	56	C3
Helsby Jn. SB	56	C3
Helston Farm No. 1	3	B1
HEMEL HEMPSTEAD	31	A3
Hemerdon GF	3	B2
Hemingfield Tunnel	58	C1
Hempstead	12	D2
Hemsworth	64	C3
Henblas (UWC)	35	B2
Hendon	76	D2
HENDON	107	B1
Hendre Waelod No.1	54	C2
Hendre Waelod No.2 (UWC)	54	C2
Hendrewen (UWC)	23	A1
Hendrewen Farm 1 (UWC)	24	D3
Hendrewen Farm 3 (UWC)	24	D2
Hendy Jn.	24	D3
Hendy Sewage Works (UWC)	24	D3
Henfaes Farm (UWC)	54	C2
HENGOED	26	C2
Henham Low Moor (CCTV)	82	D3
Henley Branch Jn.	18	D1
HENLEY-IN-ARDEN	39	B3
Henley-in-Arden SB (HA)	39	B3
HENLEY-ON-THAMES	18	D1
HENSALL	64	D3
Hensall (MCB)	64	D3
Hensall SB (H)	64	D3
Henwick (MCB)	38	D3
Henwick Hall (MCB)	64	D3
Henwick SB (HK)	38	D3
Heol-y-Deliaid (UWC)	25	A2
Hepscott (AHBC)	81	A3
Hepscott Jn.	81	A3
Herbrandston Jn.	23	A2
HEREFORD	27	B1
Hereford SB (H)	27	B1
Hereford Yard Jn.	27	B1
HERNE BAY	22	A2
HERNE HILL	112	C2
Herne Hill North Jn.	112	C2
Herne Hill South Jn.	112	C2
Herringe	14	C1
HERSHAM	111	A3
HERTFORD EAST	32	C2
HERTFORD NORTH	32	C3
Hesketh (UWC)	55	B1
Heslerton Station (AHBC-X)	71	B3
Hessay	64	D2
Hessay WD GF	64	D1
Hessel East Jn.	66	C3
HESSLE	66	C3

Hessle Road SB (HR) 65 B3
Hest Bank (MCB) 62 C1
Hest Bank Jn. 62 C1
Hestham Hall (UWC) 67 B3
HESWALL 55 B2
Hethersett GF 44 D1
Hethfelton No. 1 Crossing 8 D3
Hethfelton No. 2 Crossing 8 D3
Hett Mill (CCTV) 76 C3
HEVER 12 D1
Hever Jn. 12 C1
Hewish (AHBC) 7 A2
HEWORTH 130 A
HEXHAM 75 A1
Hexham SB 75 B2
Hexthorpe Jn. 129 A1
HEYFORD 30 C2
Heyope 1 (UWC) 37 A2
Heyope 2 (UWC) 37 A2
HEYSHAM PORT 61 B1
Heysham Power Station 62 C1
Heywood Road Jn. 16 D3
Heyworth (MCG) 64 D3
Hiams Fen House No. 20 43 B2
Hibaldstow (AHBC-X) 59 B1
Hickleton SB (H) 58 C1
Hicks Lodge GF 49 B3
High Balernoch (UWC) 83 A1
HIGH BROOMS 12 D1
High Brooms GF 12 D1
High Eggborough (MCG) 64 D3
High Ferry (AHBC) 52 C1
High Ferry Lane (AHBC) 52 C1
High Hall (UWC) 27 B3
High Lane (UWC) 62 C3
High Level Bridge Central Jn. 130 A
High Level Bridge Jn. 130 A
High Marnham Power Station (closed) 59 A3
High Meads Jn. 109 B2
High Oaks Jn. 40 D2
High Output Yard (Reading) 119 A
High Scampston (AHBC-X) 71 B3
HIGH STREET 133
High Street Jn. 133
High Street Tunnel 133
High Tor No 1 Tunnel 58 C3
High Tor No 1A Tunnel 58 C3
High Tor No 2 Tunnel 58 C3
HIGH WYCOMBE 30 D3
HIGHAM 21 A2
Higham Tunnel 21 A2
HIGHAMS PARK 20 C1
HIGHBRIDGE & BURNHAM 15 A3
Highbridge West 15 A3
HIGHBURY & ISLINGTON 109 A2
Highbury Vale Jn. 109 A2
Highdyke 51 A2
Higher Barn (UWC) 8 C3
Higher Delacre (UWC) 56 D3
Higher Doomsford (UWC) 5 A2
Higher Town Tunnel 1 B2
Highfields (UWC) 49 A2
Highover Farm (UWC) 31 B2
HIGHTOWN 55 B1
Hightown Farm (UWC) 74 D1
Highworth GF 17 A1
Highworth Jn. 17 A1
HILDENBOROUGH 20 D3
Hilgay (AHBC) 43 A1
Hillam Gates (CCTV) 64 D3
HILLFOOT 131 B1
Hillhouse No. 3 GF 61 B2
Hillhouse No. 4 GF 61 B2
Hillhouse No. 5 GF 61 B2
Hilling (UWC) 23 B3
Hillings Road 45 B2
HILLINGTON EAST 131 A2
HILLINGTON WEST 131 A2
Hillmorton Jn. 40 E
Hills (UWC) 40 D1
HILLSIDE 55 B1
Hilly Laid (TMO) 61 B2
HILSEA 10 D2
Hilton (MCG) 49 B2
Hilton Jn SB 91 B2
Hilton Jn. 91 B2
Hilton Mills (UWC) 102 D2
HINCHLEY WOOD 111 A3
HINCKLEY 40 C1
Hinderton Field Tunnel 125 B
HINDLEY 56 C1
Hindlow No. 1 GF 57 B3
Hindlow No. 2 GF 57 B3
Hindlow Tunnel 57 B3
Hindon Road Crossing 8 D1
Hinds (UWB) 40 D1
Hinksey North 30 C3
Hinksey Reception GF 30 C3
Hinksey South 30 C3
HINTON ADMIRAL 9 A3
Hinxton (AHBC) 32 D1
Hipperholme Tunnel 63 B3
Hirst Lane (MCG) 81 A3
Hirwaun (TMO) 25 B1
Hirwaun Pond 25 B1
HITCHIN 31 B2
Hitchin 'A' GF 32 C2
Hitch's No. 12 43 A3
Hitch's No. 13 43 A3
HITHER GREEN 112 D2
Hither Green TMD 112 D2
Hither Green Yard 112 D2
Hives Farm (UWC) 50 B3
Hobhole Bank (UWC) 52 C1
Hobhole Bank Bridleway 52 C1
Hochkings (UWC) 59 B3
Hockham Road 44 C2
HOCKLEY 21 B1
Hockley (CCTV) 49 A2
Hockley No. 2 Tunnel 120 B
Hockley No. 1 Tunnel 120 B
Hoe Street Tunnel 109 B1
Hoghton (AHBC) 62 C3
Hoghton East EGF 62 C3
Hoghton West EGF 62 C3
Hogs Croft 32 D2
Hogwell 21 A1
Holbeck Depot 127 B
Holbeck Depot Jn. 127 B
Holbeck Jn. 127 B
Holbrook (TMO) 50 C1
Holdingham Lane (UWC) 51 B1
Holehouse Jn. GF 78 D2
Holesmouth Jn. 118
Holgate Jn. 130 B
Hollands (Streehay) 49 B3
Holliday St. Tunnel 120 B
HOLLINGBOURNE 21 B3
HOLLINWOOD 124 C1
Holloway 108 D2
Holly Moor (UWC) 7 A1
Holme (CCTV) 42 C1
Holme (No. 31) (AHBC) 8 D3
Holme Green (R/G) 42 C3
Holme Lode (CCTV) 42 C1
Holme Road 43 B1
Holme Tunnel 63 A3
HOLMES CHAPEL 56 D3
Holmes Jn. (CCTV) 128 A1
HOLMWOOD 11 B1
Holt Lane Tunnel 58 C3
Holton Gatehouse (AHBC-X) 60 C1
HOLTON HEATH 8 D3
Holton Heath GF 8 D3
Holton-le-Moor SB (H) 60 C1
Holts (UWC) 40 D1
Holybourne Oil Terminal Sidings 18 D3
Holyhead 53 A1
Holyhead SB (HD) 53 A1
HOLYTOWN 132 D3
Holytown Jn. 132 D3
Holywell (ABCL) 76 C1
Holywell (UWC) 2 C1
Holywell Junction SB 55 A2
Holywood LC 73 A1
Holywood SB 80 C3
Home Farm (UWC) 48 D1
Homedown (UWC) 28 D1
HOMERTON 109 B2
HONEYBOURNE 29 A1
Honeybourne GF 29 A1
Honington (AHBC-X) 51 A1
HONITON 6 D3
Honiton GF 6 D3
Honiton SB (H) 6 D3
Honiton Tunnel 6 D3
HONLEY 57 B1
HONOR OAK PARK 112 C2
Hoo Jn. 21 A2
HOO JN. STAFF HALT 21 A2
Hoods Mill (UWC) 51 B3
HOOK 18 D3
Hook Moor Farm (UWC) 65 A3
HOOTON 55 B2
Hooton SB (HN) 55 B2
Hooton South Jn. 55 B3
HOPE 57 B2
Hope Exchange (UWC) 55 B3
HOPE/YR HOB 47 A1
Hopetown Jn. 70 C1
Hoplands Farm 22 C3
Hopperton Grange (UWC) 64 C1
Hopperton Old Station (UWC) 64 C1
Hoppity Tunnel 19 B3
HOPTON HEATH 37 B2
Horbury Jn. GF 127 A
Horbury Jn. SB (HJ) 127 A
Horbury Jn. 127 A
Horbury Station Jn. 64 C3
HORLEY 12 C1
HORNBEAM PARK 64 C1
HORNCHURCH (LUL) 20 D1
Horninglow Bridge Jn. 49 B2
Horrocks (UWC) 74 C2
Horrocksford Jn. SB 62 D2
Horse Fen 43 A3
Horsemoor (AHBC-X) 43 A1
Horsfall Tunnel 63 A3
HORSFORTH 64 C2
Horsforth SB (H) 64 C2
HORSHAM 11 B1
Horsham Jn. 11 B1
Horsham Road (CCTV) 12 C1
HORSLEY 19 B3
Horton (UWC) 22 C3
Horton Road (MCB) 28 C2
Horton Road Jn. 28 C2
HORTON-IN-RIBBLESDALE 69 A3
HORWICH PARKWAY 123 A1
HOSCAR 56 C1
Hoscar (AHBC-X) 56 C1
Hosegood's (UWC) 6 C3
Hospital (CCTV) 62 C3
Hospital Mill (R/G) 92 D3
Hothfield Sidings 13 B1
Hoton House (AHBC-X) 65 A3
HOUGH GREEN 56 C2
Hough Lane (AHBC-X) 51 A1
Hough Lane (Public BW) 51 A1
HOUNSLOW 111 A2
Hounslow Jn. 111 A2
HOVE 14 E
Hove Jn. 14 E
Hove Tunnel 14 E
HOVETON & WROXHAM 46 D2
How Mill (AHBC-X) 74 C2
HOW WOOD 31 B3
Howards (UWC) 60 C3
HOWDEN 65 A3
Howden (CCTV) 65 A3
Howe & Co. Siding SB (HS) 74 C2
Howey (UWC) 36 D3
Howsham 65 A1
Howsham (AHBC-X) 60 C1
Howton Court Farm (UWC) 27 A2
HOWWOOD 83 B2
HOXTON 109 A2
Hoy (AOCL) 104 C2
HOYLAKE 55 A2
Hoylake (CCTV) 55 B1
Hubbards 45 A3
Hubbards (UWC) 50 B2
HUBBERTS BRIDGE 52 C1
Hubberts Bridge (MCG) 52 C2
Hubberts Bridge SB 52 C1
HUCKNALL 50 C1
Hucknall No. 3 (R/G) 50 D1
Hucknall No. 4 (R/G) 50 D1
HUDDERSFIELD 63 B3
Huddersfield Nth & Sth Tunnels 63 B3
Huddersfield SB (HU) 63 B3
Huish (CCTV) 15 A2
HULL 66 C3
Hull Freight Yard 66 C3
Hull Paragon SB (HP) 66 C3
Hum Lane (UWC) 52 C1
Hum Road (UWC) 52 C1
Humber International Terminal 66 C3
Humber Refinery 66 C3
Humber Road Jn. 66 C3
Humberstone Road Jn. 50 B3
HUMPHREY PARK 123 B2
HUNCOAT 62 D2
Huncoat (MCB) 62 D2
HUNGERFORD 17 B2
Hungerford (CCTV) 17 B2
Hungerford GF 17 B2
HungerfordBridge 114 A
HUNMANBY 72 C3
Hunmanby Jn. 72 C3
Hunmanby Sands Lane (ABCL-X) 72 C3
Hunmanby Station (ABCL-X) 72 C3
Hunsbury Hill Tunnel 41 A3
Hunslet South Jn. 127 B
Hunslet Station Jn. 127 B
Hunter (UWC) 7 B3
Hunterston 83 A3
HUNTINGDON 42 C2
Huntingdon South Jn. 42 C2
HuntingdonNorth Jn. 42 C2
HUNTLY 101 B2
Huntly SB 101 B2
HUNTS CROSS 125 A
Hunts Cross SB (HC) 125 A
Hunts Cross W. Jn. 125 A
Hunts Path No. 1 8 C1
Hunts Path No. 2 8 C1
Huntspill (UWC) 15 A3
Hurdcott Lodge Crossing (R/G) 8 D1
Hurlford SB 83 B3
HURST GREEN 20 C3
Hurst Green Jn. 20 C3
Hutcheon St Tunnel 96 D2
Hutchings Crossing 11 A3
Hutton (AHBC-X) 66 C1
HUTTON CRANSWICK 65 B1
Huttons (UWC) 58 D2
HUYTON 125 A
Huyton Jn. 125 A
Huyton SB (HN) 125 A
Hyatts (UWC) 29 B2
Hyde (UWC) 7 B3
HYDE CENTRAL 124 D2
Hyde Farm (UWC) 7 A1
Hyde Jn. 124 D2
HYDE NORTH 124 D2
Hydrocracker (AOCL) 21 A2
Hyford (UWC) 8 C3
HYKEHAM 59 B3
HYNDLAND 133
Hyndland East Jn. 131 B2
Hyndland North Jn. 131 A2
Hyndland West Jn. 131 A2
HYTHE 33 B2
Hythe Jn. 34 C2
Hythe Station (CCTV) 34 C2
Hythe Station LC 33 B2

I

IBM 83 A2
Ickleton Mill Lane (UWC) 32 D1
Ickleton Road (CCTV) 32 D1
IFIELD 11 B1
Ifton Hill Farm (UWC) 15 B1
ILFORD 110 C1
Ilford Depot 110 D1
Ilford Depot Country End Jn. 110 D1
Ilford Depot London End Jn. 110 C1
Ilford Flyover 110 C1
Ilkeston Jn. 122 A
ILKLEY 63 B2
Immingham East Jn. 66 C3
Immingham East Jn. SB (I) 66 C3
Immingham Reception Sidings SB (IR) 66 C3
Immingham West Jn. SB (IW) 66 C3
INCE 126 C
INCE & ELTON 56 C2
Ince Moss Jn. 126 C
Inchlea (UWC) 94 C2
Inchmagranachan No. 2 (UWC) 91 B1
Inchmagranachan No. 3 (UWC) 91 B1
Inchmore (UWC) 38 C3
Inchoonans (AHBC-X) 92 C2
Inchture (AHBC-X) 92 C2
Inchyra (AHBC) 92 C2
Ingate Street (ABCL) 45 A2
INGATESTONE 21 A1
Ingatestone (MCB) 32 D3
Inkersall (OPEN) 58 D3
Inkpens No. 1 (UWC) 30 C2
Inlands Road (AHBC) 10 D2
Innerwick 82 C1
INSCH 96 C1
Insch LC 101 B3
Insch SB 101 B3
International East Jn. 109 B2
International Jn. 113
International West Jn. 109 B2
Intersection Tunnel 115
Intwood (AHBC-X) 44 D1
Inver Brora No. 1 (UWC) 103 B3
Inver Brora No. 2 (UWC) 103 B3
Inver Tunnel 91 B1
INVERGORDON 99 B1
Invergordon Distillery 99 B1
INVERGOWRIE 92 D1
Inverhaggernie No. 1 (UWC) 88 D2
Inverhaggernie No. 2 (UWC) 88 D2
Inverkeilor SB 95 A2
INVERKEITHING 85 A1
Inverkeithing Car Park FP (R/G) 85 B1
Inverkeithing Central Jn. 85 B1
Inverkeithing East Jn. 85 A1
Inverkeithing North Jn. 85 A1
Inverkeithing Tunnel 85 A1
INVERKIP 83 A2
Inverkip Tunnel 83 A2
Inverlochty No. 1 (UWC) 100 D1
Inverlochy Farm (UWC) 90 C2
INVERNESS 99 B2
Inverness SC (TCB and RETB) 99 A2
Inverpeffor (UWC) 95 A3
INVERSHIN 102 C2
INVERURIE 96 C1
Inverurie SB 96 C1
IPSWICH 33 E
Ipswich Docks 33 E
Ipswich Freight Terminal 33 E
Ipswich Goods Jn. 33 E
Ipswich Tunnel 33 E
IRLAM 123 A2
Iron Acton By-pass (TMO) 16 C1
Iron Acton Station (AOCL) 16 C1
Ironbridge Power Station Sidings 38 C1
Ironville Jn. 50 C1
IRVINE 83 A3
Isabella (TMO) 76 C1
Iscoed (UWC) 23 B2
ISLEWORTH 111 A2
ISLIP 30 C2
Islip (R/G) 30 C2
Itford (R/G) 12 C3
IVER 19 A2
Ivy Farm (R/G) 32 C1
Ivy Lane (UWC) 29 A1
IVYBRIDGE 4 C2

J

Jackie Duffin Wood (R/G) 65 A3
Jacksons (UWC) (Blythe Bridge) 49 A2
Jacksons (UWC) (Weaverthorpe) 72 C3
Jacobs Gutter (AHBC) 9 B2
JAMES STREET 125 B
Jaques Hall 34 C2

LEC (Cox's) Crossing 11 A3
Leckwith Loop Jn. North 117 A
Leckwith Loop Jn. South 117 A
Leckwith Road Bridge GF 117 A
Ledburn Jn. 31 A2
LEDBURY 28 C1
Ledbury SB 28 C1
LedburyTunnel 28 C1
Ledston 64 C3
LEE 112 D2
Lee Loop Jn. 112 D2
Lee Spur Jn. 112 D2
LEEDS 127 B
Leeds East Jn. 127 B
Leeds St. Jn. 125 B
Leeds St. Portal Central Tunnel 125 B
Leeds West Jn. 127 B
Leek Brook Jn. (former) 48 D1
Leeman Road Yard 130 B
LEICESTER 50 B3
Leicester Jn. 49 B2
Leicester North Jn. 50 C3
Leicester SB (LR) 50 B3
Leicester South Jn. 50 C3
LEIGH 12 D1
Leigh (AHBC-X) 49 A2
Leigham Court Tunnel 112 C2
Leigham Jn. 112 C2
Leigham A181 Tunnel 112 C2
LEIGH-ON-SEA 21 A1
LEIGHTON BUZZARD 31 A2
Leiston Station (TMO) 45 B3
Leith Hall (UWC) 101 B3
Leitram No.1 21 A3
LELANT 1 A2
LELANT SALTINGS 1 A2
LENHAM 21 B3
Lenham Crossover 21 B3
Lenham SR 21 B3
Lenthay Crossing 7 B2
Lenton North Jn. 122 A
Lenton South Jn. 122 A
Lentran Station (UWC) 99 A2
LENZIE 132 C1
LEOMINSTER 38 C3
Leominster (AHBC) 38 C3
Leominster SB (LE) 38 C3
Leonards No. 31 43 A2
Leri Bridge (UWC) 35 B3
Lesmahagow Jn. 132 D3
Letchworth EMU Sidings 31 B1
LETCHWORTH GARDEN CITY 31 B2
Letterston East GF 23 A1
Letterston West GF 23 A1
LEUCHARS 92 D2
Leuchars SB 92 D2
LEVENSHULME 124 C2
Leverton (AHBC) 59 A2
Levington No. 6 (AHBC) 34 D1
Lewell (No. 39) Crossing 8 C3
LEWES 12 C2
Lewes SB (LW) 12 C3
Lewes Tunnel 12 C2
Lewis Crossing (UWC) 36 E
Lewis No. 1 (UWC) 28 D1
Lewis No. 2 (UWC) 28 D1
LEWISHAM 114 C
Lewisham Vale Jn. 114 C
Ley (MCG) 28 C2
LEYLAND 62 C3
LEYTON MIDLAND ROAD 109 B1
LEYTONSTONE HIGH ROAD 109 B2
LICHFIELD CITY 49 A3
Lichfield City Jn. 49 B3
Lichfield T.V. Jn SB (TV) 49 B3
Lichfield T.V. Jn. 49 B3
LICHFIELD TRENT VALLEY 49 A3
Lidgate (UWC) 67 B3
LIDLINGTON 31 A1
Lifford East Jn. 120 A
Lifford West Jn. 120 A
Lightcliffe Tunnel 63 B3
Lillifield Lane (CCTV) 60 D1
Limbury Rd Dn. Line No. 2 GF 31 B2
Limbury Rd Up Line No. 1 GF 31 B2
Lime Kiln (AOCL) 34 D1
Lime Kiln (CCTV) 117 B
Lime Street Tunnel 125 B
LIMEHOUSE 109 B3
Limestone Hall (MCG) 67 B3
Limpsfield Tunnel 20 C3
Linby Colliery (ABCL) 50 D1
Linby Station (ABCL) 50 D1
LINCOLN CENTRAL 59 B3
Lincoln High St. (CCTV) 59 B3
Lincoln Road (MCG) 20 C1
Lincoln SCC 59 B3
Lincoln Street (CCTV) 122 A
Lindal Tunnel 67 B3
Lindridge Farm (UWC) 50 C3
Lindsey Refinery 66 C3
Linford St. Jn. 113
LINGFIELD 12 C1
LINGWOOD 45 A1
Lingwood (MCG) 45 A1
LINLITHGOW 85 A1
Linslade Tunnels 31 A2
Linwith Lane (AHBC) 65 A3
LIPHOOK 11 A1
Lipson Jn. 116 A
Lipwood (UWC) 75 A2
LISKEARD 3 A1
Liskeard GF 3 A2
Liskeard Jn. 3 A2
Liskeard SB (LD) 3 A2
Liskeard Viaduct 3 A2
Lismore Circus Tunnels 108 C2
LISS 10 D1
Liss (CCTV) 10 D1
Liss Common (AHBC) 10 D1
Lissingley (AHBC-X) 60 C2
Litchfield North Jn. 49 A3
Litchfield Tunnel 18 C3
Litlington (AHBC) 32 C1
Little Bourton (UWC) 40 C3
Little Bowden (R/G) 41 A1
Little Bullsdown Crossing 19 B3
Little Chef (UWC) 54 C2
Little Eaton Jn. 122 A
Little Genoch No. 1 (UWC) 77 A3
Little Genoch No. 2 (UWC) 77 A3
Little Harmiston (UWC) 23 A2
Little Hayes 21 B1
LITTLE KIMBLE 30 D2
Little London (AHBC) 60 C1
Little Mill (CCTV) 81 A1
Little Mill (UWC) 101 B2
Little Mill Crossovers 81 A1
Little Mill Jn. SB (LM) 26 D1
Little Mill Jn. 26 D1
Little Preston 21 A3
Little Sleeping AHBC-X) 52 E
LITTLE SUTTON 55 B2
Little Treviscoe (OC) 2 C1
Little Weir Farm 2 (UWC) 5 A1
LITTLEBOROUGH 63 A3
Littleborough GF 63 A3
Littlebury Tunnel 32 D1
Littlehampton 11 A3
Littlehampton Jn. 11 A3
Littlehampton SB (LH) 11 A3
LITTLEHAVEN 11 B1
LITTLEPORT 43 A2
Littleport By-pass (AHBC-X) 43 A2
Littleport Footpath (R/G) 43 A2
Littleton & Badsey (CCTV) 29 A1
Littleworth (MCB) 52 C3
Littleworth SB 52 C3
Litton's Mill Crossing SB 126 B
Liverpool Bulk Handling Terminal 125 A
LIVERPOOL CENTRAL 125 B
Liverpool Central North Jn. 125 B
Liverpool Central South Jn. 125 B
LIVERPOOL LIME STREET 125 B
LIVERPOOL LIME ST. (DEEP LEVEL) 125 B
Liverpool Lime Street SB (LS) 125 B
LIVERPOOL S. PARKWAY 125 A
Liverpool Street (L) IECC 110 E
LIVERPOOL STREET 110 E
LIVINGSTON NORTH 85 A2
LIVINGSTON SOUTH 85 A2
LLANABER 35 B2
Llanbadarn (ABCL) 35 E
LLANBEDR 35 B1
LLANBISTER ROAD 37 A2
Llanboidy (AHBC) 23 B2
LLANBRADACH 26 C2
Llancaiach Isaf (UWC) 26 C2
Llancillo Hall (UWC) 27 A2
LLANDAFF 117 A
LLANDANWG 35 B1
Llandanwg (UWC) 35 B1
Llandarcy GF 116 B
Llanddaniel (R/G) 53 B2
LLANDECWYN 35 B1
Llandegai Tunnel 53 B2
LLANDEILO 24 D2
Llandeilo GF 24 D2
Llandeilo Jn. 24 D3
LLANDOVERY 36 E
Llandovery (TMO) 36 E
Llandovery GF 36 E
Llandow (UWC) 25 B3
Llandre (ABCL) 35 B3
Llandre Vicarage (R/G) 35 B3
LLANDRINDOD 36 D3
Llandrindod (TMO) 36 D3
Llandrindod GF 36 D3
LLANDUDNO 54 C1
Llandudno Jn. 54 C2
LLANDUDNO JUNCTION 54 C2
Llandudno Junction SB (LJ) 54 D1
Llandudno Station SB 54 C1
LLANDYBIE 25 A1
Llandybie (AOCL) 25 A1
LLANELLI 24 D3
Llanelli Dock Jn. East GF 24 D3
Llanelli East (CCTV) 24 D3
Llanelli West (MCB) 24 D3
Llanfair (MCG) 53 B2
Llanfair SB 53 B2
LLANFAIRFECHAN 54 C2
LLANFAIRPWLL 53 B2
LLANGADOG 36 E
Llangadog (AOCL) 36 E
LLANGAMMARCH 36 E
Llangammarch Tunnel 36 E
LLANGENNECH 24 D3
Llangennech (UWC) 24 D3
Llanglan Fechan No. 2 (UWC) 36 C1
Llanglan Fechan No. 4 (UWC) 36 C1
Llangyfelach Tunnel 116 B
LLANGYNLLO 37 A2
Llangynllo Tunnel 37 A2
LLANHARAN 25 B2
Llanharan (UWC) 26 C2
LLANHILLETH 26 D1
Llanidloes Road (MCG) 36 D1
Llanion (OC) 23 A3
LLANISHEN 26 C2
Llanlliwe Farm (UWC) 23 B2
LLANRWST 54 C2
LLANRWST NORTH 54 C2
Llanrwst SB 54 C2
Llanrwst Tunnel 54 C2
LLANSAMLET 116 B
Llanstephan Footpath (R/G) 24 C2
Llantrisant West (CCTV) 26 C2
Llantrisant West GF 26 C2
LLANTWIT MAJOR 25 B3
Llanwern Exchange Sidings 15 A1
Llanwern Works East Connection 15 A1
Llanwern Works West Connection 15 A1
LLANWRDA 36 E
Llanwrda (OC) 36 E
LLANWRTYD 36 E
Lloyds & Martin (UWC) 43 A2
Llwyn Cadwgan (UWC) 35 B1
Llwyn Jack Farm (UWC) 36 E
Llwyndrys (UWC) 23 B2
Llwyndyrys (UWC) 23 B2
LLWYNGWRIL 35 B2
Llwyngwyddil 2 (UWC) 23 B2
Llwynllanc Farm 1 (UWC) 25 A1
Llwynpener 2 (UWC) 23 B2
Llwynpiod No. 1 (UWC) 36 D3
Llwynpiod No. 2 (UWC) 36 D3
LLWYNYPIA 25 B2
Llynfi Jn. 25 B2
Llynmellin Farm (UWC) 37 A3
Llysfaen Emergency GF 54 D2
LOCH AWE 87 B2
LOCH EILOUTWARD BOUND 90 C2
Loch View Farm (UWC) 104 C2
LOCHAILORT 89 A2
LOCHEILSIDE 89 B2
LOCHGELLY 92 C3
Lochiel OB (UWC) 90 C2
Lochinver Farm (UWC) 100 D1
LOCHLUICHART 98 D1
Lochluichart Station (UWC) 98 D1
Lochside (UWC) 103 B1
LOCHWINNOCH 83 A2
Lochwinnoch Crossovers 83 B2
Lock Lane (MCB) 122 A
LOCKERBIE 80 D3
Lockerbie North GSP 80 D3
Lockerbie South GSP 73 B1
Lockington (AHBC-X) 66 C2
LOCKWOOD 63 B3
Lockwood Tunnel 63 B3
Loco Yard Jn. 17 A1
Lodge Farm (OC) 3 A2
Lodge Farm (UWC) 51 A1
Logan's Road (CCTV) 132 D3
Lolham (CCTV) 51 B3
LONDON BRIDGE 114 A
London Bridge SB (L) 114 A
LONDON CHARING CROSS 114 A
LONDON FIELDS 109 A2
LONDON PADDINGTON 108 E
LONDON ROAD (Brighton) 14 E
LONDON ROAD (Guildford) 19 A3
London Road (ABCL) (Beccles) 45 A2
London Road (AHBC) (Spalding) 52 C3
London Road (TMO) (Bicester) 30 C2
London Road Jn. (Carlisle) 121 A
London Road Jn. (Derby) 122 A
London Road Viaduct 14 E
London Road Yard 121 A
London Tunnel 1 109 B2
London Tunnel 2 109 B2
LONDON VICTORIA 113
LONDON WATERLOO 113
Long Ashes (UWC) 74 C3
LONG BUCKBY 40 D2
Long Byre (AHBC-X) 74 D1
Long Dyke Jn. 117 A
LONG EATON 122 A
Long Eaton (CCTV) 122 A
Long Green FP (R/G-X) 33 B2
Long Lane (CCTV) 70 D2
Long Lanford Jn. 40 D2
Long Marsh (UWC) 67 B3
Long Plantation (UWC) 72 C3
LONG PRESTON 62 D1
Long Rock (CCTV) 1 A3
Long Salts 22 D3
Long Valley Sidings 18 D3
Longannet No. 4 (UWC) 85 A1
Longannet Power Station 85 A1
Longannet SB 85 A1
LONGBECK 71 A1
Longbeck (MCB) 71 A1
Longbeck SB (L) 71 A1
LONGBRIDGE 39 A2
LONGCROSS 19 A2
LONGFIELD 20 D2
Longforgan LC (MCB) 92 C2
Longforgan SB 92 C2
Longhedge Jn. 113
Longhirst (CCTV) 81 A3
Longlands Jn. 70 D2
Longlands Tunnel 70 D2
Longley (UWC) 100 C1
LONGNIDDRY 86 C1
LONGPORT 48 D1
Longport Jn. 48 D1
Longsight Depot Jn. 122 B
Longsight South Jn. 122 B
Longsight TMD 122 B
LONGTON 48 D1
Lonlas Tunnel 116 B
LOOE 3 A2
Lookout (UWC) 24 C3
Loover Barn 12 D2
LOSTOCK 123 A1
LOSTOCK GRALAM 56 D3
LOSTOCK HALL 62 E
Lostock Hall Depot Sdg 62 E
Lostock Hall Jn. 62 E
Lostock Jn. 123 A1
Lostock Works 56 D3
LOSTWITHIEL 2 D1
Lostwithiel (MCB) 2 D1
Lostwithiel Jn. 2 D1
Lostwithiel SB (LL) 2 D1
Lothbeg (UWC) 103 B3
LOUGHBOROUGH 50 C2
LOUGHBOROUGH JN. 112 C2
Loughborough North Jn. 50 C2
Loughborough South Jn 50 C2
Loughor Viaduct 24 D3
Lounge Jn. 50 C2
Lovers Walk Depot 14 E
Loversall Carr Jn. 129 A1
Loversall Jn. 129 A1
Low Eggborough (UWC) 64 D3
Low Ellers Curve Jn. 129 A1
Low Fell Jn. 130 A
Low Gates (MCB) 70 D2
Low Gates LC SB 70 D2
Low Gill (former) 68 D2
Low House (MCB) 74 C2
Low House Crossing SB 74 C2
Low Mill (R/G) 74 C2
Low Moor (CCTV) 62 D2
Low Moor Farm (UWC) 64 C1
Low Row (MCB) 74 D2
Low Row SB 74 D2
Low Scampston (AHBC-X) 71 B3
Low Street (CCTV) 21 A2
LOWDHAM 50 D1
Lowdham GF 50 D1
Lowdham SB 50 D1
Lower Bailey 2 (UWC) 37 A2
Lower Barn Farm (UWC) 28 C2
Lower Barn No. 1 12 D2
Lower Burton Farm (UWC) 38 C3
Lower Crianlarich 88 D2
Lower Cullernie (UWC) 99 B2
Lower Hall (UWC) 37 A2
Lower House Farm (UWC) 37 A2
Lower Radway Green (UWC) 48 D1
Lower Shakespeare Cliff Shaft 14 D1
Lower Stannage Farm (UWC) 37 B2
LOWER SYDENHAM 112 D2
Lower Trenowin (UWC) 1 A2
LOWESTOFT 45 B2
Lowestoft SB (L) 45 B2
Lowfield (UWC) 64 D3
Lowthorpe (AHBC-X) 66 C1
Lowton Jn. 56 C1
Loxley Lane (AHBC-X) 49 A2
Lucker (CCTV) 81 A1
Lucks Road (AHBC-X) 52 C3
LUDLOW 38 C2
Ludlow Tunnel 38 C2
Luffenham (CCTV) 51 A3
Lugton SB 83 B3
Lund Lane (UWC) 65 A3
Lune Viaduct 62 C1
LUTON 31 B2
LUTON AIRPORT PARKWAY 31 B2
Luton North Jn. 31 A2
Luton South Jn. 31 B2
LUXULYAN 2 D1
Luxulyan Tunnel 2 D1
Lydd Town (TMO) 14 A2
Lydden Tunnel 14 D1
Lyde Court (UWC) 27 B1
LYDNEY 27 B3
Lydney (MCB) 27 B3
Lydney (MCB) 28 C3

LYE 39 A2
LYMINGTON PIER 9 B3
LYMINGTON TOWN 9 B3
Lymn Bank (AOCL-X) 52 E
LYMPSTONE COMMANDO 6 C3
LYMPSTONE VILLAGE 6 C3
Lynchat (UWC) 94 D2
Lyneham (UWC) 29 B2
Lynwilg No. 1 (UWC) 94 D1
Lyon Crossing 37 B2
Lyons Wood Farm (UWC) 47 B2
LYTHAM 61 B3

M

M69 Overbridge (UWC) 40 D1
MacBeaths (UWC) 103 B3
Macclesfield 57 A3
Macclesfield SB (MD) 57 A3
Macclesfield Tunnel 57 A3
Machen Fach Farm (UWC) 117 B
Machen Quarry 117 B
MACHYNLLETH 36 C1
Machynlleth SB (MH) 36 C1
Macleans (UWC) 89 A1
Macraes (UWC) 94 C2
Madeley Chord Jn 48 D1
Madeley Jn (Telford) 48 C3
Madeley Jn. SB (MJ) 48 C3
Madeley South Jn. 48 C3
Madryn Farm (UWC) 54 C2
Maes (ABCL) 35 A1
MAESTEG 25 B2
MAESTEG (EWENNY ROAD) 25 B2
Maesteg (UWC) 55 A2
Maes-y-Coed Farm (UWC) 36 E
Magdelen Road LC SB (MR) 43 B1
MAGHULL 55 B1
Maghull (CCTV) 55 B1
Magor 15 A1
MAIDEN NEWTON 7 B3
Maidendale 70 C1
MAIDENHEAD 19 A2
Maidenhead East 19 A2
MAIDSTONE BARRACKS 21 A3
Maidstone East 21 A3
Maidstone East SB (ME) 21 A3
MAIDSTONE WEST 21 A3
MaidstoneWest SB (MS) 21 A3
Maindee East Jn. 117 B
Maindee North Jn. 117 B
Maindee West Jn. 117 B
Maindy Bach (UWC) 26 C3
Mair No. 2 (Accom) 13 B2
Malden (CCTV) 111 B3
MALDEN MANOR 111 B3
MALLAIG 89 A1
Mallaig GF 89 A1
Malt House (UWC) 47 A3
Maltby Colliery SB (M) 58 D2
Malting Lane (AHBC-X) 52 C2
Maltings (UWC) 32 C3
MALTON 71 B3
Malton (MCB) 71 B3
Malton SB (M) 71 B3
MALVERN LINK 28 C1
Malvern Wells SB 28 C1
MANCHESTER AIRPORT 123 B3
Manchester International Depot 122 B
Manchester North SB (MN) 122 B
MANCHESTER PICCADILLY 122 B
MANCHESTER VICTORIA 122 B
Manchester Victoria East Jn. 122 B
Manchester Victoria West Jn. 122 B
MANEA 43 A1
Manea (MCB) 43 A2
Manea SB (M) 43 A1
Mann Island Jn. 125 B
Manning Upper House (UWC) 27 B1
MANNINGTREE 34 C2
Manningtree East Jn. 34 C2
Manningtree North Jn. 34 C2
Manningtree South Jn. (CCTV) 34 C2
Manor Farm (UWC) (Langworth) 60 C3
Manor Farm (UWC) (Saltmarche) 65 A3
Manor Farm (UWC) (Oxford) 30 C3
Manor Farm (UWC) (Melksham) 16 D2
Manor Farm 2 (UWC) (Bucknell) 37 B2
Manor Farm 3 (UWC) (Bucknell) 37 B2
Manor Farm No 1 (UWC) (Banbury) 30 C1
Manor Neuk (UWC) 91 A3
MANOR PARK 110 C2
Manor Powis (UWC) 91 A3
MANOR ROAD 55 B2
Manor Way (CCTV) 20 D1
MANORBIER 23 B3
Manorbier Newton (OC) 23 A3
Manorbier Station (AOCL) 23 B3
MANORS 130 A
Manse (UWC) 102 D2
MANSFIELD 58 D3
Mansfield Jn. 50 E
Mansfield Road (CCTV) 59 A3
MANSFIELD WOODHOUSE 58 D3
Mansfield Woodhouse Jn. 58 D3
Manson (R/G) 64 C2
Mantle Lane SB (ML) 50 C3
Manton Jn. 51 A3
Manton Jn. GF 51 A3
Manton Jn. SB (MJ) 51 A3
Manton North Jn. 51 A3
Manton Tunnel 51 A3
Manton Wood 58 D2
Manuells Farm 2 (UWC) 1 C1
MARCH 42 D1
March (MCB) 42 D1
March East Jn. 42 D1
March East SB (ME) 43 A1
March South (MCB) 42 D1
March South SB (MS) 43 A1
March West Jn. 42 D1
Marchey's House (MCB) 81 A3
Marchey's House Jn. 81 A3
Marchey's House SB 81 A3
Marchington Old Station (UWC) 49 A2
MARCHWOOD 9 B2
Marchwood 9 B2
Marchwood SB (MW) 9 B2
MARDEN 13 A1
Mare Brook (UWC) 29 A1
Mares (UWC) 28 D1
Mares Close (UWC) 76 C1
Margam Abbey Works 25 A2
Margam Depot 25 A2
Margam East 25 A2
Margam Middle Jn. 116 B
Margam Moors Jn. 25 A2
Margaretting FP (R/G) 33 A3
MARGATE 22 D2
Margate SB (GE) 22 D2
Marina (ABCL) 19 A1
Maritime Freightliner Terminal 9 E
Mark Beech Tunnel 12 D1
Markdhu No. 1 (UWC) 77 B2
MARKET HARBOROUGH 41 A1
MARKET RASEN 60 C2
Market Rasen Footpath (R/G) 60 C2
MARKINCH 92 C3
Marklach No. 1 (UWC) 77 B2
Marklach No. 3 (UWC) 77 B2
Markle (AHBC) 86 D1
MARKS TEY 33 B2
Marks Tey GF 33 B2
Marks Tey Jn. 33 B2
Marlborough Road (BW) 122 A
Marley Green (UWC) 47 B1
Marley Green Emergency Crossover GFs 47 B1
Marley Lane (CCTV) 13 A2
Marley Tunnels 4 C2
MARLOW 19 A1
MARPLE 124 D3
Marple North Tunnel 124 D3
Marple South Tunnel 124 D3
Marple Wharf Jn. 124 D3
Marr House Farm (UWC) 65 B3
Marrel (ABCL) 103 B2
Marriots (UWC) 50 D1
MARSDEN 57 B1
Marsh Brook (MCB) 37 B1
Marsh Brook SB 37 B1
Marsh Farm (OPEN) 66 C3
Marsh House (CCTV) 56 C2
Marsh Junction SB (M) 60 D1
Marsh Lane (ABCL) (Aylesbury) 30 D2
Marsh Lane (AHBC) (Immingham) 66 C3
Marsh Lane (UWC) (Stowmarket) 44 C3
Marsh Lane Jn. 127 B
Marsh Mills 116 A
Marsh West Jn. 60 C1
Marshalls (UWC) 63 A2
Marshgate Jn. 129 A1
Marshmoor 32 C3
Marshwood Farm No. 2 Crossing 7 A2
MARSKE 71 A1
Marston (AHBC-X) 31 A1
MARSTON GREEN 120 A
Marston Moor 64 D1
Marston on Dove (AHBC) 49 B2
Marston Vale SCC 31 A1
Martello Tunnel 14 D1
Marth Road (UWC) 60 C3
MARTIN MILL 14 D1
Martins 43 A1
MARTINS HERON 19 A2
Martins Lane (R/G) 61 B3
MARTON 71 A1
Marton Lane (ABCL) 71 A1
Maryburgh (UWC) 99 A2
MARYHILL 131 B1
Maryhill Park Jn 131 B1
MARYLAND 109 B2
Maryland East Crossovers 110 C2
MARYLEBONE 108 G
Marylebone ASC (ME) 108 G
MARYPORT 73 A3
Maryport (CCTV) 73 A3
Maryport Station SB (MS) 73 A3
Masborough Jn. 128 A1
Masborough Sorting Sidings South Jn. 128 A1
Masons 1 (UWC) 23 B2
Masters (UWC) 16 C3
MATLOCK 58 C3
MATLOCK BATH 49 B1
Matlock GF 58 C3
Matt Pitts Lane (AOCL-X) 52 E
Mauchline SB 78 D1
Maud Foster (AHBC) 52 C1
MAULDETH ROAD 124 C2
Maxey (CCTV) 51 B3
MAXWELL PARK 133
Maxwelltown 73 A1
MAYBOLE 78 C2
Maylord (UWC) 37 A2
Maypole Rasen (UWC) 60 C2
Mays (CCTV) 19 A2
MAZE HILL 112 D2
McDougall Crossing 21 A3
McIvors (UWC) 103 B3
McNicols (UWC) 102 C2
Mead Lane FP (R/G-X) 32 C3
Meadow Croft Farm (UWC) 66 C3
Meadow Lane (CCTV) 122 A
Meadow Lane Jn. 122 A
MEADOWHALL 128 A1
Meads (R/G-X) 7 A1
Meads Farm Crossing 7 B2
Meads Lane (UWC) 72 C3
Meaford Crossing (CCTV) 48 D2
Meardsall Lane (UWC) 59 B3
Meddiant Isaf (UWC) 54 C2
Meddiant No.3 (UWC) 54 C2
Meddiant No.4 (UWC) 54 C2
Meddiant No.5 (UWC) 54 C2
Medge Hall (MCG) 59 A1
Medhurst Row (R/G) 12 D1
Medhurst Row 20 D3
Medway Viaduct 21 A3
Meir Tunnel 48 D1
Melbourne Jn. 122 A
Meldon Quarry 5 A3
MELDRETH 32 C1
Meldreth Road (AHBC) 32 C1
MELKSHAM 16 D2
Mellaig No. 1 (UWC) 102 D1
Melling Tunnel 62 C1
Mellis (AHBC-X) 44 D2
Melrose Avenue (UWC) 55 B2
MELTON 34 D1
Melton (AOCL) 34 D1
Melton Jn. & GF 50 B3
Melton Lane (MCB) 65 B3
Melton Lane SB 65 B3
MELTON MOWBRAY 50 B3
Melton Station SB 50 D2
Menadue (UWC) 2 D1
Menai Bridge North Jn. 53 B2
Menai Bridge South Jn. 53 B2
MENHENIOT 3 A2
MENSTON 63 B2
MEOLS 55 B2
MEOLS COP 61 B3
MEOPHAM 20 D2
Mercer's (UWC) 123 B3
Merchants Quay (UWC) 73 A3
Merehead Quarry 16 C3
Merehead Quarry Jn. 16 C3
Merllyn (MCG) 35 A1
Merrick No. 2 (Accom) 13 B2
Merrick No. 3 (Accom) 13 B2
Merrings (UWC) 21 A1
Merryhill (TMO) 85 A1
MERRYTON 84 C3
Mersey Tunnel 125 B
Merseyrail SB (ML) 125 A
Mersham Tunnel 14 C1
MERSTHAM 20 C3
Merstham Tunnel 20 C3
MERTHYR TYDFIL 26 C3
MERTHYR VALE 26 C1
METHERINGHAM 60 C3
Methil Dock 92 D3
Methley Jn. 64 C3
Methley North (R/G) 64 C3
METRO CENTRE 130 A
Metro-Cammell GF 120 A
Metropolitan Jn. 114 A
Meusydd Mill (UWC) 24 D2
MEXBOROUGH 58 D1
Mexborough Jn. 58 D1
MG Rover Longbridge Works (oou) 39 A2
MICHELDEVER 18 C3
Mickle Trafford SB (MT) 56 C3
MICKLEFIELD 64 D3
Micklefield Jn. 64 D2
Mickleham Tunnel 19 B3
Micklewood No. 2 (UWC) 38 C1
Mickley (R/G) 75 B2
Mid Cannock Colliery GF 49 A3
Midcalder Jn. 85 A2
Middle Drove (R/G) 42 D1
Middle Hill Tunnel 16 C2
Middle Jn. 21 B3
Middle Road Crossing 8 D1
Middle Siding East GF 119 B
Middle Stoke 21 B2
Middlemere (AHBC) 43 A2
MIDDLESBROUGH 130 C
Middlesbrough Goods Yard 130 C
Middlesbrough SB (M) 130 C
Middleton (ABCL) 45 A3
Middleton Place (UWC) 67 A2
Middleton Towers 43 B1
Middleton Towers No. 6 (TMO) 43 B1
Middleway (CCTV) 2 D1
Middlewich Loop 56 D3
MIDDLEWOOD 124 D3
Middlewood Tunnel 124 D3
Midfearn (UWC) 102 C2
Midge Hall SB (MH) 62 C3
MIDGHAM 18 C2
Midgham (CCTV) 18 C2
Midland Yard Jn. 40 C1
Midley (OPEN) 13 B2
Milburn Jn. 99 B2
Mildearie No. 2 (UWC) 101 A2
Mile Drove 22 D3
Mile End (AHBC-X) 43 B2
Miles Platting Jn. 122 B
MILFORD 11 A1
Milford (AHBC) 11 A1
MILFORD HAVEN 23 A3
Milford Jn. 48 D2
Milford Jn. 64 D3
Milford SB (M) 64 D3
Milford Tunnel 49 B1
Mill Dam (UWC) 67 B3
Mill Deeping (UWC) 50 B3
Mill Drove (AHBC-X) 43 A2
Mill Farm Crossing 7 B2
Mill Green LC SB (MG) 52 C2
Mill Hall 21 A3
MILL HILL 62 D3
MILL HILL BROADWAY 19 B1
Mill Lane (UWC) 65 B3
Mill Lane Jn. 41 A2
Mill Lane Jn. SB (M) 63 B3
Mill Path (Footpath) 8 D1
Mill Race Jn. 128 A1
Mill St (TMO) 62 E
MILLBROOK (Southampton) 9 E
MILLBROOK (Beds) 31 A1
Millbrook Freightliner Terminal 9 E
Millburn Grange (UWC) 40 C2
Millens (UWC) 90 D2
Millerhill East Jn. 86 E
Millerhill SB 86 E
Millerhill South Jn. 86 E
Millerhill West Jn. 86 E
Millerhill Yard 86 E
Millers (UWC) 67 B3
MILLFIELD 76 D2
Millfield Farm (UWC) 65 A2
MILLIKEN PARK 83 B2
MILLOM 67 B3
Millom SB 67 B3
MILLS HILL 124 C1
Millstead Crossing 21 A3
Milltown Viaduct 2 D1
Millwood Tunnel 63 A3
Milner Royd Jn. 63 B3
Milner Royd Jn. SB (MR) 63 B3
MILNGAVIE 131 B1
MILNROW 57 A1
Milnthorpe No.1 GF 68 C3
Milnthorpe No.2 GF 68 C3
Milton 18 C1
Milton Court Crossing 19 B3
Milton Fen (AHBC) 43 A3
Milton Keynes Nth Jn. 31 A1
Milton Keynes Sth Jn. 31 A1
Milton Keynes Central 30 D1
Milton No. 1 (UWC) 104 D2
Milton of Gollanfield (UWC) 99 B2
Milton of Larg No. 1 (UWC) 77 B3
Milton of Larg No. 2 (UWC) 77 B3
Milton Siding 18 E
Milton Village (MCB) 74 C2
Miltonise (UWC) 77 B2
Milverton Jn. 40 A3
Minety (MCG) 16 D1
MINFFORDD 35 B1
Minffordd Quarry (UWC) 35 B1
MINSTER 22 D3
Minster (R/G) 22 D3
Minster East Jn. 22 D3
Minster South Jn. 22 D3
Minster West SB (EBE) 22 D3
Mintholme (CCTV) 62 C3
MIRFIELD 63 B3
Mirfield East Jn. 63 B3
MISTLEY 34 C2
Mistley (Footpath) (R/G) 34 C2
MITCHAM EASTFIELDS 111 B3
MITCHAM JUNCTION 111 B3
Mitre Bridge Jn. 115
Moat Farm No 1 (UWC) 30 D2
Moat Hills (CCTV) 129 A1
MOBBERLEY 56 D2
Mobberley (MCB) 56 D2
Mobberley SB 56 D2
MOD Annan 73 B1
MOD Ashchurch 28 D1
MOD Caerwent 15 B1
MOD Ernesettle 116 A

MOD Kineton	40	C3
MOD Long Marston	39	B3
MOD Longtown	74	C1
MOD Ludgershall	17	B3
MOD Marchwood	9	B2
MOD Sidings (Chippenham)	16	D2
MOD Sidings (Redmire)	69	B2
MOD Smalmstown	74	C1
Moel Llys Tunnel	54	C2
Moira West SB (MW)	49	B3
Molewood Tunnel	32	C2
Molinnis (AOCL)	2	C1
Mona (UWC)	54	C2
MoncrieffeTunnel	91	B2
MONIFIETH	92	D1
Monk Bretton Loop	58	C1
MONKS RISBOROUGH	30	D2
Monk's Siding SB	126	B
Monkton Court	22	D3
Monkton GF	78	C1
Monktonhall Jn.	86	E
Monkwearmouth Jn.	76	D2
Monsanto GF	117	B
Monsanto/BASF (AOCL)	130	C
MONTPELIER	118	
Montpelier Jn.	14	E
Montpelier Tunnel	118	
MONTROSE	95	B2
Montrose North SB	95	A2
Montrose South Jn.	95	A2
Montrose South SB	95	A2
Moor Farm (UWC)	122	A
Moor Farm 1 (UWC)	67	B3
Moor Lane (UWC) (Elsham)	59	B1
Moor Lane (UWC) (Loughborough)	50	C3
Moor Lane Tunnels	123	A1
MOOR PARK	31	A3
Moorcock Tunnel	69	A2
Moores	43	A3
MOORFIELDS (DEEP LEVEL)	125	B
MOORFIELDS (LOW LEVEL)	125	B
MOORGATE	109	A3
Moorlands Farm (UWC)	65	A3
MOORSIDE	123	B1
Moorswater	3	A1
Moorswater (OC)	3	A2
Moorswater Viaduct	3	A2
MOORTHORPE	58	C1
Moorthorpe Jn.	58	C1
Moorthorpe SB (M)	58	C1
Moortown (AHBC-X)	60	C1
Morangie (UWC)	102	D2
MORAR	89	A1
Morar (AOCL)	89	A1
MORCHARD ROAD	5	B2
MORDEN SOUTH	111	B3
MORECAMBE	61	B1
Morecambe Jn. GF	61	B1
Morecambe South Jn.	62	C1
MORETON (Dorset)	8	C3
MORETON (Wirral)	125	A
Moreton (AHBC)	8	C3
Moreton (UWC)	23	B3
Moreton Cutting	18	E
MORETON-IN-MARSH	29	A1
Moreton-in-Marsh SB	29	A1
Moreton-on-Lugg	27	B1
Moreton-on-Lugg SB	27	B1
Morfa Main (UWC)	24	C3
MORFA MAWDDACH	35	B2
Morfa No.1 (UWC)	35	B1
Morfa-Rhydd-y-Pwll (UWC)	54	C2
Morlais Jn.	24	D3
Morlanga (UWC)	26	C3
MORLEY	64	C3
Morley Tunnel	64	C3
MORPETH	81	A3
Morpeth Electrification Depot	81	A3
Morpeth Jn.	81	A3
Morpeth North Jn.	81	A3
Morpeth SB (M)	81	A3
Morris Cowley GF	30	C3
Morris Farm No. 2	8	D1
Morris Hill (CCTV)	28	D2
Morris Motors GF	30	C3
Morse Gorse (UWC)	49	A3
Morston Hall (AHBC)	34	D2
MORTIMER	18	D2
MORTLAKE	111	B2
Mortlake (CCTV)	111	B2
Morton	58	C3
Morton Carr (AOCL)	71	A1
Morton Grange Farm No. 4 (UWC)	71	A1
Morvich No. 1 (UWC)	102	D1
Morvich No. 3 (UWC)	102	D1
Morvich No. 4 (UWC)	102	D1
Morvich No. 6 (UWC)	102	D1
Morvich No. 7 (UWC)	102	D1
Morvich No. 8 (UWC)	102	D1
Moseley Tunnel	120	A
MOSES GATE	123	B1
Moses Gate Jn.	123	B1
Mosley St GF	49	B2
Moss (MCB)	64	D3
Moss (Tip)	67	A3
Moss Lane (UWC)	124	C2
Moss Road (UWC)	83	A1
MOSS SIDE	61	B3
Moss Side (ABCL)	61	B3
Mossband Jn.	74	C1
Mossend Jns.	132	D3
Mossend Yard	132	D2
Mosset Park (UWC)	100	C1
Mossgiel Tunnel	78	D1
MOSSLEY	124	D1
MOSSLEY HILL	125	A
MOSSPARK	131	A2
MOSTON	124	C1
Mostyn Dock	55	A2
Mostyn SB	55	A2
MOTHERWELL	132	D3
Motherwell SC	132	D3
MOTSPUR PARK	111	B3
Motspur Park Jn.	111	B3
MOTTINGHAM	112	D2
Motts Lane FP (R/G-X)	33	B3
MOULDSWORTH	56	C3
Mouldsworth GF	56	C3
Moulin (UWC)	93	A2
Moulinearn (R/G)	93	B2
MOULSECOOMB	14	E
Moulton (AHBC-X)	44	D2
Mound Tunnels	85	E
Mount Bures (ABCL)	33	B2
MOUNT FLORIDA	133	
Mount Gould Jn.	116	A
Mount Pleasant (CCTV)	9	E
Mount Pleasant Tunnel (Hastings)	13	B3
Mount Pleasant Tunnel (Liverpool)	125	B
Mount Street Tunnel	112	D1
MOUNT VERNON	132	C2
Mountain (OPEN)	13	B2
MOUNTAIN ASH	26	C1
Mountains No. 29 (UWC)	51	B1
Mountfield Sidings GF	13	A2
Mountfield Tunnel	13	A2
Mountnessing Jn.	21	A1
Mountsorrel	50	C3
Mountsorrel LC	50	B3
Mow Cop (CCTV)	48	D1
Moy loop	99	B3
MPV Depot	114	B
Mucking (AHBC)	21	A2
Mucky Lane (UWC)	50	B3
Mud Lane (UWC)	15	A2
MUIR OF ORD	99	A2
MUIREND	131	B3
Muirend GF	131	B3
Muirhouse Central Jn.	133	
Muirhouse Farm (UWC)	73	B1
Muirhouse North Jn.	133	
Muirhouse South Jn.	133	
Munceys	43	A3
Munllyn (UWC)	37	A1
Murdercombe Tunnel	16	C3
Murie (AHBC)	92	C2
Murthly (AHBC)	91	B1
MUSSELBURGH	86	E
Muston (AHBC)	72	C3
Mutley Tunnel	116	A
Myremill (UWC)	78	C2
MYTHOLMROYD	63	A3
Mywars No. 2 (UWC)	36	C1
N		
Naas (AHBC)	27	B3
Nadins Swadlincote GF	49	B2
NAFFERTON	66	C1
NAILSEA & BACKWELL	15	B2
NAIRN	100	C2
Nairn East	100	C1
Nairn SB (NA)	100	C1
Nairn West	100	C1
Nairns (No. 117) (UWC)	43	A2
Nantmawr Branch Jn. (former)	47	A2
NANTWICH	48	C1
Nantwich (MCB)	48	C1
Nantwich Emergency GF	48	C1
Nantwich SB	48	C1
Nant-y-Cefn (UWC)	25	B1
Nantyci No. 2 (UWC)	24	C2
NARBERTH	23	B2
Narberth Tunnel	23	B2
NARBOROUGH	40	D1
Narborough (MCB) (CCTV)	40	D1
Narroways Hill Jn.	118	
Nashenden Crossovers	21	A3
National Railway Museum	130	B
Navarino Road Jn.	109	A2
NAVIGATION ROAD	123	B3
Navigation Road (CCTV)	123	B3
Nawlyns (UWC)	36	C1
Naworth (AHBC-X)	74	D2
Naylors (UWC)	51	A3
Neasden Jn.	108	C2
Neasden South Jn.	108	C2
NEATH	116	B
Neath and Brecon Jn.	116	B
Neath and Brecon Jn. SB	116	B
NEEDHAM MARKET	34	C1
NEILSTON	131	A3
NELSON	63	A2
Nene Carriage Sidings	42	E
NESTON	55	B2
Nether Lane (AHBC-X)	66	C1
Nether Poppleton (AHBC)	130	B
NETHERFIELD	50	E
Netherfield Jn.	50	E
Netherfield Jn. SB (NJ)	50	E
NETHERTOWN	67	A1
NETLEY	10	C2
Netwon Street Tunnel	83	A1
Neuadd (UWC)	36	D1
Neudd Farm 2 (UWC)	36	D3
Neville Hill Depot	127	B
Neville Hill East Jn.	127	B
Neville Hill West Jn.	127	B
NEW BARNET	32	C3
New Barnetby (MCG)	60	C1
NEW BECKENHAM	112	C2
New Bilton	40	E
New Bridge Lane (Footpath)	13	B1
NEW BRIGHTON	125	A
NEW CLEE	60	D1
NEW CROSS GATE	112	C2
NEW CUMNOCK	79	A2
New Cumnock SB	79	A2
New Earswick (UWC)	64	D1
NEW ELTHAM	112	D2
New England North	42	E
New England Sidings (West Yard)	42	E
New Fishbourne (AHBC)	10	D2
New Furnace Tunnel	63	B3
NEW HEY	57	A1
NEW HOLLAND	66	C3
New Holland Bulk Terminal	66	C3
New House Farm (UWC)	38	C1
New House Farm No. 43	33	A2
NEW HYTHE	21	A3
New Inn (OPEN)	66	C3
New Kew Jn	111	B2
NEW LANE	62	C3
New Lane (AHBC)	56	C1
NEW MALDEN	111	B2
NEW MILLS CENTRAL	124	D3
New Mills Central SB	124	D3
NEW MILLS NEWTOWN	124	D3
New Mills South Jn.	124	D3
New Mills South Jn. SB	124	D3
New MillsTunnel	124	D3
NEW MILTON	9	A3
New Oak Farm (UWC)	65	A3
New Place (F/P)	11	B2
NEW PUDSEY	63	B2
NEW SOUTHGATE	20	C1
New St. North Tunnel	120	B
New St. South Tunnel	120	B
New York Farm (UWC)	64	C2
NEWARK CASTLE	51	A1
Newark Castle LC SB (NC)	51	A1
Newark Crossing	59	A3
Newark Crossing East Jn.	59	A3
Newark Crossing South Jn.	51	A1
NEWARK NORTH GATE	51	A1
Newark South Jn.	51	A1
Newbold Jn.	40	D2
NEWBRIDGE	26	D2
Newbridge Jn.	85	A2
NEWBURY	18	C2
NEWBURY RACECOURSE	18	C2
NEWCASTLE	130	A
Newcastle East Jn.	130	A
Newcastle Jn.	48	D1
Newcastle Rd (AHBC-X)	48	C1
Newcastle South Jn.	130	A
Newcastle West Jn.	130	A
Newcombes (UWC)	5	A3
NEWCRAIGHALL	86	E
NEWCROSS	114	A
Newham (CCTV)	81	A1
NEWHAVEN HARBOUR	12	C3
Newhaven Harbour RC	12	C3
Newhaven Harbour SB (NH)	12	C3
NEWHAVEN MARINE	12	D3
NEWHAVEN TOWN	12	D3
Newhaven Town	12	C3
Newhaven Town SB (CCO)	12	D3
NEWINGTON	21	B3
Newland East SB	28	C1
Newlands East (MCB)	38	D3
NEWMARKET	43	A3
Newnham Barton Farm (UWC)	5	A2
Newnham Tunnel	28	C3
NEWPORT (Cambs)	32	D2
NEWPORT (Gwent)	117	B
Newport Docks	117	B
Newport East Jn.	130	C
Newport SB (N)	117	B
Newport Tunnel (New)	117	B
Newport Tunnel (Old)	117	B
NEWQUAY	1	B1
Newsham (MCB)	76	C1
Newsham North Jn.	76	C1
Newsham Road (TMO)	76	C1
Newsham SB	76	C1
NEWSTEAD	50	C1
Newstead Tilford Road (AHBC)	50	D1
NEWTON (Glasgow)	132	C3
NEWTON (Manchester)	124	D2
Newton (UWC)	49	A2
NEWTON ABBOT	4	D1
Newton Abbot East Jn.	4	D1
Newton Abbot West Jn.	4	D1
NEWTON AYCLIFFE	70	C1
Newton East Jn.	132	C2
Newton Flotman (AHBC-X)	44	D1
Newton Heath TMD	124	C1
Newton Jn. (Birmingham)	120	A
Newton Jn. (Prestwick)	78	D1
Newton Lodge (UWC)	23	A3
Newton of Struthers (UWC)	100	D1
NEWTON ST CYRES	6	C3
Newton West Jn.	132	C2
Newton, Hamilton Jn.	132	C3
Newton, Kirkhill Jn.	132	C3
Newtonhill SB	96	D3
NEWTON-LE- WILLOWS	56	C2
Newton-le-Willows Jn.	56	C2
NEWTONMORE	94	C2
NEWTON-ON-AYR	78	C1
NEWTOWN	37	A1
Newtown GF	37	A1
Newtown Tunnel	124	D3
Newtown West	117	A
Niddrie South Jn.	86	E
Niddrie West Jn.	86	E
Niffany (UWC)	63	A2
Nigg (AHBC)	102	D3
Nine Elms Jn.	113	
NINIAN PARK	117	A
NITSHILL	131	A3
Noblethorpe (MCG)	59	A1
Noose Lane (CCTV)	121	B
NORBITON	111	B2
NORBURY	112	C3
Norbury Hollow (MCG)	124	C3
Norchard Farm 1 (UWC)	23	B3
Nordans Farm (UWC)	38	C3
Normanby Park GF	65	B3
NORMANS BAY	13	A3
NORMANTON	64	C3
Normanton (AHBC-X)	50	D2
North (FP)	81	A3
North (MCB)	81	A3
NORTH BERWICK	86	C1
NORTH CAMP	19	A3
North Carr (MCG)	59	A2
North Cove	45	B2
North DownsTunnel	21	A3
NORTH DULWICH	112	C2
North Erewash (CCTV)	122	A
North Fen (AHBC-X)	43	A2
North GF	35	B2
North Green (AOCL)	45	A3
North Halling	21	A3
North Jn. (Southport)	61	B3
North Jn. (Sunderland)	76	C2
North Kelsey (AHBC-X)	60	C1
North Kent East Jn.	114	A
North Lincoln Jn.	59	B1
North London Tunnel 2 Portal	110	D2
NORTH QUEENSFERRY	85	A1
North Queensferry Tunnel	85	A1
NORTH ROAD	70	C1
North Seaton (MCB)	81	A3
NORTH SHEEN	111	B2
North Somerset Jn.	119	B
North Stafford Jn. (Crewe)	48	E
North Stafford Jn. (Derby)	122	A
North Stoke Tunnel	11	A2
North Tees (AOCL)	130	C
North Tunnel	32	C2
NORTH WALSHAM	46	D2
NORTH WEMBLEY	107	B2
North Wembley Jn.	107	B2
NORTHALLERTON	70	D2
Northallerton East Jn.	70	D2
Northallerton High Jn.	70	D2
Northam Jn.	9	E
Northam Traincare Centre	9	E
NORTHAMPTON	41	A2
Northampton North Jn.	41	A2
Northampton South Jn.	41	A3
Northampton TMD	41	A2
Northchurch Tunnels	31	A2
Northcote 2 Crossing	6	D3
Northenden Jn.	124	C3
Northenden Jn. SB (NN)	123	B3
NORTHFAMBRIDGE	21	B1
NORTHFIELD	120	A
NORTHFLEET	20	D2
Northgate Street Tunnels	126	A
Northolt Jn.	107	A2
NORTHOLT PARK	107	A2
Northorpe SB (N)	59	B2
NORTHUMBERLAND PARK	20	C1
Northwall (R/G)	22	D3
Northway (AHBC)	28	D1
NORTHWICH	56	D3
Northwich East Jn.	56	D2
Northwich South Jn.	56	D3
Northwich Station Jn.	56	D3
Northwich West Jn.	56	D3
Norton (MCB)	64	D3

Pitmain No. 2 (UWC) 94 C2
Pitmedden (R/G) 96 D1
PITSEA 21 A1
Pitsea Hall (CCTV) 21 A1
Pitsea Jn. 21 A1
Pitts (UWC) 47 A2
PLAISTOW (LUL) 110 C2
Plas Newydd (UWC) 36 D1
Plasau Clatter No. 1 (UWC) 36 D1
Plasser Works 107 B3
Plassers (AOCL) 107 B3
Plas-y-Court (AHBC) 47 A3
Platforms 20-24(oou) 113
Platts (UWC) 64 D3
Plean Jn. SB 84 D1
Pleasants (R/G) (UWC) 43 A1
PLEASINGTON 62 D3
Pleasington Golf Club No. 1 (UWC) 62 C3
Plemstall (UWC) 56 C3
Plessey Crossovers 76 C1
Plessey Road (CCTV) 76 C1
PLOCKTON 97 A3
Plot (UWC) 50 D1
PLUCKLEY 13 B1
Plucks Farm 34 C2
PLUMLEY 56 D3
Plumley West SB 56 D3
PLUMPTON 12 C2
Plumpton Crossing 12 C2
Plumpton Loop 74 C3
PLUMSTEAD 112 D1
PLYMOUTH 116 A
Plymouth East GF 116 A
Plymouth Friary 116 A
Plymouth SB (P) 116 A
Poachins (UWC) 50 B3
Poden Farm (UWC) 29 A1
Point Pleasant Jn. 111 B2
POKESDOWN 9 A3
POLEGATE 12 D3
Polegate 12 D3
Polegate SB (PG) 12 D3
POLESWORTH 49 B3
Polhill Tunnel 20 D3
Pollock (UWC) 90 D3
POLLOKSHAWS EAST 133
POLLOKSHAWS WEST 133
POLLOKSHIELDS EAST 133
POLLOKSHIELDS WEST 133
Polmadie 133
Polmadie Maintenance Depot 133
POLMONT 84 D1
Polmont Jn 84 D1
Polmont SB 84 D1
Polperro Tunnel 2 C2
POLSLOE BRIDGE 6 C3
Polyapes (UWC) 111 A3
Pond Street 46 D2
PONDERS END 20 C1
Ponsandane (UWC) 1 A3
Ponsandane Sidings 1 A3
Ponsbourne Tunnel 32 C3
Pontamman Tunnel 24 D2
PONTARDDULAIS 24 D3
PontarddulaisTunnel 24 D3
PONTEFRACT BAGHILL 64 D3
Pontefract East Jn. 64 D3
PONTEFRACT MONKHILL 64 D3
PONTEFRACT TANSHELF 64 C3
Pontefract West Jn. 64 D3
Ponthir (UWC) 26 D2
PONTLOTTYN 26 C1
Pontrilas SB 27 A2
Pontrilas Tunnel 27 A2
Pontsarn (AHBC) 26 C3
PONTYCLUN 26 C2
Pontycymmer branch 25 B2
PONT-Y-PANT 54 C3
Pont-y-Pant Lower Tunnel 54 C3
Pont-y-Pant Upper Tunnel 54 C3
PONTYPOOL & NEW INN 26 D1
PONTYPRIDD 26 C2
Pontypridd Jn. 26 C2
Pontypridd South Jn. 26 C2
Pool Hey (AHBC) 61 B3
POOLE 8 D3
Poole (CCTV) 8 D3
Poole SB (PO) 8 D3
Pooles (UWC) 28 C2
Pooley Green (CCTV) 19 A2
Pools (UWC) 28 D1
Pools No. 2 43 B2
Popham No.1 Tunnel 18 C3
Popham No.2 Tunnel 18 C3
Poplar Drove No. 30 43 A2
Poplar Farm (MCG) 44 C1
POPPLETON 64 D1
Poppleton (MCG) 64 D2
Poppleton SB 64 D1
Pork Lane (AHBC) 34 C2
Port Boundary 117 B
Port Clarence GF 130 C
Port Elphinstone GF 96 C1
Port Farm 22 C3
PORT GLASGOW 83 A2
Port of Felixstowe South Terminal 34 D2
Port of Heysham (UWC) 61 B1
Port of Seaham Sidings 76 D2
PORT SUNLIGHT 125 A
PORT TALBOT 25 A2
Port Talbot (MCB) 116 B
Port Talbot East (Taibach) 116 B
PORT TALBOT PARKWAY 116 B
Port Talbot SB (PT) 116 B
Portbury Dock 118
Portbury Terminal Jn. 118
PORTCHESTER 10 C2
Portcreek Jn. 10 D3
Portgower No. 1 (UWC) 103 B2
Portgower Station (UWC) 103 B2
PORTH 26 C2
Porth Hir (UWC) 35 B1
Porthkerry No. 1 Tunnel 25 E
Porthkerry No. 2 Tunnel 25 E
PORTHMADOG 35 B1
Porthmadog (TMO) 35 B1
Portland Street (CCTV) 61 B3
PORTLETHEN 96 D2
Portobello Jn. (Paddington) 108 E
Portobello Jn. (Wolverhampton) 121 B
Portobello Jns (Edinburgh) 86 E
PORTSLADE 12 C3
Portslade (CCTV) 12 C3
PORTSMOUTH & SOUTHSEA 10 F
Portsmouth (R/G) 63 A3
PORTSMOUTH ARMS 5 A2
Portsmouth Arms 1 (UWC) 5 A2
Portsmouth Arms 2 (UWC) 5 A2
PORTSMOUTH HARBOUR 10 F
POSSILPARK & PARKHOUSE 131 B1
Post Office Lane (AHBC) 64 D3
Post Office No. 1 (UWC) 36 D1
Post Office No. 2 (UWC) 36 D1
Potteric Carr Jn. 129 A1
POTTERS BAR 32 C3
Potters Bar Tunnel 32 C3
Potters Grange Jn. 65 A3
Potters Lock No. 1 (UWC) 122 A
Poulters (UWC) 64 D2
Poulton Jn. 61 B2
Poulton SB (PT) 61 B2
POULTON-LE-FYLDE 61 B2
Pound Lane Crossing 7 B2
Poundbury Tunnel 8 C3
Pouparts Jn. 113
Powderhall Branch Jn. 86 E
Powderham (UWC) 6 C3
Powell (UWC) 27 A2
POYNTON 124 C3
Pratts Lower (R/G) 11 B2
PREES 47 B2
Prees (MCB) 47 B2
Prees SB 47 B2
PRESCOT 56 C2
Prescot SB 56 C2
PRESTATYN 55 A2
Prestatyn SB 55 A2
PRESTBURY 57 A2
Prestbury Tunnel 57 A2
PRESTON 62 E
Preston Brook Tunnel 56 C2
Preston Docks 62 E
Preston Fylde Jn. 62 E
Preston North Jn. 62 E
PRESTON PARK 14 E
Preston Park Jn. 14 E
Preston Ribble Jn. 62 E
Preston SB (PN) 62 E
Preston South Jn. 62 E
PRESTONPANS 86 C2
PRESTWICK INTL. AIRPORT 78 D1
PRESTWICK TOWN 78 C1
Price Church Farm (UWC) 27 A2
PRIESTHILL & DARNLEY 131 A3
PRIMROSE HILL 108 D2
Primrose Hill Jn. 108 D2
Primrose Hill Tunnels 108 C2
Prince of Wales (UWC) 47 B3
Prince of Wales Colliery 64 D3
Prince of Wales SB (P) 64 D3
Princes Bridge (AHBC) 10 D1
PRINCES RISBOROUGH 30 D2
Princes Risborough Jn. 30 D2
Princes St (AOCL) 83 A3
Princess Royal Distribution Centre 115
PRITTLEWELL 21 B1
Prologis Park Siding 40 C1
Proof House Jn. 120 B
PRUDHOE 75 B2
Prudhoe (MCB) 75 B2
Prudhoe SB(PE) 75 B1
PULBOROUGH 11 A2
Pulborough SB (PH) 11 B2
Pulford (AHBC) 47 B1
Pulford (AHBC) 55 B3
Pumpfield Farm (R/G) 9 B2
Pumphouse No. 122 (UWC) 52 C2
PURFLEET 20 D2
Purfleet (CCTV) 20 D2
Purfleet Rifle Range (UWC) 20 D2
PURLEY 112 C3
PURLEY OAKS 112 C3
Purton Collins Lane (AHBC) 17 A1
Purton Common (UWC) 17 A1
PUTNEY 111 B2
Puxton & Worle (MCB) 15 A2
PWLLHELI 35 A1
Pwllheli Goods (ABCL) 35 A1
Pye Road (UWC) 92 C2
Pyewipe Jn. 59 B3
Pyewipe Road SB (P) 60 D1
PYLE 25 B2
Pylle Hill GF 119 B

Q

Quadring (AHBC-X) 52 C2
Quainton Road (site of) 30 D2
QUAKERS YARD 26 C2
Quarrington (AHBC) 51 B1
Quarry Burn (UWC) 98 C1
Quarry Hill Jn. 127 B
Quarry Tunnel 20 C3
Quay Viaduct 10 C2
Quay Ward No. 1 (UWC) 36 C1
Quay Ward No. 2 (UWC) 36 C1
Quay Ward No. 3 (UWC) 36 C1
Quay Ward No. 4 (UWC) 36 C1
Queen Adelaide (AHBC-X) 43 A2
Queen St. North Jn. 117 A
Queen St. South Jn. 117 A
Queen Street High Level Tunnel 133
QUEENBOROUGH 21 B2
Queenborough Yard 21 B2
QUEENS PARK (Glasgow) 133
QUEENS PARK (London) 108 C3
QUEENS ROAD PECKHAM 112 C2
Queens Road Tunnel 109 A2
QUEENSTOWN ROAD (BATTERSEA) 113
QUINTREL DOWNS 2 C1
Quintrel Downs (ABCL) 2 C1
Quintshill EGF 73 B1
Quoiggs No. 1 (UWC) 91 A3

R

Rabber Farm (UWC) 37 A3
Racecourse Sidings GF 18 A2
Rackheath Road (AHBC-X) 45 A1
RADCLIFFE 50 E
Radford Jn. GF 122 A
RADLETT 31 B3
Radlett Jn. 31 B3
RADLEY 30 C3
Radway Green (CCTV) 48 D1
RADYR 117 A
Radyr Branch Jn. 117 A
Radyr Jn. 117 A
Radyr Junction SB (VR) 117 A
Raigmore (CCTV) 99 B2
Raikes (UWC) 36 D3
Rainbow Hill Jn.(former) 38 D3
Rainbow Hill Tunnel 38 D3
RAINFORD 56 C1
Rainford Jn. SB 56 C1
Rainham (CCTV) (Essex) 20 D1
RAINHAM (Essex) 20 D1
RAINHAM (Kent) 21 A3
Rainham SB (EU) (Kent) 21 B2
RAINHILL 56 C2
Raiths Farm FreightTerminal 96 D2
Rallt (UWC) 36 D1
Rampart Lane (UWC) 64 D3
Ramsey Road (AHBC) 42 D1
RAMSGATE 22 D3
Ramsgate SB (HE) 22 D3
RAMSGREAVE & WILPSHIRE 62 D3
Ranelagh Road (MCG) 33 E
RANNOCH 90 D3
Ranskill (MCB) 59 A2
Ranskill Loops 59 A2
Rat Hole No. 80 (UWC) 59 A2
Ratcliffe Jn. 122 A
Ratcliffe North Jn. 122 A
Ratcliffe Power Station 122 A
Ratcliffe South Jn. (OOU) 122 A
RAUCEBY 51 B1
Rauceby SB (RY) 51 B1
Raven (AOCL) 25 A1
RAVENGLASS 67 A2
Ravenhead Jn. 56 C2
RAVENSBOURNE 112 D2
Ravensbourne Jn. 112 C2
RAVENSTHORPE 63 B3
Ravenstruther 84 D3
RAWCLIFFE 65 A3
Rawcliffe (AHBC) 65 A3
Rawcliffe Branch (UWC) 65 A3
RAYLEIGH 21 A1
RAYNES PARK 111 B2
READING 119 A
Reading Depot 119 A
Reading Lane Jn. 109 A2
Reading New Jn. 119 A
Reading SB (R) 119 A
Reading Spur Jn. 18 D2
Reading Triangle Sidings 119 A
READING WEST 119 A
Reading West Jn. 119 A
Reads GF 26 C1
Rearsby (AHBC) 50 B3
Rearsby House Farm (UWC) 50 B3
Reasby Manor (UWC) 60 C2
Recreation 21 B2
Rectory Farm (UWC) 42 D3
Rectory Jn. 50 E
Rectory Jn. SB (RJ) 50 E
RECTORY ROAD 109 A2
Rectory Road (AHBC-X) 44 D2
Red Barns Tunnel 130 A
Red Cap Lane (ABCL) 52 C1
Red Cow (CCTV) 6 C3
Red Cross Lane (UWC) 43 A3
Red Hill Tunnel (Hereford) 27 B1
Red Hill Tunnels (E. Midlands) 122 A
Red House (Kelsale) 45 A3
Red House (UWC) 37 A1
Red House Farm (Suffolk) 34 D1
Red House Farm (UWC) (Blyth) 76 C1
Red House Farm No. 1 36 D1
Red Lane 64 C3
Red Van (UWC) 94 C3
REDBRIDGE 9 E
Redcar (MCB) 71 A1
REDCAR CENTRAL 71 A1
REDCAR EAST 71 A1
Redcar Ore Terminal Jn. 130 C
Redcar SB (R) 71 A1
REDDISH NORTH 124 C2
REDDISH SOUTH 124 C2
REDDITCH 39 A2
Redford Jn. 92 C3
REDHILL 114 D
Redhill Tunnel 114 D
REDLAND 118
Redland GF 43 B3
Redmire 69 B2
Redmoor (AOCL) 43 A1
Rednal Farm (UWC) 47 A2
REDRUTH 1 B2
Redruth Tunnel 1 B2
REEDHAM (Norfolk) 45 A1
REEDHAM (Surrey) 112 C3
Reedham Jn. 45 B1
Reedham Jn. SB (RJ) 45 A1
Reedham Swing Bridge SB (RB) 45 A1
Reeds Farm (UWC) 48 C1
Reepham (CCTV) 60 C3
Regent Street (CCTV) 44 C3
Regents Canal Jn. 108 D2
REIGATE 20 C3
Reigate SB (RG) 20 C3
Renishaw Park 58 C2
RENTON 83 B1
Renwick Road Jn. 110 D2
Reston GSP 82 C2
Reston Up GF 82 C2
RETFORD 59 A2
Retford North 59 A2
Retford South Jn. 59 A2
Retford Western Jn. 59 A2
RHIWBINA 117 A
Rhiwderin (AOCL) 117 B
Rhiwlas Hall No. 2 (UWC) 36 C1
Rhiwlas Hall No. 4 (UWC) 36 C1
Rhohm Haas (AOCL) 130 C
RHOOSE 26 C3
Rhosfach (UWC) 36 C1
Rhosferig Tunnel 36 D3
RHOSNEIGR 53 A2
Rhowniar (UWC) 35 B3
Rhydllyn 2 (UWC) 37 A3
Rhydwhimen (R/G) 37 A1
Rhyd-y-Fynnon Farm (UWC) 24 D2
RHYL 54 D1
Rhyl SB (RL) 54 D1
RHYMNEY 26 C1
RIBBLEHEAD 69 A3
Ribblehead GF 68 D3
Riccarton 78 D1
RICE LANE 125 A
Richard's (UWC) 6 C2
Richborough (AHBC) 22 D3
Richborough Castle 22 D3
RICHMOND 111 A2
Richmond Hill Tunnel 127 B
Richmond SB 111 A2
Rickerscote 48 D2
RICKMANSWORTH 31 A3
Ridden's Lane Crossing 12 C2
RIDDLESDOWN 112 C3
Riddlesdown Tunnel 112 C3
RIDGMONT 31 A1
RIDING MILL 75 B2
Riggmoor (UWC) 73 B1
Rigton (MCB) 64 C1
Rigton SB (RN) 64 C2
Rillington (AHBC-X) 71 B3
Rimmell's (UWC) 27 B1
Ripe (AHBC) 12 D3
Rippings (UWC) 50 B2
Rippins Main (UWC) 50 B3
Ripple Lane Yard 110 D2
RISCA & PONTYMISTER 117 B
Risca South Jn. 117 B
Risehill Tunnel 69 A2

Ris

She

Thingley Jn. 16 D2
Third Drove (AHBC-X) 43 A2
THIRSK 70 D3
Thislington Quarry 76 C3
Thomas (UWC) 27 A2
Thomas No. 1 (UWC) 37 A3
Thomas No. 2 (UWC) 37 A3
Thompsons (UWC) 63 B2
Thoresby Colliery 59 A3
Thoresby Colliery Jn. 59 A3
Thoresby Colliery Jn. SB 59 A3
THORNABY 130 C
Thornaby Motive Power Depot 130 C
Thornally No. 47 (UWC) 60 C2
Thornally No. 48 (UWC) 60 C2
Thorne Jn. 65 A3
Thorne Moorends (AHBC) 65 A3
Thorne No. 1 (AHBC) 59 A1
Thorne No. 2 (AHBC) 59 A1
THORNE NORTH 65 A3
THORNE SOUTH 59 A1
Thorney Marsh Lane Crossing 7 B1
Thorneycroft Sidings 18 C3
Thornfield House (UWC) 64 D3
THORNFORD 7 B2
Thornford Bridge Crossing 7 B2
Thornhill LNW Jn. 64 C3
Thornhill SB 79 B3
THORNLIEBANK 131 B3
THORNTON ABBEY 66 C3
THORNTON HEATH 112 C3
Thornton North Jn. 92 C3
Thornton South Jn. 92 C3
Thornton West Jn. 92 C3
THORNTONHALL 131 B3
Thorpe (AOCL) 58 D1
THORPE BAY 21 B1
Thorpe Common (UWC) 65 A3
THORPE CULVERT 52 E
Thorpe Culvert SB (TC) 52 E
Thorpe Gates (MCB) 64 D3
Thorpe Hall (RC [MCB]) 64 D3
Thorpe Jn. 44 E
Thorpe Lane (AHBC) (Trimley) 34 D2
Thorpe Lane (CCTV) (Staines) 19 A2
Thorpe Road (AHBC) 58 D1
Thorpe Yard 44 E
THORPE-LE-SOKEN 34 C2
Thorpe-le-Soken Jn. 34 C2
Thorpe-on-the-Hill (AHBC-X) 59 B3
Thorpes Bridge Jn. 122 B
Thorrington (CCTV) 34 C2
Thorton (TMO) 61 B2
THREE BRIDGES 12 C1
Three Bridges SB (T) 12 C1
Three Gates 34 C3
Three Gates (UWC) 15 B1
Three Horse Shoes No. 1 (AHBC-X) 42 D1
Three Horse Shoes No. 2 (AHBC-X) 42 D1
Three Horse Shoes No. 3 (AHBC-X) 42 D1
Three Horse Shoes SB (THS) 42 D1
THREE OAKS 13 B2
Three Spires Jn. 40 C2
Thrumpton SB (T) 59 A2
Thrumpton West Jn. 59 A2
Thryberg Jn. 58 D1
THURGARTON 50 D1
Thurgarton (AHBC) 50 D1
THURNSCOE 58 C1
Thurrock Viaduct 20 D2
Thursdale Jn. 76 C3
THURSO 104 C1
THURSTON 44 C3
Thurston (Footpath) 44 C3
Thurstonland Tunnel 57 B1
Thurstons Crossing 9 B1
Thwaite Gates (CCTV) 66 C3
Tidal Sidings GF 117 A
Tide Mills 12 D3
Tilbury Freightliner Terminal 20 D2
Tilbury Riverside 21 A2
TILBURY TOWN 21 A2
TILE HILL 40 C2
Tile Shed (AHBC-X) 76 D2
Tiled House Farm (AHBC) 43 A2
TILEHURST 18 D1
Tilehurst East 18 D2
Tillery (OPEN) 13 B2
TIMPERLEY 123 B3
Tinsley Avesta (TMO) 128 A1
Tinsley East Jn. 128 A1
Tinsley Green Jn. 12 C1
Tinsley Park Jn. 128 A1
Tinsley South Jn. 128 A1
Tinsley Yard 128 A1
Tinsley Yard SB (TY) 128 A1
Tinsleys (UWC) 52 C3
Tinwell (UWC) 51 B3
TIPTON 39 A1
Tipton (CCTV) 39 A1
Tir Isaf (UWC) 116 A
Tir-Allen Farm 1 (UWC) 36 E
Tir-Allen Farm 2 (UWC) 36 E
Tir-Allen Farm 3 (UWC) 36 E
TIR-PHIL 26 C1
Tirydail (ABCL) 24 D2
TISBURY 8 D1
Tisbury Quarry (R/G) 8 D1
Tisbury West (AHBC) 8 D1
Tiverton Loops 6 C2
TIVERTON PARKWAY 6 C2
Tivetshall (AHBC-X) 44 D2
Toadmoor Tunnel 50 C1
Toddington (AHBC) 11 B3
Todholes No. 1 (UWC) 104 C2
Todholes No. 2 (UWC) 104 C2
TODMORDEN 63 A3
Tofthill (UWC) 92 C2
Tolans (UWC) 55 B2
Toll of Cults (UWC) 101 B3
TOLWORTH 111 B3
Tomatin Loop 99 B3
Tomich No. 1 (UWC) 102 C1
Tomich No. 2 (UWC) 102 C1
Tomlinsons (UWC) 59 B3
TON PENTRE 25 B2
TONBRIDGE 12 D1
Tonbridge East Jn. 12 C1
Tonbridge SB (PE) 20 D3
TONDU 25 B2
Tondu Jn. 25 B2
Tondu SB 25 B2
TONFANAU 35 B2
Tonfanau (UWC) 35 B3
Tongside No. 1 (UWC) 104 C2
Tongside No. 2 (UWC) 104 C2
TONYPANDY 25 B2
TOOTING 111 B2
Topley Pike GF 57 B3
TOPSHAM 6 C3
Topsham (CCTV) 6 C3
Torcoed 2 (UWC) 25 B2
Torness Siding GSP 82 C1
Torphin (UWC) 85 A2
TORQUAY 4 D2
TORRE 4 D1
Torworth (CCTV) 59 A2
Totley Tunnel 58 C2
Totley Tunnel East SB 58 C2
TOTNES 4 C2
Totnes East 4 C2
Toton Down Marshalling Yard 122 A
Toton Jn. 122 A
Toton TMD 122 A
TOTTENHAM HALE 109 A1
Tottenham North Curve Tunnels 108 D2
Tottenham South Jn. 109 A1
TOTTON 9 B2
Totton (CCTV) 9 B2
Totton West Jn. 9 B2
Totton Yard 9 B2
Towan (UWC) 1 A2
Towers Farm (UWC) 124 C3
TOWN GREEN 55 B1
Towneley (MCB) 63 A3
Towneley Tunnel 63 A3
Towney (UWC) 18 C2
Townhill Jn. 85 A1
Townsend Crossing 8 D1
Traeth Mawr (ABCL) 35 B1
TRAFFORD PARK 123 B2
Trafford Park East Jn. 122 B
Trafford Park Reversing Line 122 B
Trafford Park West Jn. 123 B2
Tram Inn (MCB) 27 B1
Tram Inn SB 27 B1
Travel's Lane (AHBC) 9 B2
Tredington (AHBC) 28 D2
Trees (CCTV) 32 D2
Treeton Jn. 128 A1
Treeton South 128 A1
Treffeddian (UWC) 35 B3
Treffoliad Farm 1 (UWC) 36 E
TREFFOREST 26 C2
TREFFOREST ESTATE 26 C2
Tregoss Moor (AOCL) 2 C1
TREHAFOD 26 C2
TREHERBERT 25 B2
Trelavour Sidings 2 C1
Tremains DPL 25 B3
Tremorfa Works GF 117 A
Trencreek (AOCL) 1 B1
Trent East Jn. (Gainsborough) 59 A1
Trent East Jn. (Toton Yard) 122 A
Trent Jn. 65 B3
Trent Lane (UWC) 50 D1
Trent Lane Footpath (R/G) 50 E
Trent SB 122 A
Trent South Jn. 122 A
Trent Valley Jn. 40 E
Trent Valley Jn. No 1. 48 D2
Trent West Jn. 59 A2
Trent Yard 122 A
TREORCHY 25 B2
Tresithney 2 (UWC) 2 C1
Treverrin Tunnel 2 D1
Treviscoe Sidings 2 C1
Trewern Farm (UWC) 23 B2
Trewern Mill (UWC) 23 B2
TRIMLEY 34 D2
Trimley (CCTV) 34 D2
TRING 31 A2
Tring North Jn. 31 A2
Tring South Jn. 31 A2
Trinity Lane (MCG) 32 C3
Troad yr Rhin (UWC) 54 C2
TROED-Y-RHIW 26 C1
Troed-y-Rhiw Fedwen (UWC) 37 A2
Troed-Y-Rhiw South Jn. 26 C1
TROON 78 C1
Trotts Lane (AHBC) 9 B2
TROWBRIDGE 16 C2
Trowell South Jn. 122 A
Trowse Jn. 45 A1
Trowse Swing Bridge 44 E
Trowse Swing Bridge SB (T.B.) 44 E
Truro 1 B2
TRURO 2 C2
Truro (MCB) 1 B2
Truro SB (T) 1 B2
Tucker's (UWC) 16 C2
Tuckwells (UWC) 30 C3
Tuebrook Sidings 125 A
Tuffley 28 C2
TULLOCH 90 D2
TULSEHILL 112 C2
TUNBRIDGE WELLS 12 D1
Tunnel 23 131 A1
Tunnel 25 131 A1
Tunnel Road Tunnel 125 B
Tunnicliffs No. 1 (UWC) 49 A2
Tunstead Church Lane 46 D2
Tunstead Market Street (AHBC) 46 D2
Turf Lock (UWC) 6 C3
TURKEY STREET 32 C3
Turnchapel Branch Jn. 116 A
Turners Lane Jn. 127 A
Turton (AOCL) 62 D3
TUTBURY & HATTON 49 B2
Tutbury (MCB) 49 B2
Tutbury Crossing SB 49 B2
Tuxford GSP 59 A3
Tuxford No. 2 GF 59 A3
Tweedmouth Crossover 82 D2
Tweedmouth SB(TW) 82 D2
Twerton Long Tunnel 16 C2
Twerton Short Tunnel 16 C2
TWICKENHAM 111 A2
Twickenham Jn 111 A2
Two Mile Bottom (AHBC-X) 44 C2
TWYFORD 18 D2
Twyford East 18 D2
Twyford West 18 D2
TY CROES 53 A2
Ty Croes (MCG) 53 A2
Ty Croes SB 53 A2
TY GLAS 117 A
Ty Mawr Farm (UWC) 36 D1
Ty Pella (UWC) 36 C1
Ty-Ddu (UWC) 37 A3
Tyddyn-y-pwll (UWC) 36 D1
Tye Green Jn. 32 D2
TYGWYN 35 B1
Tygwyn (ABCL) 35 B1
Tyminster (CCTV) 11 A3
Ty'n Llan 1 (UWC) 35 B2
Ty'n Llan 3 (UWC) 35 B2
Ty'n-Ddol (UWC) 54 C2
TYNDRUM LOWER 88 D2
Tyndrum Lower (UWC) 88 D2
Tyne Yard 76 C2
Tyneside Central Freight Depot 130 A
Tyneside SB 130 A
Tynewydd 2 23 B2
Tyning 8 D1
Tynycerig 1 (UWC) 24 D3
Tynycerig 2 (UWC) 24 D3
Tynycerig 3 (UWC) 24 D3
Tynycynllwyn (UWC) 24 D3
Tyn-y-Maes (UWC) 36 E
Tyn-y-Morfa (MCG) 55 A2
Ty'n-yr-Wtre No. 2 (UWC) 36 D1
TYSELEY 120 A
Tyseley Depot 120 A
Tyseley No.1 SB (TY1) 120 A
Tyseley North Jn. 120 A
Tyseley South Jn. 120 A
Tytherington Tunnel 16 C1
Ty-Uchaf (AOCL) 25 A1
TYWYN 35 B3
Tywyn GF 35 B3

U

UCKFIELD 12 D2
UDDINGSTON 132 C2
Uddingston Jn. 132 C3
Uffington & Barnack (MCG) 51 B3
Uffington (Swindon) 17 B1
Uffington SB (UN) (Lincs) 51 B3
Ufford (ABCL) 34 D1
Ufton (AHBC) 18 C2
Ugley Lane (UWG) 32 D2
ULCEBY 66 C3
Ulceby Jn. (MCB) 66 C3
Ulceby Jn. SB (UJ) 66 C3
Ulceby North Jn. 66 C3
Ulceby South Jn. 66 C3
Ulgham Grange (CCTV) 81 A3
Ulgham Lane (CCTV) 81 A3
ULLESKELF 64 D2
ULVERSTON 67 B3
Ulverston SB (UN) 67 B3
UMBERLEIGH 5 A1
Umberleigh (AOCL) 5 A1
Umberleigh Barton 3 (UWC) 5 A1
Underhill (UWC) 67 B3
UNITED F.C. HALT 123 B2
Universal Grindling Wheel Works 48 D2
UNIVERSITY (Birmingham) 120 A
UNIVERSITY (Tyne & Wear) 76 D2
Unthank (TMO) 75 B3
UPHALL 85 A2
Uphill Jn. 15 A2
UPHOLLAND 56 C1
Upholland Tunnel 56 C1
UPMINSTER 20 D1
UPMINSTER BRIDGE (LUL) 20 D1
Upminster East Jn. 20 D1
Upminster IECC (UR) 20 D1
Upminster LUL Depot 20 D1
Upney Jn. 110 D2
UPNEY (LUL) 110 D2
Upper Cellws (UWC) 37 A3
Upper Chapel Hill Farm (UWC) 23 B2
Upper Denton (AHBC-X) 74 D1
Upper Denton West (UWC) 74 D1
UPPER HALLIFORD 111 A2
UPPER HOLLOWAY 108 D1
Upper Holloway SB (UH) 108 D2
Upper Leigh (AHBC-X) 49 A2
Upper Llegodig (UWC) 37 A1
Upper Portland (AHBC) 50 C1
Upper Trenowin (UWC) 1 A2
UPPER TYNDRUM 88 D2
UPPER WARLINGHAM 20 C3
Upperby Bridge Jn. 121 A
Upperby Jn. 121 A
Upperby Yard 121 A
Upperby Yard GF 121 A
UPTON 125 A
Upton Lovell (AHBC) 16 D3
UPTON PARK (LUL) 110 C2
UPWEY 8 E
Urlay Nook (MCB) 70 D1
Urlay Nook SB (UN) 70 D1
URMSTON 123 B2
Urrard No. 1 (UWC) 93 A2
Urrard No. 2 (UWC) 93 A2
Usan Jn 95 B2
Usan SB 95 B2
UTTOXETER 49 A2
Uttoxeter Racecourse (UWC) 49 A2
Uttoxeter SB 49 A2

V

Vale Viaduct 12 C2
Vale Wood Crossing 11 B2
VALLEY 53 A1
Valley (MCB) 53 A2
Valley SB (VY) 53 A2
Valleyfield Colliery (UWC) 85 A1
Vange Wharf (CCTV) 21 A1
Vaseys (UWC) 70 D2
VAUXHALL 113
Vauxhall Jn. 120 B
Veals Lane (AHBC) 9 B2
Viaduct Maintenance (UWC) 32 C3
Victoria Road (CCTV) 45 B2
Victoria SB (VC & VS) 113
Victory (AHBC) 6 D1
Vine Road (CCTV) (Hounslow Line) 111 B2
Vineyard Farm No. 1 (UWC) 27 A2
Vineyard Farm No. 2 (UWC) 27 A2
VIRGINIA WATER 19 A2
Virtual Quarry GF 121 A
Vitriol Works SB 124 C1
Voltaire Jn. 113

W

Wadborough (AHBC) 28 D1
WADDON 112 C3
WADHURST 12 D1
Wadhurst GF 12 D1
Wadhurst Tunnel 12 D1
Wagon Lane (AHBC) 13 A1
Wagon Repairs GF 121 A
WAINFLEET 52 E
Wainfleet (UWC) 52 E
Wainfleet Bypass (AHBC-X) 52 E
Wainfleet LC SB 52 E
Wakefield Europort 64 C3
WAKEFIELD KIRKGATE 127 A
Wakefield Kirkgate East Jn. 127 A
Wakefield Kirkgate SB (K) 127 A
Wakefield Kirkgate West Jn. 127 A
Wakefield Road Tunnel 63 B3
WAKEFIELD WESTGATE 127 A
Wakefield Westgate South Jn. 127 A
Waldersea (TMO) 52 D3
Walesby (AHBC-X) 60 C2
WALKDEN 123 B1
Walkden SB (WN) 123 B1
Walkers (UWC) 70 D2
Walkers No. 63 (UWC) 59 B3

Wall End 22 D3
WALLASEY GROVE ROAD 125 A
WALLASEY VILLAGE 125 A
Wallers Ash 10 C1
Wallers Ash Tunnel 10 C1
WALLINGTON 112 C3
Wallington Viaduct 10 C2
Wallneuk Jn. 131 A2
Wallsend (CCTV) 13 A3
WALLYFORD 86 C2
WALMER 22 D3
Walnut Grove (UWC) 92 C2
Walpole (CCTV) 46 D2
WALSALL 121 B
Walsall North Jn. 121 B
Walsall Pleck Jn. 121 B
Walsall PSB (WL) 121 B
Walsall South Jn. 121 B
WALSDEN 63 A3
Walters Hall 22 D3
WALTHAM CROSS 32 C3
Waltham Nurseries (UWC) 67 B3
WALTHAMSTOW CENTRAL 109 B1
WALTHAMSTOW QUEENS ROAD 109 B1
WALTON 125 A
Walton Common 21 A2
Walton Jn. (Aintree Line) 125 A
Walton Street (CCTV) 66 C3
Walton Street Jn. 66 C3
WALTON-ON-THAMES 111 A3
WALTON-ON-THE-NAZE 34 D2
Wamphray GSP 80 D3
WANBOROUGH 19 A3
WANDSWORTH COMMON 111 B2
WANDSWORTH ROAD 113
WANDSWORTH TOWN 111 B2
Wansdyke (UWC) 17 B2
Wansford Road (CCTV) 66 C1
WANSTEAD PARK 110 C2
Wantage Road 17 B1
WAPPING 114 A
WARBLINGTON 10 D2
Warblington (CCTV) 10 D2
Warden (AHBC-X) 75 A1
Wards (Kent) 13 A1
Wards (UWC) (Lancs) 68 D3
Wards (UWC) (Lincs) 51 B3
Wards (UWC) (Moray) 100 D1
Wards Dyke (UWC) 52 C1
Wards Sidings GF 51 B3
WARE 32 C2
Ware (CCTV) 32 C3
WAREHAM 8 D3
Wareham SB (WR) 8 D3
Warehorne (AHBC) 13 B1
WARGRAVE 18 D1
Warkworth (CCTV) 81 A2
WARMINSTER 16 C3
WARNHAM 11 B1
Warnham Station Road (R/G) 11 B1
Warren Hill Tunnel 43 B3
Warren House 21 A3
Warren House (MWL) 50 D1
Warrenhill (UWC) 73 A1
WARRINGTON BANK QUAY 126 B
WARRINGTON CENTRAL 126 B
Warrington Central SB (WC) 126 B
Warrington North Jn. 126 B
Warrington SB (WN) 126 B
Warrington South Jn. 126 B
Warsop Jn. 58 D3
WARWICK 40 C3
WARWICK PARKWAY 40 C3
Warwickshire Oil Sidings 40 C1
Washstones (R/G) (UWC) 50 B3
Washwood Heath East Jn. 120 A
Washwood Heath SF 120 A
Wassicks (AHBC-X) 44 C3
Waste Bank Tunnel 74 D3
Waste Recycling (Claydon) 30 D1
Water Eaton (UWC) 30 C2
Water Lane (UWC) 6 C3
WATER ORTON 120 A
Water Orton East Jn. 39 B1
Water Orton West Jn. 120 A
Water Pit Lane 46 D2
WATERBEACH 43 A3
Waterbeach (AHBC) 43 A3
Waterfields No. 1 (UWC) 64 D3
Waterford (RC) 100 C1
WATERINGBURY 21 A3
Wateringbury SB (WB) 21 A3
Waterloo (AHBC) (Wokingham) 18 D2
Waterloo (CCTV) (Merseyside) 125 A
Waterloo (Llandrindod) 36 D2
WATERLOO (Merseyside) 125 A
WATERLOO EAST 114 A
Waterloo Yard (Exeter) 6 C3
Waterside 78 D2
Waterside (CCTV) 91 A3
Waterslack Quarry (UWC) 68 C3
Waterton (AOCL) 25 B3
Waterworks (UWC) 49 B3
Watery Lane S.F. (WL) 39 A1
Watery Road GF 47 A1
WATFORD HIGH STREET 31 A3
Watford Jn PSB (WJ) 31 B3
WATFORD JUNCTION 31 B3
Watford Lodge Tunnel 40 D2
WATFORD NORTH 31 B3
Watford North Jn. 31 B3
Watford South Jn. 31 B3
Watford Tunnel (Fast) 31 A3
Watford Tunnel (Slow) 31 B3
Wath (UWC) 73 A1
Watkins (UWC) 41 A1
WATLINGTON 43 B1
Watlington Road (CCTV) 43 B1
Watson (UWC) 29 A1
Watsons (UWC) 50 C3
Watten (AOCL) 104 D2
Watton (AHBC-X) 66 C2
WATTON-AT-STONE 32 C2
WAUN-GRON PARK 117 A
Waverley (East End) 85 E
Waverley (West End) 85 E
Wavertree Junction 125 A
WAVERTREE TECH. PARK 125 A
Way & Works Jn. 122 A
Weasel Hall Tunnel 63 A3
Weasenham Lane (TMO) 43 A1
Weaver Jn. (Dn) 56 C3
Weaver Jn. (Up) 56 C2
Weaverthorpe (MCG) 72 C3
Weaverthorpe SB 72 C3
Websters 32 D1
WEDGWOOD 48 D1
Wedgwood (CCTV) 48 D1
Wednesbury Town Jn. 39 A1
Wednesfield Heath Tunnel 121 B
Week Street Tunnel 21 A3
WEELEY 34 C2
Weer Lane (UWC) 49 B2
WEETON 64 C2
Weig Lane (AOCL) 36 D1
Weish Highland Railway (Flat Crossing) 35 B1
Welbeck Colliery 58 D3
Welbeck Colliery Jn. 58 D3
Welbury (AHBC-X) 70 D2
WELHAM GREEN 31 B3
Wellhouse (UWC) 99 A2
Wellhouse Tunnel 57 B1
WELLING 112 D2
WELLINGBOROUGH 41 B2
Wellingborough North Jn. 41 B2
Wellington (AHBC) (Hereford) 27 B1
WELLINGTON (Shrops) 48 C3
Wellington Crossovers (Taunton) 6 D1
Wellowgate (CCTV) 60 D1
Wellpark Tunnel 83 A1
Wells Engine 43 A2
Wells Tunnel 12 D1
Welney Road (AHBC-X) 43 A2
WELSHPOOL 47 A3
Welshpool GF 47 A3
Welsh's Bridge Jn. 99 B2
Welton (MCG) 65 B3
Welton Crossover 60 C3
WELWYN GARDEN CITY 31 B3
Welwyn South Tunnel 32 C2
WEM 47 B2
Wem (MCB) 47 B2
Wem Emergency Crossover GFs 47 B2
Wem SB 47 B2
WEMBLEY CENTRAL 115
Wembley Central GF 115
Wembley Mainline SCC (WM) 115
WEMBLEY STADIUM 107 B2
Wembley Yard 115
Wembley Yard SB (WY) 115
Wembley Yard South Jn. 115
WEMYSS BAY 83 A2
Wemyss Bay Jn. 83 A2
WENDOVER 31 A3
Wenhaston (AOCL) 45 A2
WENNINGTON 68 D3
Wennington Crossover 20 D1
Wensum Jn. 44 E
Wentloog Freight Terminal East Jn. 117 B
Wentloog Freight Terminal West Jn. 117 B
Werneth Tunnel 124 C1
Wescoehill Tunnel 64 C2
West (OPEN) 76 D3
WEST ALLERTON 125 A
West Bank Hall (AHBC) 65 A3
West Bank Terminal (Ipswich) 33 E
West Barnes(CCTV) 111 B3
WEST BROMPTON 111 B2
West Burton East Jn. 59 A2
West Burton Power Station 59 A2
West Burton SB (WB) 59 A2
West Burton West Jn. 59 A2
WEST BYFLEET 19 A3
WEST CALDER 85 A2
West Calder Goods GF 85 A2
West Cowick (R/G) 65 A3
WEST CROYDON 112 C3
WEST DRAYTON 19 B1
West Drayton (TMO) 19 A1
West Drayton East 19 A1
West Drayton Jn. 19 A1
WEST DULWICH 112 C2
WEST EALING 107 B3
West Ealing Jn. 107 B3
West Grimstead Crossing 9 A1
WEST HAM (LUL) 109 B3
West Hampstead Jn. North 108 C2
West Hampstead Jn. South 108 C2
West Hampstead PSB 108 C2
WEST HAMPSTEAD THAMESLINK 108 C2
WEST HAMSTEAD 108 C2
West Heslerton (AHBC-X) 71 B3
West Holmes Jn. 59 B3
WEST HORNDON 20 D1
West House (TMO) 45 A3
WEST KILBRIDE 83 A3
West Kinnauld No. 2 (UWC) 102 D1
West Kinnauld No. 3 (UWC) 102 D1
WEST KIRBY 55 A2
West Lodge (UWC) 74 D2
West London Jn. (Clapham) 113
West London Jn. (Willesden) 115
West London Waste Transfer Stn 107 B3
WEST MALLING 21 A3
West Midlands SC 120 B
WEST NORWOOD 112 C2
West Norwood Jn. 112 C2
West of Scotland SC (G/GG) 133
West Parade North Jn. 66 C2
West River (R/G-X) 43 A2
WEST RUISLIP 19 B1
WEST RUNTON 46 C1
West Sleekburn Jn. 81 A3
WEST ST. LEONARD'S 13 A3
West Street (AHBC) 9 B2
West Street Jn. SB (WS) 52 C1
WEST SUTTON 111 B3
West Thurrock Jn. 20 D1
WEST WICKHAM 112 D3
WEST WORTHING 11 B3
West Worthing (CCTV) 11 B3
Westborough (Public BW) 51 A1
Westbrecks (AHBC) 59 A2
Westbrook Lane (R/G) 59 B3
WESTBURY 16 C3
Westbury (AHBC) 28 C2
Westbury (AHBC) 47 A3
Westbury East Loop Jn. 16 D3
Westbury Line Jn. 119 A
Westbury North Jn. 16 C2
Westbury SB (W) 16 D3
Westbury South Jn. 16 C3
WESTCLIFF-ON-SEA 21 B1
WESTCOMBE PARK 112 D2
WESTENHANGER 14 C1
Westenhanger Crossovers 14 C1
WESTER HALLES 85 E
Westerfearn (UWC) 102 C2
Westerfearn No. 1 (UWC) 102 C2
WESTERFIELD 33 E
Westerfield Jn. 33 E
Westerfield Station (AHBC) 33 E
Westerleigh Jn. 16 C1
Westerleigh Yard 16 C1
Western Entrance (CCTV) 66 C3
Western Growers 1 A2
Western Jn. 21 B3
Westernhanger SR 14 C1
WESTERTON 131 A1
Westerton Jn. 131 A1
Westford (Footpath) (R/G) 6 D2
Westford (UWC) 7 A2
WESTGATE-ON-SEA 22 D2
Westhall (ABCL) 45 A2
WESTHOUGHTON 123 A1
Westley Road (R/G) 43 A3
Westminster Tunnel 125 A
Weston 18 C3
Weston (AOCL) 45 A2
WESTON MILTON 15 A2
Weston Rhyn (AHBC) 47 A2
Westons (UWC) 49 A2
Weston-S-M Up GF 15 A2
WESTON-SUPER-MARE 15 A2
Wests Bridge Farm (UWC) 27 A2
Westwood Sidings 42 E
WETHERAL 74 C2
WEYBRIDGE 19 B3
WEYMOUTH 8 E
Weymouth Jn. 8 E
WEYMOUTH QUAY 8 E
WHALEY BRIDGE 57 A2
WHALLEY 62 D2
Wharf Road (AHBC-X) 32 C3
Whatley Quarry 16 C3
WHATSTANDWELL 49 B1
Whatstandwell (UWC) 49 B1
Whatstandwell Tunnel 49 B1
Wheeler Street Tunnel 21 A3
Wheler Street Jn. 109 A3
WHIFFLET 132 D2
Whifflet North Jn. 132 D2
Whifflet South Jn. 132 D2
Whiley Hill (AHBC) 70 C1
WHIMPLE 6 C3
WHINHILL 83 A2
Whipps Farm 20 D1
Whisby Quarry (UWC) 59 B3
Whissendine LC SB 51 A3
WHISTON 56 C2
Whitacre GF 39 B1
Whitacre Jn. 39 B1
Whitbeck (AOCL) 67 A3
WHITBY 71 B1
Whitchester Tunnel 74 D1
WHITCHURCH (Cardiff) 117 A
WHITCHURCH (Hants) 18 C3
WHITCHURCH (Shrops) 47 B2
Whitchurch SB 47 B1
White Hart (CCTV) 111 B2
WHITE HART LANE 20 C1
White Hart Lane GF 20 C1
White House Mill (UWC) 23 B2
WHITE NOTLEY 33 A2
White Notley (ABCL) 33 A2
Whiteball Tunnel 6 D2
Whitebridge (UWC) 94 C3
WHITECHAPEL 109 A3
WHITECRAIGS 131 B3
Whitehall (R/G) 22 C3
Whitehall East Jn. 127 B
Whitehall West Jn. 127 B
WHITEHAVEN 67 A1
Whitehaven Tunnel 67 A1
Whitehills (UWC) 100 D1
Whitehouse (MCB) 130 C
Whitehouse Farm (UWC) 52 C1
Whitehouse Jn. 48 D2
Whitehouse Lane (R/G) Footpath 51 A1
Whitehouse SB (W) 130 C
WhitehouseTunnel 30 D3
Whitehurst (UWC) 47 A2
Whitehurst Tunnel 47 A2
Whitelaw Footpath (R/G) 85 B2
Whitemoor Drove (AHBC) 42 D1
Whitemoor Jn. 42 D1
Whitemoor Yard 42 D1
Whitemoss (AHBC-X) 91 B2
Whites (UWC) (Long Eaton) 122 A
Whites (UWC) (Oxon) 40 C3
Whites (UWC) (Wilts) 16 C3
White's Farm (UWC) 28 D1
WHITLAND 23 B2
Whitland (MCB) 23 B2
Whitland Jn. 23 B2
Whitland SB (W) 23 B2
Whitland Tunnel 23 B2
WHITLEY BRIDGE 64 D3
Whitley Bridge (CCTV) 64 D3
Whitley Bridge Jn. 64 D3
Whitlingham Jn. 44 E
Whitlingham Lane 44 E
WHITLOCKS END 39 B2
WHITSTABLE 22 C3
Whitterleys Farm (UWC) 37 B2
Whittington (AHBC) 47 A2
Whittle International GF 62 E
WHITTLESEA 42 D1
Whittlesea 42 D1
Whittlesea SB (W) 42 D1
WHITTLESFORD PARKWAY 32 D1
WHITTON 111 A2
Whitton Jn. 111 A2
WHITWELL 58 D3
Whitwell Tunnel 58 D3
Whitwood Jn. 64 D3
Whixley (MCG) 64 C1
Whyke Road (CCTV) 11 A3
WHYTELEAFE 20 C3
Whyteleafe (CCTV) 20 C3
WHYTELEAFE SOUTH 20 C3
Whyteleafe South (CCTV) 20 C3
Wichnor Jn. 49 B3
WICK 104 D2
Wickenby (MCG) 60 C2
Wickenby SB (W) 60 C2
WICKFORD 21 A1
Wickford Jn. 21 A1
Wickham Knights (UWC) 18 C2
WICKHAM MARKET 34 D1
Wickwar Tunnel 16 C1
WIDDRINGTON 81 A3
Widdrington (CCTV) 81 A3
Widdrington Sidings Crossover 81 A3
WIDNES 56 C2
WIDNEY MANOR 39 B2
Wig (UWC) 54 C2
Wig Farm (UWC) 54 C2
Wigan North Jn. 126 C
WIGAN NORTH WESTERN 126 C
Wigan South Jn. 126 C
Wigan Station Jn. 126 C
WIGAN WALLGATE 126 C
Wigan Wallgate Jn. 126 C
Wigan Wallgate SB (WW) 126 C
Wigston North Jn. 50 B3
Wigston South Jn. 50 B3
WIGTON 73 B2
Wigton GF 73 B2
Wigton SB 73 B2
WILDMILL 25 B2
Wilkinsons (UWC) 71 B3
Willaston (CCTV) 48 E
Willerby Carr (UWC) 72 C3

Location	Page	Grid
Willersley Tunnel	49	B1
Willesden Carriage Shed N. SB (CN)	115	
Willesden Carriage Shed S. SB (CS)	115	
Willesden High Level Jn. SB (HL)	115	
Willesden Jn. (Acton Branch)	115	
WILLESDEN JUNCTION (H.L)	115	
WILLESDEN JUNCTION (L.L)	115	
Willesden North Jn.	115	
Willesden Suburban Jn.	115	
Willesden Suburban SB (WS)	115	
WILLIAMWOOD	131	B3
Willingdon Jn.	12	D3
WILLINGTON	122	A
Willington (AHBC)	49	B2
Willoughby Road (AHBC)	52	C1
Willow Gap (UWC)	75	A2
Willow Walk (FPW)	21	A3
Willows Lane (AHBC)	52	C1
Willows Marsh (AOCL)	45	A3
Willox Bridge 1 (UWC)	27	B1
WILMCOTE	39	B3
Wilmington (AHBC)	12	D3
Wilmington Green (Footpath)	12	D3
WILMSLOW	57	A2
Wilmslow North Jn.	124	C3
Wilmslow South Jn.	57	A2
WILNECOTE	49	B3
Wilpshire Tunnel	62	D2
Wilsford (AHBC-X)	51	B1
Wilson's Crossing	21	A3
Wilstrop (MCG)	64	D1
Wilton Jn.	9	A1
Wilton South	9	A1
Wiltshires (UWC)	49	B2
WIMBLEDON	111	B2
WIMBLEDON CHASE	111	B3
Wimbledon East Depot	111	B2
WIMBLEDON PARK	111	B2
Wimbledon SB (W)	111	B3
Wimbledon Traincare Depot	111	B2
Wimbledon West Jn.	111	B2
Winchburgh Jn.	85	A1
Winchburgh Tunnel	85	A2
WINCHELSEA	13	B2
Winchelsea (AOCL)	13	B2
WINCHESTER	10	C1
WINCHFIELD	18	D3
WINCHMORE HILL	20	C1
Wincobank Jn.	128	A1
WINDERMERE	68	C2
Windmill Bridge Jn.	114	B
Windmill Lane (CCTV)	32	C3
Windmill Lane (UWC)	59	A2
Windmill Lane Tunnel	126	A
Windridge (UWC)	40	C1
WINDSOR & ETON CENTRAL	19	A2
WINDSOR & ETON RIVERSIDE	19	A2
Windsor (UWC)	59	A1
Windsor Bridge North Jn.	122	B
Windsor Bridge South Jn.	122	B
Winfrith (UWC)	8	C3
Wing (UWC)	51	A3
Wing Tunnel	51	A3
Wingfield Tunnel	50	C1
WINNERSH	18	D2
WINNERSH TRIANGLE	18	D2
Winning Jn.	81	B3
Winning SB	81	B3
Winsel (UWC)	23	A2
WINSFORD	56	D3
Winsford SB (WD)	56	D3
Winsford South Jn.	56	D3
Winterbutlee Tunnel	63	A3
Winthorpe (AHBC)	51	A1
Winwick Jn.	56	C2
Wisbech	52	D3
Wisbech Bypass (AOCL)	52	D3
Wiserley Hall (R/G)	75	B3
WISHAW	132	D3
Wishaw Central Jn.	132	D3
WITHAM	33	A3
Witham Jn. (Braintree Line)	33	A3
Withy Tree Crossing	11	A3
WITLEY	11	A1
WITTON	120	A
WITTON PARK	76	C3
Witton-Le-Wear (MCG)	75	B3
Witton-Le-Wear SB	75	B3
Wivelscombe Tunnel	3	A2
WIVELSFIELD	12	C2
WIVENHOE	33	B2
Wivenhoe Park (UWC)	34	C2
WOBURN SANDS	31	A1
WOKING	19	A3
Woking Jn.	19	A3
Woking SB (WK)	19	A3
WOKINGHAM	18	D2
Wokingham	18	D2
Wokingham Jn.	18	D2
Wokingham SB (WM)	18	D2
WOLDINGHAM	20	C3
Wolvercot Jn.	30	C3
Wolvercot Tunnel	30	C2
WOLVERHAMPTON	121	B
Wolverhampton North Jn.	121	B
Wolverhampton PSB (WN)	121	B
Wolverhampton Steel Terminal	121	B
WOLVERTON	41	A3
WOMBWELL	58	C1
Womersley (AHBC)	64	D3
Wood Ditton (AHBC)	43	B3
WOOD END	39	B2
Wood End Tunnel	39	B2
Wood Green North Jn.	108	D1
Wood Green South Jn.	108	D1
Wood Green Tunnels	20	C1
Wood Lane (AHBC)	66	D3
Wood Lane (CCTV)	111	A2
Wood Road (UWC)	65	A3
WOOD STREET	109	B1
Woodborough Sidings	17	A2
Woodborough Sidings GF	17	A2
WOODBRIDGE	34	D1
Woodburn Jn. SB (W)	128	A1
Woodburn Jn.	128	A1
Woodcroft (MCG)	51	B3
Wooden Gate	81	A2
Wooden Gate Crossovers	81	A2
Woodend (UWC)	83	A1
Woodend Jn.	58	D2
Woodfidley Crossing	9	B2
Woodgate (CCTV)	11	A3
WOODGRANGE PARK	110	C2
Woodgrange Park Jn.	110	C2
WOODHALL	83	A2
Woodhall Lane (AHBC-X)	65	A3
Woodham Fenn	21	A1
Woodham Ferrers (ABCL)	21	A1
Woodhorn (AHBC)	11	A3
WOODHOUSE	128	A1
Woodhouse Jn. SB (WH)	128	A1
Woodhouse Jn.	128	A1
Woodlands (UWC)	37	B1
WOODLESFORD	64	C3
WOODLEY	124	D2
Woodley Jn.	124	D2
Woodman Lane	64	D3
WOODMANSTERNE	20	C3
Woodnesborough (CCTV)	22	D3
Woods (UWC)	50	B3
Woods Tenement Farm (UWC)	56	D3
Woodsford (No. 37) (AHBC)	8	C3
Woodsford (No. 38) (AHBC)	8	C3
WOODSMOOR	124	C3
Woodsmoor (CCTV)	124	C3
Woodwalton Jn.	42	C1
Woofferton SB	38	C2
WOOL	8	C3
Wool Footpath (UWC)	8	C3
Wool SB (WO)	8	C3
Wool West (UWC)	8	C3
Woolascott (UWC)	47	B3
Woolaston (R/G)	27	B3
Wooley Coal Siding SB (W)	58	C1
Wooley New Tunnel (Down)	64	C3
Wooley Old Tunnel (Up)	64	C3
Wooley Tunnels	58	C1
Wooliams 1 (UWC)	29	A2
Wooliams 2 (UWC)	29	A2
Wooliams 3 (UWC)	29	A2
Woolmer Green GSP Crossover	31	B2
Woolmer Green Jn.	32	C2
WOOLSTON	10	C2
Woolton Rd. Tunnel	125	A
WOOLWICH ARSENAL	112	D1
WOOLWICH DOCKYARD	112	D1
Wootton Bassett GF	16	D1
Wootton Bassett Jn.	17	A1
Wootton Bassett West	17	A1
Wootton Broadmead (CCTV)	31	A1
Wootton Farm (UWC)	37	B2
WOOTTON WAWEN	39	B3
WORCESTER FOREGATE STREET	38	D3
WORCESTER PARK	111	B3
WORCESTER SHRUB HILL	38	D3
Worcester Shrub Hill SB	38	D3
Worcester Tunnel Jn. SB	38	D3
Worcester Tunnel Jn.	39	A3
Worget Jn.	8	
WORKINGTON	73	A3
Workington Main No. 2 SB	73	A3
Workington Main No. 3 SB	73	A3
Workington Yard	73	A3
WORKSOP	58	D2
Worksop SB (WP)	58	D2
Worksop Station (CCTV)	58	D2
Worksop West Jn.	58	D2
Worlaby (UWC)	59	B1
WORLE	15	A2
Worle Jn.	15	A2
Worlingham	45	B2
Wormleighton (UWC)	40	C3
WORPLESDON	19	A3
WORSTEAD	46	D2
Worstead (AHBC)	46	D2
WORTHING	11	B3
Worthing (CCTV)	11	B3
Worting Jn.	18	C3
Wortley Jn.	127	B
Wortley Tunnel	127	B
WRABNESS	34	C2
Wrabness (FP) (R/G)	34	C2
Wrangaton Tunnel	4	C2
Wrawby Jn.	59	B1
Wrawby Junction SB (WJ)	60	C1
WRAYSBURY	19	A2
Wraysholme (AOCL)	68	C3
WRENBURY	48	C1
Wrenbury (MCB)	48	C1
Wrenbury SB	48	C1
WRESSLE	65	A3
Wressle (AHBC-X)	65	A3
WREXHAM CENTRAL	47	A1
Wrexham Exchange Jn.	47	A1
WREXHAM GENERAL	47	A1
Wrexham North Jn.	47	A1
Wroot Road (CCTV)	59	A1
Wyberton (CCTV)	52	C2
Wybourne (AOCL)	21	A2
WYE	14	C1
Wye Crossing	14	C1
Wyfordby (MCG)	51	A2
Wyke Cop (AHBC)	61	B3
Wyke No. 2 Crossing	7	B2
Wyke Tunnel	63	B3
Wykey (UWC)	47	A2
WYLAM	75	B1
Wylam (MCB)	75	B1
Wylam SB (W)	75	B1
WYLDE GREEN	120	A
Wylds Lane Jn.	38	D3
Wylye (AHB)	8	D1
WYMONDHAM	44	D1
Wymondham (MCG)	51	A3
Wymondham GF	44	D1
Wymondham SB (W)	44	C1
WYTHALL	39	B2

Y

Location	Page	Grid
YALDING	21	A3
Yalding (ABCL)	13	A1
Yapton (AHBC)	11	A3
YARDLEY WOOD	120	A
YARM	70	D1
Yarm Tunnel	70	D1
YARMOUTH	45	B1
Yarmouth SB (Y)	45	B1
Yarnton Lane (AHBC-X)	30	C2
YATE	16	C1
Yate Middle Jn.	16	C1
Yate South Jn.	16	C1
YATTON	15	A2
Yatton GF	15	A2
Yatton Loops	15	A2
YEOFORD	5	B3
Yeovil Jn.	7	B2
Yeovil Jn. SB (YJ)	7	B2
YEOVIL JUNCTION	7	B2
YEOVIL PEN MILL	7	B2
Yeovil Pen Mill SB (YPM)	7	B2
YETMINSTER	7	B2
Yew Tree Farm (UWC)	39	B3
Ymlwch (UWC)	35	B1
Ynys (UWC) (Dyfed)	24	D2
Ynys (UWC) (Gwynedd)	54	C2
Ynys (UWC) (Powys)	35	B3
Ynys Uchaf (UWC)	24	D3
Ynysdwfnant (UWC)	25	B1
Ynyslas (AHBC)	35	B3
Ynystawleg 1 (UWC)	24	D2
Ynystawleg Farm No. 4 (UWC)	24	D2
YNYSWEN	25	B2
YOKER	131	A1
Yoker SC (YY, YH)	131	A2
YORK	130	B
York (Y) SB	130	B
York Way North Jn.	108	D2
York Yard North	130	B
York Yard South	130	B
Yorkshire Tar (TMO)	66	C3
YORTON	47	B2
Young's (UWC)	16	C2
Yrallf Cynig 2 (UWC)	36	E
Ystrad Farm (UWC)	36	E
Ystrad Fawr (UWC)	36	D1
YSTRAD MYNACH	26	C1
Ystrad Mynach South Jn.	26	C1
YSTRAD RHONDDA	25	B2
Ysyrad Mynach SB (YM)	26	C2